T0297548

Agile Systems Engineering

Agile Systems Engineering

Bruce Powel Douglass, Ph.D.

Chief Evangelist

IBM Internet of Things

AMSTERDAM • BOSTON • HEIDELBERG • LONDON
NEW YORK • OXFORD • PARIS • SAN DIEGO
SAN FRANCISCO • SINGAPORE • SYDNEY • TOKYO
Morgan Kaufmann is an imprint of Elsevier

Acquiring Editor: Todd Green
Editorial Project Manager: Charlie Kent
Project Manager: Priya Kumaraguruparan
Cover Designer: Victoria Pearson Esser

Morgan Kaufmann is an imprint of Elsevier
225 Wyman Street, Waltham, MA 02451, USA

Notices
Knowledge and best practice in this field are constantly changing. As new research and experience broaden our understanding, changes in research methods, professional practices, or medical treatment may become necessary.

Practitioners and researchers must always rely on their own experience and knowledge in evaluating and using any information, methods, compounds, or experiments described herein. In using such information or methods they should be mindful of their own safety and the safety of others, including parties for whom they have a professional responsibility.

To the fullest extent of the law, neither the Publisher nor the authors, contributors, or editors, assume any liability for any injury and/or damage to persons or property as a matter of products liability, negligence or otherwise, or from any use or operation of any methods, products, instructions, or ideas contained in the material herein.

ISBN: 978-0-12-802120-0

British Library Cataloguing-in-Publication Data
A catalogue record for this book is available from the British Library.

Library of Congress Cataloging-in-Publication Data
A catalog record for this book is available from the Library of Congress.

For Information on all Morgan Kaufmann publications
visit our website at www.mkp.com

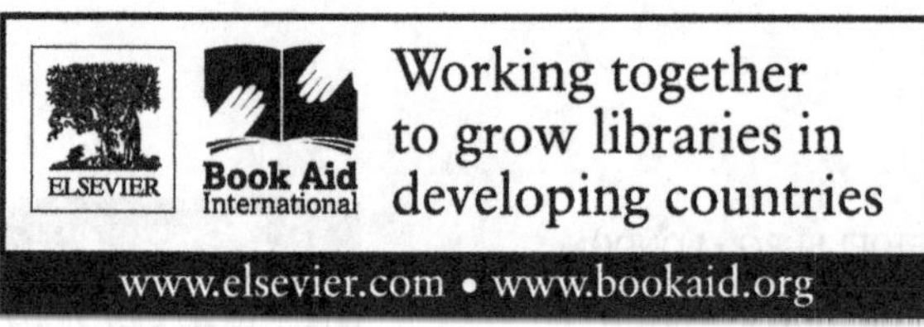

To my loving supportive mate
and Triathlon Sherpa extraordinaire,
Sarah—You're Awesome.

Contents

About the Author

Bruce was raised by wolves in the Oregon wilderness. He taught himself to read at age 3 and calculus before age 12. He dropped out of school when he was 14 and traveled around the US for a few years before entering the University of Oregon as a mathematics major. He eventually received his M.S. in exercise physiology from the University of Oregon and his Ph.D. in neurocybernetics from the USD Medical School, where he developed a branch of mathematics called autocorrelative factor analysis for studying information processing in multicellular biological neural systems.

Bruce has worked as a software developer and systems engineer in real-time embedded systems for over 30 years and is a well-known speaker, author, and consultant in the area of real-time embedded systems. He has been on the Advisory Board of the *Embedded Systems* and *UML World* conferences where he has taught courses in systems engineering, project estimation and scheduling, project management, object-oriented analysis and design, communications protocols, finite state machines, design patterns, and safety-critical systems design. He develops and teaches courses and consults in real-time systems and software design and project management and has done so for many years. He has authored articles for a many journals and periodicals, especially in the real-time domain.

He is the Chief Evangelist for IBM Internet of Things (IoT). Being a Chief Evangelist is much like being a Chief Scientist, except for the burning bushes and stone tablets. Bruce worked with UML partners on the specification of the UML and SysML standards. He developed the first UML Profile for DoDAF for the Rhapsody® modeling tool as well as other profiles such as a Fault Tree Analysis Profile and a Security Analysis Profile. He has been a co-chair of the Object Management Group's Real-Time Analysis and Design Working Group. He is the author of several other books on systems and software development, including *Doing Hard Time: Developing Real-Time Systems with UML, Objects, Frameworks and Patterns* (Addison-Wesley, 1999), *Real-Time Design Patterns: Robust Scalable Architecture for Real-Time Systems* (Addison-Wesley, 2002), *Real-Time UML 3rd Edition: Advances in the UML for Real-Time Systems* (Addison-Wesley, 2004), *Real-Time Agility (Addison-Wesley, 2009), Design Patterns for Embedded Systems in C* (Elsevier, 2011), *Real-Time UML Workshop for Embedded Systems* (Elsevier, 2014) and several others, including a short textbook on table tennis.

Bruce enjoys classical music and has played classical guitar professionally. He has competed in several sports, including table tennis, ultramarathon bicycle racing, running, and full-contact Tae Kwon Do, although he currently only fights inanimate objects that don't hit back. He has recently gotten back into racing triathlons and ultramarathon cycling and completed his first Ironman triathlon in 2014.

Bruce does extensive consulting and training throughout the world. If you're interested, contact him at Bruce.Douglass@us.ibm.com.

Preface

Products are becoming more capable and complex at an exponential rate. Additionally, the safety, reliability, and security concerns for these systems are making these systems much more difficult to engineer. Simultaneously, product development cycles are shrinking. Clearly, change in needed. We need to be able to produce more capable systems in less time and with fewer defects.

One touted solution to this problem is to eschew text as the primary means for capturing engineering data. While text is wonderfully expressive, it is ambiguous and woefully imprecise. Modeling using more formally defined languages (notably, in this context, UML and SysML) claims to improve specific engineering data. If only we could figure out how.

Another offered solution is agile methods. These have been developed in the software IT community although they have begun to be applied to embedded and real-time systems as well. However, the agile literature is (almost) entirely focused on desktop or IT software development. The development environments they consider are (almost) exclusively small co-located teams where there are no safety, reliability, or security concerns. And no co-development of electronics or mechanical parts. So the systems engineer is left to wonder, "How does this apply to ME and my work?" The agile literature offers no answer.

There are (good) books on systems engineering. There are (also good) books on SysML and Model-Based Systems Engineering (MBSE). There are books on agile methods for software (and some of those are good too). However, there is currently no book that attempts to integrate these concepts together into a cohesive, usable approach for systems engineering. This book is meant to address that need.

We start with a short introduction to the discipline of systems engineering followed by a brief discussion of agile methods, as they are discussed in the (mostly software) literature, including their benefits. Rounding out the introductory portion of the book, there is a chapter on basic SysML. With that, we are ready to start on the journey to understanding how to effectively and efficiently apply MBSE in Real Life (IRL).

The approach in the book is based on the author's Harmony Agile Systems Engineering Process. The software development aspects of this process are described in detail elsewhere[1]; this book only addresses the systems engineering concerns. The Harmony Agile Systems Engineering process is an agile, model-centric approach to developing the engineering data required of systems engineering; requirements, architectures, interfaces, and dependability analyses are the foremost among these. The Harmony process has been developed and honed by the decades of systems experience of the author in real projects that fly, drive, and otherwise perform all around the world.

There is a saying among educators—"I show you, and you see. I tell you and you hear. You do it and you understand." To that end, there are extensive examples in the book to illustrate the details of executing the engineering steps involved. These examples contain aspects from multiple engineering disciplines, including software, electronic, and mechanical engineering. The first of these examples is a high-end running treadmill. The second, and more complex, example is a wearable robotic industrial exoskeleton (known as a *waldo*) capable of carrying 1500 kg. Each of the primary activities of the Harmony Agile Systems Engineering process is discussed and then demonstrated with these and other examples. The reader is urged to construct their own solutions to the problems presented and to build the models described in these chapters.

Audience

The primary audience for this book is, naturally enough, systems engineers. This means engineers whose primary focus is the specification and design of systems that will be implemented (generally) by multiple engineering disciplines. Systems engineers specify the system properties of the product but leave discipline-specific details to the appropriate downstream engineering team. Some of those downstream engineers may find the information in this book of interest as well, especially the details of how the systems engineering data are formatted and adapted to meet their needs in the Handoff activity.

Goals

As I travel throughout the world, I am struck by the difficulty systems engineers have in applying MBSE approaches. The primary language—SysML—is daunting. SysML includes the 800-or-so pages of the UML specification and adds hundreds more. It is a highly capable but quite complex language.

[1] See, for example, *Real-Time Agility* (Addison-Wesley, 2009) or *Real-Time UML Workshop for Embedded Systems* (Elsevier, 2014).

Beyond just the language itself, as product complexity increases exponentially and product delivery cycles decrease monotonically, there is an urgent need to simultaneously increase the efficiency of systems engineering work and to improve its quality as well. More and more, we see systems taking over for humans in safety-critical, high-reliability, and secure environments, and we must be able to depend upon these systems functioning properly, all the time.

This book has a simple goal—provide enough guidance for systems engineers so that they can easily and effectively apply agile methods *and* MBSE to the development of complex systems in a world that increasingly relies on these systems for operation.

Tooling

The modeling examples in this book are all modeled with the IBM® Rhapsody™ tool. However, one of the good things about a standard is that there are multiple options for different tools. If you have a different tool that you prefer that supports the SysML standard, you should have little difficulty in building these models in the tool of your choice. This is *not* a book about Rhapsody, nor is it Rhapsody-specific.

Where to Go After the Book

If you're interested in tools, training, or consulting, see www.ibm.com. I teach advanced classes and consult worldwide on UML, SysML, MDA, DoDAF, architectural design, design patterns, requirements modeling, use cases, safety critical development, behavioral modeling, the development process improvement, project management and scheduling, and quite a bit more. You can contact me for training or consulting services at Bruce.Douglass@us.ibm.com. I also run a (free) yahoo group forum as well at http://groups.yahoo.com/group/RT-UML—come on down! My IBM Thought Leader page (http://www-01.ibm.com/software/rational/leadership/thought/brucedouglass.html) also has many white papers available for downloading on different topics that may be of interest.

Bruce Powel Douglass, Ph.D.
Summer, 2015

Acknowledgments

I want to thank my editor, Charlotte Kent, for nagging me when I clearly needed it and being supportive when I need that too. My reviewer Barclay Brown of IBM was also helpful in keeping me honest. I have no doubt that errors remain—and I claim full responsibility for those. Most of all, I want to thank my family for keeping me sane, or at least trying to, while I burned the midnight electrons, creating this book.

CHAPTER 1

What Is Model-Based Systems Engineering?

Chapter Outline

Systems engineering is an interdisciplinary activity that focuses more on system properties than on specific technologies and has the overall goal of producing optimized systems to meet potentially complex needs. This focus includes specification of necessary system properties (requirements), large-scale system organizational principles (systems architecture), definition of flows and events that travel between the system and elements in its environment as well as between large-scale architectural elements comprising the system (interfaces)—and the selection of key approaches and technologies through optimization analysis (trade studies).

In short,

> Systems engineering is an interdisciplinary approach to building complex and technologically diverse systems.

Systems engineering is involved throughout the system specification, development, and verification activities. It provides crucial systems-level oversight of the project. We will focus on the specification activities in this book, but systems engineering encompasses far more.

Systems engineering is distinct from discipline-specific engineering, known collectively as "downstream engineering." These engineering disciplines include mechanical, electronic, chemical, optical, nuclear, and software engineering. Thus, while systems engineering may define requirements allocated to these specific engineering disciplines, they shouldn't specify the design or technologies used within them, except, perhaps, at a high level.

1.1 Key Systems Engineering Activities

Figure 1.1 shows the primary aspects of systems engineering, connected in a "traditional" or "classical" flow.

There is, of course, much more to systems engineering than this, and we will cover many of them in this book. For now, this provides a useful set of high-level discussion points. For a more formal definition of systems engineering, readers are referred to the *INCOSE Systems Engineering Handbook* [1].

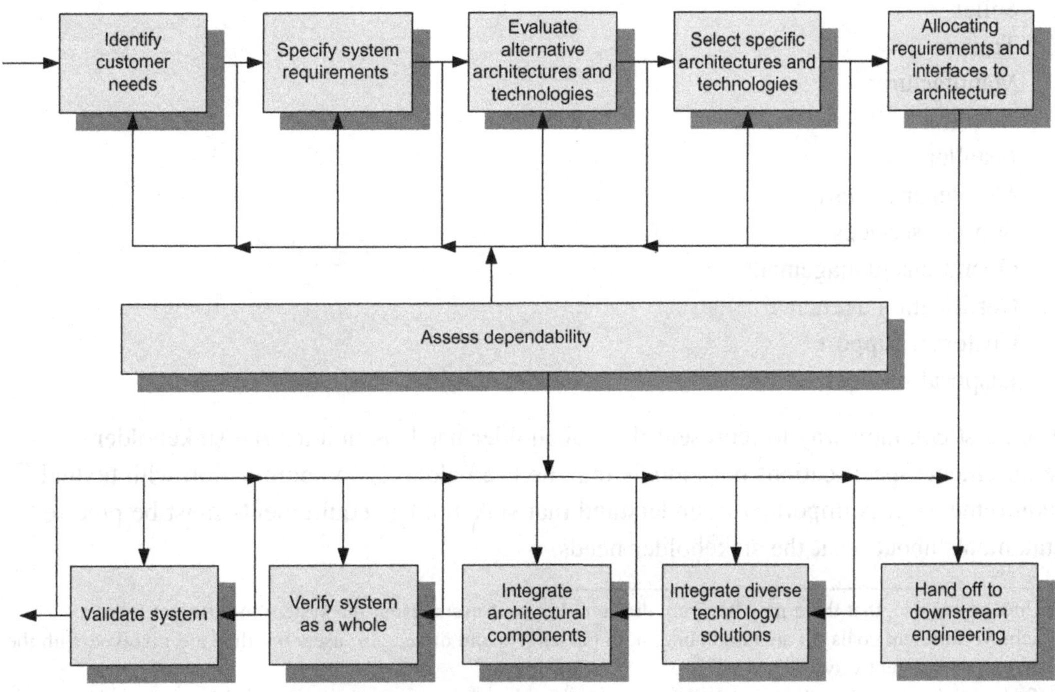

Figure 1.1
Basic systems engineering activities.

The following sections will discuss the purpose and intent of the activities but not how or when they are carried out (that will come in subsequent chapters). Since the focus of this book is to describe how the goals of systems engineering can be achieved in an agile way, how these task are performed will differ from this simplistic discussion. We'll talk about agile methods in general in Chapter 2 and detail specific best practices for agile methods in subsequent chapters.

1.1.1 Identifying Customer Needs

Ultimately, the reason we create a system is to meet a coherent set of customer's needs. This is normally captured as a set of *stakeholder requirements* or *customer requirements.* I prefer the former term because the set of stakeholders goes beyond the purchaser or even the primary user. We must satisfy the needs of a wide variety of stakeholders, such as

- Purchaser
- User[1]
- Evaluator
- Marketer
- Seller
- Trainer
- Manufacturer
- Acquirer
- Installer
- Maintenance staff
- Support services
- Operations management
- Certification agencies
- Customer support
- Disposal services

The most common way to represent the stakeholder needs is in a textual stakeholder requirements specification[2] but models may be used alone or in combination with textual requirements. It is important to understand that stakeholder requirements must be precise statements about what the stakeholder needs.

1 Understand also, that there may be many different kinds of users, using the system in different ways to achieve different goals. In an automobile, both passengers and drivers are users but they are involved with the system in different ways.

2 To be clear, when I use the term "textual xxx specifications," I am referring to *natural language specifications* and not specifications stated in precise textual languages such as mathematics, Z, SysML, and temporal logic.

1.1.2 Specifying System Requirements

Whereas stakeholder requirements are statements of stakeholder needs, system requirements are precise, testable statements of observable system properties. These most often focus on what the system *does* but may include many other kinds of requirements, such as quality of service (QoS), safety, reliability, security, durability, manufacturability, maintainability, reusability, so-called "design requirements," and parametric requirements. This topic is discussed in more detail in Chapter 4. The point is that system requirements are statements about the system behavior and properties. Obviously, to ensure we are building a system that will actually satisfy the stakeholders, we need to relate specific statements between these two kinds of requirements.

Most effort in system requirements specification is focused on two specific kinds of requirements: functional requirements and QoS requirements. Functional requirements specify *what* the system does—the behavior of the system, how it interacts with users and other systems, what capabilities it provides and what information it consumes and delivers. These are the verbs of the system. In contrast, QoS requirements specify *how well* the behavior is achieved (adverbs), such as the performance, reliability, and safety of those behaviors. In addition to QoS requirements, there are other nonfunctional requirements, including affordability, cost, system effectiveness, disposability, maintainability, packing, handling, and so on [1].

In short,

> Functional requirements specify the control and data transformations that a system performs while QoS requirements are the nonfunctional aspects of those transformations.

What system requirements don't do[3] is specify the internal architecture, design, and implementation technologies. It is a common mistake to overly constrain the internal design by specifying unnecessary constraints, limiting the flexibility of architects and downstream engineers to do their work effectively. It is completely appropriate to specify the required data or control transformation but generally inappropriate to specify the design or implementation of that transformation in the requirements.

1.1.3 Assess Dependability

The term "dependability" refers to our ability to depend upon a system in its intended environment, with its intended use, as well as when these assumptions are violated. Dependability has three primary aspects: safety, reliability, and security. You'll note in Figure 1.1, that this activity is done in parallel with all the other engineering activities. This is because dependability concerns are both intrinsic and extrinsic. Intrinsic concerns are present

[3] Or at least, shouldn't!

due to the essential nature of the system or its context. An automobile, for example, is a heavy thing whose primary role is to move, so there are inherent concerns about being able to begin, control, and end movement. These concerns are present regardless of the technology used to power the vehicle. However, in design if a gasoline engine is selected, that decision introduces concerns about gasoline flammability and fumes; if an electric engine is selected, then electrocution and hazardous material leakage are introduced. Thus, as technological decisions are made, their impact on safety, reliability, and security must be assessed.

1.1.4 Evaluating Alternative Architectures and Technologies

System requirements are detailed from a black box perspective. This means that the technological solutions within the design should not be specified. Systems engineers are tasked with identifying the system architecture and key technologies to be used. This is because the system engineers have a holistic view of the system and are in the best position to make tradeoffs that may affect multiple disciplines (e.g., electronics and software). Left to their own devices,[4] electronics engineers may make design decisions that are optimal for their design at the expense of software and mechanical designs, negatively affecting system cost or performance. However, decisions whose consequences are wholly specific to an engineering discipline are best left to the experts within that specific discipline.

Put another way, the systems engineers should not specify internal software architecture, electronic components, or mechanical parts unless the lack of such specification would negatively affect other engineering disciplines or the system as a whole.

Because the systems engineers have this holistic perspective, one of their responsibilities is to define the large-scale systems architecture. To do this, they typically must evaluate alternative approaches. This is called performing *trade studies*. In a trade study, criteria are established for defining the "goodness" of some aspect of a design. These are often known as *measures of effectiveness* (MOEs). There are usually several MOEs used to evaluate one design approach over another. In the simplest approach, each MOE is given an importance weighting factor and each solution under evaluation is given a score that identifies the degree to which that solution optimizes that criterion. The winning solution is the one with the best overall score.

A more complex but potentially useful approach is to use parametric analysis. In such an analysis, the relation between MOEs is mathematically quantified and analysis is used to find optimal parameter values. For example, one might relate battery life, weight, recharge time, available power, heat, and cost in a mathematical expression to find an optimal battery size and technology for an electric automobile.

Performing trade studies is the topic of Chapter 6.

---

[4] Pun intended.

1.1.5 Selecting Specific Architectures and Technologies

The system engineers will specify an overall architecture of the system, comprised of large-scale architectural units, known as *subsystems.* These subsystems are themselves implemented with a combination of downstream engineering disciplines and form the large-scale building blocks of the system as a whole. In large complex systems, the subsystems may themselves be recursively decomposed into sub-subsystems. Based on the systems engineer's experience and/or trade studies, a specific architecture will be defined. This may be done at different levels of abstraction from "conceptual" (outlining the architectural vision), "logical" (specifying essential aspects of the architecture), or "physical" (specifying the actual architecture as it will appear in the real world product).

These subsystems serve two primary purposes. First, they are the large-scale pieces that compose the system and hence indicate a high-level bill of materials. Secondly, they are often components that can be assigned to different interdisciplinary design teams, including subcontracting agencies, so they can serve as a focus for the project planning and scheduling. Chapter 7 will explore in more detail how this can be done in Systems Modeling Language (SysML).

1.1.6 Allocating Requirements and Interfaces to Architectures

The team tasked to design and implement a subsystem needs to know two primary things: the requirements they must satisfy and the interfaces to external systems and to their peer subsystems that they must support. The first of these goals is dealt with primarily through the *allocation* of requirements to the subsystem, although it is also common to decompose system requirements into smaller subsystem-specific requirements for allocation.

The second goal, that of subsystem interface definition, requires the definition of a set of interfaces, each of which is composed of a set of services and flows. Each service must be defined in terms of its preconditions, postconditions, required functionality, required QoS, and elements (which, in the system context, may be data, materiel, or energy) passed in and out.

The set of subsystems and interfaces is correct if and only if the required system-wide behaviors can be achieved through the collaboration of the subsystems. Analyses demonstrating the correctness of the subsystem architecture and interfaces should be performed before handing the specifications off to the subsystem teams. Chapter 7 will also discuss this topic.

1.1.7 Hand Off to Downstream Engineering

The hand off to downstream engineering provides the necessary engineering data to the subsystem teams so that they can begin their work. This process is strangely troublesome in many engineering environments. This happens because the information is specified in ways that don't meet the needs of the development teams, usually because of format, tooling, language, and/or skill sets. The hand off may also fail for process reasons, such as when it doesn't come in a timely fashion or include information necessary for the subsequent engineering to be performed.

In Chapter 8 we will discuss a model-based hand off approach that transfers the system engineering data in a simple, reliable fashion. The hand off focuses on the creation of a system "common" model that will contain elements common to more than one subsystem, and a separate model for each subsystem. A common model will contain—at this point—the physical interfaces definitions and metadata between the subsystems and the specifications of data types and subranges, known as the physical data schema.

Each subsystem model will contain the requirements allocated to that subsystem, references to the relevant items in the system common model, and the subsystem deployment architecture. The deployment architecture defines the scope of the engineering disciplines involved in the subsystem (such as mechanical, electronic, and software), the allocation of requirements to those engineering disciplines, and the definition of the interfaces between design elements of those disciplines.

1.1.8 Integrate Discipline-Specific Designs into System Composite

What we've discussed so far is the specification side of the process. Integration is all about bringing different things together into a coherent whole. This may be done within the individual subsystems by integrating the work products from different engineering disciplines together, or by bringing together preintegrated subsystems into a larger composite system. Of course, performing integration also entails some verification of the consistency of the component parts, and integration testing is a key part of this activity.

Many projects find integration troublesome because integration is typically performed rather late in the process and will uncover heretofore hidden interface, functional, and performance defects. Integration remains a hard point of many systems processes that agile methods can soften to a large degree.

1.1.9 Verify System as a Whole

To be clear, verification of a work product involves ensuring that it meets its requirements. Verification comes in two forms, which I call *syntactic* and *semantic verification.* The former is usually done by quality assurance personnel, while the second is done by subject matter experts or testers.[5]

5 In some engineering organizations, testing is a part of quality assurance, while in others they are distinct organizations. In this discussion, I will treat them as separate departments within the engineering organization. In any case, they are different personnel from the engineers creating the work products within the project.

Verification is not only applied to the completed, integrated system at the end of the project, but is also applied to all of the important work products—models, drawings, prototypes, specifications, etc.—created in the systems engineering process. This isn't shown in Figure 1.1, as it appears inside of each of the activities and is applied to the work products created or modified during that activity. Beyond that, the produced, final system is verified as well.

First, let us discuss what we mean by verification in its two forms and then we'll take about system verification as an activity.

1.1.9.1 Syntactic verification

I define syntactic verification to mean "compliance in form." This means two primary things: process compliance and work product compliance.

Audits

Process compliance means that the work done during the project adheres to project plans and guidelines. Project work normally proceeds as a set of tasks performed by workers. Each such task has a set of preconditions and postconditions, consumes expected input, produces expected outputs, performs defined steps, and follows work guidelines. Process compliance, then, means that you did the work as expected and as planned. Process compliance is assured through quality assurance audits of work to ensure that plans and guidelines are met.

Example 1: For example, if you are working in a clean room environment to reverse-engineer functionality from a competitor's product, you may have guidelines that dictate that you can have no product-related discussions with someone intimate with the product you are reverse-engineering.

Example 2: For a different example, before a design can be released to manufacturing, your process may state that it must be reviewed and approved by your department's safety assessor.

An audit verifies that the process requirements are met and produces evidence to that effect.

Syntactic reviews

Work product compliance means that the work product is properly formatted, organized, named, uses approved and appropriate vocabulary, and meets its needs. It is common for an engineering department to have standards for important work products such as requirements specifications, models, design, source code, schematic drawings, test plans, and so on. Some of these standards may be written by external agencies, such as the modeling standard DO-331, and others may be developed internally. Work product compliance verifies that the work product meets the requirements of the applicable standards, internal and external. Work product conformance may be performed by applying automation but is more commonly done by syntactic review by a quality assurance engineer.

Example 1: DO-331 requires that all nonnormative model elements are clearly identified, so the project has identified all elements of the metatype Comment or stereotyped as "nonNormative" to be treated as such. A quality assurance person reviews the model and verifies that all elements not so marked are, in fact, normative.

Example 2: Your department has a standard for requirements specification that includes in part:

- All requirements shall be uniquely numbered within the specification
- All functional requirements shall be constrained by one or more QoS requirements
- All safety requirements will be clearly labeled as such
- Requirements will be organized by use case.

A quality assurance engineer would review the specification to ensure that the (meta)requirements of this standard are achieved by your system requirement specification. Most often, checklists are created to facilitate the execution of audits and syntactic reviews and to record the compliance assessment.

1.1.9.2 Semantic verification

I define semantic verification as "compliance in meaning"; that is, "correctness." This is what is normally meant by the term "verification." There are three primary means for semantic verification: semantic review, testing, and formal methods.

Semantic review

Semantic review differs from syntactic review in a few important ways. First, the review is performed by different roles; semantic review is performed by subject matter experts while syntactic review is carried out by standards experts. Secondly, the subject is different. A semantic review focuses on the content and meaning rather than on the form. This means that deep subject matter expertise is required to perform a semantic review, whereas such knowledge is not necessary for a syntactic review. Thirdly, the degree of coverage is spotty, tends to be low, and its completeness is difficult to assess. Semantic review is, by far, the most common way to verify systems engineering work products.

The problem with semantic review—apart from its cost—as a means of verification is that it is the weakest form of semantic verification. While it adds value, it fails to find many problems and the verification of complex work products due to both the difficulty of identifying problems in complex products and in vigilance. It is not uncommon to have literally weeks of reviews and even if vigilance is high for the first few hours, it will flag before long.

Testing

Testing is done by creating a set of test cases that verify each requirement of a work product. A test case is a sequenced set of inputs to the work product with specific values and a defined, expected output. Testing is the most common means by which to verify the final system but is little applied to other system engineering work products. One reason for this is that for a work product to be tested, it must, in principle, *execute*, consume the inputs of the test case, and produce outputs and outcomes. Few system engineering work products do that in a traditional systems engineering process. However, with model-based systems engineering, we can produce precise, executable models rather than merely textual descriptions. Not only can such models be created and tested, this approach will form the foundation of the Harmony Systems Engineering process described in the rest of this book.

Testing typically provides much better coverage than semantic review. However, it is impossible to fully verify a system through testing; it just isn't possible to test all possible sequences of all possible inputs with all possible values. There are standards to determine the degree of coverage such as structure (path) testing (all paths are visited by at least one test), decision coverage (all decisions are tested in both true and false paths), and modified condition decision coverage (all inputs to all decisions are independently verified). One can get as close as desired to complete testing at increasing cost.

As an aside, there is a standard for model-based testing [2]. This standard defines a standard way to use the Unified Modeling Language (UML) as a language for specifying test cases, automatically constructing test fixtures and executing test cases to determine test outcomes. There is tool automation for this as well [3].

Formal methods

The term *formal methods* refers to a branch of mathematics used to verify various properties of systems. It requires that the specification against which a work product is verified, is specified in a mathematically precise way. Then, given a set of assumptions, properties of the system can be verified. For example, it might be desirable to verify that, given a set of assumptions, a system can reliably satisfy a request for service within a specified timeframe.

Formal methods vary in their comprehensiveness and difficulty, ranging from so-called lightweight formal methods (such as reachability analysis) to full theorem proving. In some ways, formal methods are the strongest means available for verification because the conclusions apply to all combinations of inputs. However, the difficulties in formal methods are many. For example, to apply most formal methods requires a PhD in formal methods. Creating a demonstrably correct formal specification is a daunting task; indeed, most projects that use formal methods reserve their use for critical system subsets. Additionally, the formal specification required may be unreadable by any but its author—few people are trained in formal languages such as Z or VDM. Lastly, they are vulnerable to violations of their assumptions.

1.1.9.3 System verification

System verification generally refers to the application of test cases, derived from the system requirements, to an integrated system. There is considerable work converting the requirements specification into test cases and ensuring that the test cases properly reflect the requirements both in scope and in specific meaning. Automation (test fixtures) must typically also be created although man-in-the-loop testing supplemented with limited automation is most common. System verification is not only a matter of demonstrating a set of required system properties. It is also a matter of demonstrating the absence of other properties known to be undesirable or hazardous.

System tests—just like the requirements from which they are derived—are (almost entirely) black box. Nevertheless, some standards require a degree of internal coverage corresponding to those test cases. That implies that if a part of the design or implementation cannot be verified by the test suite that represents all the requirements, then requirements must be added to justify the existence of the design elements.

Most people think of traditional system verification as taking place (hopefully) once at the end of the project. There is no reason for this to be true. In fact, agile methods create the system in a series of increments with increasing capabilities, each of which is verified. This distributes the work of verification and identifies and repairs defects earlier and at a lower cost, a subject that will be discussed in the next chapter.

1.1.10 System Validation

If system verification is ensuring the system meets its requirements, validation is about ensuring the system is usable and meets the stakeholder's needs.

As with verification, validation can be applied to work products other than the final system. Indeed, it is important to validate the system requirements well before all the design and implementation work is complete. One reason for this is that most stakeholder requirements are specified as textual statements, and such statements suffer from ambiguity, lack of precision, and lack of completeness. System engineers must interpret the stakeholder requirements to create the system requirements and validate their understanding and the statement of the requirements. As discussed earlier, the most common way to do this is with arduous review—an error prone and expensive process, to be sure. However, a model-based systems engineering approach offers an alternative; create an executable specification model of the system requirements and demonstrate that specification model to the stakeholder. Extensive experience has shown this approach greatly improves the quality and correctness of the system requirements and improves customer satisfaction with the resulting system.[6]

[6] One A&D (aerospace and defense) client reported to me an 80% reduction in requirements defects after moving to a model-based systems engineering approach. I've had similar results with other clients in A&D, automotive, and medical industries.

System validation is the process of ensuring the integrated and verified system meets the customer needs. This is often done with customer acceptance tests (often negotiated at the start of the project), delivering prototypes to the user into a sand box environment, or flight tests. The major point is that validation is distinct from verification and both are important.

In this book, we will focus mostly on the specification side of system engineering (Sections 1.1.1–1.1.7) and much less on the postdesign integration, verification, and validation side.

1.2 Systems Engineering Data

This section identifies some of the data created within the systems engineering activities. I have explicitly excluded specific engineering discipline data (e.g., source code or mechanical schematics) as belonging to downstream engineering, a topic discussed in another of my books [4].

> *Note*: Although it is common for the engineering data to be organized into documents, the interesting part is actually the data itself. Focusing on the documents (writing, signing off, etc.) often leads to poor management practices such as refusing to update a signed off document just because the data it contains have been proven to be wrong (yes, this does actually happen). If, instead, we focus on getting the engineering data correct and consistent, system engineering practice will be improved. Furthermore, the traceability we need for most projects is not between documents themselves but between statements within those documents.

1.2.1 System Development Plan

The system development plan includes the overview of how the systems engineering and downstream engineering activities will proceed. This is a key document for the coordination of many worker roles within the project. It usually includes a schedule as well as descriptions of the primary activities.

Note: In the Agile approach, planning is not only desired, it is *necessary*. A key difference between traditional and agile planning is that the former usually assumes infinite knowledge of the future and that nothing within the project scope will ever change. For this reason, I refer to this as *ballistic planning*. Agile planning, on the other hand, assumes that despite our best efforts, we don't know everything and some things will change, so plans must be maintained and updated as we learn more about the project.

1.2.2 Stakeholder Requirements

As mentioned earlier, a stakeholder requirement is a statement of stakeholder need. Collectively, we refer to the set of such statements to be the stakeholder requirements.

As will be discussed in Chapter 4, we usually organize functional and QoS requirements into use cases while other requirements are organized by purpose or subject matter.

1.2.3 System Requirements

A system requirement is a statement about the necessary properties of the system as a whole. Collectively, all such statements are system requirements. It is even more important that system requirements be organized around use cases than stakeholder requirements, as system requirements are the most essential data for systems engineering.

1.2.4 Certification Plan

In a regulated industry, such as avionics or medical devices, standards exist against which the system must be certified before it may be used by customers. Adhering to these standards is not easy and achieving certification takes serious effort. This plan outlines how the objectives of the relevant standards will be met, how the required evidence will be produced and managed, and how the procedures for achieving certification will be performed. Failure to pay adequate attention to the needs of the certification process has resulted in many failed projects.

1.2.5 Subsystem Requirements

Subsystem requirements are system requirements allocated to specific subsystems or requirements derived from system requirements to be allocable. There is a different set of requirements for each subsystem that is handed off to the subsystem team for design and implementation. Along with the subsystem requirements, the interfaces provided and required by that subsystem are also defined.

1.2.6 Discipline-Specific Requirements

During the hand off procedure, the requirements allocated to the interdisciplinary subsystem are further allocated and/or decomposed and allocated to the involved engineering disciplines, such as mechanical, electrical, chemical, and software. At the same time, the interfaces between elements of the different disciplines within the subsystem are specified. This decouples the engineers in the different disciplines, facilitating their work.

1.2.7 Safety Analysis

Safety analysis is one aspect of dependability analysis, a topic that will be discussed in more detail in Chapter 5. Safety means "freedom from harm" and safety analysis identifies hazards (conditions that lead to accidents) and combinations of events and conditions that lead to hazards. This analysis is often performed with fault tree analysis (FTA) diagrams and summarized in a hazard analysis.

Note: Dependability analysis is an ongoing and iterative activity. While it starts at, or even before, system requirements specifications, it often results in additional dependability requirements to deal with concerns that are raised with design approaches and technologies. Thus, even late in the product development cycle, it is common to create new dependability requirements.

1.2.8 Reliability Analysis

Reliability is another aspect of dependability. Reliability is a stochastic measure of the availability of system services. The most common approach to analyzing reliability is with a Failure Means and Effect Analysis (FMEA). Reliability can be specified initially to meet stakeholder needs, and such reliability requirements will constrain the design approaches, technologies, and components that can be employed. Reliability of existing designs can also be assessed in a bottom-up approach, but often issues are identified too late to have a meaningful, cost-effective impact on system reliability.

1.2.9 Security Analysis

In these days of exponentially increasing connectivity, security has emerged as the third primary aspect of dependability. Security can be defined as "freedom from undesired intrusion, interference, or theft." As systems engineering work results in interdisciplinary system designs, security concerns may be physical, cyber, or both (cyberphysical). There is no universally agreed-upon technique for performing security analysis, but I will present a model-based approach to cyberphysical security analysis in Chapter 5.

1.2.10 System Architecture

The Harmony Systems Engineering process (defined by the author and used in this book) identifies five key views of system architecture—subsystems (including interfaces), deployment, dependability, distribution, and concurrency, the last being a concern solely of the software. Of these, the identification of the subsystems and their characterization in terms of responsibilities and interfaces is probably the most important, especially in systems engineering.

1.2.10.1 Subsystems

A key view of the system architecture is the set of subsystems, along with their responsibilities (allocated requirements) and connections to peer subsystems and external actors. A *subsystem*, in this context, is a large-scale piece of the system with a coherent set of responsibilities within the larger system context and is generally realized by a combination of engineering disciplines, such as mechanical, electronic, and software. As mentioned previously, this may be done at multiple levels of abstraction, such as conceptual, logical, or physical.

An interface is a specification of how elements (such as subsystems) connect within a larger context. Most often, it defines a set of services and element (data or materiel) flows related to those services. It also should include interface related metadata, such as preconditions, postconditions, performance constraints, data schema, and any other information necessary to properly use the services.

Early on, the interface definitions are *logical*; that is, services are named and normally specified using asynchronous event or message passing with logical data definitions. Later on, these logical definitions will be refined to include physical details including exact means for communication (e.g., shared memory or bus communications messaging) and exact bit-map formats for data (known as the physical data schema).

1.2.10.2 Deployment architecture

The deployment architecture view refers to the allocation of requirements to the different engineering disciplines and the interdisciplinary interfaces between them, such as the software-electronic and electromechanical interfaces. This is largely, though not exclusively, specified within the subsystems themselves.

1.2.10.3 Dependability architecture

The dependability architecture view is largely a subset of the subsystem architecture in that it represents "redundancy in the large" to achieve safety, reliability, and security goals of the system, as well as additional elements that exist to provide, manage, or improve the dependability of the system (as opposed to providing core system functionality). All of the system elements that support dependability are either subsystems or allocated to subsystems, so the dependability view of the architecture focuses on those architectural elements responsible for the dependability properties of the system.

1.2.10.4 Distribution architecture

The distribution architecture is largely a subset of the subsystem architecture and focuses on the distribution of services across subsystems and the means by which these subsystems cooperate, coordinate, and share information, energy, and materiel. This view often focuses on bus and communication architecture and protocols and the technical realization of the subsystem interfaces.

1.2.11 Integration Test Plan

The integration test plan identifies how the system components will be integrated. It may include the integration of elements from different engineering disciplines into subsystems as well as the integration of subsystems into the coherent system. This typically includes methods, procedures, and any required automation and test benches.

Note: In an agile process, integration tests aren't applied once; as the system is incrementally implemented, the integration takes place incrementally as well. An agile practice known as *continuous integration* involved the continuous (or at least highly frequent) integration of system elements together to ensure that the final integration proceeds without major problems.

1.2.12 Integration Tests

The integration tests provide "gray box" testing of the integration of system elements together. This plan is normally done in parallel with the development plan since if integration is done incrementally, it must test features in the order in which they are introduced in the system design.

1.2.13 Verification Plan

The verification plan identifies the procedures and methods to be used for verification, including the development of test benches and automation. The verification plan is usually distinct from the Verification Tests themselves.

Note: In agile methods, the system is constructed incrementally; at the end of each iteration, a version of the system—with all the included engineering discipline elements—is ready to be verified for a subset of the requirements. Thus, verification is applied at the end of each iteration to ensure that the maturing system design meets the requirements realized so far. This may mean that for early verification, mechanical mock up and software simulations are used if some elements are not available.

1.2.14 Verification Tests

The verification tests ensure that each system requirement is met by the system implementation. If we are doing incremental system verification, then a series of elaborated test suites will be created.

1.2.15 Validation Plan

The validation plan specifies how the system will be demonstrated to meet the customer's needs. This may be done through walkthroughs, reviews, guided or free-form demonstrations, deployment in real or simulated customer environments, or flight tests.

1.2.16 Trace Matrix

The trace matrix refers to the set of trace links among the engineering data elements; for example, the relation between a stakeholder requirement, system requirement(s), architectural elements, and test cases. This can be stored in one table or many. Table 1.1 shows the recommended trace relations among different kinds of engineering data.

Although this set of connections among engineering data is referred to as the trace matrix, it needn't be a single monolithic index and may be a set of tables, each of which focuses on the relations among a pair of engineering data types.

A common question is how deep the traceability must be. If your system is undergoing certification under a specific standard, then use the specific objectives for traceability

Table 1.1: Typical engineering data trace links.

		1	2	3	4	5	6	7	8	9	10	11	12	13	14	15
1	Stakeholder requirements		R			S					R					R
2	System requirements			R	o	S	R	R	R	R		S	S		R	
3	Subsystem requirements				R	S		R	R			S	S	R		
4	SW/EE/ME requirements					S	R	R	R			S	S	R		
5	Dependability analyses						R	R	R	R	S	S	S			
6	System architecture							R	R	S		S	S	R	S	
7	Control model(s)								o	R		S	S	o	S	
8	Integration tests									o		S	S	R	o	
9	System verification tests											S	S		R	
10	System validation tests												S			R
11	Certification plan												S	S	S	S
12	QA records															
13	Integration results															
14	Verification results															
15	Validation results															

R, recommended; S, recommended for safety critical systems; o, optional.

within that standard. In general, single requirements, design elements (class, data structure, function, mechanical or electronic part), and test cases form the recommended "units" of traceability.

1.2.17 Integration Test Results

The integration results include the outcomes for each integration test performed. They also need to include the configuration version and revision numbers for the integrated elements, the date performed, and other test result metadata.

1.2.18 Verification Results

The verification results include the outcomes for each verification test performed. They also need to include the configuration version and revision numbers for the integrated elements comprising the build, the date performed, and other test result metadata.

1.2.19 Validation Results

The validation results include, naturally enough, the outcomes for each validation test performed. They also need to include the configuration version and revision numbers for the integrated elements, the date performed, and other test result metadata.

1.3 Lifecycles of the Systems Engineer

It turns out that there are different sequences and procedures for executing the tasks of systems engineering. The most prevalent is the V-Cycle, largely because it is simple to plan; the primary concern with it is that, at best, it only roughly approximates how the project will unfold. It assumes that all of the work products can be created once, in its entirety and more-or-less without defect. Section 1.3.1 discusses this traditional V-model lifecycle. The other extreme is the fully agile incremental approach, as discussed in Section 1.3.2. In the fully agile incremental view, systems and downstream engineering can take place in time-demarcated epochs known as iterations (known in Scrum as "sprints"). The upside of this approach is that you incrementally create the engineering data and verify and validate them throughout the project, improving system quality and engineering efficiency. The downside of the fully incremental approach is that it doesn't really take into account that the work in some engineering disciplines (e.g., mechanical parts) has long lead times and cannot be designed well on partial information. The hybrid approach, described in Section 1.3.3 uses both approaches and varies when and how the increments are done to the nature of the problem.

1.3.1 V-Model Lifecycle

The V-model is an extended (or perhaps "bent") waterfall lifecycle in which the activities on the left side of the "V" stipulate two different but related work products: a specification and its means of verification. The specification is consumed by the next activity in the V while the tests are applied at the corresponding step on the right side of the V.

Figure 1.2 shows this workflow, the relations between activities on opposing sides of the V and activities that go on through multiple activities of the V. The ellipse drawn around the activities on the left side indicate the focus of this book (specification activities).

The V-model is a "breadth-first" approach in that each work product is assumed to be created in one activity and is expected to be complete, accurate, and correct at that point

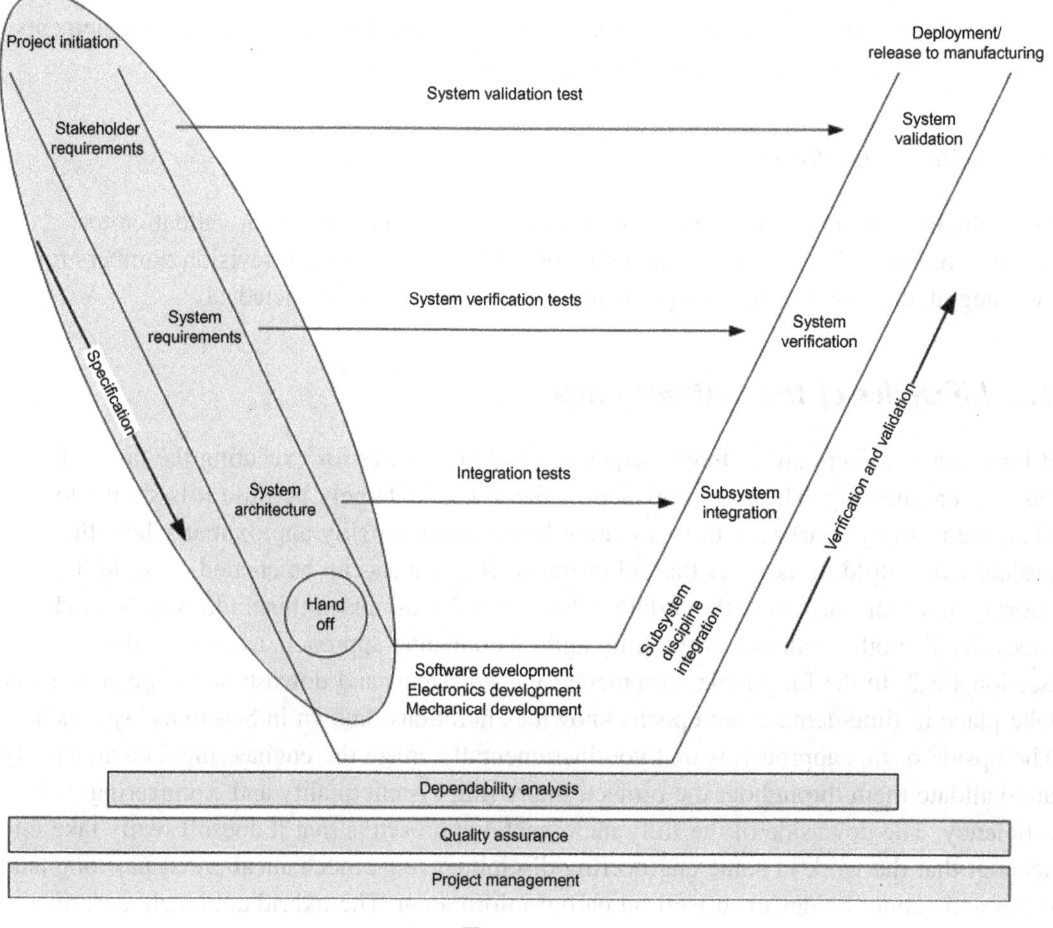

Figure 1.2
V-model lifecycle.

and forever more. This, of course, problematic, because it is very difficult to create flawless specifications with limited information. In actual fact, projects planned using the V-model generally run with cycles of correction and addition to many or all documents.

There are a number of well-known problems with this approach. The first big issue is the quality of the work products. Generally, each activity in Figure 1.2 is considered a "phase" and transition into and out of each phase is rigidly controlled, requiring approval and sign off of the work products. However, for most system engineering data, the only means for verification used is semantic (and sometime syntactic) review—the weakest form. This means that approved, signed-off work products are released but many, if not most, defects there aren't discovered until subsequent phases. There is a natural reluctance to change approved work products because their approval process is cumbersome, expensive, and time-consuming. In addition, even if corrections are incorporated in the work products, their quality still tends to be less than with the other lifecycles discussed here because of the long delay between the creation of a work product and its verification. Some of the quality concern can be mitigated through the application of model-based systems engineering and the creation of verifiable engineering data, but model-based systems engineering (MBSE) cannot entirely eliminate it on its own.

This additional work—updating the already-approved engineering work products—is unscheduled work so it becomes difficult to estimate how close to release a product actually is. The unplanned cycles of defect repair occur at the end of the project after the project plan has determined the project should be completed. This makes project planning difficult because you have to estimate defect rates and cost for updates for data that have not yet been created. Again, the V-model lifecycle assumes infinite depth, breadth, and stability of knowledge when the plans are created.

Not only are there unknowns when planning, some of the things you do know will change later. The V-model lifecycle is notoriously resistant to changing customer needs, requirements, technologies, and staffing.

1.3.2 Incremental

The fully incremental lifecycle (Figure 1.3) takes a fundamentally different approach. A relatively narrow slice of functionality through all activities to produce a version of the system that is then verified and validated, before incrementally adding the next slice of functionality. This is a "depth-first" approach that takes coherent sets of requirements (use cases or user stories) at a time. To work effectively, the incremental approach makes a few assumptions:

1. The use cases or user stories implemented in one iteration are independent from those in other, unrealized use cases or user stories.
2. The amount of work necessary to refactor existing designs and implementation to accommodate the new functionality is much less than to implement the new functionality.

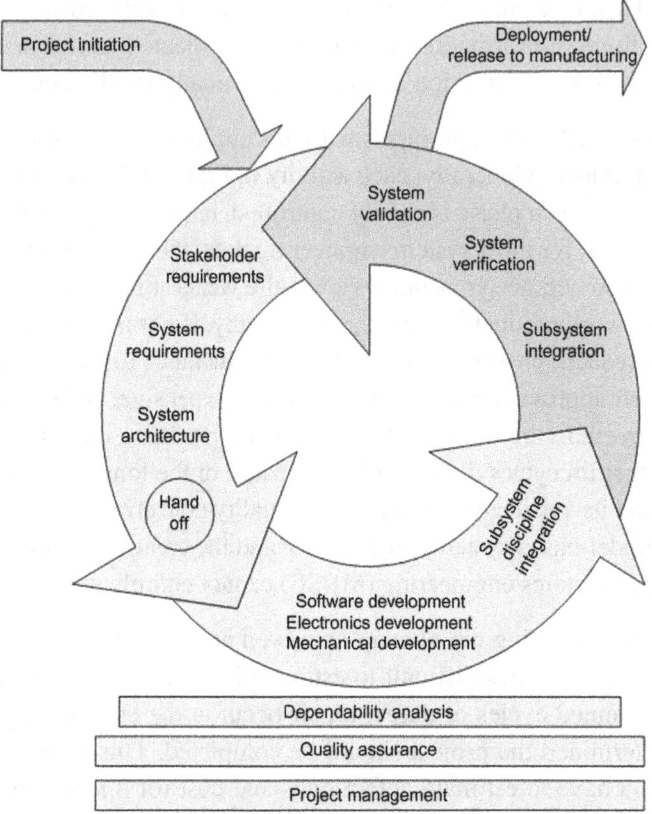

Figure 1.3
Incremental lifecycle.

The first assumption is simple to meet. It means that you must create use cases or user stories that represent coherent system functionality and a given requirement should only map to a single use case or user story. It is not necessary that they don't have design elements in common.

The success of incremental and agile methods in software development is due largely to the ease with which software can be refactored, so with software, the second assumption is met. However, it is less true of mechanical and electronic engineering because of physical real-world constraints (such as heat, weight, and power) and because of the long lead times to create physical parts. For example, imagine a use case in which you design an automotive power system to meet the needs of the radio and later come to find out that you also have to power the engine. A system with significant new hardware generally cannot be effectively developed purely incrementally because the necessary refactoring of the design may require too much work.

1.3.3 Hybrid

The hybrid lifecycle is shown in Figure 1.4. It appears as three interconnected cycles with hand offs between them. Exactly how many cycles of the systems specification cycle are performed depends on the nature of the system being developed and the degree of risk[7] of the project. We can see in the figure that system engineers can continue to work on the next system iteration while downstream engineers design and implement the current iteration and test engineers verify and validate the previous iteration.

1.4 Model-Based Systems Engineering (MBSE)

So far, we've talked about the activities and outcomes of system engineering. In traditional systems engineering,[8] all of the engineering data are represented either as textual specifications or possibly as schematic drawings. In the last 20 years, models have been introduced as a better way of creating, managing, and verifying engineering data than textual specifications. With the initial release of the UML in 1995, systems engineers had a standard language in which they could express requirements, architectures, designs, and other kinds of engineering data. However, there was widespread belief that the UML itself was too "software-oriented" for general use in systems engineering, which led to the development and release of the SysML[9] [5] in 2006.

The UML has built-in mechanisms for extension and specialization of the languages. A set of coherent extensions is called a *profile*. SysML is such a profile, simultaneously subsetting the UML language, specializing it in some ways, and extending it in others. An overview of the key SysML features and views is provided in Chapter 3, although for a detailed language description and overview, the interested reader is referred to other books[10] [6,7].

Basically, what is true in the UML is also true in SysML, although we cleverly changed the names of things to make it sound more appealing to systems engineers; for example, a big

---

7 In this context, I mean "risk that the project won't be successfully completed (project risk)" rather than "risk that the product in use will harm people (safety risk)." The term risk is used in both situations but has significantly different meaning.

8 Systems engineering is a relatively new discipline, so when we talk about "traditional systems engineering," remember that we are speaking of far less than 100 years of tradition.

9 I had a hand in developing both specifications, although Sandy Friedenthal was the lead for the SysML specification work.

10 The specification is the definitive source of detail, but is sometimes referred to as the "hairy underbelly" of the SysML and reading it isn't for the weak of heart.

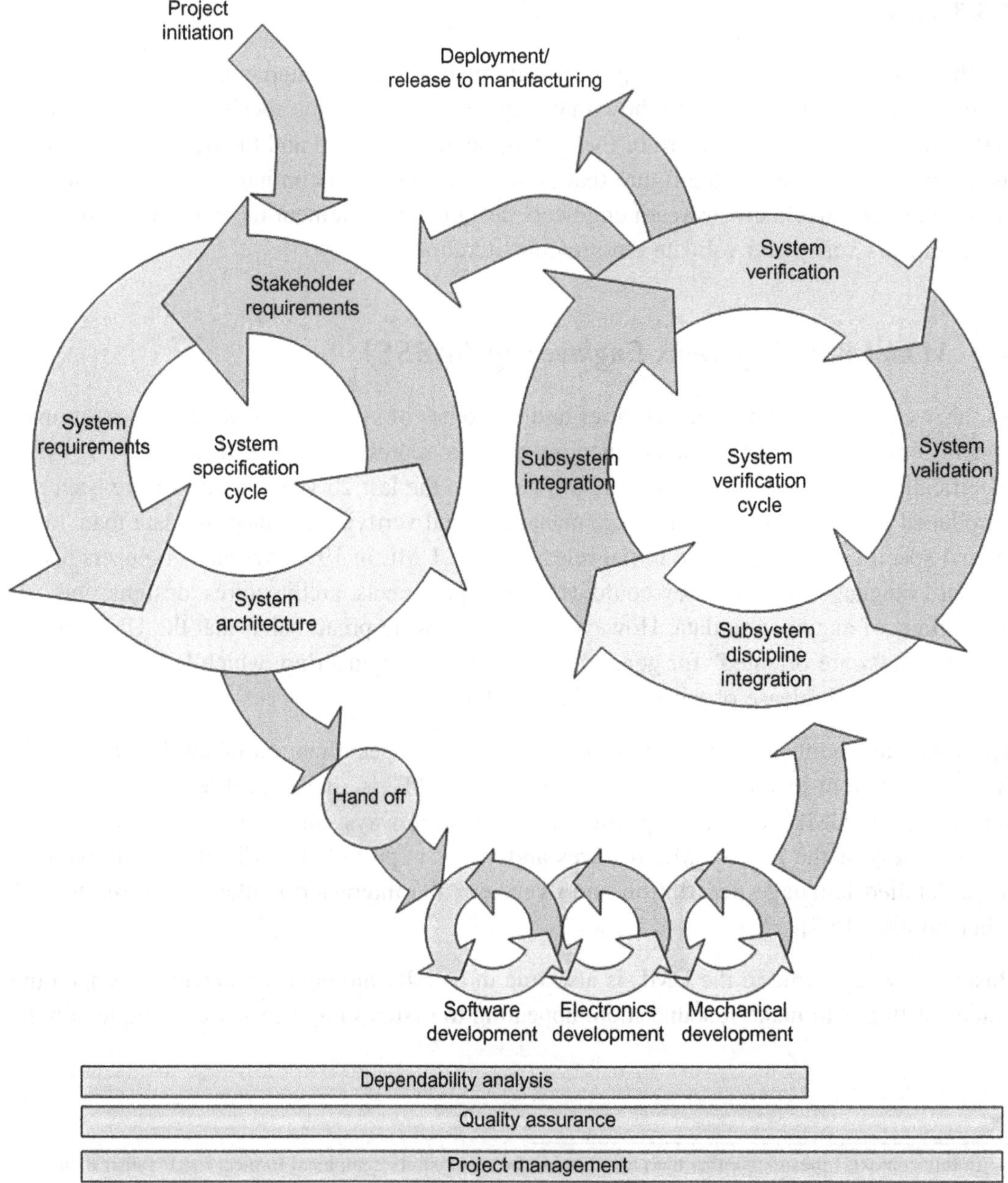

Figure 1.4
Hybrid lifecycle.

obstacle was overcome with the simple change of the term *class* to *block*. Having said that, there are some important semantic improvements in SysML that improve its applicability to systems engineering beyond name changes, such as:

- The introduction of the *Requirement* model element type
- Extensions of interfaces to include material and energy flows as well as information flows
- Extensions of the UML *port* concept
- Extension to activity diagrams to include behavior that is continuous in both time and value[11]
- Addition of parametric diagrams to support trade studies.

To be clear, SysML models (one of the primary foci of this book) are not the only kinds of models that are created. Safety models, threat models, performance models, physics models—are all useful kinds of models that are created as work products by system engineering activities. We will focus on SysML models to a large degree, but much of what is said about models applies to all kinds of models.

1.4.1 The Modeling Advantage

There are a number of important benefits to be gained from modeling well.[12] The most important of these are listed here.

1.4.1.1 Precision of engineering data

In traditional systems engineering, most engineering data are ultimately captured in textual statements in textual documents. Text is wonderfully expressive; most of the poetry I've written has been done in English.[13] However, natural language suffers from both imprecision and multiple interpretations. The SysML is more precise and less ambiguous than equivalent natural language statements, resulting in superior specifications.

1.4.1.2 Data consistency across work products and engineering activities

Models provide formal traceability links among engineering data both within the same model and stored in separate models and work products. The SysML provides specialized trace links that identify the kind traceability relations among the data, such as

- «copy» Specifies that one requirement is a read-only copy of another and its use is to support the reuse of a requirement in a different context. The arrow points to the originating requirement.

[11] All behavior in the UML is fundamentally discrete in both time and value.

[12] Notice the implied caveat.

[13] While I find poems I've written in state machines to be better received than poems I've done in Z or temporal logic, state machines are nevertheless not a natural language for expressing poetic imagery. Trust me.

- «deriveReqt» This is a relation between requirements stating that one requirement is derived from another.
- «satisfy» This relation is used to show that one element satisfies the need specified by another, generally how a design or implementation element satisfies a requirement. The arrow points to the requirement being satisfied.
- «verify» This relation shows how a test case verifies a requirement, or design or implementation element. The arrow points to the requirement or design element.
- «allocate» Arguably this isn't a trace relation, but it is used to show that one element is allocated to a context. Common uses are the allocation of a requirement to a use case or design element; allocation of a behavior to a structural element (block); one component (part) allocated to a structural element (block). The arrow points in the direction of the allocation (i.e., to the allocated context).
- «trace» (from UML) The relation is used in SysML models when there is a trace link between elements that is other than one of the more specialized ones above.

Common trace links among engineering data are shown in Table 1.1.

Beyond just ensuring the consistency of disparate engineering data, traceability also allows us to perform impact analysis to assess the effect of changes in data. For example, it is common that each requirement has trace links to architectural elements, design elements, implementation elements, test cases, and various kinds of analyses, such as safety, reliability, and security. If a requirement changes, impact analysis identifies all of the now related "suspect" elements that will require at least examination, if not complete replacement. This permits a cost assessment of a proposed change[14] and the identification of the related elements that will require modification should the change request be approved.

1.4.1.3 A common source of engineering truth

Because modeling *is not* the same as drawing (see Section 1.4.5, number 9, below), a model contains a single source of engineering truth. All the functional, QoS, behavioral, and structural semantics of the system are represented in a precise way within the model. We can reference this information to do various kinds of analyses—such as performance, safety, or reliability—and we can create consistent views of that information, such as diagrams and tables, with assurance that the information in one view or analysis is consistent with the information in another. This is not only *not* true in traditional text-based approaches to systems engineering, it is also a key source of confusion and error.

---

[14] "Yes, you can have tail fins but it will cost $120K more in development and delay the project 5 months."

1.4.1.4 Improved visualization and comprehension of engineering data

Visualization of engineering data is difficult in traditional text-based approaches. It is a little like seeing the transistor-level design of a processor and trying to assess from it, system-wide behavior. It *can* be done—if you have unlimited time and resources—but it is very, very hard.

In contrast, models hold engineering data in a model repository (see Section 1.4.1.3). From this engineering data repository, we can construct views of the information relevant to questions we have and analyses we wish to perform (see Section 1.4.5, number 4, below). We can construct as many of these views (diagrams or tables) as we have questions to answer and because the information source is a data repository, we can be assured of the consistency of that information across all such views.

The fact that we can create views to answer specific questions and that the information in these views is guaranteed to be consistent enables a deeper understanding of the semantics of our system as well as understanding to a broader range of stakeholders. I can create views that focus on externally visible behavior, system interaction, architecture, collaboration design, detailed design, safety, reliability, security, performance, . . . the list goes on. That means that I can understand the impact of the technical decisions made in a way not otherwise easily attainable. Further, I can create views for nontechnical stakeholders that answer their questions about the system.

1.4.1.5 Ease of integration of disparate engineering data

Because of the traceability links possible in models, integrating information from different sources (possibly different models) can be easily done in models. Sometimes this is done by modeling the disparate information in different parts of the same model and then creating relations and views among them, and sometimes this is done by modeling the information in different models or kinds of models and integrating the models together. For example, SysML tools typically have limited ability to directly do performance analysis of behavior. However, the UML has two standard profiles—the UML Profile for Schedulability, Performance and Time (known as the SPT profile) [8] and the UML Profile for Modeling and Analysis of Real-Time and Embedded Systems (MARTE) [9]—that specify ways that modeling and analysis tools may interact. Rational Rhapsody™, for example, has interfaces with tools such as ChronVal™ (www.inchron.com) and RapidRMA™ (http://tripac.com/rapid-rma) for performance and schedulability analysis and Medini Analyze™ for safety analysis (http://www.ikv.de/index.php/en/products/functional-safety).

1.4.1.6 Improved management and maintenance of engineering data

Naturally, the engineering data in the models are configuration-managed; modern modeling tools have good integrations with CM tools for versioning and management of consistent sets of engineering data. Beyond that basic set of facilities, we still need to manage all the data within a configuration or version. Modeling helps here in a variety of ways. The single source of truth means that we don't have a "dual maintenance" problem with changes not propagating properly throughout the engineering viewports. Traceability links enable us to ensure the consistency of related but different kinds of engineering data. Advanced tools like Rational Engineering Lifecycle Manager (RELM)™ (http://www-03.ibm.com/software/products/en/ratiengilifemana) permit the integration of referenced engineering data from widely diverse engineering sources such as requirements, PLM, mechanical and electrical CAD, and software designs.

1.4.1.7 Early verification of the correctness of engineering data

I believe this to be *the* key benefit, the gem that outshines all the other not-insignificant benefits of MBSE. I can verify engineering data *as I created them* to ensure that I have good requirements, architectural, and other specifications. This really isn't possible with textual-based systems engineering approaches.

As I discussed in Section 1.1.9.2, there are three means for semantic verification of engineering data—(semantic) review, testing, and formal methods. These are listed in order of their "strength" from weakest (review) to strongest (formal methods). In traditional systems engineering approaches, you are limited to the weakest form for most data. This means that in traditional SE approaches, the requirements and architectures generally contain significant errors that will require late, downstream identification, rework, and reverification. This is expensive and generally manifests at a time when the project schedule expects us to be done. However, through this we can use models to construct executable, verifiable specifications to ensure that the SE data are complete, consistent, and correct before handing them off to downstream engineering activities. The techniques and practices of agile model-based system engineering (aMBSE) will be the subject of most of this book.

1.4.2 High-Precision Modeling with UML and SysML

In order to achieve the benefits outlined in the previous section, it is not enough to draw pictures and call it a model. This belies a fundamental truth:

1.4.2.1 The fundamental truth of modeling: drawing≠modeling

Another term used for drawing, as used here, is "napkin modeling." It means that we

- Sketch out an idea
- We don't worry if we "misuse" a modeling concept because—hey—it's just a picture on a napkin
- We don't worry about the details, we're just trying to get the basic concept down
- We might discuss the drawing with a peer, before using the napkin to wipe the barbeque sauce off our chin and throw it away

- We then do the *real work* in some other tool or approach.

That, my friends, is *not* what I mean by modeling. When I model, I use a precise language to specific the deep semantics of the element(s) of concern to gain an understanding, answer a question, or perform some reasoning. I may create graphic views (diagrams) to represent those semantics, but it is in a formal language. This *is* the real work of systems engineering and not some throw-away artifact. Napkin models are a great way to *start* a conversation, but a terrible way to *end* one. *Don't make me come over there.*

In this book we will create different models for different reasons. We'll create models of requirements. We'll create models of architecture. We'll create safety analysis models, reliability analysis models, and more. All of them will be precise enough in detail to achieve their purpose. In general, though, a model is precise enough if its contents can be verified through testing or formal mathematical analysis and not just a semantic review.

When I talk about testing the model, I don't mean testing other work products created as a result of the model; I especially don't mean that we verify the requirements model by building the system and then figuring out if we built the right system or not. While I agree that's important, that's verification of the *system* not of the *requirements.* What I mean by "verifying the requirements model" is that we show that the requirements model (and its contained requirements) is itself consistent, complete, accurate, and correct. By doing this before we hand off requirements to downstream engineering we greatly reduce the work and cost of identifying incorrect requirements late in the process, throwing design work away, and redoing it. This is true in an iterative, incremental context as well; the set of requirements dealt within the current iteration can be demonstrated to be, within their scope, complete, consistent, accurate and correct.

People fail at modeling for all kinds of reasons (i.e., they don't adhere to the rules—see Section 1.4.5) and not understanding the difference between just drawing and modeling is one of the key reasons. The other primary reason has to do with how they choose to adopt modeling—the topic of Section 1.4.4.

1.4.3 Modeling Is Essential for Agile Systems Engineering

There a second fundamental truth regarding the application of agile methods to systems engineering:

1.4.3.1 The fundamental truth of agile systems engineering: verifiable models are required for agile systems engineering

I make the assertion that modeling is essential to apply agile methods to systems engineering because one of the key ideas of agile is continuous verification of engineering data. Of course, almost all agile books focus on IT software and not systems or embedded software[15] and they typically use small collocated teams for their example. Nevertheless, we can (and will) extend the core ideas from agile for IT software to systems engineering in this book. The next chapter will explore this in some detail and the details of the application of agile practices will populate the remainder of this book.

Agile methods—the focus of the next chapter—are almost exclusively applied to the development of software source code. A core idea is the best way to have defect-free software is to avoid defects in the first place, rather than put them in and remove them later. This is accomplished through a couple of key practices: Test Driven Development and Continuous Integration.

Test Driven Development (TDD) means that the tests of your source code are written at the same time—or slightly before—a small amount of source code is written. Immediately thereafter, the tests are applied and any noncompliance is repaired. Then you write the next set of tests. Rinse and repeat. As a guideline, this means that you should never be more than a few minutes away from demonstrating—through testing—that the software is correct so far.

The practice of TDD can be applied to *any* data that you create, provided that you can make them testable (i.e., that they can be made to execute). This includes requirements, architectures, designs, control models, etc. This cannot be done with textual statements about those work products because of the lack of precision and executability. High-precision models are, however executable, and can therefore be developed using the TDD practice.

Another agile practice used to avoid late defect identification and rework is continuous integration. A leading source of project failure is that certain defects are not easily visible until the components of the system are brought together; if this happens late in the project, then these defects are identified late, resulting in significant rework and delay. The continuous integration practice brings incomplete (but demonstrably correct) software components early and often,[16] resulting in the early resolution of integration problems. Like TDD, this practice also requires testability and execution of the components.

For systems engineering, it is common to have many engineers work collectively on coherent sets of engineering data—requirements, architectures, designs, etc. Applying the continuous integration practice to the creation of these work products means that we bring together and demonstrate the interoperability and consistency of those data as they are being created, not *ex post facto*. Again, the idea is one of avoidance of defects, rather than late identification and repair.

It should be noted that, to a large degree, agile methods aren't so much about doing different activities as they are about modifying the order in which those activities are done.

[15] Reference [4] is an exception to this general statement.

[16] Most commonly daily.

Traditional projects also do integration and testing; they just do them at the end of the project. Agile methods mix those activities into the development activity so that we can avoid defects in the first place.

I think of agile practices as hygienic. Imagine a situation in that I think that brushing my teeth is a good idea so that every year on December 31, I give them a good solid cleaning. That is similar to how traditional projects approach integration and testing. Then, at the end of the year, I deal with the defects (cavities and gum disease) at a high cost. The agile approach is to move the brushing activity to around when I use my teeth (such as after meals); this "continuous brushing" practice improves the quality of the teeth and gums and to a large degree avoids defects. I think I like the hygienic agile approach better for both my tooth care and my systems engineering.

1.4.4 Adopting Modeling in Your Organization or Project

Change is hard. Doing something in a fundamentally new way, using new and unfamiliar languages, with new and unfamiliar tools to create engineering data represented in new and unfamiliar ways is, well, *hard.* The fact that there are real benefits to be had doesn't make it any easier.

As it turns out, there are better and worse ways to adopt MBSE. Here are some of the worst.

1.4.4.1 Antipatterns of adopting MBSE

I've worked on literally hundreds of projects that have used modeling. I've seen triumphant successes and catastrophic failures. Getting to the point where you and your organization are *good* at modeling and realize the benefits requires that you don't do these things:

- Avoid planning the adoption of the technology and approach
- Change everything you do—all at once
- Change things that are already working well for you
- Avoid measuring the success of adoption—it doesn't hurt if you close your eyes
- Continue to do it, even if it fails. It'll eventually work
- Do it on your own, you weenie
- When you fail, don't blame your approach—blame modeling (or the tool, or the consultant, or the manager, or the engineer).

1.4.4.2 Recommend approaches for adopting MBSE

Alternatively, I recommend a thoughtful, evidence-based approach to adopting MBSE:

- Use an agile approach to adopt aMBSE
- Assess your organization's strengths and weaknesses
- Create an adoption plan for an incremental, continuously verified adoption.

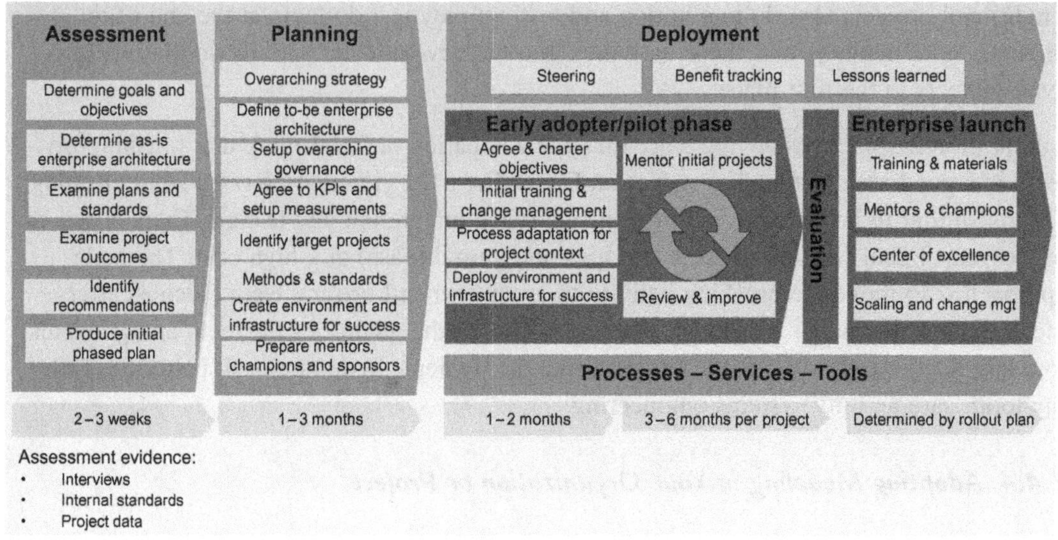

Figure 1.5
Adoption of agile MBSE.

Figure 1.5 shows the approach I use when helping engineering organizations adopt model-based development approaches, including aMBSE. There are four overlapping phases: assessment, planning, pilot, and deployment.

Assessment

I greatly prefer beginning any adoption of technology and process with what I call an "R&D Capability Assessment." This assessment looks at three kinds of information to understand where, as an organization, strengths and weakness lie with respect to the development of complex systems. In most cases, the gathering of this information takes around 1 week; this is followed by another week of analysis of the gathered data. A fourth kind of information—objectives—is also discussed during this assessment.

I generally start with interviews of staff—including engineering managers, project managers, team leads, architects, systems engineers, software developers, electronics engineers, mechanical engineers, safety and reliability specialists, quality assurance assessors, integrators, testers, and support staff. From each, I gather their perspective on what the organization does well, what it does poorly, and what obstacles they face in successfully achieving their goals.

The second kind of information I review in detail is what the organization thinks it is doing. These are typically codified as process, procedures, standards, guidelines, and policies documentation. Usually, these are thick unread tomes on the shelves of the engineering staff. It is nevertheless important to understand the lies that the engineers and managers are telling each other.

The third kind of information is what actually happens during projects. This always differs from the process and procedures documents in either small or large ways. I generally look at data records from one or two projects, consisting of:

- Project schedules (planned)
- Project schedules (actual)
- Requirements data
- Systems architecture
- Interface specifications
- Software design
- Electronics design
- Mechanical design
- Quality assurance records
- Unit test plans
- Unit test results
- Integration test plans
- Integration test results
- Test plans
- Test results
- Defect reports
- Change requests
- Safety assessment (FTAs, hazard analyses)
- Reliability assessment (FMEAs, for the most part)
- Security assessment (threat analyses).

Analysis of this third kind of data provides a view into the effectiveness of the process and how well the staff enacts that process.

The last kind of information gathered during the assessment is obtained in meetings with senior and mid-level engineering management: where do you want to be? How much capability do they want to achieve and how much are they willing to invest in achieving it?

The outcome of this assessment is a detailed report of usually 30–40 pages outlining what has been found and, based on the stated goals and objectives of the organization, a prioritized list of recommended remediation actions.

If aMBSE is seen as a solution, this assessment will identify what issues aMBSE needs to address and the priority of when those issues will be addressed. For example, if an organization has strong architectural skills but is weak in requirements specifications, early MBSE efforts should focus on improving the ability of the projects to define good requirements models. If the interfaces are poorly managed, but requirements are done well, then early MBSE improvements will concentration there. If SE is generally good but information is lost in the hand off to downstream engineering, let's fix that first. If architectural aspects from different engineers don't integrate well, focusing attention here will improve the capability of the team. The assessment provides focus, direction, priority, and urgency to the adoption plan.

Planning for adoption

The planning step is a negotiation between the people responsible for improving the engineering capability and the people who are either paying for it or who are going to have to participate in it. Key to this is understanding the gap between where the organization is today and where it wants to be in the future. The plan exists to reduce this gap by detailing which remediation actions will be taken, when they will be done, who will participate in it, the expected cost, effort, and time for each action, and how and when success of those actions will be measured.

In practice, this is generally done as a phased incremental activity. The plan for each phase outlines the key concerns to be addressed. For example, for one company I created a plan with three phases: near term (3 months), mid-term (3–6 months), and long term (6–12 months). The near-term plan included introduction of the team to the Harmony process for systems and software developers, 1 week training in the Rational Rhapsody tool, a 1-week systems engineering workshop for functional analysis, and an update to the policies and procedures related to requirements definition and management. The mid-term phase focused on improvements in the manager's ability to accurate schedule projects and the adoption of agile planning methods, the use of Key Performance Indices (KPIs) to monitor engineering progress, and fix what was a broken work product review process. The long-term phase concentrated on reworking the core engineering process to be more usable and efficient (including moving from textual process documents to Rational Method Composer), and broadening the use of UML and SysML across other projects.

Much of the time, the remediation actions revolve around 1) improvements in skill via training on techniques and tools, 2) using tools to automate difficult or error-prone activities, 3) mentoring on practices and methods during real engineering work, 4) gaining real experience using the methods and tools on real projects and 5) expert review of created engineering data and work products.

In my experience, one of the keys to success with an improvement project, such as adoption of MBSE, is deciding on how to measure improvement. KPIs—sometimes referred to as *metrics*—allow us to create evidence of the degree of success we achieve. Remember that a plan is theory, and all theories require evidence to support them. We start the process improvement with a plan, a theory, and rather than say "Oh god, I hope this works," a KPI-based approach measures the degree of success. If it is less than desired, we can tweak the approach, techniques, or tools to make it better. But we can't do that if we're not paying attention. For example, suppose that a key problem we are trying to address is defects in the requirements. A reasonable metric would be the defect density of the requirements. So as we create the requirements, an independent assessor looks for requirements defects; the ratio of defects to total number of requirements is the defect density. As we employ model-based requirements models and their functional analysis, we would expect this number to sharply decline. If it does not, perhaps we can change how we are working to improve it.

Pilot

The most common call I get for process improvement or MBSE adoption work usually starts with:

Caller	OMG, we're all gonna die!
Me	What? Again?
Caller	We've got this make-or-break project. If it fails, we'll have to shut the company down. We're already late, we've got flight tests in 6 months, and our system architecture doesn't work at all.

In such a situation, you don't have time for a gentle improvement to your methods, or running a pilot to gain skills to be used on later projects.

This is not my preferred approach. What I prefer is that we plan—long before catastrophes occur—for engineering capability improvement. Ahead of time, we assess and understand the set of concerns we want to address, we plan on acquiring the skills, tools, and techniques, and then we apply them to a modest project with a few people for a short period of time. The pilot should be simple enough to be done in a reasonable time but large and complex enough to demonstrate the effectiveness of the new improved approach and to allow the participants to hone their new skills. Once the pilot is complete, the team members can serve as experts to others in the enterprise-wide deployment of the new methods. An ideal pilot project is usually around 6–10 people for 6 months, but the size varies with the organization.

Deployment

At this point, we've got the skills; we've got the tools; we've practiced and honed our art (a bit a least); we've tweaked the approach to be highly effective in our target environment. Now, we can deploy these methods across the larger organization, including other teams and engineering sites. Since a number of people have honed their skills on the pilot programs, they can serve as evangelists to other project teams to help them come up to speed. We still have the original training and mentoring materials to help deploy the solution throughout the organization.

Adopting aMBSE isn't stumbling into the engineering environment, throwing practices and tools at problems that may or may not be real. Adopting aMBSE is itself an incremental agile project, with assessment, planning, piloting, and deployment phases.

1.4.5 The Rules (of Modeling)

This section gives a short list of modeling rules and guidelines. Feel free to add more, as you desire.

1. Every model should have purpose, intent, scope, language, accuracy, fidelity, and completeness. Let's be clear: we don't model so as to pick up girls, guys, or even cuddly pets.[17] We model for a reason. Each model should have a clear purpose and intent. What do you want to get out of this model? Better understanding of the requirements? Clear architectural specification? A platform to support simulation and analysis? The purpose and intent should lead to a clear scope (what's in the model and what's out). Models are specified in some language appropriate to their purpose, such as SysML or mathematics. To achieve their purpose, models have a need for a certain level of precision and fidelity. And finally, to achieve its purpose, enough of the scope of the model must be represented so that its intent may be realized.
2. Deploy and follow a modeling standards guideline. Modeling standards define standard ways of doing things in the model. You might start with naming conventions and model organizational templates but go on to provide guidance to improve readability and maintainability of the model, or its accessibility by various stakeholders. The greater the number of people using the models, the greater the benefit of modeling guidelines.
3. Use a core subset of the modeling language and extend only when necessary. UML and SysML—and any other modeling language complete enough to be generally useful—are complex. However, much of that complexity just gets in the way. Usually a relatively small subset of the language will be enough for most of your work; this is known as the 80/20 rule: 80% of the work can be done using 20% of the modeling language. This is a topic we'll discuss in more detail in Chapter 3.
4. Every diagram should answer a single question, support a specific analysis, or show a singular concept. In the process of MBSE, you will create models, all of which have too many elements to be shown in one diagram.[18] So you have to decide how to show the relevant model elements in subsets. One approach popular in the 1980s was to apply the 7 ± 2 rule,[19] which was just silly. The rule we recommend in the Harmony process is that every diagram should try to show a singular concept and should have all the model elements on it to support that mission.

---

[17] Although "Want to come up to my room and see my UML models?" is effective a *surprising* percentage of the time.

[18] Although I remember seeing hallways in the 1980s lined with A4 plotter paper in 4-pt font, 10s of meters in length attempting, unsuccessfully, to render entire aircraft models in a single diagram. Don't do that. It's a waste of our rainforests.

[19] This rule was that you should have 7 ± 2 elements on a diagram; any more and you should add levels of diagram hierarchy; any less and you should throw a few more unrelated elements on to the diagram. This was based on a 1957 study that showed people could remember 7 ± 2 things if you showed them a list and then took it away. This has *no relation whatsoever* to what we do when we model and has resulted in some horrendously unusable models.

5. Create as many diagrams as you have questions. This is a consequence of the previous rule. It's perfectly ok to have the same element on multiple diagrams (see "It's not about the diagrams, stupid," below).
6. Document your models. Models are *not* self-documenting. Diagrams should have comments on them describing their mission or purpose, preconditions, and postconditions. Model elements should have a description that gives us information as to their use, purpose, and scope.
7. Create a "Model Table of Contents" diagram at the top of your model with links to important parts. Modeling tools typically have a model element browser on the left side of the display. This is essentially an index of the model elements that is organized however you organized your models (typically in packages in SysML). You also need a table of contents to allow you to easily find areas of interesting and related data and views. This is best achieved with a Model Overview diagram that identifies these areas and has hyperlinks to important views related to that topic. The diagrams can also have "See also . . ." hyperlinks in comments to point to related elements of diagrams that might be of related interest. As models get larger, building in this kind of model navigability becomes increasingly important.
8. It's not about the diagrams, stupid (I might have a little energy on this topic :-)). It is common for neomodelers to focus on the diagrams; after all, it's how they enter in information into the model and it's how they usually view it. However, diagrams are just views of sets of elements that are held in the model repository. It is the repository that has the definitions and deep semantics of the system. The repository is truth. Diagrams are just shadowy reflections of truth. Ask Plato.
9. Drawing≠Modeling. I said it before and I'll say it again; this is one of the most important rules. To paraphrase Bruce Lee[20]: "Drawing is like a finger pointing to the moon [slaps the student]. Don't concentrate on the finger or you will miss all of the heavenly glory."
10. Be precise. Being precise means making statements in some language so that they accurately and unambiguously convey information with an appropriate exactness. When I say, "The control surfaces should flutter so the plane don't crash," I'm not being very precise. "Flutter the control surfaces at a rate of 50 ± 2 ms" is much more precise. The degree of precision is, of course, problem-specific. In requirements, this generally means that each functional requirement ("flutter the control surfaces") should be constrained by one or more QoS requirements ("at a rate of 50 ± 2 ms").
11. Be complete (enough). The model should have a clearly defined scope. It is important to stay within that scope in order to get all the work done in a timely fashion. However, within that scope, all relevant data should be included. For example, a requirements specification should generally avoid design information (out of scope) but should include all the functional and QoS requirements.

[20] *Enter the Dragon* (1973). A classic.

12. Be correct first; optimize later. Some people tend to focus far more on design efficiency and optimality than basic correctness. I believe this to be a fundamental error. A system needs to be *fast enough, light enough, cool enough* but beyond that I don't care so much. I've seen far too many systems that were very fast at doing the wrong thing. Don't let your system be one of those.
13. Focus initially on the normal case, but don't neglect errors, faults, and the general mayhem that may descend upon your system on a rainy day. Most people naturally focus on the normal behavior of the system but others become paralyzed by the myriad of ways that a system can fail. Focus first on normal, correct behavior and then incrementally add error and fault behaviors.
14. Be semantically complete. This means include things like preconditions, postconditions, invariants, assumptions, QoS, and constraints where applicable. Most requirements specifications omit this information entirely, necessitating the downstream engineers—with inadequate context—to make important system-level decisions.
15. Organize like you want to find things. While it doesn't matter greatly how you organize simple models, complex models and integrated sets of models require careful consideration as to how they are organized. This is important so that relevant information can be found and managed. It is crucial for the long-term management of the models. We will talk about this topic more at the end of Chapter 3.
16. Connect related views with navigable links. When working with models, you usually have to manipulate views and elements that are related in some important way. If you project links for these relations within your model, this will simplify the effort of making coherent updates to the models. Some of the relations are automatically built in; for example, the state machines of blocks on a block diagram are usually only a click away. Others may not be automatically created; a set of sequence diagrams that show the interactive behavior of a cooperative set of blocks may be linked to the block diagram by adding your own hyperlinks or dependency links.
17. Configuration manage your models. This is basic hygiene. As a model reaches various stable points, we can baseline the model and give it a configuration name or version number. This supports basic team collaboration and more advanced notions such as product line engineering.
18. Verify your models—early and often. Verification of models is a key message of this book. We do verification at three levels: unit, integration, and system. Unit verification should be done every few minutes—no longer than an hour between verification cycles. Integration of work from collaborating engineers should be done frequently as well—usually once per day. Verification of larger assemblies can be done weekly or monthly. Verifying your work frequently means that we can avoid much of the rework that plagues traditional systems engineering.

19. Break up large models into collaborations of related models. We talk about the systems engineering model but we typically mean a set of integrated models, each focusing on a different aspect, such as requirements, architecture, or safety, or at different levels of abstraction (such as system context, system, subsystem, or component). Within each of those areas of interest, large models can be broken down into smaller models to facilitate work. A basic recommendation is that once you get to 10 people working on a single model, consider breaking it down into a set of collaboration models.
20. Incrementally adopt modeling in small, verifiable steps. Not only should you verify your models, you should do it—more or less—continuously. Just like you brush your teeth after each meal and don't wait for the winter solstice for cleaning your teeth, perform model hygiene through verification every hour or even more frequently.

1.5 Summary

We haven't talked that much about agile methods yet but it is important to understand the scope and breadth of systems engineering as well as to understand a bit about the advantages of modeling. The next chapter will talk about agile methods in general and specifically about how it can apply to systems engineering. Following that, we'll have a brief introduction to SysML and then we'll get into the detail of what all this means and how to actually do it.

References

[1] INCOSE Systems Engineering Handbook. <http://www.incose.org/ProductsPublications/sehandbook>.
[2] UML Testing Profile. <http://utp.omg.org/>.
[3] IBM Rational Rhapsody Test Conductor Add On. <http://www.btc-ag.com/de/SID-186CB68E-779F203B/3005.htm>.
[4] B. Douglass, Powel Real-Time Agility, Addison-Wesley, 2009. <http://www.amazon.com/Real-Time-Agility-Harmony-Embedded-Development/dp/0321545494>.
[5] OMG Systems Modeling Language (SysML). <http://www.omg.org/spec/SysML/>.
[6] M. Friedenthal, R. Steiner, A Practical Guide to SysML, 2nd Edition: The Systems Modeling Language, OMG Press, 2011. <http://www.amazon.com/Practical-Guide-SysML-Second-Edition/dp/0123852064/ref=sr_1_2?ie=UTF8&qid=1404271802&sr=8-2&keywords=sysml>.
[7] T. Weilkiens, Systems Engineering with SysML/UML: Modeling, Analysis, Design, OMG Press, 2004. <http://www.amazon.com/Systems-Engineering-SysML-UML-Modeling/dp/0123742749/ref=sr_1_3?ie=UTF8&qid=1404271802&sr=8-3&keywords=sysml>.
[8] The UML Profile for Schedulability, Performance and Time. <http://www.omg.org/spec/SPTP/>.
[9] The UML Profile for MARTE: Modeling and Analysis of Real-Time and Embedded Systems. <http://www.omgmarte.org/>.

CHAPTER 2

What Are Agile Methods and Why Should I Care?

Chapter Outline

Agile methods are largely a response to increasing regimentation of software development and work that was only tangentially related to the development of the software itself. It is also a reaction to the fact that despite the burden of this additional work, the quality of the software is low and the software far too often doesn't meet the needs of its intended users. Although agile was originally conceived for small software projects, we will see that there is much to recommend it for other endeavors, including (and of great interest here) systems engineering.

From an overview perspective, agile methods are really about optimizing development along two dimensions—product quality and engineering efficiency. Many people think it's about what you DON'T do—you DON'T plan, document, fill out paper work, design, analyze, or create requirements. In actuality, agile is more about what you DO and the order in which you do them. Agile methods are meant to be adaptive and responsive to different situations and changing needs using objective evidence to guide how work it done.

Put another way, it isn't so much that you do different things when you do agile methods as much as the order and sequence of those things is changed. This facilitates early feedback as to the correctness and adequacy of the work and work products you create. For example, traditional methods[1] do a "breadth-first" approach to creating work products and defer the verification of those work products at least until they are complete, and often much later. Agile, on the other hand, incrementally verifies the work products as they are being created. That provides more immediate feedback as to the correctness of the work product and how well your process is helping you achieve your engineering goals.

I liken the agile approach to dental hygiene. Imagine that you want to ensure your "tooth quality" by applying the "tooth brushing quality step." Because you view this as important, at the end of every year, on December 31, you do a good and thorough job of brushing your teeth and verifying their quality, and then going to a dentist for tooth quality problem remediation. Much to your dismay, your tooth quality is pretty low and requires extraordinary measures (and no small amount of discomfort) to bring the quality up. That is how the traditional approach works with deferred verification.

Imagine instead performing this quality improvement and assessment step immediately after using your teeth (i.e., after meals). Through constant application of quality methods, the quality of your teeth remains high throughout the year. This is a more hygienic approach and avoids big quality problems more than identifying them late for defect removal.

[1] See Section 1.3.1 V-Model Lifecycle in the previous chapter.

In either case, you're performing quality assurance activities to both improve and verify quality but what is different is *when* those activities are performed. Agile methods perform quality assurance activities throughout the development of important work products rather than after they are completed. That is, when these activities are performed, we optimize defect avoidance rather than defect identification.

Oh, and Agilistas DO plan, document, fill out paper work, design, analyze, and create requirements. We'll talk about how those activities can be done in an agile systems engineering environment in some detail in this book.

2.1 The Agile Manifesto

A good place to start to understand agile methods is with the agile manifesto.[2] The manifesto is a public declaration of intent by the Agile Alliance, consisting of 17 signatories including Kent Beck, Martin Fowler, Ron Jeffries, Robert Martin, and others. Originally drafted in 2001, this manifesto is summed up in four key statements:

- Individuals and interactions over processes and tools
- Working software over comprehensive documentation
- Customer collaboration over contract negotiation
- Responding to change over following a plan.

A thing to note about the manifesto is that it states an emphasis, not an exclusion. We emphasize working software over documentation, but that doesn't mean that we don't write documentation. We emphasize responsiveness to change over dogmatically following a plan, but that doesn't mean that we don't plan. The point is to pay more attention to the things that really matter. Paying attention to meeting the customer's needs and creating correct software is more important than following the plan and writing the documentation, but it doesn't mean that these other aspects don't get any attention at all.

To support the statements of the manifesto, the Agile Alliance give a set of 12 principles. I'll state them here to set the context of the following discussion:

- Our highest priority is to satisfy the customer through early and continuous delivery of valuable software.
- Welcome changing requirements, even late in development. Agile processes harness change for the customer's competitive advantage.
- Deliver working software frequently, from a couple of weeks to a couple of months, with a preference to the shorter timescale.
- Business people and developers must work together daily throughout the project.

[2] http://agilemanifesto.org.

- Build projects around motivated individuals. Give them the environment and support they need, and trust them to get the job done.
- The most efficient and effective method of conveying information to and within a development team is face-to-face conversation.
- Working software is the primary measure of progress.
- Agile processes promote sustainable development. The sponsors, developers, and users should be able to maintain a constant pace indefinitely.
- Continuous attention to technical excellence and good design enhances agility.
- Simplicity—the art of maximizing the amount of work not done—is essential.
- The best architectures, requirements, and designs emerge from self-organizing teams.
- At regular intervals, the team reflects on how to become more effective, then tunes and adjusts its behavior accordingly.

Again, you can see the emphasis is on "solving the problem" by getting continuous customer and quality feedback rather than "following the plan." A plan is a good thing, but a plan is a theory and it needs to be supported with evidence. Agile methods are the epitome of an evidence-based approach rather than a theory (plan)-based approach. Of course, theories are good because they allow us to make predictions. But without evidence as to the correctness of our theory, they can lead us into all kinds of problems.

It is glaringly apparent that the agile manifesto and the 12 principles are about software development, and specifically about the development of IT, rather than embedded real-time software.[3] Somewhat predictably, the typical example is a team of three people working in a garage on a web site. It's not easy to see how an approach that works for them can be applied to other engineering domains, such as systems engineering.

The biggest obstacle for applying agile methods to systems engineering is that systems engineering is not software development. This is a more profound difference than might be obvious because the outcome of software engineering is *implementation* but the outcome of systems engineering is *specification.*[4] Furthermore, software implementation executes and is therefore testable. Specifications are generally written in natural language text and are therefore too ambiguous and imprecise to test directly. What does it even mean to "test a requirement" as a requirement anyway?[5] Additionally, software development teams can be very insular. They may interact with customers for IT systems (and agile methods encourage this) but they often don't interact with nearly as many different roles as does systems engineering.

---

[3] See Ref. [1] for an exception.

[4] Some SEs might be tempted to argue that the outcome of systems engineering is a *system* but we are focusing on the specification side of the systems engineering work, as discussed in Chapter 1. We won't be focusing on system integration, system verification, and system validation in this book.

[5] In this case, I don't mean to test that the resulting system correctly realizes the requirement but to show that the requirement itself correctly represents what the system must do to meet the customer need.

Another barrier to the application of agile methods in the systems engineering space is that agile methods have a very different approach to planning, Traditional planning usually completes before the start of systems engineering and outlines a detailed (and almost-by-definition incorrect) plan for system development. Traditional planning makes a number of invalid assumptions that lead inevitably to erroneous plans:

- Availability of all information relevant to the plan
- Infinite fidelity of plan-related information
- Invariance of plan-related information.

The resulting plans make assumptions about what work items will need to be done, how long they will take, and the level of quality and rework that will have to be performed. All of this is largely unknown at the start of the project. I refer to this planning approach as *ballistic planning* because it is like aiming and shooting a firearm at a (very) distant vaguely identified erratically moving target.

The agile alternative to this type of planning is to create a plan only detailed to the actual degree of information we have but is also reworked as we get a deeper understanding about the work to be done and as things change. In agile methods, we plan to replan. I call this approach *dynamic planning* because we have the expectation that we will refine our plans as more and better information becomes available. We will talk more about dynamic planning later in this chapter.

Since the Agile Manifesto and the 12 principles are so software-centric, let's restate the Agile Manifesto with a systems engineering focus:

- Individuals and interactions over processes and tools
- Verifiably correct specifications over comprehensive documentation
- Customer collaboration over contract negotiation
- Responding to change over following a plan.

The restated 12 principles for systems engineering might read like this:

- Our highest priority is to satisfy the customer through early and continuous delivery of specifications and systems that demonstrably meet their needs.
- Welcome changing requirements, even late in development. Agile processes harness change for the customer's competitive advantage.
- Deliver verified systems engineering work products frequently, from a couple of weeks to a couple of months, with a preference to the shorter timescale.
- Business people and systems engineers must work together daily throughout the project.
- Build projects around motivated individuals. Give them the environment and support they need, and trust them to get the job done.
- The most efficient and effective method of conveying information to and within a development team is face-to-face conversation or work products that execute (or simulate).

- Verified engineering data are the primary measure of progress.
- Agile processes promote sustainable development. The sponsors, engineers, and users should be able to maintain a constant pace indefinitely.
- Continuous attention to technical excellence and good design enhances agility.
- Simplicity—the art of maximizing the amount of work not done—is essential.
- The best architectures, requirements, and designs emerge from self-organizing teams.
- At regular intervals, the team reflects on how to become more effective, then tunes and adjusts its behavior accordingly.

2.2 Benefits of Agile Methods

The primary goal of agile systems engineering is to develop specifications that can drive downstream engineering to create a system that meets the customer's needs. It isn't to produce documentation. It isn't to attend meetings. It isn't to create schedules. It isn't to create productivity metrics. You may do all of these things during the pursuit of your primary goal, but it is key to remember those activities are secondary and only performed as a means of achieving your primary goal. Too often, both managers and systems engineers forget this and lose focus. Many projects spend significant effort without even bothering to assess whether that effort aids in the pursuit of the development of the system engineering data.

The second most important goal of an agile project is to enable follow-on systems development. This means that the previously developed system must have an architecture that enables the next set of features or extensions, documentation so that the follow-on team can understand and modify that system, support to understand and manage the risks of the development, and an infrastructure for change and configuration management.

The key benefits of agile methods to systems engineering are:

- Improved quality of engineering data
- Improved engineering efficiency
- Early return on investment (ROI)
- Satisfied stakeholders
- Increased project control
- Responsiveness to change
- Earlier and greater reduction in project risk.

Improved Quality of Engineering Data

As a systems engineer, this is the most obvious and important benefit of applying agile methods. Because agile methods employ practices for early and continuing verification of engineering data and specifications, they will contain fewer and less significant defects. Remember, true progress in systems engineering is not the production of work products just like true progress in software development is not the generation of more lines of code. True progress is the generation of *demonstrably correct* work products, just as true progress in software is the production of *demonstrably correct* implementation.

Improved Engineering Efficiency

Because of the emphasis on continuous verification of engineering work products, there is far less rework than in traditional approaches. Rework (known in lean methods as "waste") is the leading cause of inefficiency. Having to isolate the defects in the work product, throw existing work away and reengineer it is expensive.

Early Return on Investment (ROI)

Agile methods provide earlier ROI than traditional approaches because demonstrably correct engineering data and specifications are actionable, whereas data of unknown quality are not. In a traditional approach, when a Systems Requirement Specification (SRS) is completed, a System Requirements Specification Review (SRRS) is performed. In this task, hundreds to tens of thousands of requirements are evaluated by a team over a period of days to months. There are two big problems with this: first, reviewing thousands of requirements looking for defects is neither an effective nor efficient way to improve requirements. Furthermore, any defects identified are found after weeks to months of work and defect repair means not only rewriting the defective requirements but also looking at all related requirements that may be impacted. Because this effort is deferred, it is not only a larger effort, it is also more error-prone. Early feedback about the number of correct requirements is more valuable than late feedback.

Satisfied Stakeholders

Ultimately, we build systems to satisfy stakeholders, so this is an objective we would like to optimize. Stakeholders include not only the ultimate system users but purchasers, maintainers, testers, trainers, and manufacturing. Satisfaction is greatly improved by improving the quality of the work products and by working with relevant stakeholders throughout the process.

Increased Project Control

Many systems projects are out of control, at least to some degree. This is often because we are working with violated assumptions and data of questionable correctness. In traditional approaches, we track projects on the basis of conformance to plan rather than achievement of project objectives.[6] Agile methods track progress more against objectives than against the plan, giving us earlier indications when the project goes off the rails or when the plan is flawed.

---

[6] And no, they're not exactly the same thing.

Agile methods track with a variety of metrics (aka Key Performance Indices (KPIs)). A common agile metric is *defect density*—the number of defects per unit of work product or *velocity*—the amount of work (verified functionality) accomplished per unit time. By instrumenting your systems engineering project with appropriate metrics, you can gain a true understanding of the state of the project, giving you a much greater degree of control over it.

Responsiveness to Change

One of the things that traditional projects assume—which is known to be patently false—is that nothing will change. This assumption is so ingrained that most traditional projects have extremely heavyweight practices in place to handle the inevitable changes to requirements, needs, platforms, and environments. If you live in a volatile environment, then your approach should optimize your ability to adapt to change. Agilistas assume not only that they don't know everything but at least some of what they know will change in the future, so agile methods handle change much more gracefully than traditional approaches.

Earlier and Greater Reduction in Project Risk

Your lead engineer quits. Your server crashes, losing your design work. The effort to incorporate new technology is far higher than you expect. Hardware you are expecting to use in your design goes end-of-life. "Project risk" refers to things that threaten the successful completion of the project, and is always about things that you don't already know. While good traditional processes use risk reduction methods, in my experience most projects do not adequately address project risk.

Agile methods use a *risk list* or *risk management plan* to identify and manage these risks to improve the likelihood of project success; indeed one useful metric of progress is the Risk Burndown List. Since risk is always about stuff you don't know, agile methods employ work tasks—known as *spikes*—to learn that relevant information and then replan as necessary. It is intrinsic to the responsiveness to change that agile methods embody.

2.3 Applying the Agile Manifesto to Systems Engineering

In order to get the proposed benefits from agile methods in our systems engineering work, there are some key technologies and approaches we must incorporate. These core ideas will be realized by more precisely stated practices in subsequent chapters in this book, but I think it's useful to understand the overarching ideas.

2.3.1 Work Incrementally

Traditional waterfall and V lifecycles are, as previously mentioned, "breadth first," in that they complete all work in some area of concern before moving on. Incremental engineering approaches have been around for a long time (Barry Boehm calls this "spiral development" in Ref. [2]). The foundational concept of incremental engineering is to break up a big problem into a series of small problems that can be (mostly) independently verified. These increments are typically 4–6 weeks long, although in modern agile software development they are trending down to 1–2 weeks. At the end of each iteration, the work product(s) are verified and repaired (if necessary) and then more capability is added in the next iteration.

By providing feedback on progress, completeness, quality, and velocity on a regular basis, the incremental engineering approach improves both project control as well as product quality. The key points to properly realize incremental engineering are:

1. The work must be *linearly separable* into parts that may be verified more-or-less independently (that is, if some body of work is completed and then verified, subsequent iterations will require, at most, minor reworking of work already completed)
2. Divide the work up into five or more iterations, ideally each iteration being 2–4 weeks in length
3. Verify the quality of the work products at the end of each iteration and repair any major defects (minor defects may be repaired in subsequent iterations).

As a side note, most Agilistas believe that it is important to have a regularity to the increment timeframe, whether it is 2 weeks or 4 weeks. This forms a project "heartbeat" that should be precisely maintained throughout the project. The advantage is that this does ensure steady project progress. However, I prefer to vary the iteration length as much as ±25% so that coherent units of work can be performed.[7] This approach also ensures steady progress, but eases the verification by ensuring that the work progresses in coherent steps. Readers should feel free to use whichever approach they prefer.

2.3.2 Plan Dynamically

Three major problems with traditional planning are that (i) it assumes we know everything at the beginning, (ii) those things will never change, and (iii) "optimistic schedules"[8] are a useful way to motivate engineers. It is important to remember that planning is important but only if it is accurate.

Because we do know some things with some degree of accuracy, we can do some planning, but planning beyond the fidelity and scope of information we have is worse than a waste of time—it is actively misleading. And optimistic schedules are, to put it as kindly as I can, "management malfeasance."

[7] Not all use cases are exactly the same amount of work, after all.

[8] A euphemism for "intentionally wrong schedules."

Dynamic planning, as discussed here, is a two-tier planning approach during which the plan is expected to be evolved and refined throughout the project. The upper tier constitutes the major work units—the iterations, while the lower tier focuses on the work within the iterations.[9]

If we're going to enact the project as a series of increments, our plan should reflect that; that is, the plan should be organized primarily around the increments. The plan should identify the proposed work for the iteration as a part of its mission statement (see Section 2.4.8) and estimates for effort. This is the upper tier of the two-tier plan. The lower tier is a more detailed plan done for each iteration. This lower tier is created just prior to the initiation of the iteration.

It is crucial to understand that an engineering plan is like a scientific theory, and theories need to be supported and proven with evidence. We have an idea about what work needs to be done, how long it will take, how many people we have to put on it, and their relative skills and efficiencies. All of these ideas—except in hindsight—are approximate at best, and completely wrong at worst. One of the fundamental assumptions is the expected velocity of the project—how much work gets done per unit time. Usually, management overestimates the velocity and underestimates the amount of work, resulting in actual project execution that bears little resemblance to planned schedules. However, in the dynamic planning approach, we adjust these assumptions based on project evidence which means that our schedule 2 months into the project will generally be much more accurate and realistic than the original schedule.

2.3.3 Actively Reduce Project Risk

As mentioned earlier, project risk is all about stuff we don't know that can negatively impact our project.

Risk is defined to be the product of the severity of an outcome and its likelihood. In a risk management plan, we list the most likely and severe hazards to the successful completion of the project, do our best to quantify the risk of each and address them in priority order, highest risk first. We address risk with risk mitigation activities, commonly known as *spikes*. Since risk is all about things we don't know, a spike is an experiment used to verify or improve our understanding of the issue. If, after we have understood the issue, the risk of failure of that part of the plan is too high, we replan the portion of the project affected by the issue.

[9] By the way, it is perfectly reasonable to have some planned milestones at the end of selected iterations. For example, you might have a Preliminary Design Review (PDR) at the end of iteration 4 (of, say, 12 planned iterations), and a Critical Design Review at iteration 7. To schedule such milestones, it is enough to decide at what point enough information is known and verified to meet the objectives of the milestone.

For example, we might want to use a new high-speed 1000-Gbit bus being developed in a separate lab, but there is a chance that it won't be ready in time to use in our designs and the error rates of the technology may not be good enough for our needs. A suitable spike might be to use hand-built hardware components for a portion of the system design to test error rates while we simultaneously look at the factory schedule and the factory board drop-out rates to see if it is sufficiently likely to work for our project. If not, then perhaps we can rework our design to use multiple 100-Gbit buses to give us enough bandwidth.

2.3.4 Verify Constantly

> Law of Douglass #30: the best way not to have any defects in your system is not to put defects in your system.

The relevant question about Law #30 is "How do I do that?" The agile approach is *Test Driven Development* (TDD). As discussed in Chapter 1, TDD comes from agile software development wherein the (unit) tests for a piece of software are written before or at the same time as the software, and then the tests are applied as the software is developed. This is done continuously, so that every 20–60 min, the developing software is being verified. This can be applied in systems engineering as well, improving the quality of the work products, provided that we develop *testable work products*. That's the key and that's why I assert that modeling is essential for aMBSE since models can be made testable.

We verify our work products at three distinct levels. Unit-level verification is done by the originator (or sometimes a peer) and tests the work product statements individually. This is "in the small" testing and can be applied to systems requirements, architectures, interfaces, and control models. The second level is integration level, where related work components, usually developed by different engineers, are brought together to ensure that they are consistent with each other (see the next section). The third level is system-level verification where the entire work product is verified as a coherent whole. This is normally done incrementally, so that at subsequent increments, the work product becomes increasingly complete. The previous system-level tests become regression test cases and new system-level tests are added to verify the new content.

2.3.5 Integrate Continuously

Integration, in this context, means to bring different parts of a work product or different work products together and verify that they are consistent. In software, this is straightforward because software defines interfaces, and integration testing largely consists of testing data and control flows that exercise those interfaces. With models, there may be explicit interfaces or there may be implicit relations that must be verified to ensure consistency.

Consider the example of two use cases.[10] Good use cases are independent in terms of the requirements allocated to them; that is, a requirement is only allocated to a single use case. However, sometimes use cases are only mostly independent and there may be subtle relations between them that result in inconsistencies.

2.3.6 Use Case 1: Find Tracks in Airspace

Req 1.1: The system radar shall return radar hits every 10 ms.
Req 1.2 The system shall maintain a complete log of data available to the navigation system for every identified track up to a maximum of 60 min.

2.3.7 Use Case 2: Perform Periodic Built in Test (PBIT)

Req 2.1: The system shall perform a system PBIT every 10 s that shall result in turning off radar tracking for no more than 500 ms.
Req 2.2 The PBIT shall zero out track history data so that hardware memory tests can be performed.

In this quick example, requirements 1.1 and 2.1 are in conflict, as are requirements 1.2 and 2.2 even though they are in different use cases.

In a system of thousands of requirements, these subtle conflicts might be missed with a semantic review. However, they can be caught by verification through testing of the requirements themselves.

The normal way we verify a use case through testing is to construct an executable model for each use case. Then through execution or simulation, we demonstrate that the outputs and outcomes of the system executing the use case achieve objectives stated by the requirements. This wouldn't find the conflicts above, however, because each use case model is executed separately. However, if we think there is a possibility of conflict we can execute the two use case models integrated together. A conflict means that by definition some outcome or output will be incorrect if we execute these two models together. The conflict between Req 1.1 and 2.1 will be discovered when we see the break in radar hits that happen when the PBIT is executing. The conflict between Req 1.2 and 2.2 will show up when we find that we can no longer access history data after the PBIT.

Similarly, such an integration test can be applied to architecture or other work products that can be made testable.

---

[10] We'll talk a lot about use case modeling in Chapter 4.

2.3.8 Validate Frequently

Validation is distinct from verification. *Verification*, in this context, means that a work product contains what we think it should, in whatever language we state it. *Validation* means that the work product meets the users' needs. Because requirements may be incorrect, it is possible for a fully verified system to not provide the expected value to the stakeholders of the system. The traditional method of validation of systems engineering work products is to review textual specifications with the customer. As with system verification, while this approach has some value, it is problematic as well and will not generally find all defects and issues. Showing the users the technical specification (model) is even more unlikely to be helpful because most stakeholders are not systems engineers or savvy in the ways of techjitsu.

However, since we are building executable specifications, we can show them the execution of those models without revealing all of the hairy innards of the technical specification. We can capture simulation runs as sequence diagrams, for example, which can be easily consumed by non-technical stakeholders. We can use the simulation runs to explore "what if" scenarios as to what exactly requirements state or how exactly the components of the architecture interact in possible obscure situations. Based on this feedback, we can then refine the requirements, so that the final resulting system will be one more suitable to their needs. This progressive refinement of engineering data is one thing that distinguishes traditional and agile systems engineering.

2.3.9 Modeling Is Essential for aMBSE

As we've discussed, constant verification and frequent validation are key aspects of an agile process. To implement an agile systems engineering approach, we must create work products that are precise enough to ensure that we are building the right system. We must be able to ensure this with not only semantic review, but also testing and formal analysis. That means we need precisely stated models that allow for simulation, execution, test, and mathematical analysis.

2.4 Agile Best Practices for Systems Engineering

We've talked about the agile manifesto and principle and how this impacts how we do our work. In this section, we'll discuss in more detail a number of key practices for aMBSE. These practices are not entirely independent and together they coalesce into the Harmony Agile Systems Engineering Process.

2.4.1 Incremental Development of Work Products

This practice focuses on the incremental development, verification, and validation of work products. This incremental development of work products occurs in step with the product

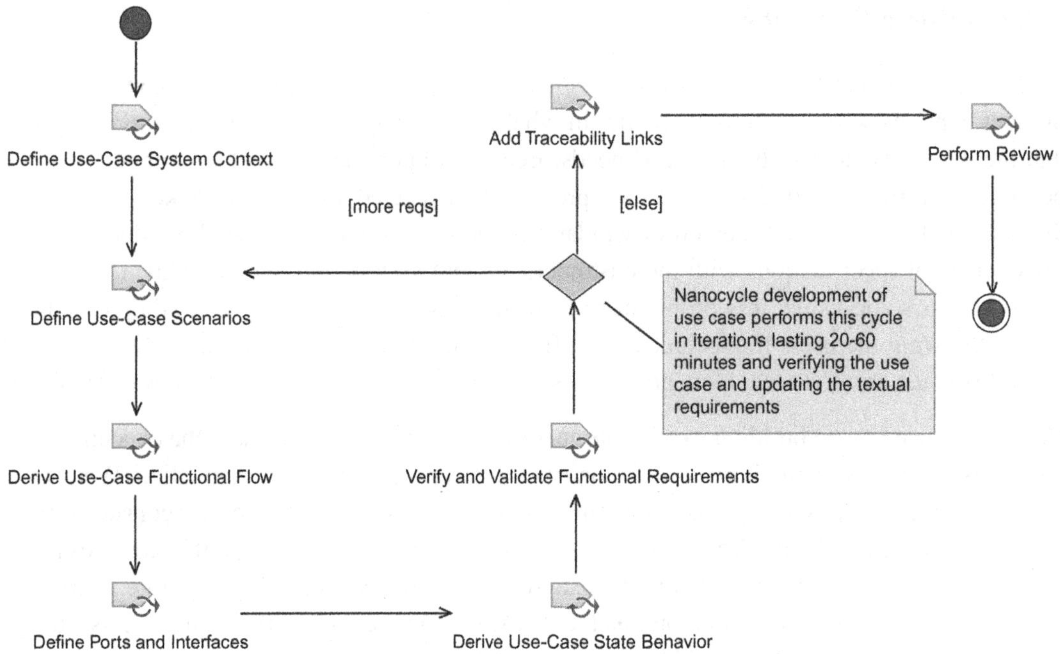

Figure 2.1
Nanocycle development of system requirements.

iterations. At the end of each systems engineering iteration, some work products are produced, such as a set of requirements, a use case model, an architectural definition, a set of interfaces, and so on. The system is not yet complete, but because of the linear separability, these work products can be verified that they are individually correct and that the integration of those elements works as expected. Further, these evolving products can be validated with the stakeholders using a combination of semantic review and execution/simulation. Questions as to the exact meaning of a stakeholder need or how those needs have changed can be addressed far earlier than in a traditional process. This reduces waste and rework while improving quality.

2.4.2 Continual Verification of Work Products

Just as brushing one's teeth is a highly frequent quality activity, continual verification of engineering data and the work products that contain them is nothing more than hygienic behavior. If the best way to avoid having defects in a system or work product is to simply not put it in there in the first place, this is the practice by which that is accomplished.

For example, Figure 2.1 shows a part of the Harmony aMBSE process for analyzing and refining requirements.[11] During the activity *Scenario-Based Use Case Analysis Workflow*, an

[11] This process will be discussed in detail in Chapter 4.

executable use case context is defined. This models the actors and the use case under analysis as SysML blocks and identifies the appropriate relations among them to support model execution. Then we develop some scenarios, derive a functional flow model, add or refine ports and interfaces in the context model, derive state-based behavior, and verify—through execution—that we've modeled the system behavior properly. *Then we add more*—more requirements, more details on the existing scenarios, more states, etc. This workflow is a very tight loop known as a *nanocycle*, and is usually anywhere from 20–60 min in duration. This constant verification of our models—and our understanding of the requirements—improves the requirements and the models because they are updated, elaborated, and modified as our understanding deepens and we discover mistakes and defects in the requirements and models. In practice it is fairly hard to get a complex use case model right if you defer its verification but it is relatively easy to do so with continual verification.

2.4.3 Executable Requirements Models

As a consequence of the need to perform continual verification of the models as well as verify the models at the end of each iteration, we must build verifiable things. Free text is very difficult to verify, but well-formed models are easy. Thus, we capture the information stated in the requirements free text as formal models to support the verification of the correctness of those requirements and to deepen our understanding of them.

Since functional requirements focus on a system's inputs, the required transformations of those inputs, and its outputs, a state machine is an ideal representation of functional requirements. The inputs can be represented as events on the state machine, complete with values passed from the external actors. Actions on the state machine provide the means to specify both the input–output transformations and the delivery of the output events (along with any necessary data). Alternatively, an activity model can be used if desired although activity models are better at specifying deterministic flows than they are at receiving and processing asynchronous events, which are typical of most systems.

We group requirements into use cases, so each use case will have its own state machine or activity model.

For a state behavioral example, consider an anti-lock braking system (ABS) as shown in Figure 2.2. This diagram shows the related requirements for the use case.

These requirements don't specify the inner workings of the system but they do specify externally visible behavior, as well as inputs and outputs of the system while executing the use case. Figure 2.3 shows the associated state machine representing those requirements.[12]

[12] Note that the chXXX events are UML/SysML change events and are initiated when the relevant parameter changes.

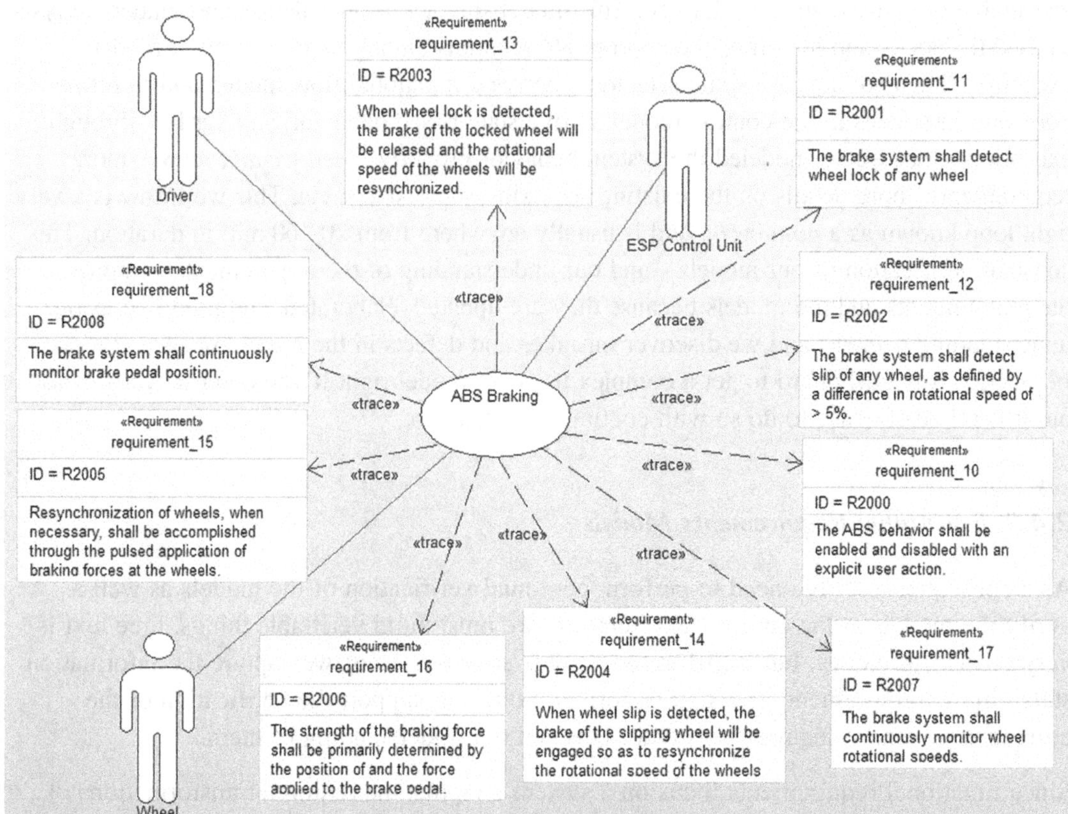

Figure 2.2
ABS braking use case.

For an activity example, consider an automotive wiper blade system with a use case wipe automatically (Figure 2.4).

This might be expressed by the following executable activity model (some requirements are shown on the diagram) shown in Figure 2.5.

In either case, the behavioral model represents the requirements, not the implementation. The advantage is that the behavioral model can be verified through execution and formal analysis, which helps to uncover defects in the requirements early, when the cost of their repair is far lower than later in the project.

2.4.4 Model-Based Specification Linked to Textual Specification

Text can be very expressive, however it suffers from imprecision and ambiguity. Text is wonderful at explaining why something should be done, providing rationale, and providing

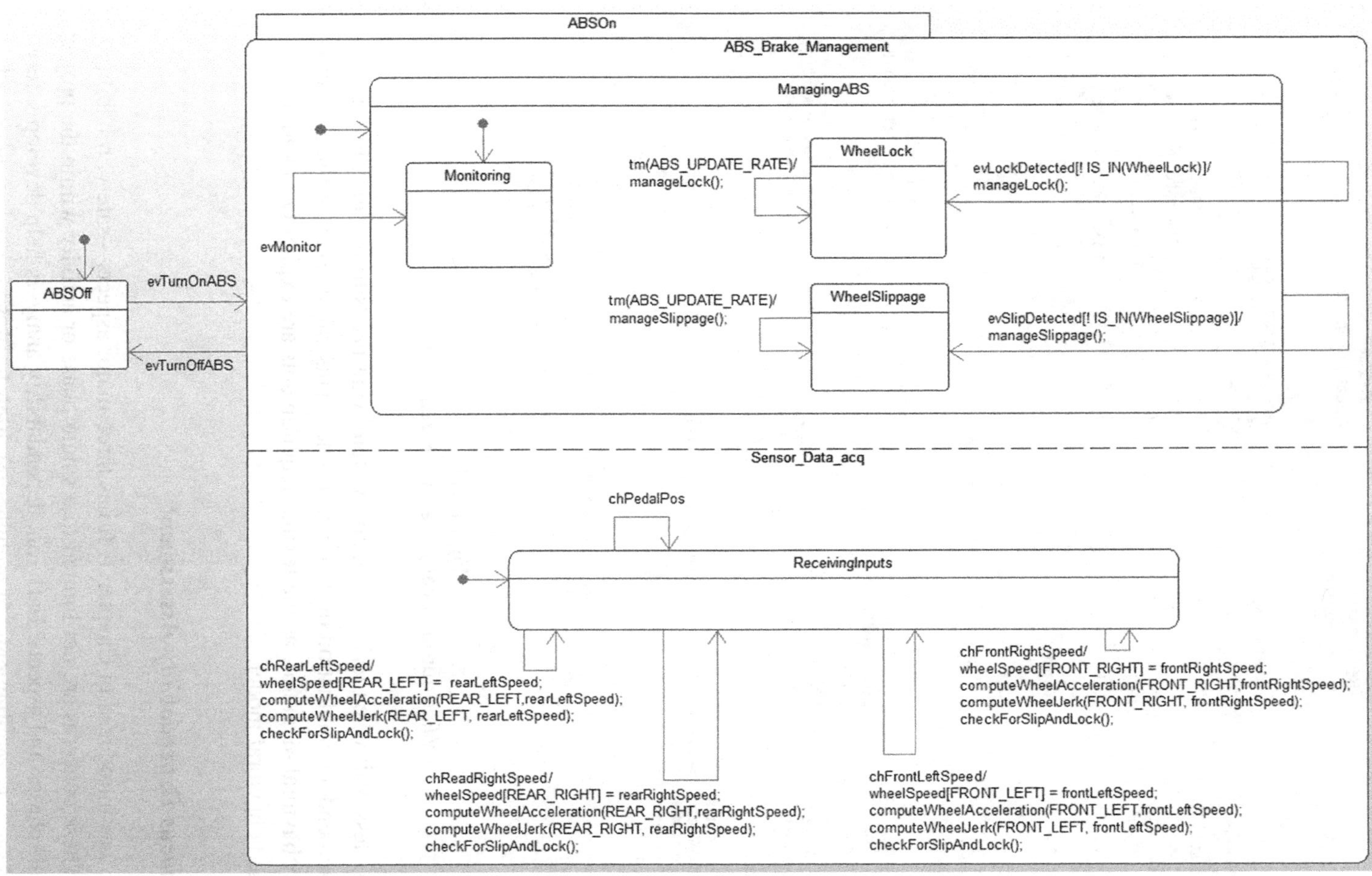

Figure 2.3
ABS braking use case state machine.

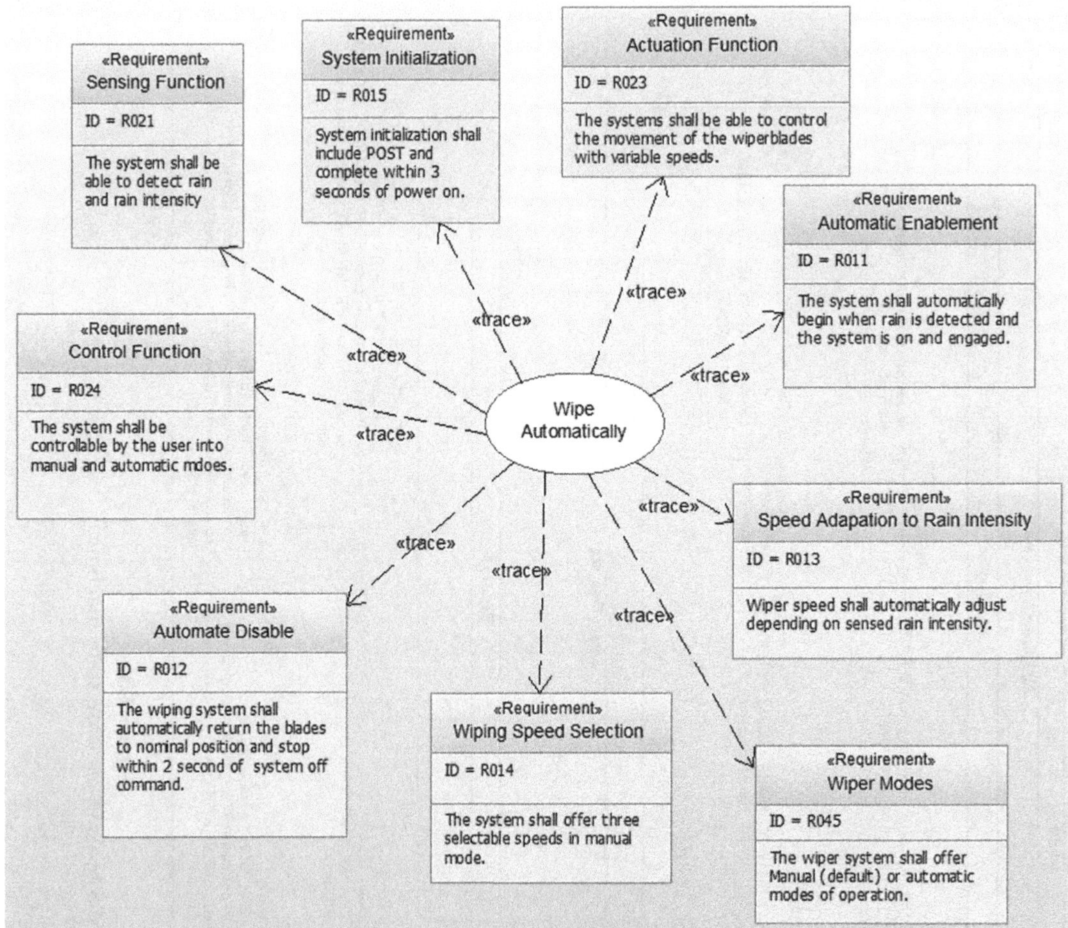

Figure 2.4
Wipe automatically use case & requirements.

context. It fairs less well when trying to precisely state what needs to be done. For this reason, I recommend a combination of both approaches. This can be seen in the previous use case and behavioral diagrams, as the textual requirements are explicitly linked to elements in the behavioral model.

2.4.5 Continuous Dependability Assessment

Dependability was introduced in Chapter 1. It has three major aspects—safety, reliability, and security. These concerns are not limited to a single phase or activity within the project but permeate all phases and aspects. Early on, dependability analyses help develop safety, reliability, and security requirements. In architecture, high-level design decisions must be

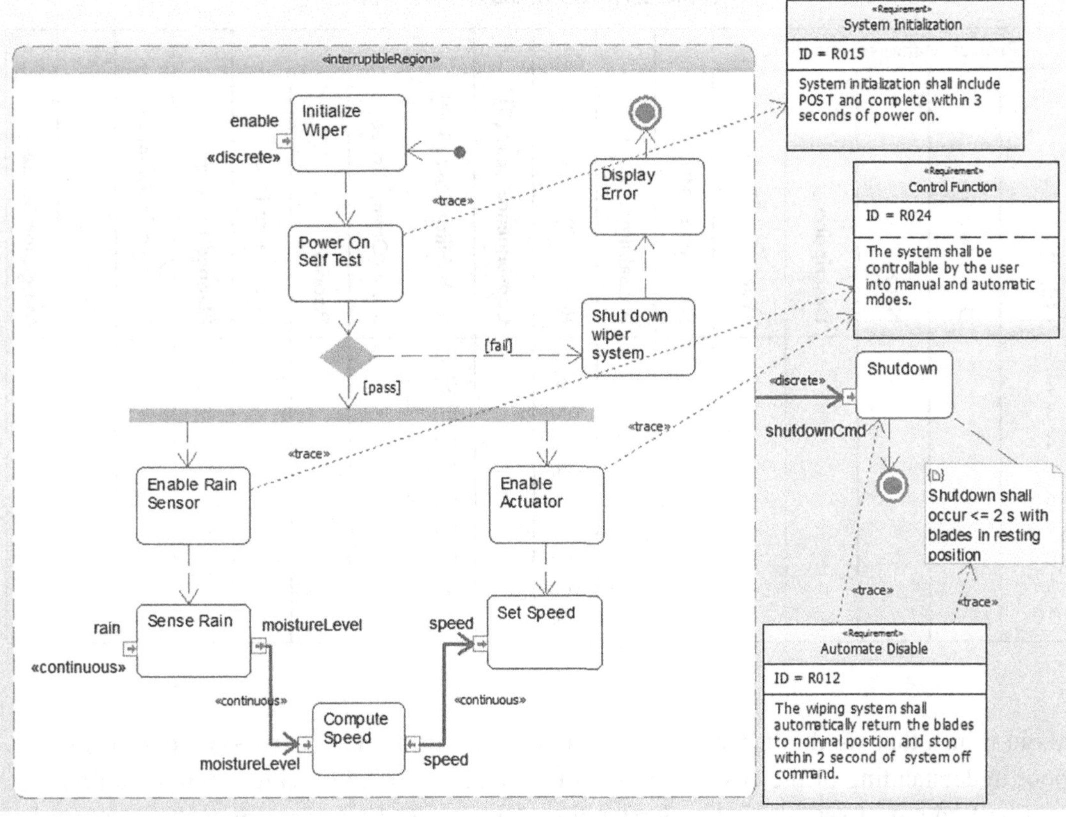

Figure 2.5
Wipe automatically use case activity model.

assessed for their impact on the dependability, and very often this analysis results in additional requirements being added. Even after the hand off to downstream engineering, the detailed design and implementation can also impact dependability and may again result in additional requirements to ensure that the resulting system is safe, reliable, and secure.

2.4.6 Active Project Risk Management

I've been involved in hundreds of projects, in a variety of roles, such as project manager, team leader, architect, safety assessor, systems engineer, and software developer. I've seen projects succeed victoriously and I've seen projects fail catastrophically. In my experience, the leading cause of project failure is poor project risk management.

In this context, project risk is the possibility that the project will fail in some way, such as failing to be a system which meets the needs of the stakeholders, exceeding budget, exceeding schedule, or being unable to get necessary safety certification. Risk is always

Table 2.1: Risk management plan

Project Management Plan																		
Risk ID	Date Identified	Name	Description	Type	Severity (1–10)	Probability (0.0–1.0)	Risk (S*P)	Consequence Cost ($)	Probability Cost ($*P)	State (Open, Closed)	Priority	Occurrence Date	Planned Iteration	Impacted Stakeholder	Owner	Mitigation Strategy		
1							0%		0.0									
2							0%		0.0									
3							0%		0.0									
4							0%		0.0									
5							0%		0.0									
6							0%		0.0									
7							0%		0.0									
8							0%		0.0									
9							0%		0.0									
10							0%		0.0									

about things that we don't know. This includes missing or misunderstood requirements, poor understanding of the cost and time of development, not knowing when a required part will go out of service, not understanding the impact of using a new technology, and so on. Active risk management identifies such concerns, quantifies them, and then undertakes activities—known as spikes—to improve our understanding so that we can account for them.

In its most basic form, risk is the product of two values; the likelihood of an undesirable outcome and its severity:

$$\text{Risk} = \text{likelihood}^{*}\text{severity}$$

The Risk Management Plan (also known as the Risk List) identifies all known risks to the project above a perceived threat threshold. This is usually modeled within a spreadsheet with fields such as those shown in Table 2.1.

The columns in the risk management plan provide additional data about the risk:

- Type may be: (Business, Resource, Technical, Schedule, Certification, Manufacturing)
- Severity is scaled from 1 (low risk) to 10 (blocking)
- Probability is scaled from 0.0 (impossible) to 1.0 (certain)
- Risk is the product of the Severity and the Probability

- Consequence cost is the dollar value (if any) associated with the risk
- Probability cost is the probability of the risk times the consequence cost
- State may be: (open, scheduled, closed, avoided, obsolete, mitigated}
- Priority is optional, as most often the risks are ordered by risk magnitude. This column exists when priority may be some other value than this
- Occurrence data is when the spike (risk mitigation activity) was completed
- Planned iteration is in which iteration the spike is scheduled to be executed
- Impacted stakeholder identifies which stakeholders are potentially affected
- Owner is the person assigned to perform the spike
- Mitigation strategy describes how the risk will be mitigated.

Practically this means that

1. Initially, there will be an effort to identify and characterize project risks during project initiation
2. Risk mitigation activities (spikes) will be scheduled during the iteration work, generally highest risk first
3. At least once during each iteration, risks will be reassessed to update the states for risks addressed during the spike and looking ahead for new project risks.

2.4.7 Model-Based Hand Off to Downstream Engineering

I've seen that in many companies, systems engineers work very hard creating engineering data to hand off to downstream engineering (typically electronics, mechanical, hydraulics, pneumatics, and software). This hand off is performed as a "throw over the wall" and the system engineers then scamper for cover because the format of the information isn't particularly useful to those downstream of systems engineering. I propose that if we systems engineers spend effort to create precise and accurate engineering data in models, then we should hand off models, and not just textual documents generated from them.

The problem is, however, that we can't just hand them the systems engineering models. The implementation disciplines need different information or information represented in different forms than systems engineers. For the reason, the handoff to downstream engineering isn't an event; rather, it is a workflow where we convert and organize the relevant systems engineering data into data needed and consumable for detailed design and implementation. Chapter 8 is devoted to the discussion of this workflow.

2.4.8 Dynamic Planning

Traditional project planning usually amounts to organizing an optimistic set of work estimates into a linear progression with the assumptions that everything is known and accounted for and there will be no mistakes or changes. This is why traditional project planning has such a poor track record. Often, the "correct answer" is predefined, independently of the work required. As Capers Jones puts it

> "Arbitrary schedules that are preset by clients or executives and forced on the software team are called 'backward loading to infinite capacity' in project management parlance. The essence of the phrase is that irrational schedules trigger more disasters than any other known phenomenon." [3]

A plan is a theory, and theories need to be supported with evidence. The big lie of traditional planning is that it is something that can be performed once, and then you're done. Plans make all sorts of assumptions in the face of incomplete data, such as the work that needs to be done, obstacles that will appear along the way, quality of developed work products and engineering data, and efficiency (known as *velocity* in agile-speak) of generating those data. For this reason, I refer to traditional planning as *ballistic* in nature. A bullet, once fired, goes where it will subject to forces we may or may not have accounted for, and our ability to modify its flight path is strictly limited.

An alternative approach is dynamic planning, or what I also call *guided project enactment.* In this approach we make a plan (or several) but not beyond the fidelity of information that we have. We do try to identify what we don't know and plan to upgrade the plan when that information becomes available. In this way, planning is continuous throughout the project and is dynamically updated based on evidence.

Being modified on evidence also means that we have to seek such evidence. We do this through the application of project metrics—measurements made to verify our assumptions and gather information about how the project is actually proceeding, rather than just assuming that it will follow a correct ballistic path. This is called dynamic planning because we plan to dynamically replan as we learn more and as things change.

Agilistas tend to avoid Gantt charts and PERT diagrams and prefer to estimate relative to other tasks rather than provide hours and dates. Methods such as Planning Poker (see Refs [4] or [5]) are used to obtain consensus on these relative estimates.

That's understandable but unacceptable in many business environments. I personally like Gantt charts but use statistical methods to improve estimation and then update the schedules based on actual evidence of project success. To construct an initial schedule I basically do the following:

- Identify the tasks that need to be performed
- For each task
  - Identify the 50% estimate—that is, an estimate that you will beat 50% of the time
  - Identify the 80% estimate—that is, an estimate that you will beat 80% of the time (also known as the pessimistic estimate)

- Identify the 20% estimate—that is, an estimate that you will beat only 20% of the time (also known as the optimistic estimate)
- Compute the used estimate as $E_{working} = \frac{E_{20\%} + 4E_{50\%} + E_{80\%}}{6} E_c$ where E_c is the *estimator confidence factor*, the measured accuracy of the estimator
- Identify task dependencies
- Assign resources (workers) to tasks

- Construct the "working schedule" from the $E_{working}$ estimates
- Construct the "customer schedule" from the estimates using $E_{80\%}{}^{*}E_c$
- Construct the "goal schedule" from the estimates using $E_{20\%}{}^{*}E_c$.

That is the starting point for project planning. We have a working schedule which is as accurate as we can make it (and we expect to update based on measured velocity and quality). We have a schedule we give to the customer that we will make 80% of the time (far better than industry average). We have a goal schedule that we are unlikely to meet but we can incentivize.

Now as we enact the project, we monitor how we're doing against project goals and against the project plan. If, for example, we find that we average 20% slower task completion rates than in our working schedule, we adjust the E_c factor and recompute the schedule. As we discover tasks that we missed in the initial plan, we add them and recompute the schedule. As we adapt to changes by modifying the tasks or performing rework, we update and recompute the schedule.

We won't talk much about project management in this book beyond this section. This book focuses on the technical aspects of model-based systems engineering and performing those tasks in an agile way.

2.5 Putting It All Together: The Harmony Agile MBSE (aMBSE) Process

A process is a set of practices integrated with a definition of worker roles and work products. The Harmony aMBSE process integrates the practices discussed in the previous section. This section shows the overview of the process with little description, as the process details are delved into as we go through the remainder of the book, starting in Chapter 4. Nevertheless, outlining the process here provides a map of how the practices and workflows all fit together.

Figure 2.6 shows the overall structure of the Harmony Agile Model-Based Systems Engineering process. After project initiation, we see the normal system engineering activities (which will be detailed below): define stakeholder requirements, systems requirements definition and analysis, architectural analysis, architectural design and handoff to downstream engineering. A difference between this process and a traditional V process is the path labeled "[more reqs]"; if there are more requirements, this loop of activities is done

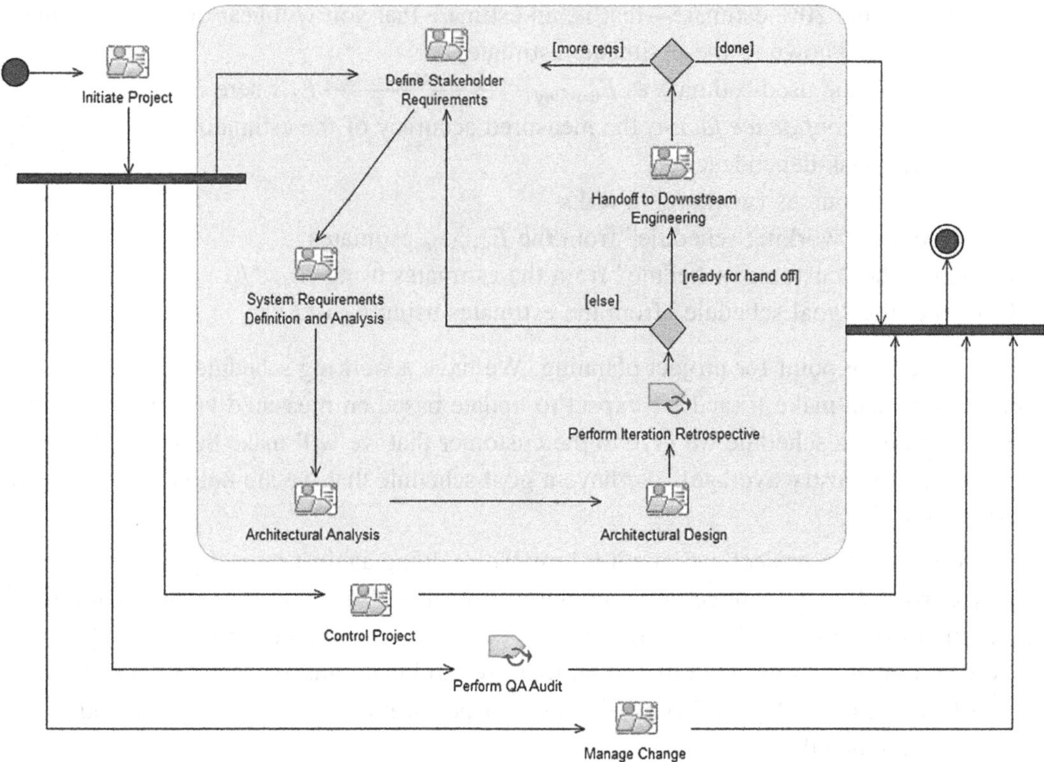

Figure 2.6
Harmony aMBSE delivery process.

again. In fact, a traditional V process is simply this process cycle done once. However, the power of the approach is that we can do this many times, handing off incrementally developed engineering data to downstream engineering for development.

The amount of work done per iteration loop can vary widely. One extreme, as discussed in Chapter 1, is to just do it once. The other extreme is to do an iteration for each use case (the incremental approach identified in Chapter 1). For the most part, projects I've been involved with have been somewhere in the middle; a small number of use cases are developed and handed off together—a hybrid incremental approach. The nature of the project will determine the best strategy and the size of the increments. Generally speaking, the greater the risk associated with the hardware, the larger the size of the system engineering increments.

Many inexperienced agile practitioners look at Figure 2.6, and think "WATERFALL!" but that doesn't take into account the loops that occur at different timeframes. The most obvious loop in the figure is the big one that iterates over the requirements one use case (or

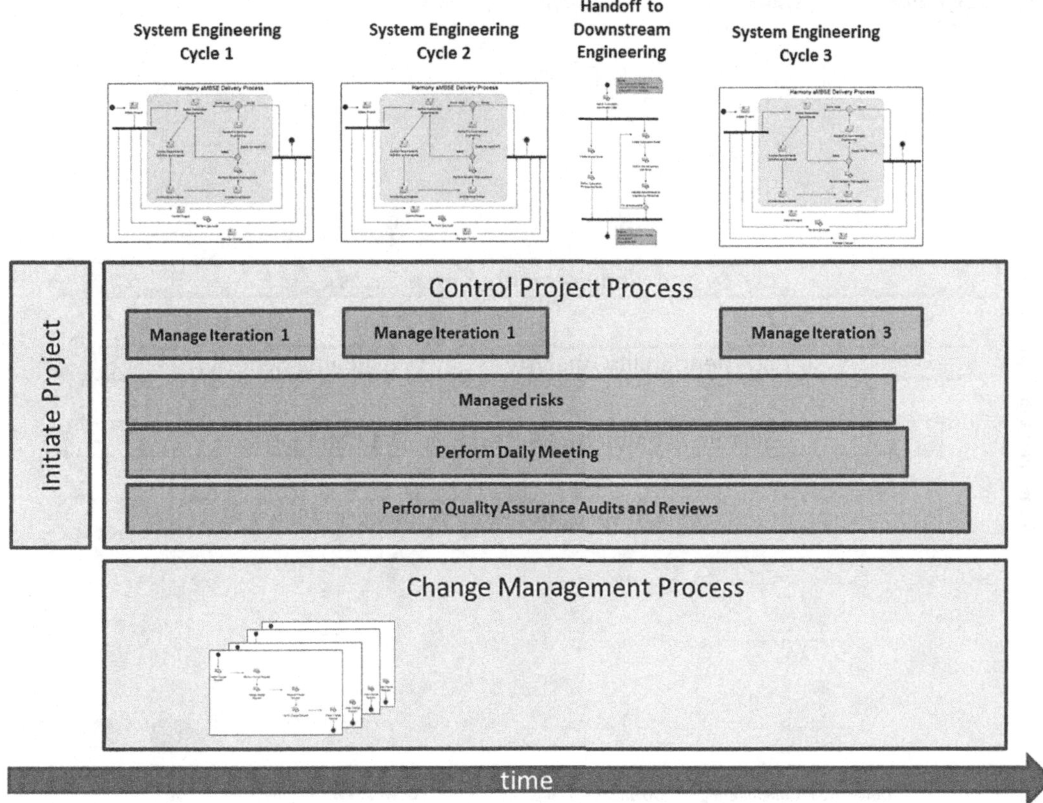

Figure 2.7
System engineering iteration timeline.

a small number of use cases) at a time, optionally hands off to development teams, and works on the next set of capabilities, features, and use cases. Figure 2.7 shows how Figure 2.6 might look if we add the time dimension.[13] In the figure, a handoff doesn't occur until iteration 2. In the meantime, the activities of project management, risk management, and quality assurance activities proceed in parallel. The change management process is also in parallel but is more episodic and is done whenever a change in existing data or need is determined.

The integration of the system engineering workflow with downstream engineering (electronic, mechanical, and software design) is better seen in Figure 2.8, which "unrolls the loop" to show how the system engineering work takes place in iteration cycles, updating

[13] I like to thank Barclay Brown of IBM for his recommendation to add the time dimension leading to Figures 2.7 and 2.8.

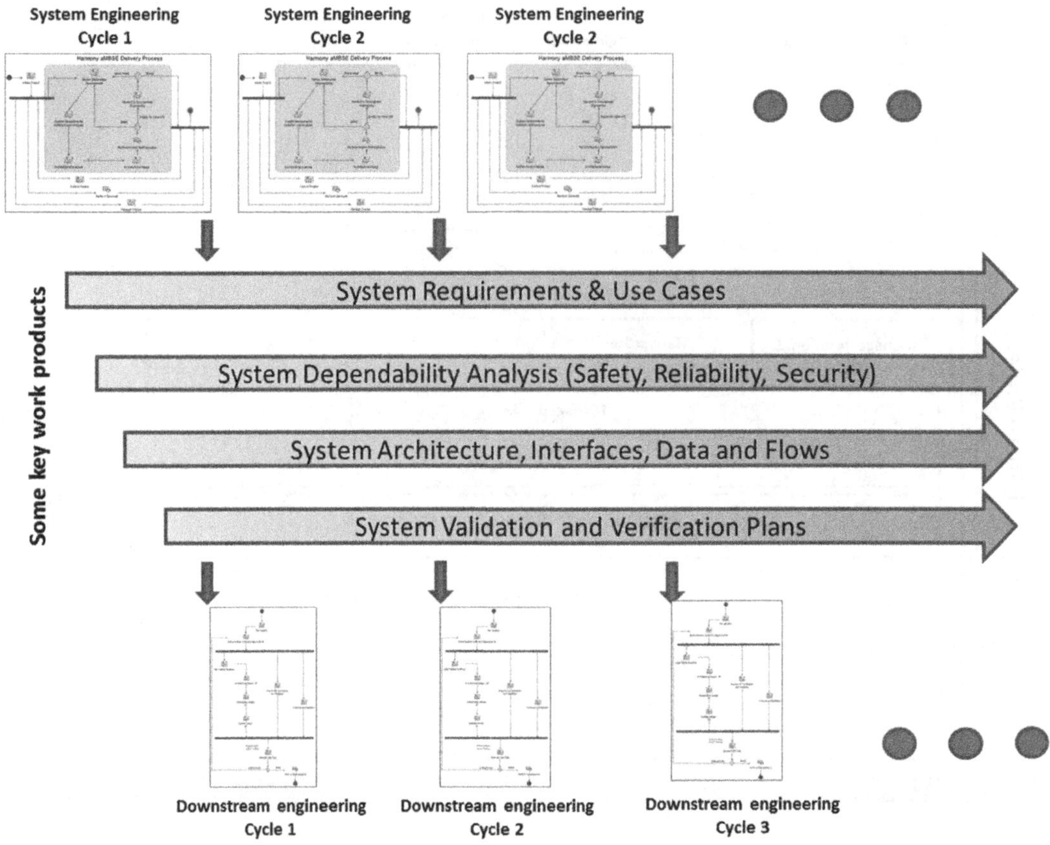

Figure 2.8
Overall project timeline.

evolving engineering data sets (such as requirements, architecture, dependability analyses, and test plans) and these engineering data are used to guide the development activities by "downstream engineering."

In this book, we'll detail the activities within the system engineering iteration. The details of the downstream engineering cycle are discussed elsewhere [1].

2.5.1 Initiate Project

The initiate project activity consists of a set of largely parallel tasks, as shown in Figure 2.9.

On the left we see the tasks to identity stakeholder use cases and then prioritize them. This can be done after stakeholder requirements are identified but I prefer to do some high-level thinking about the use cases first, although this does mean that I may have to add or

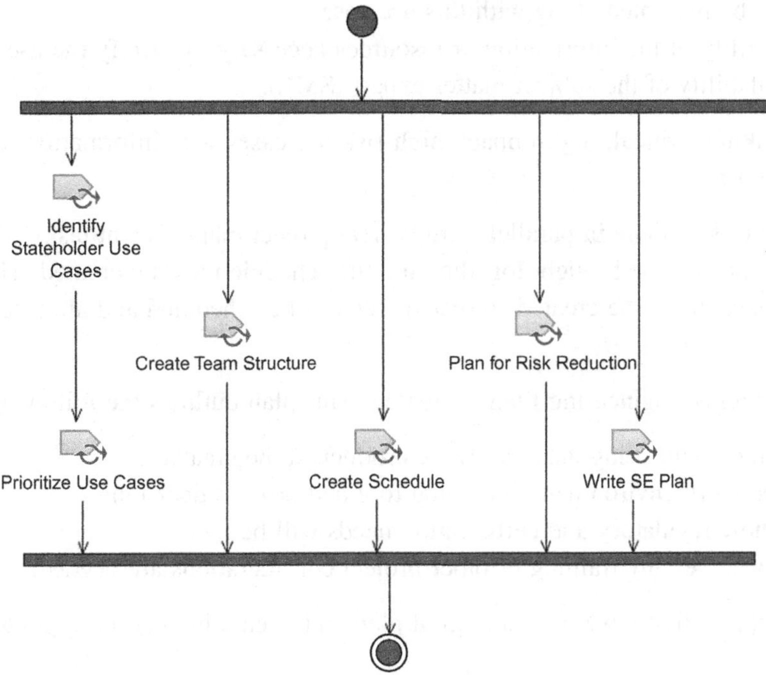

Figure 2.9
Initiate project activity.

remove use cases later as I start the requirement gathering process. At this point, I identify the use cases relevant to all the identified stakeholders and create a mission statement for each one (the requirements themselves will come in the next activity).

The use case mission statement format I like to use is

- Use case name
- Purpose—what is the value to the stakeholder(s)?
- Description—what kind of input–output data and control transformations are needed?
- Preconditions—what is true before these set of behaviors run?
- Postconditions—what do we need to be true after these behaviors have run?
- Invariants—what assumptions are we making?

Modeling tools provide a description field for the use cases and I populate that description with this use case data.

The priority determines the order in which use cases will be specified and possibly developed and delivered to the customer. As for priority, there are a number of factors to consider, such as:

- The benefit to the stakeholder(s), such as useful, important, or critical
- The architectural impact of the use case, such as none, extension, reorganization

- The risk to be mitigated along with this use case
- The availability of the information or resources necessary to specify the use case, such as the availability of the subject matter expert (SME).

Generally speaking, critical, high-impact, high-risk use cases with information available should be done first.

The next three tasks—done in parallel—are typical project management tasks. The team to perform the work must be brought together and the schedule must be created. The risk management plan should be created so that spikes can be scheduled and allocated to team members.

Finally, the Systems Engineering Plan is created. This plan outlines the following:

- Identifies the engineering data and work products to be created
- Defines the work environment, including tool and process decisions
- Specifies how regulatory and certification needs will be met
- Identifies whether any training or other project considerations are needed.

At the end of this activity, we have an initial plan and a team hungering to get to work. So, let's do it.

2.5.2 Define Stakeholder Requirements

The workflow for the define stakeholder requirements activity is shown in Figure 2.10.

The first task is to identify all of the relevant stakeholders. Typical stakeholders include:

- Primary users and operators of the system
- Secondary users and operators of the system
- Personnel responsible for
  - System installation
  - On-site system integration
  - System configuration
  - System maintenance
  - System decommissioning
  - System disposal
  - System manufacture
  - System certification
- Purchaser (customer)
- Testers.

These are the people the system must satisfy and you must work with these stakeholders if you want to meet their needs. Remember, however, that the scope of this activity need not

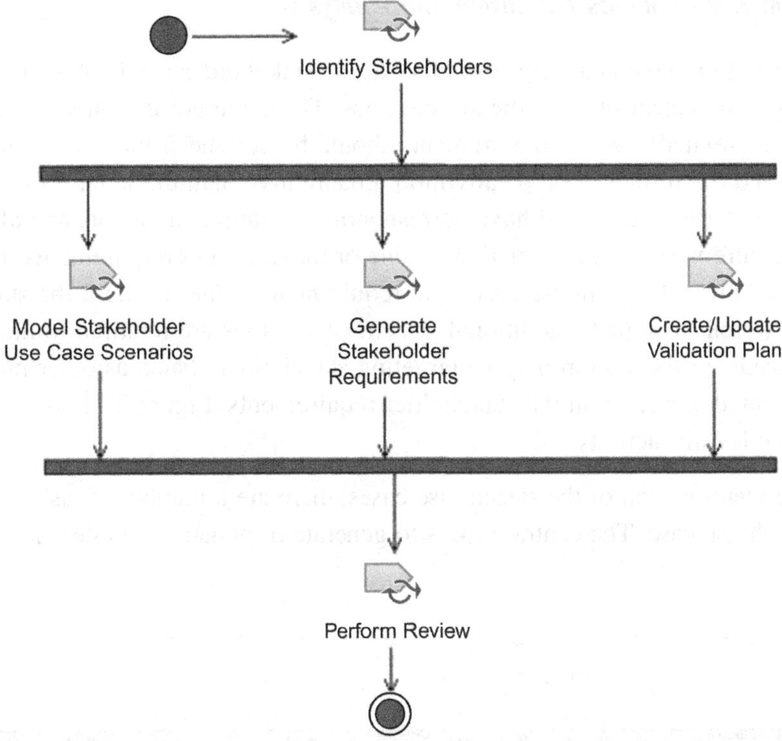

Figure 2.10
Define stakeholder requirements.

be the entire system. In fact, it is usually applied to one or a small number of use cases at a time. This means you might well focus on operational (functional) requirements early and later on add in use cases and requirements to facilitate system maintenance.

Following stakeholder identification, there are three tasks that go on in parallel for the set of selected use cases. On one hand, we use scenarios to understand the interesting set of interactions of the system executing the use case in question and the actors. As we identify messages in and out and the system transformations that they imply, we execute the parallel task generate stakeholder requirements. We focus first on primary scenarios but also add in secondary and "rainy day" (error) scenarios. Each scenario contains a sequence containing input events and data, transformations, and output events and data. All of these are represented both as elements in the scenario and as textual requirements with traceability links between them.

In parallel with these two tasks, we can also define how we might validate that the system meets these stakeholder needs in the validation plan.

2.5.3 System Requirements Definition and Analysis

A stakeholder requirement is a statement of what the stakeholder needs. A system requirement is a statement of what the system does. Those are not the same thing but they ought to be related! System requirements should be derived from the stakeholder requirements and the former are typically more quantitative than the latter. For the most part, all stakeholder use cases will have corresponding system equivalents and all stakeholder requirements will be satisfied by one or more system requirements. However, there may be additional system use cases and requirements either because the stakeholder requirements weren't complete, additional system capabilities are required to meet the stakeholder needs, or the system may be targeting stakeholders (such as other markets) that are not represented explicitly in the stakeholder requirements. Figure 2.11 shows the high-level workflow for this activity.

Following the identification of the system use cases, there are a number of tasks that go on in parallel for each use case. The central task is to generate or update the system requirements.

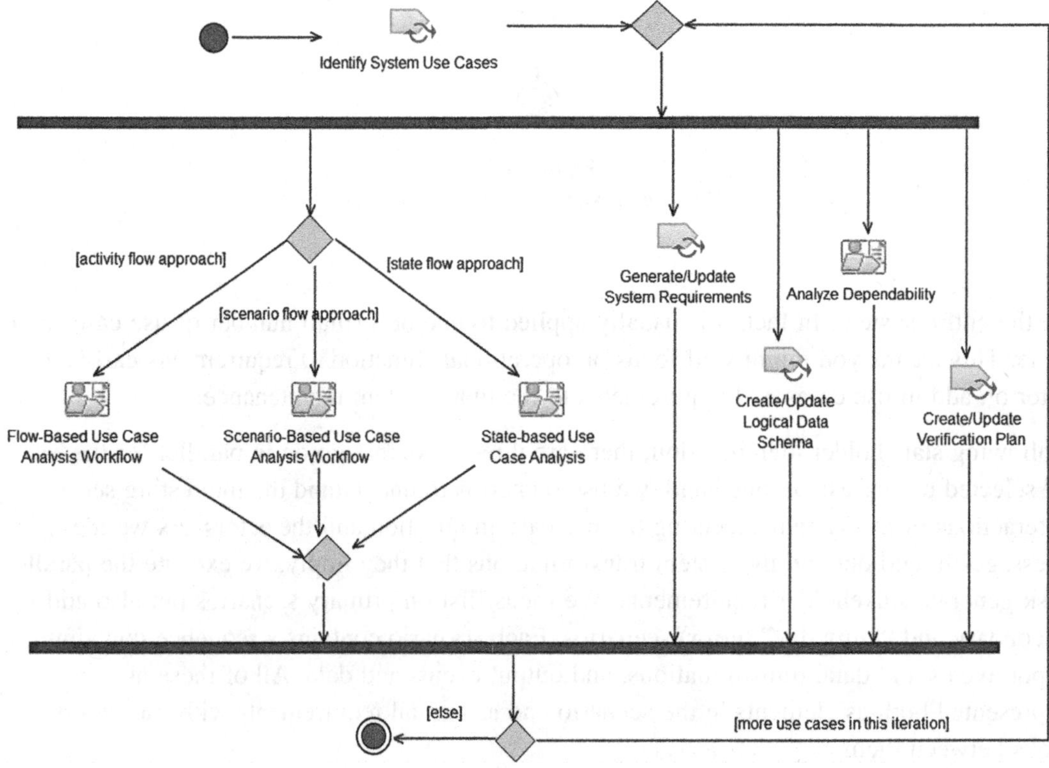

Figure 2.11
System Requirements Definition and Analysis.

In parallel with that task, the set of requirements allocated to the use case are modeled and analyzed using one of three approaches. It should be noted at the outset that these different workflows all end up in the exactly the same place but differ in their starting point.

2.5.4 Approach 1: Flow-based Use Case Analysis

The flow-based approach begins with an activity model of the various flows within the use case. Once the flows are defined, scenarios are derived by finding the set of branching paths within the activity model. Then a normative state machine specification is constructed and verified through execution or formal methods. As can be seen in Figure 2.12, the creation of these modeling views is done in very short cycles known as *nanocycles*, each taking 20–60 min. That means we *don't* create a complete and possibly very complex activity model before we move forward, but do only part of it, then derive the scenarios and state machine, verify that we got that much right, update the system requirements (see Figure 2.11 for the parallel generate/update system requirements task) and do some more analysis. I've worked this way with many teams and using these small iterations greatly speeds up the work and greatly reduces the errors introduced.

This is a common approach and is preferred by many systems engineers.

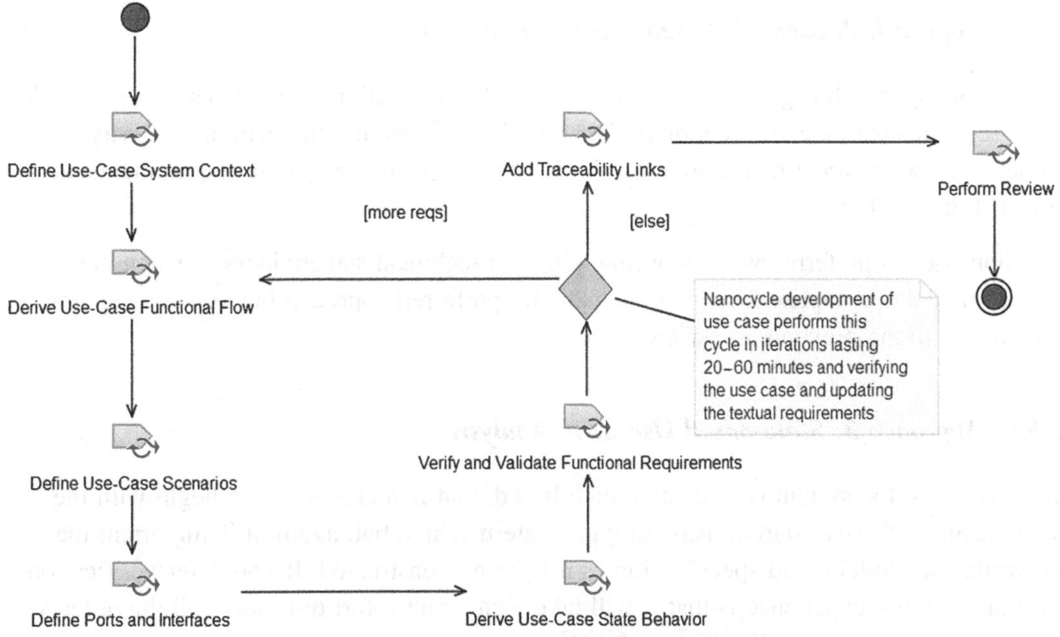

Figure 2.12
Flow Based Use Case Analysis.

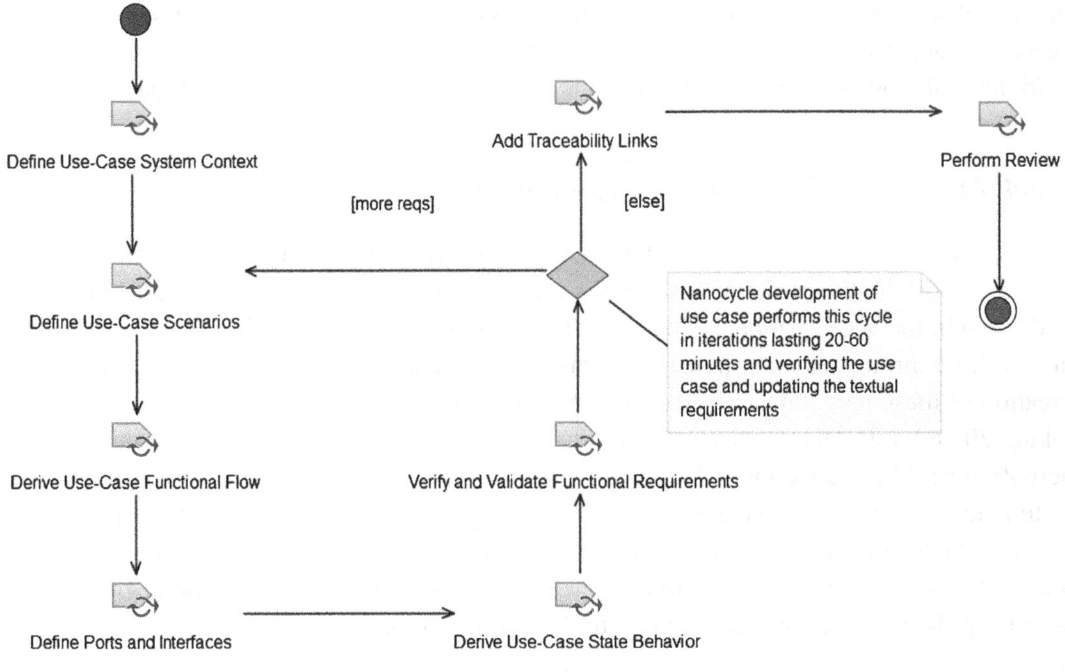

Figure 2.13
Scenario-based use case analysis.

2.5.5 Approach 2: Scenario-based Use Case Analysis

The second approach begins with scenarios instead of the activity model. That is, we model some scenarios (or parts of scenarios), then add these flows into the evolving activity model, then create a normative state machine, verify, update the system requirements, and repeat (Figure 2.13).

This approach is preferred when working with non-technical stakeholders or when the activity model is complex. This is my personally preferred approach but you can see how similar it is to the previous workflow.

2.5.6 Approach 3: State-based Use Case Analysis

In some cases, the system is so clearly state-based, that is makes sense to begin with the state machine. We can start constructing the state machine but, again, it is important that we verify the model-based specification as it is being constructed. If you defer verification until the end, my experience is that it will take significant effort to remove all the defects that you didn't remove earlier (Figure 2.14).

While I am fond of this approach as well, it is technically the most challenging and requires systems engineers who are highly adept with state machines.

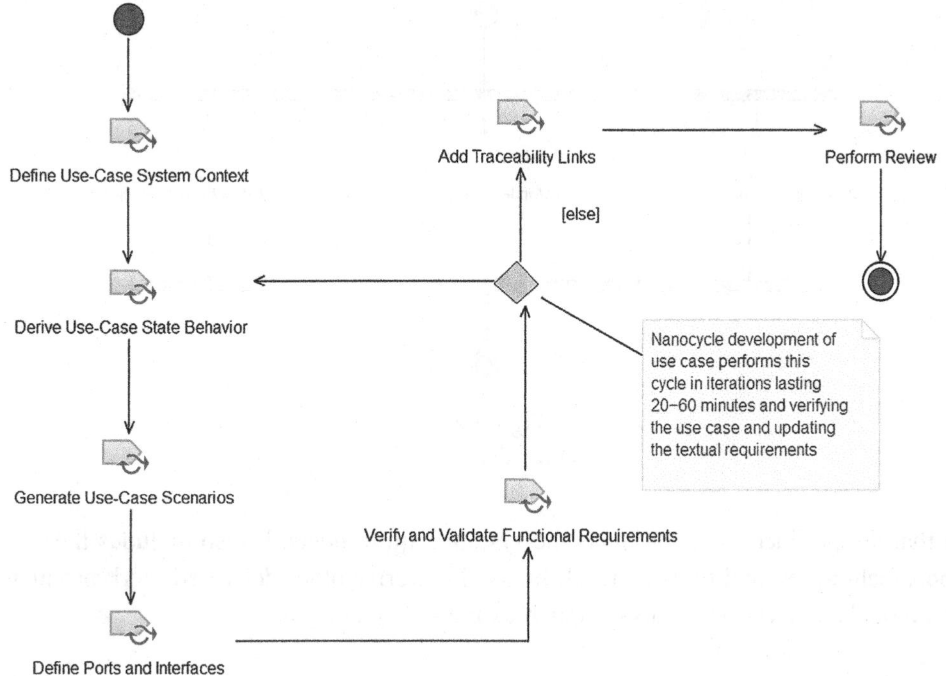

Figure 2.14
State-based use case analysis.

These three approaches are described in detail in Chapter 5.

Beyond the use case analysis and the generation of the textual system requirements, there are other activities going on in parallel as well. We must understand the required properties of the information and flows of the system. We call this the *logical data schema.* We don't care about the physical format or representation of the data, but we care a lot about the required range, accuracy, and precision of the data. If I'm specifying that I want a radar track, I need to know the value range for how far away the radar target can be (such as 10 m to 100 km), how accurate the distance is (such as ± 2 m), the units (such as meters and kilometers), and how quickly I can process the image (such as <100 ms). I don't care whether the distance to the target is represented using a scaled integer or a floating point value. At some point, people will care about how it is represented—that will be when we create the *physical data schema.*

Figure 2.11 also shows a parallel activity analyze dependability. As we identify functional and non-functional requirements, we must continuously analyze their effect on the safety, reliability, and security of the system. The simple parallel workflow is shown in Figure 2.15. This topic is explored in detail in Chapter 5.

The last task in the system requirements definition and analysis activity is create/update verification plan. This plan outlines the methods, techniques, and tools that will be used to

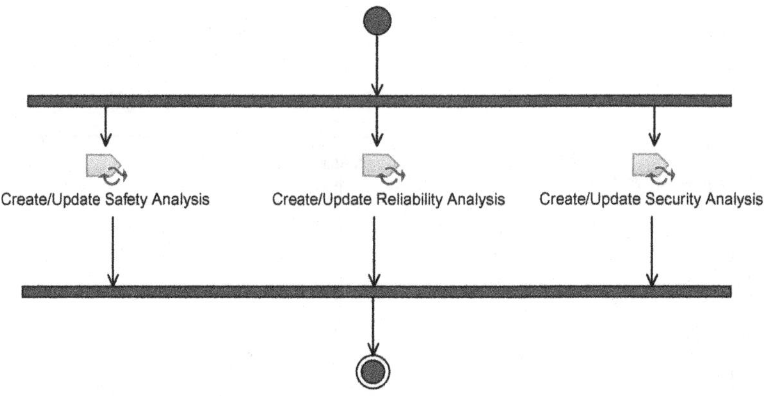

Figure 2.15
Analyze dependability.

verify that the produced system meets the system requirements. It also includes the methods, techniques, and tools that will be used to verify other delivered work products, such as models and various analyses (such as the safety analysis).

2.5.7 Architectural Analysis

Architectural analysis looks at candidate architectures and selects from among them (Figure 2.16). The approach is to first identify key system functions, then suggest candidate architectures that might fulfill the system needs. In the trade study workflow (Figure 2.17), we define the criteria by which we will judge the fitness of the solution (the assessment criteria), and how important each criterion is. We may need to define utility curves for the criteria that are nonlinear in nature. These criteria are also known as *measures of effectiveness* (MOEs). We assess each candidate solution against each criterion and look for which solution is the best fit. Sometimes a combination of architectural solutions will end up as the recommended architectural solution.

Architectural analysis is the subject of Chapter 6.

2.5.8 Architectural Design

In architectural design, we implement the selected architecture (Figure 2.18). Here we focus on key system architectural aspects:

- Identification of the subsystems
- Allocation of requirements to the subsystems
- Definition of the interfaces between subsystems.

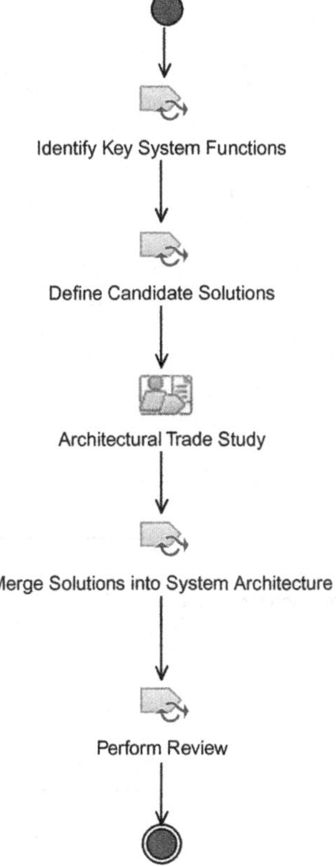

Figure 2.16
Architectural analysis.

A *subsystem* is a large-scale piece of a system that provides a set of coherent functionality and is typically implemented with a combination of engineering disciplines (for example, mechanical, electronic, and software). Subsystems are opaque to their peers, but offer and require services via interfaces. Interfaces are definitions of discrete or continuous flows of energy, materiel, or information (control and/or data) that are sent to or from a system element. Because different subsystems are often developed by different teams, specifying the interfaces well is crucial to system integration and operation. As an aside, the interfaces defined in this activity are *logical* rather than physical since we want to focus on the essential properties of the flows and not on their physical manifestation (at least for now). We will derive the physical interfaces during the hand off workflow discussed in Chapter 8.

The nested activity on the left side of Figure 2.18 allocates use cases and requirements to the subsystems. It is extremely rare that a system-level use case can be directly allocated to

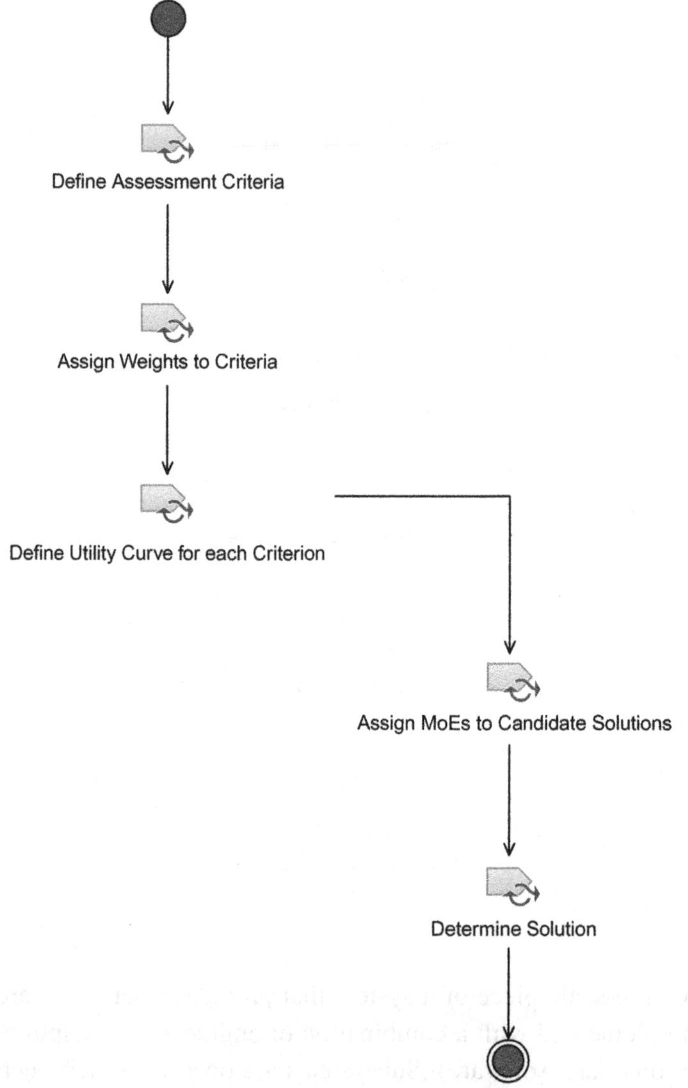

Figure 2.17
Perform trade study.

a subsystem; rather, we must allocate parts of the system use case to different subsystems so that they collectively provide the behavior of the system use case. As we see in Figure 2.19, there are two workflows to accomplish this. The first, shown on the left, I think of as "bottom up." The system-level use case scenarios include messages between the system use case[14] and the actors. To perform this task, we examine each such message and

[14] Which is just another way to say "the system when running the use case of concern."

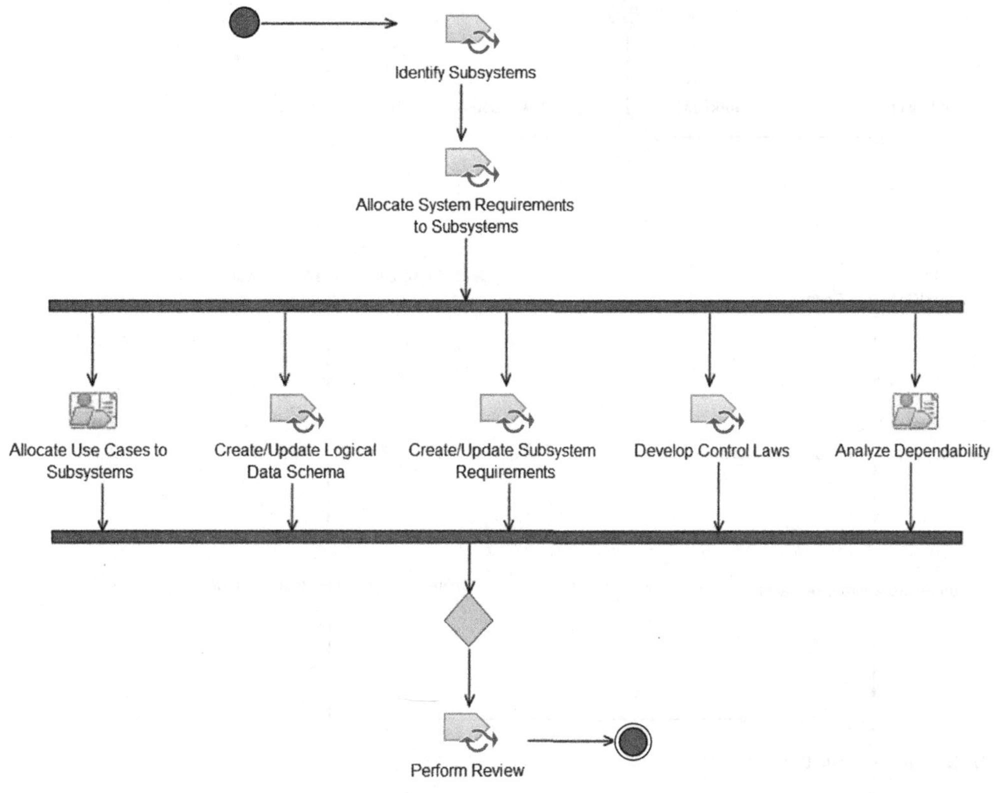

Figure 2.18
Architectural design.

identify the roles the subsystems will play in its execution. This results in a message sent among the subsystems, resulting in an equivalent, but more detailed scenario that shows how the subsystems interact to perform the single system-level behavior. We call these detailed scenarios "white box scenarios" because they show the interaction of the large-scale internal system elements. Once this is done, we can group the subsystem services we've identified (and the requirements associated with those services) into subsystem-level use cases.

The alternative, shown on the right side of the figure, I call "top-down." We start by thinking at a high level what use cases a subsystem must provide to fulfill its role within the system-level use case. That is, we decompose the system-level use case into a set of collaborating subsystem-level use cases. Once that is done, we then elaborate the white-box scenarios.

In either case, we end up with white box scenarios and subsystem-level use cases which we can detail using the same techniques that we applied to the system-level use cases.

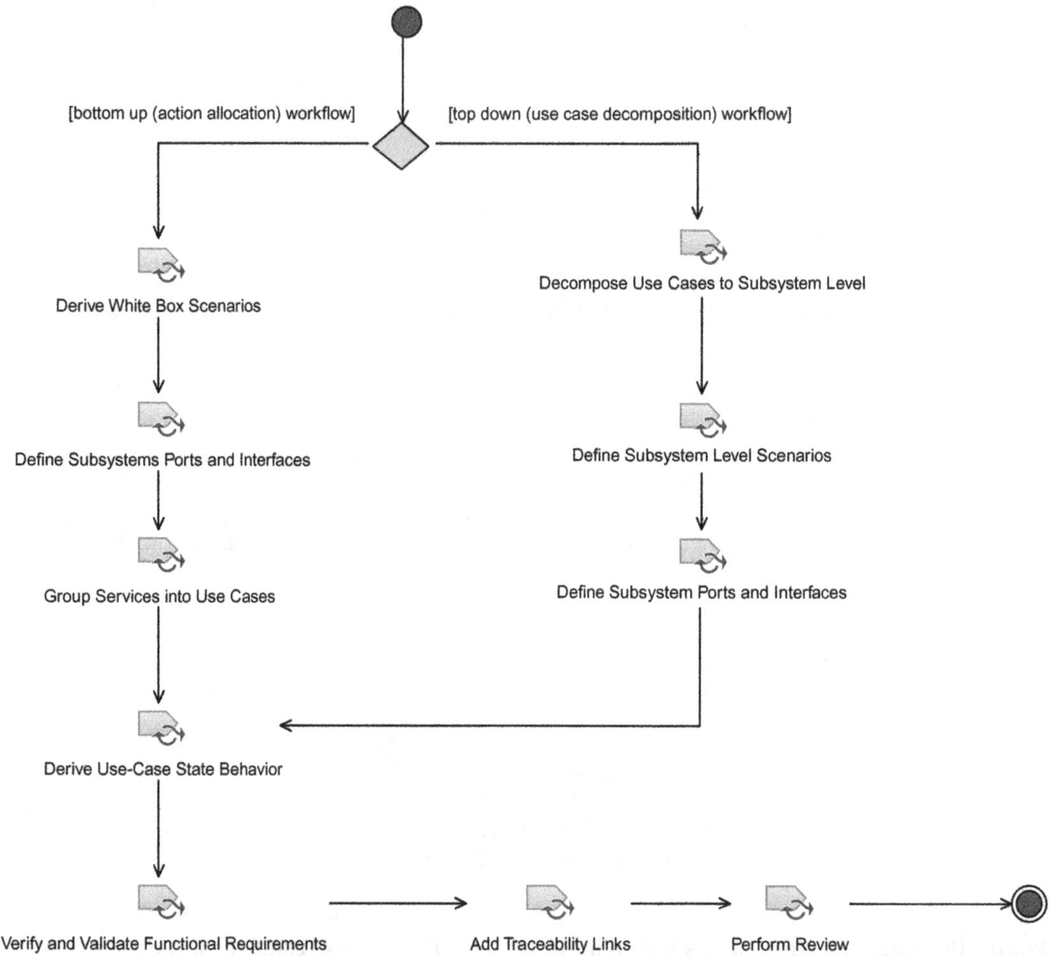

Figure 2.19
Allocate use cases to subsystems.

Parallel with the allocation of requirements and use cases, we allocate textual requirements to the subsystems. Some requirements may be directly allocated to a subsystem-level use case while others will need to be decomposed into derived requirements which may be so allocated.

As a result of this activity, we must usually update the logical data schema and analyze the effect of this deeper understanding of the system on its dependability.

Beyond that, in Figure 2.18, we see the task develop control laws. For systems that exhibit continuous behavior via control laws that cross subsystem boundaries, we must define these control laws and allocate behavioral and interface requirements to the subsystems.

2.5.9 Perform Iteration Retrospective

The iteration retrospective has four objectives:

- Measure project performance against project objectives
- Measure project performance against plan
- Identify areas of improvement for the project, such as methods and tools
- Adjust plan, methods, and procedures to improve project performance.

We explicitly do this during each iteration to maximize the likelihood of project success. Note that this is where the *dynamic* part of *dynamic planning* takes place. We adjust the plan based on measured success even as we try to improve our methods.

2.5.10 Handoff to Downstream Engineering

As I travel around the world teaching and consulting, I get the most questions about the hand off from systems engineering. The workflow, shown in Figure 2.20, illustrates that the handoff is not an event but a workflow. We take the system engineering data and transform it to data needed by the implementation engineers. There are two primary parallel flows.

On the left, we create and organize information shared by at least two subsystems; that is, the interfaces and shared data and resource definitions. We'll put this information in a separate model, called the *shared model* (for obvious reasons). Most of the effort in this flow will be transforming the logical interfaces and data schema to the physical definitions needed for implementation.

The path on the right is repeated for each subsystem. For each subsystem, we create a separate subsystem model and we import our requirements specification from the systems engineering model. The next step is to allocate the requirements to the involved engineering disciplines. As with the subsystems, some requirements may directly map to one discipline, such as electronics, mechanical, or software but others must be decomposed into derived requirements which can be so allocated. In addition, we must define the physical interfaces between the engineering disciplines, such as the software–electronic and electro–mechanical interfaces. These interfaces are frozen in configuration management, to be thawed and renegotiated only if defects or missing properties are discovered.

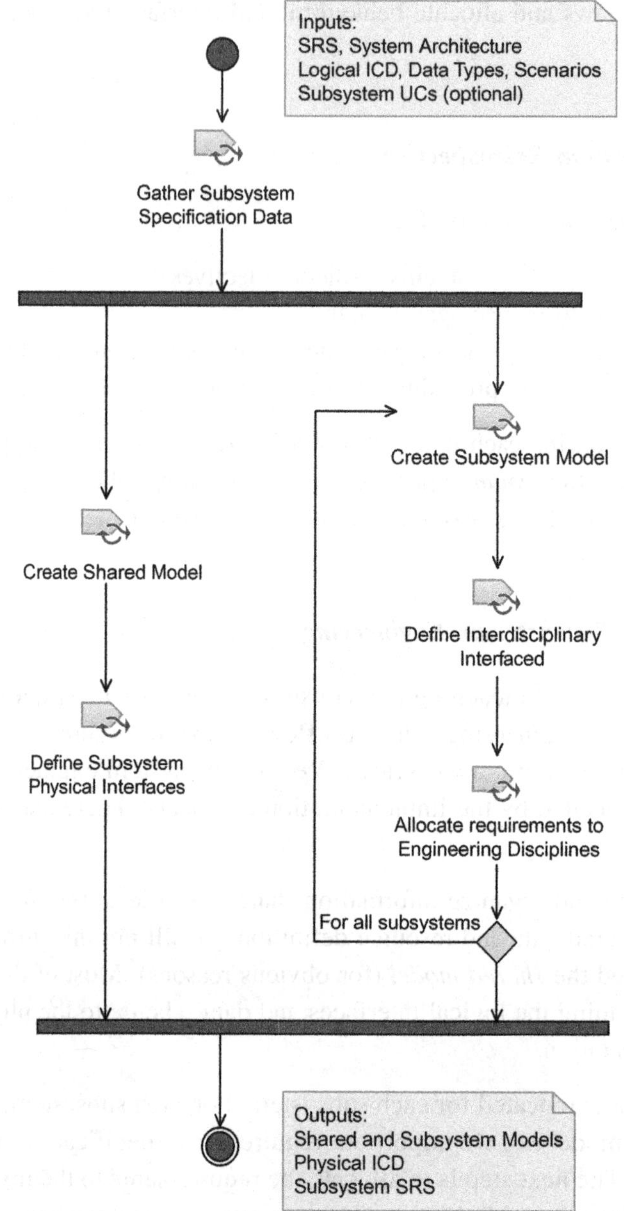

Figure 2.20
Handoff to downstream engineering.

At the end of the hand off, the subsystem teams and discipline-specific engineers are ready to begin their work.

The hand off is the topic of Chapter 8.

2.5.11 Control Project

In parallel with the above iteration activities, there are some ongoing activities as well. The first of these is the control project activity. It consists of three nested, parallel tasks. The manage iteration task includes tracking project progress, applying metrics, and handling project issues. The manage risk task looks after the risk management plan including updating it as spikes are performed and adding new risks as they are uncovered.

The last task is perform daily meeting. This task is a short meeting of the team members in which each team member provides three key statements:

- What I accomplished yesterday
- What I plan to do today
- What roadblocks are in my way.

As mentioned, this is meant to be a short meeting, so discussions about removing roadblocks or whether what they plan to do is appropriate take place outside this meeting. The purpose of the meeting is to share status with the team and make short-term commitments (Figure 2.21).

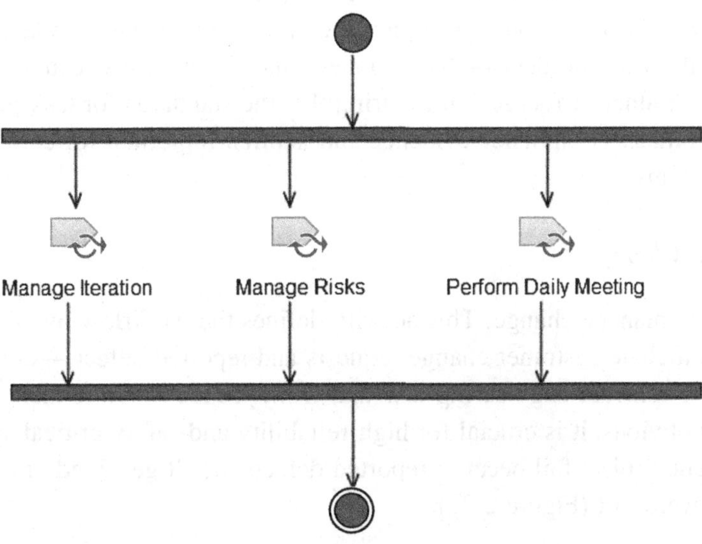

Figure 2.21
Control project.

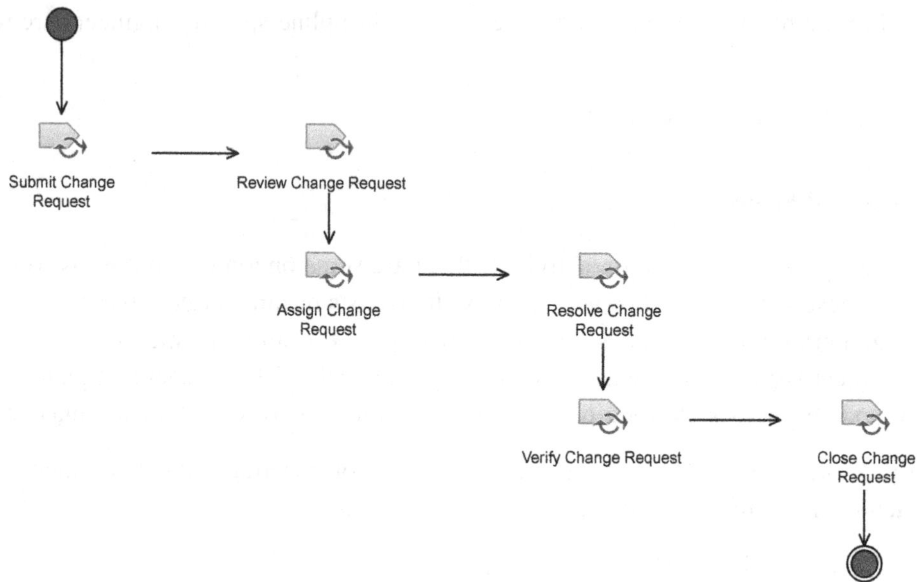

Figure 2.22
Manage change.

2.5.12 Perform Quality Assurance Audits

We discussed audits briefly in Chapter 1. To review, an audit is work done by a quality assurance engineer to demonstrate conformance of work to plan and standards. This is not about reviewing the work products—that is done in the review tasks scattered about in the above workflows. Rather, it focuses on ensuring that the standards for task performance are met. This task produces compliance evidence and is often important for certification of safety-critical systems.

2.5.13 Manage Change

The last activity is manage change. This activity defines the workflow by which change requests—which include customer change requests and reported defects—are processed and result in change to relevant engineering data and work products. While the workflow is clear and mostly obvious, it is crucial for high-reliability and safety-critical systems. I've seen more than one project fail because reported defects didn't get fixed or customer change requests were lost (Figure 2.22).

2.6 Summary

At its core, agile is about being efficient, focusing on delivering quality in the work products, and being adaptive to change. Agile methods originated in the software industry (although they have much wider applicability) and were largely a result of a rebellion against "big process"—the definition of heavyweight and burdensome methods for developing software supported (but not required) by standards such as CMMI and ISO 9001. Agile changed the focus from adhering to a process to meeting the need, from writing documentation to producing verifiably correct work products, from rigorously negotiating contracts to collaborating with the customer, and from following a plan to responding to change. Again, this is a matter of focus, because even in agile projects, you still have a process, you still use tools, you still write documentation, and you still follow a plan (more or less).

For model-based systems engineering, agile has great potential, and I've seen significant benefits where I've applied it with my customers. Some key practices required to achieve these benefits include:

- Incremental development of engineering data and work products
- Continual verification of the correctness, accuracy, and fidelity of the engineering data
- Use of verifiable modeling, especially in the creation of verifiable (executable) models for specifications and design
- Continuous dependability assessment to ensure the system remains safe, reliable, and secure
- Active project risk management to improve the likelihood of project success
- Model-based handoff to downstream engineering to make sure they have all the information they need for the implementation and in a form they can consume
- Dynamic planning so that we can adjust our plans based on project ground truth and respond quickly and correctly to change.

I developed the Harmony aMBSE process specifically to provide strong effective guidance for doing the system engineering activities with models and doing them in an agile way. This chapter provides an overview of the process. It may appear daunting because of the number of work tasks but process workflows simply provide a template for what tasks need to be done, in which order they are done, and how to use modeling to perform them. The most important of these activities will be discussed in far more operational detail in the coming chapters, starting with Chapter 4. Next, however, we'll have a light discussion of the SysML language that we will use in our modeling efforts.

References

[1] B.P. Douglass, Real-Time Agility, Addison-Wesley, MA, USA, 2009. <http://www.amazon.com/Real-Time-Agility-Harmony-Embedded-Development/dp/0321545494>.

[2] B. Boehm, A spiral model of software development and enhancement, ACM SIGSOFT Software Engineering Notes, ACM 11 (4) (1986) 14–24.

[3] C. Jones, Applied Software Measurement 3rd Edition: Global Analysis of Productivity and Quality, McGraw-Hill Osborne Media, NY, USA, 2008.

[4] M. Cohen, Agile Estimation and Planning, Prentice Hall, NJ, USA, 2006.

[5] Grenning, J. Planning Poker <http://www.objectmentor.com/resources/articles/PlanningPoker.zip>.

CHAPTER 3

SysML Introduction

Chapter Outline

This chapter is meant as a lightweight review of the SysML language. It is most certainly not an in-depth tutorial on the language. Just like a book on writing poetry in French might provide an overview of the syntax and semantics of the French language but really focus on writing good poetry, this book provides a quick SysML review but will spend most of its time instructing on writing poetic SysML (or at least properly capturing engineering data). If you're new to SysML or UML, I strongly recommend you study up on the language before trying to digest this chapter. In this chapter, we'll mostly overview the SysML language but at times we'll dive a little deeper to address misunderstandings that I find make life difficult for novice modelers.

The section *The Rules of Modeling* in Chapter 1 provides some basic guidelines of good modeling and I urge you to reread that section before you start modeling on your own.

3.1 SysML at 30,000 Feet

As briefly mentioned in Chapter 1, SysML is a profile[1] of the UML. That means that SysML inherits all of the underlying meta-architecture of UML (and there's a lot of it) but it omits some parts of the UML and extends the meta-classes for others. In a profile, you may not add a fundamentally new kind of thing but you can stereotype (sort of "meta-specialize") elements within the UML as well as add new relations, add new kinds of features and properties to these metaclasses,[2] constraints, model libraries, and customized diagrammatic representations. This is because UML contains within itself a number of key mechanisms for language extension: stereotypes, tags, constraints, model libraries, diagrams, and profiles.

---

[1] A *profile* is a coherent collection of specializations to the UML language usually to address a specific topic or user need.

[2] A metaclass is an element of the UML metamodel. If you want to know more, check out the UML Infrastructure specification [1].

Before we discuss UML's extension mechanisms, let's discuss something even more basic—the type–instance dichotomy. Understanding this underlies all effective modeling and it is something frequently misunderstood by engineers new to modeling.

A `Bicycle` is an example of a type (which we can represent as a block). The specific bicycle on which you rode to work today is an *instance* of the block `Bicycle`. You can give the instance a name (I call mine `Rocinante`[3]). You can refer to the instance using the format <instance name>:<type name>, such as `Rocinante:Bicycle`.

If I define a SysML *Block* (equivalent to a UML *Class*) called `Motor`, I've specified a design element type that I can use in the design of my system. I can create instances of this block in a specific system, such as `LeftFrontMotor:Motor` or `RightRearMotor:Motor`. That is, once I define a design type, I can use it to specify the properties, such as structure and behavior, of any number of instances that will appear in the actual physical system. A *metatype* is the type of design element. The UML defines lots of metatypes, such as Class, Operation, Type, Package, Signal, and so on. These elements form the vocabulary in which you cast your design with elements like `Motor`, `enable()`, `scaledInteger`, `DesignPakage`, `powerOnEvent`, and so on. These design elements still exist only at design time, but the instances that are created from these specifications exist at run-time, that is, in manufactured physical systems operating in the real world. Yeah, this can be a bit confusing.

Figure 3.1 shows the relations between metaclass (equivalent to a metatype), stereotype, class (equivalent to a type), and an instance. The metaclass level defines the basic language in which you will specify your design. The stereotype level (optionally) specializes the language a bit. The design level is your system design. The instance level is some particular operational system manufactured from your design specification. You—as a system engineer—will spend most of your time and effort at the design level, using UML or SysML to specify your design, so that you can create instances of systems produced in a manufacturing plant. The stereotype level is not considered a true level in the metalevel hierarchy, but it makes sense from the system engineer's point of view to consider these stereotypes at the metaclass level—that is, defining the language in which you cast your design.

While understanding the "hairy underbelly" of the UML and SysML isn't crucial to creating good system designs, a firm understanding of the Block (Class) and Instance levels is. A *block* is the specification of a design element, along with various important properties. An *instance* is a specific implementation of that Block specification. Consider the simple case of modeling an elevator panel. You might be tempted to model it as shown in Figure 3.2 but that would be *wrong*.

[3] After Don Quijote's horse, if you're interested.

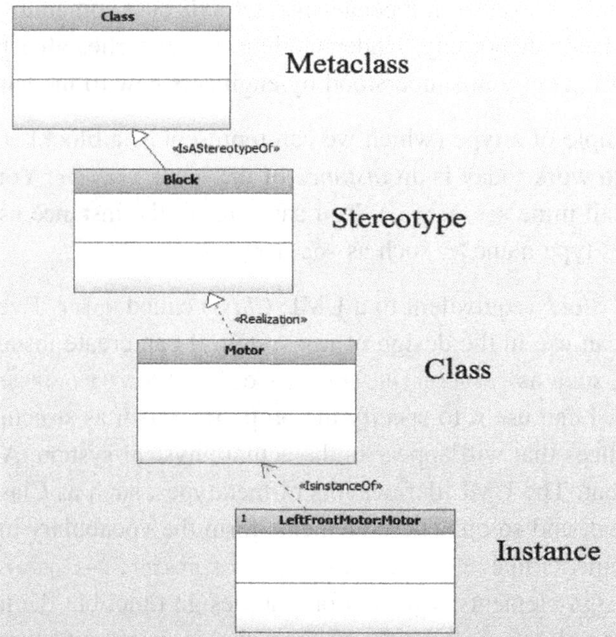

Figure 3.1
Metatype–stereotype–type–instance.

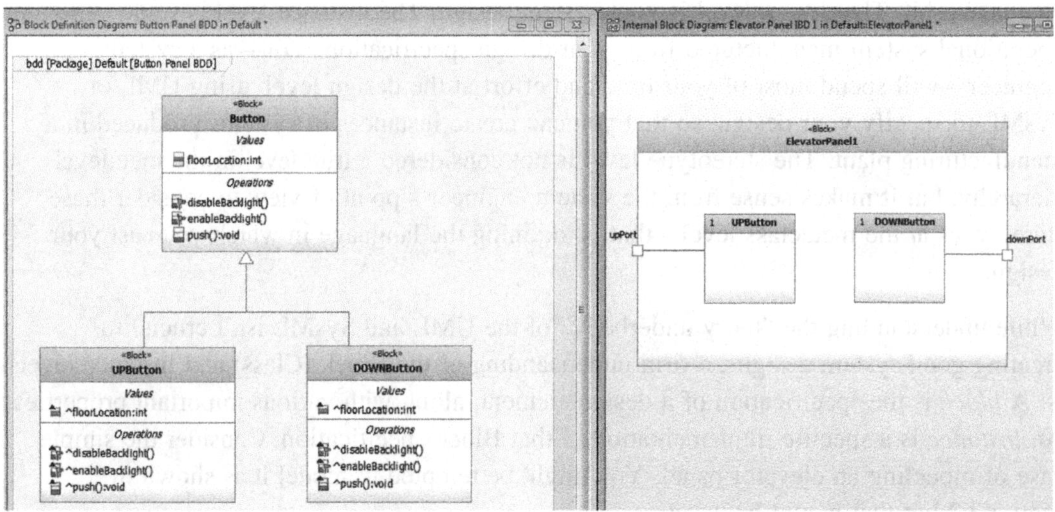

Figure 3.2
Elevator button panel model 1.

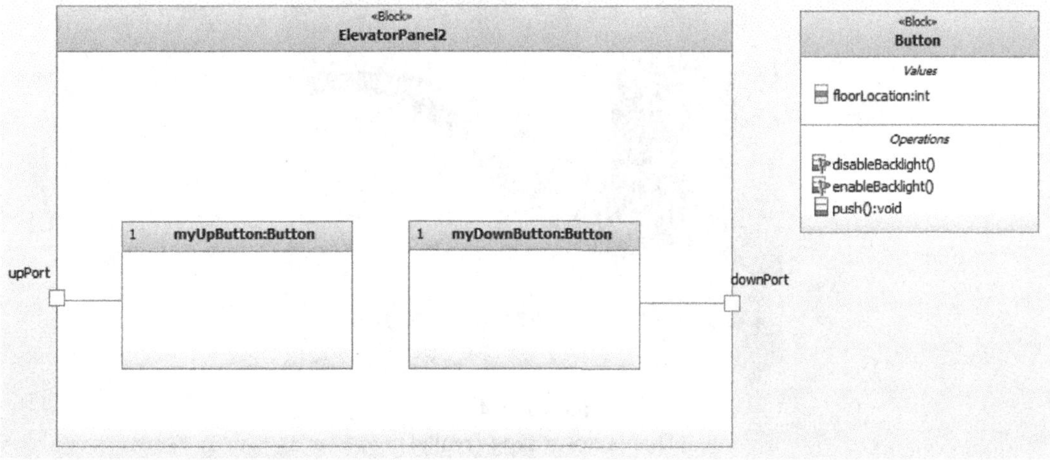

Figure 3.3
Elevator button panel model 2.

Figure 3.2 shows the UP and DOWN buttons as specialized kinds of `Button`; that is, `UPButton` and `DOWNButton` are Blocks (type specifications). On the right-hand side of the figure, we see these as parts of the `ElevatorPanel1` block.

When the `UPButton` is pressed, the event is interpreted by the elevator signal as a request for an elevator going in the up direction, but note that the structure and behavior of the button itself is identical to that of the `DOWNButton`. What we really want is for the `UPButton` and `DOWNButton` to be two different instances of the block `Button`. The semantically correct model is shown in Figure 3.3.

Figure 3.3 shows a single block, `Button`, that specifies two parts (contextualized instances) within the `ElevatorPanel2` block. Structurally and behaviorally, the two `Button` instances are the same but they are wired to different ports and so differ in context and usage, not type.

The bottom line is that it is crucial to understand the different between a new kind of design element (a new Block) and different instances of it within your design (a new Block Instance or Part).

Another thing that beginning modelers struggle with is the difference between diagrams and models. A *model* is a semantic web of interconnected specifications of various types, such as blocks, associations, events, states, and so on. The model is held within the modeling tool's repository. *Diagrams*, on the other hand, are nothing more or less than visualizations of some portions of a model. Diagrams are great ways to both define that semantic information (data entry) and to view/understand that semantic information, but they are not

Figure 3.4
This is not a pipe (really!).

the information itself. It's like if you paint a picture of a pipe and you say "This is not a pipe" because it is actually a *painting* of a pipe not an actual pipe [see *The Treachery of Images* (Figure 3.4) by Rene Magritte]. The visualization of a thing is distinct from the thing being visualized.

> Models are (engineering) data; diagrams are *visualizations* of data.

The distinction becomes important when I add a block with the same name as a block on another diagram. Am I referencing that same block in the repository or creating a new block in some other part of the repository? When I use diagrams to add or expose element properties, am I adding a property to an existing element (to be merged with other element properties) or am I defining a property for a new element?

We use diagrams for two primary purposes in UML and SysML. First, we use diagrams to enter modeling information that is then stored in the model repository. Second, we use diagrams to visualize some portion of the contents of that repository to understand, reason about, or communicate model information.

3.2 UML Extension Mechanisms

SysML is UML in sheep's clothing, in the sense that it is really UML underneath the façade even though SysML has extended the language in a number of ways using stereotypes, tags, constraints, new diagrams, and model libraries.

A *stereotype* is like adding a new word in your vocabulary that you can then use in your poetry. Unlike adding a fundamentally new meta-element, a stereotype must be based on an existing element (specifically, a metaclass that already exists in the language).[4] Once added into the language, you can use that element just like it was predefined in the language.

For example, consider an `ActivityEdge` in the UML metamodel for activities. UML defines two kinds of `ActivityEdge`—a `ControlFlow` and an `ObjectFlow`. Both of these are fundamentally discrete *in time* in that they are sent at some rate and such events sent take place at some instant of time. But what if you want to model something that is truly continuous, such as water flow down a pipe or energy flow along a wire? It is true that the UML doesn't place restrictions on the rate of such flows and so you can approach continuous flow by setting the time between the incoming events as arbitrarily short but that is a hard way to model something which for you is fundamentally continuous. You could create a stereotype of `ActivityEdge` called «continuous» for modeling such flows. Then, where you have flows in your activities that are discrete you can use the original control flows and where they are continuous you can use your new term, «continuous». SysML does just that.

Stereotypes often provide additional metadata known as *named properties* but more commonly referred to as *tags*. For example, suppose you stereotype a class (or block, since we're focusing on SysML here) to represent a hazard—a condition known to be unsafe as it leads to an accident or loss. You might want to add properties relevant to all hazards such as *likelihood* of the hazard manifestation, *severity* (level of concern), and Safety Integrity Level to meet some standard should it manifest.

Figure 3.5 shows a simple example in which I've defined three stereotypes for modeling the safety of a system—«Hazard», «Fault», and «LogicFlow»—and then use those stereotypes to model the relation of a fault event to the manifestation of a hazardous condition.[5]

A *model library* is a kind of package that contains elements that are expected to be widely reused in other packages. For example, you might create a package of common types of values (such as weight, length, area, and volume) and units (such as pounds, kilograms, meters, $meters^2$, and $meters^3$) (and SysML does just that too).

The UML comes with a set of predefined diagrams, although diagrams are really second-class citizens in the UML (did I mention that models are really just the data?). What is

---

[4] Such as the term *techjitsu* which is a stereotype of *technical* and *ju-jitsu*.

[5] This is, in fact, a greatly simplified version of the UML Fault Tree Analysis (FTA) Profile which I authored to model safety and reliability analysis and has tabular views [such as Hazard Analysis and Fault Means and Effect Analysis (FMEA)] and graphical views [such as FTA and Safety Analysis Diagrams (SAD)]. We'll be seeing the profile in use starting in Chapter 5.

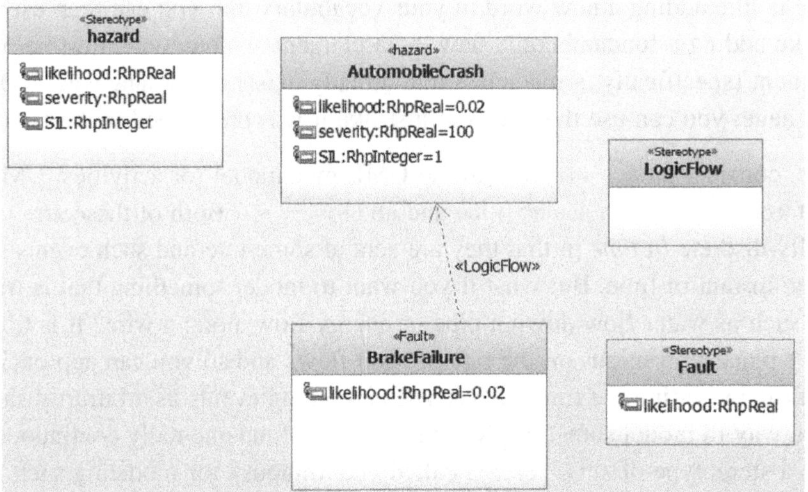

Figure 3.5
Example of stereotypes and tags.

important to the creators of the UML (and ought to be important to modelers too) is *what is being said* and only secondarily how it looks. Nevertheless, UML and SysML are graphical modeling languages, so if you are specializing the UML, it is common to add specialized forms of diagrams as well.

A *Profile* is a coherent collection of extensions—commonly stereotypes (with or without tags), constraints, model libraries, and specialized diagrams, intended for some specialized use or industry application. SysML is just a profile; it is UML specialized for systems engineering.

Finally a quick note: many people like to add lots and lots of stereotypes in their models, complicating their models without adding a great deal of value. Even though I've authored or participated in authoring many profiles, it is almost always better to *model* than to *metamodel.* If I want to write a book, it is almost always better to write using the existing vocabulary of the language than it is to define lots of new words and then use them to write your book. Having said that, sometimes it *is* better to add new words or even define your own language, but I recommend you model the concept first and only extend your language if it really simplifies your model or its application.

3.2.1 SysML Model Elements

For the most part, UML elements have the same, renamed, or slightly modified correspondents in the SysML. A UML *Class* becomes a SysML *Block*, an *association* between classes becomes an *association* between blocks, class *attributes* become block

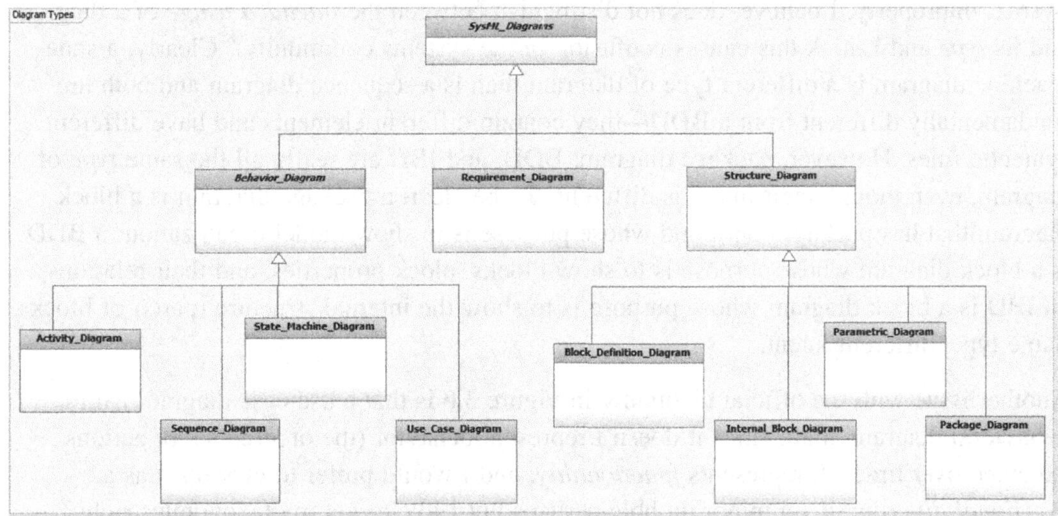

Figure 3.6
SysML diagram types.

values in SysML, and so on. There are also new things added such as *Requirement*[6]—a new element in SysML (a stereotype of Class)—and *Constraint blocks*, used to represent performance and reliability model constraints in SysML in *Parametric diagrams* (a new kind of diagram). Overall, about 80% of UML is reused and available without much, if any change, in SysML. Some elements, such as Nodes (used on deployment diagrams) and timing diagrams are not reused.[7] There are also some new elements that bear little resemblance to their base metaclass from UML. We will introduce the key elements used in SysML modeling starting in Section 3.4 but we won't discuss or use some advanced or little used SysML features.

3.2.2 SysML Diagrams

Figure 3.6 shows the various types of diagrams defined within the SysML language. Most of the diagram types are the same as their UML counterparts (e.g., sequence diagram, use case diagram, state machine diagram, and package diagram). Some are constrained from their UML counterparts [block definition diagram (BDD), internal block diagram (IBD)], while an activity diagram is extended from its UML version. A couple (requirement and parametric diagrams) are new.

---

6 Although requirement should arguably be a part of the UML base language.

7 However, most SysML tools also support UML so those diagrams and language features are there if you want to use them.

SysML improperly, I believe, does not distinguish between the *intended usage* of a diagram and its *type* and I think this causes confusion in the systems community.[8] Clearly, a state machine diagram is a different type of diagram than is a sequence diagram and both are fundamentally different from a BDD—they contain different elements and have different syntactic rules. However, package diagram, BDD, and IBD are really all the same *type* of diagram, even though their intent is different. To be clear, a package diagram is a block diagram that has packages on it and whose purpose is to show model organization; a BDD is a block diagram whose purpose is to show blocks, block properties, and their relations; an IBD is a block diagram whose purpose is to show the internal structure (parts) of blocks. Same type, different intent.

Another issue with the official taxonomy in Figure 3.6 is that a use case diagram isn't a behavioral diagram at all, since it doesn't represent behavior (the ordered set of actions executed over time). It represents *functionality*, and I would prefer to classify it as a *functional diagram*. It's a minor quibble perhaps but I like to get my taxonomies right.[9]

You'll notice that in Figure 3.6, all the elements are enclosed within a diagram frame. SysML provides diagram frames which are generally optional. While they may provide some value (such as showing the name of the diagram), I find them to clutter my visual space. However, they are particularly useful for activity diagrams (since activity parameters are attached to the frame) and IBDs for a specific block (since ports show on the diagram frame).

With those caveats in mind, let's briefly look at the defined SysML diagrams.

3.2.3 Behavior Diagrams

Behavior is defined as the change of state or value over time. SysML provides different ways of defining and visualizing behavior. All of these diagrams are essential and so all will be detailed more in Section 3.4.

3.2.3.1 Activity diagram

Activity diagrams have a more prominent place in SysML than they do in UML. Many system engineers are familiar with extended functional flow block diagrams (EFFBDs) and activity diagrams are semantically similar if visually distinct. SysML activity diagrams are significantly extended from their UML parent through the addition of flows that are continuous in value and continuous in time. Activity diagrams are *semantically complete* in the sense that they specify *all* the behavior of one or more elements.

[8] To be fair, UML has the same problem as well.

[9] I tell my wife that I'm not pedantic, I'm *precise*. She is quick to point out that's a pedantic thing to say.

Activity diagrams are a place where the SysML diagram frame actually has semantics; a diagram frame on an activity diagram represents the activity itself and can include flow and data connection points (activity parameters). While you may elide the diagram frame, if the activity has parameters then I recommend you include it.

You might remember an activity diagram from the previous chapter (see Figure 2.5).

3.2.3.2 Sequence diagram

Sequence diagrams represent specific interactions, commonly known as *scenarios*, among elements. A scenario is a specific interaction among a set of elements, characterized by a specific set of messages arriving among the modeled elements in a specific order. Change the order or change the messages, and you have a different scenario. Sequence diagrams are used to express interactions of external elements with the system realizing a use case, interesting specific interactions among elements within the system design, or specify test cases using the UML Testing Profile [2].

They really only apply to discrete messages and don't represent continuous time or value well. However, if the elements exchange discrete messages in some way—whether it is in mechanical, electronic, or software systems, sequence diagrams allow you to focus on specific scenarios of interest. Sequence diagrams are said to be *partially semantically complete* because each typically only elucidates part of the behavior of the related elements.[10]

3.2.3.3 State machine diagram

Finite state machines represent the crisp[11] discrete behavior of a single element—such as a block or use case—in SysML. The state is a condition of existence of that element—defined by its current set of owned values, its current behavior, and the reachability graph of subsequent states. I am personally a huge fan of state machines and use them more than many systems engineers. For a quick example, see Figure 2.3 in the previous chapter.

3.2.3.4 Use case diagram

Although SysML refers to the use case diagram as a behavioral diagram, it doesn't show behavior. What use case diagrams really show is collective functionality as coherent units (use cases) and their relations with elements outside the system scope (actors). Use cases are going to be a critical view in our agile system engineering approach and will be used extensively in the discussion of requirements engineering in the next chapter. Figure 2.2 from the previous chapter shows a common usage.

---

[10] Although in UML 2.x (and in SysML), it is possible to create fully complete specifications within a single sequence diagram using nested interaction operations. That is generally not recommended, however, because such sequence diagrams become unreadable quickly.

[11] In the mathematical sense.

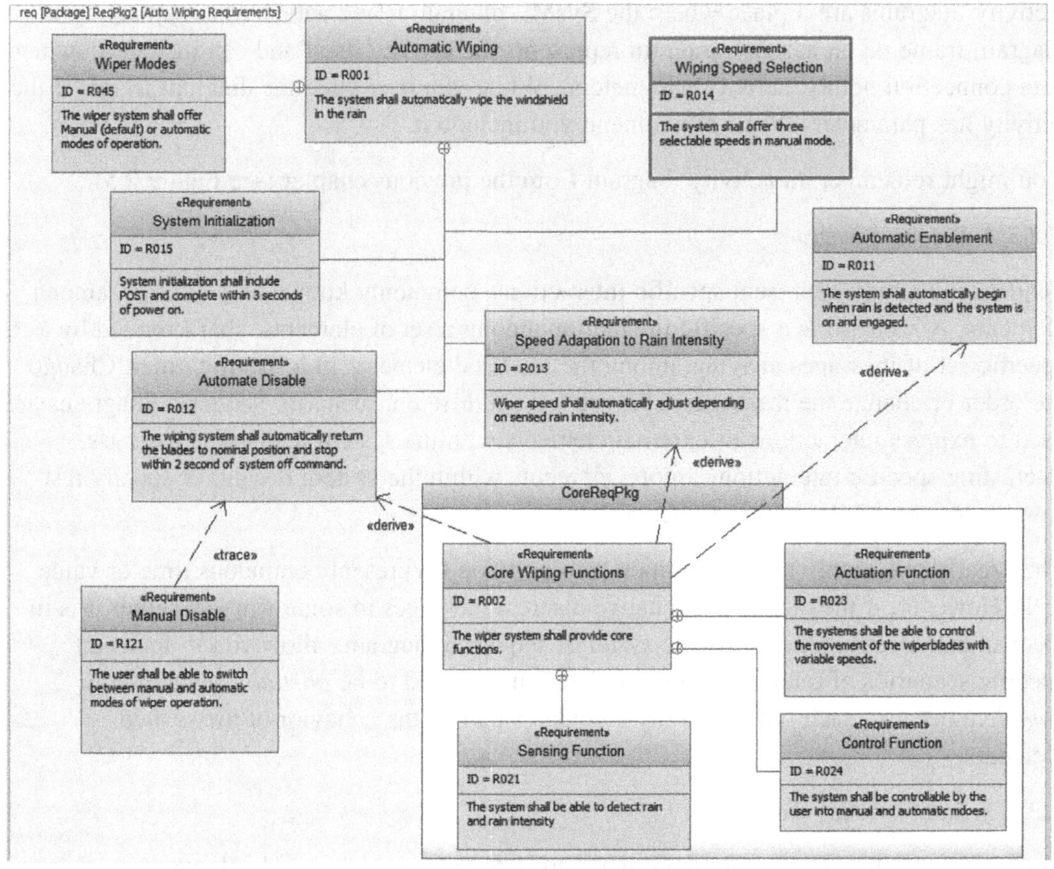

Figure 3.7
Requirement diagram.

3.2.4 Requirement Diagram

A requirement diagram is a diagram meant to show sets of requirements and their relations. SysML added the new Requirement stereotype and new kinds of relationship «contain», «refine», «satisfy», «allocate», and «verify». I use requirement diagrams sparingly but I do put requirements on other diagrams quite a bit. For example, I commonly create a use case diagram with a single use case surrounded by requirements allocated to it (see Figure 2.4 in the previous chapter).

Figure 3.7 shows a typical requirement diagram. The relationship with the circular crosshairs is the «contain» relation, and provides a means of decomposing abstract requirements into more concrete parts.[12] The requirement at the crosshairs logically

[12] It should be noted that this is a "design-time" relation that has no impact on run-time, unlike the composition relationship between blocks and their parts.

R001	[ ] Automatic Wiping	The system shall automatically wipe the windshield in the rain
R002	[ ] Core Wiping Functions	The wiper system shall provide core functions.
R011	[ ] Automatic Enablement	The system shall automatically begin when rain is detected and the system is on and engaged.
R012	[ ] Automate Disable	The wiping system shall automatically return the blades to nominal position and stop within 2 second of system off command.
R013	[ ] Speed Adapation to Rain Intensity	Wiper speed shall automatically adjust depending on sensed rain intensity.
R014	[ ] Wiping Speed Selection	The system shall offer three selectable speeds in manual mode.
R015	[ ] System Initialization	System initialization shall include POST and complete within 3 seconds of power on.
R021	[ ] Sensing Function	The system shall be able to detect rain and rain intensity
R023	[ ] Actuation Function	The systems shall be able to control the movement of the wiperblades with variable speeds.
R024	[ ] Control Function	The system shall be controllable by the user into manual and automatic mdoes.
R045	[ ] Wiper Modes	The wiper system shall offer Manual (default) or automatic modes of operation.
R121	[ ] Manual Disable	The user shall be able to switch between manual and automatic modes of wiper operation.

Figure 3.8
Requirement table.

contains the requirement at the other end of the relation. Two other relations are also depicted. The «derive» relation points towards from the base requirement towards the derived requirement and the «trace» relation is just a navigable traceability relation.

Requirements diagrams depict relations among requirements but this is, relatively speaking, of little concern. The requirements themselves are the things of importance. For the most part, requirements are best shown in a requirements table, such as that shown in Figure 3.8. Even if you use requirement diagrams as a data entry mechanism, in my experience, you will spend more time visualizing them in tabular format generated from the data so entered.

A problem I see in the application of SysML in engineering organizations is too much attention to decomposing relations among requirements and too little focus on ensuring the requirements themselves are correct. My recommendation is only to add relations to requirements when it helps clarify, understand, or verify the requirements. Don't add relations just because they're in the toolbox.

3.2.5 Structure Diagrams

The SysML defines four structural diagrams that we'll discuss in this section.

3.2.5.1 Package diagram

Models can get very large, so we need some way to subdivide the model into parts and organize it to allow multiple people to work on it. *Models* and *packages* are the means by which models are organized in the SysML. A model is a collection of elements that represent other elements, specified in terms of properties and features relevant to the purpose of the model. Organizationally, large model can always be divided into submodels. This is most useful when the submodels have limited relations among them. Models can relate to other models in two primary ways—by *reference* and by *copy*. "By reference" means that I can define a relation of some elements in one model with elements in another. If I make changes to the referenced model, the referencing model may be affected. "By copy" means that I make a copy of one model and place it within another. I am free to change the copy I've made, but such changes are not reflected back in the original referenced model. A model is graphically depicted as a package (tabbed folder) with a triangle, and, in fact, a model is just a special kind of package in SysML.

A *package* can be thought of as a folder or chapter of an owning model. Packages have no semantics other than design-time containment and provide a namespace for the elements they contain. They also serve as the primary units of configuration management; that is, it is most common to check in and check out a package with all its contents at a time.

I particularly recommend the creation of a model overview diagram at the top level of the system that shows the package structure of the model and contains hyperlinks to important diagrams as an aid to understanding and navigating the model.

The use of packages to organize models is discussed in more depth in Section 3.3.

3.2.5.2 Block definition diagram

Blocks[13] are core elements in SysML. They represent elements that, in general, have values, services, behavior, constraints, and relations with other such elements. A BDD (a kind of class diagram)[14] is one of two key diagrams for visually showing blocks, their features, and their relations. They can also show other things such as requirements, and even activities. Figure 3.9 is a simple BDD for an automotive wiper systems.

The primary purpose of the BDD is to show sets of blocks, some of their properties, and their relations. The BDD will be discussed in more detail in Section 3.4.

3.2.5.3 Internal block diagram

If BDDs are the SysML equivalent of the UML's Class diagram, then the IBD is the SysML equivalent of the UML's Structure Diagram. The IBD is really a usage of a BDD where the purpose is to show the internal part structure of a block. I say that it is a usage of a type rather than a type of diagram because I can show internal parts on a BDD as well, if desired. However, it is a common enough usage that it was reified as a type of structural diagram in the SysML.

---

13 Class in UML.

14 Class diagram in the UML.

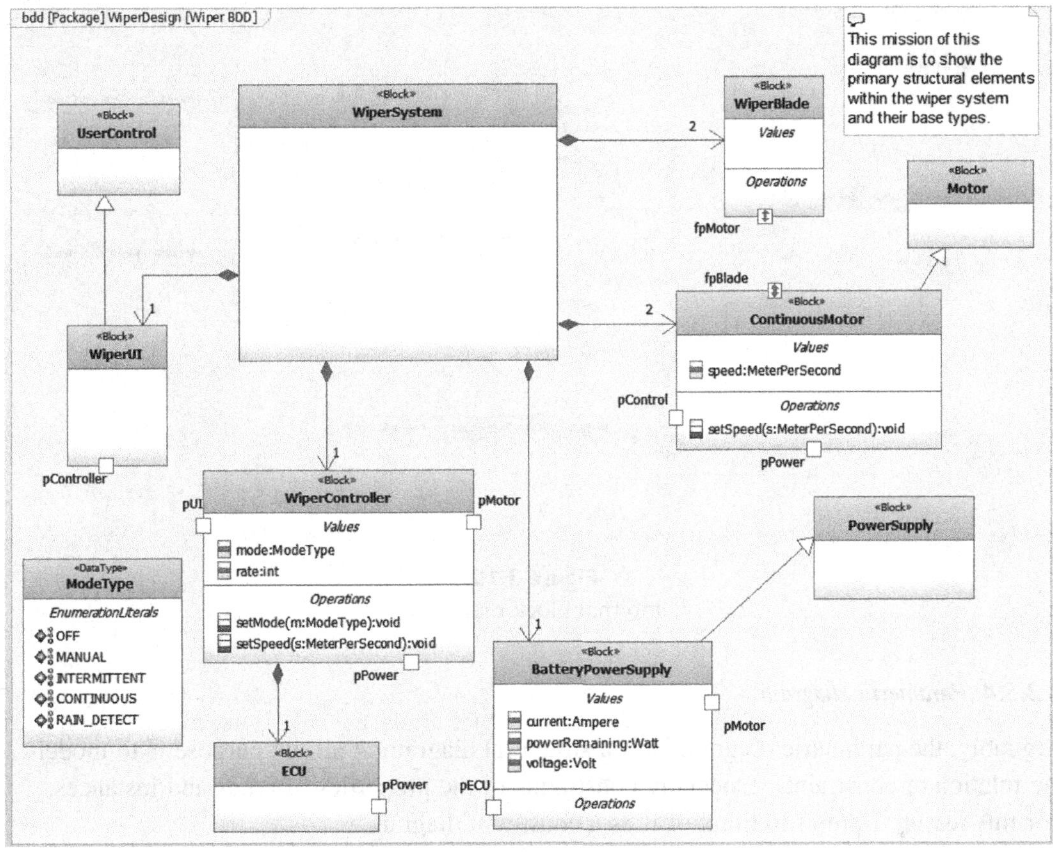

Figure 3.9
Block definition diagram.

Figure 3.10 shows the elements in the previous figure as an IBD. I added some flows on the diagram (electricity and commands) to illustrate something often done by system engineers.

Note that the names on the parts are in an *instance-name:block-type* format. This way we can see the names of the instances as well as their type. If desired, we can also show other features and properties such as their nested parts, as I did in the case of the `WiperController`.

We couldn't show the relations between the ports in Figure 3.9 because the connector relation is not a relation between blocks (which are types) but really relations between block instances or parts. We'll talk a bit more about different ways to connect blocks and parts later in this chapter.

The IBD is a crucial view because systems engineers structure systems as layers of whole-part decompositions, and this is the intent of this diagram.

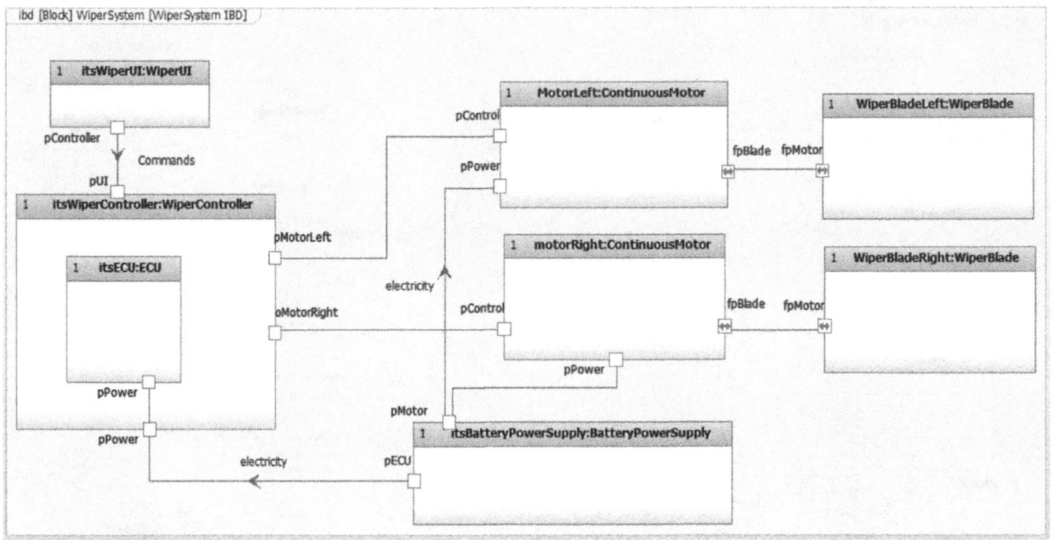

Figure 3.10
Internal block diagram.

3.2.5.4 Parametric diagram

Arguably, the parametric diagram isn't a structural diagram at all; its purpose is to model the relation of constraints, especially constraints of the properties of types and instances. For this reason, I prefer to think of it as a constraint diagram.

Parametric diagrams allow you to create systems of equations or inequalities to constrain various properties of blocks. The constraint blocks themselves may be defined and decomposed on BDDs but they are related to each other in interesting ways on the parametric diagram.

Parametric diagrams are useful so that we can compute aggregate properties of a system (such as total mass), ensure aggregate properties are reasonable (such as not exceeding a total weight constraint), and perform trade studies to find the best from a set of potential solutions.

In Figure 3.11, we've characterized the motor of the wiper system in terms of power. Given that it uses a certain current at a specific voltage with a (controllable) duty cycle, we can calculate average power usage. The upper part of the figure defines the Constraint Block `PowerUsage` to be a property of the Block `Motor` in a BDD. Then in the lower part of the figure, the constraint parameters within the constraint block are bound (via binding connectors) to value properties of the motor. In tools such as IBM®Rational® Rhapsody®, the constraint blocks can be evaluated by mathematical tools, such as Modelica, for rapid calculation.

That completes the overview of the SysML diagrams. Next, let's talk about using packages to organize our models.

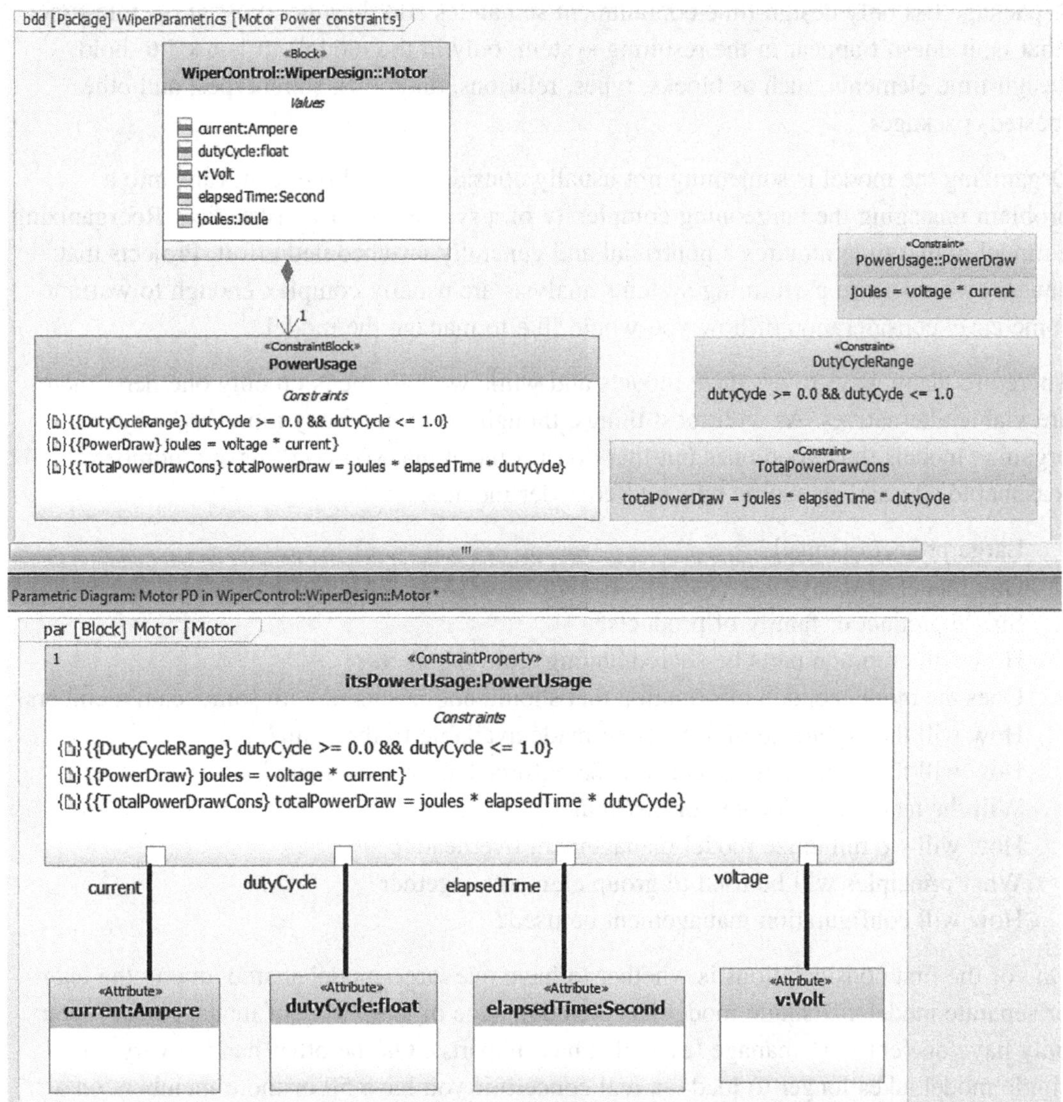

Figure 3.11
Parametric diagram.

3.3 Organize Your Models Like It Matters

In SysML, as in UML, the *package* is the key mechanism for model organization. In fact, a model itself is a kind of package within the defining metamodel of the UML. A package also serves as the primary basis for configuration management—that is, you normally check in and check out portions of a model or a package at a time.

A package has only design-time containment semantics and does not exist at operate-time (that is, it doesn't appear in the resulting system, only in the model). It is used to hold design-time elements, such as blocks, types, relations, diagrams, stereotypes, and other (nested) packages.

Organizing the model is something not usually considered until the team runs into a problem managing the burgeoning complexity of a system under construction. Reorganizing a model at that time requires a nontrivial and generally unscheduled effort. Projects that have a systems team performing systems analysis are usually complex enough to warrant some early consideration of how you would like to manage the model.

There are many ways to organize models and while we will focus on only one here, there are viable alternatives. As with most things, though, there are many more *bad* ways to organize models than good ones but that doesn't mean that you don't have a number of reasonable alternatives. Some points to consider include:

- Large project or small?
- One model or many?
- Single product or family of products?
- How will common parts be shared among team members?
- Does the model contain information that should not be shared with some team members?
- How will the architectural aspects be made available to the team?
- How will the architectural decisions be enforced among the team?
- Will the team be co-located or distributed?
- How will we minimize model management overheads?
- What principles will be used to group elements together?
- How will configuration management be used?

One of the first considerations is whether to have one large model shared among the team or separate models. A single model has the advantage of simplicity of management—you only have one entity to manage (even if it has subparts). On the other hand, a vary large single model takes longer to load—a real concern if you have 50 or more members on a team—and finding things to facilitate sharing and collaboration in a large monolithic model can be difficult. Multiple models have the advantage that system complexity can be divided across many different models and each model is smaller, more manageable, and takes less time to load than a larger single model. On the other hand, significant thought should be put into what the submodels should be, what criteria should be used to locate model elements in the various models, how the models will interrelate, and how the models will be shared across multiple stakeholders.

As a recommendation, for teams of 15 or fewer members, a single model may be a good choice; for teams of 20 or more, multiple connected models are probably a better choice.

Table 3.1: Model stakeholders.

Group	Purpose	Scope of concern
Systems engineers	• Construct a discipline-independent model of requirements and architecture • Map requirements and functionality to subsystems • Specify interfaces between subsystems	• System requirements • System architecture
Subsystem team	• Create a deployment architecture for the specific subsystem • Create software and hardware specifications (submodels)	• Single subsystem • Mapping of subsystem requirements to engineering disciplines
Engineers (SW, mechanical, electronic, chemical)	• Perform analysis and design of a specific subsystem within their discipline	• Model elements within their discipline for a single subsystem
Design architect	• Oversee architectural design for the set of subsystems	• Common architectural model for entire system • Discipline-related architecture for each subsystem
Testers	• Subsystem-level testing • Integration testing • Verification testing • Validation testing	• Subsystem—normally done within the subsystem team • Integration—normally done with system-level scope • Verification—system scope • Validation—normally done at system-level scope

Of course, the properties of the system under development impact the decision. If the model is linearly separable (i.e., able to be broken into a number of more-or-less independent pieces), management of multiple models is easy. If the system is not linearly separable, it may be much more difficult to create multiple models. If, in order to work on one model one must import all the other models as well, breaking the system up into multiple models won't help you.

The primary reasons to break up large models are to (i) decrease load/save time, (ii) provide smaller but sufficient models to teams who have narrow focus, (iii) better support collaborative engineering, and (iv) protect information. The typical stakeholders for a system model are shown in Table 3.1.

Figure 3.12 shows a typical recommended model organization for a medium to large project.[15] The icon for a model is a package that contains a nested triangle. This figure shows a systems engineering model (`SE_Model`), a model holding shared elements

[15] This same organizational architecture holds for very large models, by simply making some of the packages within the models into separate models themselves. I worked with one customer whose (very large) project consisted of 1200 interconnected models.

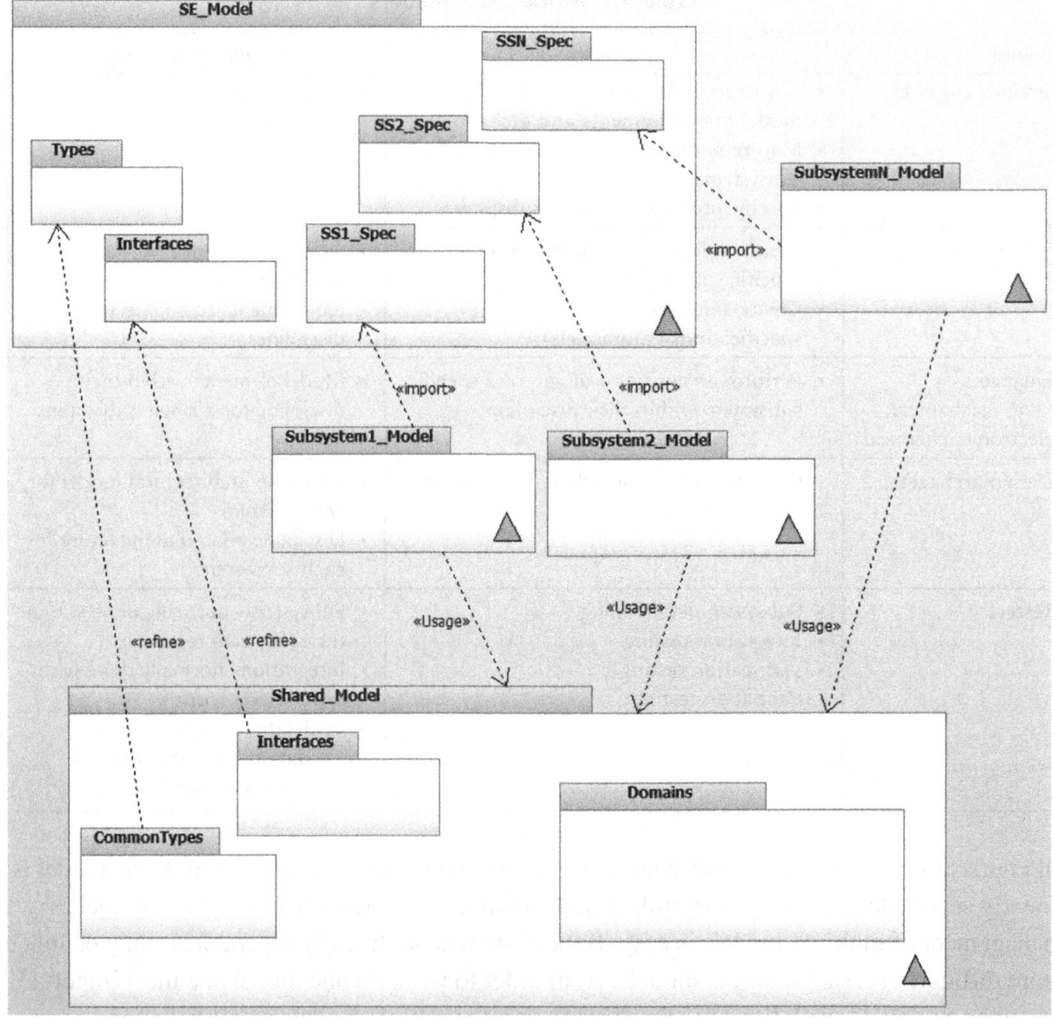

Figure 3.12
Recommended large project organization.

(`Shared_Model`), and a set of subsystem models. Each of these models has internal packages, only some of which are shown. In actual fact, any of these models can be split into multiple models; for example, there might be multiple SE models focusing on different use cases.

The models are related in three different ways. The subsystems «import» a *copy* of their specification package while they *reference* (via the «usage» relation) elements that are used by at least two subsystems. The «refine» relation indicates that the logical elements (types and interfaces) must be *refined* into physical elements; this is done during the hand off from systems to downstream engineering (see Chapter 8).

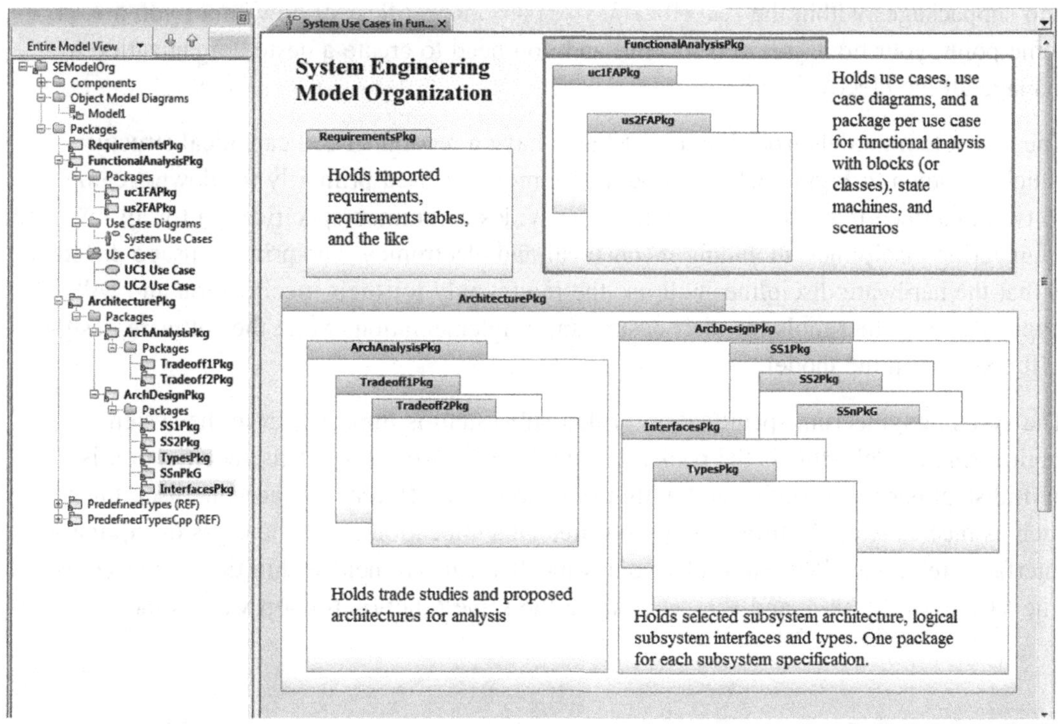

Figure 3.13
Canonical system engineering model organization.

The Harmony process recommends a canonical system engineering model organization. This is shown in Figure 3.13. The organization can be seen both in the browser at the left or as a package diagram on the right.

The highest-level packages are `Requirements`, `Functional Analysis`, and `Architecture`. The `Requirements` package holds the requirements, use cases, and use case diagrams. The `Functional Analysis` package contains one nested package per use case for functional analysis—a process we will describe in some detail in Chapter 5. The `Architecture` package is divided into two packages, one for architectural trade off analysis and one for elaborating the selected architecture (`ArchDesignPkg` in Figure 3.13). This package holds the architectural specifications that will ultimately be handed off to downstream engineering; one package per subsystem holds allocated requirements and subsystem-level use cases and their specifications for that subsystem. There are also separate packages to hold the subsystem interfaces and the user-defined logical types used by those interfaces.

It should be noted that more packages can be added as necessary. If you have 10 use cases, then a single package to hold them (`FunctionalAnalysisPkg`) is fine. If you've got 500, as you might for a very large system such as an aircraft, then you will want to organize them into subpackages within the `FunctionalAnalysisPkg`. Regardless of how smart you are, at some point, your brain just gets too full and you need to create a nested organization to manage all the pieces.

The subsystem models from Figure 3.12 also have a recommended canonical structure, which is shown in Figure 3.14. Although this model is used primarily for downstream software engineering of the subsystems, it provides a common specification for all involved engineering disciplines, including mechanical and electronics. The primary usage difference is that the hardware disciplines will use the model only for their specification and will (typically) use other tools for their design and implementation, while the software design will continue in the model.

The system engineering specification of that subsystem is imported from the system engineering model—this is the package named `SubsystemSpecPkg`. This specification is multidisciplinary and is allocated within this model to different engineering disciplines, such as mechanical, electronic, and software. This allocation—and the cross-disciplinary interfaces (e.g., sw-electronics, electronics-mechanical) are held within the `DeploymentPkg`. The `SWReqsPkg`, `SWFAPkg`, and `SWArchPkg` serve the same function for software as the

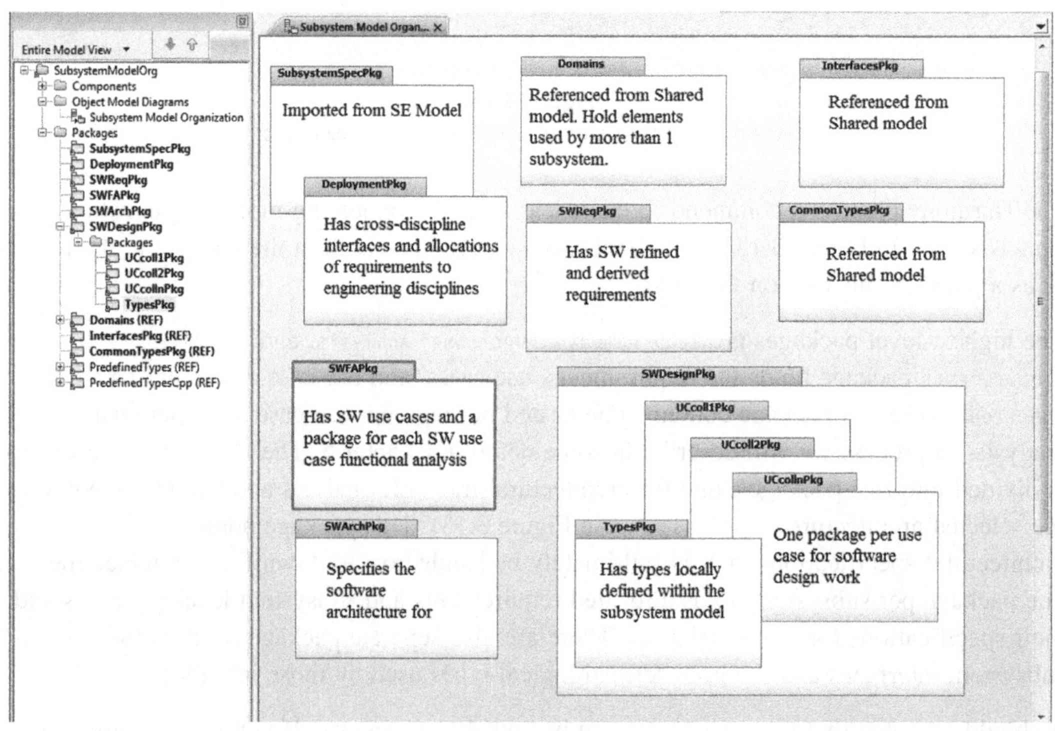

Figure 3.14
Canonical subsystem model organization.

RequirementsPkg, FunctionalAnalysisPkg, and ArchitecturePkg, respectively, did for systems in the system engineering model. The software analysis and design are held within the SWDesignPkg, which—outside of a TypesPkg package for widely used types—are organized by internal packages holding the collaborations for each of the use cases. Lastly, there are three packages referenced from the shared model. The InterfacesPkg and CommonTypesPkg packages reference system and subsystem interfaces and types used by those interfaces. The Domains package holds software-specific elements that are used by multiple subsystems so they don't have to be defined everywhere they are used.

3.4 Key SysML Views and Core Semantics

There are five diagrams that are used more than any others in SysML—block definition, internal block, activity, sequence, and state. These are the core set of conceptual modeling views used for MBSE. Let's discuss those views and the elements they depict.

3.4.1 Blocks, Relations, Interfaces, and Ports

3.4.1.1 Blocks

Let's begin with the most basic element of SysML, the *Block.*

A block is a design-time specification of pieces of the system. These pieces can be electronic, mechanical, software, or any other kind of modular element, including one that has combined these types. Blocks specify both structure and behavior of block instances as well as other properties of interest in the same way that the blueprint for an engine specifies the structure and behavior of the actual engines in different cars.

One of the most basic properties of a block is the values that it owns. Each of these values may be a simple scalar or something complex (and itself typed by a block). It is common to use either basic types (integer, float, complex), or SysML SI definitions of dimensions (length, mass, or time) or units (ampere, meter, kilogram) to type values. Figure 3.15 shows the block Motor in two different forms on the left side of the figure. The upper form shows Motor as an undifferentiated rectangle while below it, the Motor's values and operations are shown. Each value in the *value compartment* is typed. For variety, we see values typed by a basic integer (int), a couple typed as rotational speed units (RPM), one as torque units (NewtonMeter), and one as a structured type (LED) that is actually defined by the block LED (not shown). Yes, blocks can contain values typed by other blocks.

The lower compartment of the Motor block shows the *operations* it owns. An operation is the specification of an invocable behavior that may take input values (called *arguments*) and may produce a *return value*. These may be software, electronic, mechanical, or even abstract functions.

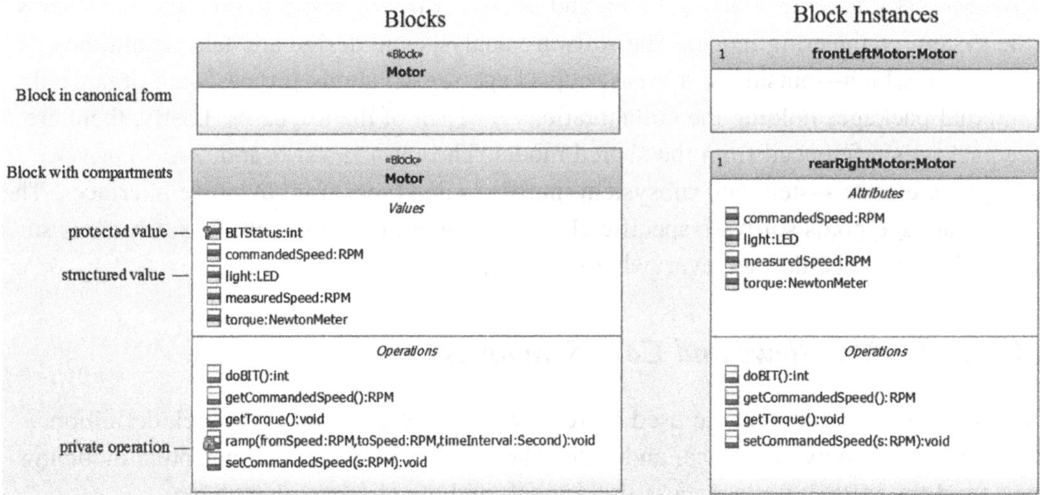

Figure 3.15
Block.

Values and operations are said to be *features* of a block. Features have a property called *visibility* that defines who may access them. In Figure 3.15, the unadorned (i.e., not otherwise annotated) features are said to be *public*. This means that any element that can access the block instance can access the feature. Thus, any other block instance that can find the instance of Motor can command it to `doBit()` or read or write the value `commandedSpeed`. The `ramp()` operation is said to be *protected*. This means that the feature can only be accessed by Motor itself or any subtypes derived from Motor (we'll talk about generalization and specialization shortly). The value `BITStatus` is said to be private, which means that *only* the Motor is allowed to access the feature internally.

3.4.1.2 Block instances

A *Block Instance* ("object" in the software world) is the implementation of a block specification. The right side of Figure 3.15 shows two different instances of the same block. The upper is in canonical form, exposing no internal features. The one below shows the compartments, although only exposing the public features in this case (just to show that it can be done).[16] The left and right side of the figure look remarkably similar; however the text in the block name is different. The syntax for showing a block instance is <instance name>:<type name>. The upper instance is named `fronLeftMotor` and is typed by the block `Motor`. The lower instance is similarly typed but given the name `rearRightMotor`.

[16] In fact, you needn't show all features all the time. You can always select which features are appropriate to display on any given diagram.

Of course, we design systems with lots of connected parts. In the SysML, blocks and block instances are connected through various relations, and the most important of these are association, aggregation, composition, and generalization.[17]

3.4.1.3 Association

An association is a navigable connection between blocks. Behaviors in one block may dereference that association to access values or invoke operations of other blocks. This allows instances of the different blocks to communicate and collaborate. This communication takes one of two forms, and sometimes a combination of the two. First, the collaboration may be *discrete*; that is, one block may invoke a service of another by synchronously invoking an operation or by sending the block a synchronous or asynchronous event. It is discrete in the sense that the communication happens at some point in time, takes finite time to complete, and then it's done. Alternatively, the communication can be *continuous*, such as the continuous flow of energy or material from one instance to another, such as a pump delivering a fluid flow. Digital software only models the first kind of communication—discrete—while systems must, in general, contend with both. Associations are the conduits over which these communications flow. Basic associations are shown in Figure 3.16.

Associations, by default, are bidirectional. That means that if two blocks are connected with an association, communication can be initiated by either. Associations can also be unidirectional by adorning them with an open arrowhead on one end, as between the `Controller` block and the `Motor` block in Figure 3.16. That means that the `Controller` can send messages to the Motor but not vice versa.

You will notice in the figure that the association has a name at each navigable end. These *association ends* are the means by which the block instance is referenced. For example, for the Controller to invoke the `zero()` operation of the `Motor`, you might use a statement within the `Controller` such as:

```
itsMotor->zero();
```

where `itsMotor` is the reference by which the `Controller` knows the `Motor` block instance to which it is connected.

The *multiplicity* of an association end is the number of block instances that fulfill that role in the operating system. By far, the most common is 1; that is, a single instance fulfills the role. However, it can be optional, meaning it may or may not be there (0, 1), a fixed integer when there are one or more (such as the two instances of the Battery block in Figure 3.16), zero or more with no fixed upper bound (denoted as *) or one or more (shown as 1..*).

[17] There are also many different kinds of a more generic relation known as a *dependency*. We'll discuss the most important of these as they come up naturally in the conversation.

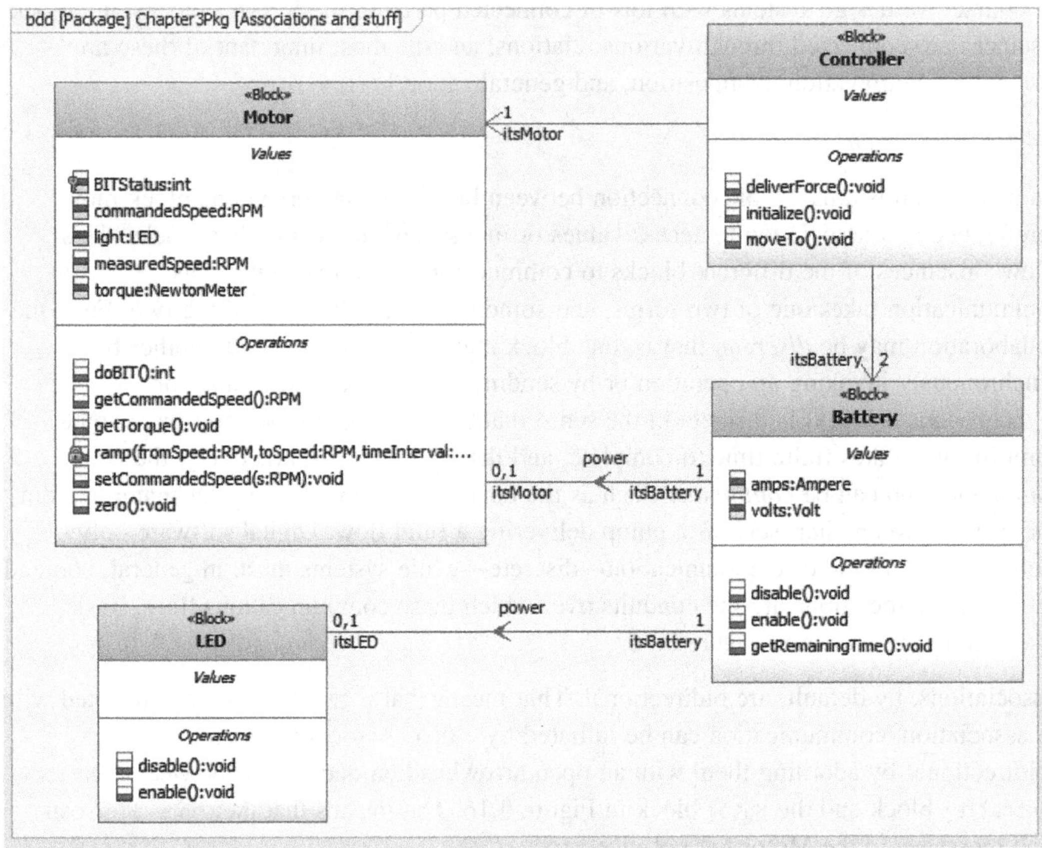

Figure 3.16
Association relation.

3.4.1.4 Flows

The last feature of interest in Figure 3.16 is the arrows in the middle of the association. These denote *flows*. While they can denote information flow—typically used in software—in systems, they more often denote energy or materiel flow. In the case of the figure, the flow is labeled `power`, to indicate the electrical energy is flowing. The flow is defined in terms of *flow items*, which can be typed in the same way that block attributes of types—by simple types, dimensions, units, or even blocks.

3.4.1.5 Aggregation

It turns out that the UML (and therefore SysML as well) defines three types of association—"normal" association, aggregation, and composition. Aggregation is an association that denotes not only a conduit of communication but also that one—the aggregator—collects one

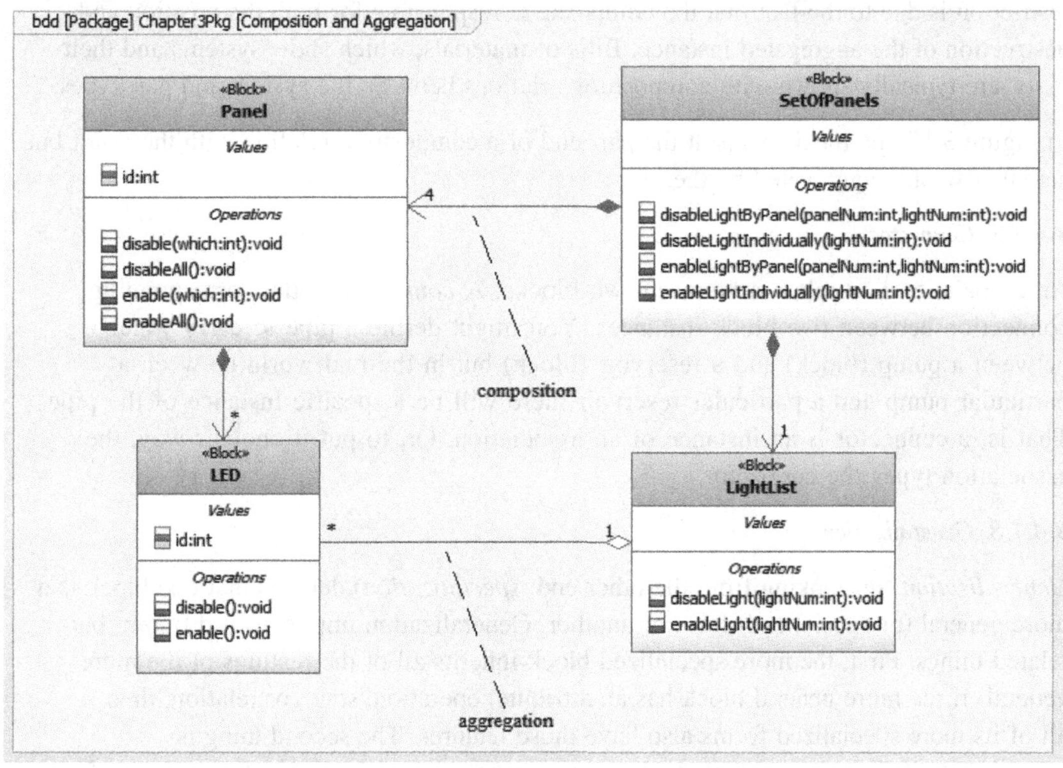

Figure 3.17
Aggregation and composition.

or more of the other—the aggregate. This is a weak form of aggregation that is also known as *shared* or *catalog aggregation*. It is weak in the sense that aggregated instances can be aggregates of more than one aggregator. For example, the same instance of a book can simultaneously be in different lists organized by name, title, ISBN number, or subject. The book in question belongs to each list. Aggregation is shown with an empty diamond at the site of the aggregator on the association, as in Figure 3.17.

3.4.1.6 Composition

Composition is the strong form of aggregation. It is shown with a filled diamond at the aggregator end of the association. It is strong in the sense that an aggregated instance can have at most a single composite owner. This doesn't mean that the same block (type) cannot be aggregated into different composites—an engine (block) can define a part for both an automobile and a boat, after all. Additionally, the same instance can be a part of a composite but still be the subject of a weak aggregation with another element. Composition just means that a given instance can only have a single composite owner. This semantic restriction is due to the fact that the composite is responsible for both the creation and destruction of the aggregated instance. Bills of materials, which show systems and their parts, are typically shown with composition relations between the system and part types.

In Figure 3.17, the block `LED` is at the part end of a composition relation with the `Panel` but also it is weakly aggregated by the `LightList`.

3.4.1.7 Connector

An association is a relation between two blocks. A *connector* is the corresponding connection between two block instances. You might define a pipe to carry water between a pump (block) and a reservoir (block) but in the real world between a particular pump and a particular reservoir there will be a specific instance of the pipe. That is, a connector is an instance of an association. Or, to put it another way, the association types the connector.

3.4.1.8 Generalization

Generalization (or, looking from the other end, *specialization*) denotes that one block is a more general (or specialized) form of another. Generalization implies two different but related things. First, the more specialized block inherits all of the features of the more general. If the more general block has an attribute, operation, state, or relation, then all of its more specialized forms also have those features. The second thing is "substitutability"—that means that whenever you can use an instance of the general form, you can also use an instance of any of its more specialized forms.

Specialization is useful in a number of circumstances. For example, you might want to reuse a core set of features (such as a state machine, attributes, and/or operations) but specialize them for different uses. Or, you might want to support different implementations in the different specialized blocks, such as in a continuous motor versus a stepper motor.

Specialization can be done using either (or both) of two methods. The first is to actually specialize a behavior—that is, provide a different implementation of a behavior defined in a more general block. The other is that you can add new features to the specialized block not contained within the general block, including new states and transitions, new attributes, and new operations. Generalization is a powerful tool that is underutilized by systems engineers.

Figure 3.18 shows a simple use of generalization. Generalization is shown as a line with a *closed arrowhead*; this distinguishes it from a directed association which uses an open arrowhead. The arrowhead points to the more general block. In the figure, we see that the `Sensor` block defines a set of values (`id` and `value`) and some operations. The subclasses (another term for the specialized blocks) inherit all these properties and can specialize the behaviors and new features as well. The `FilteredSensor` block adds a low and high filter limit and an operation to set them. The `RedundantSensor` adds a second copy of the sensed

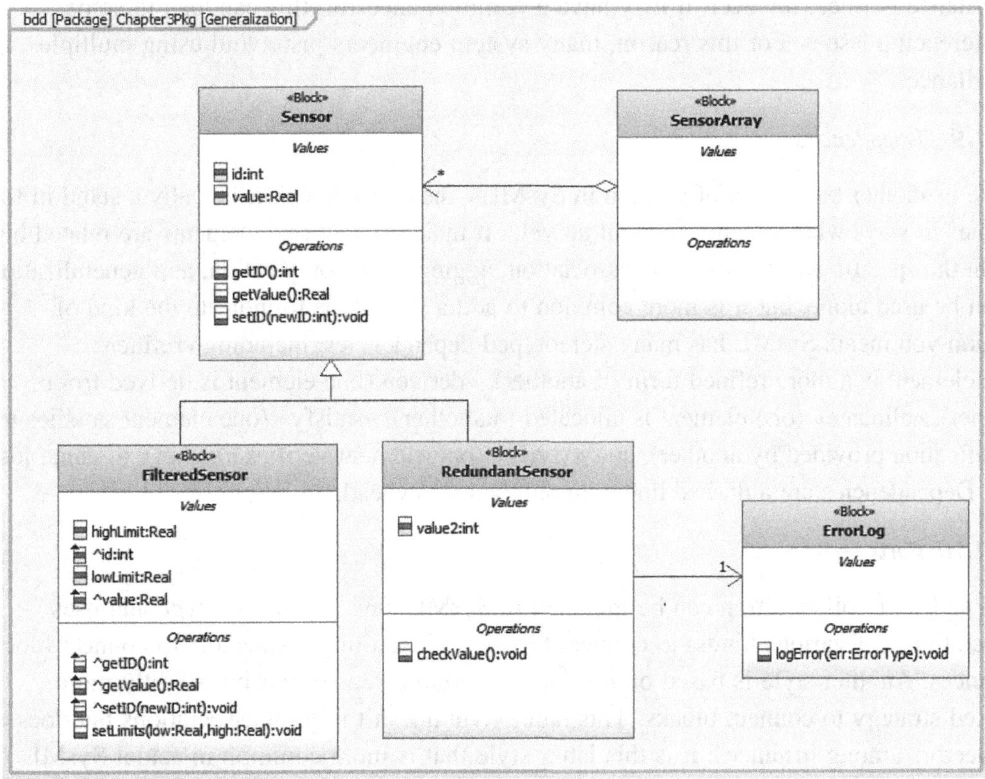

Figure 3.18
Generalization.

value so that if the original value should be corrupted via EMI (for example), that corruption can be detected. This second subclass also has a relation to the `ErrorLog` block to register when such an error has been detected.

Note that in both cases, the subclasses inherit all the features of the base block, and, although I've chosen to only show the inherited features for the `FilteredSensor`, they are still present in the `RedundantSensor`.[18] Also note that the `SensorArray` block can aggregate instances of all three kinds of blocks—`Sensors`, `FilteredSensors`, and `RedundantSensors`, because the latter two *are* kinds of the first.

It is possible for a block to be a specialized form of more than one block, a situation known as *multiple inheritance*. If the two blocks have no common ancestor between them, multiple

[18] You needn't show all the features of a block on the diagram. Remember, a diagram is just a visualization of the sets of elements and features in the model repository that you want to see in this specific context.

inheritance is fine. However, if they have a common ancestor, this can lead to some dereferencing issues. For this reason, many system engineers just avoid using multiple inheritance.

3.4.1.9 Dependencies

There is another basic kind of relation in SysML—the dependency. It is really a stand in for "relates in ways what we ain't thought up yet." It indicates that two elements are related but not in the specific ways defined by association, aggregation, composition, and generalization. It can be used alone, but it is more common to add a stereotype to indicate the kind of relation you mean. SysML has many stereotyped dependencies, including «refine» (one element is a more refined form of another), «derive» (one element is derived from another), «allocate» (one element is allocated to another), «satisfy» (one element satisfies the specification provided by another), and «verify» (one element verifies another), to name just a few. Dependencies are a dashed line with an open arrowhead.

3.4.1.10 Ports

Two styles of collaboration can be modeled in SysML; one is based on *type* and uses associations (of various kinds) to connect blocks and resulting connectors to connect block instances. Another style is based on *interface compliance*, a similar but slightly more relaxed strategy to connect blocks. This latter style doesn't rely on associations but does use connectors among instances. It is this latter style that is more common in actual SysML practice and it entails the use of ports.

A port is shown as a small rectangle on the boundary of a block, and specifies a connection point. SysML changed and enhanced ports in UML and in SysML 1.3 they were changed even more radically. Standard ports are identical (more or less) to UML ports and are typed by *interfaces*. *Flow ports* were added to SysML to model continuous flows and are an extension to UML ports, and are typed by *flow specifications*. In SysML 1.3, flow ports and flow specifications are deprecated[19] and are replaced by proxy ports and full ports.

Standard ports

Standard ports (from UML) are supported in SysML but really only support discrete messaging. In practice, this means that you can have function calls (synchronous messaging) and signal events (asynchronous messaging). Standard ports are typed by interfaces (see below). One of the primary purposes for a port is to expose services from an internally nested block to the clients of its owner block, without exposing the internal structure of the composite block. The client just knows that the `Ventilator` provides a

[19] Meaning they're still in the definition of the language should you want to use them, but they may be removed in some future release of SysML. However, I think this is unlikely because they are very useful in multitool simulations, such as with Rhapsody™ and Simulink™ co-simulation.

setRespirationRate(r: int) service but not which element inside the Ventilator block is doing the actual providing (Figure 3.19). To do this, a port *provides* an interface; that means that a block (or one of its internal parts) will implement the named service. You can also conjugate the interface, that is, another block (perhaps the UI wanting to configure the Ventilator) may *require* the interface, meaning that it expects to be connected to some element that will implement the service.

By the way, ports can have multiplicity as well, if you need an array of ports. Bracket notation is used and the specification with the brackets is the same as with multiplicity on associations.

Interfaces

An *interface* is shown as a block with the stereotype «interface». An interface is a specification of communication that identifies the operations called or the events received. An interface is different from a block in that it can have no implementation; it really is just a specification of services. A block that *realizes* with the interface implements the operations and event receptions to provide the response behavior for the events from the interface.

If you look at Figure 3.19, you see that the Ventilator block has a port named pMedical which provides the services specified in the interface iResp. However, the Ventilator block

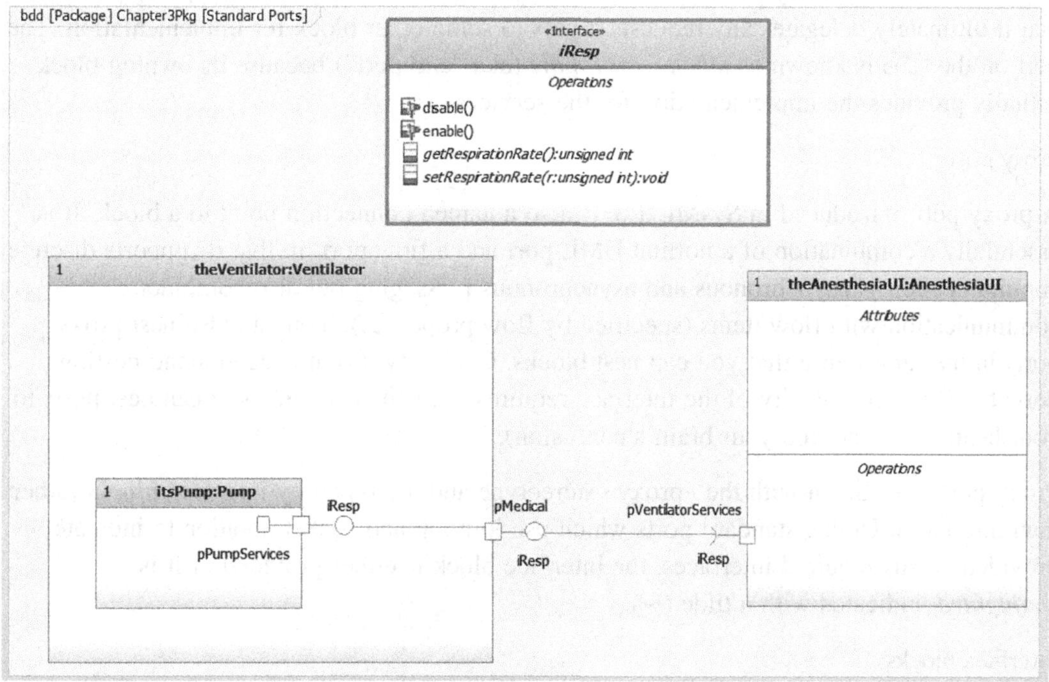

Figure 3.19
Standard ports.

itself doesn't implement those services; that nested block instance `itsPump` (typed by block `Pump`) does. Nevertheless, the `Ventilator` can provide those services to its clients by providing a port that delegates the request off to the internal part that provides the implementation. The lollipop on the port shows that the `iResp` interface is *provided*. At the other end of the connector, the `AnesthesiaUI` block has a port that *requires* the services from `iResp` (as indicated with the socket notation on the port). The `AnesthesiaUI` block knows that it can connect to the `Ventilator` block to get that need fulfilled but doesn't know anything about how the `Ventilator` block provides it.

As an aside, you can only connect block instances (not blocks) with connectors between ports. That is why the diagram shows instances of `Ventilator` and `AnesthesiaUI` not their block types themselves. This is an inherent characteristic of using the interface compliance approach rather than the type approach, which just uses associations. Some people find this a bit confusing and want to connect ports on blocks and not just on interfaces. There are good metamodeling technical reasons for this but we won't go into them here. Sorry.

The figure also shows the `iResp` interface details and you can see that it contains both synchronous operation calls (such as `setResirationRate(r: unsigned int)`) and asynchronous events (such as `enable()`).

The port on the boundary of the `Ventilator` block is known as a *delegation port*, meaning that it ultimately delegates any requests it gets to some other block for implementation. The port on the `Pump` is known as a *behavioral port* (aka "end port") because its owning block actually provides the implementation for the services.

Proxy ports

A proxy port, introduced in SysML 1.3, is also a named connection point to a block. It is essentially a combination of a normal UML port and a flow port, in that it supports discrete communication via synchronous and asynchronous messaging but also continuous communication with flow items (specified by flow properties). You can also nest proxy ports in the same sense that you can nest blocks. Generally, I don't recommend nesting ports but if the complexity of the interface requires such shenanigans, you can nest ports to your heart's delight (and your brain's confusion).

Proxy ports are shown with the «proxy» stereotype and are typed by *interface blocks* rather than interfaces. Unlike standard ports which use lollipop and socket notation to indicate provided versus required interfaces, the interface block is either provided or it is *conjugated*, indicated with a tilde (~).

Interface blocks

Interface blocks permit the externalization of the features of a block. Like an interface, it doesn't provide implementation but, unlike an interface, it can expose elements beyond services, including flow properties, standard ports, flow ports, proxy ports, and even parametric diagrams for modeling constraints. Yes, interface blocks can themselves have ports defined by other interface blocks. However, interface blocks cannot have *full ports* (which we'll discuss in a little bit) or implementation.

Interface blocks can have *directed features*, such as operations and attributes.[20] An operation provided as a directed feature via an interface block is shown with the keyword *prov* while an operation required via an interface block is shown with the keyword *reqd.* Directed features can also be used in normal blocks as well; a reqd directed feature (such as an attribute or operation) is provided by some other element than the block that declares it to be reqd.

Flow properties and flow items

The flow properties model is, well, *things that flow* between blocks, such as information, material, or energy. Flow items are the specific things that flow in a specific usage of a flow property. A good example is a flow property might specify fluid as the thing that is flowing, but the usage of the property might show that water or natural gas are the things that are actually flowing among the block instances.

Figure 3.20 shows a simple example of the use of proxy ports, directed features, flow properties, and interface blocks. The `TempController` block interfaces with the `User` block to get the `commandedTemp` and to the `Sensor` block to get the `currentTemp`. The proxy port to interface with the `User` block (`pUser`) is typed by the interface block `ibUser`; similarly, the proxy port that interfaces with the `Sensor` block (`pSensor`) is typed by the interface block `ibSensor`. Note that the unconjugated form is used for the ports on the `TempController` block and, for interface correctness, the conjugated form must be used on the `User` and `Sensor` blocks. For interface compatibility, interface blocks must be conjugated at one end.

`currentTemp` is defined as a flow property with a direction In at the site of the `TempController`, and Out at the site of the `Sensor`.

Full ports

Full ports are essential externalized parts. That means that a full port is not really a port as much as it is an internal part that you are exposing to the world. Generally, this is a bad idea, and so I don't recommend the use of full ports except when the internal part is an interface device. If you're building an automobile that has a router to connect to the interwebz, then exposing the router is ok because its inherent purpose is to interface things. Full ports are shown with the stereotype «full».

[20] In Rhapsody, at least, it isn't obvious how to make a feature directed. You must add the stereotype ≪directedFeature≫ and then you can set it as prov or reqd.

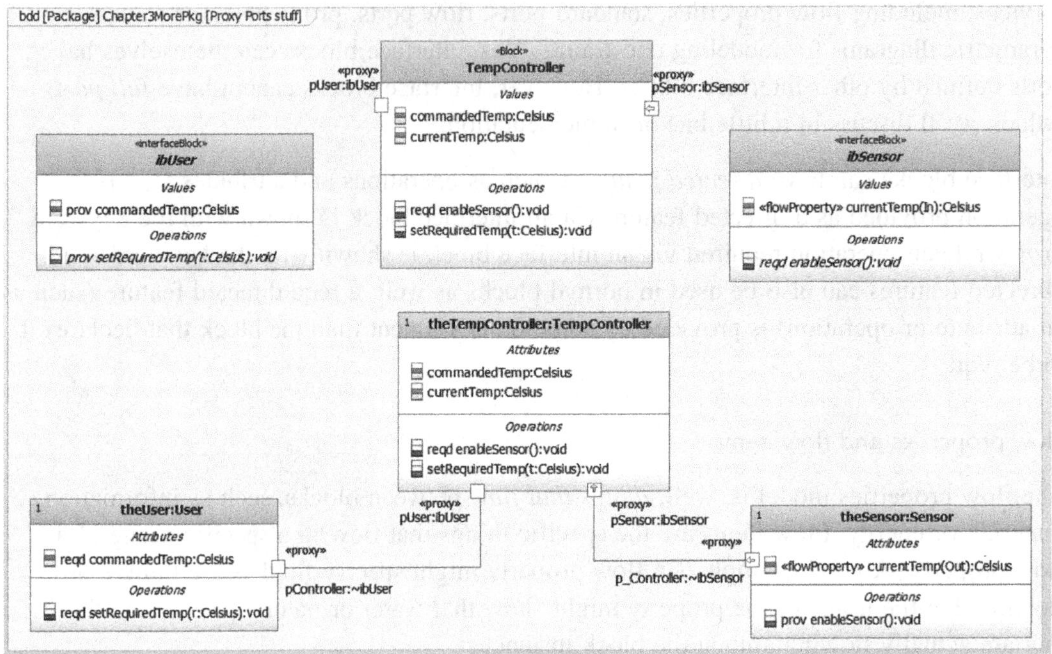

Figure 3.20
Proxy ports and interface blocks.

3.4.1.11 Parts

Blocks can be decomposed into subelements, each of which is known as a part (and each part is sort-of an instance of some (other) block). Strictly speaking, a part is a typed slot into which an instance will play the role provided by the slot. Confused yet?

To really grok parts, it is essential to understand the difference between a block, an instance, and a part. A block is a type that defines a number of features and properties. If you look at Figure 3.21, Pump is represented in all three forms.

On the upper right hand side of the figure, you see `Pump` as a block, including that it has a value called `serialNumber`, which is unique for every instance. We cannot provide a specific value for the serial number within the block because each instance has a different value.

On the left hand side, we see `itsPump:Pump` as a part within the `Ventilator` block. This `Ventilator` block is a design specification of the `Ventilator`. The internal part is not a block because it fulfills a specific role within the context of the `Ventilator` design. A part is really then the role which an instance of the block will play. We still cannot give this `Pump` a specific serial number value because we could put any of a number of Pump instances here, and in fact we'll do just that when we build a specific instance of a `Ventilator`.

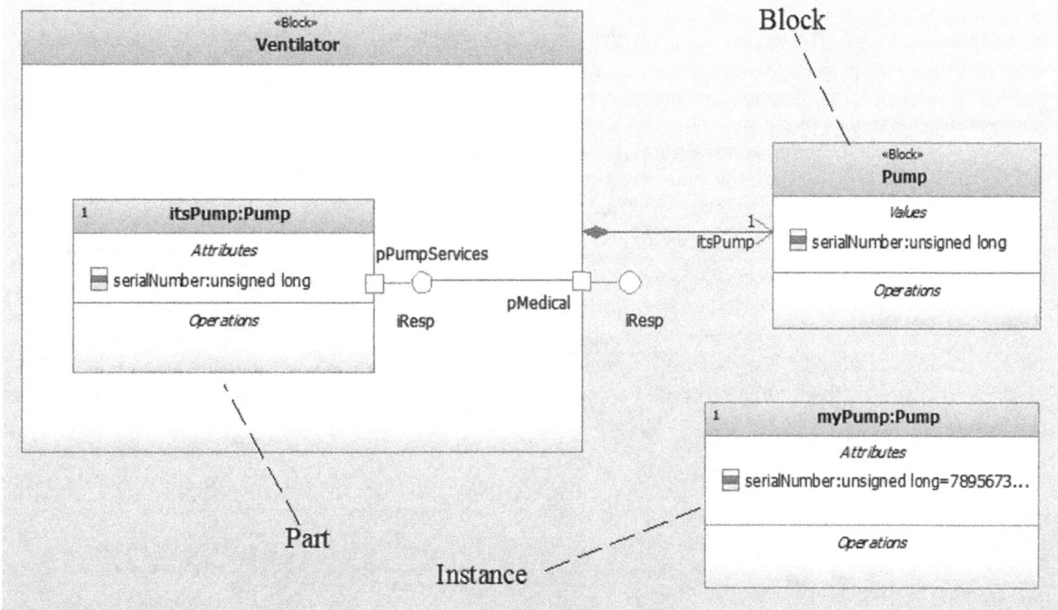

Figure 3.21
Blocks, parts, and instances.

Finally, on the lower right of the figure we see a true instance, `myPump:Pump`. This is a unique instance and so it has a specific value for its `serialNumber`. It may in fact be the very instance we use to make the first or second `Ventilator` in our factory run.

The utility of parts is that they allow us to create reusable building blocks and use them to construct more complex assemblies. A pump could be used in a ventilator, but it can just as well be used in a gas mixer or a medical infusion pump. We can define these building blocks recursively down to whatever level of detail we find useful; at each level, a part is defined by a block that specifies its important properties.

3.4.2 Sequence Diagrams

Sequence diagrams in SysML are identical to their UML counterparts. Sequence diagrams are a great way to show the flow of communications among sets of blocks in a particular case or scenario.

Sequence diagrams depict instance roles—which might represent instances subsystems, systems, parts, or even use cases—interacting over time. The vertical lines in Figure 3.22 are called *lifelines*, and represent the instance (or instance role). Instances (or instance roles) can both send and receive messages. Messages are shown by the arrowed lines going from one lifeline to another.

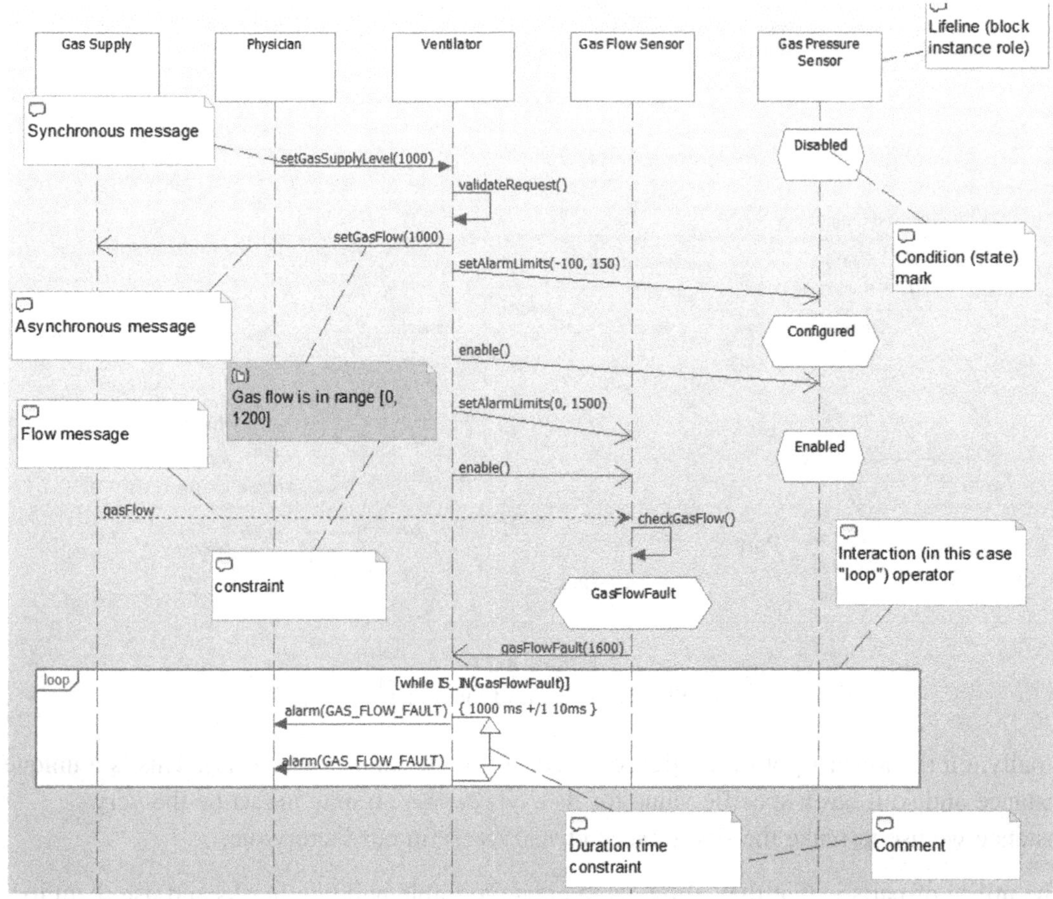

Figure 3.22
Sequence diagram.

The sequence diagram shows an *exemplar* or "sample execution" of some portion of the system under specific conditions. Such an exemplar is commonly called a *scenario*, and a single sequence diagram generally shows a single scenario.[21] The messages may be synchronous (shown with a solid arrowhead), asynchronous (shown with an open arrowhead), or flow (shown with a dashed arrow line). Time on a sequence diagram flows, more or less, from the top of the page downwards. Additionally, state or condition of the lifeline can be shown, as can constraints. In Figure 3.22, a time duration constraint is shown

[21] With the use of interaction operators, it is possible to express many scenarios on a single sequence diagram but this often results in unreadable sequence diagrams. General rule: don't nest interaction operators more than three levels deep. If you find yourself doing that, instead make multiple sequence diagrams showing the different variants of flow.

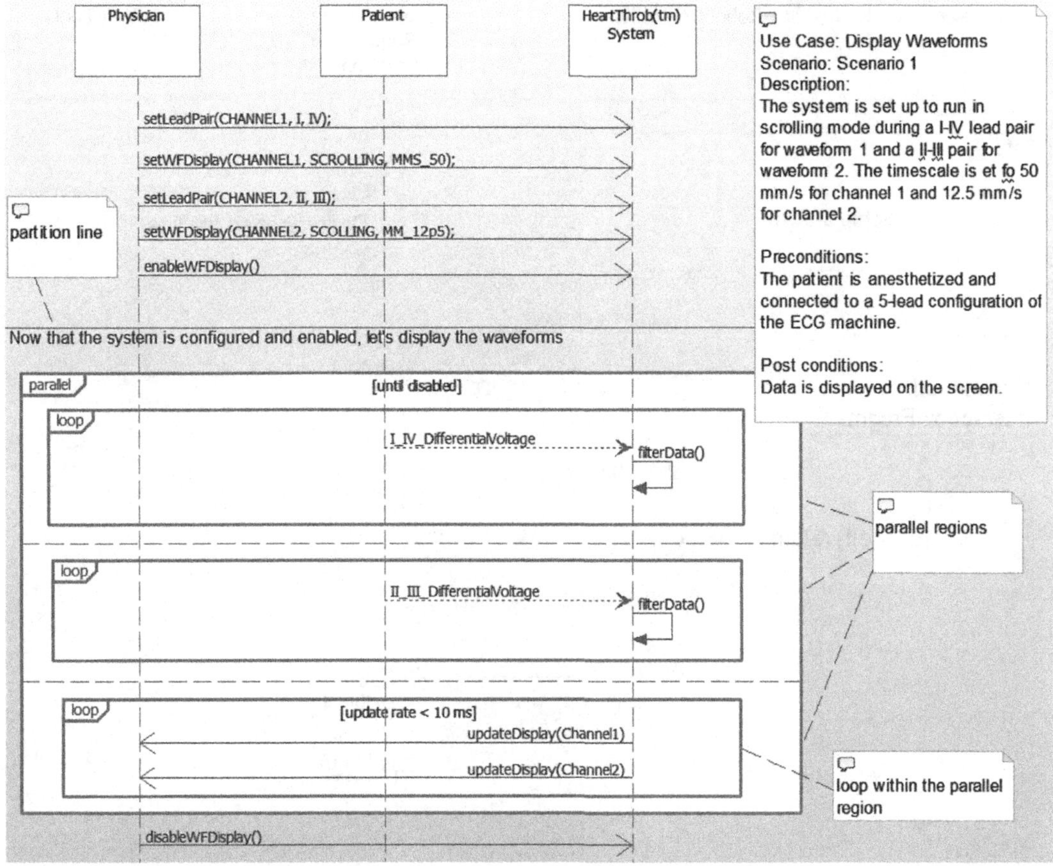

Figure 3.23
Interaction fragments.

clarifying the rate of update of the alarm message set to the Physician. A more general constraint is shown anchored to the `setGasFlow()` message, denoting the valid range of values for the message.

Sequence diagrams may contain, essentially, subdiagrams called *interaction fragments.* Each interaction fragment can have an operator, such as `loop`, `opt` ("optional"), `alt` ("alternative"), `ref` ("reference"), `para` ("parallel"), and so on. These interaction fragments and operators greatly enhance the ability of sequence diagrams as specification tools. Figure 3.23 shows four interaction fragments in total. One has a parallel operator indicating that it contains regions that execute concurrently. Within that interaction fragment are nested three more.

Sequence diagrams can be decomposed into multiple subdiagrams. This can be done either "horizontally" by using an interaction fragment with the `ref` operator, or "vertically" by

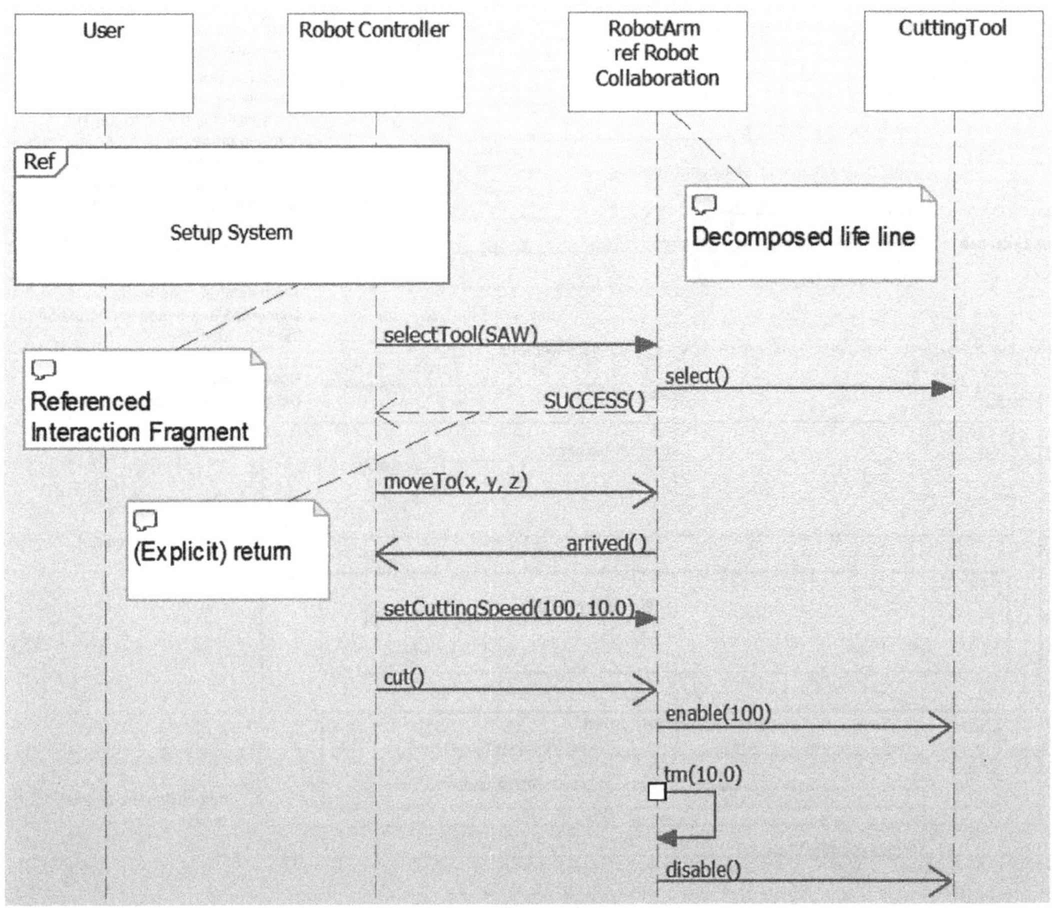

Figure 3.24
High-level sequence diagram.

setting a reference from one lifeline to a separate sequence diagram that shows the same scenario at a more detailed level of abstraction. The next three figures show how these decomposition mechanisms can be used.

Figure 3.24 shows the "high-level" sequence diagram for an industrial robot system. The user sets up the system and based on the task plan, the controller commands the robot to achieve the tasks. The robot itself has internal parts—two angular joints (called the knee and the elbow) and a rotating manipulator, which can grab and control tools. This high-level sequence diagram contains two references to more detailed interactions. The first of these is the `Setup System` referenced interaction fragment. If we open up that diagram (a right-click in Rhapsody), we see the details shown in Figure 3.25.

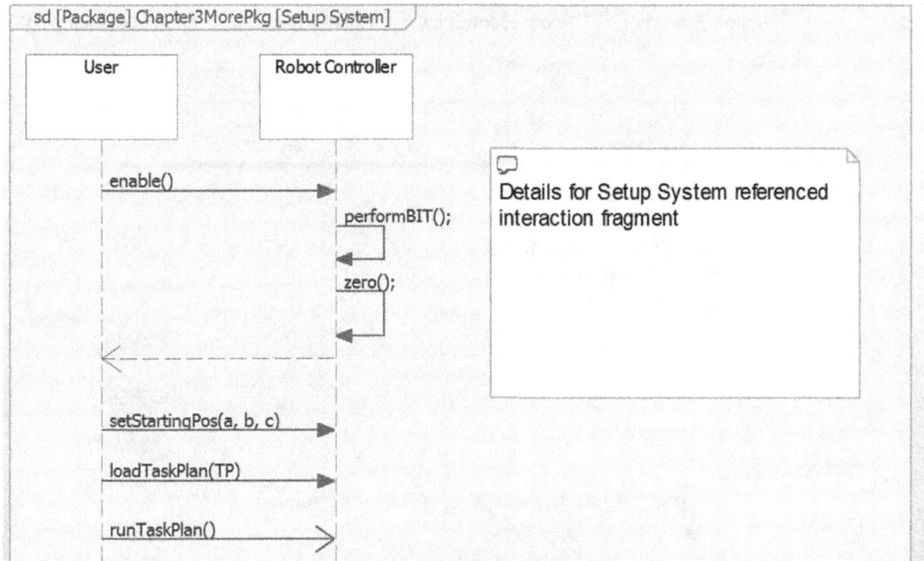

Figure 3.25
Referenced interaction fragment.

Even more valuable, is the ability to decompose the lifeline. This mechanism allows the same scenario to be viewed at many different levels of abstraction without overwhelming the viewer by putting everything on a single, huge diagram. Figure 3.26 shows the details of how the internals of the Robot interact to achieve their roles in this same scenario. The `ENV` lifeline provides the connection between the high- and low-level interactions. At the high level, a message going to the Robot lifeline comes *out* of the `ENV` lifeline on the more detailed diagram. Conversely, a message going *into* the `ENV` lifeline on the more detailed diagram comes out of the `RobotController` lifeline on the higher-level sequence diagram.

3.4.3 Activities, Actions, and Activity Diagrams

Activity modeling sequences and specifies flows among activities and actions, similar to an EFFBD [3]. They play a prominent role in systems engineering because the sequencing and flow of behavior and materiel are a crucial aspect of system behavior. This functional flow modeling (of either data or control) can be done at different levels of abstraction including the system context, system architecture, or detailed system design. SysML makes some important extensions to UML activity diagrams, especially in support of behavior that is continuous in both value and time.

In application, activity diagrams normally show the behavior within a limited scope. In requirements analysis, this scope might be the set of requirements represented or flows

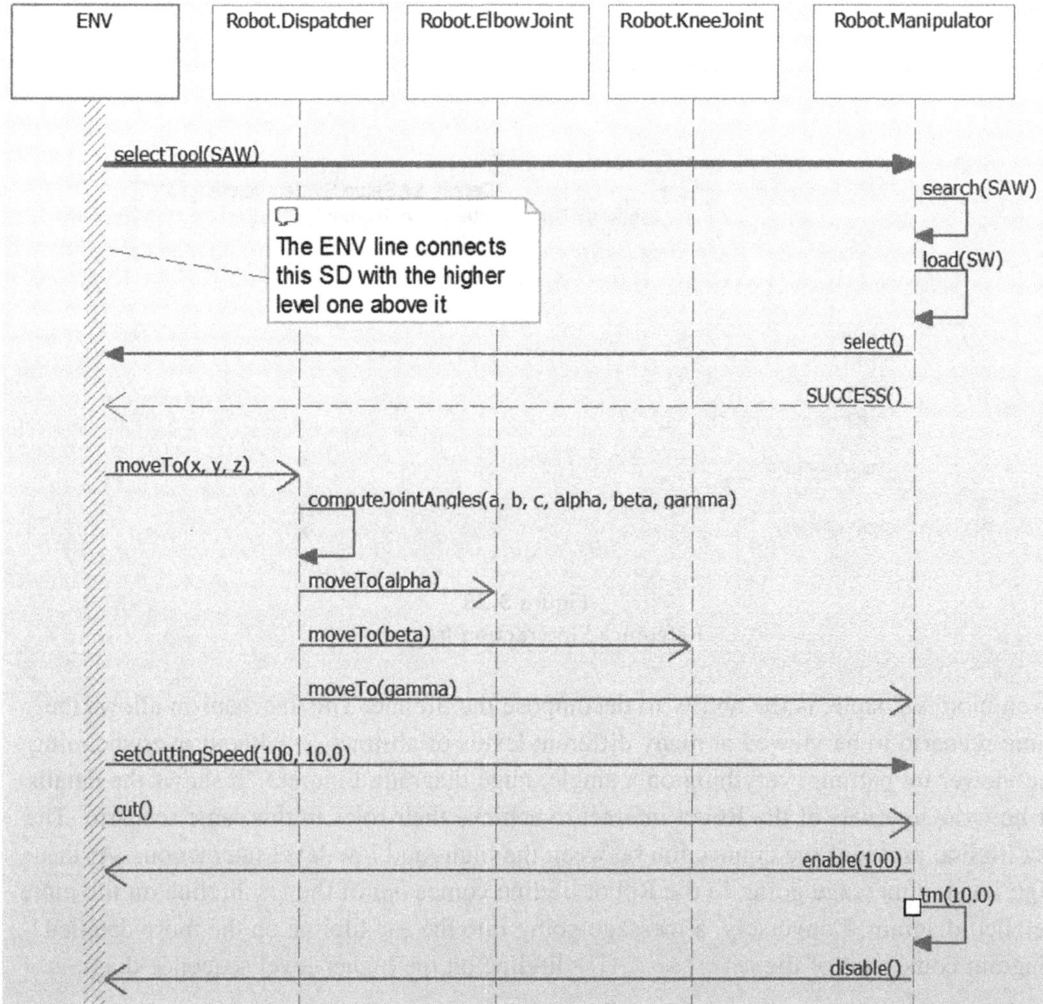

Figure 3.26
Decomposed lifeline.

within a use case. Inside the architecture, the scope might focus on flows around different key system functions, such as delivering power through the drive shaft or controlling the movement of the power windows in a vehicle. Primarily, activity diagrams are used to show flow of behavior; that is, once the behavior is kicked off, the activities are executed one after the other in the prescribed sequence based on the completion of previous actions. It doesn't have to be this way, as SysML activity diagrams to allow the reception and creation of events, but for the most part, activity diagrams are used to model flow of control behavior in which an action is started following the completion of the action that precedes it.

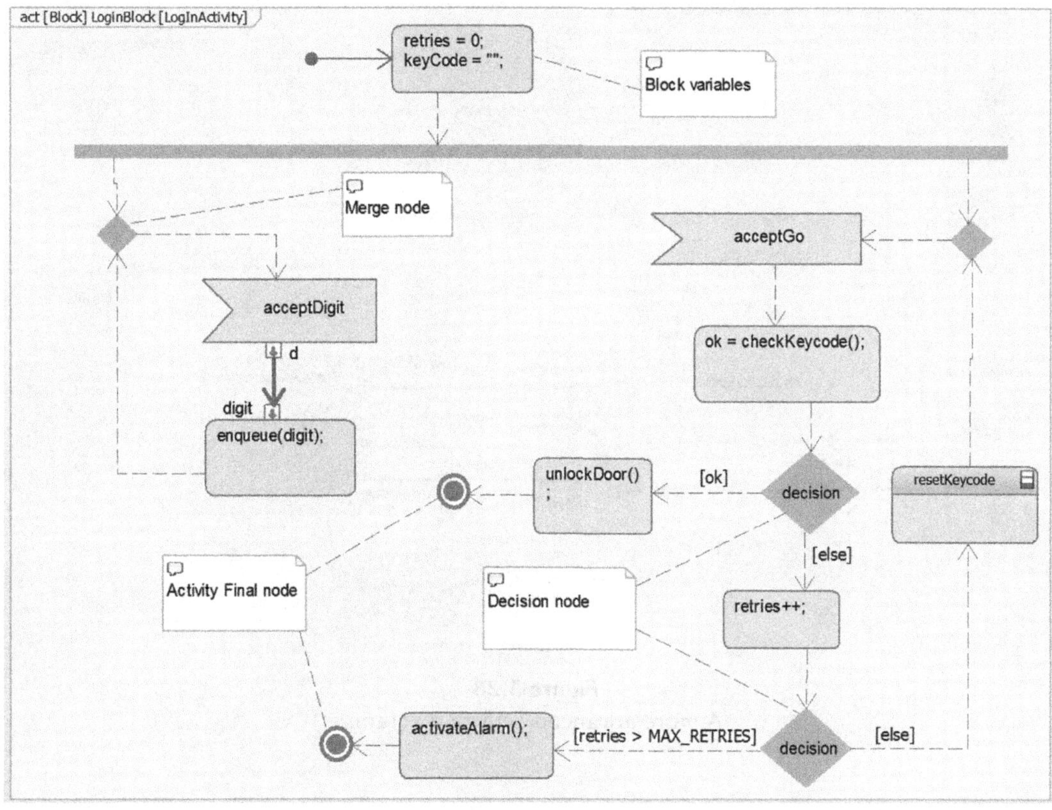

Figure 3.27
Basic activity diagram.

In Figure 3.27, the diagram represents an activity comprised of a set of actions (the rounded rectangles), and control flows (the dashed arrowed lines). In addition, the pentagons represent event receptions, where the flow waits for a specific event to occur. The small rectangle on the `enqueue(digit)` action is called an *action pin* and represents a parameter of the action. The arrow within the pin indicates whether the flow at the pin is in, out, or in-out. The wide bar is a *fork*, and depicts a branching concurrency; in this case, that the `acceptDigit` event reception proceeds in parallel with the `acceptGo` event reception. The diamonds are either decision branch points of which at most one branch can be taken or they are "merge nodes" where multiple input flows combine into one. The branches are selected on the basis of the guard conditions on the branches exiting the decision point. Unfortunately, merge nodes are the same shape as decision nodes even though their semantics are quite different. You can always tell the difference because one will have multiple input flows (merge) and the other will have multiple output flows (decision).

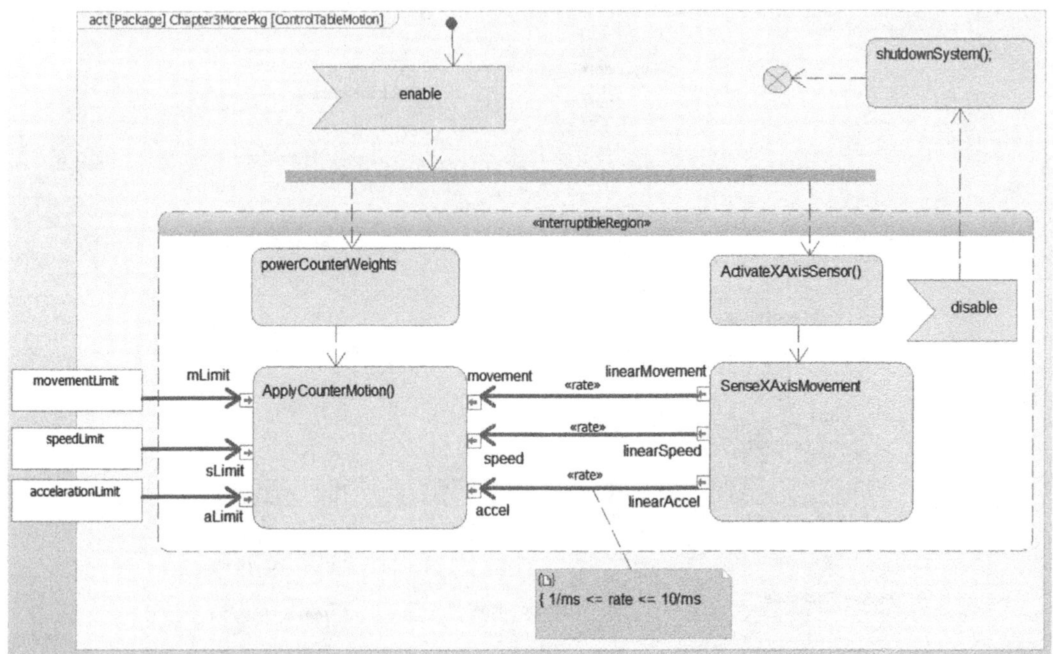

Figure 3.28
A more advanced activity diagram.

So, the correct interpretation of Figure 3.27, is that this activity starts with some initialization and then waits on two events. Digits can be entered (on the left); when a digit it entered, it is put into the Digits string. When the Go button is pressed, the code is examined and if it is ok, then the door is unlocked. If not, then the retries value is augmented and, if not too many attempts have been made, the digits string is emptied and the user can try again. If too many retries have been attempted, an alarm is sounded. The double circle at the *Activity Final* and indicates that the activity completes at that point.

Figure 3.28 shows a slightly more elaborate activity diagram. First, we note that the activity has *activity parameters* on the left; these provide data or objects for the activity to process. In this case, the purpose of the activity is to stabilize a table from linear motion by analyzing its movement, velocity, and acceleration and applying counter motion within the specified limits. Once the activity is enabled, control forks into two parallel branches. The one on the right senses linear displacement, speed, and acceleration and provides this information periodically with a rate between once and 10 times per millisecond. The parallel branch on the right receives those data, then computes and applies countermotion to stabilize the platform.

Most of the actions in the activity in Figure 3.28 are within an *interruptible region*. This allows an incoming event (in this case, the `disable` event) to force the activity to stop what it is doing and shutdown the system.

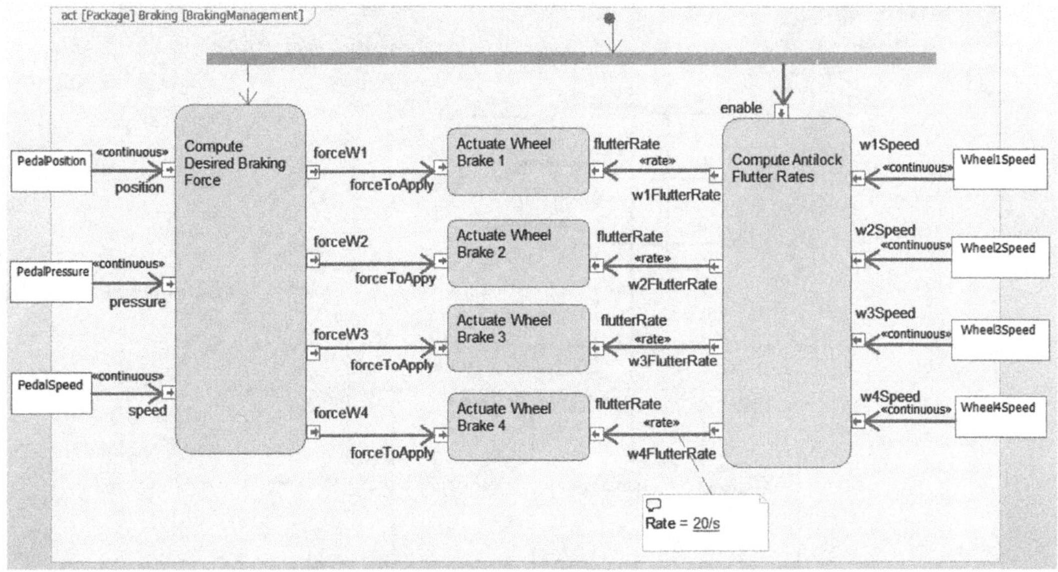

Figure 3.29
Continuous behavior with activity diagrams.

The «rate» stereotype on flows is one of the important extensions in SysML to the UML activity diagrams. Along with «continuous» (for continuously flowing items) and «stream» (for streaming items), these extensions permit the modeling of continuous behavior, something that UML activity diagrams cannot do.

Figure 3.29 brings «rate» and «continuous» flows together to model the activity `BrakingManagement`. In that activity, pedal position, pressure, and speed are continuously fed into the `Compute Desired Braking Force` action while at the same time the speed of each continuously flows into the `Compute AntiLock Flutter Rates` action. This results in discrete flows from the former action and periodic flows from the latter action to the various `Actuate Wheel Brake` actions.

The last activity diagram in this section is shown in Figure 3.30. This activity diagram shows the flow for an activity of a robot to grasp an object at a position provided by three coordinates, *x*, *y*, and *z*. The flow depicted can be summarized as follows:

1. From the *x*, *y*, and *z* coordinates, compute the angles at each of the four robot arm joints necessary to achieve the position and store these in local data stores (variables).
2. Validate that the position is achievable and not illegal (such as in the middle of the robot operator's head).
3. If it is not valid, then display an error and exit.
4. If it is valid, then move each arm joint in parallel to achieve the required joint angles, and then grab the object at the location.

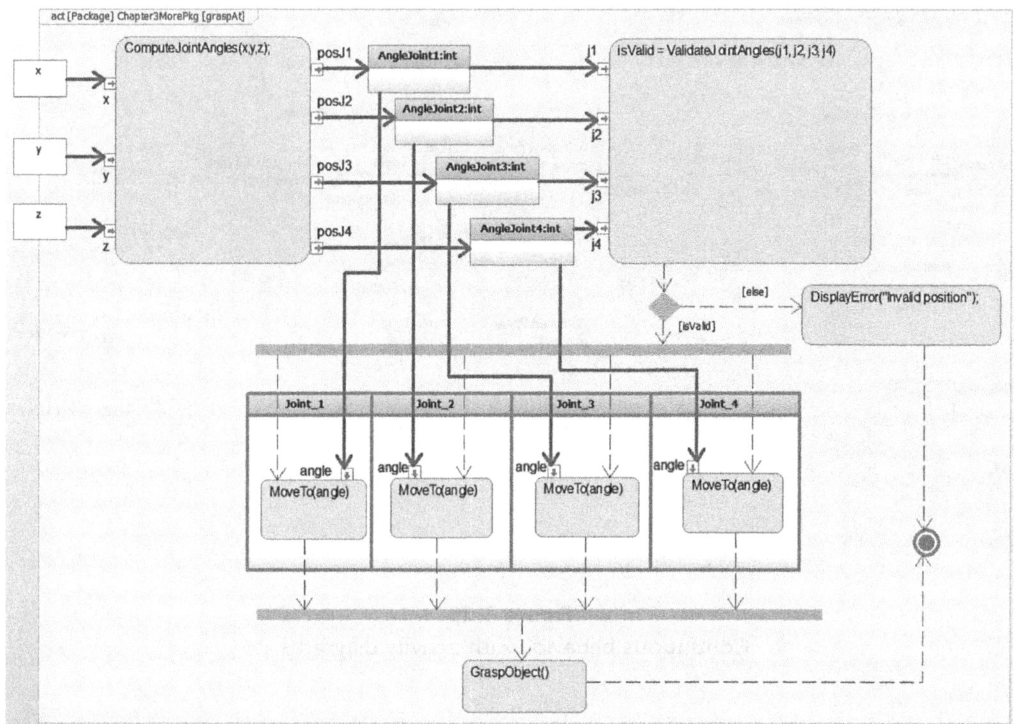

Figure 3.30
GraspAt activity.

This activity diagram adds something not yet discussed but fairly common in activity diagrams: *activity partitions*. An activity partition (also known as a *swim lane*) is a way of depicting what block instance in the system is performing that action. In the case of Figure 3.30, each arm joint is responsible for moving to its assigned angular position.

3.4.3.1 Some subtle semantics

Activity diagrams are not without their subtleties. First, did you wonder why we needed the merge node in Figure 3.27? The reason is that if we ran the looping control flow back directly to the `acceptDigit` event reception, then it would never fire! An action can only be active when there is an input token at *all* of its input flows; if there was a flow down from the fork and a flow back from the end of the loop both entering the `acceptDigit` event reception, there would be no way to get tokens on both of those input flows.

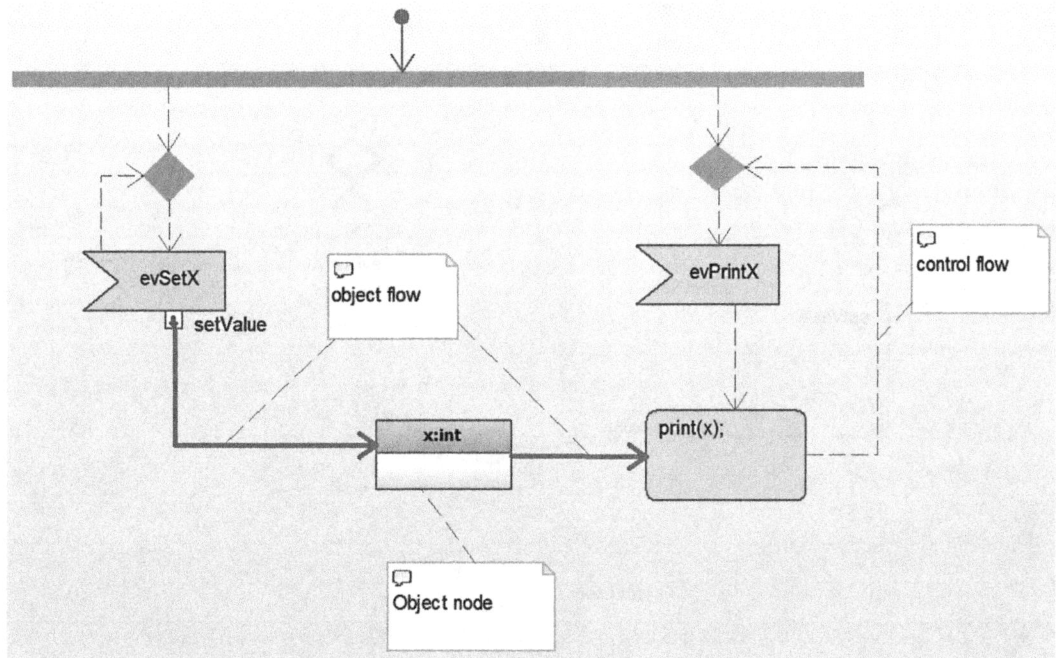

Figure 3.31
Subtle activity diagram semantics.

An activity diagram uses pins to show points of data exchange. They also contain an *object node*[22] that can store object flows (such as, but not limited to, data), but this is no simple scalar store. It is actually a token queue and this has ramifications for interpretation and execution. Consider the simple activity diagram in Figure 3.31.

In this figure, we have two parallel flows, one that sets the object node *x* (passing parameter received along with the `evSetX` event) and the other prints out its value. You might expect the following behavior: `evSetX(100)`, followed by `evSetX(200)`, followed by `evSetX(300)`, followed by `evPrintX` would result in the display of the value 300. You would be wrong; it will actually display the value 100. A snapshop of the running activity diagram in fact shows that there are two more tokens awaiting the print action (Figure 3.32)[23] and the one containing the value 300 is the second of those.

What do you think would happen if the very first thing you did when running the activity diagram was to send the `evPrintX` event? Print the initial value of x? Nope—the activity diagram will just sit there, waiting for a token to arrive from the object node (because the object node hasn't received a token yet). If you then send an `evSetX(75)` event, suddenly

[22] To be clear (and not pedantic *at all*), pins are actually object nodes and as such can queue multiple tokens.
[23] Rhapsody shows the number of waiting tokens on actions when you run activity diagrams.

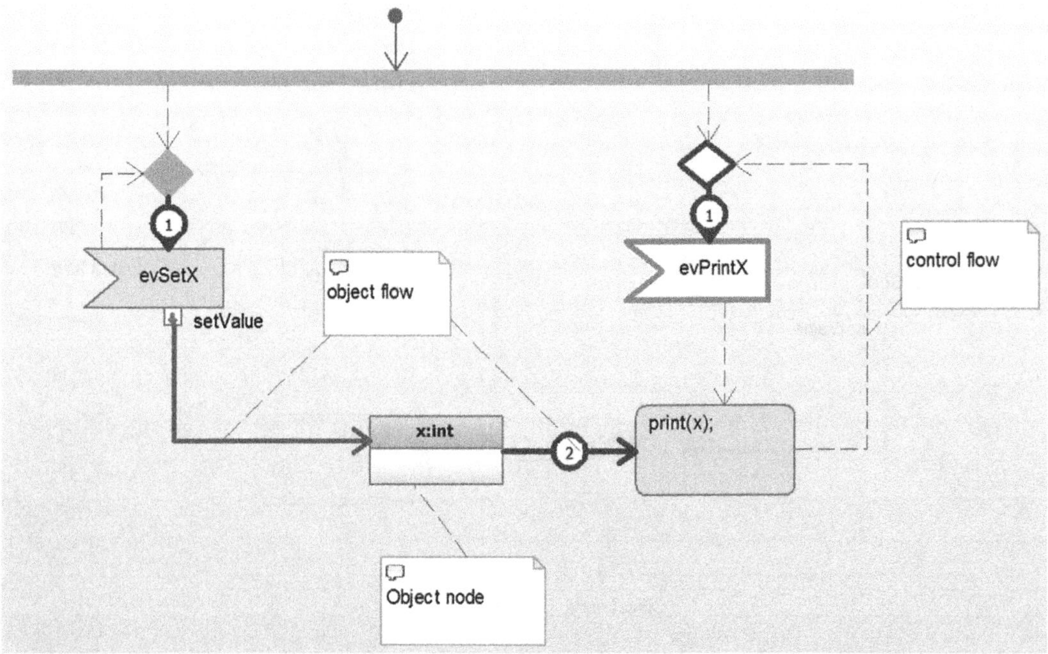

Figure 3.32
Running the subtle activity diagram.

there are tokens on all of the action's inputs and it will now print the value 75. Also, if an action has multiple output flows, a token is put on *every* output flow when that action completes not just one of them.

As I said: *subtle.* If you want a simple data store, you'll have to create a variable outside the activity diagram per se (typically owned by a block) and then you can manipulate it in your activity diagram.

3.4.4 State Machine Diagrams

While activity diagrams focus on the actions performed and their sequencing, state machines instead focus on states (and their sequencing). An action is a primitive behavior, while a state is an existential condition. It is a significantly different way of looking at dynamic behavior and some people find it counter-intuitive. This, more than anything, I believe accounts for the popularity of activity diagrams over state machines with systems engineers.

Nevertheless, state machines are an extremely powerful tool for specifying behavior. I've taught a popular class "Advanced Behavior with State Machines" for well over a decade all over the globe and have found that it just takes some thinking—and more importantly, practice—to be able to use state machines effectively. I'm a huge fan of state machines myself and use them extensively on a daily basis.

Because of the huge benefits that can be obtained through their use and the observable difficulty people having in achieving them, I'll spend a little more time talking about state machines than some of the other SysML diagrams.

3.4.4.1 Definitions

First, let's start with a few definitions:

state: a distinguishable, disjoint, orthogonal condition of existence of an element that persists for a significant period of time.
event: an occurrence of interest which may optionally carry data.
transition: a response to an event of interest moving the instance from a state to a state.
action: a primitive behavior often associated with the processing of an event. Actions may be specified as entry, exit, transition, or reaction actions.

3.4.4.2 Basic state machines

These elements are put together in a basic form in Figure 3.33.

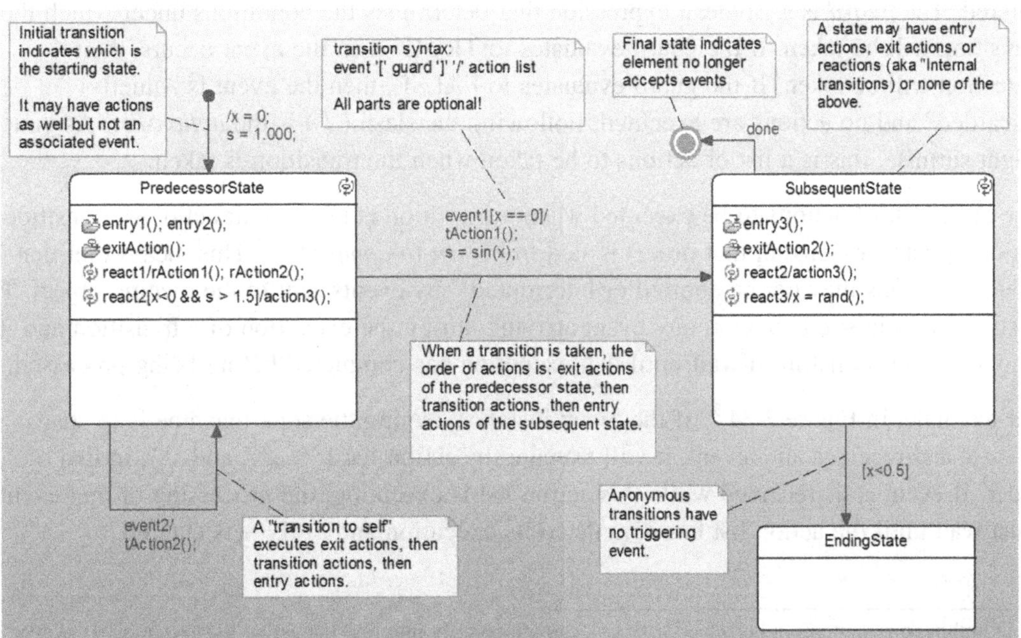

Figure 3.33
Basic state machine.

Figure 3.33 shows a simple state machine. The rounded rectangles are state (conditions) that an instance of a block can assume. Common state names are things like "Off," "Running," "Configuring," "Configured," and "Shutting Down." They present a condition that (generally) persists until some event of interest induces the instance to change its state. These states are also known as OR-states because when running, the instance must be in exactly one of these states, no more and no less.

Three key properties of states are entry actions, exit actions, and internal transitions. *Entry actions* are a list of actions that are executed whenever a state is entered, regardless of which transition path is taken to enter the state. *Exit actions* are actions taken whenever a state is left, regardless of which exiting transition is taken. An *internal transition* (also known as a "reaction") means that the actions associated with the event are taken but there is no state change. The instance assumes the state after completing the state's entry actions.

The arrowed lines are transitions, which denote that when the instance is in the predecessor state and the event on the transition occurs, that path is taken to a new state. The syntax for a transition has three fields in it, all of which are optional:

event '[' guard ']' '/' action-list

The *event* is an occurrence of interest that may trigger a transition on a state machine. The event on the transition is optional; if omitted, the transition fires as soon as the state is entered. The *guard* is a Boolean expression that determines the conditions under which the transition will be taken. If the guard evaluates to TRUE when the event occurs, then the transition will be taken. If the guard evaluates to FALSE, then the event is "quietly discarded" and no actions are executed. Following the slash ('/') is the *action-list*. As you might surmise, this is a list of actions to be taken when the transition is taken.

The entire list of actions to be executed when a transition is taken (exit actions—transition actions—entry actions, in that order) is said to be *run-to-completion*. This means that that chain of actions may not be aborted or interrupted[24] by events sent to the owning object. To ensure deterministic behavior, any event arriving during the execution of a transition and its associated action list must wait until that execution has completed before being processed.

For example, in Figure 3.34,[25] if the block instance owning the state machine is in state `state_0` and receives an `e` event, it will execute the action list f`()`, `g()`, and `h()`, in that order. If event `e2` is received while this action list is executing, the processing of that event must wait until the action list has completed its execution and `state_1` is entered.

[24] In multitasking systems, a higher-priority task can temporarily interrupt the action list execution. However, when the object owning the state machine resumes operation, the action list behavior picks up where it left off.

[25] I know we haven't talked about nested states yet, but we will shortly.

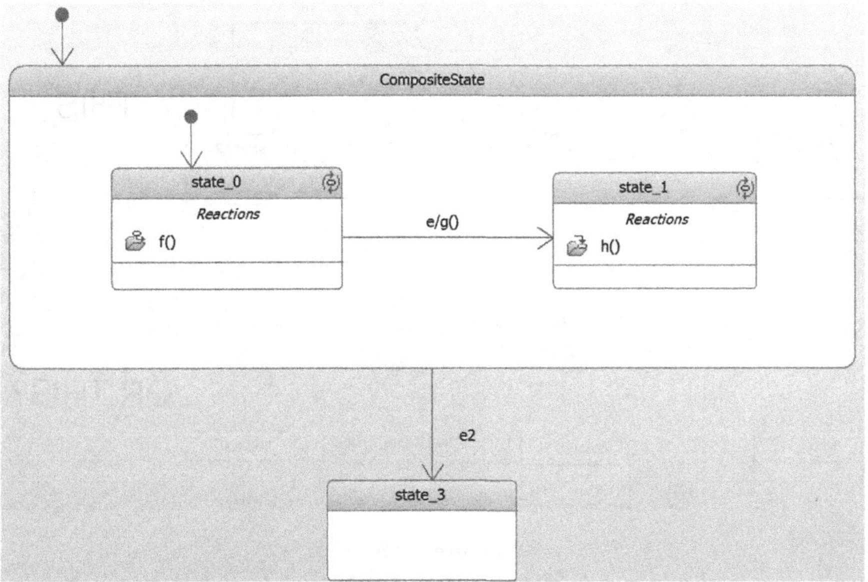

Figure 3.34
Run-to-Completion example.

Also on Figure 3.33 is the *initial transition* (also known as the default transition); this transition has a ball on its originating end and is used to indicate which state the element enters when it begins its behavior. The final state (ball inside a circle) depicts the ending of all behavior of the element.

Events are one of four types:

- Asynchronous—an event that is sent asynchronously by its sender; that is, the sender sends the event and does not wait for the behavior to initiate or complete. Asynchronous events require a mechanism for queuing the events when they cannot be handled immediately.
- Synchronous—an event that is sent synchronously by its sender; that is, the sender waits until the event processing is complete before it progresses. Synchronous events require some mechanism for blocking incoming events when they cannot be handled immediately.
- Time—an event based on elapse of a duration within a state. This is indicated by either after(duration) or tm(duration). When a state has an existing timeout event, it logically starts timing when that state is entered. If the element is still in that state when the timeout occurs, then the transition is activated. If the element changes state before the timeout duration elapses, then the timeout is discarded.
- Change—an event due to the change of a state-relevant value (little used).

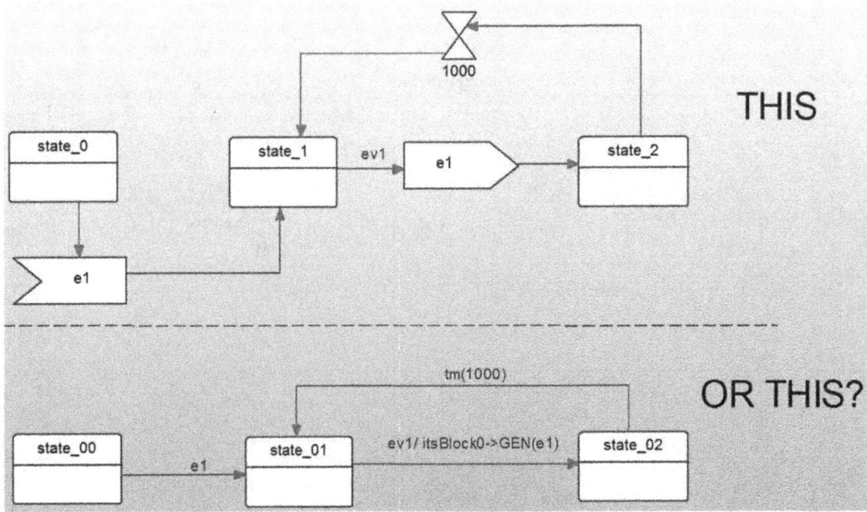

Figure 3.35
State notation options.

There are a couple of ways to show these events on a state machine diagram, as shown in Figure 3.35. The upper form uses the graphical notation for event reception, event generation, and timeout event reception as we find on an activity diagram. The lower part of the figure uses an abbreviated notation that is entirely equivalent. The only unobvious thing used in the lower form is the use of the action language statements to dereference an association from the current block to `itsBlock0` and the use of the `GEN(event)` macro to generate the event. My personal preference is the lower form because I prefer its parsimoniousness but the forms are semantically identical.

The bottom line is that state machines move from state to state based on internally or externally generated events received by the element, and actions are performed along the way.

> *A note about passing data with events.* The standard UML/SysML syntax for passing data with an event it to list the data just like a function call, such as `event(data)/x = data`. In this book, I'm using the Rational Rhapsody™ tool which uses a slightly peculiar syntax. Rhapsody doesn't show the data in the event signature on the transition but it is still there (if defined). To use it, you must reference it in a structure called `params`. The Rhapsody equivalent to the above transition signature would be `event/x = params->data`.

Let's look at a simple example of building a state machine. Suppose you have the following behavior description:

- The pacemaker may be Off (not pacing or sensing) or executing the pacing mode of operation. The system shall change between modes as a result of receiving a user command.
- The cardiac pacemaker shall pace the Atrium in Inhibit mode; that is, when an intrinsic heart beat is detected at or before the pacing rate, the pacemaker shall not send current into the heart muscle.
- If the heart does not beat by itself fast enough, as determined by the pacing rate, the pacemaker shall send an electrical current through the heart via the leads at the voltage potential specified by the Pulse Amplitude parameter (nominally 20 mv, range [10–100] mv) for the period of time specified by the Pulse Length (nominally 10 ms, range [1–20] ms).
- The sensor shall be turned off before the pacing current is released.
- The sensor shall not be re-enabled following a pace for the period of time it takes the charge to dissipate to avoid damaging the sensor (nominally 150 ms, setting range is [50–250] ms). This is known as the *refractory time*.
- When the pacing engine begins, it will disable the sensor and current output; the sensor shall not be enabled for the length of the refractory time.

Figure 3.36 shows what the state machine realizing this behavior might look like. Note the `heartBeatDetect` transition on the `Sensing` state. If the pacemaker is still in the `Sensing` state

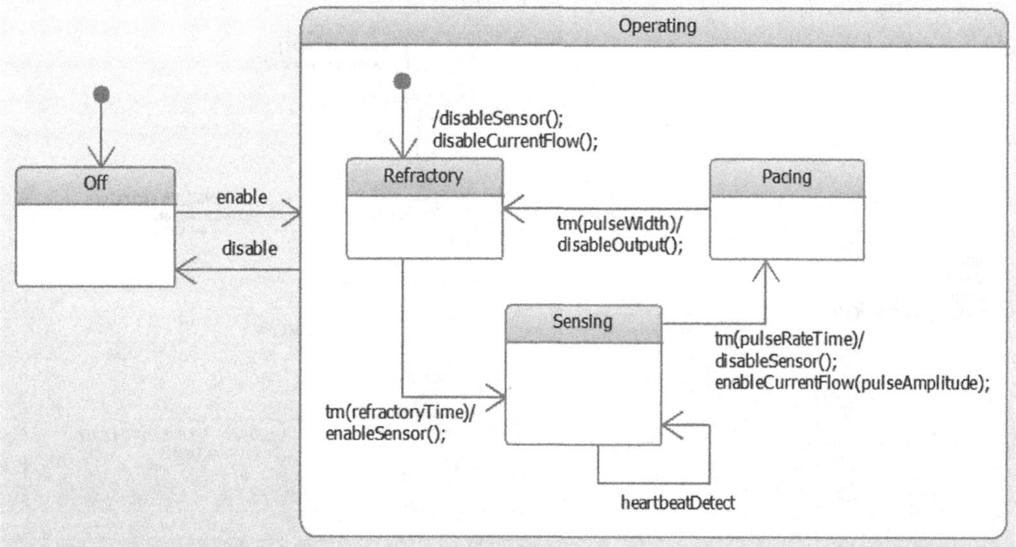

Figure 3.36
Simple state example.

when the `pulseRateTime` duration has elapsed, then the pacing engine transitions to the `Pacing` state. However, if, while in the `Sensing` state, an intrinsic heart beat is detected, the state machine takes the transition from the `Sensing` state back to the `Sensing` state. The only behavioral effect of this is that this restarts the timeout transition. This means that as long as the heart beats fast enough on its own, the pacemaker only monitors the heart. It only paces the heart if the heart doesn't beat fast enough on its own and the timeout transition can fire.

3.4.4.3 Nested states

As we've seen in some of the preceding figures, states can be nested. Although common parlance is to call the containing state a *superstate* and the nested state a *substate*, I prefer the nomenclature of *composite* and *nested* states so as not to conflict with object-oriented vocabulary.

Figure 3.37 shows a typical state machine with nested states, this time for a home alarm system. First, note that there are two ways to transition from the `Off` state to the `Armed` state. The first, triggered by the event `evImmediateActivation`, goes to the default state within the

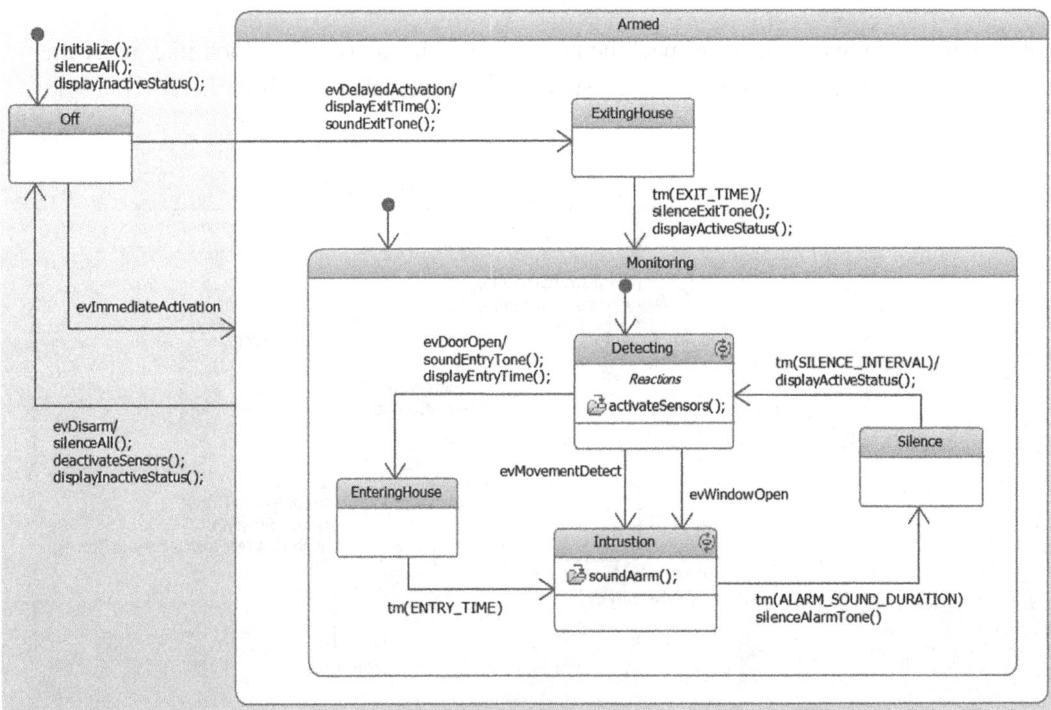

Figure 3.37
Composite and nested states.

Armed state (namely, Monitoring), and to the default nested state within Monitoring (namely, Detecting). You must identify the default state at every level of nesting.

On the other hand, you can bypass the default when appropriate. When you're setting the alarm while still in the house, you need time to exit before the system begins active monitoring. This is the transition triggered by the event evDelayedActivation.

Also note that whenever the system is in the Armed state, if can be disarmed by sending the system the evDisarm event. Without using nested states, this transition to the Off state would have to be replicated for each of the nested states to get the same behavior. Nesting states within a composite mean that events that should be processed for all nested states can be shown using a single transition, simplifying the diagram.

It is also possible to query the state machine to see whether it is in a particular state. In Rational Rhapsody™,[26] this is done with the IS_IN(state) macro. If the system is currently in the Detecting state, the IS_IN(Detecting), will return TRUE. Similarly, IS_IN(Armed) will also return TRUE because Detecting is nested within the Armed state.

3.4.4.4 Submachines

When the internal structure of a composite state becomes too complex, then it can be put onto another state machine diagram (called a *submachine*), leaving the composite state only on the original diagram. This means that complex state machines can be decomposed and spread across multiple diagrams should that become useful.

Consider the state machine for a Tetris-like game in Figure 3.38. All the states shown have to do with piece or game management not about actually running of the game. That behavior is hidden within the runningGame submachine, shown in Figure 3.39.

There are a few special connectors (known as *pseudostates*) that are noted on the diagram, including the entry, exit, conditional, and deep history connector. We'll discuss the first two pseudostates here and we'll defer the discussion on the others for now.

Because a submachine has a default transition, transitions going to the submachine's default state or exiting the composite state need no special annotation. However, we can bypass the defaults by adding a transition directly to a nested state or exiting from a nested state if the nested state is on the same diagram. If it is put into a submachine, the internal states are no longer visible on the main diagram, so we need some way to direct a transition to a specific nested state (the entry pseudostate) or from a specific nested state (the exit pseudostate). They are essentially "off diagram connectors." In Figure 3.38, PAUSED is an entry pseudostate and GAME_OVER and DONE are exit pseudostates.

[26] Although this book isn't intended to be Rhapsody-specific, I want to give you enough information to properly interpret the diagrams herein.

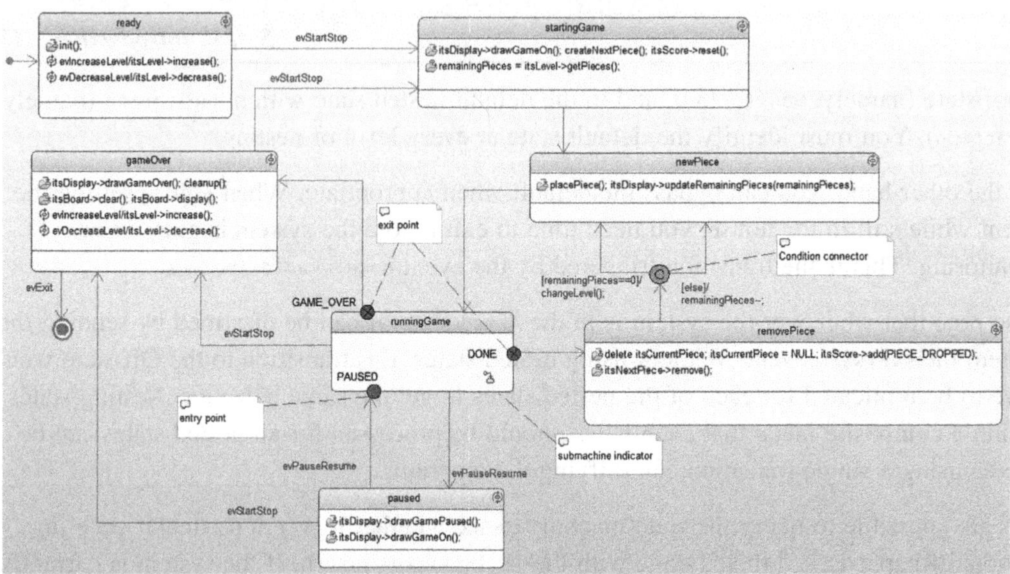

Figure 3.38
Game control state machine.

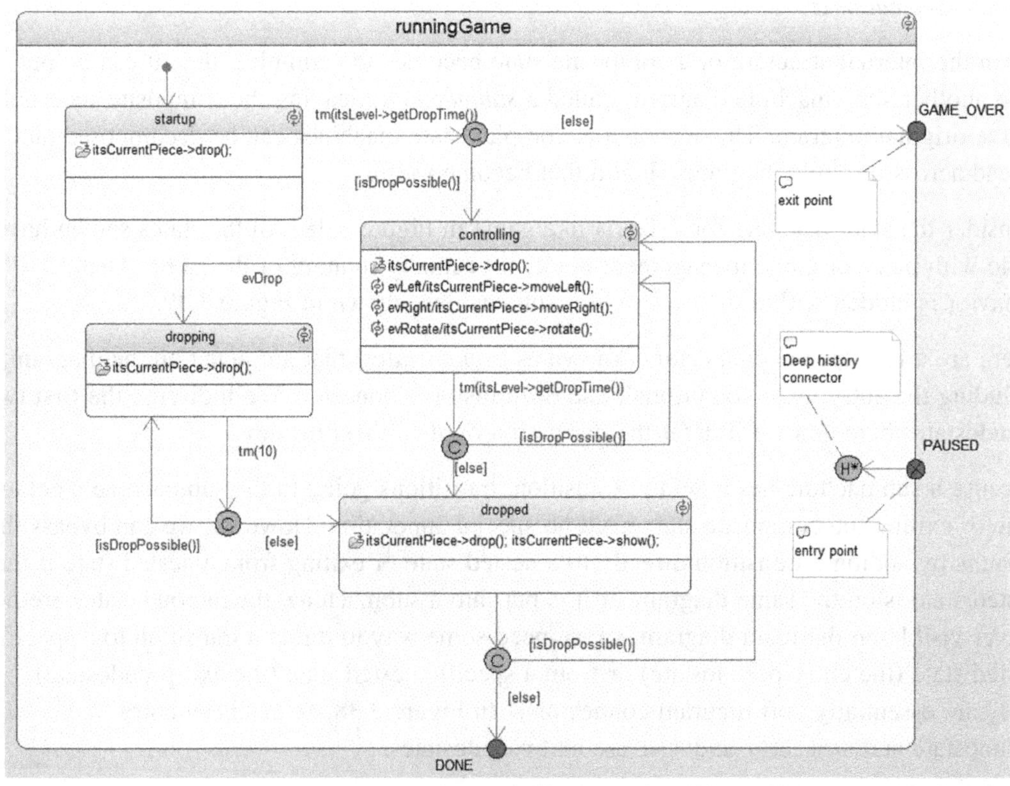

Figure 3.39
Submachine.

3.4.4.5 AND-states

All the states we've talked about so far are OR-states; within a given level of nesting, an object can be in no more than one OR-state. UML/SysML state machines extend the notion of states to include states that can be simultaneously true, known as AND-states. Of course, this works best with properties that are at least mostly independent.

Consider a light that can assume three colors (red, green, and yellow) and simultaneously show the light in a steady fashion, slowly flashing or quickly flashing. To draw all possible conditions requires computing the cross product of the two state spaces, resulting in states such as `Red_FlashingQuickly` and `Green_Steady`. With AND-states, the two independent aspects of color and flashing rate can be represented independently, as shown in Figure 3.40. When the light is in the `On` state, it must be in exactly one nested state in the `Color` region and one in the `Rate` region.

While the AND-states are logically independent, they can process the same events if desired. In the figure, the `evEmergency` event is in process in both AND-states. Logically, each AND-state is free to respond or discard every event received by the instance independently from all the other active AND-states. If the light is in states `Green` and

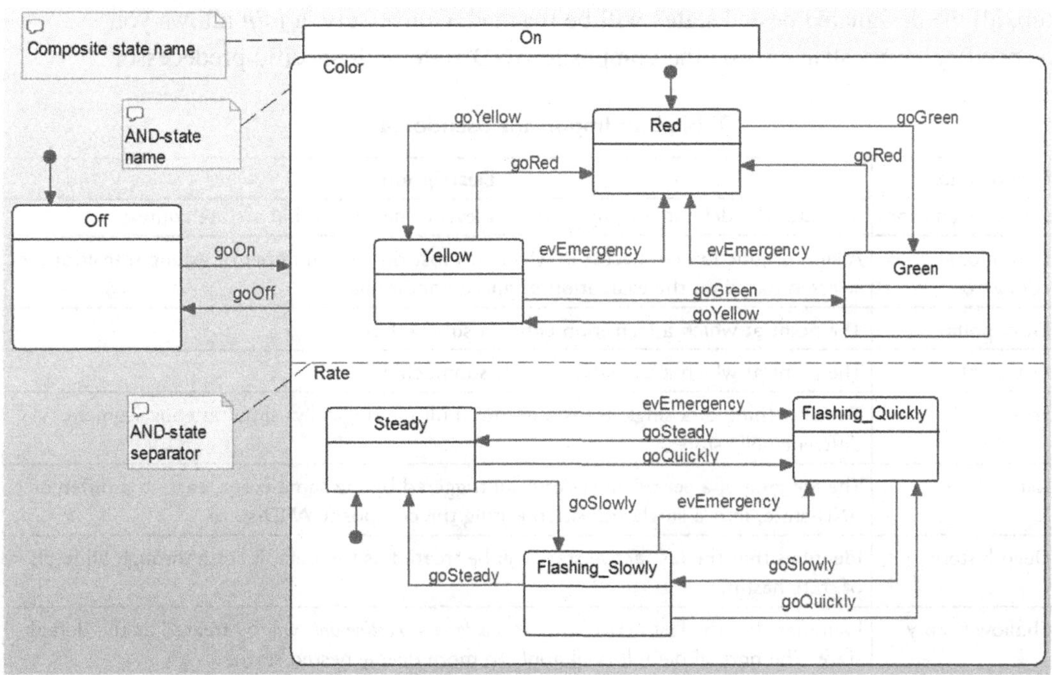

Figure 3.40
AND-states.

`Flashing_Slowly` and then receives the event `evEmergency` event, it will transition to states `Red` and `Flashing_Quickly`. However, it cannot be known *in principle* which transition will be taken first. What is known is that by the end of the state machine execution step, both target states will be entered.

3.4.4.6 Pseudostates

State machines in SysML are not just states, transitions, and actions. As we've seen, there are a number of "annotations of special semantics," known by the misleading name of pseudostates (since they are neither pseudo nor states). The most important pseudostates are shown in Table 3.2.

Many of these pseudostates are shown in Figure 3.41, including default, condition, fork, join, deep history, shallow history, and terminal. Fork and join are particularly useful with AND-states. Every separate AND-state region must have its own default. With nested states, bypassing the default is done by simply drawing a transition to the desired nested state. With AND-states, there are multiple destinations to specify, and a *fork* allows the transition to simultaneously branch to multiple nested states. The rules are that: (1) the nested state targeted by transitions exiting the fork must be in different AND-states, (2) any AND-state region not specified will use its default state, and (3) it is not specified which nested state will be arrived at first, only that by the end of the state machine execution step, all the designated nested states will be reached. Conversely, a *join* allows you to specify a target state outside the composite AND-state with specific predecessor

Table 3.2: Important pseudostates.

Pseudostate	Description
Default transition	Indicates the default starting state at a level of nesting within a state context
Conditional connector	A kind of junction connector in which at most one of a number of exiting transitions is selected based on the evaluation of guard conditions
Entry point	The point at which a transition enters a submachine
Exit point	The point at which a transition exits a submachine
Fork	The branching of a single transition into multiple (logically) simultaneous segments in different AND-states
Join	The merging of a set of transitions, all triggered by the same event, each in a different AND-state, into a single transition exiting the composite AND-state
Deep history	Identifies that the last active state will be treated as the default state through all levels of state nesting
Shallow history	Identifies that the last active state *in this level of nesting only* will be treated as the default state. The normal defaults will apply to more deeply nested states
Junction	Allows a transition to be broken up into segments and for different transitions to be merged together

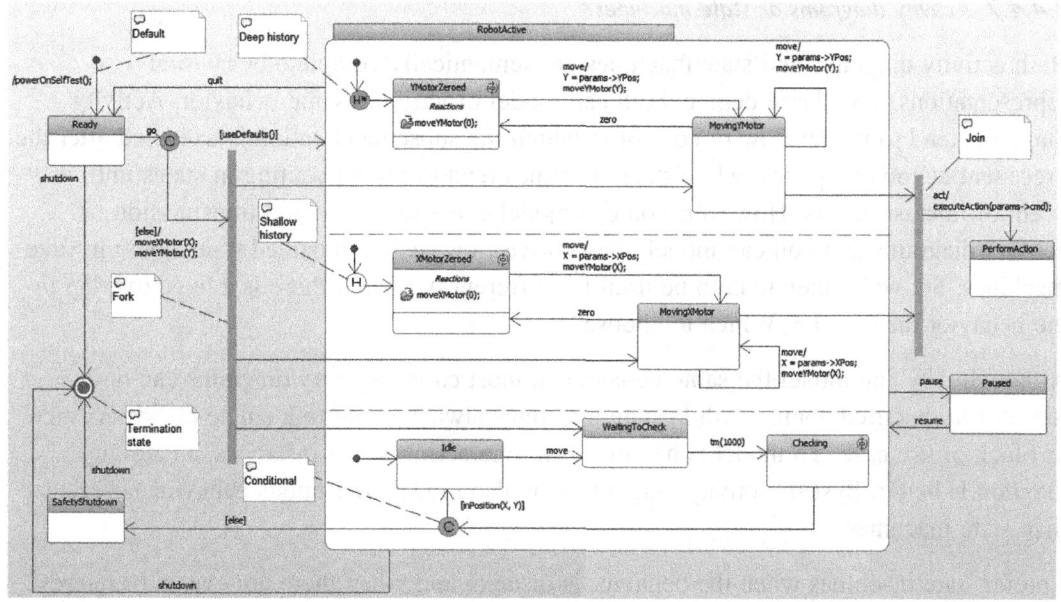

Figure 3.41
Pseudostates.

AND-states. In the figure we see the in order to get to the state `PerformAction`, the instance must be in *both* `MovingYMotor` and `MovingXMotor` states (which state in the bottom region isn't specified, so it doesn't matter). If both of the states are not active when the event `act` is received, then the event is discarded and the transition is not taken.

Also shown in Figure 3.41 are history connectors (shown as an encircled 'H'). The shallow history connector, specified in the middle AND-state region, means that if the `RobotActive` state is left and then reentered, the default state for this region will be the last active state. The reason there is a transition shown from the history connector to the nested state is that before the instance has gone to `RobotActive` state, there is no history, so that condition must be handled. The semantics of the shallow history are that if the state machine transitions out of the `RobotActive` state and later returns, the default state for this middle region will be the last active state; however, if any of those states has internally nested states themselves, the defaults for those subnested states will be used.

The upper region uses the *deep history connector* (usually shown with an encircled 'H*'). The semantics for this pseudostate are the same except that the last active state becomes the default *through all levels of nesting.*

For example, if the instance is currently in `MovingYMotor`, `MovingXMotor`, and `WaitingToCheck` states and the `pause` event is received, it will transition to the `Paused` state. Following the `resume` event, the system enters the states `MovingYMotor`, `MovingXMotor`, and `Idle`.

3.4.4.7 Activity diagrams or state machines?

Both activity diagrams and state machines are semantically complete behavioral representations. To a large degree, both can model exactly the same behavior. Activity diagrams tend to model flow of control in which the subsequent action is executed after the precedent action completes, while state machines tend to model waiting in states until an event of interest occurs. However, you can model event reception and transmission in activity diagrams and you can model consecutive flow (using unnamed transitions) in state machines. So, while they tend to be used for different purposes, there is a huge overlap in the behavior they model. Which to choose?

Although they can model the same behavior in most cases, activity diagrams can have a loose or unspecified context, while state machines always relate to a single classifier, such as block or use case. To model behavior for an interacting set of instances, an activity diagram is better. SysML activity diagrams can also model continuous behavior far easier than state machines.

I prefer state machines when the behavior is discrete and when there are events of interest. For modeling the discrete behavior of individual blocks or use cases, I strongly prefer state machines. I prefer activity diagrams either when the behavior, once begun, is not event-driven, or when the flows are continuous rather than discrete. When modeling a complex activity that is executed as an action on a state machine, I model the higher behavior as a state machine and model the action with an activity diagram.

Having said that, either technique can be used to model most of the system behavior you will come across.

3.5 Minimal SysML Profile

SysML is a rich (and therefore complex) language that many beginning modelers find intimidating. To address this, I've created a Minimal SysML Profile (MSP) that provides only the most useful and common SysML diagrams and elements. It eliminates some diagrams and reduces the set of elements that can be put onto the remaining diagrams. If—and only if—a more advanced feature of SysML is needed, then it can be introduced into the model.

3.5.1 Diagrams

The MSP provides the following diagrams:

- Use case diagram,
- Block definition diagram,
- Internal block diagram,

- Activity diagram,
- State diagram,
- Sequence diagram.

It eliminates the requirements, package, and parametric diagrams. Note that the intention of the first two can be achieved on a BDD.

Not only is the number of diagrams reduced. Each diagram is simplified as well by removing some less frequently used or complex elements (Table 3.3).

Table 3.3: Minimal SysML diagrams.

Diagram	Supported elements	Removed elements
Use case	Use case Actor Association Generalization «include» «extend» Requirement Dependency	Package Boundary Flow
Block definition	Block Part Interface block Proxy port Association Aggregation Composition Connector Generalization Dependency Requirement «allocate»	Flow Interface Standard port Flow port Full port Constraint block Problem Rationale Binding connector
Internal block	Block Part Interface block Proxy port Association Aggregation Composition Connector Generalization Dependency Requirement «allocate»	Flow Interface Standard port Flow port Full port Constraint block Problem Rationale Binding connector

(Continued)

Table 3.3: (Continued)

Diagram	Supported elements	Removed elements
Activity	Action Action pin Initial flow Control flow Object flow Fork Join Merge (decision) Dependency Requirement «allocate»	Call behavior Call action Interruptible tegion Object node Swim lane
State	State Transition Default transition And-line Conditional connector Fork Join Termination state Requirement Dependency	Shallow history Deep history Junction Entry point Exit point Send action Accept event action Accept time event
Sequence	Lifeline Synchronous message Asynchronous message Timeout Condition mark Time interval Interaction operator	System border Reply message Create message Destroy message Data flow Execution occurrence Lost message Found message Destruction event Action block

If you find you need any of the elements omitted in the MSP, feel free to add it in to your own version of the MSP. The point is to remove the little-used items and support 80% of the work with a reduced feature set.

3.6 Summary

This chapter is intended to provide a basic introduction to the SysML so that we can use it in our discussion of doing agile systems engineering. SysML is actually more complex than this and you are referred to Ref. [4] or other books that deal solely with the language itself for additional detail.

SysML is a profile of the UML in which UML is simultaneously subsetted and extended. Classes and software-sounding things were renamed with more "systemy" nomenclature but more importantly, extensions were added to better support systems engineering.

3.6.1 Copied from the UML

The SysML also provides all the expressive power of UML's sequence and state machines. In addition, all the behavior of classes and their relations are retained, if renamed, in SysML.

3.6.2 Modifications

On the structural side, ports were extended to support flows with flow ports and proxy ports, and interfaces were extended to add interface blocks. Since much of systems engineering deals with things that flow—such as energy and materiel—this is a significant extension.

In activity diagrams «continuous», «rate», and «stream» modify flows from the realm of the discrete to that of the continuous. This extends UML's discrete behavioral modeling in to a continuous world, allowing it to be applied to energy and material systems.

3.6.3 New Elements

A key new element is the Requirement and associated relations including «allocate», «satisfy», «verify». Also new is the parametric diagram and quantified constraint modeling, useful for calculations and trade studies. Lastly, the SysML provides model libraries of standard types and supports the definition and use of dimensions and units in modeling.

Now that we have a basic understanding of the language we will use in our MBSE approach, let's move on to applying this language in agile systems engineering. That part of our journey begins in the next chapter, "Agile Stakeholder Requirements Engineering."

References

[1] OMG Unified Modeling Language (OMG UML) Infrastructure Version 2.4. 1. Available from: <http://www.omg.org/spec/UML/2.4.1/Infrastructure/PDF>.

[2] UML Testing Profile Version 1.2. Available from: <http://utp.omg.org/>.

[3] C. Block, UML2 Activity Model Support for Systems Engineering Functional Flow Diagrams, US National Institute of Standards, 2003. Available from: <www.mel.nist.gov/msidlibrary/doc/sysmlactivity.pdf>.

[4] OMG SysML Specification version 1.3. Available from: <http://www.omg.org/spec/SysML/1.3/PDF>.

CHAPTER 4

Agile Stakeholder Requirements Engineering

Chapter Outline

4.1 Objectives

The objective of this activity is to identify stakeholder requirements. Stakeholder requirements are fundamentally statements reflecting stakeholder needs. System requirements differ in that they specify what the system will do and how well it must do it. There is a need to demonstrate traceability between these sets of requirements but they differ both in context and in their degree of precision.

Generally speaking, stakeholders may be (although are not necessarily) domain experts but are not usually system engineering experts. Most stakeholders will be comfortable communicating requirements via text and few will be capable of using more formal languages, such as activity or state diagrams. The good news is that scenarios—captured in sequence diagrams—are easily taught to nontechnical stakeholders and serve as a valuable tool for capturing any requirements.

This chapter will discuss the identification of stakeholder needs, and capturing them as textual requirements and scenarios on sequence diagrams. Requirements will be clustered into coherent sets called *use cases*. A great deal of what we talk about here applies equally well to system requirements, the topic of the next chapter; however, for system requirements, we will also perform more rigorous analysis that goes well beyond the initial capture of stakeholder needs.

A note about use cases

A use case is traditionally considered to be a set of flows into and out of the system that, in sequence, define a useful, self-contained, coherent usage of a system from a stakeholder's perspective. Each use case can have many such sequences, which may differ in value, quantity, sequence, and outcomes–these are referred to as *scenarios* of the use case.

In this book, I've described a use case in this way, but I've also said that a use case is a "cluster of requirements" or "a system capability." I believe that *all* these descriptions of a use case are true, and, if not exactly the same, then at least roughly equivalent. In practice, they are entirely equivalent, and just identify different perspectives on the same thing; and that's how we'll treat them in this book.

4.2 The Stakeholder Requirements Workflow

Figure 2.6 shows the high-level view of the Harmony Agile Model-Based Systems Engineering (MBSE) process. In Figure 2.9, the details of the *Initiate Project* activity include two tasks particularly relevant to this chapter: *Identify Stakeholder Use Cases* and *Prioritize Use Cases.* This is done before the actual definition of the use case contents so that preliminary project planning can take place.

At the point of entering the *Define Stakeholder Requirements* activity, an initial set of stakeholder use cases has been identified and each has been qualified with a mission statement that consists of:

- Use case name.
- Purpose—what is the value to the stakeholder(s)?
- Description—what kind of input–output data and control transformations are needed?
- Preconditions—what is true before this set of behaviors runs?
- Postconditions—what do we need to be true after these behaviors have run?
- Invariants—what assumptions are we making?

In addition, the use cases are prioritized. To be clear, the priority of a use case defines the order in which it will be detailed. The priority of the use cases is best defined as a weighted sum of a number of independent factors, such as:

- The *importance* of the capabilities to be provided by the use case.
- The *urgency* of the features provided by the use case, especially in a phased delivery program.

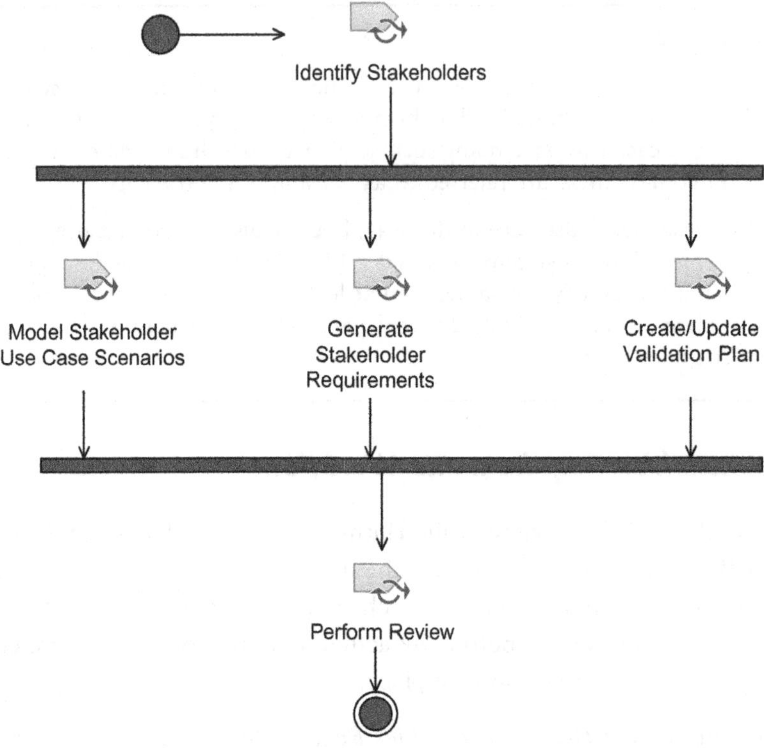

Figure 4.1
Define stakeholder requirements.

- The *project risk* associated with the capabilities, features, or technologies required to deliver the capability modeled by the use case; generally speaking higher-risk use cases should be tackled first.
- The availability of information necessary to define the requirements associated with the use cases. Sometimes the domain experts or technical information necessary to do the requirements definition may not be immediately available.

So, as we begin the stakeholder use case and requirements definition, we have already identified a prioritized set of use cases, each with a mission. This is just a starting point and we may well find that we've missed a use case or misinterpreted its priority, but being agile means that we can adapt after we start working.

The workflow for defining stakeholder requirements is shown in Figure 4.1.

4.2.1 Remember—This Is Agile MBSE

The workflow in Figure 4.1 exists within the larger context of the system engineering iteration (see Figure 2.6). This means that we need not detail all the stakeholder requirements on any particular iteration. For example, you might have identified 25 stakeholder use cases and created a project plan that includes eight iterations. The first iteration might focus on use cases 1, 2, and 3, while the second iteration elaborates use cases 4 and 5, and the third iteration might use cases 6, 7, 8, and 9 (and so on). The point is, not all the requirements need be detailed in this Define Stakeholder Requirements workflow in each iteration.[1] In fact, it's even possible to do the "sunny day" scenarios (normal, expected operation) in one iteration and add the "rainy day" scenarios (unusual, exceptional, or fault operation) in the next. The project plan identifies which use cases are planned to be detailed in which iteration as well as identifying the set of use cases and their priorities. Of course, the plan is revisited on each iteration, so it can be adjusted when needed, but we still have a plan!

4.2.2 So, What Is a Use Case?

Before we get too far down the road, it is necessary to understand what a use case is and what it is not. There are a number of ways to think about what constitutes a use case:

- It is a named operational capability of a system.
- It is a collection of related specific usage scenarios of a system.
- It is a collection of requirements around a system usage.
- It is a coherent set of interactions of the system with a set of external elements (actors).

In my experience, I have found that use cases are the most misused part of SysML. The point of use cases is to understand not just individual requirements but also the interactions of those requirements and their consequences. We do this by modeling the flows into and out of the system that are relevant to the usage in question. What are the acceptable input flows and the associated control and flow transformations (functional requirements) and their limitations (quality of service (QoS) or nonfunctional requirements)? How does the system respond in different ways to different collections, orders, and timings of input events and flows? Use cases raise the level of comprehension from small individual statements about specific functionality to a gestalt understanding of how the system must behave in possibly highly complex interactions with various elements in its environment.

4.2.2.1 General properties of good use cases

I don't believe in hard and fast rules (including this one) but good use cases have a set of common properties.

[1] Indeed, a traditional "V Model" development process is just a degenerate form of this workflow where there is only a single iteration.

Coherence

All the requirements within a use case should be tightly coupled in terms of system behavior. For example, if you create a use case focusing on the movement of aircraft control surfaces, you would expect to see it represent requirements about the movement of the rudder, elevator, ailerons, and wing flaps. These requirements might define the range of movement, the conditions under which they move, the timing requirements for movement, the accuracy of the movement, and so on. All of these are relevant to the movement of the control surfaces. You wouldn't expect to find requirements about communication of the aircraft with the ground system or internal environmental controls also associated with the use case.

Note: The coherence property also means that QoS requirements (such as performance requirements) are allocated to the same use case as the functional requirements they constrain.

Independence

Good use cases are independent in terms of the requirements. This is an important characteristic because we want to be able to reason independently about the system behavior with respect to the use cases. This means that, in general, each requirement is allocated to at most one use case[2]—we call this the *linear separability* of use cases. There are cross-cutting requirements allocated to multiple use cases but they are usually nonfunctional rather than functional requirements.[3] This independence allows the independent analysis of use cases to proceed without introducing subtle errors. Use cases that are not independent must be analyzed together to ensure that they are not in conflict.

Coverage

All functional requirements and their modifying QoS requirements should map to use cases. If a requirement specifies or constrains a system behavior, then it should be allocated to some use case. In addition, requirements about error and fault handling in the context of the use case must also be included. For example, in a use case about movement of airplane control surfaces, requirements about handling commanded "out of range errors" and dealing with faults in the components implementing such movement should be incorporated.

Size (10–100 requirements, 3–50 scenarios)

Getting the size of use cases right is a problem for many beginning modelers. The point of use cases is to have independent coherent sets of requirements that can be analyzed together.

---

2 We will see in Section 4.4.1 that not all requirements are allocated to use cases.

3 For example, "The system must comply with DO-178C level B" applies to all use cases and is an example of a cross-cutting requirement.

Far too often, I see a use case with just one or two requirements. As a general rule, each use case should have a minimum of 10 requirements and a maximum of 100. While these numbers are approximate, it gives the idea that a use case is a *cluster* of related requirements not a requirement itself. If a use case is too small, then that use case should be absorbed into another use case. If a use case is too large, it can be decomposed into smaller use cases with use case relations (see below).

For example, should *Start Up* be a use case? In some cases, starting a system is no more complex than pushing a button—one requirement, and a single message on a sequence diagram. In this case, the *Start Up* use case should be merged with the *Initialize* use case which takes care of initializing sensors and actuators, setting up communication paths, and so on. In another case, starting up a system is a complex activity with multiple flows interacting with potentially many actors (i.e., lots of requirements). In this latter situation, *Start Up* is a very reasonable use case.

Exception for large systems

A small system, such as a medical ventilator, may have 6–25 use cases containing a total of between 100 and 2500 requirements. If your system is much larger, such as an aircraft with 500 use cases and over 20,000 requirements, then you need some taxonomic organization to your requirements. This can be done with packages in some cases, but it is very common to create a use case taxonomy. Some typical use case sizes are shown in Figure 4.2.[4]

We will see examples of building use case taxonomies to manage requirements later in this chapter.

Return a result visible to an actor

Functional requirements, as will be described in Section 4.5.1, are about specifying input–output control and data transformations that a system performs. That means that functional requirements must return an output that is visible to some element in the system's environment (actor). If you are specifying some behavior that is in no way visible to the actor, you should ask yourself "Why is this a requirement?"

4.2.2.2 Some things to avoid with use cases

As I mentioned, use cases are often suboptimally applied. Some common mistakes are highlighted below.

[4] Although I hate to use lines of code as an indication of size, it does provide one way to look at the relative sizes of the systems depicted in the figure.

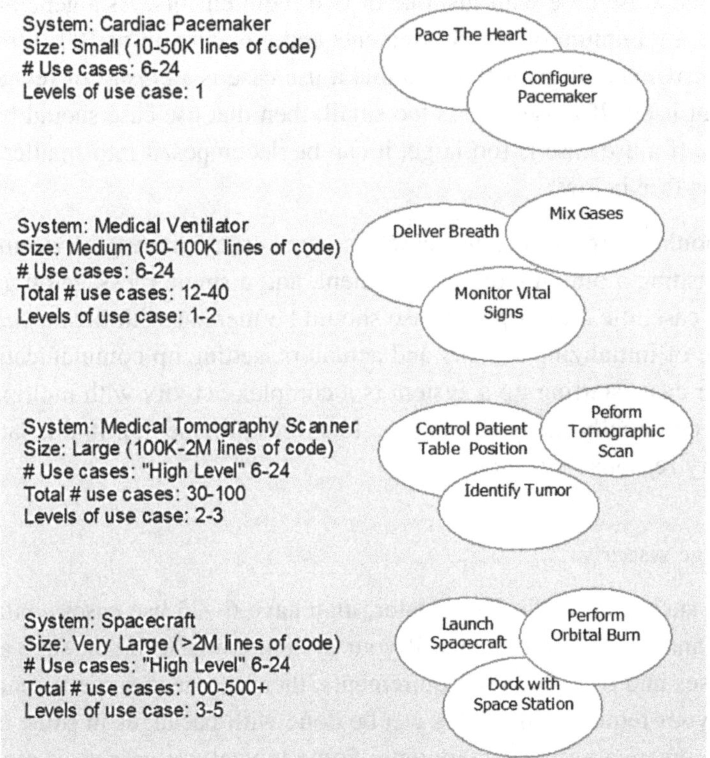

Figure 4.2
Use case sizes.

Implying or revealing internal system structure

Many engineers are trained in designing systems but far fewer are trained in specifying requirements for them. At the scope of concern at which a use case is applied, the perspective should be black box—that while you can characterize the input–output transformations being performed by the use case, exactly how the transformations occur and what internal elements are performing them should be invisible. It is necessary to characterize the transformations but not the computational or structural elements by which those transformations are achieved. For example, it is completely ok to specify an equation that defines the relation of input values to computed output values, but whether that computation is done by software running on an embedded CPU or by a mechanical difference engine should not be apparent in the use case model.

Using use cases to decompose system internals

Similarly, some people try to apply use cases to depict internal design. If you look at Figure 4.2, the `Pace the Heart` use case seems completely appropriate, while use cases such as `Charge The Pacing Capacitor` and `Enable Reverse Biasing Diode` would not be since they are design-specific.

Use cases that are too small

It is also common for use cases to be overly decomposed into units too small to be useful. I've seen many use case models that included use cases that contained a single message. The point of use cases is to understand the interaction of many requirements in coherent sets organized around system uses. Each use case should have a minimum of three scenarios of interest and each scenario of interest should have at least several messages. If you find this to be not true, consider merging your use cases together.

Dependent use cases

I've already said that good use cases should be independent of each other. That means that they are independent in terms of the requirements but not necessarily in terms of the design. Consider two use cases for an intersection light controller [1]. If we have a use case `Control Traffic`, it uses configuration data such as the length of the green light time, the length of the yellow light time, and the sensitivity of the car sensor to make decisions about controlling the lights. On the other hand, the use case `Configure Traffic Control` sets these configuration values. These use cases are independent because how we change the light colors to control traffic is independent from how we set the configuration values, even though they are coupled in terms of design (both access the same stored configuration values).

If those use cases are independent, what about the use cases `Control Vehicular Traffic` and `Control Pedestrian Traffic`? These use cases are clearly *not* independent because you have to control cars and pedestrians together or *bad things* will happen (mostly to the pedestrians). It would be far better to combine these two use cases into a singular `Control Traffic` use case because of that tight coupling. On the other hand, it might be very reasonable to have different modes of operation such as `Fixed Cycle Mode` (system controls traffic as a function of time), `Responsive Traffic Mode` (system responds to arrival of cars), and `Adaptive Mode` (varies light times based on observed traffic density) modeled as different use cases.

Too many relations among use case

SysML defines a number of relations among use cases that we'll talk about shortly. However, they should be used only when they simplify the use case model, either by clarifying the relation among use cases or supporting an organizational taxonomy to manage the requirements. Too many engineers add relations in pursuit of "completeness" that either add no value or complicate the use case model.

Associations between use cases

No, no, no.

Remember that use cases are independent (with the exception of a few relations). If you have an association between use cases you are unambiguously declaring that you failed in the quest for that independence. The other relations among use cases – «include», «extend», and generalization—have fundamentally different semantics than associations and are far more likely to be appropriate. An association provides a conduit for the exchange of messages and use cases should *not* be exchanging messages amongst themselves. Exchanging messages with the actors is fit and proper, but having associations between use cases defeats their intent.

In a small number of situations, it might possibly make sense to do a simulation of two use cases when it just wasn't possible to make them independent. In that case, such an association might be justified. However, this is an extremely rare (<1%) occurrence.

4.2.3 Use Case Diagrams

It is possible to use the notion of use cases without the graphical view. For example, use cases can be the chapter headings for a requirement specification as a way to organize the requirements. While this has some value, a great deal of the benefit is missed when use cases are applied in such an informal way.

4.2.3.1 An example: the Speed Demon Treadmill

Being an Ironman™ triathlete, I spend a fair amount of my time running and, in poor weather much of this running is done on a treadmill. So I thought it would be a useful example to create a use case model for a treadmill that I would actually like to own (see Figure 4.3). This treadmill is highly featured; not only can you manually control elevation and speed, you can also define and execute exercise protocols such as the Bruce protocol.[5] Of course it monitors athlete information like heart rate, stride rate, (computed) calorie output, SpO_2 (with the optional finger cuff), and respiration rate (with the optional Darth Vader respiration mask). Not only that, you can buy and play both music and movies. Of course, this being a *serious* treadmill, it accommodates multiple athletes and stores demographic and workout data on a personal data card. Lastly, you can race other athletes running on other treadmills connected over the internet. The Speed Demon Treadmill will show up throughout the remainder of the book as a relatively simple system example for illustrative purposes.

Each of these large-scale capabilities constitutes a use case. It is easy to imagine several to dozens of requirements for each of these use cases.

4.2.3.2 Use cases

A use case is an operational usage of a system. It is not the same as a system function because a use case contains multiple system functions. In the example in Figure 4.3, the `Play Video` use case includes system functions to turn on and off the video player, change

---

[5] Swear to god this is a real thing. It's a diagnostic test of cardiovascular function. Honest! http://en.wikipedia.org/wiki/Bruce_protocol

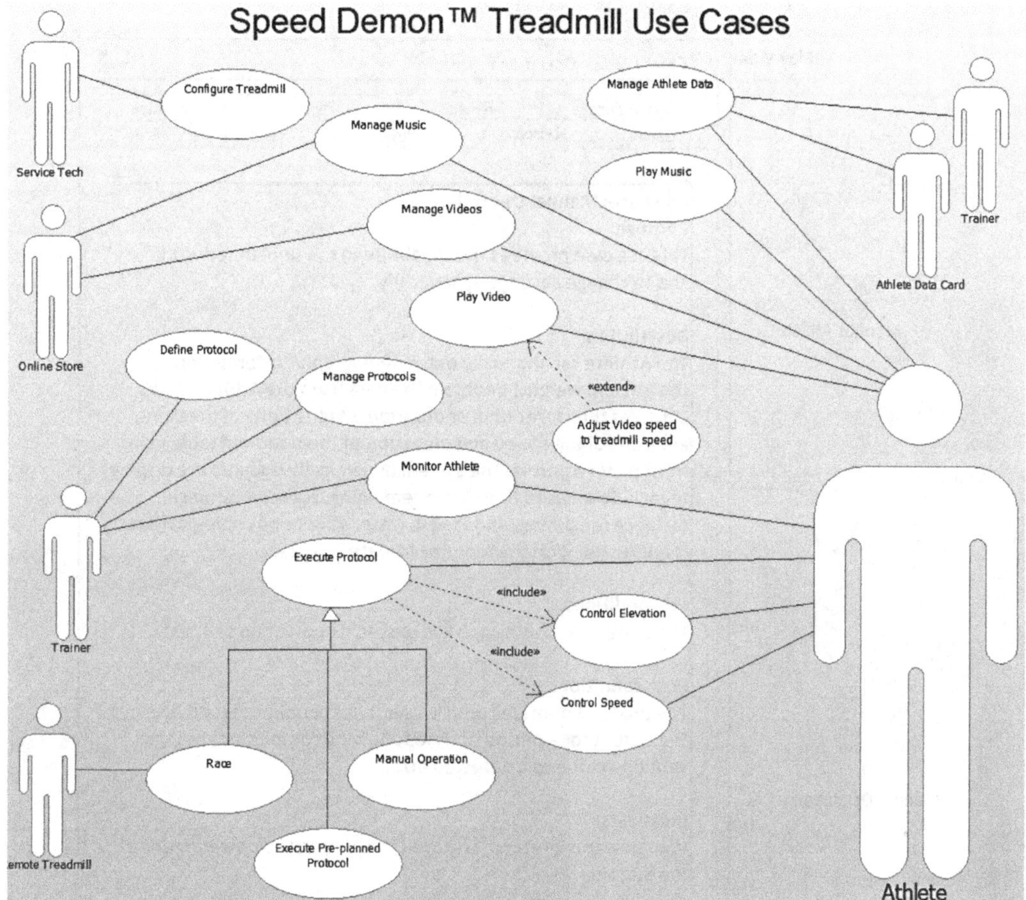

Figure 4.3
Use case diagram.

the volume, select the chapter, pause, advanced, and rewind—oh yes, and actually play the video. The use case `Control Elevation` includes system functions to raise and lower the front of the treadmill, and monitor and display the angle of elevation.

Each use case should have a statement that describes the scope of the use case. I call this the *Use Case Mission* and recommend the format shown in Figure 4.4. This information is normally put in the use case description field in the modeling tool and is in addition to the formal allocation of requirements to the use case.

4.2.3.3 Actors

Actors are elements outside the scope of the system with which the system interacts. The Speed Demon Treadmill identifies a number of actors, some of which are people

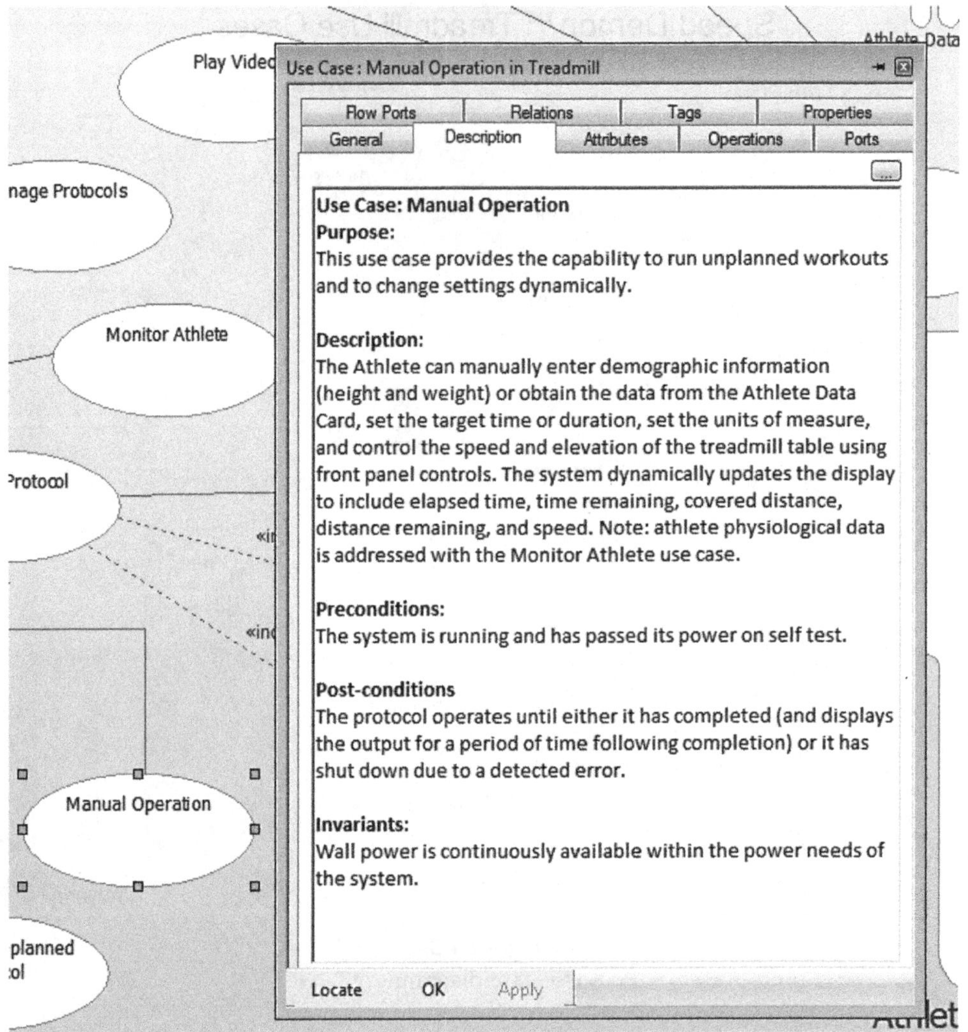

Figure 4.4
Use case description.

(Athlete, Service Tech, and possibly the Trainer[6]), devices (Athlete Data Card), and other systems (Online Store, Remote Treadmill). In use case analysis, we only care about how actors interact with our system of interest and their other properties and interactions (such as with other actors) are out of our scope of concern. We may model specialization among actors because more general actor forms may have different modes of interaction in addition to the more specialized forms but we, in general, never model associations between actors.

[6] If you had my coach, you'd understand the use of the phrase "possibly a person."

4.2.3.4 Relations

The use case diagram has a number of key relations that is depicts, as well as some minor ones. The most important of these are discussed here.

4.2.3.5 Association

The association is the most important relation on use case diagrams and appears on almost every use case diagram. Specifically, associations between an actor and a use case should be interpreted to mean that *while the system executes this use case, messages are exchanged between the actor and the system.* It may be a directed association (indicated with an open arrowhead) if the message flow is only one way, but bidirectional flows are most common.

4.2.3.6 Generalization

Sometimes, a use case may be specialized either in terms of the actors with which it associates, the technology or approach realizing the use case, or in the way the operation plays out. In principle, specialized ("subclassed") use cases can always be combined with their parent as variants of the scenarios but this is a technique by which use case size can be controlled. In Figure 4.3, `Execute Protocol` is the parent ("superclass") use case and `Race`, `Executed Preplanned Protocol`, and `Manual Operation` are the specialized use cases. Generalization is shown with a closed arrowhead pointing to the more general use case.

Although it is usual for each use case to have an associated set of requirements, sometimes a use case is a placeholder that serves only to help organize the use cases. Consider the `Execute Protocol` use case. It includes the use cases `Control Elevation` and `Control Speed`. It is subclassed into three types: `Race`, `Execute Preplanned Protocol`, and `Manual Operation`. Are there any requirements common to all three subuse cases? If so, they should be allocated to the `Execute Protocol` use case; if not, then all the requirements are allocated to either the included use cases or to the specific subtypes. If this is the case, `Execute Protocol` would be a *virtual use case* and serves solely to organize the others and provide common features (relations, in this case) to the others.

4.2.3.7 «Include»

This relation is a containment-style relation in that the included use case is logically a part of the larger use case but is extracted out for some reason. It may be separately identified to manage the size of the larger use case or to create a reusable use case that can be included by other larger use cases. «Include» is a stereotype of SysML's dependency relation and is shown with an open arrowhead and a dashed line.

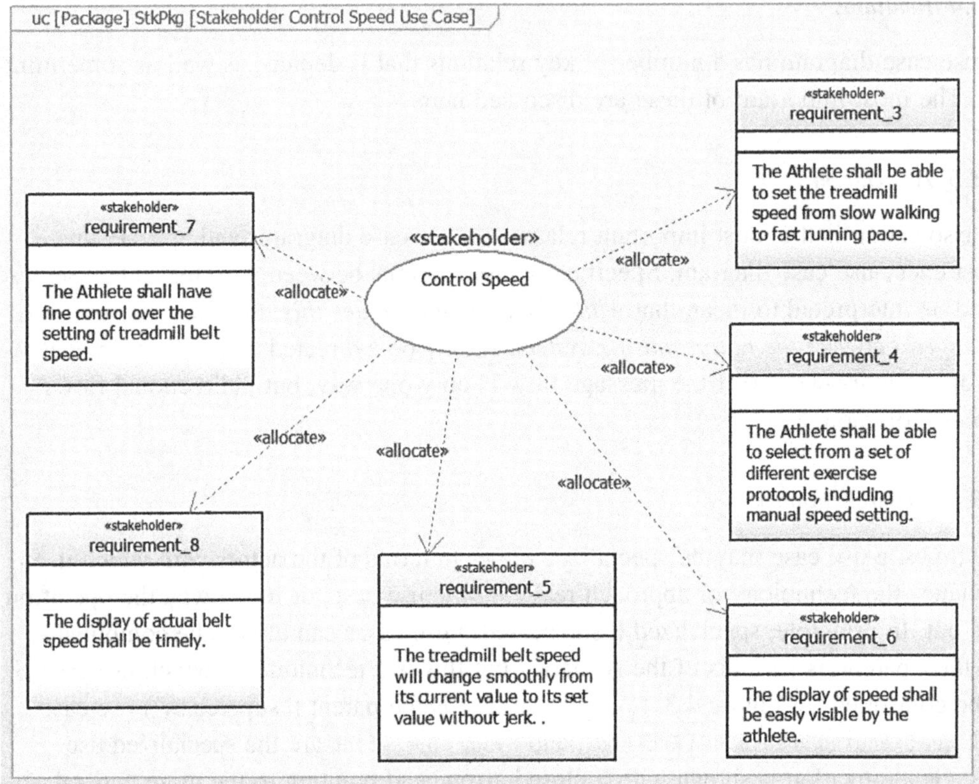

Figure 4.5
Allocation of requirements to use cases.

4.2.3.8 «Extend»

This relation is similar to the «include» relation in that it identifies "part use case" but differs in two ways. First, unlike in the «include» case, the arrow points towards the larger use case. More significantly, it is meant to represent an optional, occasional set of scenarios. Remember that included or extensed use cases are still use cases and should still meet the criteria for good use cases expressed above. In the case of Figure 4.3, being able to dynamically adjust the speed of play of the video to match treadmill speed is an extension to the `Play Video` use case.

4.2.3.9 «Allocate»

I like to use this relation to allocate requirements to use cases. I generally create a separate diagram for each use case and show the allocation on the diagram. Figure 4.5 shows an example. Note that I've indicated the use case and requirements are from the stakeholder perspective by explicitly stereotyping them. An alternative to the «Allocate» relation is to use the more common «trace» relation.

4.3 The Example Model: T-Wrecks, the Industrial Exoskeleton

At this point, it makes sense to introduce the system we will use as a running example through the rest of the book. Welcome to T-Wrecks, an industrial robotic exoskeletal waldo (Figure 4.6). This system is "worn" by the user and "driven" to perform tasks requiring greatly augmented strength and carrying capacity. It is meant to be an all-terrain power loader capable of lifting and moving loads of up to 1500 kg while support normal movement of walking, turning, and even running.

Figure 4.6
T-Wrecks industrial exoskeleton.

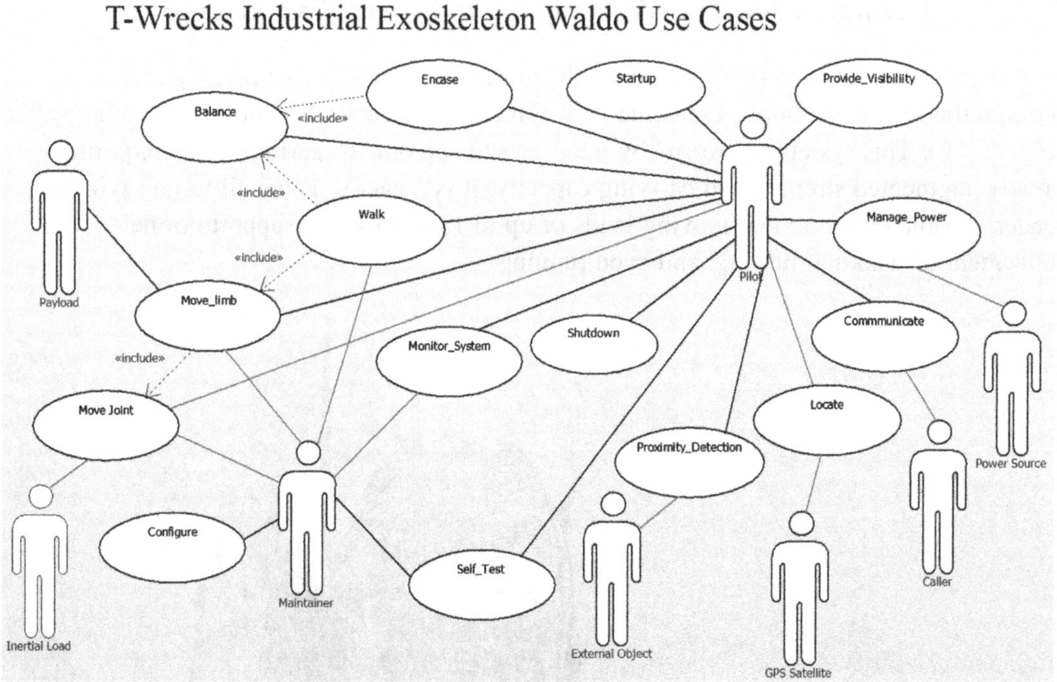

T-Wrecks Industrial Exoskeleton Waldo Use Cases

Figure 4.7
T-Wrecks use case diagram.

Appendix A provides a simple set of stakeholder requirements while Appendix B provides the corresponding system requirements. The use cases are shown in Figure 4.7. We will use some of these use cases to illustrate our techniques and methods on a more complex example throughout this book.

4.4 Identifying Stakeholders

Now that we have an understanding of what a use case is, let's start going through the workflow in Figure 4.1. The first task is *Identify Stakeholders*.

A key part of identifying stakeholder needs is knowing just who the stakeholders are. This is a step often omitted from initial requirements definition and, as a result, necessary functional and nonfunctional properties are forgotten. They can be added in later, but usually at a much higher cost and with significant rework.

As mentioned in Chapter 2, typical stakeholders include:

- primary users and operators of the system,
- secondary users and operators of the system,

- personnel responsible for
  - system installation,
  - on-site system integration,
  - system configuration,
  - system maintenance,
  - system decommissioning,
  - system disposal,
  - system manufacture,
  - system certification,
- purchaser (customer),
- testers.

You can see from this list that all users are stakeholders but not all stakeholders are users.

Each of these roles (with the possible exception of the purchaser) will interact with the system with particular points of views and workflows that they need to support. Although we tend to focus on the primary users of the system, many systems have special requirements for installation, commissioning, decommissioning, maintenance, configuration, and so on. At a minimum, people who will play these roles should contribute to the set of requirements as each of these roles will have their own sets of needs.

We will talk about two specific techniques in this chapter for the elicitation of requirements: interviewing the stakeholders and writing down what they say (Section 4.5) and using scenarios (Section 4.6). In both cases, textual requirements are written down within the use case section of the stakeholder requirements specification.

Let's identify the stakeholders relevant to our T-Wrecks system:

4.4.1 Pilot

The pilot is clearly an important stakeholder, as the primary user/operator of the system.

He or she will be responsible for the operation of the system in the field and will require training on the system to understand and use its capabilities. The bulk of the functional and QoS requirements will arise from this stakeholder and their interaction with the system. Beyond just normal usage, does the system need to provide simulation and training modes of operation?

4.4.2 Fleet Manager

It is likely that a large organization might deploy many of these systems in a given location or across multiple locations. Are there features that should be added that would help the management of fleets of these systems, or help in the coordination of multiple systems in use?

For example, does the fleet manager need to be able to locate all systems at once through a GPS location capability? Do they need to be able to inspect fleet status at a glance? Provide summary reports of hours of use?

Are there ancillary support systems—such as multisystem charging or repair stations that a fleet manager is likely to need? Are such systems parts of this project or another?

4.4.3 Maintainer

Another key player is the staff that will configure, maintain, and repair these systems in the field. What access to information or physical parts are required for this stakeholder to be successful? Is any additional support equipment needed for this role?

4.4.4 Purchaser

The purchaser has a need they are trying to meet with the acquisition of this system. What are those needs beyond simple operation? What are the cost and delivery constraints on the project?

4.4.5 Installer

The installer of this system will likely perform a number of activities such as initialization of the system hydraulics, installation of factory boards, and custom accessories purchased as factory options. What support should the system provide for these activities?

4.4.6 The T-Wreckers Testing Team

Systems verification testing ensures that the system needs its (system) requirements. What access to information do they need to facilitate the verification of the system? What test points and internal health data should be provided for this purpose?

4.4.7 Manufacturing Engineer

The system assembly process should be smooth and simple. The design of the system should support reliable and robust manufacturing. Can existing parts and devices be reused?

4.5 Generating Stakeholder Requirements

Stakeholder requirements are statements about stakeholder needs. This task in the process identifies those needs in clear, unambiguous, and testable ways.

4.5.1 What's a Requirement?

A requirement is a statement of a necessary or expected system property, feature, characterization, or usage. There are different kinds of requirements as depicted in Figure 4.8. In use cases—and in this book—we will focus on functional (what the system does) and QoS (how well it does it) requirements. Nevertheless there are other requirements such as

- Operational (such as environmental conditions within which the system will function).
- Logistics, such as how the system will support business logistics flow or the logistics information provide by a system.
- Usability—requirements about the ease of use and level of required skill and training of users.
- User interface—requirements about how information or control features are presented to and controlled by the user; this includes languages and labeling.
- Parametric requirements—requirements about static properties of the system such as weight or color.

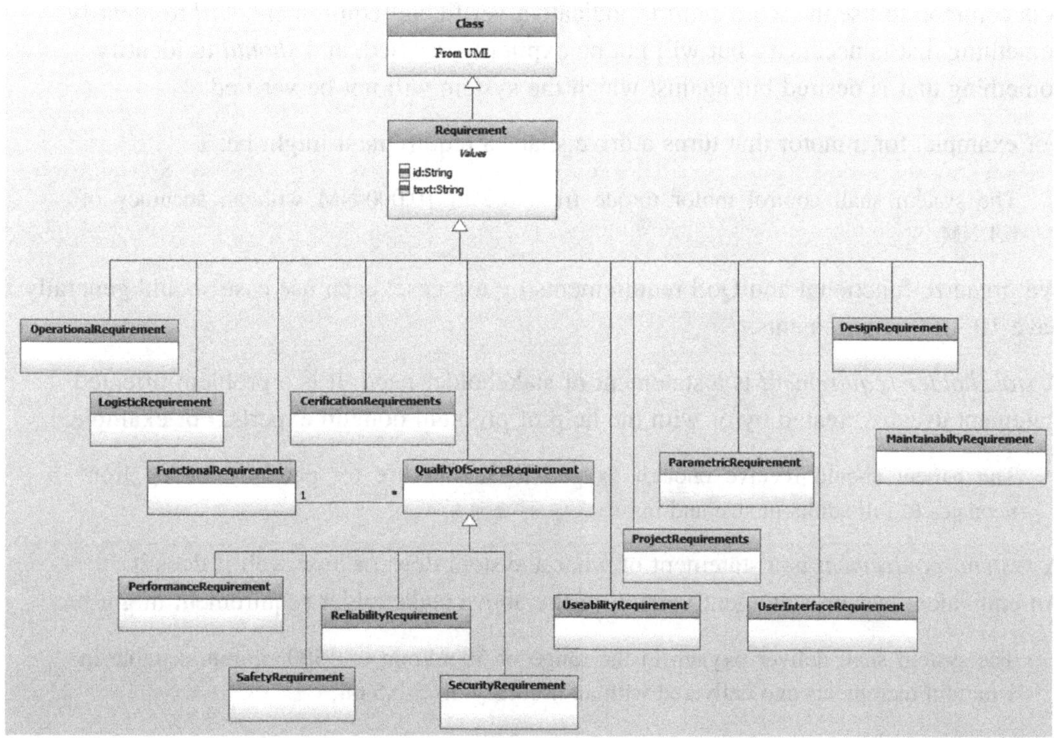

Figure 4.8
Requirements types.

- Maintainability requirements—requirements about the maintenance, repair, and upkeep of the system.
- Certification requirements—requirements about what standards must be met and how the system will meet and be certified against them.
- Project requirements—requirements about the development of the system itself, such as time, cost, and deliverables.
- Design requirement—these are constraints levied against the design, such as materials or the reuse of existing designs.

It's not so much that we need to adhere to a particular way of classifying requirements as it is important to understand that there are different kinds of requirements that must be captured and against which the system must be verified in some way.

Good stakeholder requirements are unambiguous, understandable, and verifiable statements about the needs a system must satisfy. Ambiguous or unclear requirements are clearly not very useful, and the same is true of unverifiable statements. Requirements should also be "black box" from the scope at which they are stated and focus on external observable properties. The internal properties hidden from view will be specified in design.

It is common to use the word *shall* to indicate a verifiable requirement, *will* to identify something that is necessary but will not be explicitly verified, and *should* to identify something that is desired but against which the system will not be verified.

For example, for a motor that turns a drive shaft, a requirement might be:

> The system shall control motor torque from 0.0 to 10,000 NM with an accuracy of 0.1 NM.[7]

We organize functional and QoS requirements by use case; each use case should generally have 10–100 requirements.

A *stakeholder requirement* is a statement of stakeholder need. It is a problem-oriented statement usually created by or with the help of problem domain experts. For example:

> The patient should receive enough oxygen to sustain life for patients ranging from neonates to full adults in size and mass.

A *system requirement* is a statement of what a system does or how well it does it. An equivalent system statement version of the above stakeholder requirement might be:

> The system shall deliver oxygen in the range of 50 ml/min to 1500 ml/min, settable in 1 ml/min increments and delivered with an accuracy of $\pm$0.5 ml.

[7] The statement arguably contains three requirements; one about the requirement to provide torque, another to specify the range of permitted values, and another to specify operational accuracy.

System requirements tend to be more quantitative than their stakeholder counterparts. Stakeholders may not understand the capabilities of the solution technologies even if they are problem domain experts, so system engineers provide or search for technical expertise where appropriate.

4.5.2 Performance and Other QoS Requirements

If functional requirements are verbs, then QoS requirements are adverbs. QoS requirements define how much, how fast, or how well a required functional behavior will be performed. Sadly, stakeholder requirements often fail to state important QoS constraints even though they are essential properties. For example, it is rare for a system to provide a function where no one cares how long that function takes to execute, how often it might fail, or with what accuracy the service must be delivered.

Common QoS constraints include:

- Flows
  - Extent—what is the range of permitted values? Are all values within this range permitted or are there explicitly excluded values? What should happen if these ranges are violated?
  - Accuracy—what is the level of precision required for specification, control, and delivery?
- Performance
  - Worst case performance—what is the longest time this behavior should take to perform?
  - Average performance—on average, how long should this behavior take to perform?
  - Bandwidth—what is the rate of information or materiel transfer?
  - Throughput—what is the rate of successful information or materiel transfer?
  - Maximal delay—what is the longest time this behavior can be delayed?
  - Jitter—what variability in performance is allowed?
  - Signal-to-noise ratio—what is the proportion of the signal that is information?
- Safety
  - Criticality—how critical is this system property?
  - Is there an appropriate safety objective (such as a Safety Integrity Level) required by a relevant safety standard?
- Reliability
  - Error rate—what is the rate at which unhandled errors may occur?
  - Mean time between failure—on average, how long should the system operate before failing?
  - Availability—what is the percentage of time the system aspect is available?

- Security
  - Value of assets—what is the value of features of the system that should be protected from interference, intrusion, or theft?
  - Threats—what threats should the system handle?
  - Vulnerability—how easy should it be to attack aspects of the system?
  - Assurance—what is the level of guarantee that the system will not be successfully attacked?

Because QoS requirements are adverbs, they should be clustered in the same use case with the verbs (functional requirements) they constrain.

4.5.3 Visualizing Requirements

There are a number of ways to visualize there requirements. Certainly, a requirements diagram (see Figure 3.7 from the previous chapter) is one way, particularly when you want to depict the relations among requirements.

A requirements table is a good summary view of the requirements. A partial example for an aircraft surface control system is shown in Figure 4.9.

Another useful view of requirements is to put them on other diagrams to show the allocation of requirements. Such a use case diagram for the same aircraft *Manage Control Surfaces* system (that interacts with the aircraft's *Attitude Management* and *Pilot Display* systems) is shown in Figure 4.10.

This diagram not only shows the allocation, it also supports traceability, as the relations are navigable and searchable links. Of course, the traceability of the requirements to various elements can be summarized in matrix form as well, as shown in Figure 4.11.

4.5.4 Requirements Management Tools

For systems with many requirements, especially when the cost of system specification defects is high, the use of requirements management tools is very common. IBM Rational DOORS™ is the pre-eminent such tool but there are others in the market. While these tools manage textual requirements for the most part, they still offer significant advantages over using traditional word processing or spreadsheet software to capture and manage requirements.

First of all, a word processor treats text as, well *text*. Such tools have no concern of semantics or identifiable elements made up of text (other than perhaps sentences and paragraphs). A requirements management tool however knows what a requirement *is* and treats it as an object. As an object, it can be assigned properties, such as the type of requirement, when or in what version of a system it will appear, and criticality. As an

Name	ID	Specification
requirement_0	R000	The software shall independently control the following control surfaces: the left elevator, the right elevator and the rudder. Each of these elements shall be referred to as a "control surface."
requirement_1	R001	Each control surface shall be independently controlled by commands from the Attitude Management System.
requirement_10	R010	The off-normal maximum and minimum control values for each control surface is provided in Table 3. Control Surface Minimum Value (degrees) Maximum Value (degrees) Rudder -35 +35 Left Elevator -30 +30 Right Elevator -30 +30
requirement_11	R011	The range of accuracy for commanded and measured positions shall be +/- 0.5 degrees.
requirement_12	R012	The maximum time from a transition from minimum position to maximum position or from maximum position to minimum position shall be 3.0 seconds.
requirement_13	R013	The ACES shall maintain a total elapsed time for all states except OFF since last cleared. This data shall persist between power cycles of the ACES.
requirement_14	R014	The system shall be able to detect a loss of communication with a control surface within 1.0 seconds and report an error to both the Pilot Display and the Attitude Management System in that case.
requirement_15	R015	The system shall report an error if the system has not achieved the commanded position +/- 0.5 degrees of a control surface within 3.0 seconds and shall enter FAILSAFE_STATE.
requirement_16	R016	Upon initial power up, the ACES shall default to battery power.
requirement_17	R017	Upon initial power up, each control surface shall be positioned to it's minimum range and its position verified. If the position achieved is less than 1 degree off specification or requires more than 3.0 seconds to compl
requirement_18	R018	Following successful achievement of minimum position following an initial power up, each control surface shall be commanded to its maximum position. If the position achieved is less than 1 degree off specification re
requirement_19	R019	Following successful achievement of maximum position following an initial power on, each control surface shall be commanded to its zero position. If the position achieved is less than 1 degree off specification requir
requirement_2	R002	At least every second, the measured position of each control surface shall be reported to the Attitude Management System.
requirement_20	R020	Following successful achievement of zero position, the system shall perform a software Built In Test (BIT) to check the integrity of the loaded software, that the hydraulic pressure in each control surface is within 5% c
requirement_21	R021	The system shall not automatically perform minimum, maximum, and zero position tests during a restart, where "restart" is defined to be starting up within 5 minutes after being enabled, or being operational. Rationale:
requirement_22	R022	The system can be commanded into a restart mode from the OFF_STATE by the Attitude Management System.
requirement_23	R023	Prior to shut down, each control surface shall be set to its zero position and the power removed from all actuators and sensors.
requirement_24	R024	Prior to shut down, the ASES shall transition to receive power from the airframe battery.
requirement_25	R025	Prior to shut down, all measured and command data shall be stored in non-volatile memory.
requirement_26	R026	OFF_STATE. In this state, the system shall be without power and the system has attempted to zero the position of all control surfaces.
requirement_27	R027	BIT_STATE: In this state, the system is performing an automatic or requested Built In Test. The system is not permitted to transition to this state directly from OPERATIONAL_STATE with a pilot override action.
requirement_28	R028	WARM_STATE. In this state, the system has successfully passed initial boot sequence, all control surfaces are zeroed, and the system is ready to begin operation, but has not yet been commanded to do so.
requirement_29	R029	OPERATING_STATE: In this state, the system is actively accept commands to position the control surfaces and is actively reporting measured control surface positions.
requirement_3	R003	At least every second, the ACES operational state and hydraulic pressure shall be reported to the pilot display (see States and Modes).
requirement_30	R030	FAILSAFE_STATE: In this state, the system has detected an error condition and it attempting to perform nomal function, but may not be able to do so.
requirement_31	R031	FAIL_STATE: In this state, the system has detected an error condition and is disallowing transition to any start other than OFF_STATE or BIT_STATE.
requirement_32	R032	MAINTENANCE_MODE: In this mode, the system will accept all commands including commands to retrieve and reset persistent historical data, including elapsed time in states. The system shall only permit transition
requirement_33	R033	The following error codes are defined as a bit set. Code Name Description 0x00 <no error> No detected errors 0x01 Internal comm error Communication error detected within the ACES 0x02 External comm error Communication error detected between the ACES and an external system 0x04 BIT fail Built In Test failure 0x08 Rudder fail Rudder movement out of spec 0x10 Left elevator fail Left elevator movement out of spec 0x20 Right elevator fail Right elevator movement out of spec 0x10000 Hydraulic under pressure Hydraulic pressure too low 0x20000 Hydraulic over pressure Hydraulic pressure too high 0x40000 reserved unused 0x80000 reserved unused
requirement_34	R034	The software for the ACES shall be implemented in the C language for ease of certification.
requirement_35	R035	The software for the ACES shall be developed with Rational Rhapsody tool.
requirement_4	R004	Any detected error or failure condition shall be reported to both the Attitude Management System and the Pilot Display within 0.5 second of detection.
requirement_5	R005	The ACES shall interface with the electrical power system via the aircraft alternator, the aircraft APU, and the aircraft battery.
requirement_6	R006	The ACES shall monitor provided current and voltage from its selected power source and automatically transition if the current or voltage exceeds nominal values by more than 10% for more than 30 seconds, or by m

Figure 4.9
Requirements table.

object, it can relate to other objects, such as requirements within the current specification or others as well as other kinds of elements such as design and test elements. These properties and relations can be viewed, searched, and manipulated in any number of ways.

Some of the things that a requirements management tool enables are:

- Impact analysis. If a requirement changes, what are the related elements (derived requirements, design elements, test cases, etc.) that may also require modification? What verification steps will need to be repeated?
- Design justification. Justification of the existence of design elements can be obtained by tracing backwards to the requirements that is satisfies. This is especially important for safety critical systems because most safety standards disallow design elements that do not satisfy at least one requirement.
- Design completeness assessment. Are all the requirements satisfied by design or implementation elements?

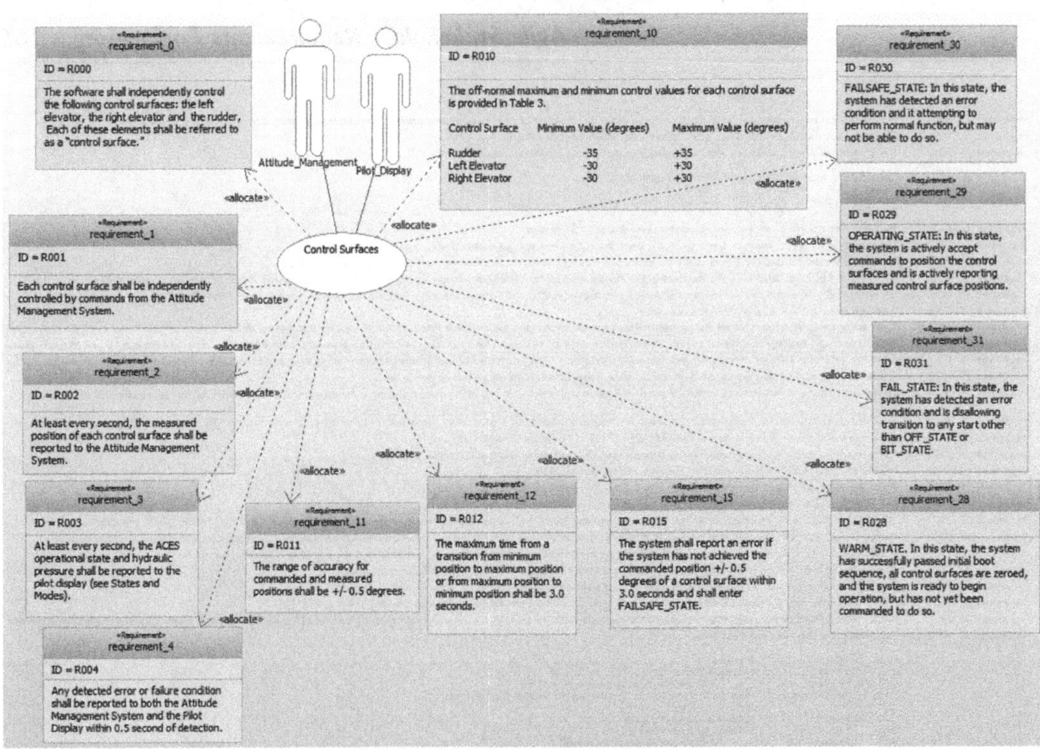

Figure 4.10
Use case requirements allocation.

To: Requirement Scope: SpecModel

	Control Surfaces	Display Data	Manage Data	Manage Power	Start Up	Shut Down	Communicate with external devices
requirement_0	requirement_0						
requirement_1	requirement_1						
requirement_2	requirement_2						
requirement_3	requirement_3						
requirement_4	requirement_4						
requirement_5				requirement_5			
requirement_6				requirement_6			
requirement_7		requirement_7					
requirement_8							requirement_8
requirement_9							requirement_9
requirement_10	requirement_10						
requirement_11	requirement_11						
requirement_12	requirement_12						
requirement_13			requirement_13				
requirement_15	requirement_15						
requirement_16				requirement_16	requirement_16		
requirement_17					requirement_17		
requirement_18					requirement_18		
requirement_19					requirement_19		
requirement_20					requirement_20		
requirement_21					requirement_21		
requirement_22					requirement_22		
requirement_23						requirement_23	
requirement_24						requirement_24	
requirement_25						requirement_25	
requirement_26						requirement_26	
requirement_27					requirement_27		
requirement_28	requirement_28						
requirement_29	requirement_29	requirement_29					
requirement_30	requirement_30						
requirement_31	requirement_31						
requirement_32			requirement_32				
requirement_33							requirement_33

Figure 4.11
Use case–requirement matrix.

- Verification completeness assessment. Which test cases verify or validate which requirements? Are all requirements verified by at least one test case?
- Project status assessment. How many of the requirements are satisfied by design or implementation elements? How many requirements have been verified so far?

Good requirements management tools integrate with other tools in the system engineer's environment, including modeling and verification tools. While you can certainly perform some level of traceability in most modeling tools, requirements management tools are optimized for that purpose.

4.5.5 Organizing the Stakeholder Requirements Specification

There are a number of ways to organize stakeholder requirement specifications. Probably the most common is to organize the specification into chapter by the type of requirement (usability, user interface, function, performance, safety, reliability, security, etc.). While this works, it doesn't support the larger-scale analysis and reasoning supported by use case analysis, so I recommend that functional and QoS (performance, safety, reliability, and security) be grouped together within the use cases and the use cases should be the primary organizational schema. Chapters for other kinds of requirements (such as usability, logistics, and parametric) are still appropriate ways to handle those kinds of requirements. This is true without regard to how you've chosen to represent the requirements—in text, as requirements objects in a requirements management tool, or in a model.

Again, in this book, we'll focus on the functional and QoS requirements for the most part.

4.6 Modeling Stakeholder Use Cases Scenarios

In my experience, if the system engineering team builds the wrong system because the stakeholders did a poor job of stating their needs, the stakeholders will still blame the system engineers. It is our job to ensure all the relevant needs of the stakeholders are represented within, and ultimately satisfied by, the system we develop. It behooves us to ensure that we extract a complete set of the correct requirements. Of course, a set of requirements is a still a theory—the stakeholders *believe* that a system that satisfies these requirements will meet their needs—so we must still perform *validation* activities to ensure that the incrementally specified and developed system does, in fact, meet their needs. So while this theory (the requirements) isn't proof, it's still the best place to start.[8] We use use case scenarios as a tool to explore the requirements by explicitly representing the permissible (and sometimes impermissible) interactions of the system with elements in its environment. The result of this analysis is the identification of missing, incorrect, or inconsistent requirements.

[8] Law of Douglass #109: *Theorize* but *verify*.

4.6.1 What Is a Use Case Scenario, Exactly?

A use case scenario is a *specific* interaction between a system executing a use case and the actors in its environment. By *specific*, I mean that it has a specific set of messages and flows that arrive in a specific order with specific values and with specific timing. These messages and flows come from the actor to the system and also arise from the system and are sent to the actors. Each message, sequence, value, and timing relates to one or more requirements. Scenarios provide a means for *requirements solicitation*—if we need to add a message on the sequence diagram for which we have no requirement, that implies a missing requirement (so add it!). As we explore how the stakeholder expects the system to interact with its environment, we identify and deepen our understanding of these requirements. Just as important, we also identify alternative flows (scenarios) that identify so-far unstated requirements by asking questions about the sequence, the values, the messages, and the timing.

Sidebar: A couple of misconceptions about scenarios

Some authors state that all scenarios start with a message from an actor.

WRONG! We often build autonomous systems that generate their own behavior.

Some authors think that Time should be represented as a lifeline on a sequence diagram.

WRONG! Time events should be indicated as a "message to self" because they are internally generated by a system timing mechanism.

Consider the following conversation between myself and a doctor specifying the behavior he wants from a patient ventilator:

Doctor — So, I want to turn the Respiration Rate knob to set respiration rate, see the value change, and push the button in to set the value. Then I want to see both the set value and the actual measured value above the button.

Me — Ok. What about tidal volume?

Doctor — That should work in the same way—turn the Tidal Volume knob, push in to confirm, and display the set and actual values.

Me — Ok. That's pretty easy. (Thinking...) Hmmm what if the user turns the respiration knob but doesn't push it in before turning the tidal volume knob?

Doctor — Well, let's see. (Thinking...) In that case, the original set value should be retained for respiration rate since it wasn't confirmed.

Me — Doesn't that mean that the user can't see the actual set value because it now displays the unconfirmed but changed value?

Doctor — That's a good point. Ok, then as soon as the user turns the tidal volume knob, the unconfirmed respiration rate will just revert back to its current confirmed value and the change should be discarded.

Me	Ok, should there be any visual indication that the value is pending and not yet confirmed, such as with color or flashing text?
Doctor	Flashing would be good, and then solid once it's confirmed.
Doctor	Once the ventilation settings are all updated, then I want to push the Deliver Ventilation button to start the therapy.
Me	You mean, like this (see Figure 4.12)?

As I do this scenario exploration of the stakeholder's needs, I start identifying the textual requirements and put them in either my requirements management or modeling tool:

> The respiration rate shall be set by the turn of a dedicated knob to select the desired value.
>
> When the respiration rate control has not be turned or changed or after it has been confirmed, it shall display the current set value with a steady color.
>
> When the respiration rate control has been turned or changed, but not yet confirmed, the proposed selected value shall be displayed flashing.
>
> The proposed respiration rate value shall be confirmed by pressing the respiration rate control knob in.
>
> The tidal volume shall be set by the turn of a dedicated knob to select the desired value.
>
> When the tidal volume control has not be turned or changed or after it has been confirmed, it shall display the current set value with a steady color.

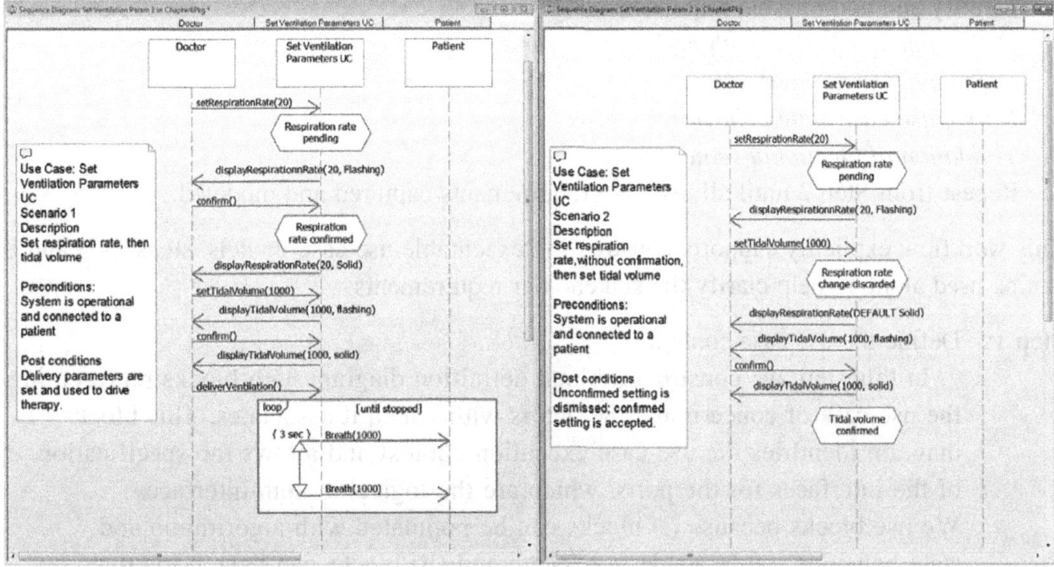

Figure 4.12
Use case scenarios.

When the tidal volume control has been turned or changed, but not yet confirmed, the proposed selected value shall be displayed flashing.

The proposed tidal volume value shall be confirmed by pressing the tidal volume control knob in.

When the tidal volume value is confirmed, the display shall show the new set value with a steady color.

Of course, we go on to talk about other ventilator parameters, ranges of permissible values, and other requirements. The point is that scenario modeling like this can be used with nontechnical stakeholders to describe the desired interaction of the system with them and its environment. And as I do that, I deepen my understanding of the stakeholder's needs and identify missing, incorrect, or ambiguous requirements.

4.6.2 Scenario Analysis Workflow

I tend to follow a specific workflow when doing scenario analysis. While the details of the workflow are more critical when you create executable use cases (something often only done during system use case analysis rather than stakeholder use case analysis), it is nevertheless applicable while trying to clarify the stakeholder needs (steps that are optional in stakeholder scenario analysis are italicized):

1. Define use case context.
2. Define use case scenarios.
3. Identify and add missing requirements.
4. *Define functional flow with activity diagrams.*
5. *Define ports and interfaces.*
6. *Derive use case state behavior.*
7. *Validation of functional requirements.*
8. Repeat from Step 2 until all use case requirements captured and modeled.

This workflow explicitly supports constructing executable use case models, steps 1–3 and 8 can be used alone to help clarify the stakeholder requirements.

Step 1: Define the use case context

In this step, we construct a block definition diagram with blocks representing the use case of concern and the actors with which it associates. This block diagram identifies the use case execution context and allows the specification of the interfaces for the ports, which are the logical system interfaces. We use blocks because (i) blocks can be populated with algorithmic and state behavior and be made to execute and (ii) blocks can have ports that are typed by their interfaces, and this aids in the specification of the system interfaces.

Step 2: Define use case scenarios

The activity in this step is to capture the flow of data and service requests between the actors and the use case (more specifically, the system executing the use case). Every message between an actor and a use case is there to at least partially represent one or more requirements.

Note: I recommend that for the purpose of system engineering, we use asynchronous events to depict discrete messages between the use cases and the actors. This will simplify the execution later and it means that we don't have to consider blocking semantics (asynchronous messages are automatically queued). If a message to or from an actor needs to carry data, just add the data as an event parameter. For continuous interactions, use flows on the sequence diagram or use continuous flows on an activity diagram.

Step 3: Identify and add missing requirements

As we work with the stakeholders to reason out the scenarios, missing requirements will be identified and a deeper understanding of the stakeholder's needs will be achieved. These missing requirements are then added to the stakeholder requirements set.

Step 4: Define functional flow with activity diagrams

Model the scenarios together in an activity diagram using decision points, forks, and joins to combine the different flows into an overall view of the use case behavior. *Note*: This step is optional in stakeholder scenario analysis.

Step 5: Define ports and interfaces

Add a port on the use case block for every actor with which the use case associates and add a port on the actor block for connecting to the use case block. The messages in the scenarios sent between the use case and the actor blocks form the logical interface for the system executing the use case. *Note*: This step is optional in stakeholder scenario analysis.

Step 6: Define use case state behavior

This is where we build an executable requirements model. Construct a state machine for the use case block where incoming messages are events on the state machine and messages to the actors are (send) actions on the state machine. The execution of this state machine is fully generative, meaning that it can generate all possible scenarios for the use case. This will be heavily used in system requirements specification and is optional here.

Step 7: Validation of functional requirements

The execution of the state machine (from the previous step) is used to verify our understanding of the allowed and disallowed interactions between the actors and the system running the use case. The outcome of these executions can be shown to the stakeholders and validated with them. Additionally, requirement exploration (as in "What happens if C happens and then B and finally A, rather than the usual A, B, then C?") can be done by simply executing the requirements model. This is a great way to identify missing or incorrect requirements. This step is also optional for stakeholder requirements.

Step 8: Repeat from step 2 until all use case requirements are captured and modeled

We needn't do *all* scenarios in step 1 before we proceed to step 2. In fact, we prefer to do only one or even a partial scenario before proceeding to the next step. These form very short iterations called *nanocycles* that usually last 30–60 min. When I work with stakeholders, I often perform 10 or more iterations in a day and identify many previously unstated requirements.

This workflow is very effective with discrete messages between the actors and the system use case. It works less well, as we will see later, with continuous flows—such as continuous pressure, fluid flow, or energy exchange. In that case, SysML activity diagrams are preferable to sequence diagrams for modeling the behavior.

4.6.2.1 How do you know when you're done?

This is a question I get in almost every consulting engagement that deals with requirements analysis: how much is enough?

There are an infinite number of possible scenarios for any worthwhile use case because of the possible different values messages can carry, the different sequences that are possible, all the things that can possibly go wrong, and that messages can be repeated (looped). We will stop when we have captured and modeled all the functional and QoS requirements. Three criteria must be met to complete the use case scenario analysis:

1. All functional and QoS requirements for the use case are represented in at least one sequence diagram.
2. All "interesting variants"[9] of scenario flow are captured, including error and exception scenarios (known as "rainy day" scenarios).
3. All messages are reconciled with the requirement(s) they represent.

Usually, meeting the completeness criteria above requires anywhere from 5 to 50 scenarios, depending on the size and complexity of the use case.

Scenarios represent requirements not only by identifying service invocations and their performance properties. They also represent requirements in terms of allowable and disallowed sequences of those services. After all, lowering the landing gear *after* the plane touches down is commonly known as a "crash" rather than a "landing."

[9] In this context, an "interesting variant" is one that adds at least one new requirement, including, possibly, the same messages but in a different sequence, messages passing different values when those values invoke different behaviors (such as "go left if $x < 0$ and go right if $x >= 0$"), or when changes in timing result in different system responses.

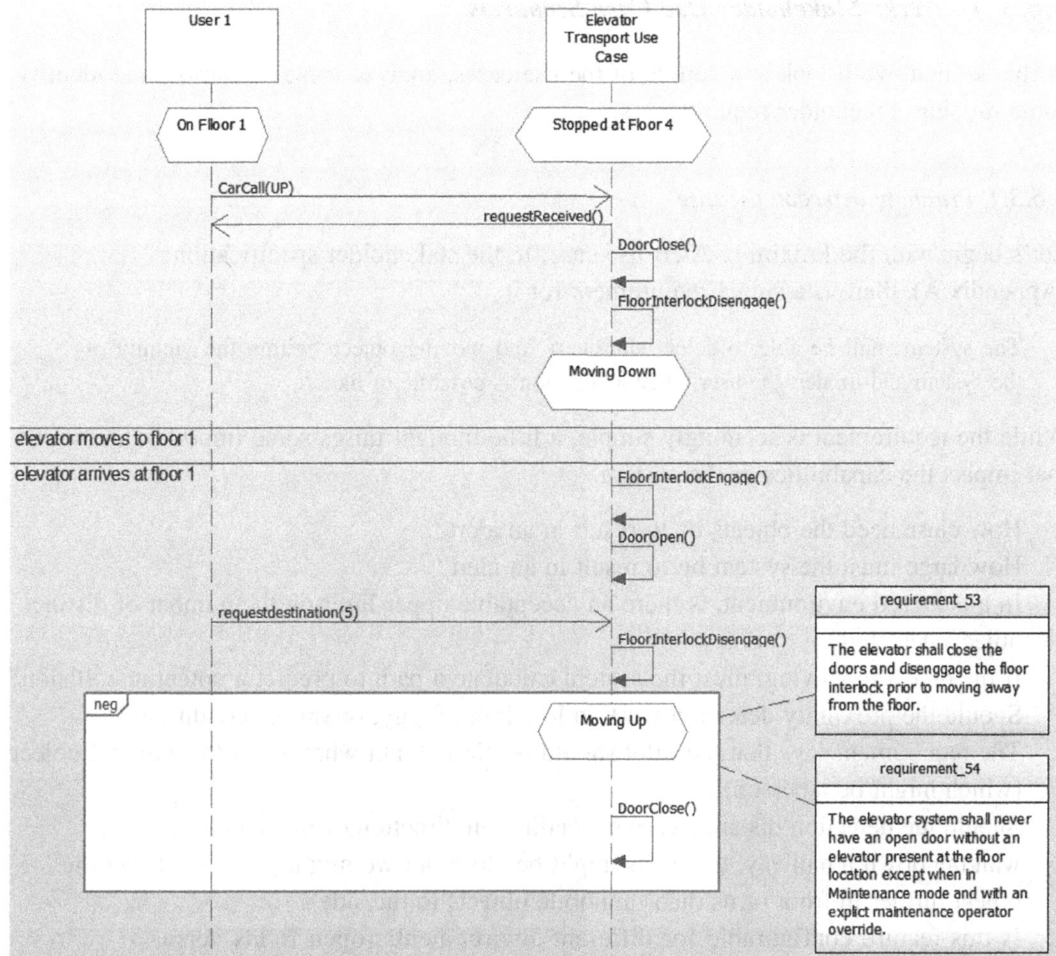

Figure 4.13
Showing disallowed flows.

Note: To show a specifically disallowed sequence, draw the sequence and annotate it with a *neg* (negate) operator, such as in Figure 4.13. Showing 100 scenarios where the door always closes before the elevator moves is not the same as explicitly disallowing leaving the door open.

It isn't necessary to create a new scenario for every fault condition. It is enough to identify and capture all fault classes. A *fault class* is a set of faults that are treated in the same way. For example, a medical gas mixer might treat running out of input gas, a failure in a valve, and an intern standing on the intake gas hose all in the same way. It is enough to draw the scenario once and in a constraint or comment (and ultimately in a requirement), list the members of the fault class. This reduces the number of scenarios you must draw to a potentially large but still manageable set.

4.6.3 T-Wrecks Stakeholder Use Case Scenarios

In this section, we'll look at a couple of the use cases, analyze some scenarios, and identify some missing stakeholder requirements.

4.6.3.1 Proximity detection use case

Let's begin with the Proximity Alert use case. In the stakeholder specification (Appendix A), there is a single requirement for it:

> The system shall be able to detect stationary and moving objects within the vicinity of the system and to alert the user when a collision is possible or likely.

While the requirement is seemingly simple, a little thought raises some important questions that impact the capabilities of the system[10]:

- How close need the objects be to result in an alert?
- How large must the system be to result in an alert?
- In a cluttered environment, is there an acceptable upper limit on the number of distinct objects detected?
- If the object is moving, must the system calculate a path to predict a potential collision?
- Should the proximity detection work in low light, foggy, or smoky conditions?
- The requirement says that the pilot should be alerted, but what about the external object (which might be a person)?
- Should the detection distance vary depending on direction of movement (e.g., in walking down a hallway, the walls might be close but we might prefer to detect the object further in front of us than immobile objects to the side)?
- Is this feature configurable for different environments (open fields versus warehouses)?
- Can the system expect humans in the area to be wearing active detection devices (as is commonly done in proximity systems used in the mining industry)?

In conversations with the stakeholders, we use sequence diagrams to frame the conversations. In the first such scenario, shown in Figure 4.14, we see the system handle three objects within its detection range. We also see that a pilot action results in the enablement and the disablement of the proximity detection capability and that the system will add criticality to the pilot alert in some fashion. As a result of creating this scenario, additional requirements have been identified and added to the Stakeholder Requirements Specification.

[10] Many of these will be resolved in the system requirements rather than the stakeholder requirements, but all the questions are valid concerns.

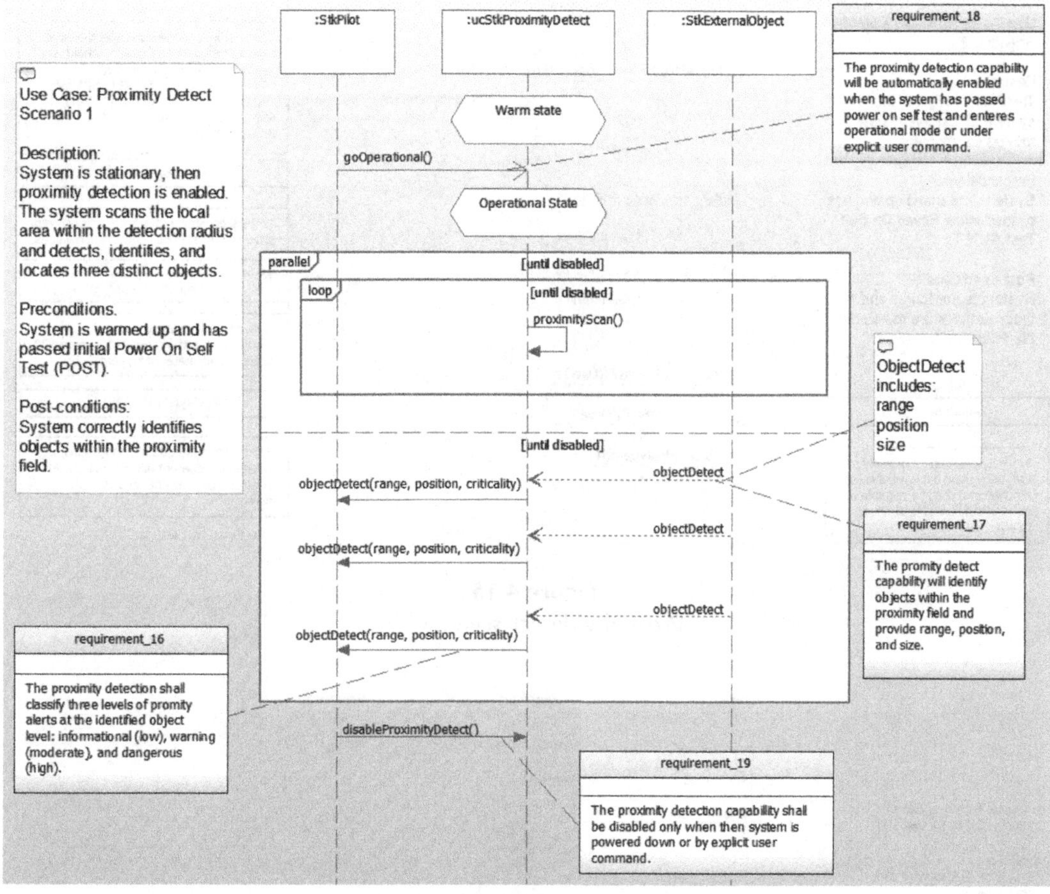

Figure 4.14
Proximity detect scenario 1.

In this next scenario, the pilot configures the proximity detection capability for a cluttered but slow-moving environment and then individually tailors the settings. This adds a number of new requirements that elucidate more about this intended capability, including the configurable properties (Figure 4.15).

Let's do one more scenario. In this scenario (Figure 4.16), a fault in the proximity sensor occurs while the system is operating. The system detects the fault and alerts the user. Two missing requirements are identified.

4.6.3.2 Move joint use case

Next, let's start thinking about modeling the required movement behavior of the system. We'd like to work up to complex behaviors such as `Walk` but that requires coordinated

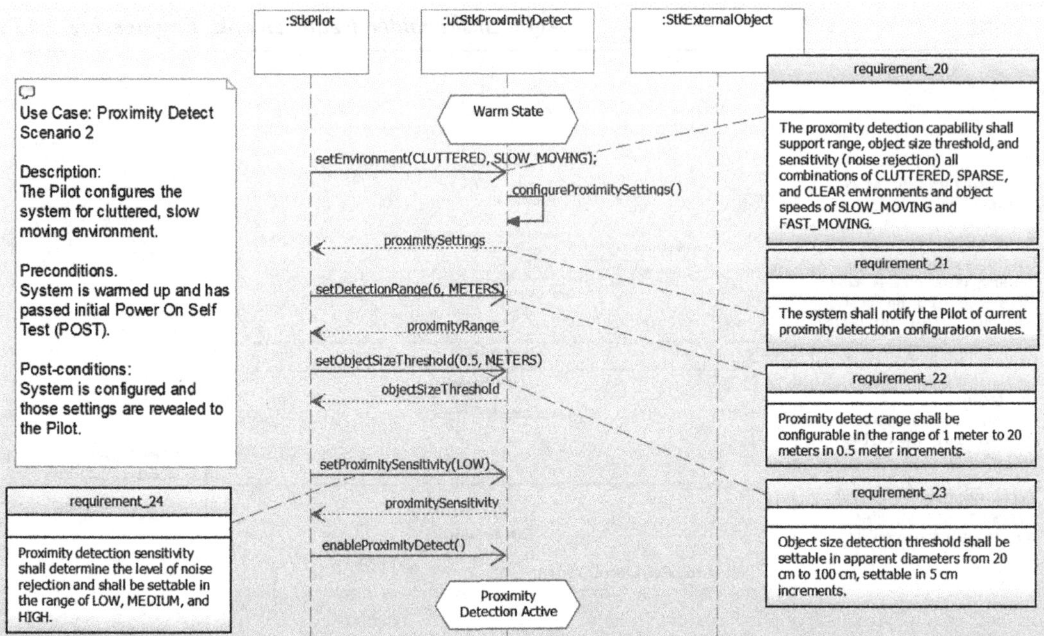

Figure 4.15
Proximity detect scenario 2.

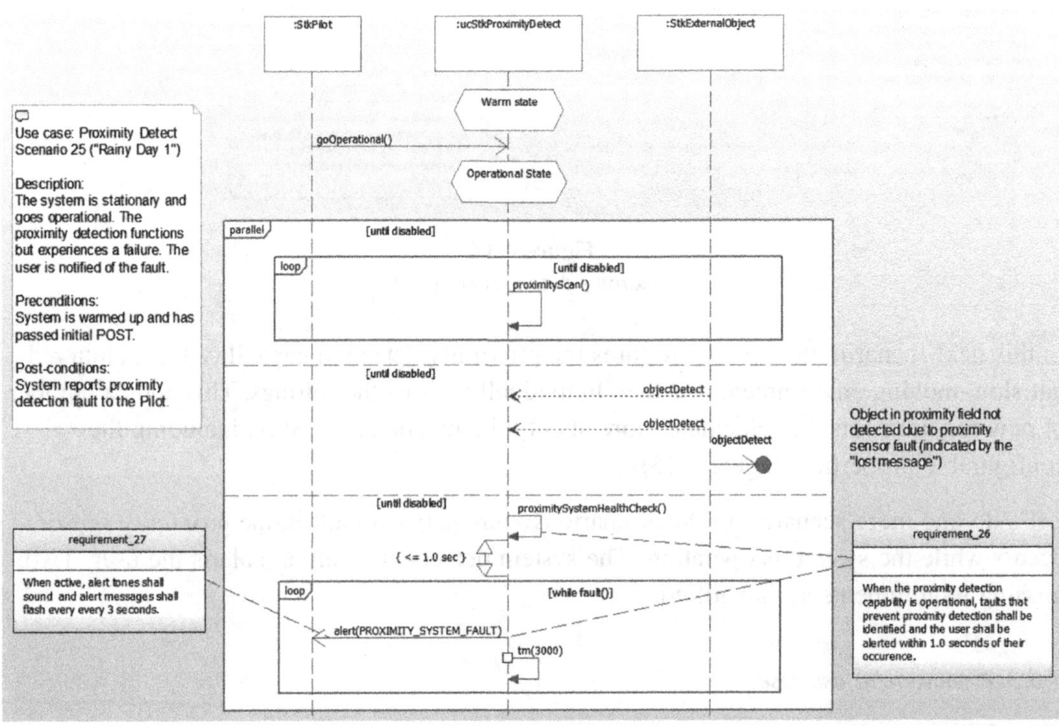

Figure 4.16
Proximity detect rainy day scenario.

movement of multiple limbs. You can see in Figure 4.7 that the `Walk` use case includes the `Move Limb` use case. Of course, each limb has multiple joints so coordinated limb movement requires control over joint movement, so we see that `Move Limb` includes the use case `Move Joint`. Let's start there.

Let's analyze some use case scenarios for the T-Wrecks system use case `Move Joint`. Within this use case, the operator can grip payloads, move the system's knee, hip, elbow, shoulder, and gripping joints (and possibly others as well, such as potentially wrist, foot, and multiple torso joints, depending on the system design).

Before we start doing any deep thinking about limb movement, we need to define our vocabulary in which we will describe movement. Following standard anatomic planes, we will define motion in terms of motion as the summation of movement within three perpendicular planes. Movement in the *sagittal* plane is forward and backward; movement in the *coronal* (also know as *frontal*) plane is side to side (*abduction* is movement away from the middle in the coronal plane and *adduction* is movement towards the middle); movement in the *transverse* plane is up and down (see Figure 4.17). For convention, forward movement will be considered positive and rearward negative. Likewise, abduction will be considered positive and adduction negative, and up will be positive and down will be negative.

Joints may move in a single plane (such as the knee joint) or in all three planes (such as the hip or shoulder joints). However, movement of limbs is not unrestrained; all joints have a fixed point on the body, therefore even if the limb can move in three dimensions, it is enough to think about movement in two planes and compute the movement in the third plane. Figure 4.18 shows how the T-Wreck's leg is comprised of multiple joints.

Let's think of some scenarios for the `Move Joint` use case:

- Exerted pressure of Pilot moves the joint forward.
- Exerted pressure of Pilot moves the joint rearward.
- Exerted pressure of Pilot abducts the joint (away from the centerline of the body in the coronal plane).
- Exerted pressure of Pilot adducts the joint (towards the centerline of the body in the coronal plane).
- Exerted pressure of Pilot abducts the joint while moving forward.
- Exerted pressure of Pilot adducts the joint while moving backwards.
- Joint movement (in all possible directions) reaches maximal position.
- ...

Figure 4.19 shows the first scenario. It shows an `enableMovement` event sent to the system use case, followed by some movement flows, and completing with a disable event. What we see is that the user sends an event to enable movement, then produces pressure in the forward and rearward directions, and the system responds (with "messages to self") by

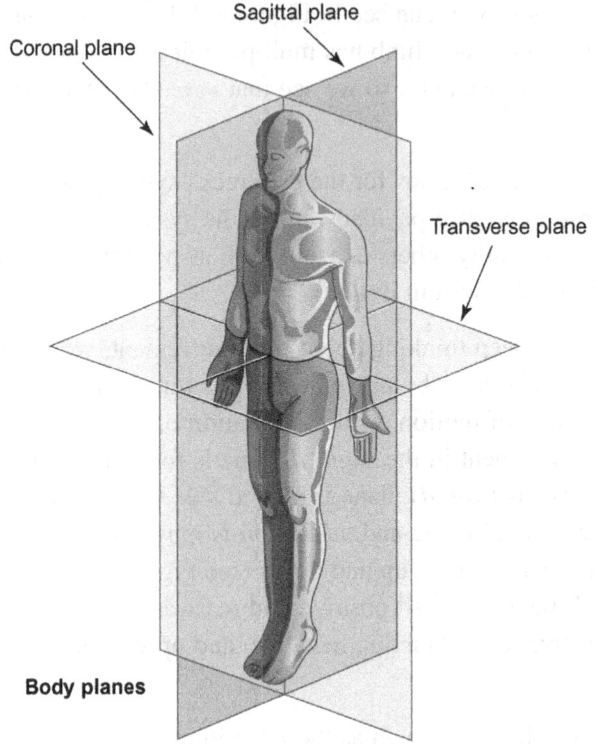

Figure 4.17
Anatomical planes.[11]

producing movement in the sagittal and coronal planes. This diagram is not very satisfying because unlike events, these flows occur over some period of time and assume continuous values over that time. While we could, in principle, just show the flows when the pressure changes, in reality, the pressure applied by the user is continuously changing. Even if we limit to a specific sampling rate (say, every 100 ms), this is problematic—there would be dozens to hundreds of very similar messages. This wouldn't really improve our understanding of the requirements. This illustrates that while sequence diagrams are great for showing the sequence of discrete events, they don't fare well for continuous flows and behavior.

The situation isn't improved for coordinated movement (multiple joints on the same limb) either (Figure 4.20). Most use cases that deal with discrete flows of control or data work well with sequence diagrams, but you can see that continuous flows are not represented well in sequence diagrams.

[11] From http://en.wikipedia.org/wiki/Anatomical_terms_of_location

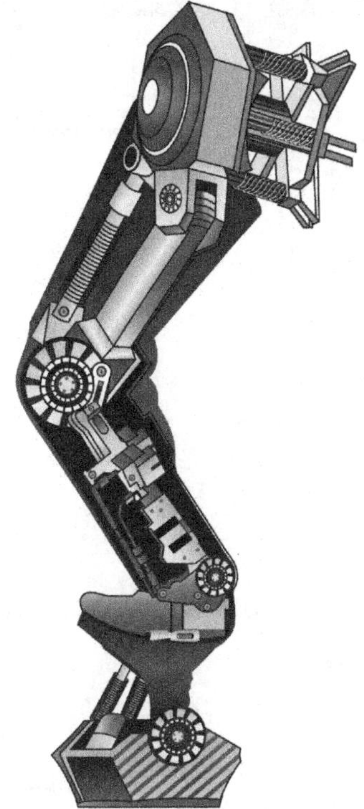

Figure 4.18
Limbs and joints.

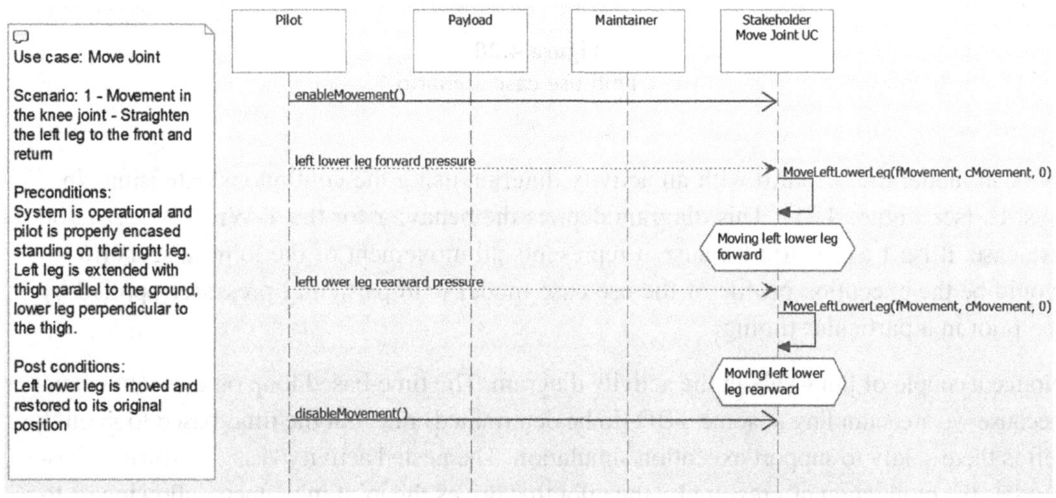

Figure 4.19
Move joint use case scenario 1.

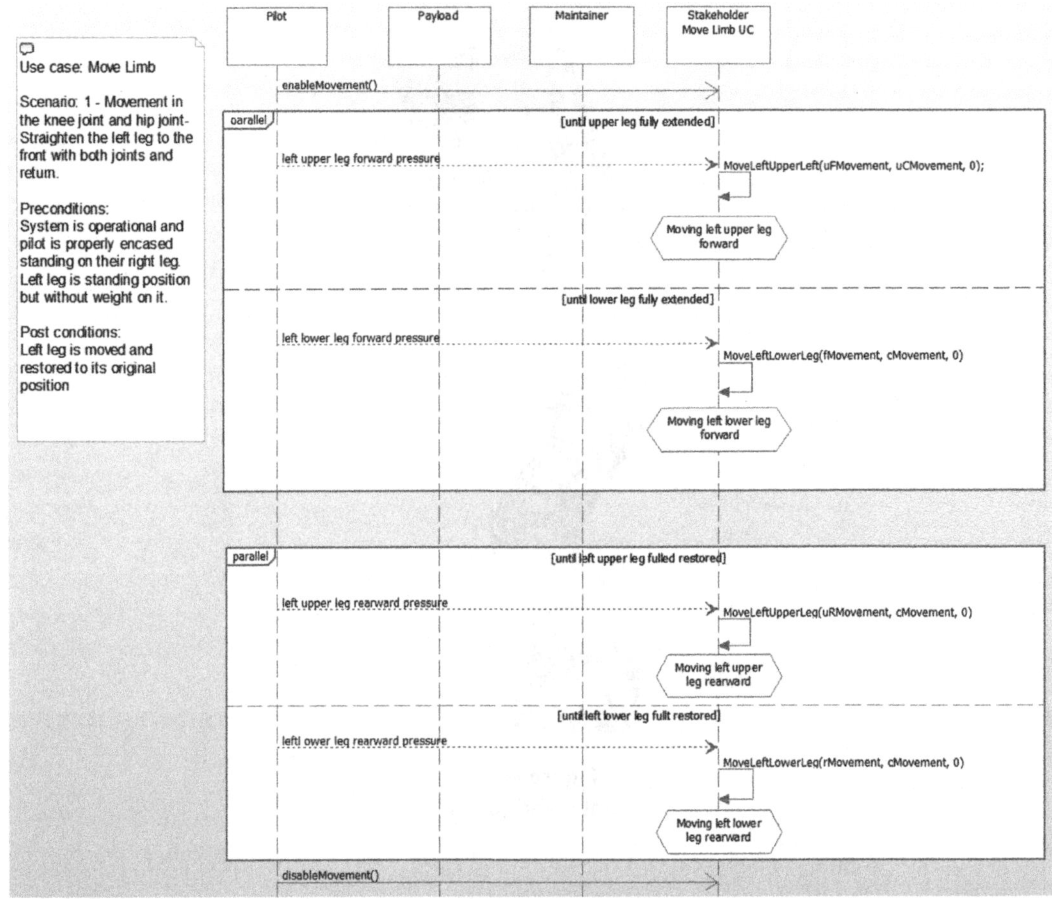

Figure 4.20
Move limb use case scenario 1.

We can model the scenario with an activity diagram using the continuous extensions in SysML (see Figure 4.21). This diagram depicts the behavior for the T-Wreck's `Move Joint` use case. It isn't a scenario because it represents all movement of the joint; a scenario would be the execution profile of the use case model with particular pressures applied by the pilot in a particular timing.

Notice a couple of things about the activity diagram. The time-based loop on the right occurs because we are sampling at some TBD (to be determined) rate, but the time-based loop on the left is there solely to support execution/simulation. The nested activity `ProduceJointPressure` models the production of pressure by the pilot that drives the joint movement, allowing us to simulate different scenarios. Secondly, the `JointDisable` event reception terminates the `MoveJoint` activity (the entire region is identified as an interruptible region).

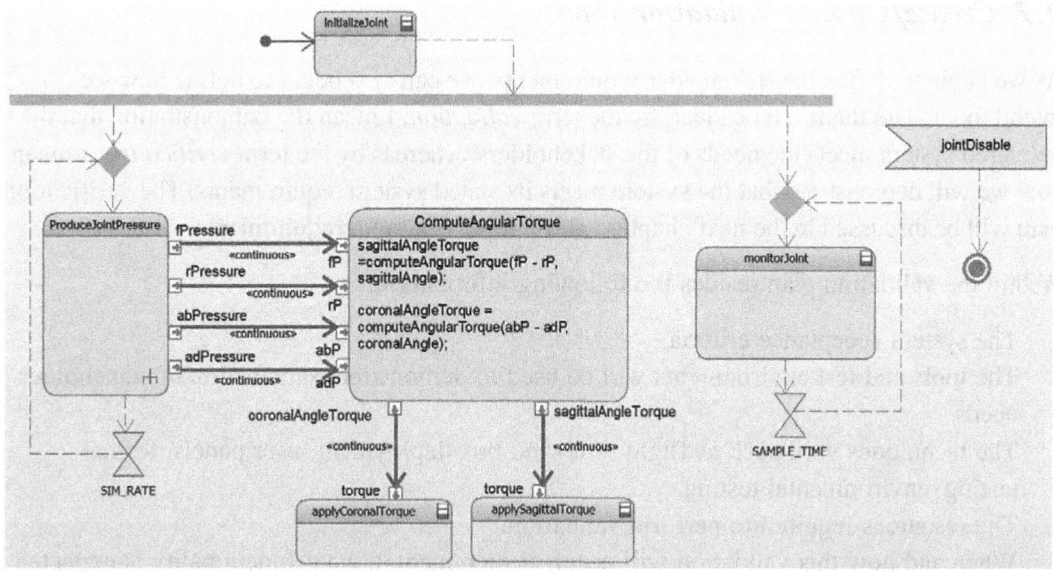

Figure 4.21
Activity diagram for move joint use case.

This kind of detail (and more) certainly belongs in the system use case model, but does it belong in the stakeholder model? Many stakeholders will not be able to effectively follow the flows, dynamics, and consequences on the activity diagram even though sequence diagrams are relatively easy to understand. However, such a diagram, even if simplified, will help the engineer ask the right questions to derive the stakeholder needs.

Also notice what does *not* appear in the activity model. We've specified that the exoskeleton responds to pressure provided by the pilot, but we've not identified the kinds of motors or sensors, nor their number, power, response times, and strength. That kind of analysis must come out of system analysis but it is not a part of requirements analysis where we concern ourselves exclusively with externally visible system properties.

Locally coordinated movements are the job of the `Move Limb` use case. It should be noted, that for pilot-driven motions, there need not be much in the way of coordination of movement on the part of the T-Wrecks system because the pilot is simultaneously controlling and coordinating the limbs. It is only when autonomous complex behavior is required that the system must coordinate the movement to a large degree.

4.7 Create/Update Validation Plan

As we begin to define the stakeholder requirements, we can also begin to define how we intend to validate them. To be clear, by the term *validation,* I mean the demonstration that the delivered system meets the needs of the stakeholders, whereas by the term *verification*, I mean how we will demonstrate that the system meets its stated system requirements. The verification plan will be discussed in the next chapter, whose topic is system requirements.

Within the validation plan resides the following information:

- The system acceptance criteria.
- The tools and test environments will be used to demonstrate satisfaction of stakeholder needs.
- The techniques used such as flight test, sand box deployment, user panels, formal testing, environmental testing.
- The resources required to perform validation.
- When and how this validation will occur; if incremental, what functionality is expected to be validated at each validation point.
- Who is responsible for different aspects of validation, such as creating the detailed validation test cases and/or analyses, procuring or creating the validation test tools and environments, running the actual validation procedures, assessing the outcomes of the validation procedures, and accepting or rejecting the delivery.
- Transition to Manufacturing—how the validated design elements will be conveyed to manufacturing.
- Transition to Customer—how manufactured systems will be delivered, installed, commissioned, and configured at the customer site(s).
- How the system will be managed, tracked, and otherwise supported in its operational environment.
- How the information within the validation plan will be controlled—that is, configuration and change management of the information within the validation plan.

4.8 Summary

This chapter is all about specifying the needs of stakeholders in a fashion that is both agile and model-based. We organize requirements around use cases—coherent operational capabilities of the system. Each use case typically contains anywhere from a few up to several dozen requirements. Because the *Define Stakeholder Requirements* activity is part of an iterative approach, only some of the identified stakeholder user cases will be addressed at a time, while others will be deferred until later iterations.

Figure 4.1 shows the overall workflow for this activity. For a small number of selected use cases (which might be as few as one), we perform the following tasks:

4.8.1 Identify Stakeholders

There are many stakeholders for the system, not all of which are interested in every use case. This task identifies the relevant stakeholders for the use case(s) under consideration and works with them to elucidate their requirements in the subsequent tasks.

The next three tasks are performed in parallel.

4.8.2 Generate Stakeholder Requirements

A number of stakeholder requirements are identified and explicitly stated so as to be clear, unambiguous, and testable. Most stakeholders will start with an idea of what their needs are so collaborating with the stakeholders is crucial.

4.8.3 Model Stakeholder Use Case Scenarios

Requirements can be complex. They can be ambiguous. And—most common of all—they can be unstated. We use scenario analysis to reason about the requirements by constructing sequence diagrams showing the expected interactions of the system executing the use case and the elements in its operational environment (actors). Messages—flows, control messages, and data—are shown in sequenced sets, representing the required behavior of the system unfolding. As we create these scenarios, we can clarify our understanding of the messages, the conditions under which they are valid or invalid, and the properties of the exchange of information and other flows. This almost always results in not only the clarification of the stakeholder's stated needs but also in additional, as-yet-unstated requirements. Scenario analysis is a powerful tool for the elicitation of requirements from the stakeholders.

Sequence diagrams are the primary means for representing scenarios. But, as we have seen, they work best for discrete messages that occur between the actors and the system. For continuous flows, other representations, such as activity diagrams, are superior.

The key outcome of use case scenario analysis is the identification of all the stakeholder needs around the use cases.

A common question is which comes first—the textual stakeholder requirements or their use case and scenario representation? The answer is that it doesn't particularly matter. If the stakeholders hands you an initial specification and you begin to reason about it with use case identification and scenario analysis, that's fine. If the workflow starts with a discussion of the use cases and scenario analysis is used to elicit the textual requirements, that's great too. By the end, there needs to be a consistent set of textual stakeholder requirements and corresponding use cases and scenarios.

4.8.4 Create/Update Validation Plan

Validation is about ensuring that the system meets the needs of its stakeholders. Verification is about demonstrating that the design or implementation meets the requirements. These are not precisely the same thing. During this activity, we begin to develop the notions for how we will validate the system and various work products. While we focus on the validation of the final resulting system, we also must identify how all deliverables—such as specifications—will be demonstrated to meet their needs.

Furthermore, if we are engaged in agile systems development, that means we will not only perform incremental specification of the system, we will also perform incremental design and implementation as well. The intermediate, partially complete implementations give us opportunities to validate our work earlier than with traditional methods. This means that the validation plan will address the use cases under concern for the current (and previous) iterations and will be added to as the project progresses.

The key information at this point is the acceptance criteria that indicate the stakeholder satisfaction but other information is important as well, including the validation approaches, when validation will occur for different work products, and if validation will be performed incrementally or "big bang."

4.9 Moving On

The next chapter is arguably the most important of the book—how system requirements are identified and how functional analysis yields the requirements that drive the design and implementation of the system. It starts from the basis of having good stakeholder requirements—the subject of this chapter—but focuses on the system properties and behaviors necessary to meet the stakeholder needs. This will include a deeper dive into use case functional modeling (and building executable requirements models) but will also touch on data and control analysis, updating the dependability analysis, and ensuring consistency of requirements.

Reference

[1] B.P. Douglass, Real-Time UML Workshop, Second ed., Elsevier, Waltham, MA, USA, 2014.

CHAPTER 5

Agile Systems Requirements Definition and Analysis

Chapter Outline

5.1 Objectives

The objective of this activity is rigorously to identify and characterize system requirements. As stated in the previous chapter, while stakeholder requirements are statements about stakeholder needs, system requirements are statements about what the system does and how well it performs those things.

We'll start from the stakeholder requirements, organized within stakeholder use cases. From there, we'll define system use cases and system requirements corresponding to, but elaborating upon, those stakeholder needs. As a part of this workflow, we will subject them to detailed model-based analysis, analyze the data and dependability requirements of the system, and begin writing the system verification plan. These activities will change from the perspective of stakeholder needs—a problem-oriented point of view—to the system requirements—a solution-oriented perspective. The system will still be treated as a black box and design concerns are not the focus of this activity. Instead, we will concentrate on characterizing required system properties and the set of input–output control and data transformations performed by the system without regard to exactly how those transformations will be performed.

5.1.1 Let's Get Technical

To a superficial eye, the techniques used in this chapter look very much like the ones used in the previous chapter to define stakeholder requirements. Indeed, that chapter contains some important discussions that define the core terms and methods we will use here, such as *requirement*, *use case*, and *scenario analysis*. The stakeholder requirements definition activity results in two primary work products: the textual stakeholder requirements (which may repose in a textual document or a requirements management repository or even within the stakeholder requirements model) and a stakeholder requirements model.[1]

Apart from the difference in perspective between stakeholder and system viewpoints alluded to above, there are also technical differences. The analysis will be more rigorous and while executable models were mentioned in the previous chapter, they will be in full use here. Beyond that, we'll use block definition diagrams to characterize the logical data schema for information and flows passed between the system and its actors. We'll also apply dependability analysis to understand the safety, reliability, and security needs of the system. While these activities might be begun in stakeholder requirements definition, it is here where the full capabilities of SysML are brought to bear.

5.2 The Systems Requirements Workflow

Figure 2.6 shows the high-level view of the Harmony Agile MBSE process. At the point of entering the *System Requirement Definitions and Analysis* activity, stakeholder use cases have been identified and some of them have been detailed with textual stakeholder requirements and use case scenarios. This activity creates matching system use cases and requirements.

In general, for every stakeholder use case, there is a corresponding system use case. There may be additional use cases identified as a result of deeper analysis but the use cases identified to meet the stakeholders will be enough to cover most of the system behavior. The primary difference between the stakeholder and system requirements models are:

1. They are different models
2. System use cases have system requirements allocated to them while stakeholder requirements have stakeholder requirements
3. System use cases will be subjected to deeper analysis and we will create executable use case models for each system use case
4. Logical system–actor interfaces will be detailed in the system requirements model
5. Data and flows carried across the system interfaces will be characterized by defining a logical data schema, resulting in additional system requirements
6. Initial dependability analysis will result in safety, reliability, and security requirements
7. Traceability links will be added between stakeholder and system requirements.

---

1 For small and simple systems, the stakeholder requirements model may be a package in a systems engineering model. For larger and more complex systems, it will probably be one (or possibly more) separate models.

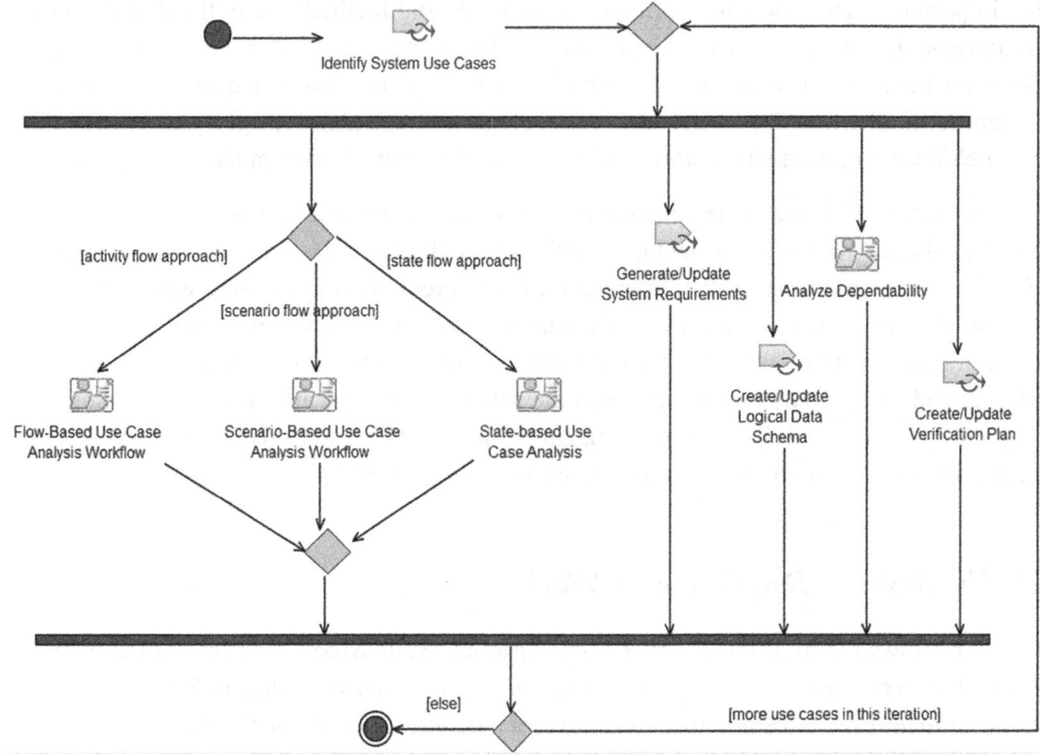

Figure 5.1
System requirements definition and analysis.

The workflow for defining and analyzing system requirements is shown in Figure 5.1. Because Harmony is an agile MBSE process, this activity will be performed on a small set of use cases at a time. The activity is iterated to include other use cases.

Let's briefly discuss the primary elements of this activity before we drill down in detail.

5.2.1 Identify System Use Cases

This task creates system use cases. For the most part, these correspond directly with the stakeholder use cases. However, it often happens that capabilities not yet identified rear their head (usually because not all stakeholders have been considered). This is especially true for capabilities specifically required by regulatory standards or secondary capabilities such as error and fault management and self tests. In addition, deeper system thinking may demonstrate the some system use cases are too large or complex to be defined within a single iteration, and require decomposition in some fashion to get them to a manageable size. This decomposition may be either via the «include» or «extend» relations (creating aggregation taxonomies) or via the generalization relation (creating type taxonomies). As we identify new system use cases, they will be added to the system engineering iteration plan for analysis during either the current iteration or a future one.

In any event, the stakeholder use cases are a great place to start.

5.2.2 Generating/Updating System Requirements

In the use cases under consideration in the current iteration, every stakeholder requirement will result in one or more corresponding system requirements. The system requirements are generally more quantitative and typically have more QoS constraints (which are also requirements) than their stakeholder counterparts. The system requirements are normally put into a different repository than their stakeholder antecedents and trace links are defined between the requirements sets.

5.2.3 Perform Use Case Analysis

Although the textual stakeholder requirements are the best place from which to start to define the system requirements, they tend to be an incomplete source. Even though the stakeholders may be problem domain experts, their understanding of system engineering is typically limited. Use case analysis is required to detail the requirement, ensure we understand what they mean, and to identify missing, incomplete, and inconsistent requirements.

The Harmony process provides three alternative approaches for performing this analysis. They are largely equivalent and provide alternatives that might prove to be superior approaches for a given capability, tool set, engineering skill set, or even personal preference. It is important to remember though, that in all cases, you end up in basically the same place and will have identified the same requirements (in the parallel *Generate/Update System Requirements* activity). In all these alternatives, activity diagrams, scenarios, state machines, requirements, connections between the system use case and the actors, and logical interfaces are specified.

5.2.3.1 Flow-based approach for use case analysis

The flow-based approach begins with activity diagrams to capture flows. From there, scenario flows are derived as paths through the activity diagram. Based on the analysis of those scenarios, the connections, events, messages, data, and flows are captured in logical system interfaces and an executable state machine requirements model is constructed and the requirements are evaluated in terms of correctness, precision, accuracy, coverage, and consistency. Consequent and Parallel to this analysis, requirements are added or updated.

5.2.3.2 Scenario-based approach for use case analysis

An alternative approach is to start with scenarios on sequence diagrams and incrementally add these scenarios to the use case activity diagram. From there, we create logical system interfaces and construct the executable state machine model. Execution of this yields a better understanding of the system requirements and, again, results in new and updated system requirements in the (parallel) *Generate/Update System Requirements* activity.

5.2.3.3 State-based approach for use case analysis

The last alternative is less frequently used because it is most applicable to specific kinds of system behavior and requires a more technically skilled system engineering staff. Nevertheless, when the capability is clearly state-based or highly modal and when the engineers are skilled in the state machine constructed, then it may make sense to start with the definition of the state machine. Scenarios can be generated by executing the state machine with different sequences of incoming events, and, if desired, the activity diagram can be created by incrementally adding those scenarios together.

5.2.4 Create Logical Data Schema

Most system interfaces either carry data or provide flows.[2] These flows must be at least logically characterized. By "logically characterized," I mean that permissible ranges, acceptable values, and unacceptable regions must be identified. We must also understand the relations among data and flows. We'll do this by creating a logical schema that represents the essential properties and relations of those elements.

5.2.5 Analyze Dependability

Dependability has three core pillars: safety (freedom from harm), reliability (availability of services), and security (freedom from undesired outside interference). In today's world in which artificial systems are taking over and providing capabilities that previously required human intervention and decision-making, the need for our ability to depend upon the systems we create is rapidly increasing. This activity will analyze the nature of the stakeholder needs and the system requirements to identify additional dependability-related requirements.

[2] I'm using the term *flow* here to refer to flows of not only information but also of materiel and energy.

5.2.6 Create/Update System Verification Plan

Just as the stakeholder requirements process began the specification of how the system would be demonstrated to meet the stakeholder needs, system requirements activities will being the definition of how we will verify that the resulting system meets its (system) specification. This is done with the System Verification Plan.

We're got a lot to do, so let's get this party started.

5.3 Identify System Use Cases

For the most part, the system use cases map 1:1 to stakeholder use cases. That is, for every stakeholder use case, there is a system use case of the same name and focus. They differ in a number of two minor ways:

- System use cases are held within the system model, while stakeholder use cases are held within the stakeholder model
- System requirements are allocated to system use cases, while stakeholder requirements are allocated to stakeholder use cases.

The stakeholder use cases will cover the vast majority of the requirements. However, stakeholders are not, generally speaking, technologists. They will not consider what is needed to perform the engineering to create the system; they instead (appropriately) focus on their concerns within their domains of expertise. As system engineers, however, we must consider the information that we need to successfully create a solution that will meet the stakeholder needs. We will consider, for example, system states and modes, information consistency, reuse of existing engineering intellectual property (such as existing designs), the needs for product line engineering, dependability concerns, compliance with regulatory objectives, limitations of technology, error and fault handling, and management of use case size for engineering and development purposes. For the most part, these concerns will result in the addition of system requirements within already-identified use cases but often will result in the identification of new use cases. These use cases may be completely new (such as the addition of a Fault Management use case which may not have been considered by the stakeholders) but most will be related to existing use cases.

5.4 Generating System Requirements

Much like the corresponding activity for stakeholder requirements, *Generating System Requirements* is probably the most key task in this activity. As stated in the previous chapter, requirements are clear, unambiguous and testable statements of system properties. Although there are a number of different kinds of requirements, we tend to focus mostly on functional requirements (what the system does) and quality of service (QoS) requirements (how well it does those things), both of which we represent in use cases.

There are a few differences between system and stakeholder requirements:

- System requirements focus on system properties, while stakeholder requirements focus on stakeholder needs.
- System requirements are stated in engineering language, while stakeholder requirements are specified in problem-domain language
- System requirements tend to be more quantitative than their corresponding stakeholder requirements.

In both cases though, requirements should be "black box" and neither reveal nor imply internal structure or realizing technology. If the point is to create a diesel engine car, then having requirements about the diesel engine is ok. If however, the point is to create a self-powered platform, then the requirements should characterize the needs (stakeholder) and externally visible properties (system) and let the design activity select the appropriate technology.

As with stakeholder requirements, the requirements themselves can be stored as model elements in a modeling repository, as requirements objects in a requirement management tool, or even as textual statements in a word processing tool.

Regardless of exactly how they are stored, the major difficulty with textual requirements is that the analysis of their completeness, consistency, accuracy, and correctness is difficult. The most common way to check the quality of the requirements is by visual inspection ("review") and this is problematic, error-prone, and expensive. That is not to say that reviewing requirements is a bad thing, but relying on review as your sole means for ensuring requirements quality is unsatisfying.

Hence, we will rely on modeling the requirements to verify the requirements as requirements before we use them to drive architectural, technical, and project decisions. From an agile perspective, we must be able to continuously demonstrate the adequacy and correctness of our engineering data, and to do that, we need models.

5.4.1 Allocating Requirements to System Use Cases

Just as with the stakeholder requirements, system requirements must be allocated to requirements. Figure 5.2 shows the allocation for the Speed Demon `Control Speed` system use case.

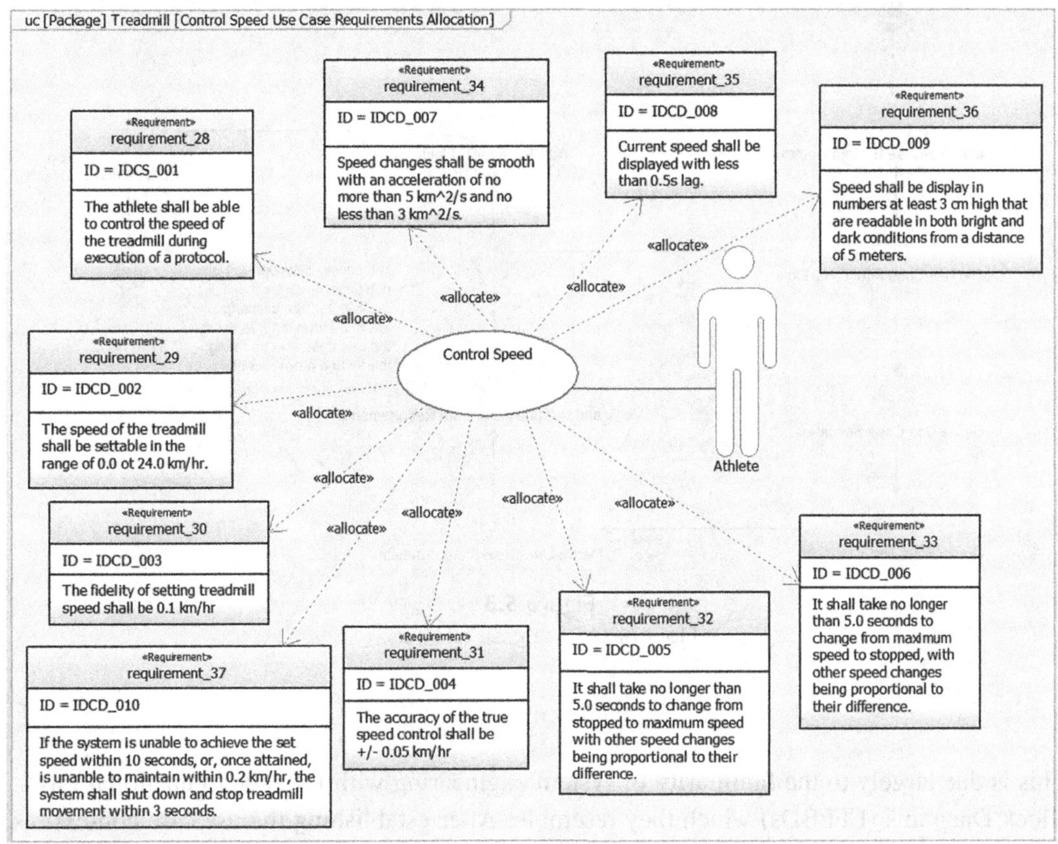

Figure 5.2
Allocation of system requirements to system use case.

5.5 Analyzing Use Cases

At the heart of the MBSE approach is use case modeling of requirements. There are three similar workflows for analyzing use cases—one that starts with activity diagrams (flow-based), one that starts with sequence diagrams (scenario-based), and one that starts with state diagrams (state-based). They are not only similar approaches, they basically all end up in the same place—with a set of scenarios, an executable state diagram, (optionally) an activity diagram, and an updated set of textual requirements. The following sections discuss these approaches in more detail.

5.5.1 Flow-Based Use Case Analysis

The flow-based approach for use case analysis is the most common and popular approach for MBSE.

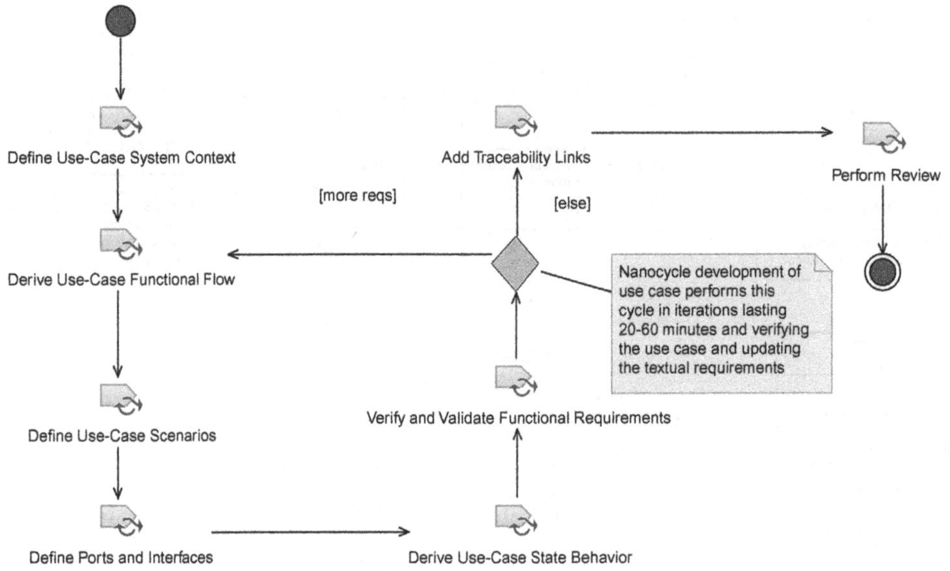

Figure 5.3
Flow-based use case analysis.

This is due largely to the familiarity of system engineering with Extended Functional Flow Block Diagrams (EFFBDs) which they resemble. After establishing the use case context (as a block diagram, with blocks representing the use case and its associated actors), an activity diagram is created depicting the actions and activities the system must perform—along with actions and activities that might be allocated to the actors. Sequence diagrams are then derived from this workflow that illustrate various sequences of interactions between the use case and the actors. Finally, an executable state machine is created that represents all possible scenarios of the use case. This analysis results in correction of poorly stated requirements and identification of missing textual requirements. Following this, traceability links are added between the model elements and the requirements, and between the system requirements and other related work products.

Figure 5.3 shows the workflow of tasks for flow-based analysis.

5.5.1.1 Define the use case context

In this task, we will create a block diagram that represents the system use case as a block and represents an addition block for every actor with which it interacts. We use a block diagram—rather than the original use case diagram—for this for two reasons: (1) blocks support execution and (2) blocks can have explicit ports and interfaces.

Steps

1. Create a package to hold the functional analysis of the use case
2. Add a block diagram within the created package
3. Add the actors and use case as blocks
4. Add port pairs for each use case—actor connection
5. Add an interface (for normal ports), flow specification (for «flow» ports), or interface block (for «proxy» ports)[3]
6. Make instances of the added blocks and connect them with connectors.

Notes:

Packages

First, remember from Chapter 3 and especially from Figure 3.12, that the functional analysis of the use cases takes place in a package called `FunctionalAnalysisPkg` (or `FAPkg`, if you like shorter names). Within this package we'll have one package per use case analyzed. All of the elements for that analysis will be contained within that package.

Actor blocks

We'll create blocks for the use case and its associated actors. I use "uc" as a prefix for the use case block and "a" as a prefix for the actor blocks. In addition, I add some special code that indicates for which use case the actor block is to be used, such as `aTTO_Radar` for the block representing the `Radar` actor for a `Track Tactical Objects` use case. The reason is simple: while in principle, we can create a single actor block and use it for all use case analyses, in practice that wastes a lot of time and adds unnecessary dependencies to the analysis work. Another team working on another use case that needs that actor would be adding behaviors to that actor that do your analysis no good, just as the behaviors you add for your analysis will likely do the other use case analysts no good. So instead, we will create actor blocks that are specific to the needs of the use case analysis at hand. So if there is an `Initialize Sensors` use case that initializes the `Radar` actor, our actor block for that analysis would be `aIS_Radar`. Because we will be creating executable models, we want to only model the things relevant to our purpose.

Activity and state

Although we'll use the blocks in the use case block context diagram for the lifelines on the sequence diagrams and to hold the state behavior, we'll actually create the activity diagram for the use case itself. Because both an activity diagram and the state machine are both fully constructive behaviors, we need to assign them to different model elements. So the use case owns the activity diagram and the use case block owns the state machine.

---

[3] If you're using SysML 1.3, I just recommend using «proxy» ports.

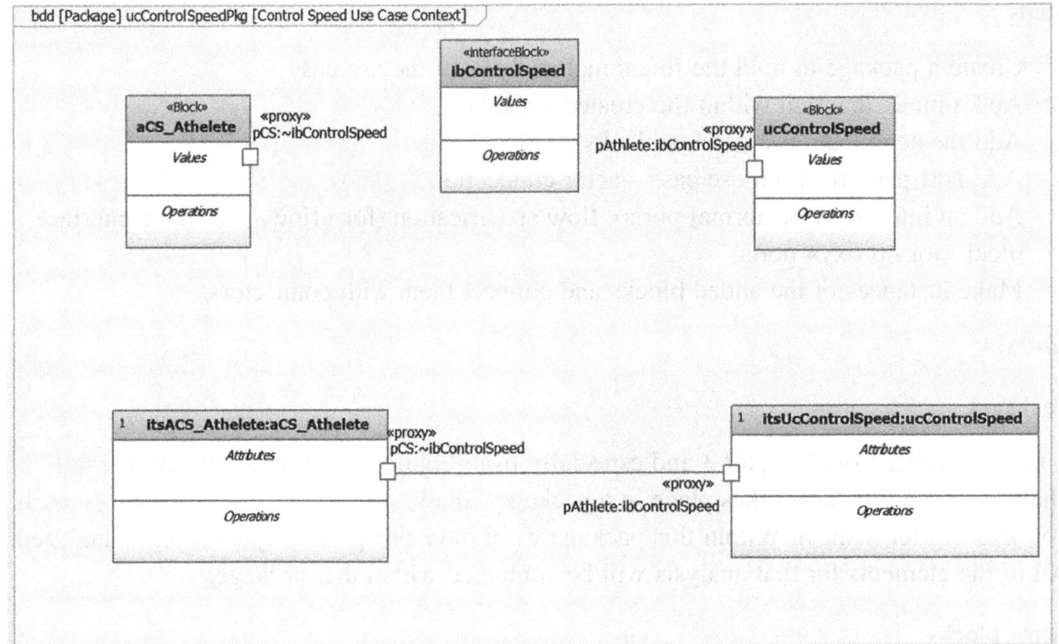

Figure 5.4
Control Speed block context.

In this section, we'll use the Speed Demon™ Treadmill example from the previous chapter. If we do this for the `Control Speed` use case, we'll create a block diagram that looks something like Figure 5.4. The actor block (Athlete) is named `aCS_Athlete` and the use case block is named `ucControlSpeed`. Below the blocks are shown connected instances of those blocks typed by a (currently empty) interface block called `ibControlSpeed`. The subsequent steps in the analysis will flesh out the missing details.

5.5.1.2 Derive use case functional flow

The next step is to define the use case activity diagram. As mentioned above, the activity diagram is defined for the use case itself, rather than the use case block. The point of the activity diagram is to identify the primary and secondary flows of behavior of the system. Alternative flows are depicted with decision points and parallel flows are shown with forks and joins.

Consider the `Control Speed` use case. The Athlete can set the speed by entering in a value, augment or reduce it by a set increment, activate or deactivate the belt, and Pause. For the latter, if the Athlete hits pause, the `driveRunningBelt` activity stops; if they hit the Pause button again, it restarts; if they wait 5 s, then it deactivates. The behavior is shown in Figure 5.5.

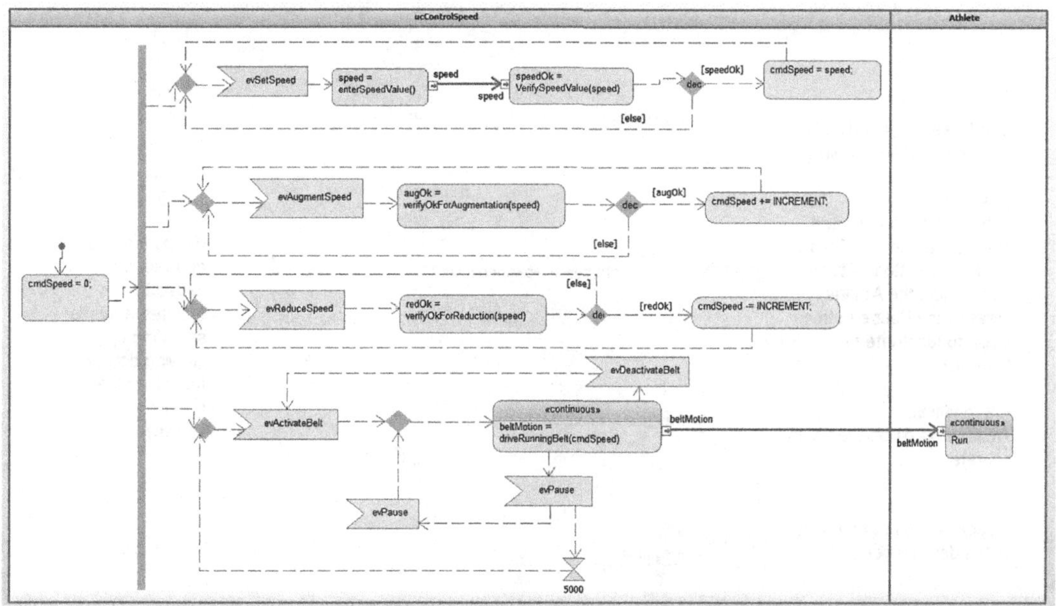

Figure 5.5
Control Speed use case activity diagram.

5.5.1.3 Define use case scenarios

Deriving the scenarios from an activity diagram is conceptually very simple. Each parallel flow constituted a separate scenario set. Each flow from a decision point within a scenario set constitutes a different scenario. In Figure 5.5, we can easily identify four scenario sets, one for each of the parallel flows. Each of the first three scenarios has a single decision point with outgoing flows, resulting in six scenarios. The last adds three more branches (deactivate, Pause-Pause, Pause-Timeout) for a total of nine scenarios—if we ignore different data values and combinations of the other flows (such as set a speed, wait 4 s, augment it twice, pause for 2 s and restart). If we were treating this as a real project, we would create at least a dozen or so scenarios. Remember the criterion for minimal completeness—each requirement is represented in at least one scenario.

As we draw the scenarios, we'll use the blocks from the use case context diagram (Figure 5.4) as the lifelines. You'll notice that I added the *continuous* interaction type[4] to depict an ongoing behavior (in this case, driving the running belt) (Figure 5.6).

The utility of the scenarios is largely due to the fact that they are easily consumable by the stakeholders, which may not be true for the activity or state diagrams. They do not show

[4] It's not part of the SysML standard, but its use is obvious enough, I think.

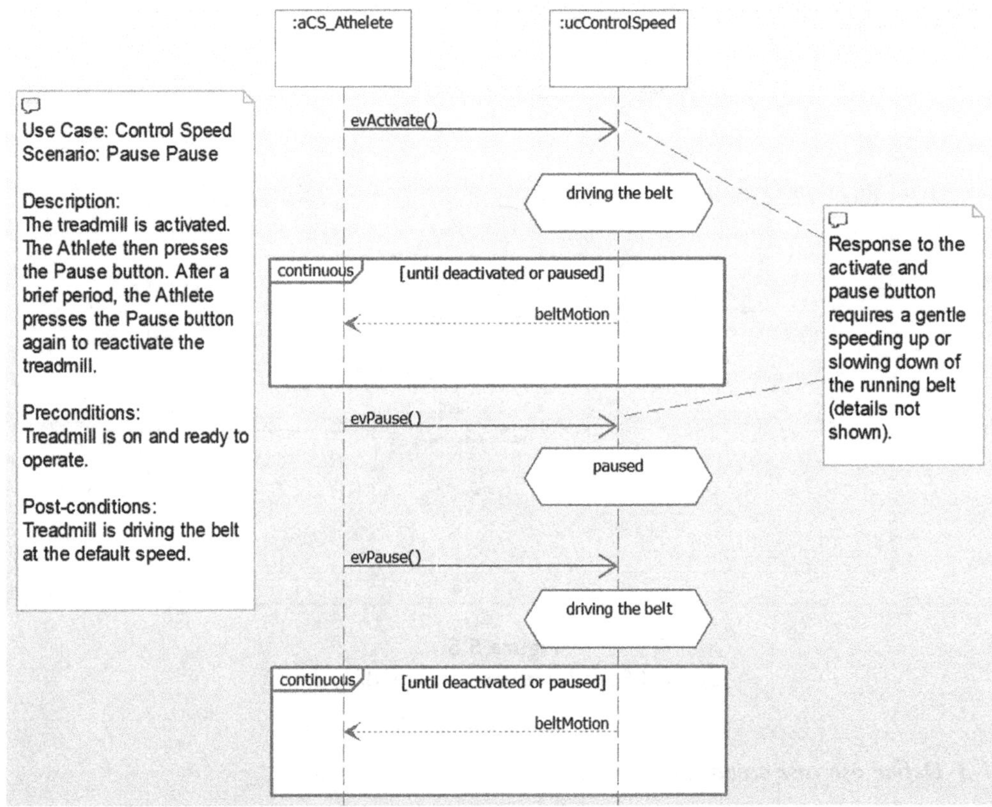

Figure 5.6
Control Speed use case "Pause Pause" scenario.

continuous behaviors well, but excel at depicting discrete interactions. For continuous flows, I used asynchronous events for the discrete messages and flows for the continuous flows, as well as the above-mentioned continuous interaction operator.

5.5.1.4 Define ports and interfaces

If we do all the (interesting) scenarios for the `Control Speed` use case we end up with an interface control block that defines the event set (for the discrete messages) and the flow property `beltMotion` for the continuous (out)flow. Note that the interface is conjugated at the Athlete end, meaning that they receive the `beltMotion` but also generate the discrete events of interest (Figure 5.7).

This—along with the interface blocks for the other use cases—defines the logical system interfaces. There is other information required to fully characterize the logical interfaces of the system including the (logical) data schema and dependability analysis.

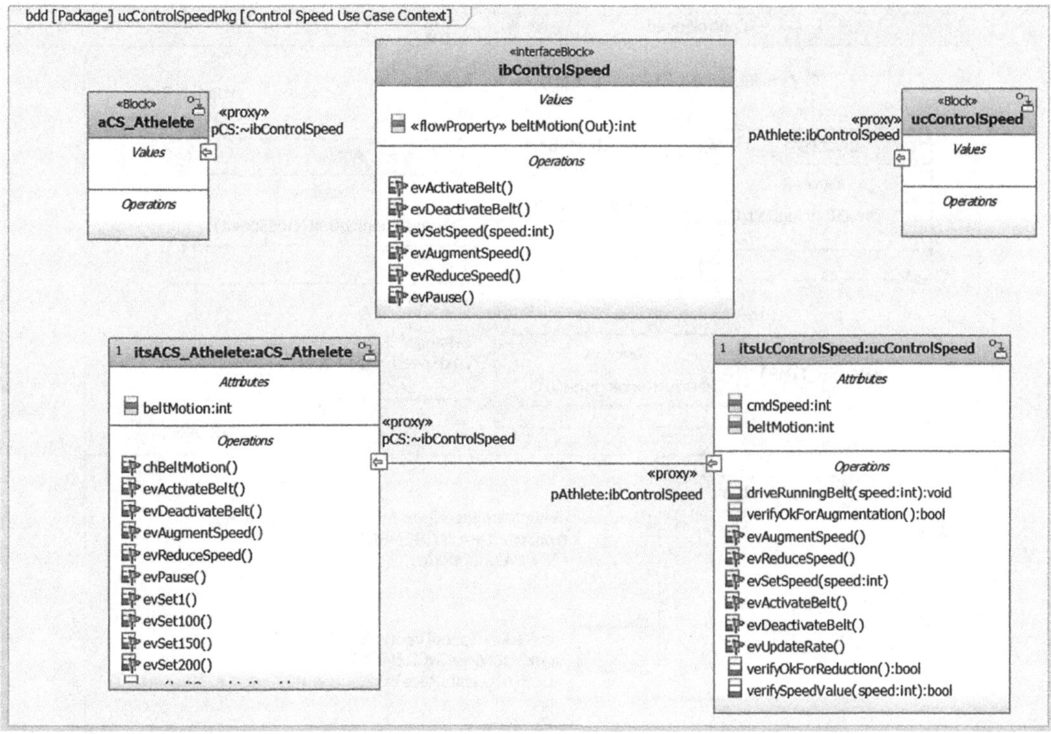

Figure 5.7
Control Speed Interface Block.

5.5.1.5 Derive use case state machine

If I have an activity diagram, why do I need a state machine?

1. Activity diagrams usually only show primary flows, therefore they don't represent all the requirements (although they theoretically *could*).
2. State machines better represent system states and modes than activity diagrams.
3. There is a stronger connection between the system interfaces, the state behavior, and the sequence diagrams than with an activity diagram.
4. State machines scale to complex behaviors better than activity diagrams, which is why the use case activity diagram usually shows only the primary flows and the use case state machine shows the entire behavior.
5. Executable UML/SysML tools provide better support for state machine execution than for activity diagram execution.

Both activity diagrams and state machines execute and their specific execution flows can be captured as sequence diagrams. As sequence diagrams, they can be validated with the customer and they can be used as specifications of test cases. In general, for behaviors

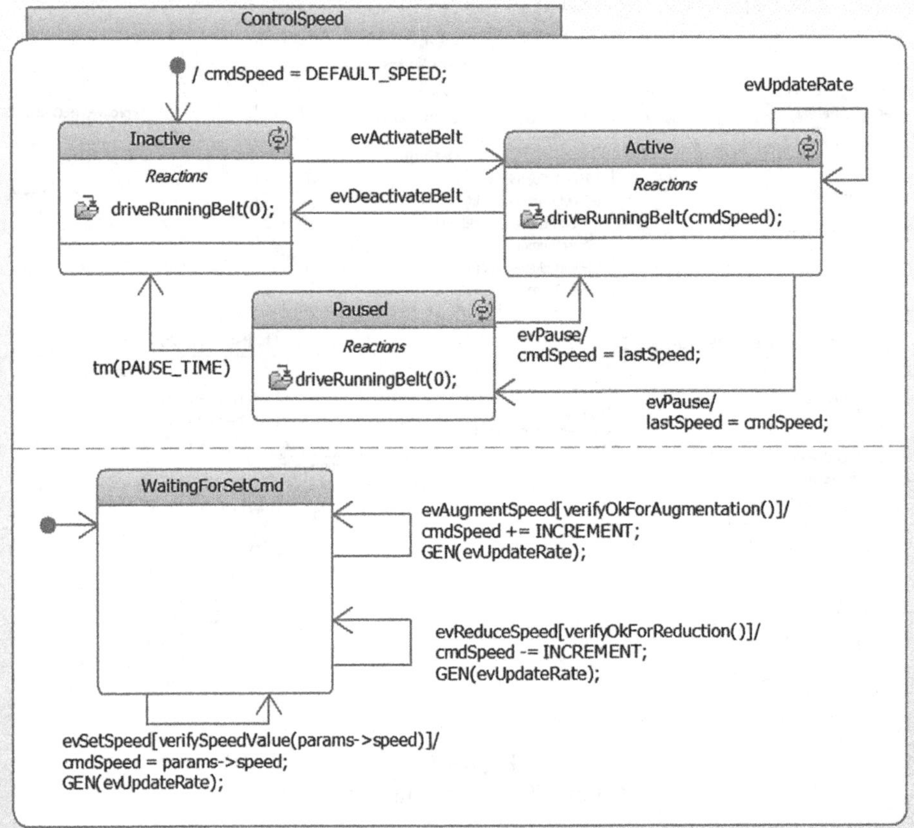

Figure 5.8
Control Speed use case state machine.

which are heavily event-based (the majority of use cases), state machines are the preferred choice for validation and verification. Activity diagrams are preferable when there is a preponderance of parallel flows, sequences that are mostly flow-based (actions are started when the previous actions complete), and especially when there are continuous behaviors and flows. Having said that, in most cases either can be used.

We can easily construct a state machine for the `Control Speed` use case (Figure 5.8). This is behaviorally equivalent to the activity diagram we created earlier (Figure 5.5).

To run a simulation, we need to give the actor block `aCS_Athlete` some behavior (Figure 5.9) as well as create a local variable `beltMotion` and bind it to the flow property of the same name in the interface block. That way, when the invocation of the `driveRunningBelt()` operation is invoked and sets the value of `beltMotion`, this value is conveyed to the actor block.

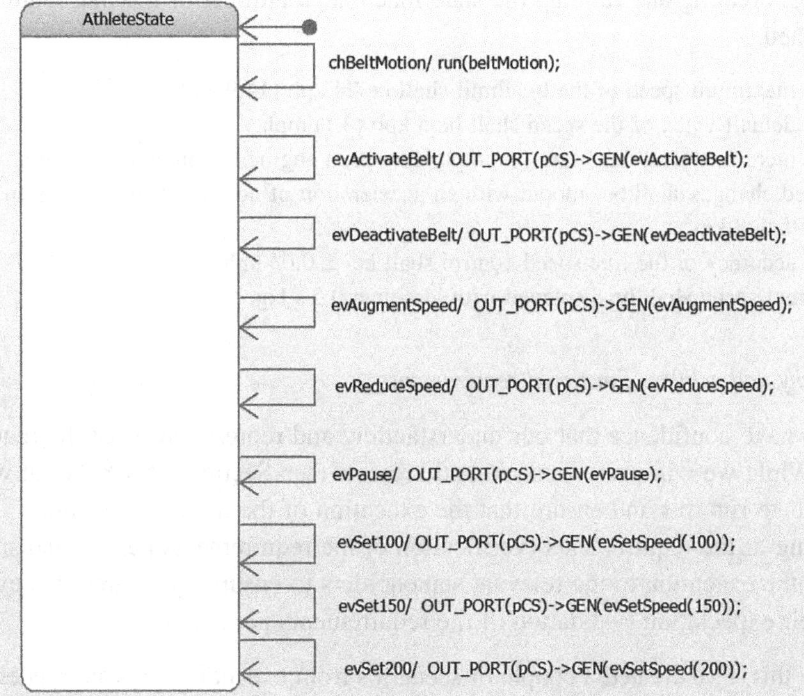

Figure 5.9
State machine for Athlete actor block.

Another execution point is that state machines rely on execution actions, rather than continuous activities.[5] Thus, the action `driveRunningBelt()` is modeled as an entry action in the Active state in Figure 5.8. This entry action is triggered whenever the Active state is entered—such as when the actor's `evAugmentSpeed` event generates the `evUpdateRate` event. Internally, this operation sets the value of the flow property `beltValue` and this change is propagated to the actor block. The state machine for the actor block shows an event `chBeltMotion` which is a *change event* and is created when the value of `beltMotion` changes. This event triggers the corresponding transition on the actor state machine causing the `run()` action to execute.

Once again, the best way to construct this state machine is in small incremental steps of 20–60 min. Add a little behavior, get it to run, add more behavior, . . . and repeat until done. Figure 5.8 is the end result of several such nanocycles.

5 Yes, there is a "doActivity" option for states defined in the UML metamodel, but there is no tool with which I am aware that actually implements executable behavior for it.

As a result of creating and running the state machine, a number of missing requirements were identified.

- The maximum speed of the treadmill shall be 24 kph (14.9 mph).
- The default value of the speed shall be 5 kph (3.1) mph.
- The increment shall be 1 kph (0.6 mph) for speed augmentation and reduction.
- Speed changes shall be smooth with an acceleration of no more than 5 km^2/s and no less than 3 km^2/s.
- The accuracy of the true speed control shall be ± 0.05 kph
- Current speed shall be displayed with less than 0.5 s lag.

5.5.1.6 Verify and validate functional requirements

We want to have confidence that our understanding and representation of the requirements is correct. While we will perform a semantic review (see Section 5.5.1.8), what we really want to do is to run this and ensure that the execution of the model meets our understanding of the requirements (verification of the requirements per se) and show the outcome of the execution to the relevant stakeholders to ensure they agree this execution matches their expectation (validation of the requirements per se).

To illustrate this, I've created a couple of scenarios from executing the state model in Figure 5.8. In the first one, the Athlete pushes augment twice (upping the command speed from the default of 3 to 4 mph), and then the Athlete sends the `evActivateBelt` event, setting the treadmill belt in motion. The flow captured from the execution of this scenario is shown in Figure 5.10 (treadmill speeds are scaled up by 10). This sequence diagram was not manually drawn but was actually generated from the execution of the state model above.

The second scenario shows the Pause–Pause scenario discussed earlier (Figure 5.11). Because the Athlete pressed the Pause button quickly enough, the timeout transition was avoided and the treadmill returned to its previously set running speed.

5.5.1.7 Add traceability links

The previous steps are generally iterated a number of times before you get to this point in the workflow. At this point, the use case requirements are fairly stable and traceability links can be added. This is not only true for the original requirements, but also for any corrected or new requirements. The trace links connect the system requirements to the system use case and to their stakeholder requirement counterparts. Note that I could have added the «trace» stereotype to the dependencies but I decided that it added little value.

The requirements diagram in Figure 5.12 graphically shows the trace links between the stakeholder and system requirements for this use case. This can also be shown in tabular format, as in shown in the automatically generated table in Figure 5.13.

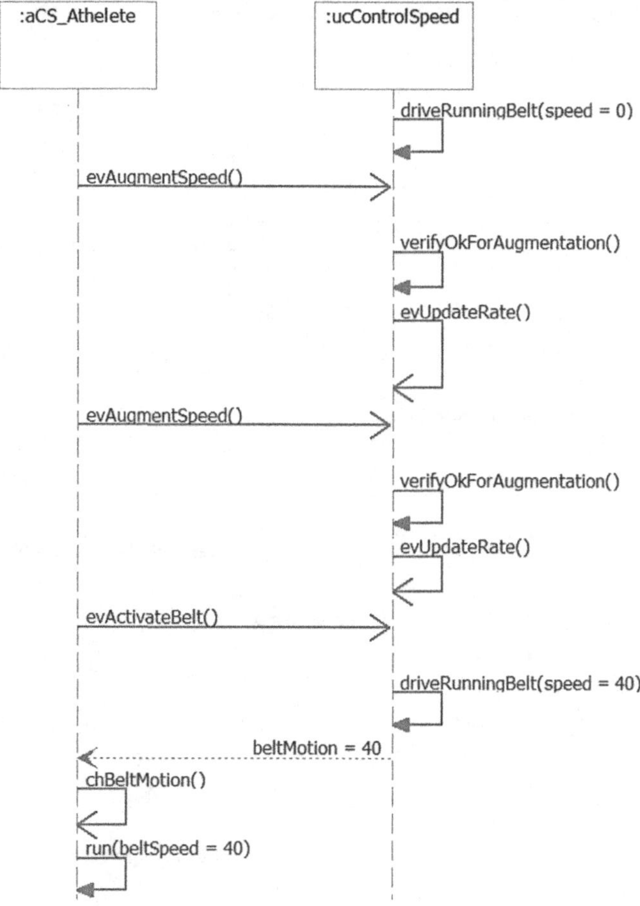

Figure 5.10
Execution of control speed scenario 1.

5.5.1.8 Perform review

Although I emphasize the use of execution to support both verification and validation of the engineering data (models and requirements), reviews do add value. Syntactic reviews—performed by quality assurance personnel—ensure that the engineering data are well formed and in the appropriate format. Semantic review gives stakeholders and subject matter experts a chance to look at the engineering data to ensure they are complete, consistent, accurate, and correct.

5.5.1.9 T-Wrecks flow-based use case analysis

Let's apply this flow-based workflow to the T-Wrecks use case `Move Joint`. Again, we won't show the multiple short iterations that take place to save some trees.

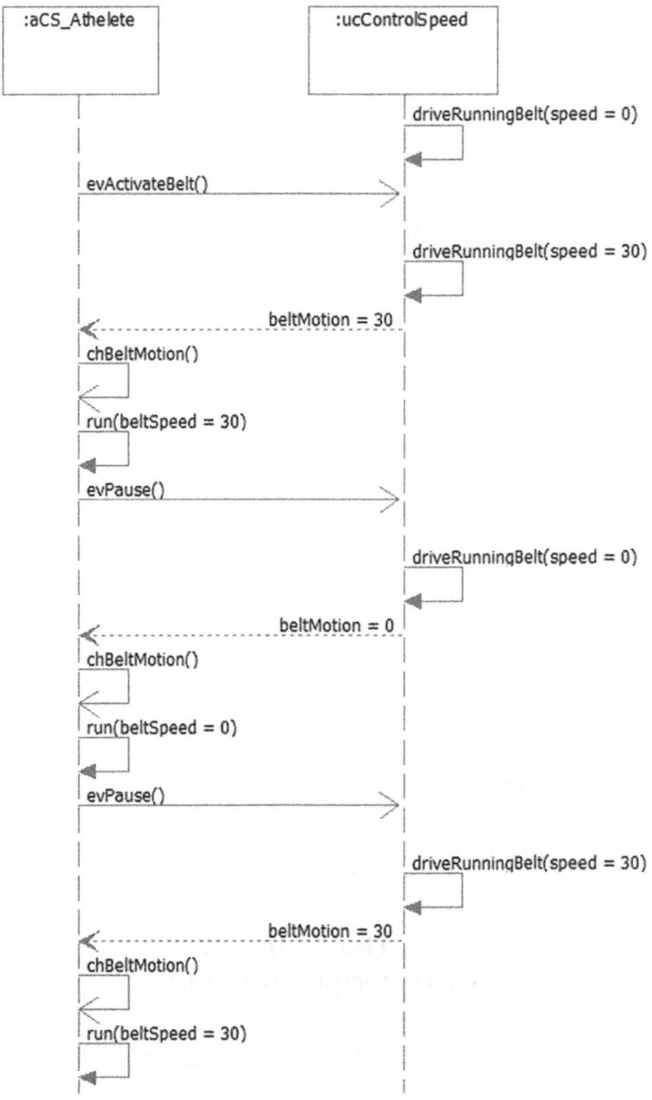

Figure 5.11
Execution of control speed scenario 2.

Step 1: Use case execution context

Figure 5.14 is straightforward and shows the use case and actor blocks with (empty) interface blocks to define the proxy ports. Note the naming convention in effect. Actor blocks have "a" and "MJ" (for Move Joint) prefixed to their names so that there is no naming conflict with actor blocks used for other use cases. The interface blocks are prefixed with "ib" and "MJ" to also uniquely name them within the functional analysis package. Notice also that the port definitions are conjugated at the ports on the actor blocks.

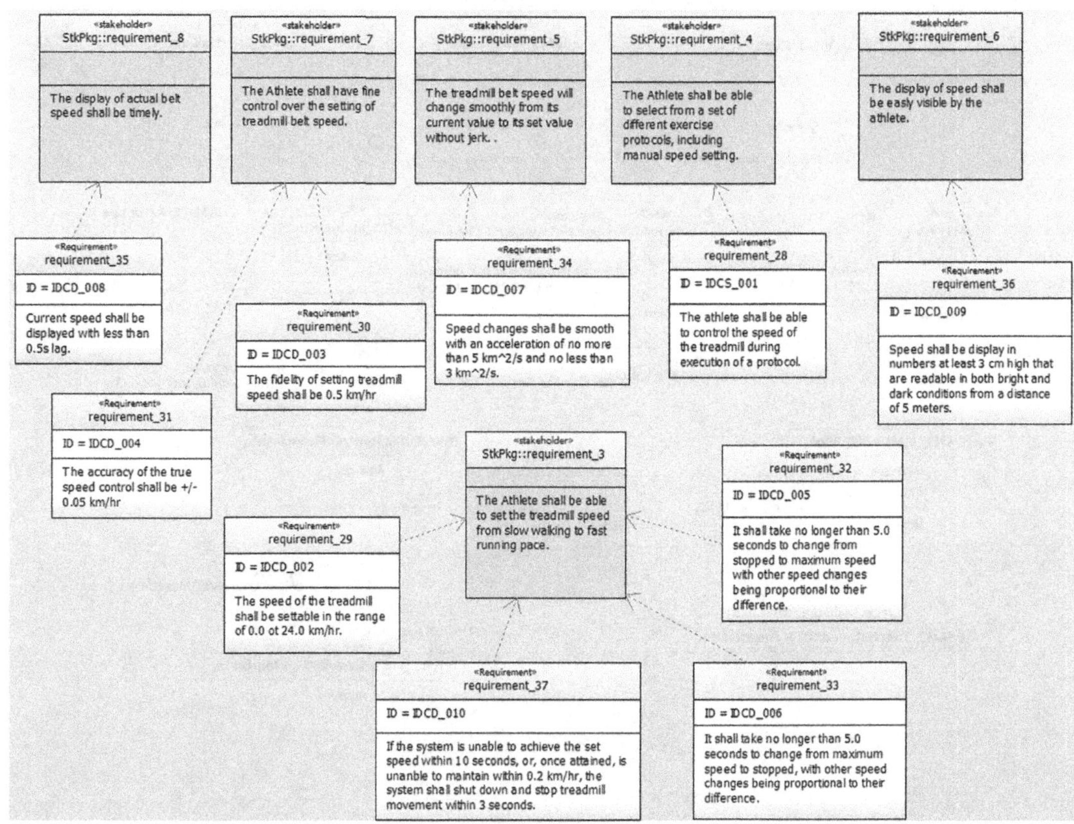

Figure 5.12
Requirements traceability.

	requirement_3	requirement_4	requirement_5	requirement_6	requirement_7	requirement_8
requirement_24						
requirement_25						
requirement_26						
requirement_28		requirement_4				
requirement_29	requirement_3					
requirement_30					requirement_7	
requirement_31					requirement_7	
requirement_32	requirement_3					
requirement_33	requirement_3					
requirement_34			requirement_5			
requirement_35						requirement_8
requirement_36				requirement_6		
requirement_37	requirement_3					

Figure 5.13
Generated System-Stakeholder requirements matrix.

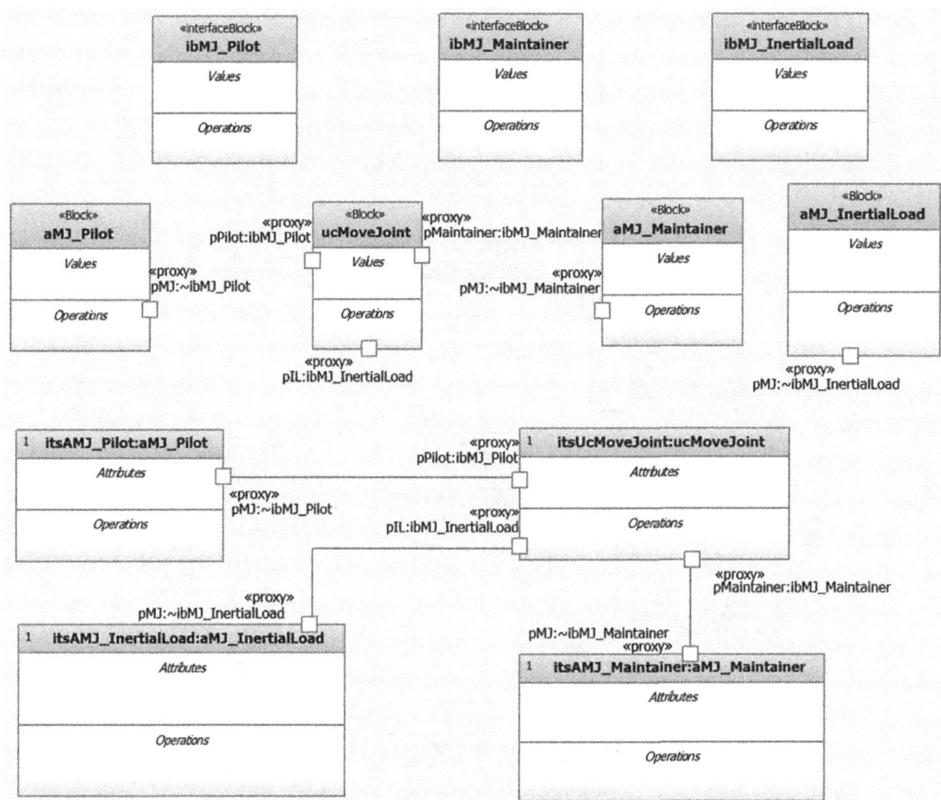

Figure 5.14
T-Wrecks Move Joint use case execution context.

Step 2: Derive use case functional flow

In the previous chapter, we performed the slightly unusual step of making an activity diagram for the stakeholder use case of the same name. This activity diagram is quite similar to that. However, having thought about it a bit more from an engineering point of view, we see that we should add the remaining plane (to account for all joints) and that the application of torque produces motion and this motion in turn creates a resistance to movement ("inertial load") that must be compensated for. This resistance will be the result of a number of factors including direction of the gravitational vector, limb weight, and limb drag.

The `ProduceJointPressure` activity is used to drive the execution of the activity diagram. I coded up in an action language[6] an action that produces sine waves for the pressures in the four directions of interest (forward, backwards, abduction, and adduction) and use this to drive the `ComputeAngularTorque` activity in Figure 5.15. I send the pressures and resulting output torque to standard output for examination.

[6] In this case C++ but other action language can be used.

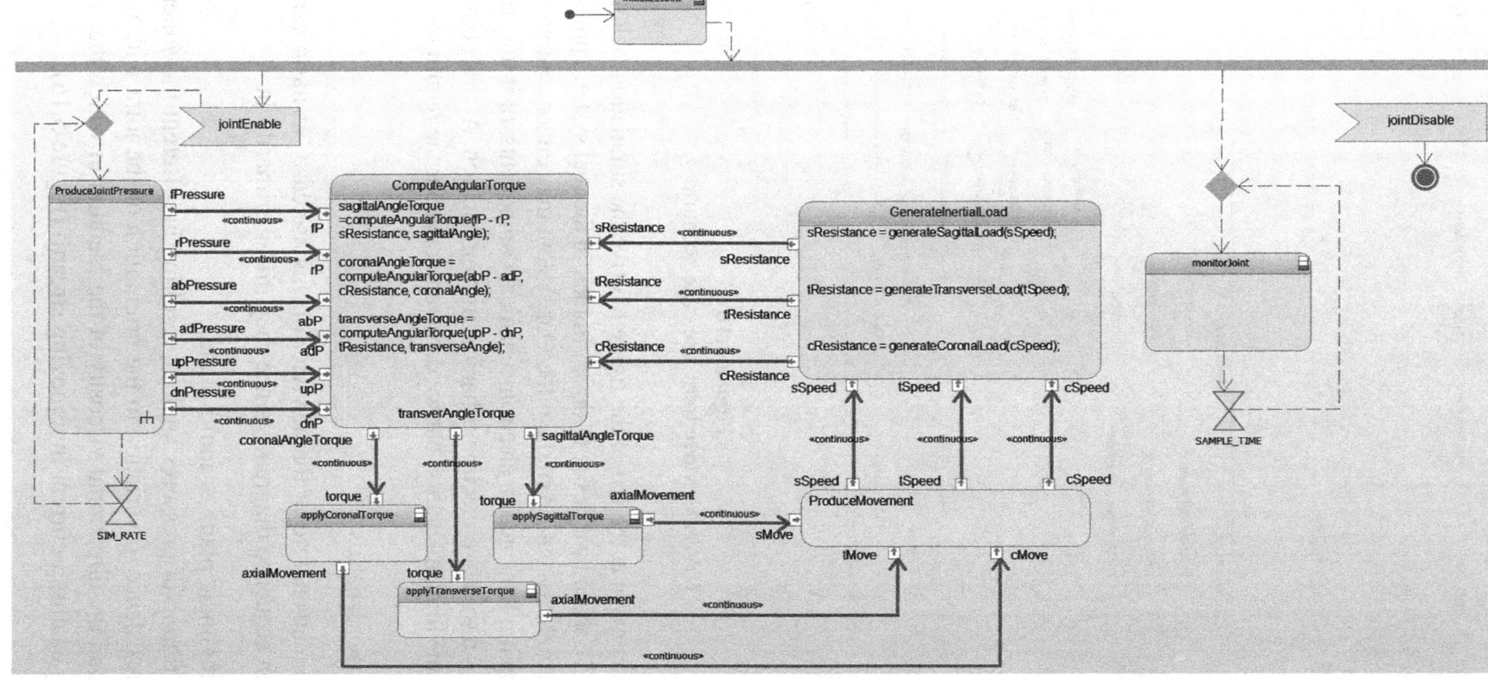

Figure 5.15

T-Wrecks Move Joint use case activity diagram.

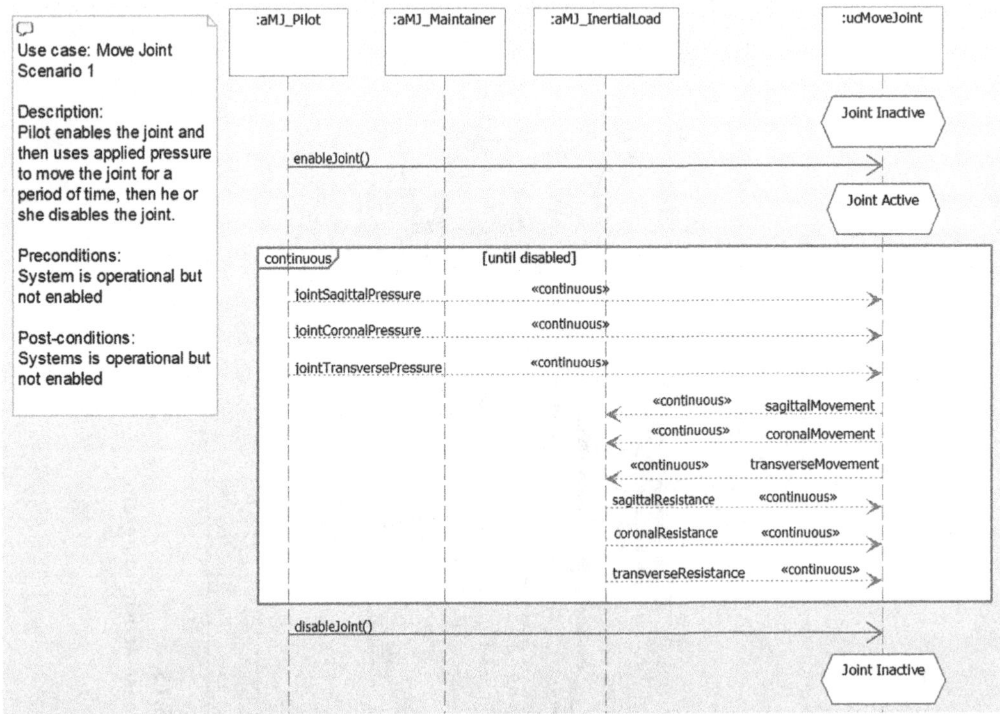

Figure 5.16
T-Wrecks Move Joint use case scenario 1.

We only need the timer event at the left of the figure to drive the simulation (see the SIM_RATE timeout in Figure 5.15), should we desire to do so. In fact, in the real system, pressure is continuously applied to the system from the pilot. Our system may either continuously respond via a PID control loop implemented in electromechanical components, or it may respond with a discrete period such as a software-electromechanical implementation. At this point, we neither know nor care about the implementation but we do care a lot about the requirements.

Step 3: Define use case scenarios

Because of the continuous nature of the behavior of this use case, scenario variants are difficult to express in sequence diagrams, since they differ primarily in

- The type of joint (single plane or multi-plane)
- The degree and timing of pressures applied, resulting in different movements
- The amount of resistance to variation in the orientation of the joint with respect to gravity normal and the directional viscosity of the medium in which the suit is moving (such as moving against a current in a moving stream) (Figure 5.16).

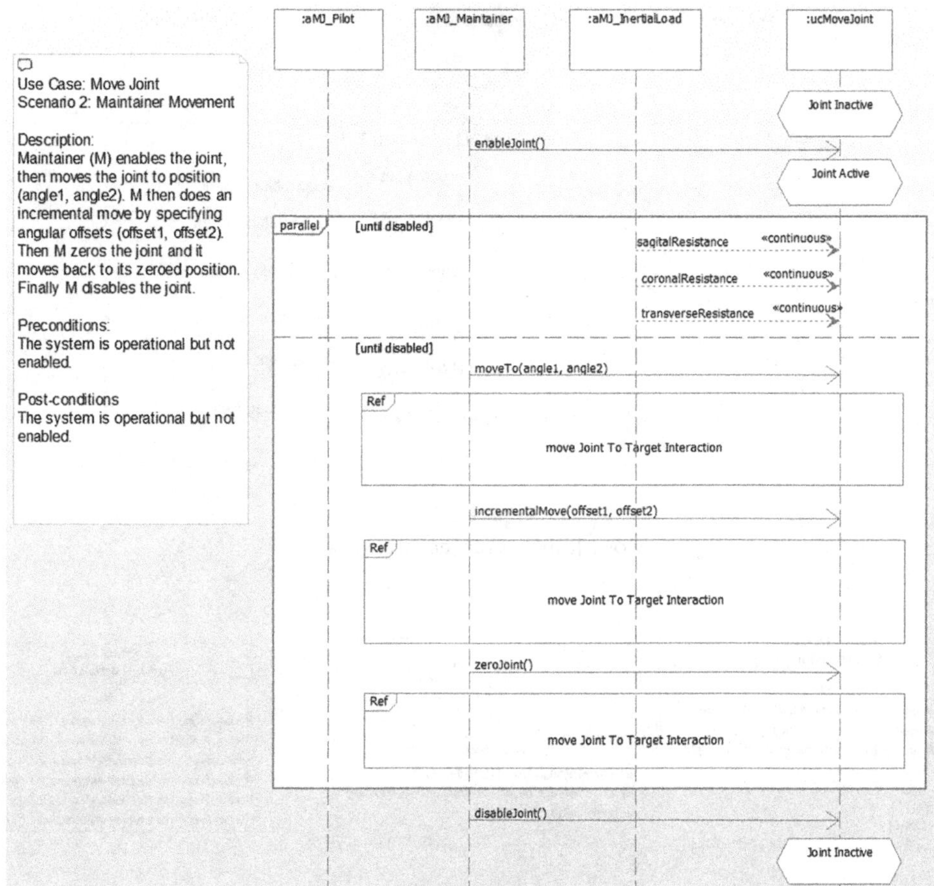

Figure 5.17
T-Wrecks Move Joint use case scenario 2.

The second scenario (Figure 5.17) involves the system `Maintainer` using their maintenance tool to enable the joint, move it to a position, do an incremental movement, zero the joint, and then disable the joint. It uses a referenced sequence diagram ("move Joint to Target Interaction") whose detail can be seen in Figure 5.18.

Step 4: Define ports and interfaces

The flows shown in the activity diagram show the interfaces necessary for the system. The input flows will ultimately be generated internally via some sensor and the output flows (movements in various planes of motion) will result from internal actuators. Nevertheless, we can characterize the interfaces (Figure 5.19).

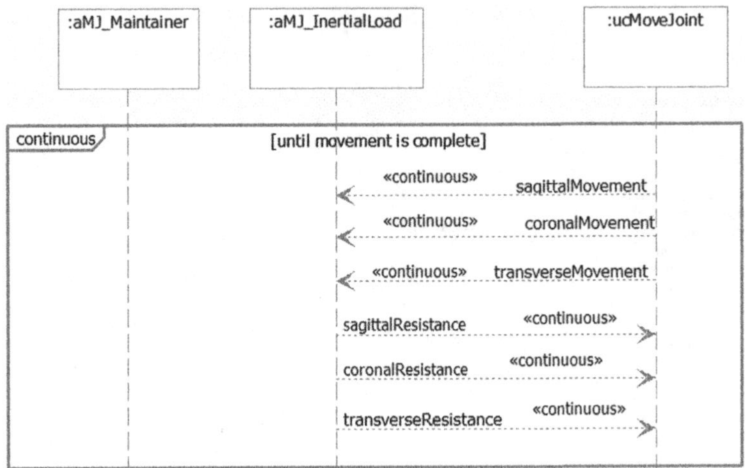

Figure 5.18

Move Joint to target interaction.

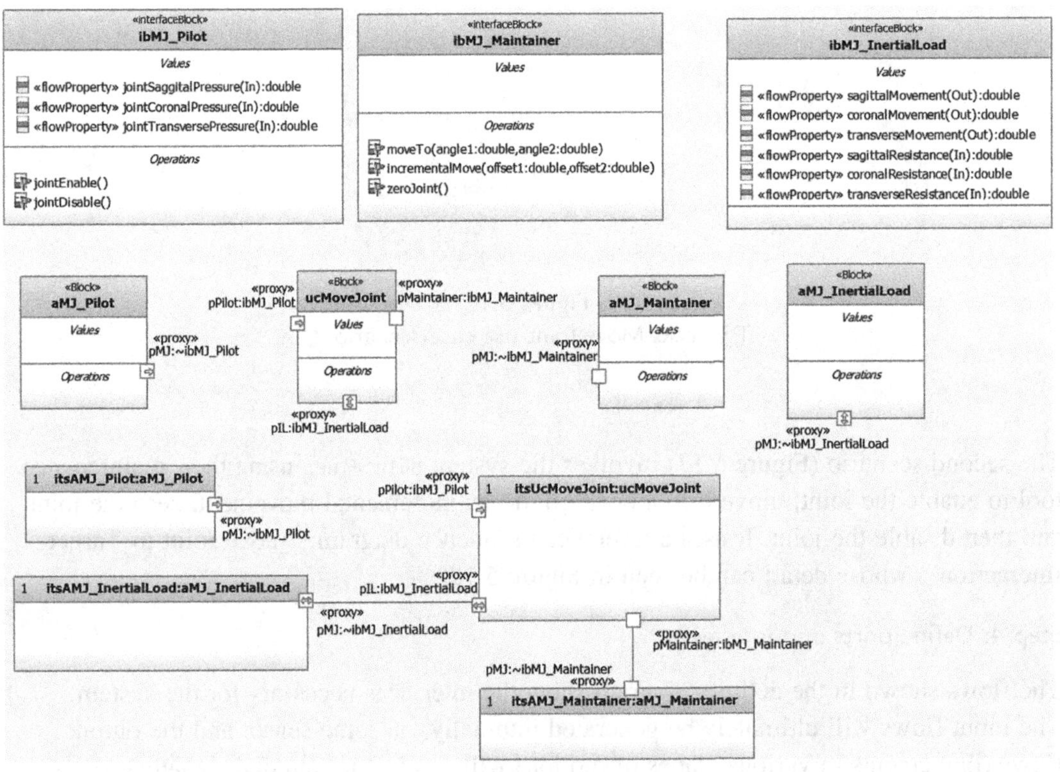

Figure 5.19

Interface blocks for Move Joint use case block.

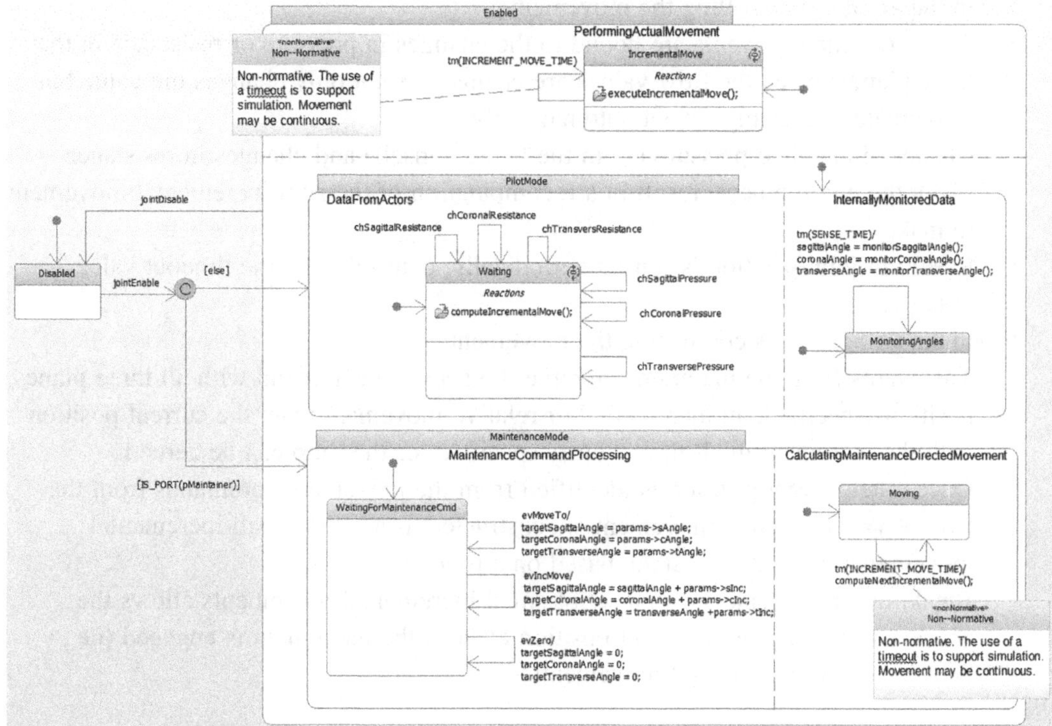

Figure 5.20
Move Joint use case block state machine.

Step 5: Derive use case state behavior

Figure 5.20 shows a state machine that represents the behavior of the `Move Joint` use case. State machines are fundamentally discrete, so continuous flows must be turned into either periodic flows or change events for execution and simulation.

There are a number of interesting aspects of this state machine that bear comment, such as:

- Different transition branches are taken depending on whether the `jointEnable` event came from the `pMaintainer` port or the `pPilot` port, using the macro `IS_PORT()` to identify the source of the event
- Once enabled, the system always executes small incremental movements (see the uppermost AND-state), even those these movements may be zero in length. This is done based on a timeout controlled by the setting of the `INCREMENT_MOVE_TIME` value
- Comments are added (with stereotype «nonNormative») to indicate that the timing loops are really just there to support simulation

- When the Pilot is controlling the movement
  - The chXXX change events are bound to the changes in pressure or resistance in the three planes; when the flow values are changed, it not only changes the value but also creates the change event automagically
  - Changes in applied pressure (from the Pilot himself) and changes in resistance (from the environment) result in a recomputation of the next incremental movement to make
  - Resulting joint position is sensed periodically, controlled by the timeout value SENSE_TIME
- When the Maintainer is controlling the movement
  - The events from the maintain can either be a moveTo command with all three plane positions specified, an incremental or relative movement from the current position with the increment in all three planes specified, or the limb can be zeroed
  - Once a new target position is identified from the movement commands from the Maintainer, the actual movement is constructed as a set of small incremental movements in the Moving state, based on a timeout
  - Breaking the movement into a set of small incremental movements allows the Maintainer to change the target position even as the movement is engaged (i.e., between small incremental movements).

Step 6: Verify and validate functional requirements

Execution was done with the help of the Webify toolkit in Rhapsody. It allows you to mark various events and values as "web-enabled" and during execution constructs a web page to see and change values and to create events. It can be done with internal facilities, but this makes driving the simulations a bit easier. The web page to drive Pilot behavior during the simulation is shown in Figure 5.21.

The generated sequence diagrams resulting from the state machine execution are quite lengthy so only a portion of one is shown here, in Figure 5.22.

However, the ability to simulate the interaction of the system with the actors allows us to understand the individual requirements—and more importantly—the interaction of the set of requirements much more easily than the standard textual review of requirements. With the simulation, we can see the need to specify the ranges of pressures, the amount of gain involved, and do computations for stress loading of limbs. This means that we can identify missing and inconsistent requirements easily.

Step 7: Add traceability links

Following the completion of the workflow, we can add trace links to the stakeholder requirements, as we did for the Speed Demon Treadmill example previously.

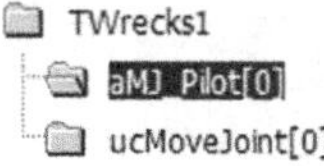

aMJ_Pilot[0]	
jointSagittalPressure	75
jointCoronalPressure	35
jointTransversePressure	-60
evPEnable	Activate
evPDisable	Activate
incSP	Activate
incCP	Activate
incTP	Activate
decSP	Activate
decCP	Activate
decTP	Activate
zeroP	Activate

Figure 5.21
Web page to drive the simulation.

Step 8: Perform review

When we perform our review, we can review the textual requirements along with the model. It is not uncommon to ask "what if" kinds of questions during such a requirements review and with an executable model, the easiest way to answer those questions is often to run the model to find out!

5.5.2 Scenarios-Based Use Case Analysis

This workflow for performing use case analysis is my favorite when working closely with stakeholders to elicit and understand their needs. Even when I'm dealing with subject matter experts who are also systems engineers, I find this approach is generally the fastest way to get a solid understanding of the requirements. The workflow, shown in Figure 5.23, is similar to the flow-based approach. The primary difference is that the order of scenario identification and activity diagram is swapped; in this workflow, rather than derive the scenarios from the activity flows, the activity diagram is constructed by adding together flows identified in the scenarios.

Let's walk through this workflow with the `Execute Protocol` use case from the Speed Demon Treadmill. The requirements allocated to the use case are shown in Figure 5.24.

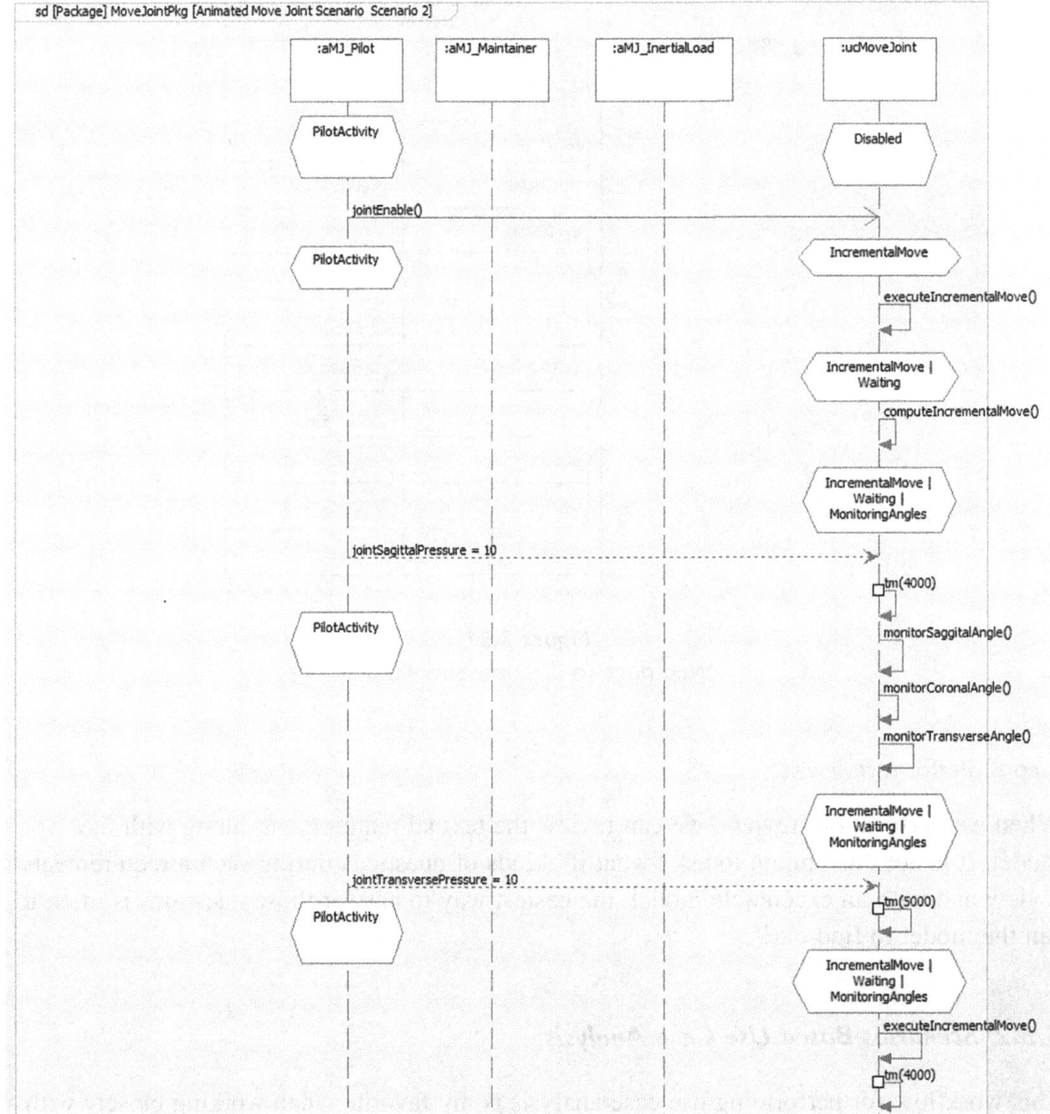

Figure 5.22
Portion of execution scenario of Move Joint use case.

Note that there are three subclassed use cases. Requirements specific to those use cases are allocated directly to the more specific use case, but it is important to remember that the most specific use cases inherit the requirements allocated to their base use case. That is, all requirements allocated to use case `Execute Protocol` are also, if indirectly, allocated to `Race`, `Execute Pre-planned Protocol`, and `Run Factory-Defined Protocol`.

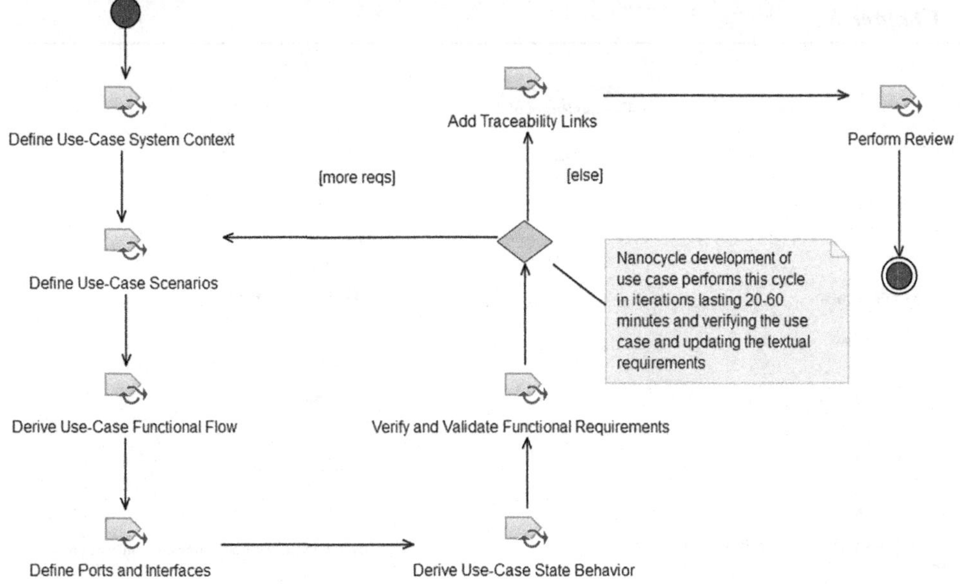

Figure 5.23
Scenario-based use case analysis.

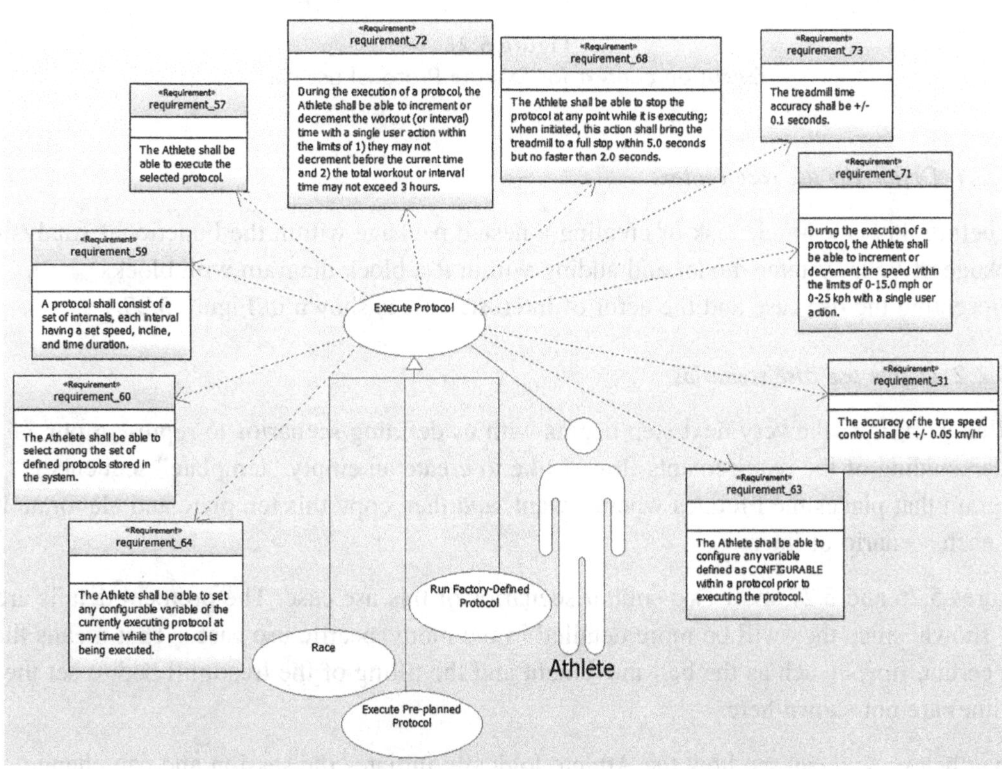

Figure 5.24
Requirements allocated to Execute Protocol use case.

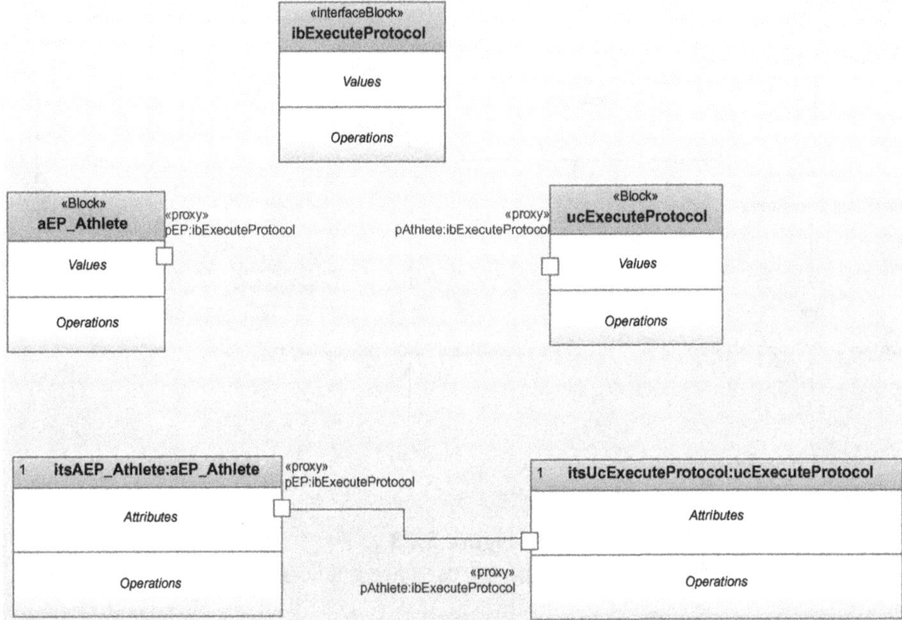

Figure 5.25
Execution context for Execute Protocol use case.

5.5.2.1 Define the use case context

As before this is a simple task of creating a nested package within the Functional Analysis package of your systems model and adding within it a block diagram with blocks representing the use case and the actor of interest. This is shown in Figure 5.25.

5.5.2.2 Define use case scenarios

In this workflow, the very next step begins with us defining scenarios to represent our understanding of the requirements flow. I like to create an empty "template" sequence diagram that places the lifelines where I want, and then copy this template and elaborate it for each scenario of interest.

Figures 5.26 and 5.27 show two similar scenarios of this use case. The protocol details are not shown, since they will be more detailed in the more specific use cases. That means that the certain flows (such as the belt movement and the tilting of the treadmill bed to set the incline) are not shown here.

Nevertheless, you can see how the Athlete logically initiates the session and can change values, such as speed or time, during the protocol execution. In the former case, the protocol runs to completion while in the latter, the Athlete terminates it early.

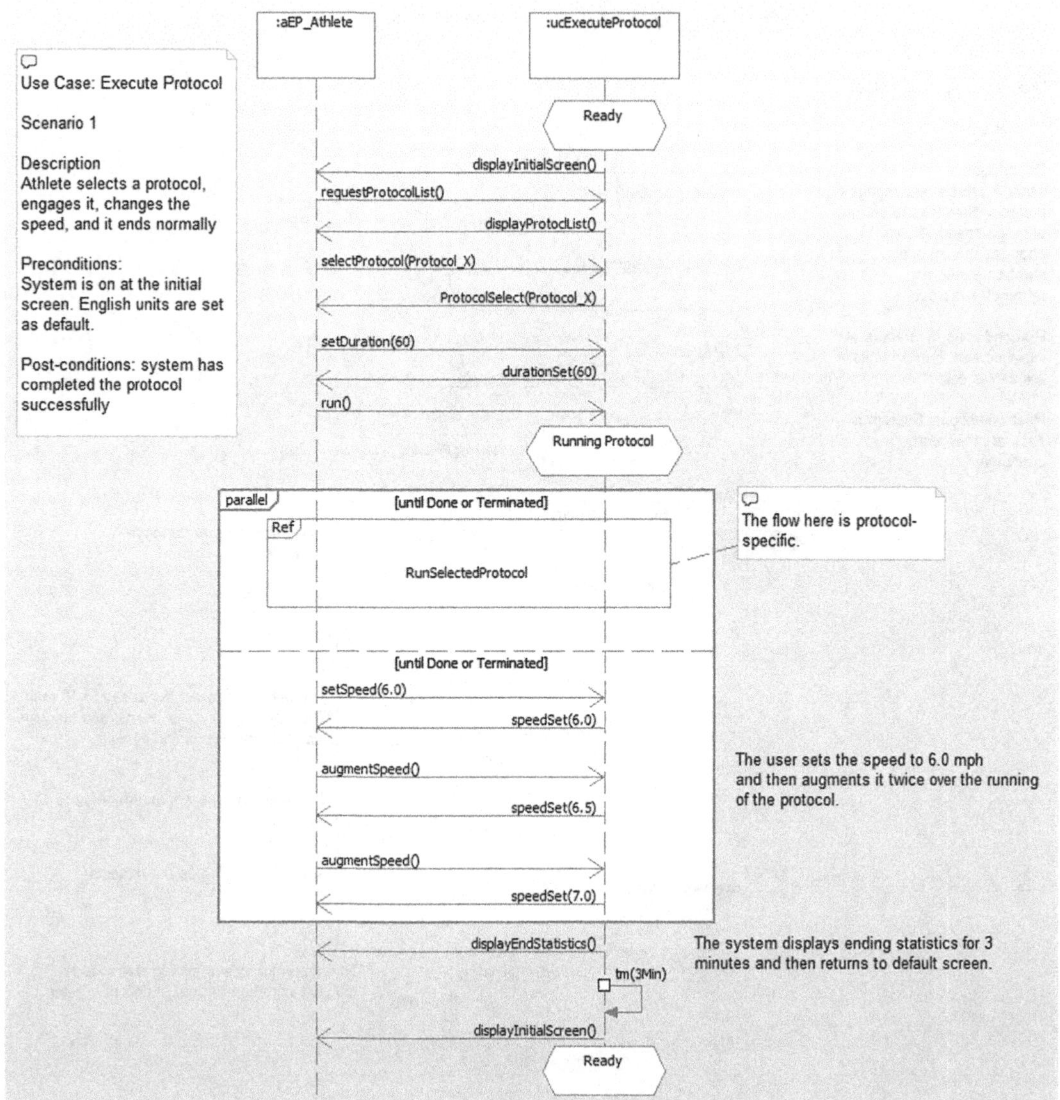

Figure 5.26
Execute Protocol scenario 1.

5.5.2.3 Derive use case functional flow

In this workflow, the creation of an activity diagram is optional. If you decide to do this, you will incrementally create the activity diagram as you add more scenarios of interest. Scenarios will usually be added as either alternative flows (using the decision node) or will run in parallel (using forks and joins).

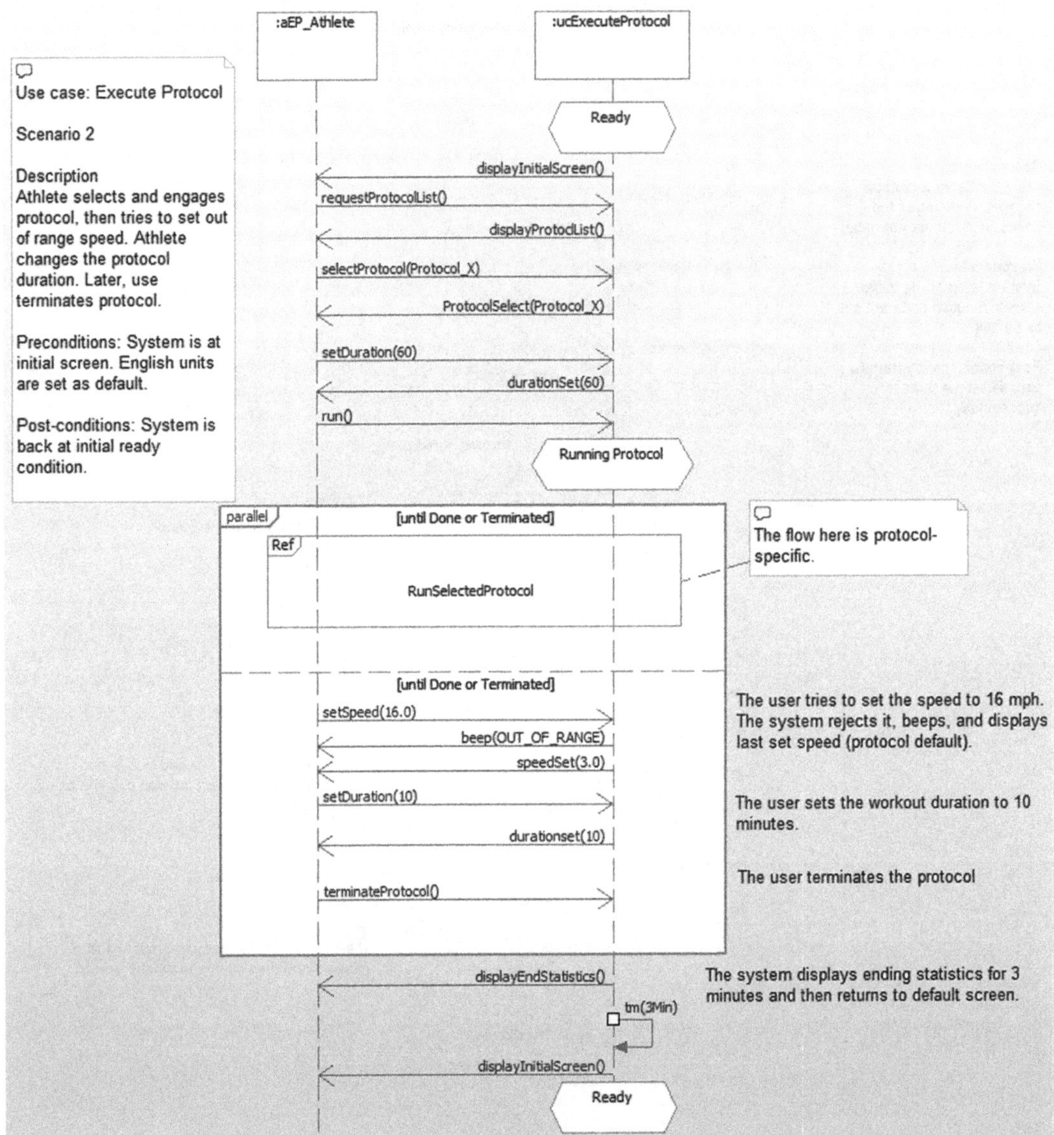

Figure 5.27
Execute Protocol scenario 2.

Activity diagrams and sequence diagram are not completely isomorphic because scenario flows really show interaction (request and response sets) while the activity flows focus on the behavior performed. Nevertheless, the relation between the sequence diagrams above and the activity diagram in Figure 5.28 is clear.

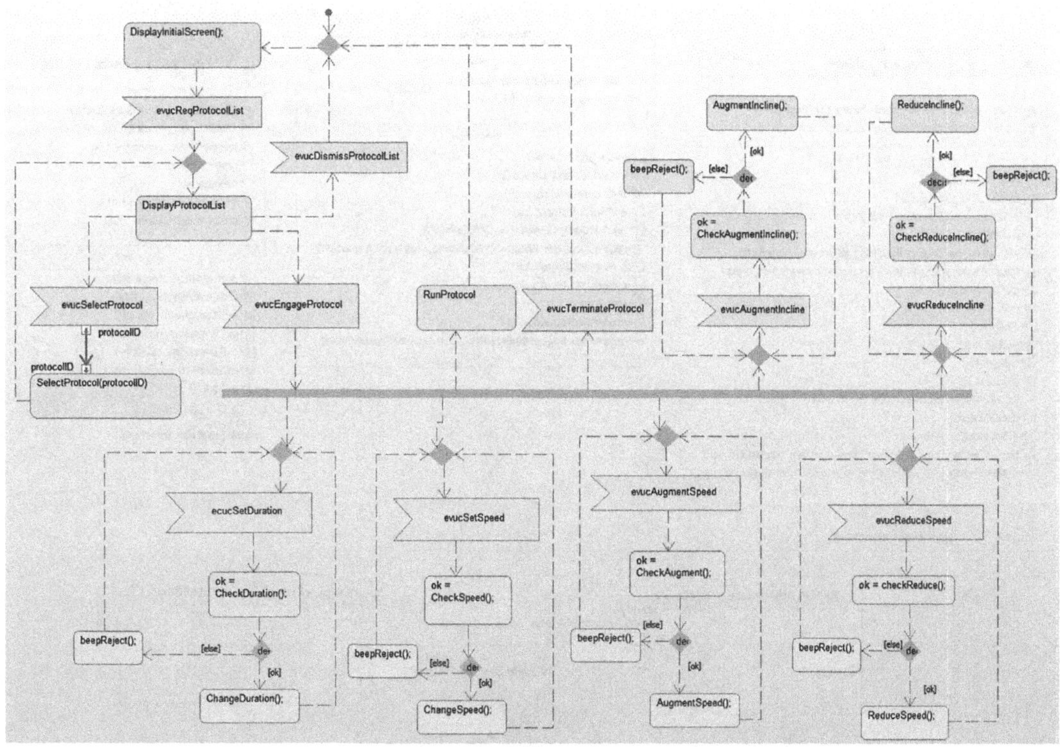

Figure 5.28
Activity diagram for Execute Protocol use case.

5.5.2.4 Define ports and interfaces

Based on the incoming (and in the case of `Beep`, outgoing) events and the physical flows of `beltMotion` and `incline`, the ports can be elaborated (Figure 5.29).

5.5.2.5 Derive use case state machine

The next step is to build an executable state machine for the block `ucExecuteProtocol` that represents the scenario flows and requirements. The state chart was constructed using a number of short nanocycles. The end result of one of them, shown in Figure 5.30, just shows the `Athlete` state machine (on the left) driving the `Execute Protocol` system use case state machine (on the right) to select the protocol. Getting this to work resulted in captured sequence diagrams, one of which is shown in Figure 5.31.

Quite a number of nanocycles later, the complete (and executable) state machine specification for the Execute Protocol use case is shown in Figure 5.32.

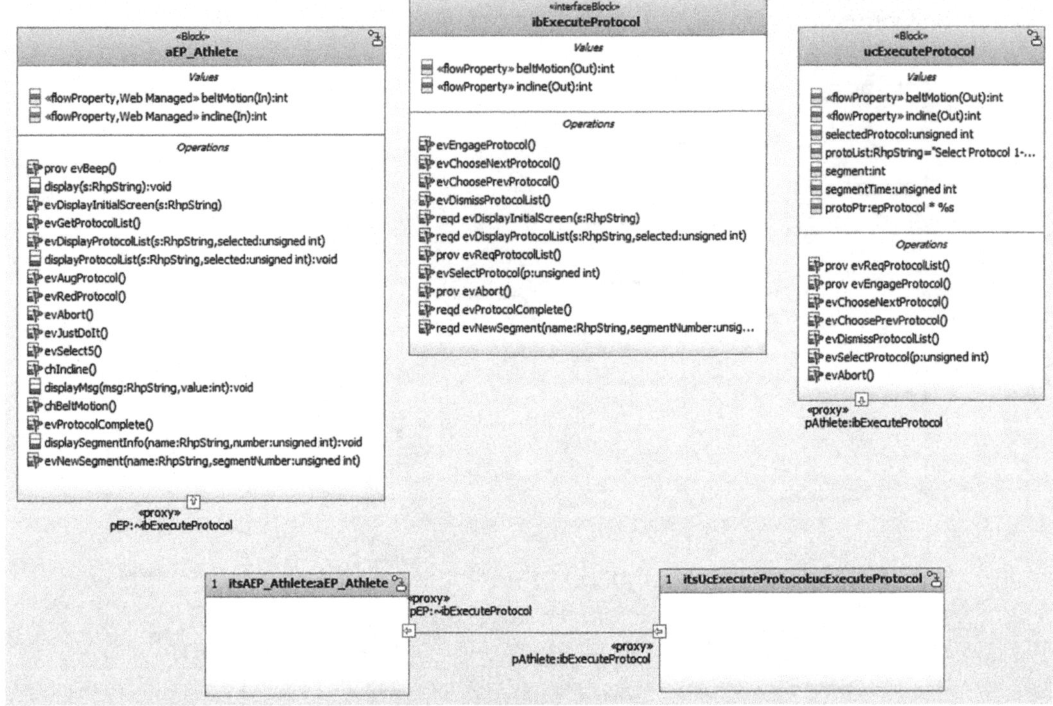

Figure 5.29
Interface block for Execute Protocol.

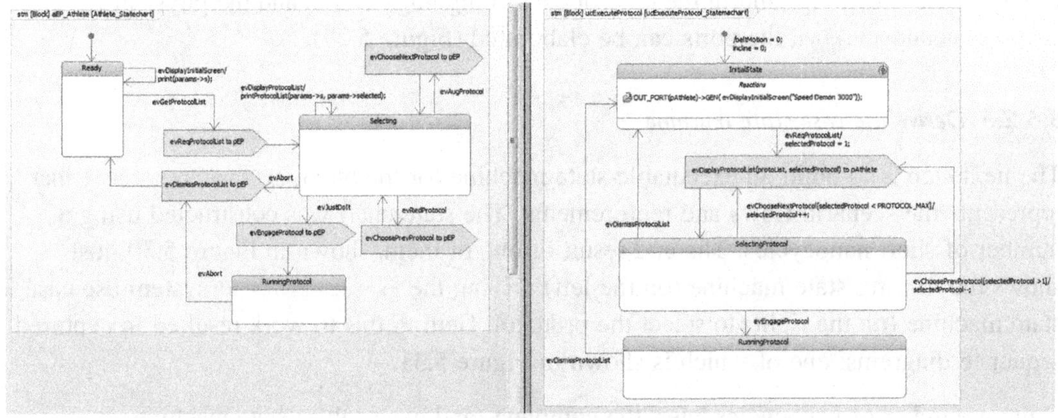

Figure 5.30
Execute Protocol state machine in an early nanocycle.

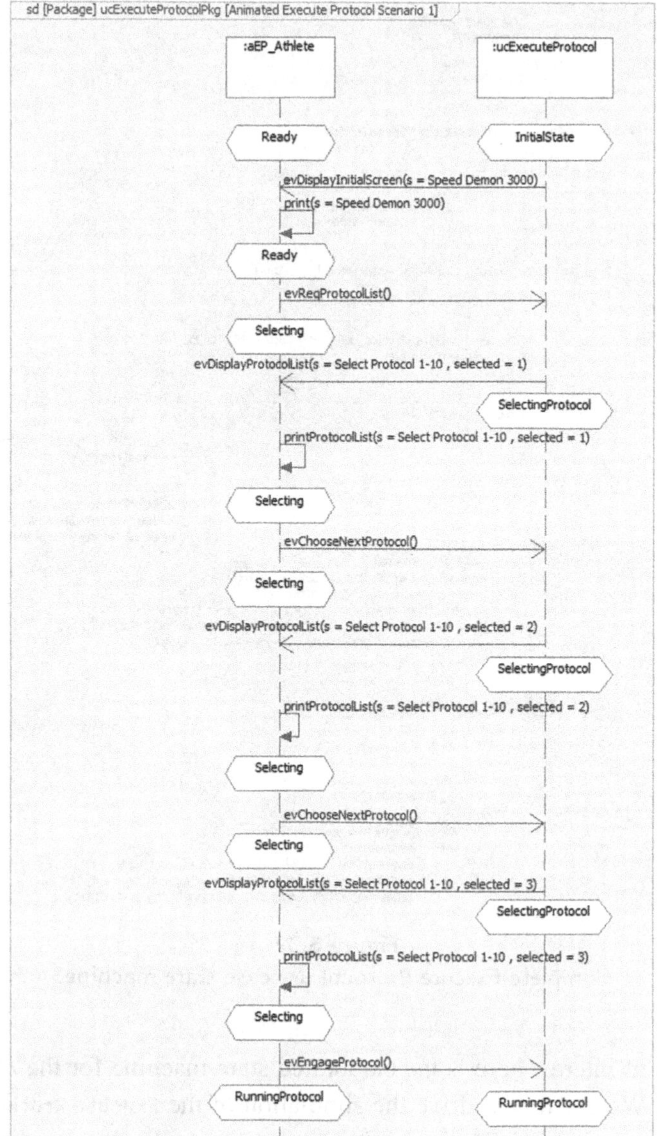

Figure 5.31
Sequence diagram captured from previous figure.

The upper part of the state machine in Figure 5.32 is very similar to that in Figure 5.30. What is added in the former state machine is the execution of the exercise protocol. To support this level of simulation, I added some blocks to describe the logical data schema for representing protocols (something we'll discuss in more detail in Section 5.6). For now, see Figure 5.33.

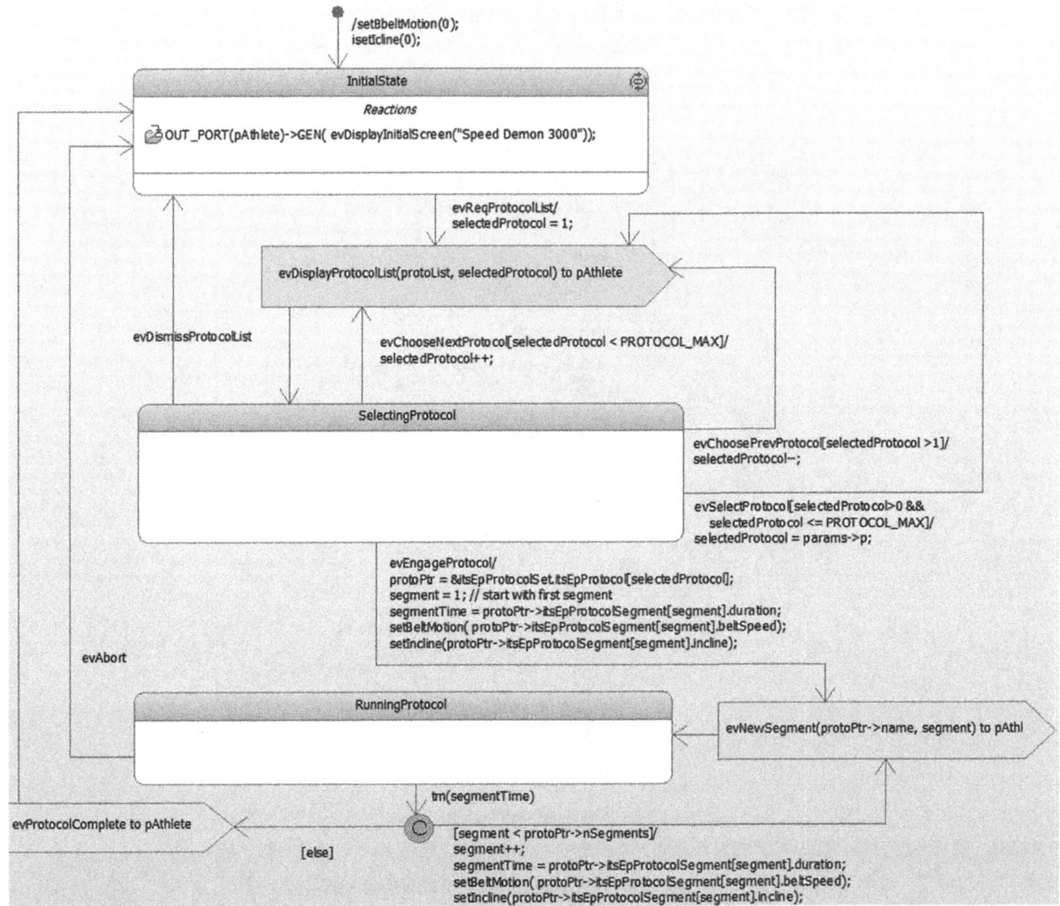

Figure 5.32
Complete Execute Protocol use case state machine.

The other diagram of interest here is the elaborated state machine for the `Athlete` actor block `aEP_Athlete`. We use this to drive the simulation of the `Execute Protocol` use case and also display simulation information. It has operations to display interval information (the protocol name and the interval segment number), to display belt speed and incline, and to display the protocol list. This state machine is shown in Figure 5.34.

When we simulate the requirements by running the model, we can capture various scenarios to understand the interactive and dynamic behavior that we are specifying. A portion of such an execution is shown in Figure 5.35. I removed the initial part of the scenario where the protocol was selected to focus on the part where the protocol is actually run. I also added a few comments but every message and state shown on the sequence diagram in the figure was actually generated and captured by running the model.

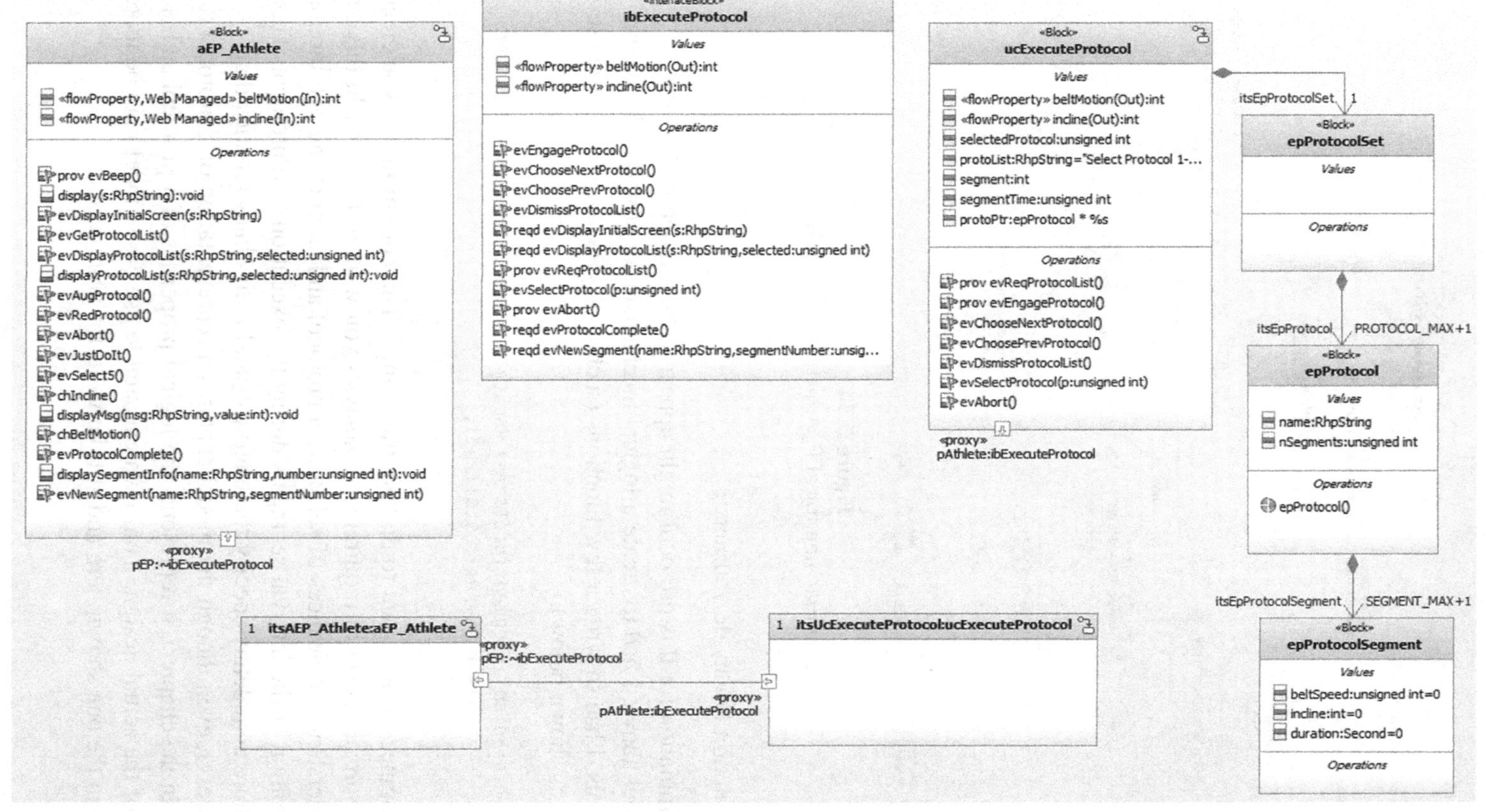

Figure 5.33
Updated execution context for Execute Protocol.

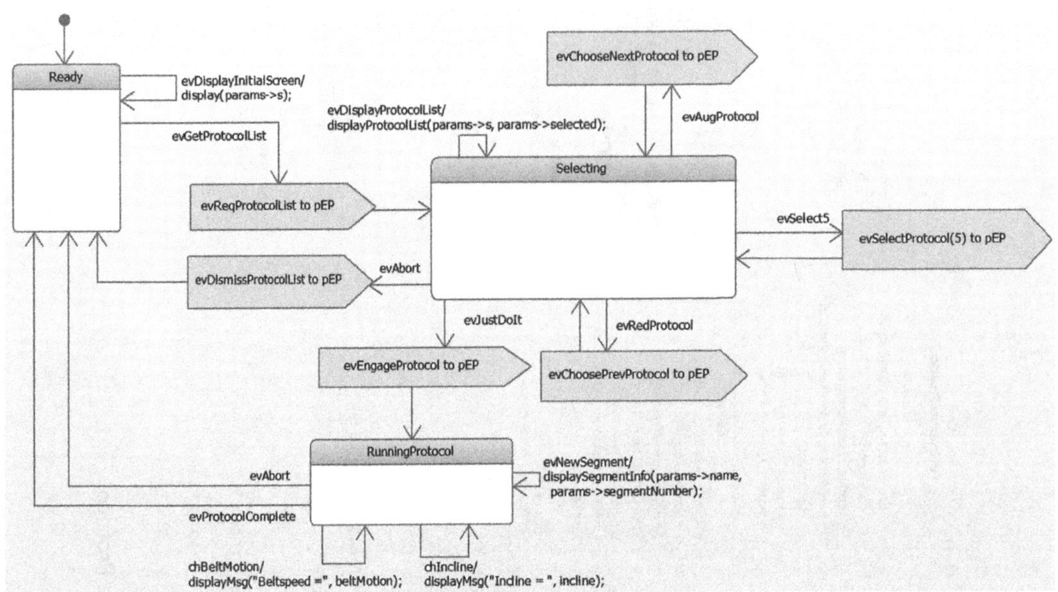

Figure 5.34
State machine for aEP_Athlete actor block.

How much simulation fidelity do you need?

The level of simulation for this protocol might appear to be too detailed. In the executable model above, I had to create a logical mechanism for stored and "playing" exercise protocols. I had to write a few functions (such as `displaySegmentInfo` whose implementation is shown below).

```
void aEP_Athlete::displaySegmentInfo(const RhpString& name, unsigned int number) {
  std::cout << " " << name << number << std::endl;
}
```

Most system engineers don't want to do "programming." The bottom line is you create a model that supports the level of requirements analysis you want to perform. In this case, I wanted to understand the nuances of selecting a protocol and capture the belt motion, incline, and duration of the interval segments during the execution of a protocol. This allows me to more completely specify the interfaces and their characteristics than otherwise. However, even though the model captures a representation of a protocol (to be discussed later in the chapter), it represents the logical properties of a protocol and is not representative of the actual design. Your own executable use case model may be more or less detailed than the one shown here and still be valid for your needs.

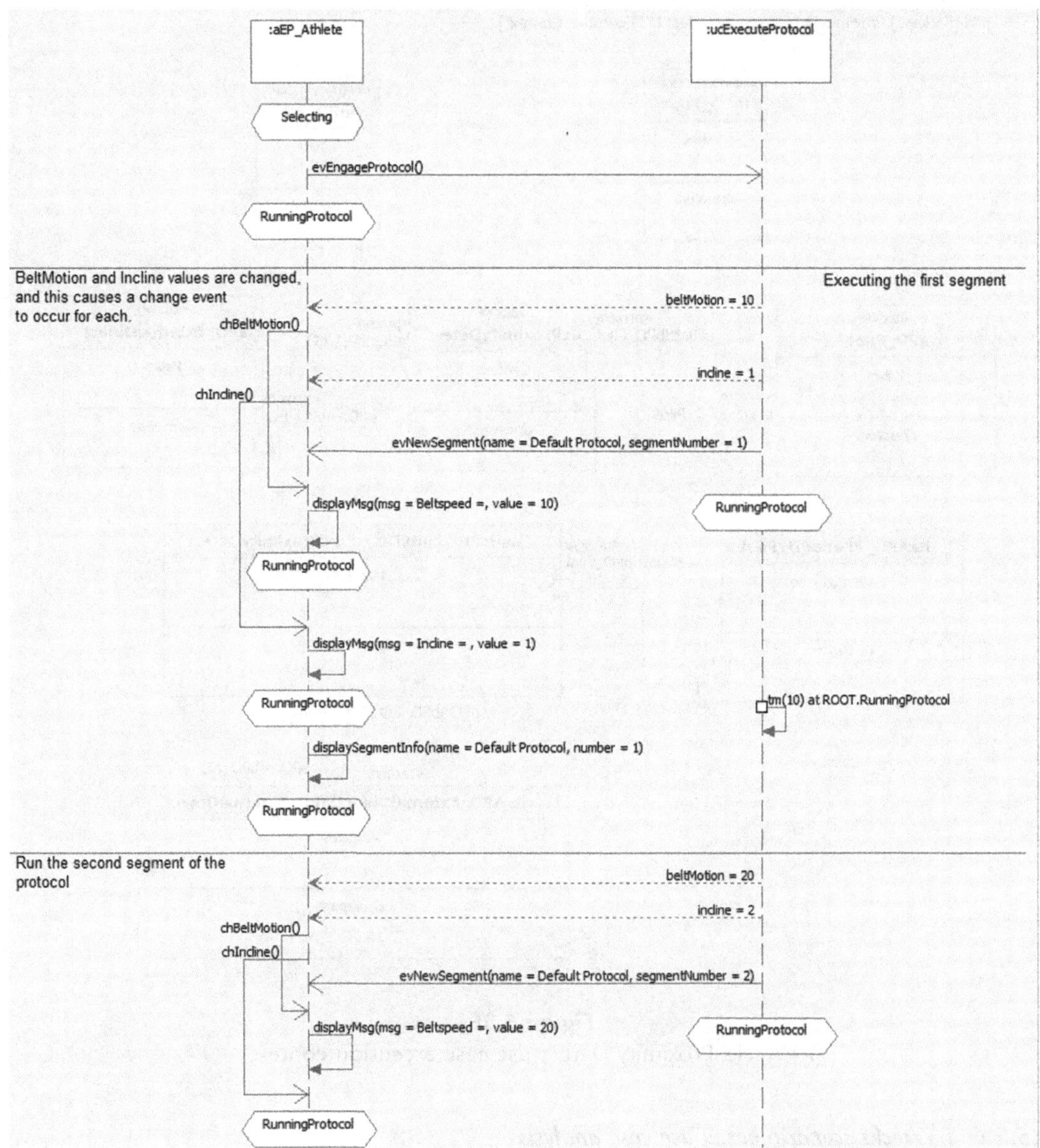

Figure 5.35
Portion of simulation scenario from Execute Protocol use case.

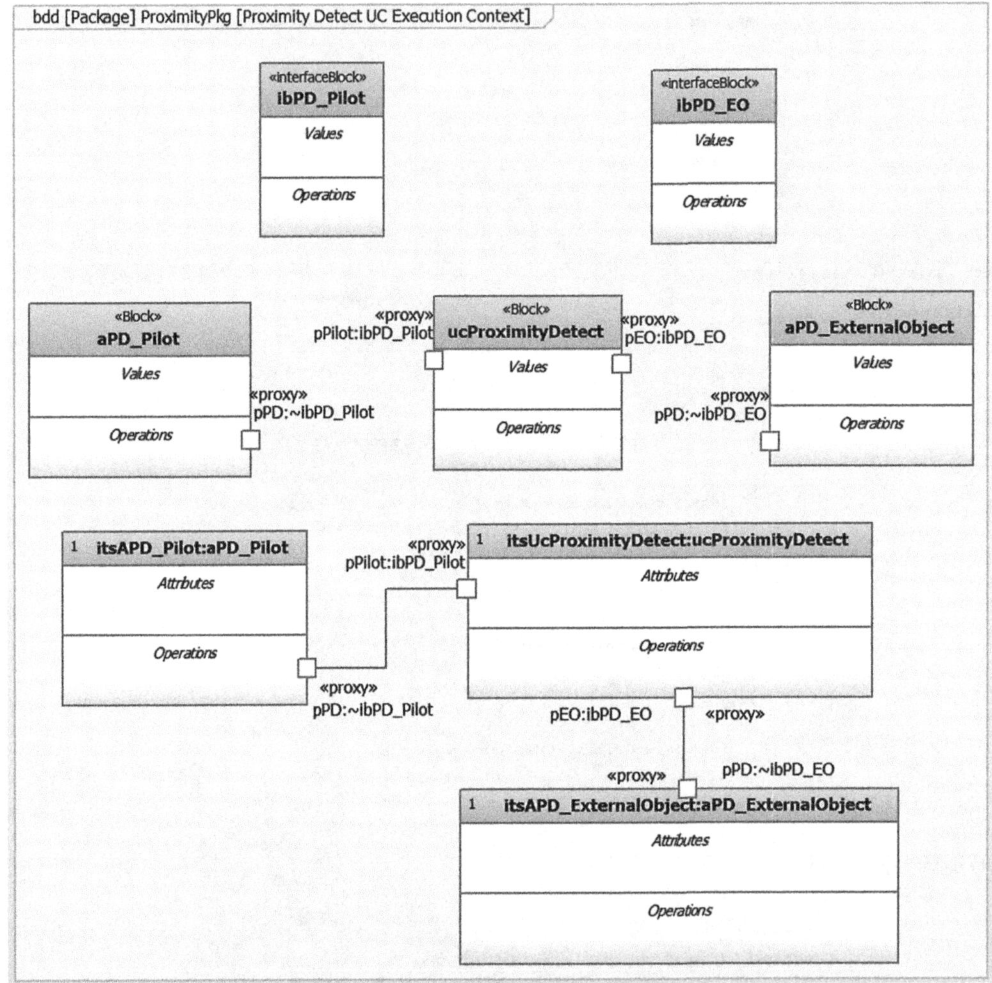

Figure 5.36
T-Wrecks Proximity Detect use case execution context.

5.5.2.6 T-Wrecks scenario-based use case analysis

Let's apply this flow-based workflow to the T-Wrecks use case `Proximity Detection`. Again, we won't show the multiple short iterations that take place to save some trees.

Step 1: Use case execution context

Figure 5.36 is straightforward and shows the use case and actor blocks with (empty) interface blocks to define the proxy ports.

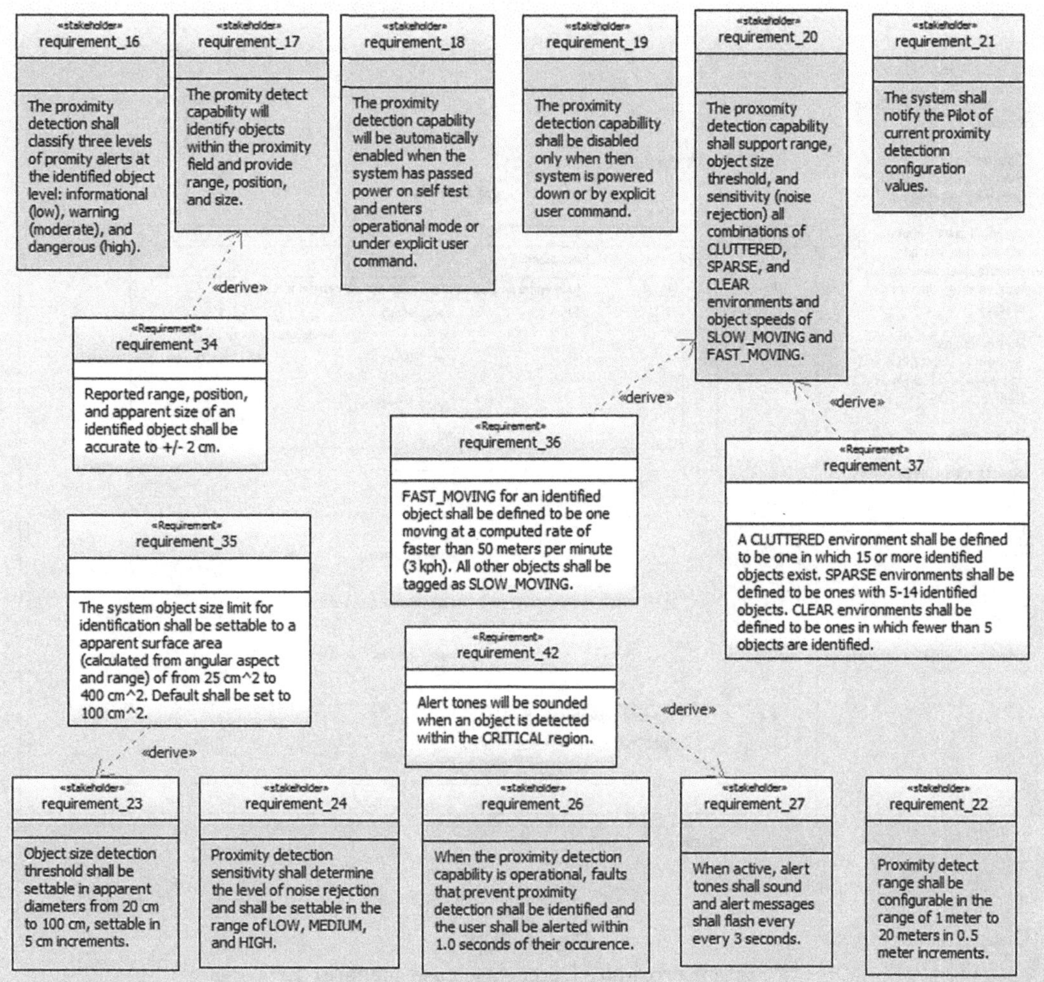

Figure 5.37
Proximity Detect derived system requirements.

Step 2: Define use case scenarios

The stakeholder requirements for this use case are pretty good. We do identify some derived requirements—quantitative specifications of value ranges—and these are shown in Figure 5.37.

Looking at the stakeholder scenarios, we see that they are a bit overly simplistic. For example, in Figure 4.14, the system performs a `proximityScan()` and identifies objects from flows from the External Object. In reality, the system might produce a great many range bursts to paint the environment and from the return from these bursts, the system will identify the presence of external objects and, based on the properties of the return of the

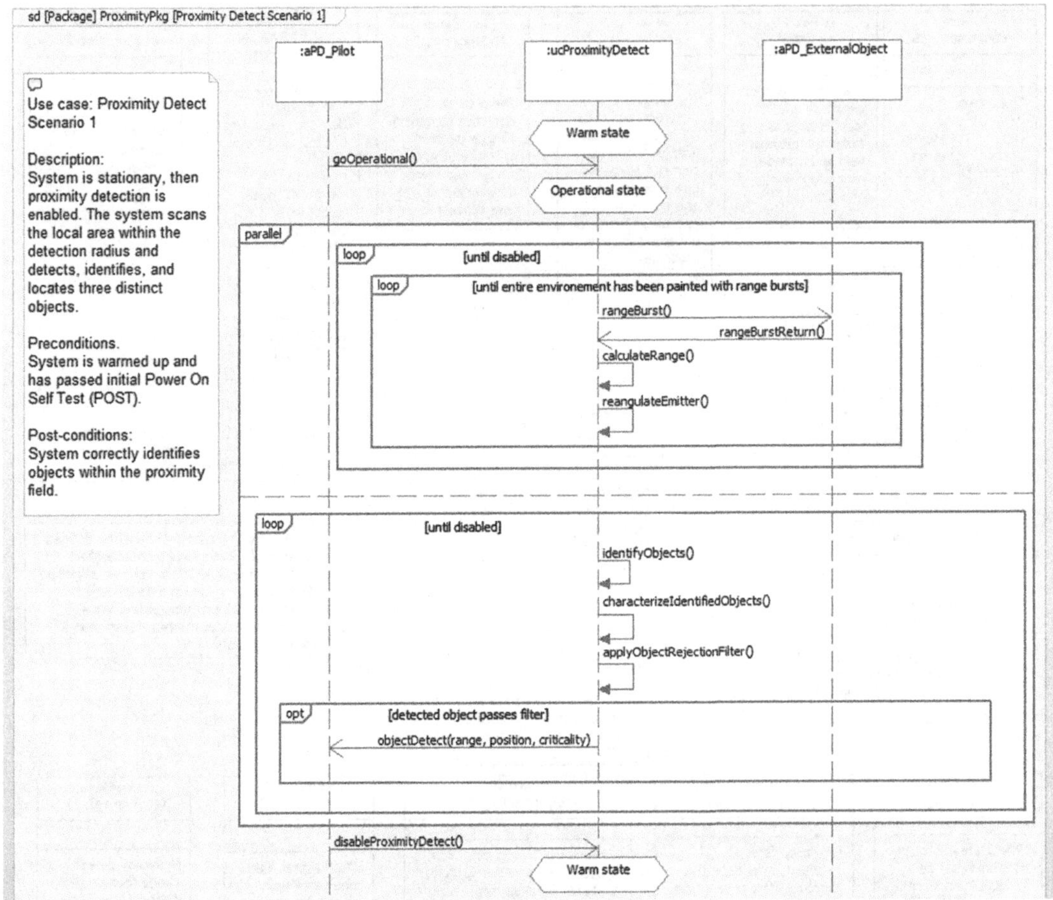

Figure 5.38
System Proximity Detect use case scenario 1.

range bursts, will characterize the objects. Following that, the object sensitivity filters will reject objects that are either too small or too far away; the remaining objects will be reported to the `Pilot`. This flow is shown in Figure 5.38.

It is instructive to compare Figure 4.14 with Figure 5.38. They both describe basically the same scenario, but the latter does so from a system engineering, rather than a stakeholder, perspective.

Similar elaborations (not shown) are made for the other stakeholder scenarios in Chapter 4.

It is important to note that we are *still* not designing the system, but we are defining properties that must be true *in every possible acceptable solution* (we call those properties *requirements*). We know that we must do active scanning and that means producing a range burst and listening for the return. We have not specified whether this is a burst of physical

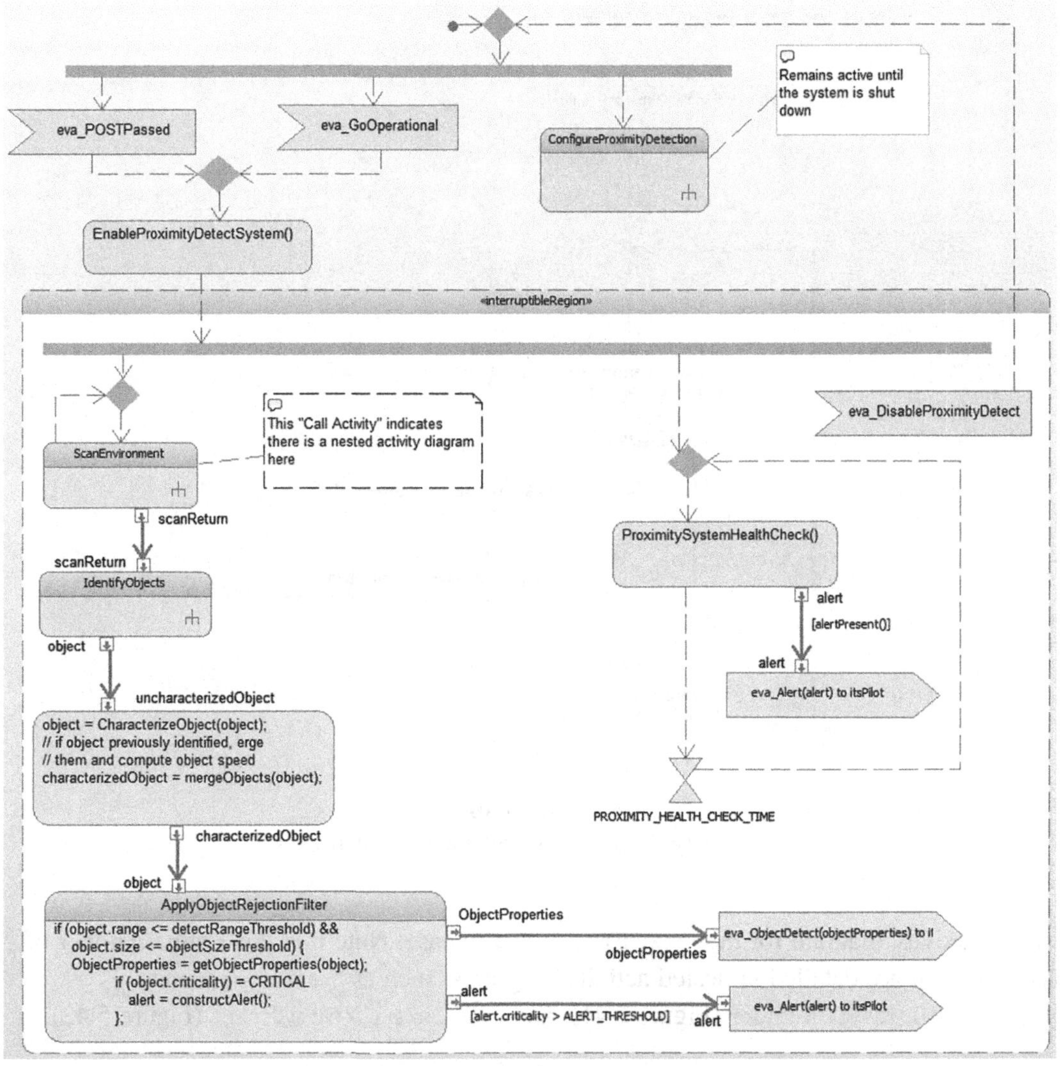

Figure 5.39

Proximity Detect use case activity diagram.

light, infrared radiation, microwave radiation, or even sound waves. We haven't specified whether we send out one pulse at a time or multiple pulses simultaneous, possibly at different frequencies. Those decisions will be made in the design phase (although technical options may be evaluated in a trade study during architectural analysis (see Chapter 6)).

Step 3: Derive use case functional flow

In this step, we will create an activity diagram that represents all of the primary flows of the use case, as identified in the aforementioned sequence diagrams. Figure 5.39 shows the

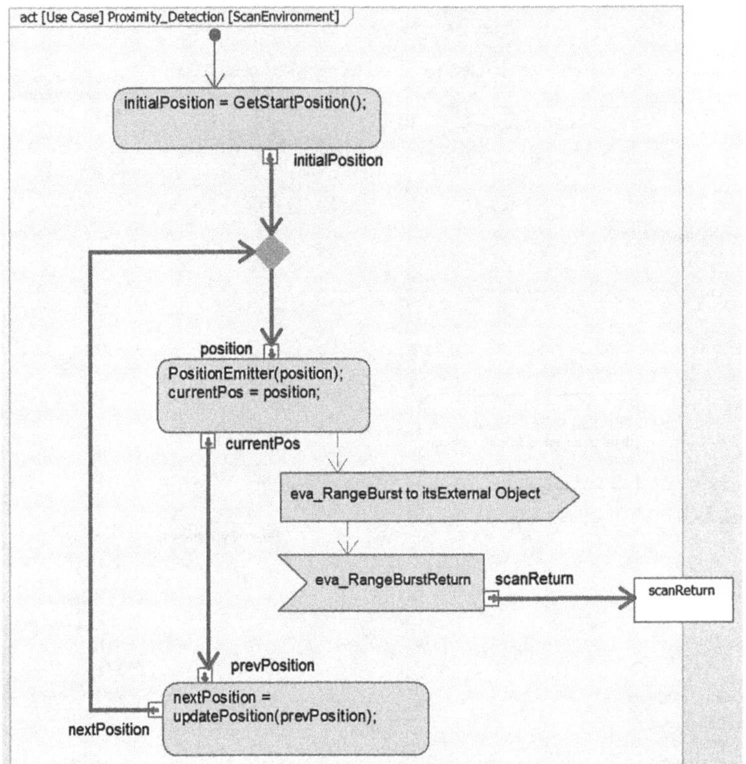

Figure 5.40
Activity diagram from ScanEnvironment.

overall activity diagram for the `Proximity Detect` use case. Note that there are a number of activities that are detailed in nested activity diagrams, such as `ScanEnvironment` (Figure 5.40), `IdentifyObject` (Figure 5.41), and `ConfigureProximityDetect` (Figure 5.42).

Step 4: Define ports and interfaces

Figure 5.43 shows the interfaces for this use case, captured in interface blocks. The blocks that use the interfaces are shown as well—after all, they must provide implementations of those interfaces. The number of services provided and offered demonstrate the need to iteratively define the services—define some interfaces, develop and implement the state machine, add more interfaces, enhance the state machine, . . . repeat until done. Otherwise the probability that you'll get them all correct before you define and run the state machine is fairly small. Iterations allow you to progressively define the interfaces and ensure that they are correct.

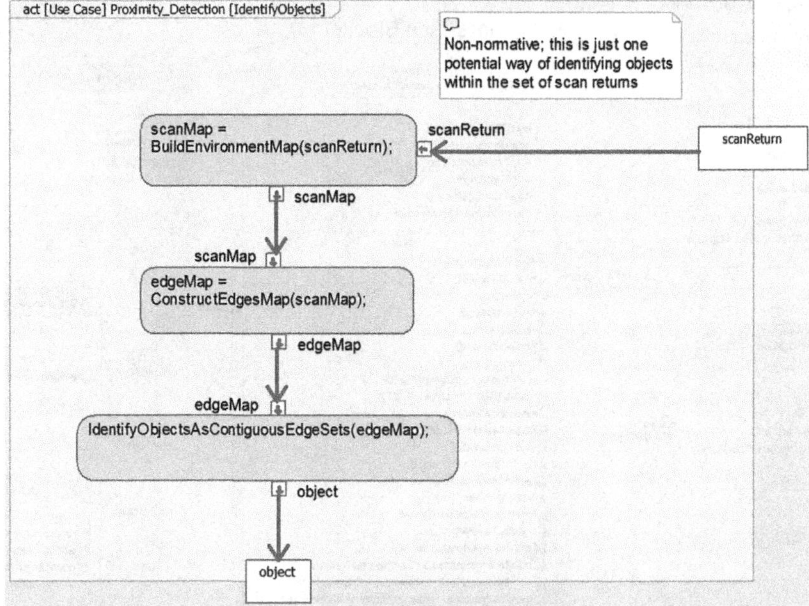

Figure 5.41
Activity diagram for IdentifyObjects.

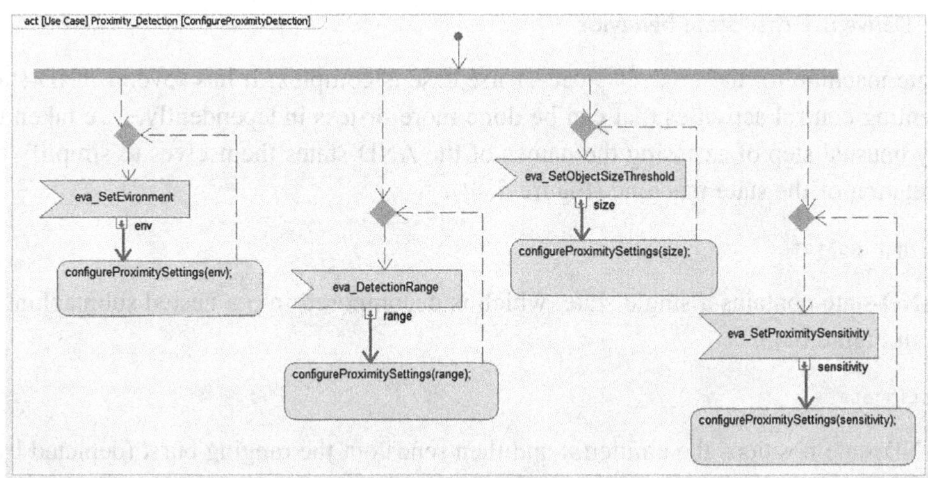

Figure 5.42
Activity diagram from ConfigureProximityDetect.

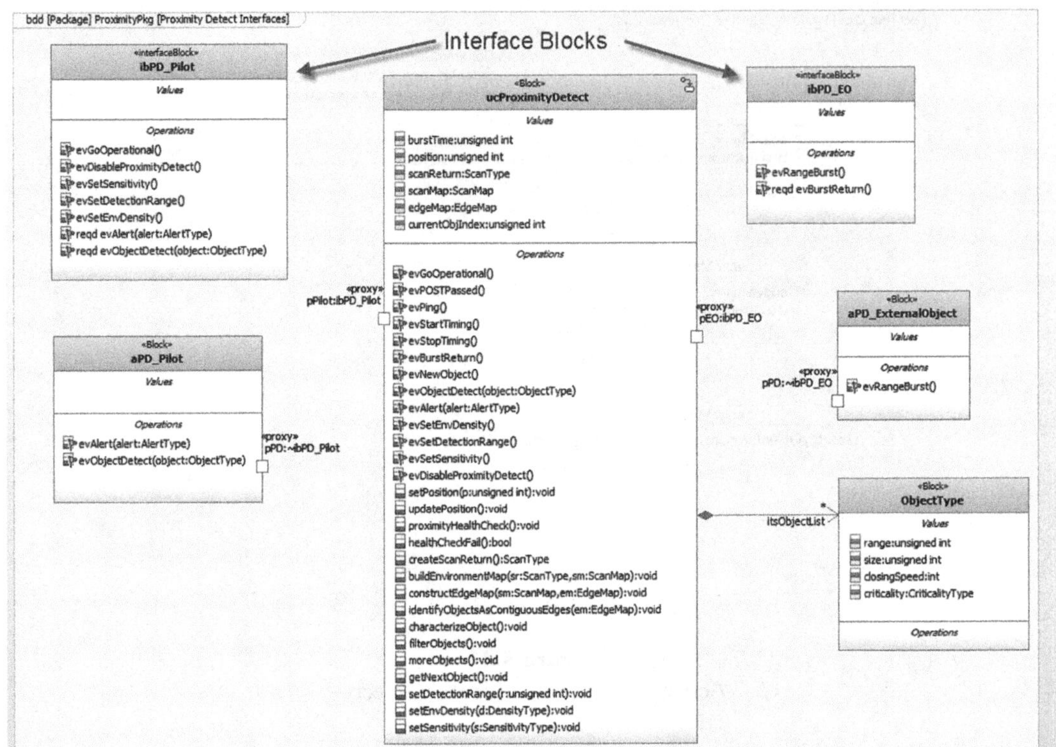

Figure 5.43
Interface Blocks for Proximity Detect use case.

Step 5: Derive use case state behavior

The state machine for the `Proximity Detect` use case is complex. It has several AND-states representing control activities that can be done more-or-less independently. I've taken the slightly unusual step of exposing the names of the AND-states themselves to simplify the interpretation of the state machine (Figure 5.44).

`ConfiguringState`

This AND-state contains a single state, which is decomposed into a nested submachine, shown in Figure 5.45.

`EmittingState`

This AND-state positions the emitter(s) and then sends out the ranging burst (depicted by sending the event `evRangeBurst` to the port `pEO`, which is in turn, connected to the `ExternalObject`). After sending the burst, it sends an event (to itself) to start timing and stops when the burst return is detected. Then it updates the position and sends the next burst.

`TimingBurstState`

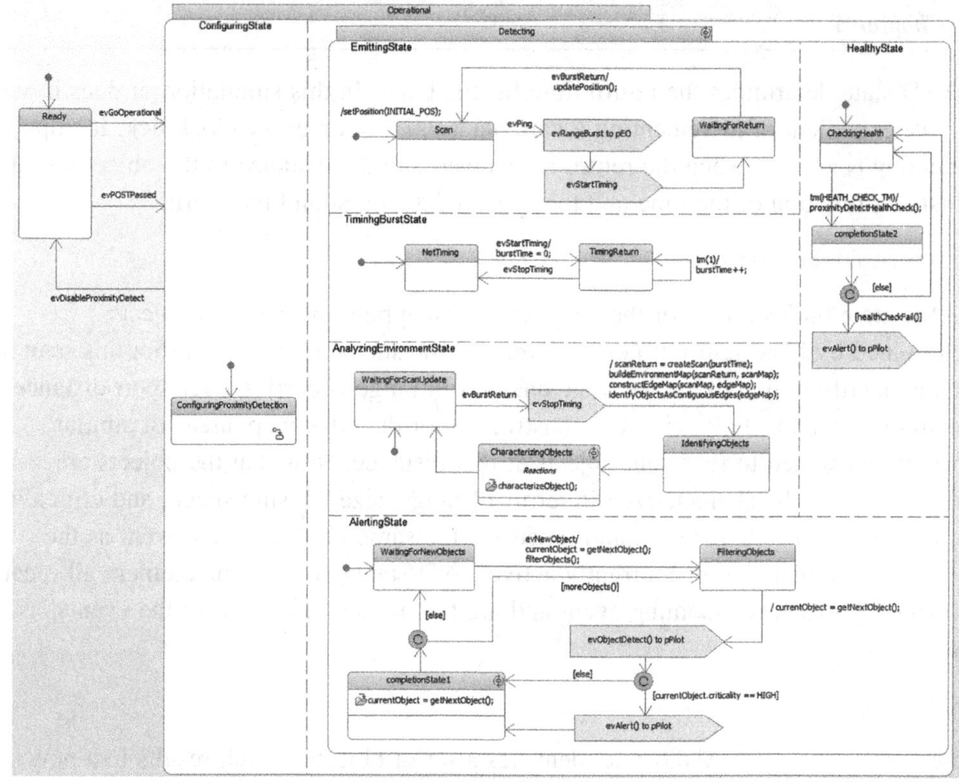

Figure 5.44
Proximity Detect use case state machine.

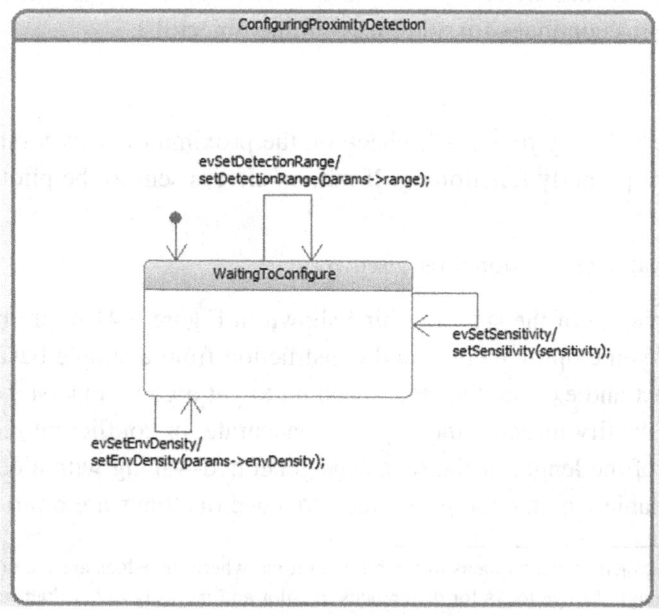

Figure 5.45
ConfiguringProximityDetection submachine.

This AND-state determines the return time for the burst. In this simulation, it does it with the simple expedient of incrementing a variable `burstTime` on every clock tick. It stops incrementing `burstTime` when the return is received and the distance to the object returning the burst is a function of the time and the speed of the burst and its return.

`AnalyzingEnvironmentState`

This AND-state builds a map of the environment, mapping distances to objects (as determined by burst return times) to a map of the surrounding area. From this scan map, edges are identified by looking for large changes in range occurring over short distances in the environment map.[7] Following the construction of the edge map, areas of similar distance are presumed to represent objects at that distance. Now that the objects are identified, they can be characterized in terms of range, size, closing speed, and criticality. Note that this AND-state receives and processes the same `evBurstReturn` event as the `EmittingState`. Remember, concurrently active AND-states of the same element all receive their own copy of every incoming event and are free to act on or discard the events, as they see fit.

`AlertingState`

The previously described AND-state identifies a set of objects, which results in a new set of `ObjectTypes` (available to `ucProximityDetect` block via `itsObjectList` relation) (see Figure 5.43). The system can walk the list, applying the alerting filters to determine which objects are interesting enough with which to bother the Pilot. The interesting ones result in a detection notification and the really interesting ones (the ones whose criticality is HIGH) result in an alert. This continues for all objects in the object list.

`HealthyState`

This AND-state periodically runs a self check on the proximity detect components to ensure that it appears to be properly functioning. If not, an alert is sent to the pilot.

Step 6: Verify and validate functional requirements

The size and complexity of the state machine shown in Figure 5.44 might be a little intimidating but if you employ incremental construction from a simple basis, it's not difficult to construct and execute the state machine to get a good understanding of the requirements and identify missing, incomplete, inaccurate, or conflicting requirements. In this case, because of the length of the scenarios generated—along with a desire to keep the chapter to a reasonable length—the generated sequence diagrams are omitted.

---

[7] Interestingly, this is exactly what happens in the human retina, where the edges are identified by convolving a Gaussian filter, although the eye looks for differences in color and intensity rather than return time. (I KNEW that PhD in neurocybernetics would come in handy at some point!)

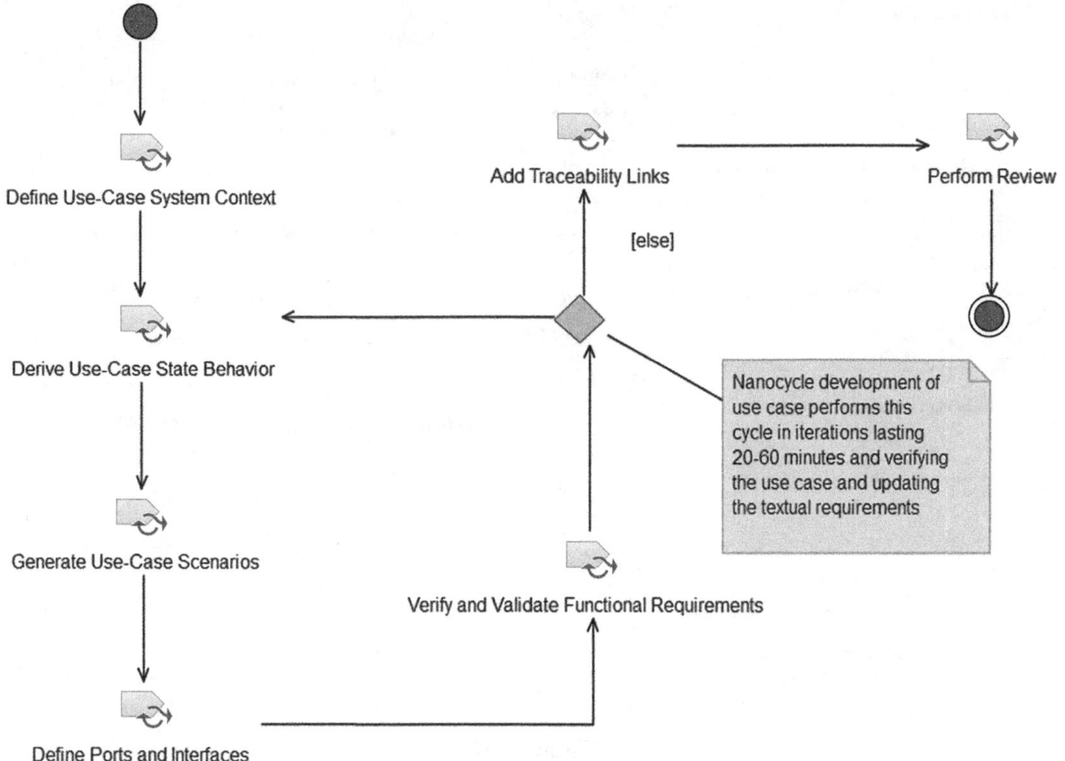

Figure 5.46
State-based use case analysis.

5.5.3 State-Based Use Case Analysis

The last of the three alternative approaches develops the state machine first and from this generates the scenarios as different paths through the state machine. The scenarios are still valuable because they can be reviewed with the stakeholders and subject matter experts and may also be used as the basis for system verification test cases. To use this approach requires the engineers to be skilled in state machine thinking and creation. It also helps if the use case is clearly stateful and/or modal.

Figure 5.46 shows the workflow for state-based use case analysis. One obvious difference between this and the other workflows (other than beginning with the state machine) is the omission of the creation of the activity diagram. Generally, when this workflow pattern is appropriate, the activity diagram is not particularly helpful and is usually omitted.

So what do we mean by the term "stateful"? In general, the term refers to behavior that is dependent upon both current value(s) and the path taken to achieve it (them). However, in this context, a more useful definition would be that a stateful system contains sets of

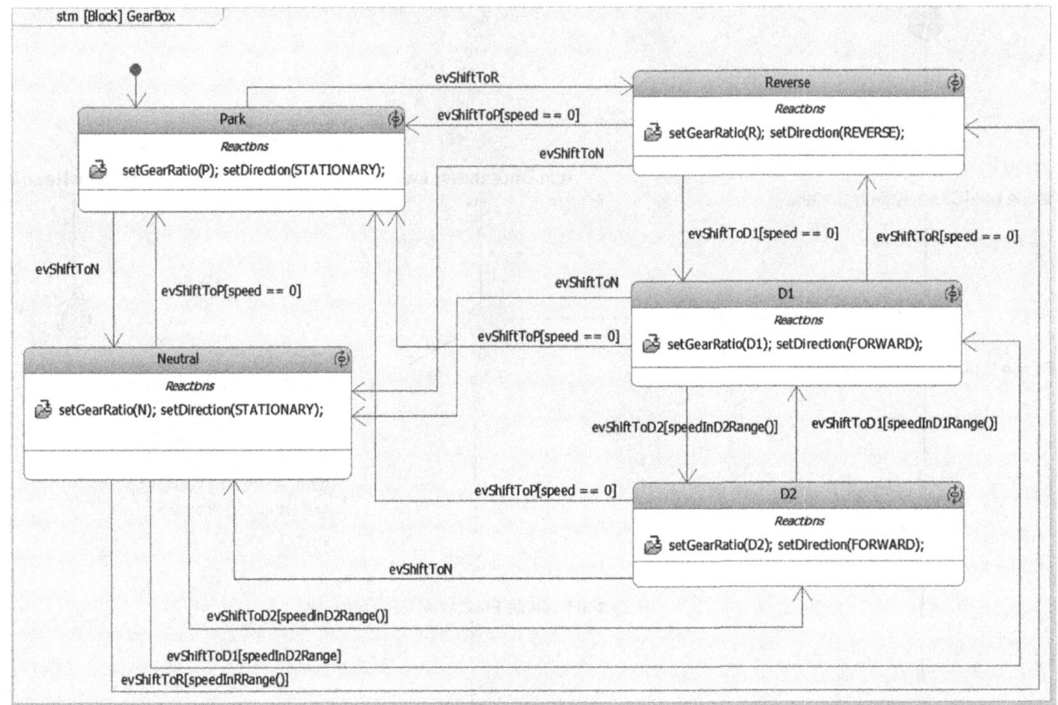

Figure 5.47
Stateful Gearbox.

behaviors that are distinguishable and non-overlapping. Probably the prototypical example of a stateful system is a manual automotive gear box. Figure 5.47 shows a somewhat simplified version. The important point is that the states are non-overlapping (you can't be in `Reverse` and `Neutral` at the same time) and distinguishable. The behavior performed in those states is similar (driving the transmission within a rotational speed range) but they differ in terms of the gear ratio and the direction of rotation. Guards control whether the event should trigger the transition or be discarded. Also notice that some transitions are disallowed, such as from `D2` directly to `Reverse`.

In such situations, it might make sense to start by constructing the state machine. Then scenarios, such as `Park → Reverse → Neutral → D1 → D2 → D1 → Park`, can be created by executing paths through the state machine.

5.5.3.1 Define the use case context

As usual, we start with defining the use case execution context, and reify the use case and its associated actors as blocks. For our example of this workflow, let's use the Speed

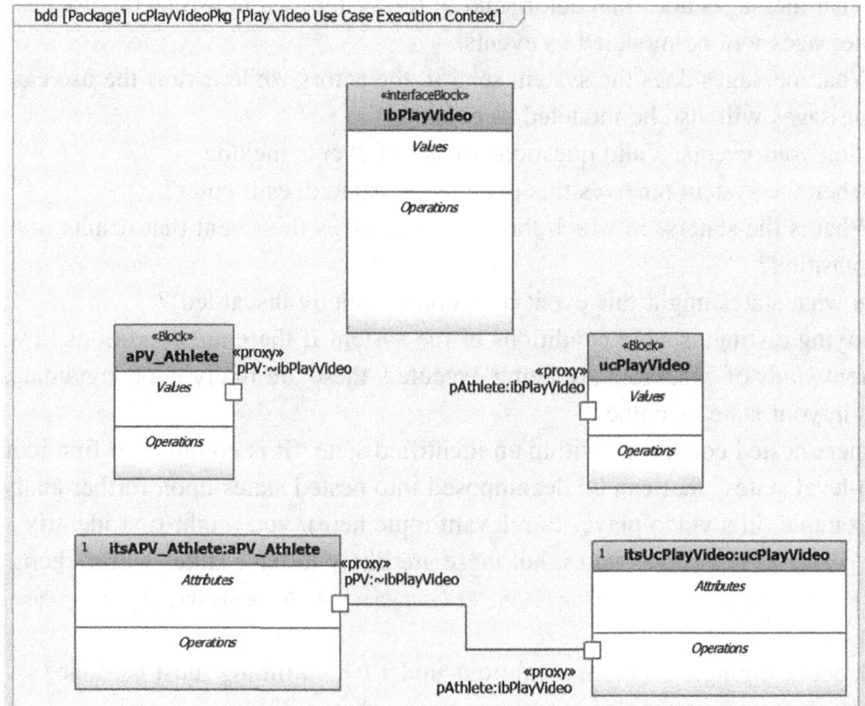

Figure 5.48
Play Video use case execution context.

Demon `Play Video` use case. In this case, the video is already loaded (presumably via the `Manage Videos` use case). Why this use case? Well, it seems to me that it is stateful—having non-overlapping states like selecting a video, playing a video, selecting a chapter, and so on.

Following the same approach as before, I've created two blocks—`ucPlayVideo` and `aPV_Athlete` and one interface block, `ibPlayVideo`, to define the interfaces between them (Figure 5.48).

5.5.3.2 Derive use case state machine

Starting with the state machine, the states may not be as obvious as when previous thinking has been done about the use case behavior. There are a number of strategies you can employ to help you identify the states:

- Start with the events. Sometimes you know the events of interest and that can give you a starting point to begin to identify the states. Since we are specifically modeling state machine for use cases, the only candidates for event sources are the relevant actors and other parts of the use case state machine. For each actor

- What messages does that actor send to the system while it runs the use case? Those messages will be modeled as events.
- What messages does the system send to the actors while it runs the use case? Those messages will also be modeled as events.

- Question your events. Valid questions to ask of events include
  - When the system receives this event, what state does it enter?
  - What is the state(s) in which the system receives this event that results in a valid transition?
  - In what states might this event be ignored (quietly discarded)?
- Identifying distinguishable conditions of the system If there are conditions in which different *kinds* of behaviors are being executed, these are likely good candidates to be states in your state machine
- Are there nested conditions within an identified state? It is common to first identify "high-level states" that can be decomposed into nested states upon further analysis. For example, in a video player (a relevant topic here), you might first identify `Selecting` and `Playing` as high-level states, but these are likely to have states within them, such as `Showing Videos`, `Showing Video Details`, `Playing Normal`, `Backing Up`, `Skipping Ahead`, and so on.
- Think about timing. Are there conditions under which timing must be done?
  - The timeout must be done in some state—what is it?
  - When a timeout occurs, the system enters some state—what is that?

Not to beat a dead horse,[8] but it is particularly important to construct the state machine in an iterative fashion, and the importance of iteration grows with the complexity of the behavior. In my development of the state machine for this use case, I first got the video selection behavior working (and even that was done in several nanocycle increments), followed by the video play behavior.

You can see in Figure 5.49 that there are three high-level states nestled within a larger state (added to reduce the number of transitions and thereby simplify the diagram). The two states on the right, Selecting and Playing, are both further decomposed with submachines, as indicated by the submachine icon in the lower right hand corner of the state.

To support the notion of "selecting" a video from a list, it was necessary to create Video blocks that have metadata, such as the video name, description, total play time, and number of chapters. This was added to the execution context (see the section on ports and interfaces, Figure 5.55).

The use case state machine receives events from the actor to select a video, display its description, and play it. All this behavior is held within the `Selecting` state submachine

[8] Although nobody wants it to rise as a zombie horse.

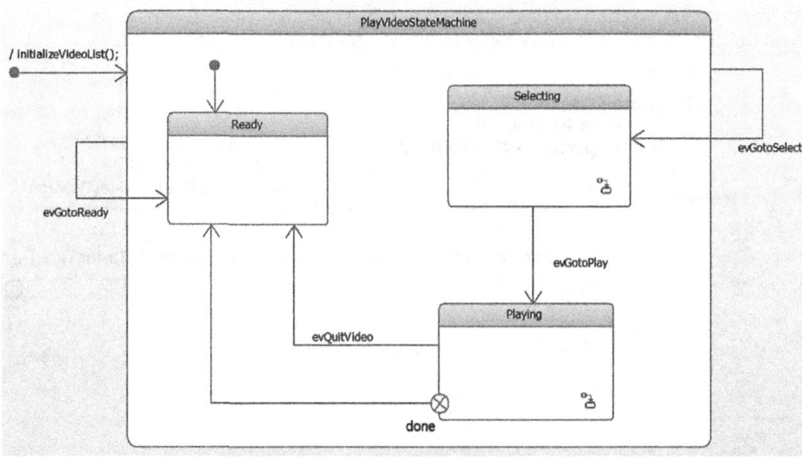

Figure 5.49
Play Video use case state machine (main).

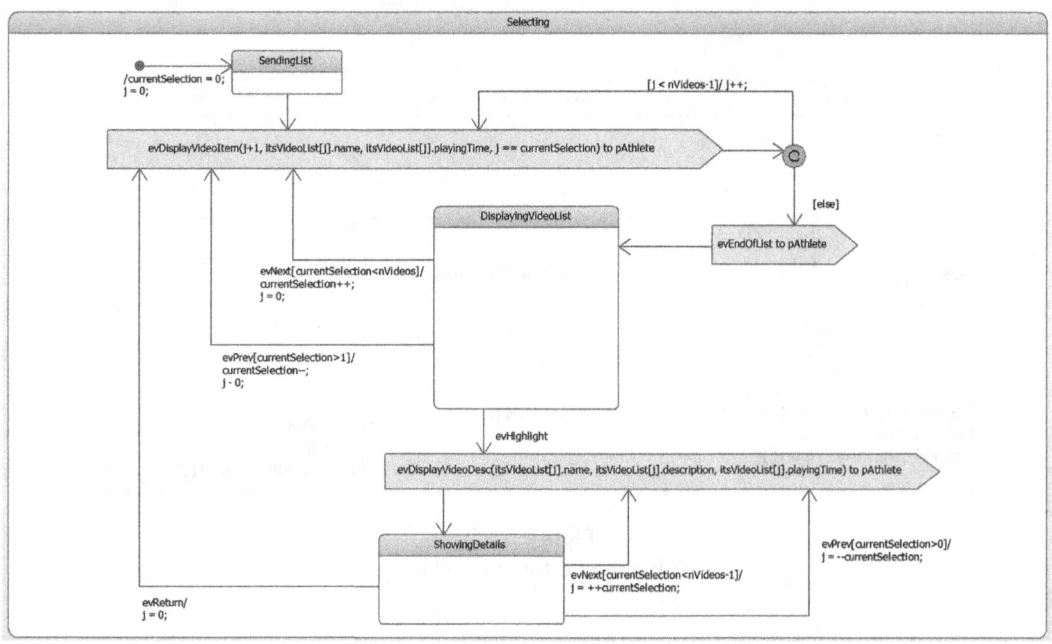

Figure 5.50
Submachine for state Selecting.

(Figure 5.50). The behavior for playing the video, including sending blocks of AV to the `Athlete` (by updating the flow property `AVSignal`) and processing commands from the `Athlete` to advance or retreat a chapter or quit. The `Playing` state submachine performs all this behavior (Figure 5.51).

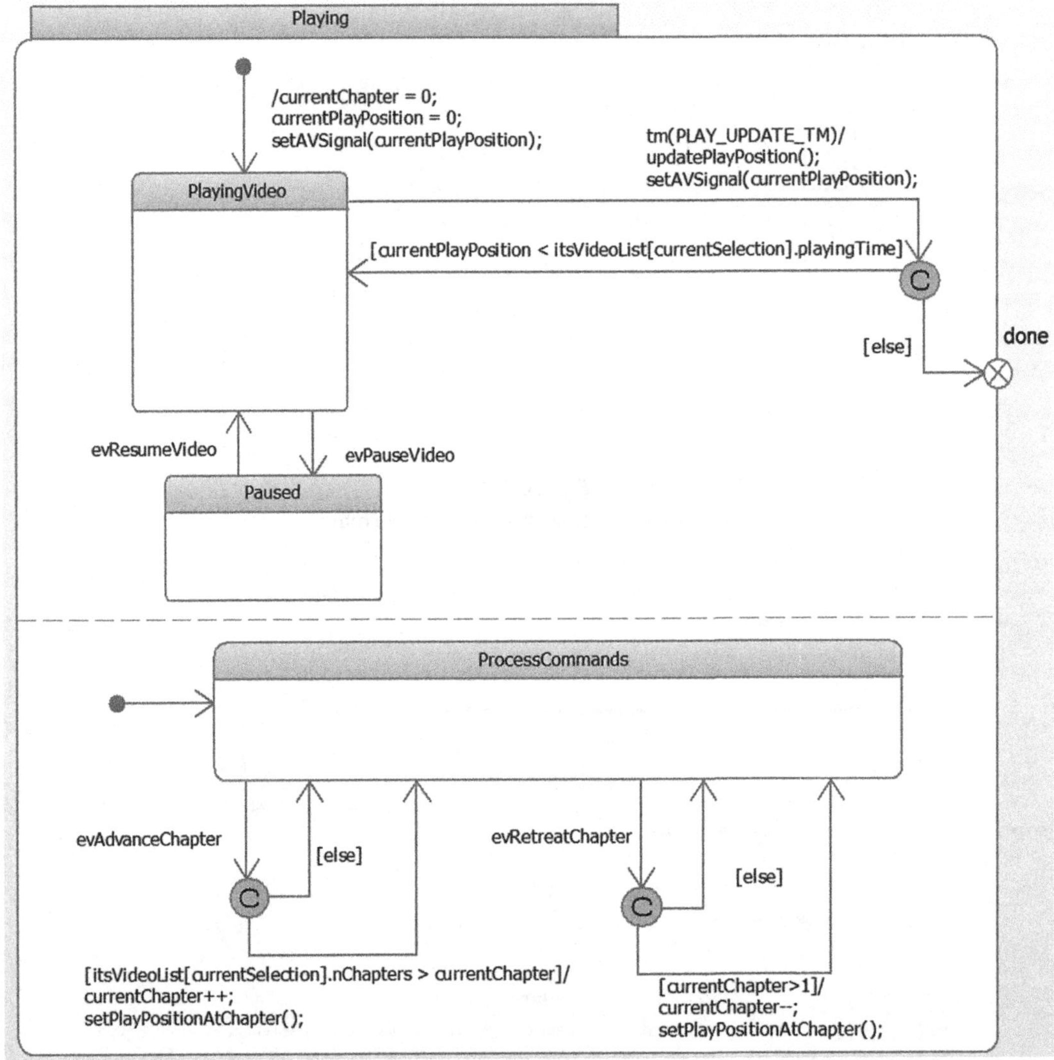

Figure 5.51
Submachine for state Playing.

Finally, the state machine for the `Athlete` actor block is shown in Figure 5.52. Creating such a state machine for the purpose of simulation support is known as "instrumenting the actor." You can see in the figure that the `Athlete` sends all the appropriate events to the use case state machine. It also receives video information which it sends to standard output (so that the person running the simulation can see it). Also note that changing the flow property `AVSignal` results in change events (`chAVSignal`) which end up invoking the `watch()` operation.

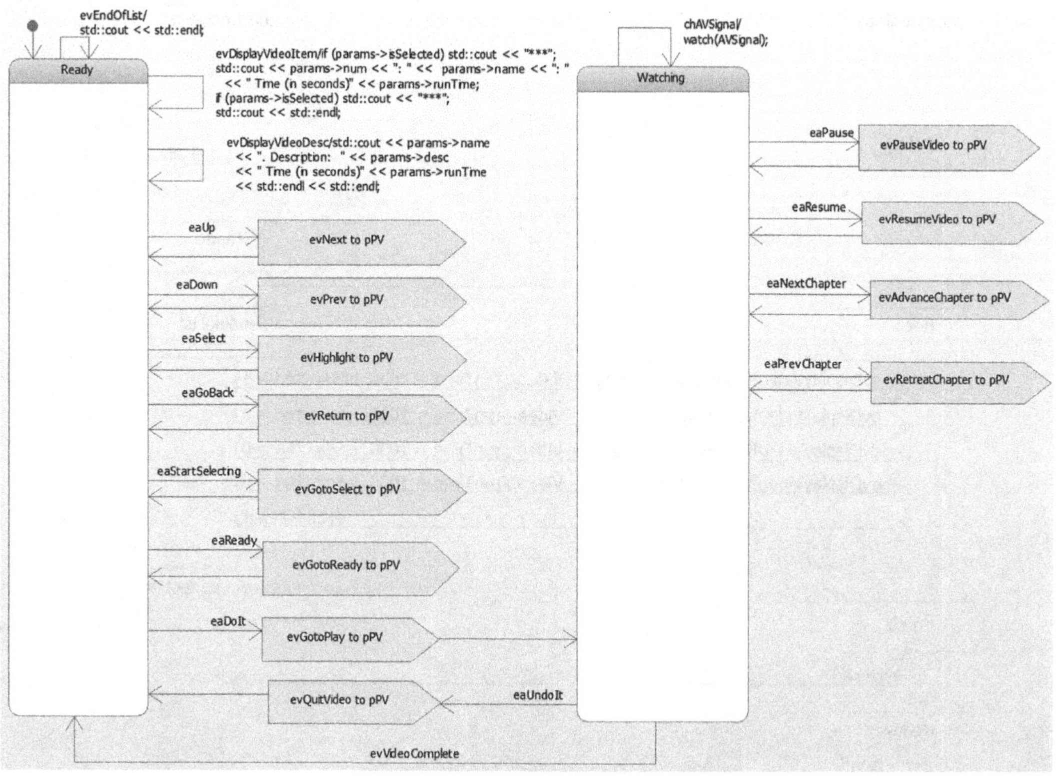

Figure 5.52
Athlete actor block state machine.

5.5.3.3 Define use case scenarios

It is perfectly reasonably to define scenarios, even at this stage, to improve your understanding of the expected system behavior and add them into the state machine. However, it is more common with this strategy to *generate* them by running the state machines and varying the input events and values. For this use case, one can imagine that a few dozen scenarios would be necessary to achieve the minimal spanning set.[9] I will leave that as an exercise for the reader. I will provide you with one scenario, broken up into two figures. Figure 5.53 shows the interaction between the `Athlete` and the `ucPlayVideo` use case block for the selection of the video. In the scenario, the `Athlete` views the list, advances the selection, and then initiates its play.

In the second part of the captured scenario, shown in Figure 5.54, the video is played. This is simulated by sending an "AV block" called `AVSignal` every so often (in this case, the timeout is set to a generous 1000 ms to keep the number of messages down). You can see

[9] Which, if you recall, means that each transition in the state machine is represented in at least one scenario.

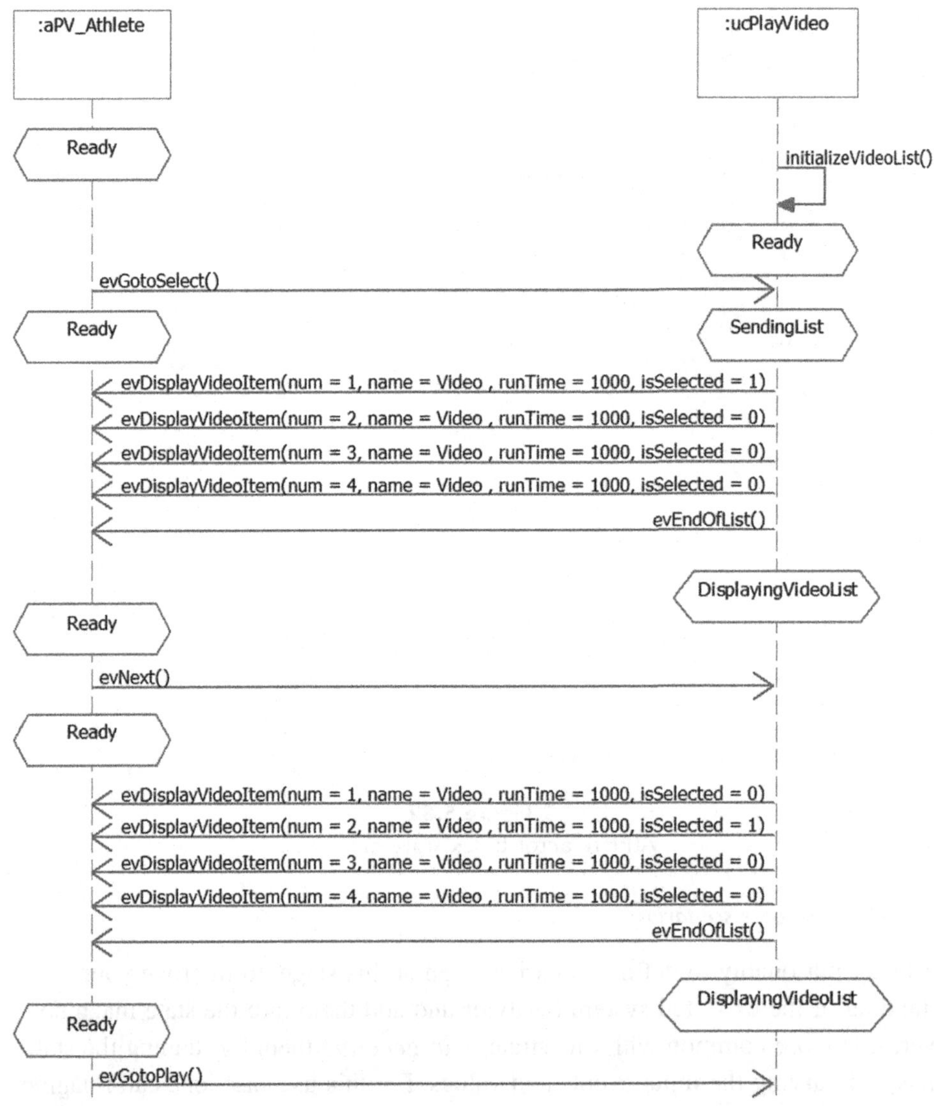

Figure 5.53
Play Video scenario part 1.

the special dashed arrow indicating a flow when the `AVsignal` is changed; this results in a `watch()` behavior on the part of the `Athlete`. Later in the scenario, the `Athlete` pauses and then resumes video play and finally quits the video at the end of their workout. *Note*: the AVSignal is modeled very simply as we are not trying to recreate video processing (that will be done in design) but to address our need to understand the requirements and the necessary interactions of the system with the actor.

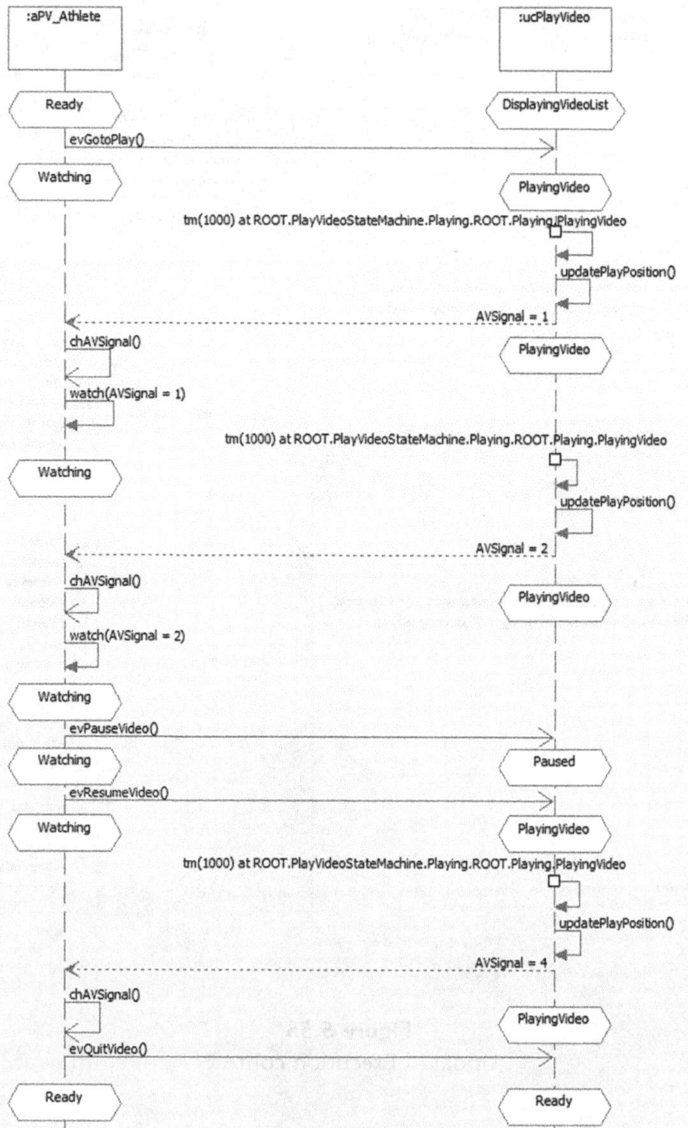

Figure 5.54
Play Video scenario part 2.

5.5.3.4 Define ports and interfaces

Having incrementally constructed and executed the state machine, the interface block `ibPlayVideo` was likewise incrementally constructed. As new events and flow properties were added to the state behavior of the `Athlete` and use case actor blocks, they were also added to the interface block to support that execution. Figure 5.55 shows the interfaces,

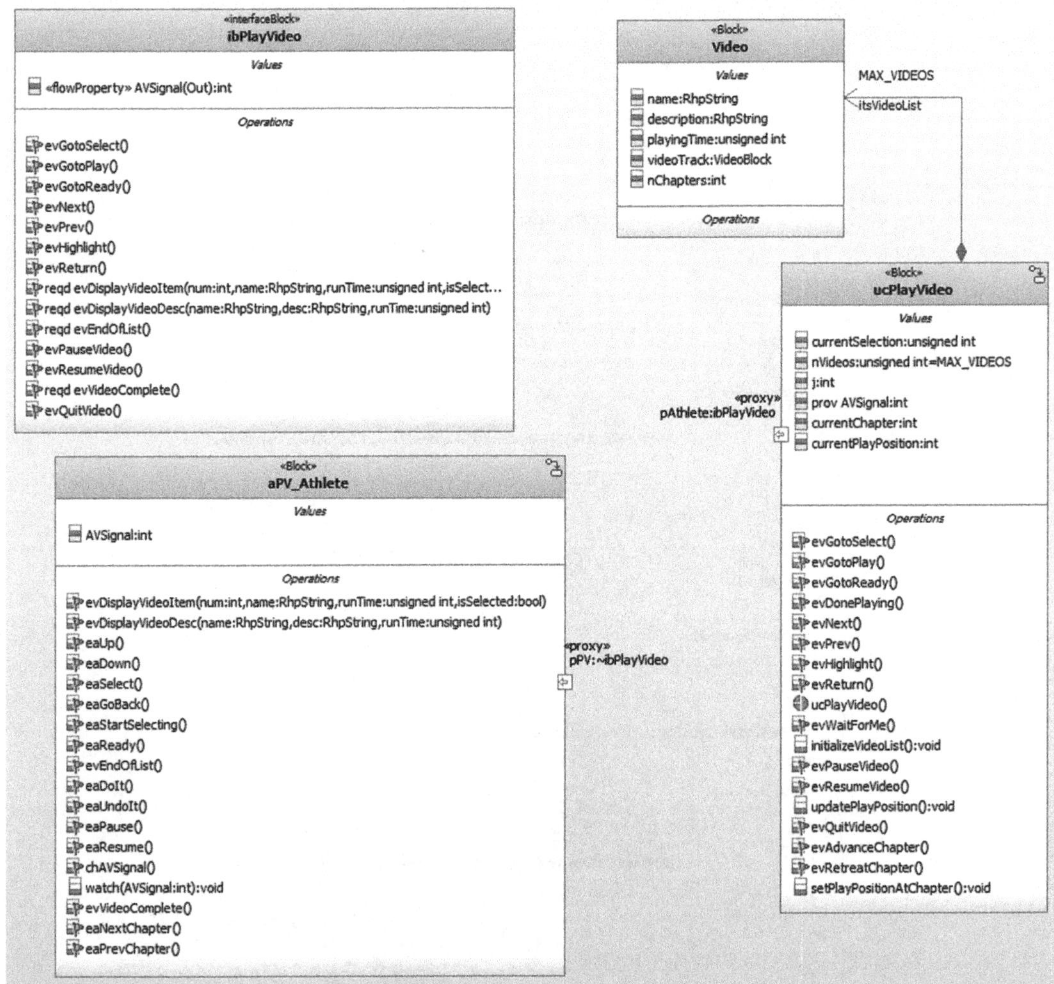

Figure 5.55
Updated Execution context.

data, and flows for the system. The interface block defines the logical interface for the system whilst running the `Play Video` use case. Note that the interface block is conjugated at the `pPV` proxy port of the `Athlete`, so events that it wants to receive must be specified as directed features with the "required" (or `reqd`) mark.

5.5.3.5 T-Wrecks state-based use case analysis

Let's apply this state-based workflow to the T-Wrecks use case `Locate` which interacts with the constellation of GPS satellites to determine system position.

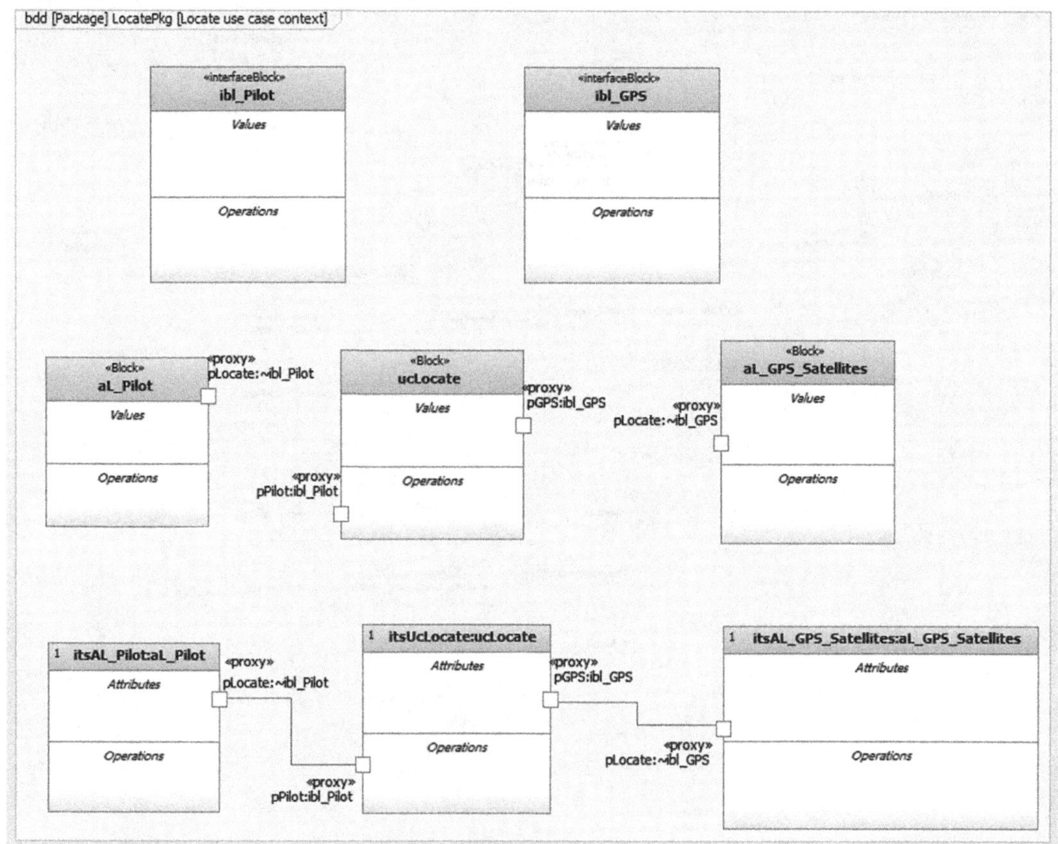

Figure 5.56
T-Wrecks Locate use case context.

Step 1: Use case execution context

Figure 5.56 is straightforward and shows the use case and actor blocks with (empty) interface blocks to define the proxy ports.

Step 2: Derive use case state behavior

Using GPS for location is algorithmically complex (which will be detailed in downstream detailed design) but is modal in nature. Figure 5.57 shows that there are several high-level states: `Disabled` is clear enough. `UnabletoLock` is the state in which the system is unable to obtain lock on enough satellites (four are required) to derive the system location. Within the `Enabled` state there are three nested AND-states: `GettingSatelliteData` receives the 50-bps 1500-bit GPS satellite message that includes satellite time information, ephemeris data[10]

[10] Satellite orbit information.

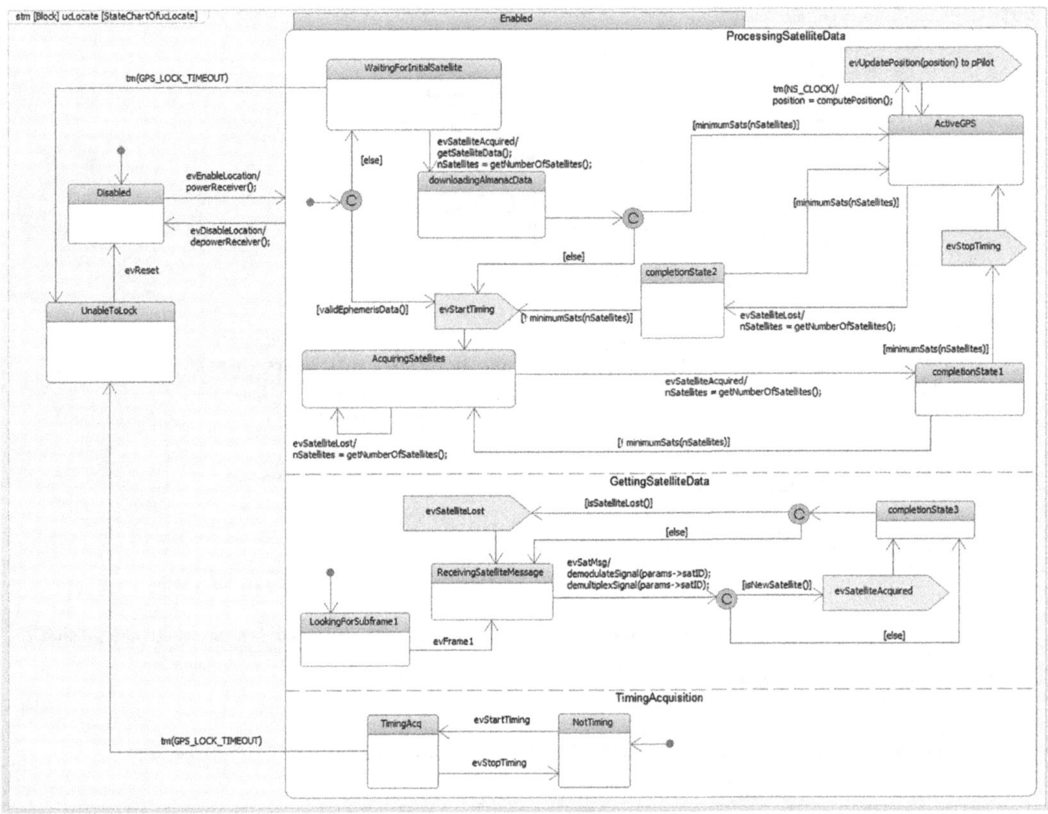

Figure 5.57
Locate use case state machine.

and the satellite almanac.[11] It demodulates and demultiplexes the signal.[12] From there, it can determine whether a new satellite is detected or an old satellite is lost.

The `ProcessingSatelliteData` AND-state keeps track of whether we have enough satellites to determine position and actually solves the equations (in `computePosition()`) to get the system position and sends it to the `Pilot`.

The lower-most AND-state is used to time the acquisition of satellites and will time out if too few satellites are detected within the lock timeout period.

Simulation note: This is not about simulated actual GPS messages but is about specifying the interfaces. The states in the state machine—such as `AcquiringSatellites`—are essential

[11] Orbit and status information of the other GPS satellites.

[12] The GPS satellites all transmit on the same frequency, so their frames must be extracted from the CDMA message.

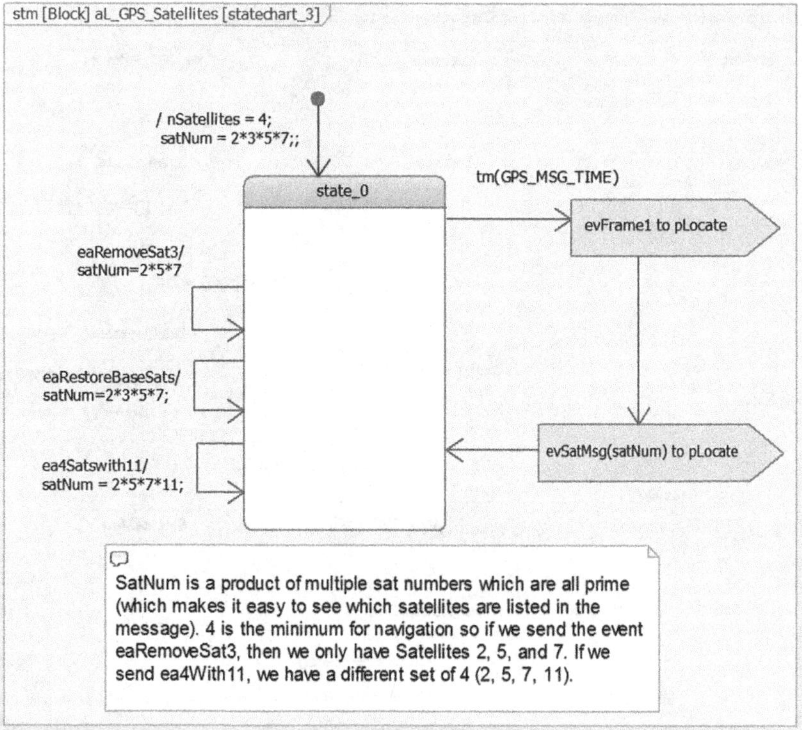

Figure 5.58
aL_GPS_Satellites state machine.

for any possible solution and so should be a part of the requirements simulation. To achieve this, I modeled the GPS message as a simple product of prime numbers (2, 3, 5, 7, 11, and so on). I can determine whether a satellite is detected by simply checking if that satellite number factors within the solution by checking whether the modulus of the message value by the satellite number is zero (that is, whether the passed data evenly divide the message value). This allows me to simulate adding new and losing satellites by passing different products. For the actual data message, I would refer to the GPS message specification. The `aL_GPS_Satellites` actor block state machine to support the simulation is shown in Figure 5.58.

Step 3: Create scenarios

Figure 5.57 is a fairly complex state machine with many different possible scenarios. I've shown one here—generated from running the state machine—divided across three figures (Figures 5.59–5.61). In this scenario, redundant messages have been removed to shorten the sequence to be put into the book.

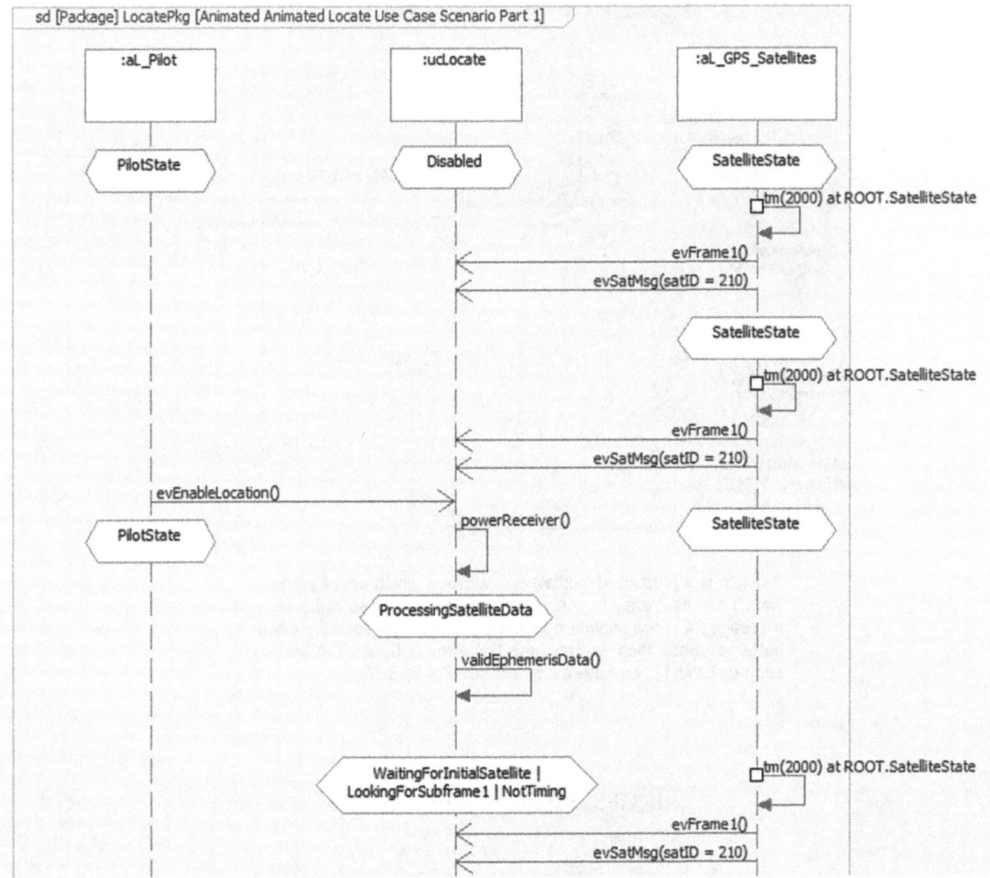

Figure 5.59
Locate use case scenario part 1.

Figure 5.59 shows the first part of the scenario. We see the Frame 1 and GPS message arriving from the `Satellite`[13] and the `Pilot` enabling the location services.

Part 2 of the scenario (Figure 5.60) shows the processing of the message that culminates with the display of position to the `Pilot`.

Part 3 (Figure 5.61) shows the computational update on position (done on the `NS_GPS` clock) to the `Pilot` and the `Pilot` disabling the location service.

As a result of this analysis, we identify additional requirements for location, as shown in Figure 5.62.

13 Yes, I know it's all one message but I didn't want to get bogged down in parsing the message which requires 750 seconds (12 and ½ minutes) to fully receive.

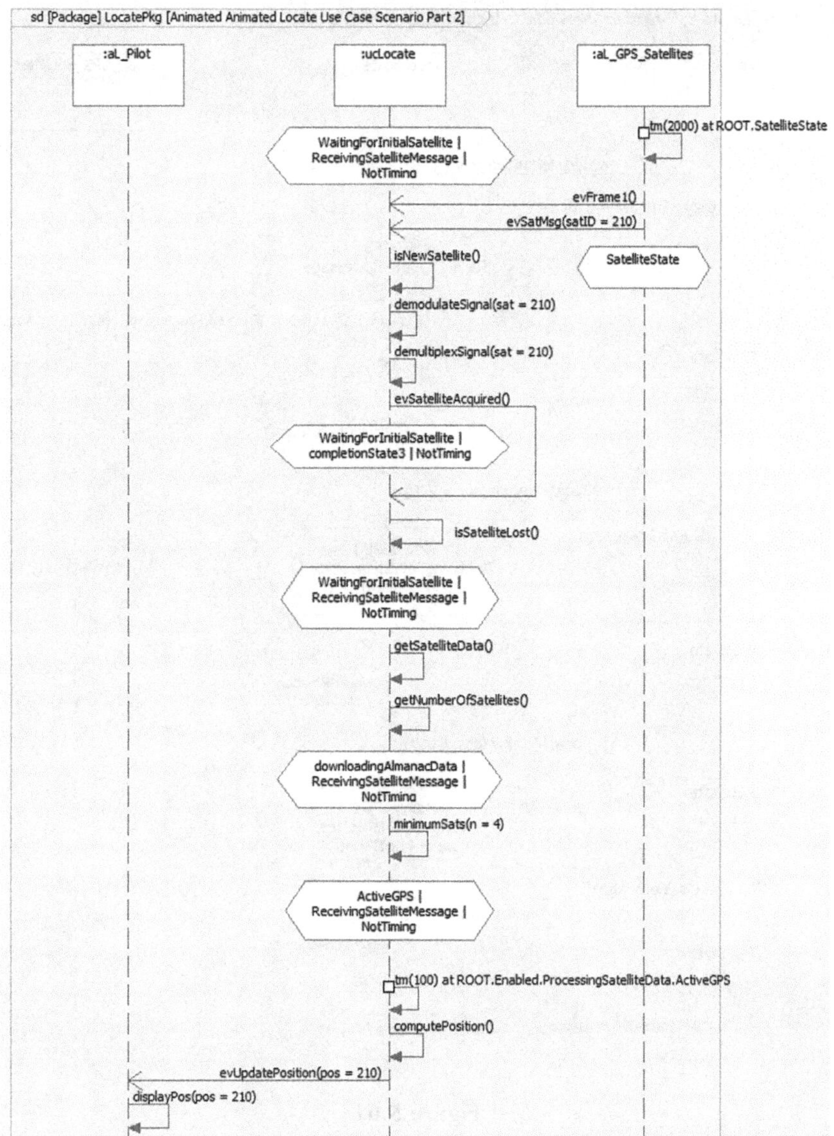

Figure 5.60
Locate use case scenario part 2.

Step 4: Define ports and interfaces

Along with building up and executing the state machine, we identify the logical interfaces between the system and the `Pilot` and GPS satellites to support the location services (Figure 5.63).

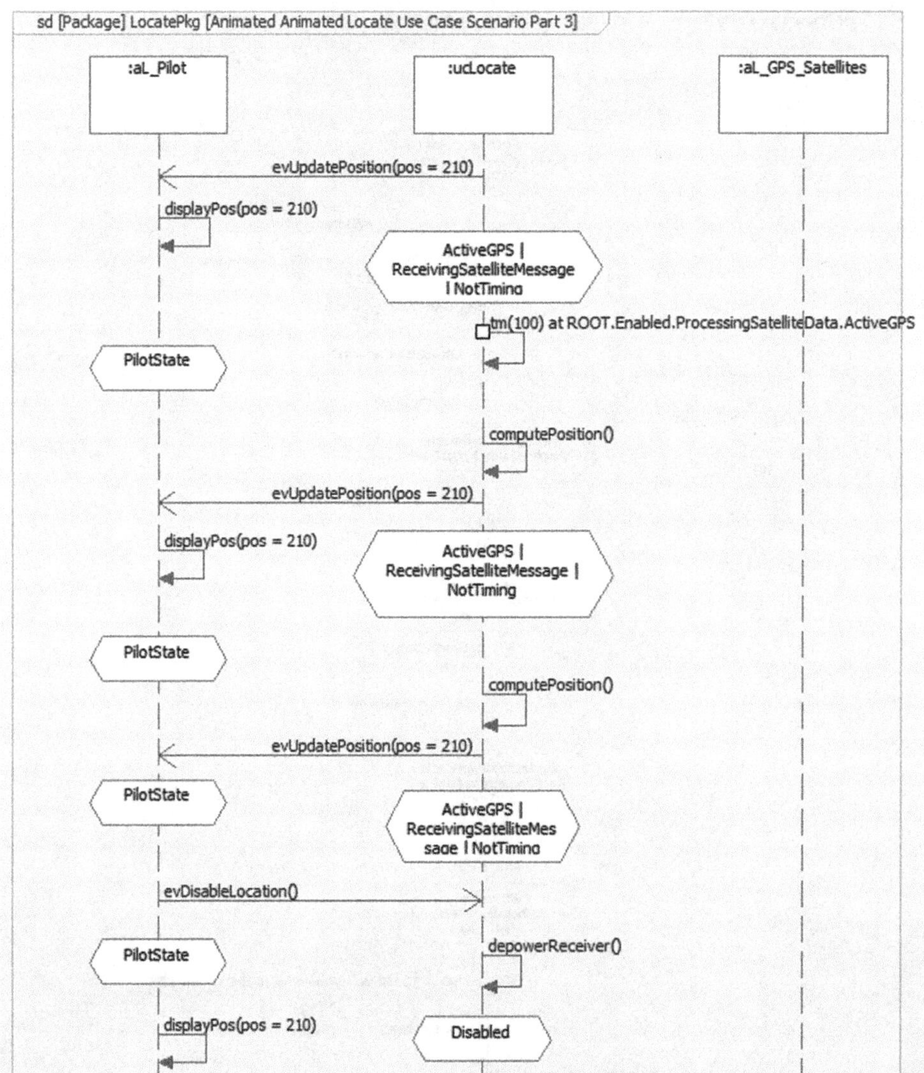

Figure 5.61
Locate use case scenario part 3.

Step 5: Verify and validate functional requirements

The fact that the state machine is executable allows us to explore the interaction of the requirements and do "what if" analysis for various sequences. We can save these execution sequences as sequence diagrams and show them to the stakeholders to ensure that they agree with the behavior.

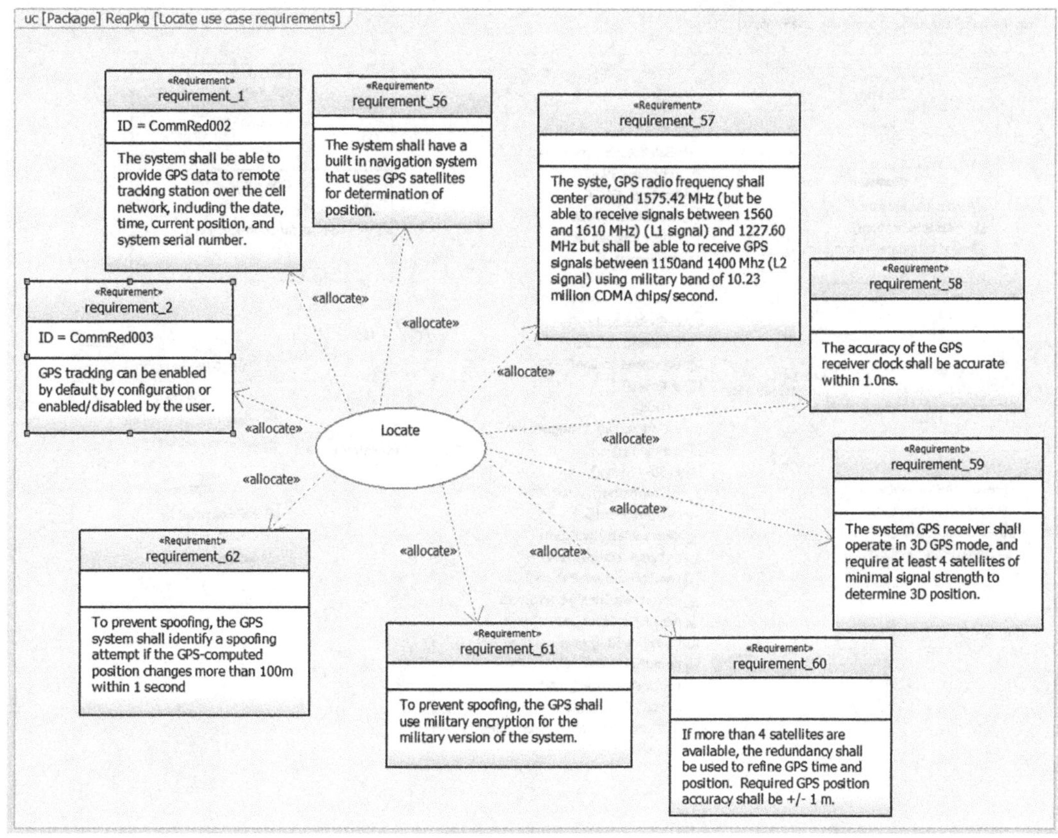

Figure 5.62
Locate use case updated requirements.

5.6 Create/Update Logical Data Schema

It is crucial for system engineers to understand the essential nature and properties of flows—both real and informational—of the system. This is called the *logical data schema* even though its use extends well beyond the informational content per se. In simple command systems, this may be relatively obvious and uninteresting, but for flow- and data-rich systems, this view is imperative.

The flows and data properties that require deep understanding depend, naturally enough, on how those flows are used by the system and the actors. Generally, though, data and flows should be characterized with

- Volume/amount/mass
- Flow rates/frequency

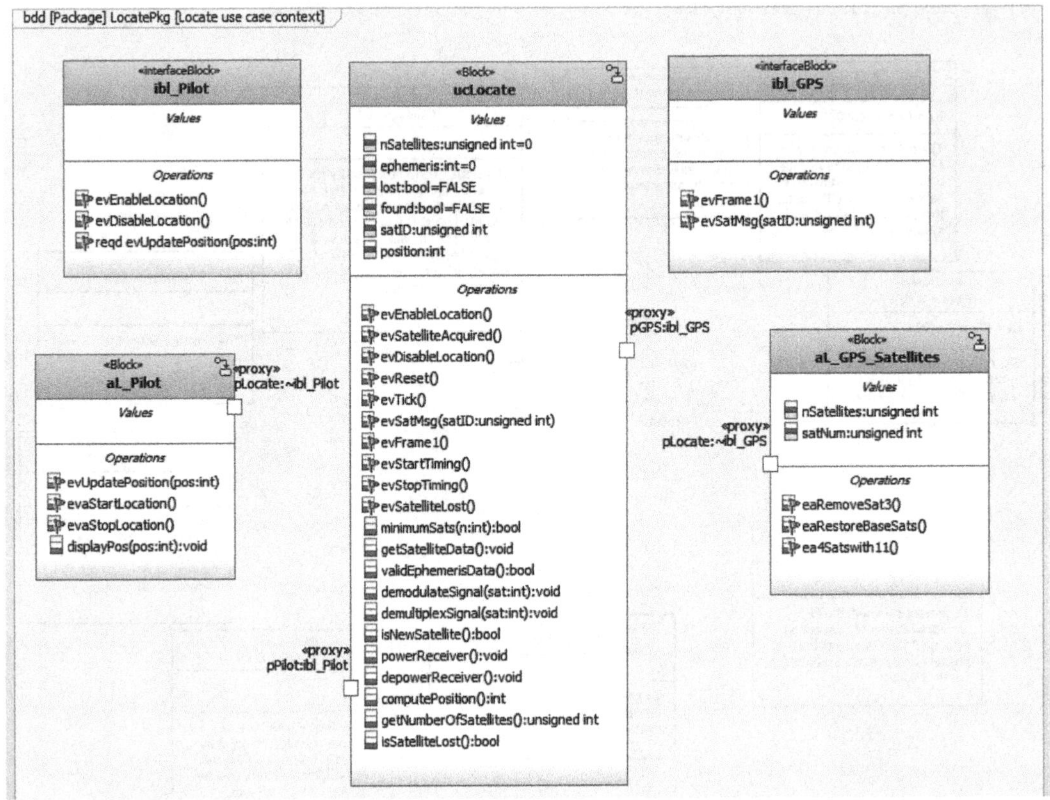

Figure 5.63
Interfaces for Locate use case.

- Bandwidth/throughput
- Extent—valid ranges of values
- Fidelity—accuracy required
- Error tolerance
- Availability.

As system engineers, we generally *do not* care about bit-representation of information. This is defined in the *physical interface* but we do care about the logical properties of the data and flows. For example, we may characterize a data element as an integer scalar with valid ranges between 0 and 12,000, a fidelity of ± 5 and an accuracy of 1, but we don't care if its stored as doubles, integers, unsigned longs, or even as analog voltages. Figure 5.64 shows an example of a logical data schema for aircraft data.[14] Note that all

[14] Note that some of the values are typed with C++ types such as double and long but these are because the tools require all data to be typed. The selected types are non-normative in this case.

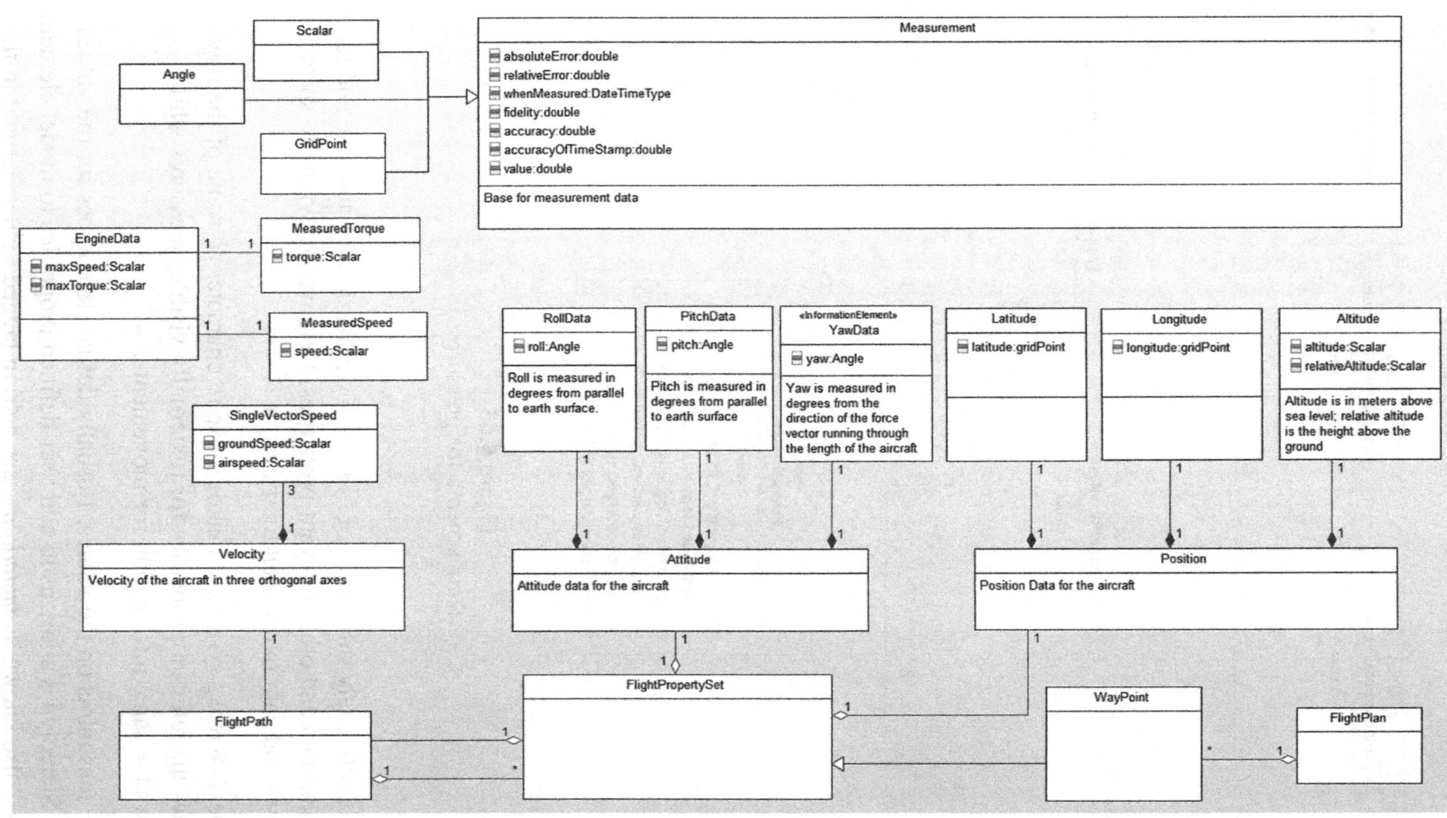

Figure 5.64
Example Logical Data Schema for Aircraft nav data.

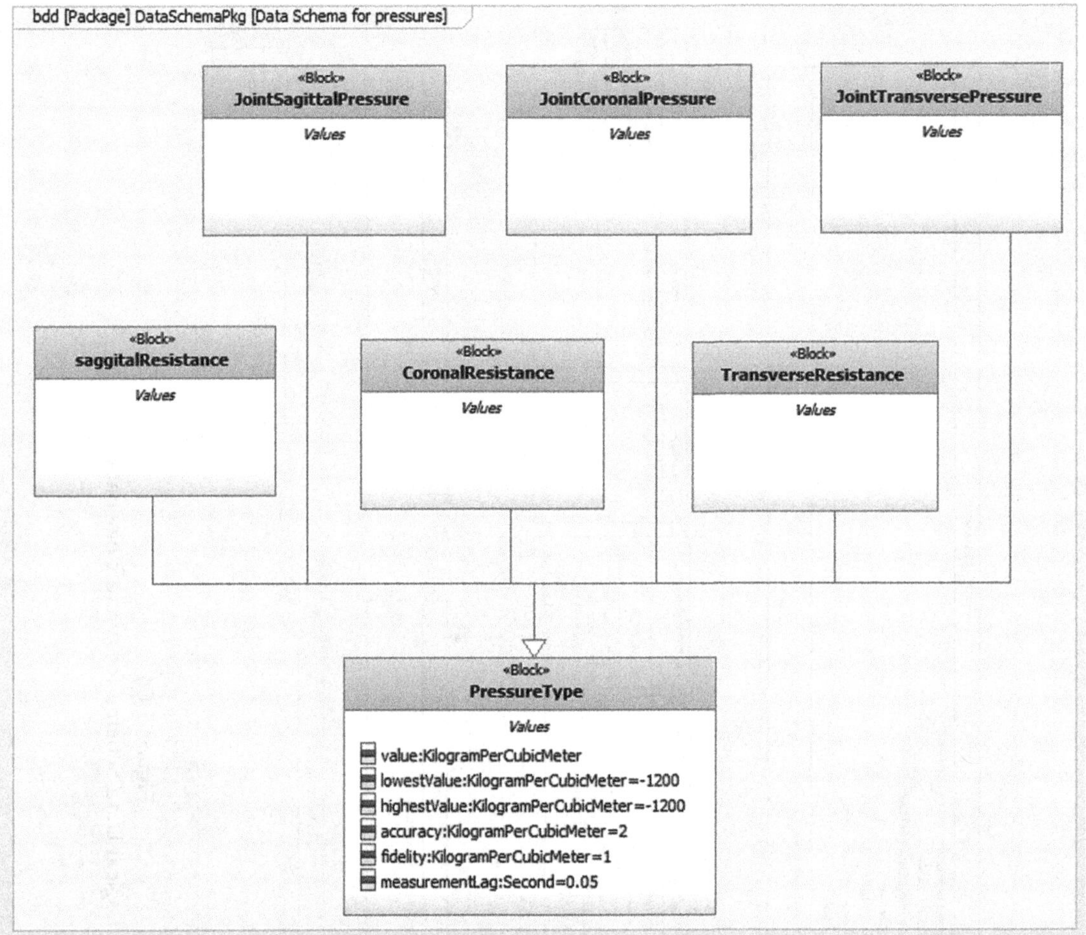

Figure 5.65
Data schema for pressures.

measurements are ultimately subclasses of `Measurement`, that defines absolute and relative error and data measured and other relevant properties. Here we are typing to specify the nature of the flows and data rather than their design.

In the case of the T-Wrecks system, it makes sense to characterize some of the flows. Figure 5.65 shows the relevant properties for (externally visible) pressures while Figure 5.66 shows the same information for movements.

To represent the constraints on the values, I usually define stereotypes for the values to hold the information. Stereotypes allow us to add user-defined properties to model elements. These properties—also known as *metadata*—are held in tagged values defined in the

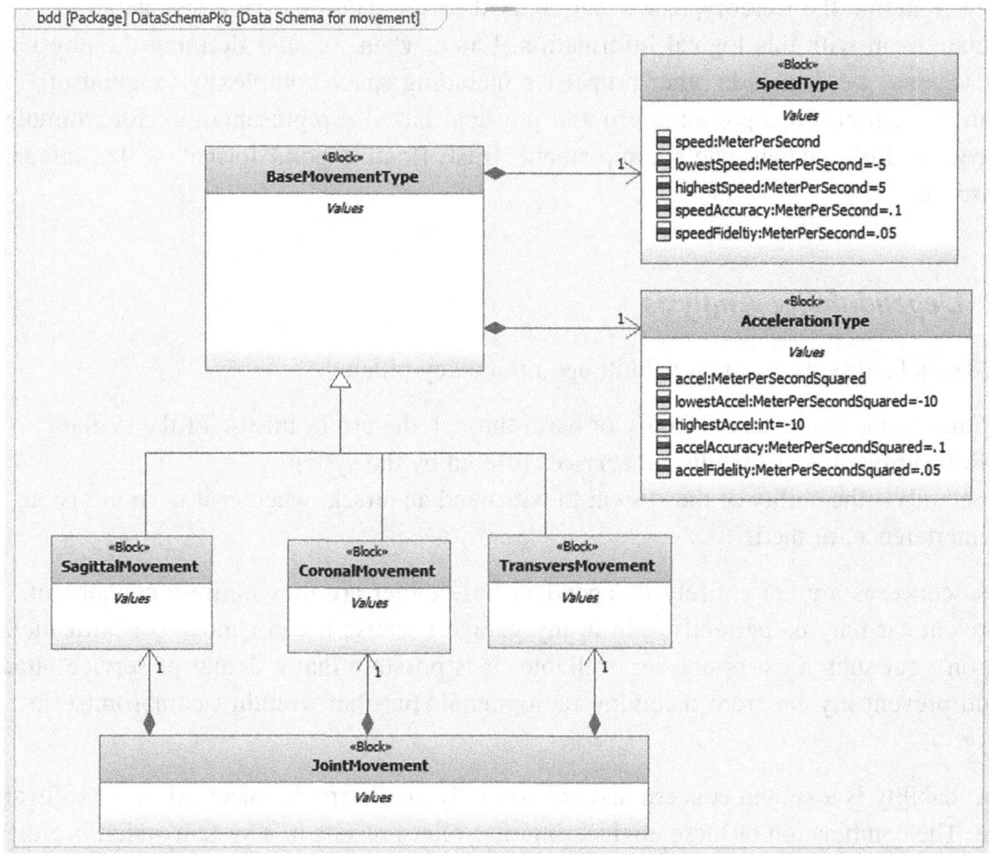

Figure 5.66
Data schema for movements.

stereotype. In the case of the data schema, I want to add various properties such as those in the bulleted list above. A typical stereotype for a numeric value would add tags such as

- Lower range limit
- Upper range limit
- Accuracy
- Update rate.

In SysML, it is common to have the units as a part of the data typing itself; if units are not so used (and the numeric value is not unitless), then units should be added as a tagged value as well. After all, a range of 1 to 100 kilometers is not the same as a range of 1 to 100 miles.[15]

[15] This confusion may lead to the loss of your $125 million Mars orbiter (http://www.cnn.com/TECH/space/9909/30/mars.metric/).

Once we define the stereotype, we can apply it to the data or flow elements and populate them with this logical information. Later, when we start defining the physical data schema, we'll include other properties including space complexity (amount of resource required for representation) and physical bit-wise representation (for example, big endian, little endian, one's complement, IEEE floating point format, scaled integer, and so on).

5.7 Dependability Analysis

The dependability of a system is built upon three key pillars:

- Safety—the avoidance of injury or harm through the use or misuse of the system
- Reliability—the availability of services offered by the system
- Security—the ability of the system to withstand an attack, whether it is an intrusion, interference, or theft.

These concerns are not entirely independent but neither are they entirely concordant. A broken car may be perfectly safe in my garage because it can't move (or burn fuel, or turn on), but such a car is not very reliable. It is possible that a denial of service attack would prevent my car from receiving radio signals but that wouldn't compromise its safety.

Dependability is a system concern and not specially an electronic, mechanical, or software issue. The combination of these engineering disciplines results in a system which is either adequately dependable or not. Some people think that dependability is solely a concern during the initial specification of requirements, but that is naïve. Even when the requirements properly specify the safety, reliability, and security needs, technical decisions that follow the requirements specification can profoundly influence the system's dependability.

Stakeholder requirements for an automobile may address concerns about passenger capacity, maximum speed, braking distance, and so on. If, in design, we opt for a diesel engine, then we introduce safety concerns of flammable fuel. If we instead decide on an electric engine, then we introduce safety issues about electrocution and hazardous chemicals. If we select mechanical locks, then we have issues about how mechanical locks can be defeated; electronic-only locks have issues about being hacked. As we make design decisions, we typically must add additional dependability requirements to ensure that we adequately address the introduced concerns. These new requirements result in control measures that enable our system to meet its dependability needs. In short, as we make technical decisions, dependability must be reassessed and new requirements added to ensure the system remains safe, reliable, and secure.

Different approaches are used to model the different aspects of dependability. Safety is most often addressed with Fault Tree Analysis diagrams and Hazard Analysis; reliability with Fault Means and Effect Analysis (FMEA); and security with threat analysis. We will discuss each independently.

5.7.1 Safety Analysis

A safe system is one that does not incur too much risk of loss, either to persons or equipment. A *hazard* is an undesirable event or condition that can occur during system operation. *Risk* is a quantitative measure of how dangerous a system is and is usually specified as:

$$Risk = Hazard_{severity} {}^{*} Hazard_{likelihood}$$

The failure of a jet engine is unlikely, but the consequences can be very high. Overall, the risk of flying in a plane is tolerable because even though it is unlikely that you would survive a crash from 30,000 feet, such an incident is extremely unlikely. At the other end of the spectrum, there are events that are common, but are of lesser concern. A battery-operated radio has a hazard of electric shock but the risk is acceptable because even though the likelihood of the hazard manifestation is relatively high, its severity is low [1].

Assessing the safety is commonly done with safety analysis (such as Fault Tree Analysis (FTA)) [2]. FTA uses logical operators to connect conditions (some of which may be undesirable) with events, such as failures. The notational elements of the FTA[16] are shown in Figure 5.67.

Logical operators[17] combine events and conditions with *logic flows* to form either intermediate *resulting conditions* or *hazards*. The combinations of events and conditions that result in safety concerns are called *cut sets*. The logical flows allow us to reason about where we need to add safety control measures to either decrease the likelihood of a hazard or decrease its severity.

Figure 5.68 shows a simple example of an FTA. An AND operator combines the required condition `Mixer is Operating` with the `Power Loss` hazardous event; when both are `TRUE`, the resulting condition is `Pumping Stops`. Since this is a medical gas mixer, if the pumping stops, this results in the hazard `Hypoxia`. However, there are two other conditions that can result in `Hypoxia` as well (hence the use of the OR operator; the output of OR is `TRUE` if any of its inputs are `TRUE`, while the output of the AND operator is true only if all its inputs are TRUE). If we run out of breathing gas (fault `Gas Supply Exhausted`), this also results in `Hypoxia`. Additionally,

16 The FTA diagrams in this book are snapshots of my FTA Profile for UML/SysML. Other tools may use slightly different notations.

17 The transfer operator is a special operator used to connect across diagram boundaries.

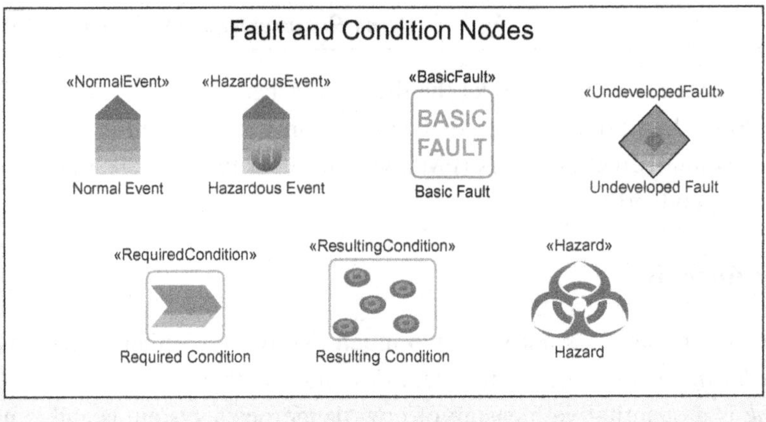

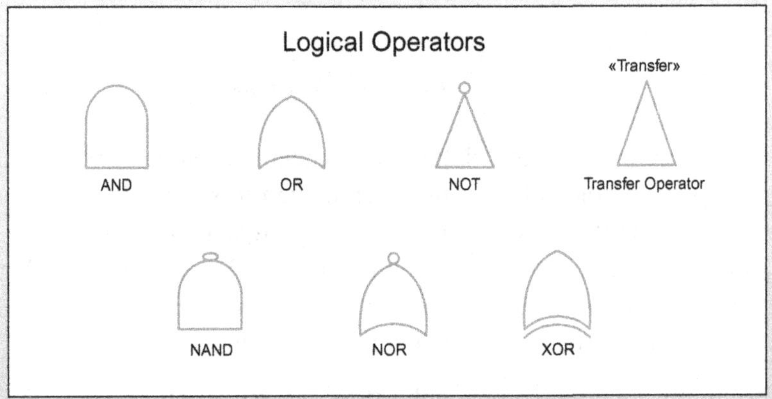

Figure 5.67
FTA notational elements.

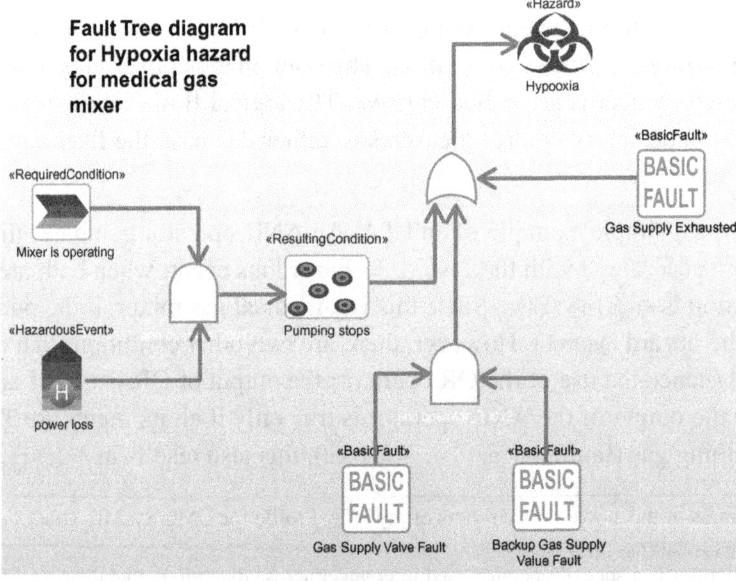

Figure 5.68
Example FTA.

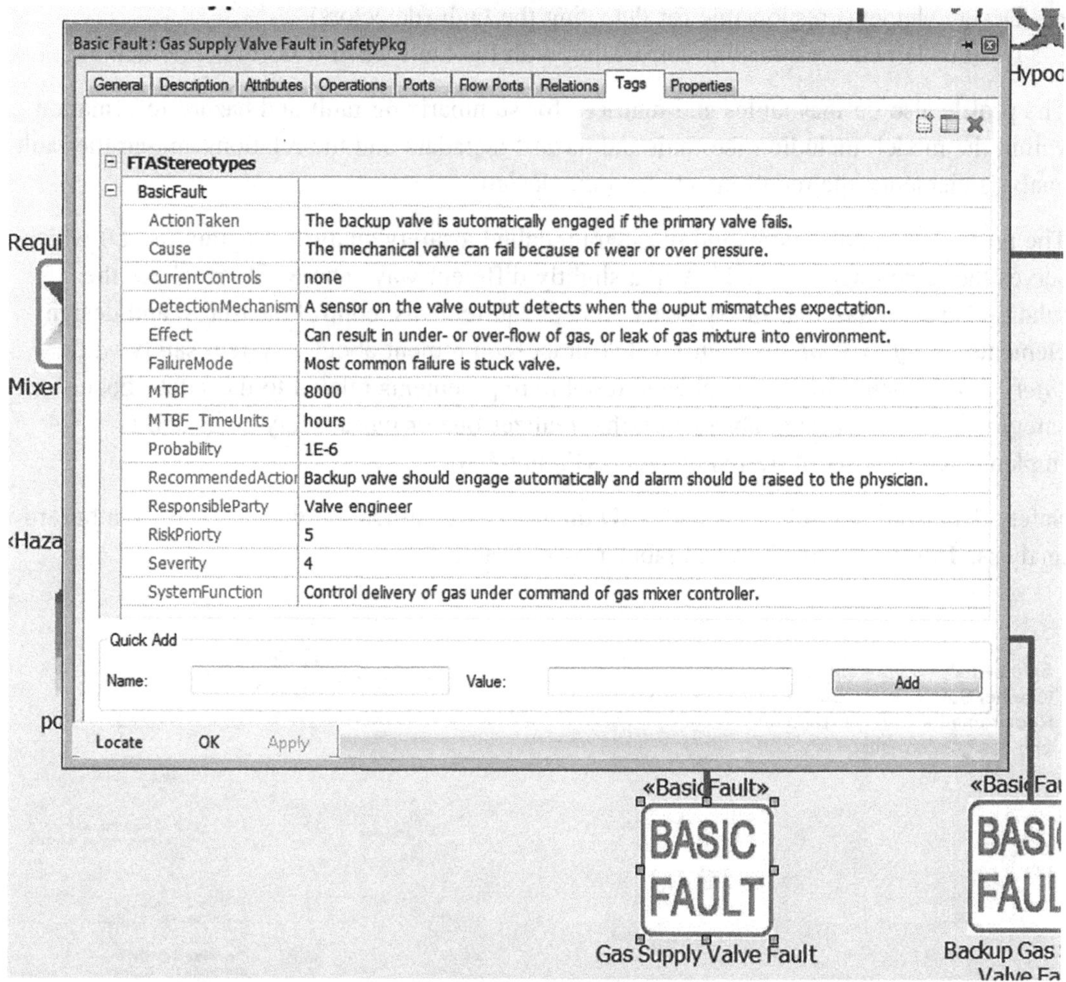

Figure 5.69
Safety relevant metadata.

if the gas supply valve and its backup valve both fail, this will result in `Hypoxia`. The backup valve is an example of a safety control measure because it decreases the likelihood of `Hypoxia` by requiring two independent faults to occur before the hazard can manifest.

The event and condition nodes of the FTA diagram are annotated with safety metadata. In the FTA profile, these are stored as *tags* defined by the stereotype «`BasicFault`» (see Figure 5.69). This same information is used to populate the FMEA for reliability analysis as well.

The profile extends the content of the standard FTA to permit explicit links to requirements and design elements, including links to:

- Requirements dealing with the fault, condition, or event
- Design elements that could cause the fault (manifestors)

- Design elements responsible for detecting the fault (detectors)
- Design elements responsible for dealing with the fault when it occurs (extenuators).

The profile also defines tables and matrices for summarizing fault and hazard information within the model, including the fault and hazard metadata and the relations among the fault analysis elements, the requirements, and the design.

The profile also adds a new kind of diagram called a safety analysis diagram (SAD) which serves the same intent as the FTA in a slightly different way. The SAD visualizes the relation between hazards, safety goals, safety requirements, control measures, and design elements. A *safety goal* is a high-level abstract requirement about a system safety while *safety requirements* are more concrete testable requirements related to the safety goal. A safety measure is a design abstraction that realizes one or more safety goals and is implemented by a set of design elements (Figure 5.70).

Safety data from multiple FTA and SAD diagrams are gathered together to create a hazard analysis. This is usually shown in tabular form (Table 5.1).

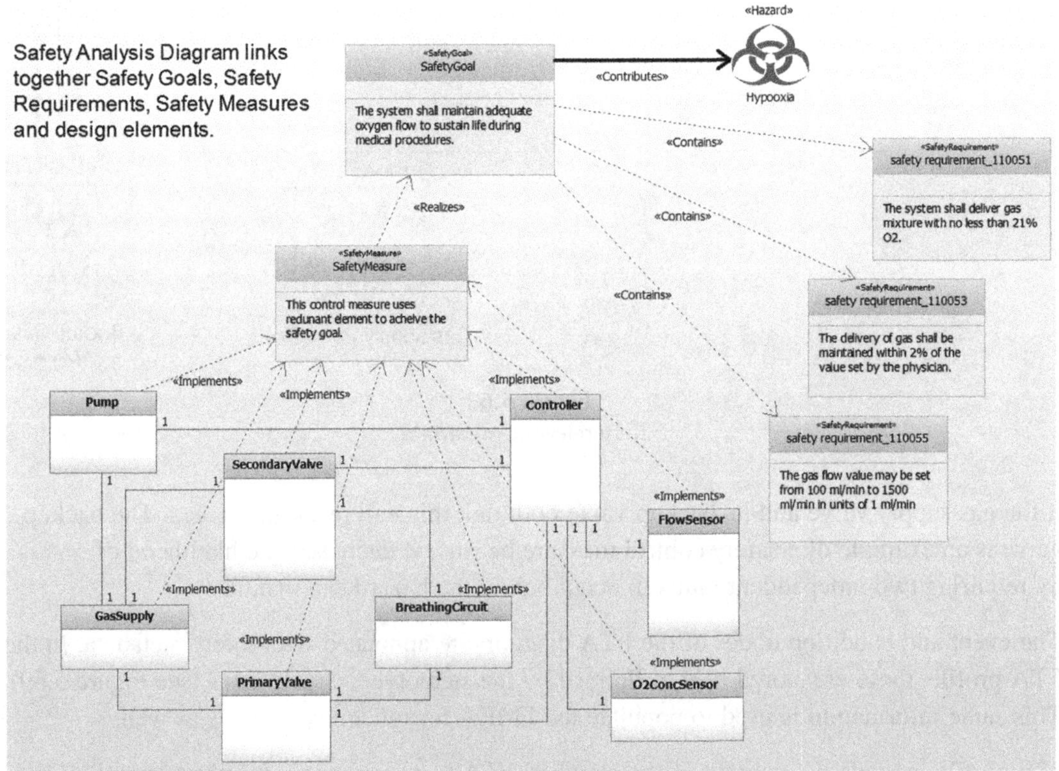

Figure 5.70
Safety analysis diagram.

Table 5.1: Hazard analysis (partial).

Hazard	Fault or Cause	Severity	Likelihood	Risk	Time Units	Tolerance Time	Detection Time	Control Measure	Action Time	Exposure Time	Safe?
Collision due to failure to brake	Brake pedal stuck	8	3	0.24	Ms	500	0	Recommended inspection of brake pedal assembly on regular maintenance; dashboard reminder of due maintenance	0	0	Y
	Brake pedal sensor fault	8	4	0.32	Ms	500	200	Periodic query of sensor by brake control unit; raise dashboard alarm on fault detect	100	300	Y
	Wheel brake actuator fault	8	3	0.24	Ms	500	200	Periodic query of actuator by brake control unit; raise dashboard alarm on fault detect	100	300	Y
	Worn braking surface	8	7	0.56	Ms	500	150	ABS braking flutters the brake actuation to maintain vehicle stability	50	200	Y
	Internal communication fault resulting in failure to brake	8	4	0.32	ms	500	10	Use of message CRC and ACK response to ensure reliable message delivery	30	40	Y
	Braking force computation fault	8	2	0.16	Ms	500	200	Braking force is computed by two dissimilar methods and compared	50	250	Y
	Differential wheel slippage due to road conditions	8	9	0.72	Ms	500	150	ABS braking flutters the brake actuation to maintain vehicle stability	50	200	Y
	Collision (any cause)	8	–	–	–	–	20	Air bags to deploy within 50 ms of detected collision	30	50	Y

(*Continued*)

Table 5.1: (Continued)

Hazard	Fault or Cause	Severity	Likelihood	Risk	Time Units	Tolerance Time	Detection Time	Control Measure	Action Time	Exposure Time	Safe?
Collision due to steering fault	Steering mechanism mechanical fault	7	2	0.14	ms	300	0	Recommended inspection of steering assembly on regular maintenance; dashboard	0	0	Y
	Drive-by-wire comm fault	7	4	0.28	ms	300	10	Use of message CRC and ACK response to ensure reliable message delivery	30	40	Y
	Wheel turn fault	7	2	0.14	ms	200	50	Wheel position sensor reports wheel orientation; engine output automatically decreased and braking engaged	50	100	Y
	Turn control gain fault results in lack of steering control	7	2	0.14	ms	200	50	Wheel position sensor reports wheel orientation; engine output automatically decreased and braking engaged	50	100	Y

During stakeholder requirements specification, we can only address intrinsic faults that arise due to the nature of the system we are developing but not faults due to its design. For example, the whole point of a plane is to fly, so there are intrinsic safety concerns about avoiding crashes, midair collisions, attitude (roll, pitch, and yaw) management, and the maintenance of passenger environmental conditions (air pressure and temperature). Once we add technical solutions for engines, attitude sensors, communication infrastructure, and the like, additional safety concerns will be raised.

5.7.1.1 Reliability analysis

As mentioned earlier, reliability refers to the availability of system services. Reliability analysis—most often captured in a FMEA—identifies the requirements for availability of system services and then examines how the availability of services from internal components propagates through the system to achieve system-level reliability. This results in reliability specifications at the component level. In general, reliability is improved through a combination of two design approaches. First, individual components may be engineering to be individually reliable. This is sometimes accomplished by choosing more robust materials, algorithms, and methods, even if they are more expensive. The other primary approach to improve reliability is by introducing component redundancy so that if a component fails there are other components ready to deliver the required component services. It is important to begin to consider reliability during requirements capture because these requirements will drive later development technology, materials, and approaches.

The most common way to represent reliability metadata is in a FMEA.[18] Key to the concept of reliability are the probability or failure, the availability of services, and the time between failures (which are all correlated). This information can be represented as quantitative (for example, a component might have a failure probability of 0.05% in the first 2 years) or qualitative ("relatively likely"). While quantitative values give the appearance of higher fidelity, they are only as good as their source information. The metadata are often shown with and without the mitigation, so the effects of the design change are apparent.

FMEAs are most commonly represented as tables.

Steps to creating a FMEA

- Identify the key services under consideration of the reliability analysis. These will form the sections of the FMEA.
    1. For each service, identify the failure mode (externally visible or detectable condition) that could prevent the successful delivery of the service.

[18] A FMEA, per se, does not have any indication as to the severity of a failure and so cannot be used in safety analysis. However, a Failure Mode Effects and Criticality Analysis (FMECA) adds this information and so is relevant. Modern usage of the term FMEA often is intended to refer to a FMECA.

a. For each failure mode, identify the visible effects of the failure.
b. Identify the internal faults that could result in the failure mode. These form the rows in the table.
c. Fill out the information related to each internal fault.
   - Identify the mission phase, if relevant
   - Identify the likelihood of this failure. This is often a normalized value between 1 (impossible) and 10 (certain)
   - (FMECA) Identify the worst-case severity of the failure. This is often a normalized value from 1 (no effect) to 10 (catastrophe)
   - Determine the detectability of the fault. This is often a normalized value between 1 (certain to be detected with current measures in place) and 10 (undetectable)
   - Compute the risk priority number (RPN = likelihood × severity × detectability). This value is used to prioritize reliability engineering work
   - Identify existing (if any) control measures to be used to reduce the likelihood (or severity)
   - Identify recommendations (if any) to improve reliability with respect to this fault
   - Identify the responsible party or engineering role
   - Record actual actions performed with regard to mitigation of this fault
   - Identify resulting severity, likelihood, and risk *after* the control actions are implemented.

The actions taken include (but are not limited to) design actions, such as adding redundancy to make the system failure less likely or less severe or by making the individual components more robust. For example, the FMEA in Table 5.2 adds lubrication in a sealed piston to the braking pedal to make the pedal less like to jam, but also adds to additional pedal position sensors to provide redundancy in the event of a sensor failure.

5.7.1.2 Security analysis

The third tier of dependability is *security*. Security in the context of systems is about the prevention, detection, and response to unintended behavior caused by outside influences. Such unintended behavior includes theft (of information or of physical things), causation, prevention, or modification of system behavior, or interruption in the delivery of system services.

As more systems are connected, the risk of compromise increases exponentially because of the ability to remotely penetrate the system. In times past, to hack into a nuclear power plant required the perpetrator to be on the premises with a crowbar. However, now it is

Table 5.2: Example FMEA for automotive braking system.

Failure Means and Effect Analysis														
				Pre-action								Post-action		
Service/Function	Failure Mode	Faults	Failure Effects	Likelihood (1 = impossible, 10 = certain)	Severity (1 = no effect, 10 = catastrophe)	Detectability (1 = certain, 10 = no detection)	RPN (=sev * likely * detect)	Existing Control Measures	Recommendations	Responsible	Actions	Likelihood	Severity	RPN
Braking	Pedal nonresponsive	Pedal stuck	Pedal doesn't move; No braking action occurs	3	9	10	270	none	Make pedal assembly self lubricating	Joe	Added sealed piston with lubrication	2	9	180
		Pedal position sensor fails	Pedal depresses; No braking occurs	4	9	8	288	start up comm check with sensor	Use 3 pedal position sensors	Susan	Added 2 more sensors with voting	2	9	144
	Comm fault	CAN Bus failure	Braking message not conveyed	3	9	2	54	continuous monitoring of CAN bus	none	n/a				
		Loose bus connector	Braking message not conveyed	4	9	9	324	continuous monitoring of CAN bus	update monitoring to send lifeticks to every node on bus	Samuel	updated lifetick protocol	2	9	162
	Processing fault	Braking ECU Failure	No braking occurs	2	9	2	36	Lifeticks every 1.0 s	none	n/a				
	Wheel actuator fault	Brake actuator processing failure	No movement of brake master cylinder	2	9	10	180	none	Include in lifetick poll	Samuel	updated lifetick protocol	1	9	90
		Brake hydraulic pressure low; O-ring leak; gasket leak	reduced or no braking force	7	9	10	630	none	Add hydraulic pressure sensor; Alert driver	Joe	Added sensor; updated periodic driver messages	3	9	270
		Push rod fracture	Hydraulic pressure not increased on braking	1	9	10	90	none	none	n/a				
		Vacuum boost leak	Reduced braking force	6	4	6	144	sensor on pressure differential valve	none	n/a				
		Brake pads worn	Reduced braking force	9	4	10	360	none	Add periodic driver reminder for service every 6 months	Samuel	updated periodic driver messages	4	6	240

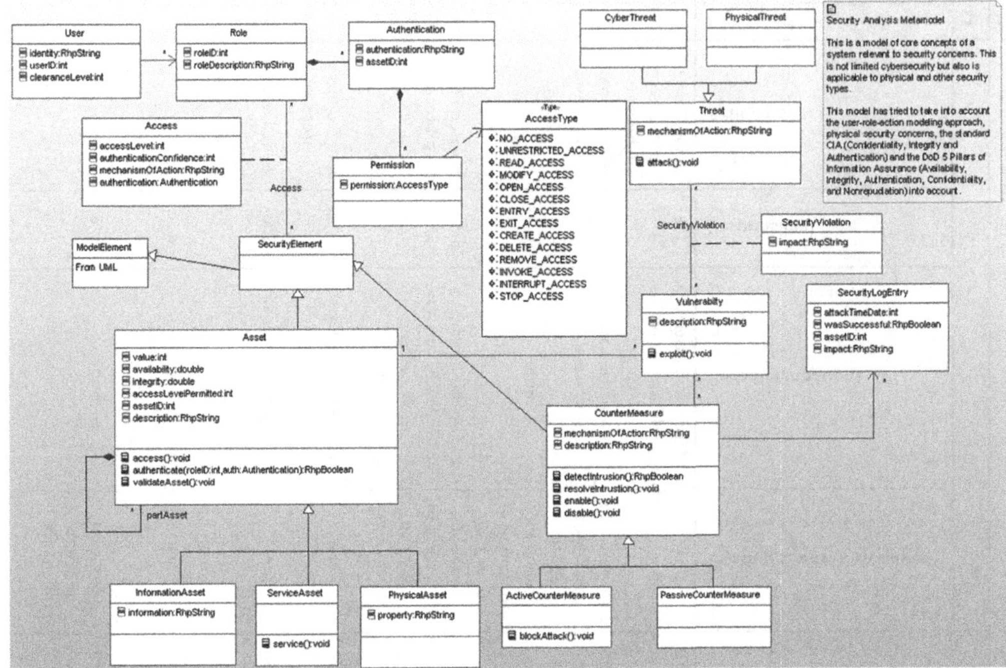

Figure 5.71
UML/SysML security profile metamodel.

possible to hack into and damage, take control, or steal information from civil power networks, automobiles, and medical devices. We must all be concerned about security as complex devices evolve.

Although in complex systems a security solution may be as simple as adding a physical lock, most focus is on cybersecurity as we construct the internet of (billions of) things. The analysis of the means by which security can be penetrated is known as *threat analysis*. Similar to FTA or FMEA, threat analysis leads to control actions to maintain and improve the security of devices.

I've create a security analysis profile for the UML that allows the analysis of assets, threats and countermeasures. The profile is based on the metamodel shown in Figure 5.71 and Table 5.3 describes the key metaclasses of the profile.

Workflow for threat modeling is straightforward.

1. Identify assets that you want to protect
2. Assign values to the asset meta-attributes such as the *asset value*. This is important because it makes sense to spend more effort and cost protecting more valuable assets

Table 5.3: Key metaclasses for security metamodel.

Metaclass	Description
Asset	Assets are security-relevant features of a system, including the value, availability, and the required authentication for access. The different kinds of assets are: • **Information assets**—refers to information that should be kept secure, such as: user credit card information, classified data • **Service assets**—for example: life support service (e.g. cardiac pacemaker or patient ventilation), power delivery service (e.g. power grid), credit authorization service • **Physical assets**—meant to refer to physical elements and infrastructure, such as cash, paintings, automobiles • **Currency assets** • **Resource assets** • **Security assets**—countermeasures may themselves have vulnerabilities and be attacked Assets may be "nested", that is, assets may contain part assets with different levels of required authentication and security
Authentication	The means by which an asset may be accessed. For example, a physical key, password, retinal scan, or encryption key. An authentication has a set of permissions
Countermeasure	Features added to a system to ensure its security; specifically addresses vulnerabilities • Active countermeasure looks for, detects, and acts on attempts to penetrate vulnerabilities. For example, motion detector alarm, authentication check • Passive countermeasure prevents access via a vulnerability, for example, door, removing an access port, lock, enclosure, data encryption
Role	Represents the usage of a user within the security context that is granted permission to access some set of assets through a set of authentications
Threat	The means by which a vulnerability is exploited
User	Represents an actual human or system instance; may have a permission or security level that grants level of access to all its roles
Vulnerability	The means by which an asset may be inappropriately accessed. It may be a physical, system, or software vulnerability

3. For each asset, identify means by which the asset can be compromised; these are the vulnerabilities
4. For each asset above some threshold, or for each of its vulnerabilities, identify the attack vectors (threats), that is, the means by which the vulnerability can be exploited
5. For each threat, identify a countermeasure to prevent the attack.

The profile is meant to facilitate this reasoning so that the engineers can identify what countermeasures are appropriate and where they are needed. This is similar to safety and reliability analysis but is expressed towards security concerns.

Consider a medical ventilator. Such a device has a number of assets worthy of protection: (information assets) patient demographic data, patient medical data, ventilator

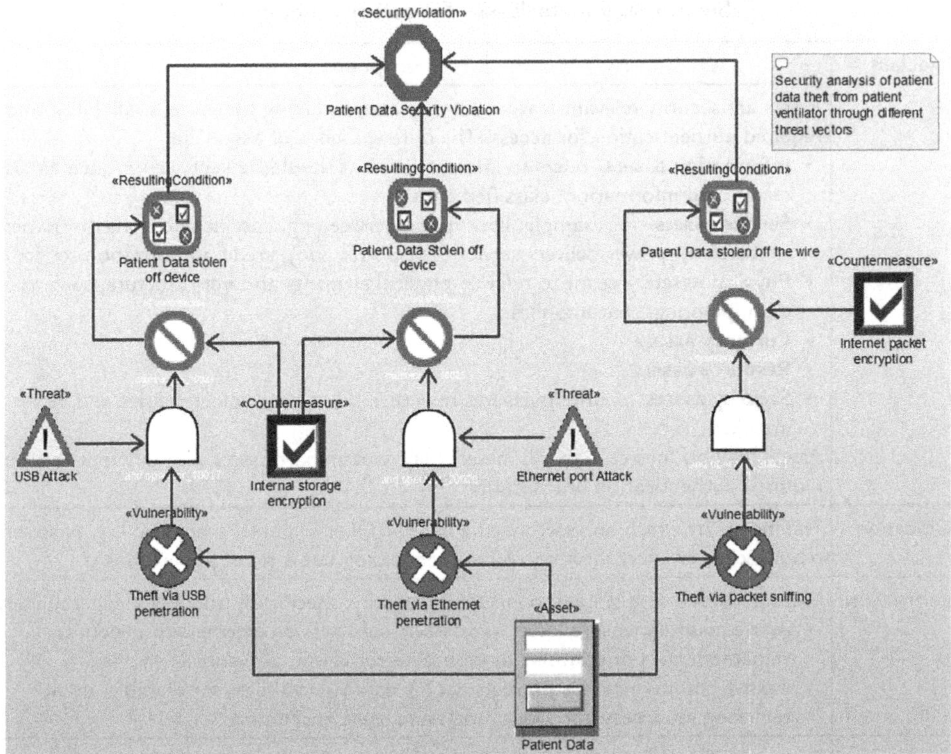

Figure 5.72
Security analysis of patient data theft.

configuration settings; (service assets) gas mixing, delivery of ventilation, device mode; (resource assets) O_2, He, and N_2 gas supplies. Figure 5.72 shows a model-based threat analysis for patient data.[19]

During this analysis, it behooves you to check for known threats and vulnerabilities to similar systems or to systems using similar technologies. The Mitre Common Weakness Enumeration [3] is a good place to start as it identifies common vulnerabilities and threat vectors. Additional guidance for dealing with security risks can be found at SEI. They have developed a methodology known as OCTAVE (Operationally Critical Threat, Asset, and Vulnerability Evaluation) [4].

Just as the hazard analysis and FMEA, summary tables can be easily constructed for the security-relevant metadata to support ranking the vulnerabilities and threats. Table 5.4 shows such a table format.

19 If you don't appreciate the icons, they can be replaced with boxes as with normal block diagrams. The metatypes can be identified via stereotypes on the boxes.

Table 5.4: Threat analysis table.

Asset value is the value of the asset to be protected (1 = very low, 10 = very high)										
Likelihood is the probability of the attack (1 = very low, 10 = certain)										
Reproducability refers to how easy it is to reproduce the attack (for example, does it depend on timing or other circumstances?) (1 = hard, 10 = very easy)										
Exploitability refers to how easy it is to launch the attack (1 = very easy, 10 = very hard)										
Breadth is a measure of the extent of the attack. How widespread is it or how many systems are affected (1 = few, 10 = very many)										
Discoverability is how easy is it for outsiders to find out about and exploit the vulnerability (1 = very easy, 10 = very hard)										
Threat priority is the product of the above values and is used to prioritize the threats for countermeasures										
			These are in the range of 1–10							
Asset	**Vulnerability**	**Threat Vector**	**Asset Value**	**Likelihood of Attack**	**Reproduc-ability**	**Exploitability**	**Breadth**	**Discoverability**	**Threat Priority**	**Counter Measure**
Patient Demo-graphic Data	Access via ethernet	Input validation weak	4	7	9	4	1	9	9072	Internal encryption
	Access via USB	Auto execution of USB SW	4	7	9	3	1	9	6804	Internal encryption
	Access via packet snooping	Messages sent in plain text	4	7	9	5	1	8	10080	Message encryption

Name	Description	Probability	Severity	Risk	SafetyIntegrityLevel	FaultToleranceTime	FaultToleranceTimeUnits
Collision	The Collision hazard occurs when the system collides with an element in its environment.	0.8	0.8	.64	4	0	seconds
Grapper Crushing	The grabber is capable of causing damage or injoru with the application of too much pressure.	.4	.6	.24	3	10	miliseconds
Pilot Injury	This hazard has to do with Pilot injury due to encasement fault, such as internal crushing injuries or resultant from restricted breathing.	.2	0.8	.16	4	1000	miliseconds
Toppling	System toppling presents an opportunity for crushing damage.	.4	.8	.32	4	0	

Figure 5.73
T-Wrecks initial hazards.

5.7.2 T-Wrecks Initial Dependability Analysis

5.7.2.1 T-Wrecks safety

The safety of the T-Wrecks system can be thought of as manifesting in four hazards. Figure 5.73 shows the hazard table with the safety metadata for the hazards, including the descriptions and initial estimates for the probability and severity (both normalized to values between 0 and 1). The Safety Integrity Level (SIL) refers to the level one might use with a safety standard such as IEC 61508 [5].

Figure 5.74 shows the initial FTA for the Collision hazard. We see that a Collision hazard can arise when the system and object have relative motion (at least one of them is moving) and either a failure to alarm (based on proximity detection) has occurred or there is a failure to adequately control the system movement. Undeveloped Faults are used where we think it is likely that further decomposition of the fault may occur and Basic Faults are used when the fault is unlikely to be further decomposed. We also see that additional requirements, with trace links to the fault elements, have been created as a result of this analysis.

5.7.2.2 T-Wrecks reliability

The point of reliability specification this early in the process is to drive later technical choices. At this point, no internal structural elements are known so it is adequate to identify the key system functions and characterize their required aggregate reliabilities. The required reliability can be either provided as availability (percentage of time the service can be provided) or time between unavailability (such as Mean Time Between Failures, or MTBF).

Table 5.5 identifies the key system functions for the two use cases we've considered so far, Proximity Detection and Move Joint. Added are estimates (now requirements) of the reliability needs, expressed as MTBF for the key functions identified within those use cases. If we consider a typical 5-day week, 8 h per day of usage, the configure proximity scanner is allowed to fail, on average, once every year, while the ability to detect proximal objects is allowed to fail only once every 4 years. For the use case Move Joint, the movement is only allowed to fail, on average, once every 2 years.

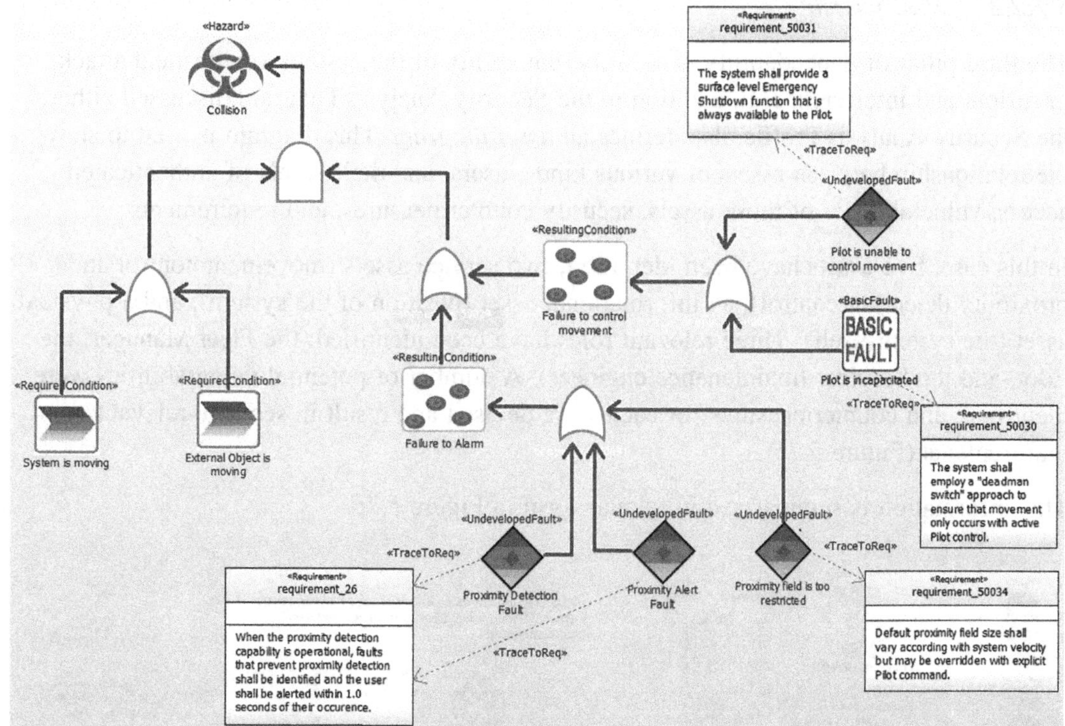

Figure 5.74
FTA for collision hazard.

Table 5.5: Stakeholder reliability requirements.

Use Case	System Function	Required MTBF	Time Units
Proximity Detection	Configure proximity detection	2000	Hours
	Proximity scan	8000	Hours
	Alert user of proximal object	8000	Hours
	Proximity system health check	4000	Hours
	Enable proximity scan	8000	Hours
	Disable proximity scan	8000	Hours
Move Joint	Detect pilot pressure	4000	Hours
	Compute angular torque	4000	Hours
	Monitor joint movement	4000	Hours
	Apply angular torque	4000	Hours

5.7.2.3 T-Wrecks security

The third pillar of dependability is security, the ability of the system to withstand attack, intrusion, and interference. In addition to the Security Analysis Diagram discussed either, the Security Analysis Profile also defines an *asset diagram*. This diagram is used to show the relationship between assets of various kinds, users, and their levels of authenticated access, vulnerabilities of those assets, security countermeasures, and requirements.

In this case, five assets have been identified; two service assets (movement control and proximity detection control), an informational asset (position of the system), and a physical asset (the system itself). Three relevant roles have been identified: the Fleet Manager, the Pilot, and the Servicer (maintenance engineer). A number of potential vulnerabilities were identified, and countermeasures for each were devised and result in security-relevant requirements (Figure 5.75).

This information is summarized in tabular form in Figure 5.76.

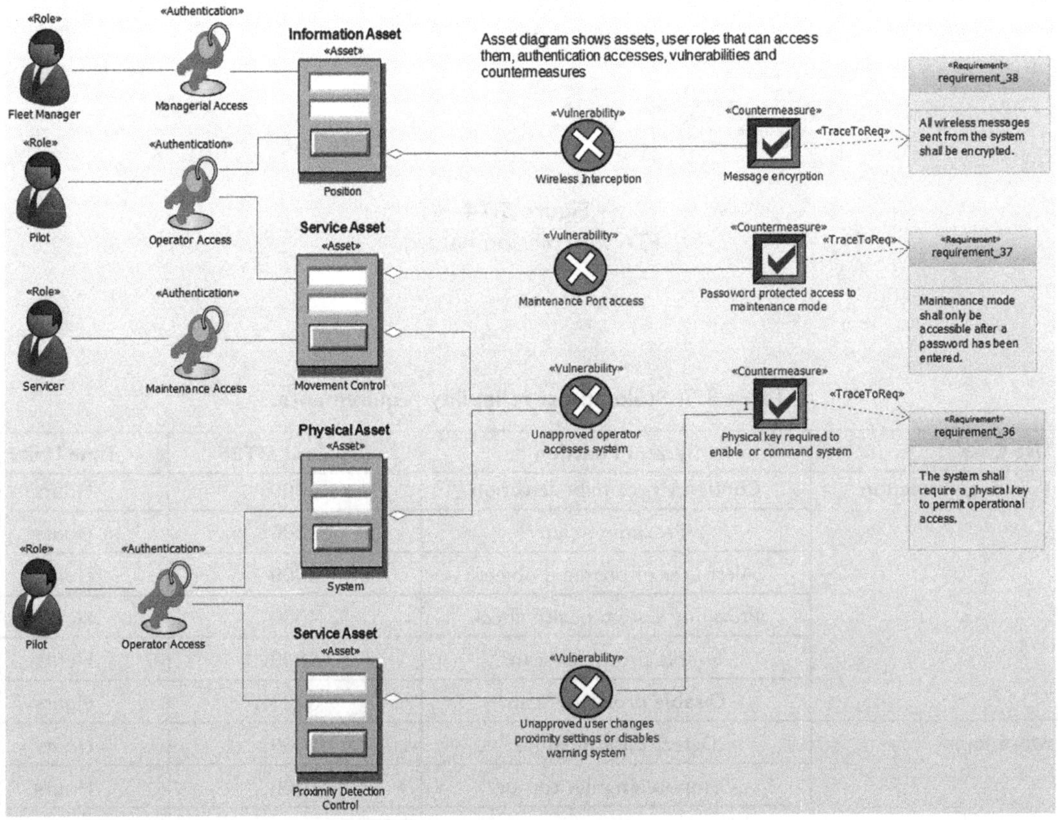

Figure 5.75
T-Wrecks asset diagram.

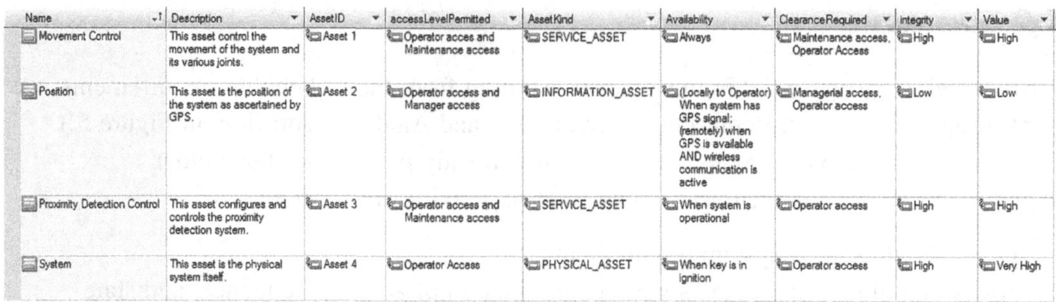

Name	Description	AssetID	accessLevelPermitted	AssetKind	Availability	ClearanceRequired	integrity	Value
Movement Control	This asset control the movement of the system and its various joints.	Asset 1	Operator acces and Maintenance access	SERVICE_ASSET	Always	Maintenance access, Operator Access	High	High
Position	This asset is the position of the system as ascertained by GPS.	Asset 2	Operator access and Manager access	INFORMATION_ASSET	(Locally to Operator) When system has GPS signal; (remotely) when GPS is available AND wireless communication is active	Managerial access, Operator access	Low	Low
Proximity Detection Control	This asset configures and controls the proximity detection system.	Asset 3	Operator access and Maintenance access	SERVICE_ASSET	When system is operational	Operator access	High	High
System	This asset is the physical system itself.	Asset 4	Operator Access	PHYSICAL_ASSET	When key is in ignition	Operator access	High	Very High

Figure 5.76
Asset metadata.

At this point, the key benefit of the analysis of safety, reliability, and security is to ensure all the stakeholder needs are represented in requirements.

5.8 Create/Update Verification Plan

As we begin to define the system requirements, we can also begin to define how we intend to verify that the developed system meets these requirements.

Within the verification plan resides the following information:

- The system acceptance criteria
- The tools and test environments will be used to demonstrate satisfaction of system requirements
- The techniques used such as flight test, lab testing, wind tunnel testing formal testing, environmental testing, formal (mathematical) analysis, reachability testing, materials testing
- The resources required to perform verification
- When and how this verification will occur; if incremental, what functionality is expected to be verified at each verification point
- Who is responsible for different aspects of verification such as creating the detailed verification test cases and/or analyses, procuring or creating the verification test tools and environments, running the actual verification procedures, assessing the outcomes of the verification procedures, and accepting or rejecting the delivery
- Transition to Manufacturing—how the verified design elements will be conveyed to manufacturing
- Transition to Customer – how manufactured systems will be delivered, installed, commissioned, and configured at the customer site(s)
- How the system will be managed, tracked, and otherwise supported in its operational environment
- How the information within the verification plan will be controlled—that is, configuration and change management of the information within the verification plan.

5.9 Summary

Whew. We've covered *a lot* in this chapter. Starting from the stakeholder requirements, we went through the System Requirements Definition and Analysis workflow in Figure 5.1. This involves identifying any new use cases not already part of the stakeholder requirements model and then performing a set of activities in parallel:

- Generating/updating system requirements
- Analyzing those requirements with a combination of activity, sequence, and state diagrams using one of three potential workflows:
  - Flow-based analysis, which starts with the activity diagram
  - Scenario-based analysis, which starts with sequence diagrams
  - State-based analysis, which starts with the state machine
- Analyzing dependability, focusing on requirements for system safety, reliability, and security
- Creating/updating the logical data schema
- Creating/updating the Verification Plan.

We emphasize building executable models to support simulation of our requirements model and this allows us to verify the correctness, consistency, accuracy, and completeness of our requirements. As we discover more requirements or defects in existing requirements, we update the textual requirements. Once the requirements for the use case stabilize, we add trace links from the system requirements to the stakeholder requirements and also to the verification plans.

Getting the requirements right is a lot of work but it pays off in not having to throw away engineering work later when you discover missing or bad requirements during downstream engineering.

5.10 Moving On

In this agile iterative lifecycle, at the end of this activity, we have identified and characterized requirements for a small number of use cases—remaining use cases will be dealt with in future iterations. Now it is time to start thinking about architectural approaches for the system architecture that allow us to optimize properties of the system that we care about—such as reliability, safety, performance, development cost, manufacturing cost, and maintenance. That is what we mean when we talk about architectural analysis and that is the subject of the next chapter.

References

[1] N. Leveson, Safeware: System Safety and Computers. Addison-Wesley, 1995.

[2] The Fault Tree Handbook NUREG 0492. Nuclear Regulatory Commission, 1981. Available from: <http://www.nrc.gov/reading-rm/doc-collections/nuregs/staff/sr0492/>.

[3] <cwe.mitre.org>.

[4] <www.cert.org/resilience/products-services/octave>.

[5] Functional Safety of Electrical/electronic/programmable electronic safety-related systems EN 61508. BSI Corporate, 2010.

[6] B.P. Douglass, Real-Time UML Workshop, second ed., Elsevier Press, 2014.

[7] <http://www.fmeainfocentre.com/>.

CHAPTER 6

Agile Systems Architectural Analysis and Trade Studies

Chapter Outline

6.1 Objectives

At this point, we have a set of use cases and allocated requirements[1] so, for some important portion of the system, we have a decent understanding of the requirements. The next step in the iterative process is to look at some architectural alternatives, evaluate them for "goodness" and select an architectural approach that meets our needs in an optimal way. The primary objective of this activity is to develop an optimal system design that meets the requirements. We will do this by identifying a set of assessment criteria for our candidate solutions and determining how well each candidate solution optimizes that criterion. The quantification of a specific assessment criterion against a key system property is called a measurement of effectiveness, or MOE.

More specific subgoals are:

1. Make sure we understand the assessment criteria by which we will judge our system.
2. Quantify the relative importance of our various criteria.
3. Identify the set of reasonable alternative architectures we can use to design the system.
4. Characterize each solution as to how well it rates against our selected criteria; that is, compute or estimate the set of MOEs for each candidate solution.
5. Select a solution architecture that has the best weighted overall MOE ranking.

It is important to understand that architecture is not essential in the sense that requirements are. A system simply must meet our requirements (that is why they're referred to as, well, *requirements*). There are always multiple architectures that can meet the requirements, so defining architectures is always an exercise in optimization. The primary difficulty with architectural selection arises because of the need to simultaneously optimize different (often conflicting) optimization criteria. Some common optimization criteria include:

- cost,
  - recurring (manufacturing),
  - engineering (development),
  - operational (deployed system),
  - maintenance (deployed system),
- time to market,
- size,
- capacity,
- weight,
- power,

[1] But probably not all—did I mention that we're doing an agile iterative approach to systems engineering specification?

    - mechanical power, instantaneous,
    - mechanical power, sustainable,
    - electrical power available,
    - electrical power, utilization,
- power/weight,
- performance,
    - worst-case,
    - average-case,
    - throughput,
    - bandwidth,
- accuracy,
- tolerances,
    - machined,
    - computational,
    - environmental,
- heat generated,
- reliability,
- safety,
- security,
- usability,
- longevity.

The benefit of the approach outlined here is that it provides a stepwise approach to selecting one architecture from a sea of possibilities. It's repeatable. It is model-based. And it is supported by existing engineering tools.

At the end of this activity, we have a selected optimal architecture that we will detail in the next activity, to be described in Chapter 7.

> *Tool note*: The analysis approach here is strict SysML, but I will be doing the examples in Rational Rhapsody with the parametric constraint evaluator (PCE) profile linked to the open source Maxima symbolic mathematic evaluation tool (version 5.22.1) to evaluate the mathematical expressions, perform the mathematical analysis, and produce graphical plots. For more information on Maxima, see Ref. [1].

6.2 Architecture Analysis Workflow

Figure 6.1 shows the workflow for the activity Architectural Analysis. Although we will walk through these steps in more detail later in the chapter, I'll provide an overview of the tasks here.

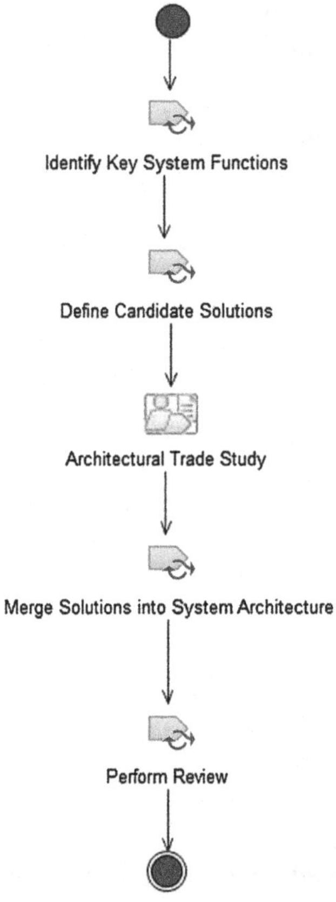

Figure 6.1
Architectural analysis.

6.2.1 Identify Key System Functions

While not all of the architectural decisions will directly relate to system functions (such as, perhaps, the choice of titanium or steel materials for casing), most will, so it behooves us to identify the behaviors we want to optimize. Others may relate to some key system property (such as total weight) that we want to optimize.

6.2.2 Define Candidate Solutions

This task identifies viable alternatives for the functions or properties identified in the previous task.

6.2.3 Perform Architectural Trade Study

This is an activity containing a number of subtasks and will be explored shortly, in conjunction with Figure 6.2.

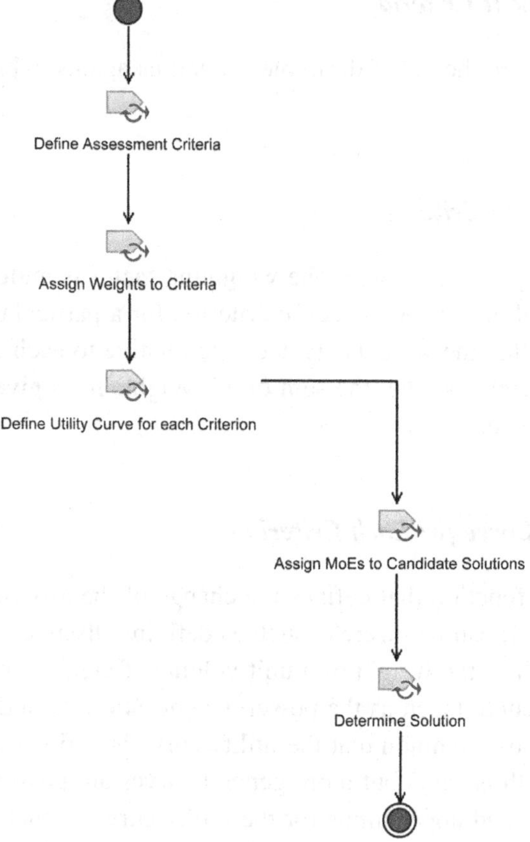

Figure 6.2
Architectural trade study workflow.

6.2.4 Merge Solutions into Systems Architecture

This defines the system architecture as the sum of its aspects. In most cases, this task is simply additive; however, in cases where determined optimal solutions for different system functions or properties are in conflict, further analysis may be required. From the set of candidate solutions, one is selected and taken forward into the next activity, Architectural Design.

The workflow shown in Figure 6.1 has an activity, *Architectural Trade Study*, which is further decomposed into a set of tasks. Figure 6.2 shows the tasks nested within this task. This activity is repeated for each key system function or property of concern. This nested activity contains the following tasks, described at a high level.

6.2.5 Define Assessment Criteria

The assessment criteria are the set of desirable properties against which you wish to evaluate the solution.

6.2.6 Assign Weights to Criteria

Not all criteria are of equal importance. The weighting factor is multiplied by the MOE to provide a weighted MOE score for a specific criterion for a particular solution. The crucial part of the weighing is that the weights are accurate relative to each other. To help achieve this, normalizing the weights so that the sum of all weights for a given criteria add up to 1.0 is a common technique.[2]

6.2.7 Define Utility Curve for Each Criterion

The utility curve is the function that defines the change of the assessment criteria as some other property changes. It can be discrete, such as defining discrete assessment values for different materials (such as the weight of a unit volume of aluminum, titanium, and steel) or it can be a continuous curve (such as the power/weight ratio over a defined range of weight). It is perhaps most common that the utility curve is defined as a straight line (mostly because the math is easy) but more general curves are possible. It is important to define reasonable lower and upper limits for the utility curve so that we restrict consideration to only reasonable solutions.

Similar to the assessment weights, it is common (though not required) to normalize the utility curve so that it ranges from 0 to 10, with the higher score being more favorable.

6.2.8 Assign MOEs to Candidate Solutions

This task assigned the weighted MOEs to the candidate solutions for all the criteria under consideration. Normally, these scores are put into a table to facilitate side-by-side comparison of candidate solutions.

---

[2] Normalizing does provide a standard way of looking at a range of values, but it also often overemphasizes differences when the range is very small. Normalizing cost from \$0.00 to \$1000 to a scale of 0–10 is different than normalizing a cost range of \$995, \$997, and \$1000. One might reasonably say "these values are all the same" but if normalizing the range so that \$995 gives a "0" and \$1000 gives a "10" puts a lot of emphasis on what might be an insignificant difference.

6.2.9 Determine the Solution

The "best" solution is determined by adding up all the MOEs assigned to the candidate solutions and comparing the overall total sums, with the best solution having the highest total weighted score. This nested workflow is repeated for all key system functions and/or properties.

6.3 Assessment Methodology

First, I'll describe a simple, low-effort (and relatively low-fidelity) approach to performing a trade study. Following that, I'll get into a higher-effort but also higher-fidelity model-based approach using parametric diagrams and constraint properties.

6.3.1 The Easy Way

In this approach, we'll use a simple spreadsheet to construct a table of MOEs and calculate the overall resulting score. The approach is actually very useful when you don't have a mathematical objective function to optimize. Suppose our optimization criteria are things like

- ease of use,
- ease of learning,
- appearance of quality,
- ease of maintenance,
- development cost,
- etc.

To be clear, it *is* possible to construct mathematically objective utility functions for these criteria. For example, ease of use can be assessed by creating limited-functionality mockups and performing usability studies and then doing a least-squares best-fit analysis to match the data to an appropriate curve. However, it may be cost- or time-prohibitive to do so. So as an alternative, one might do a simple voting poll among a set of stakeholders to estimate such a curve, perhaps in a method reminiscent of planning poker[3] [2,3]. Or, more commonly, a single engineer might just apply their best judgment. Like I said, this approach tends to be low effort, but its conclusions are of less assuredness as well.

Just as important as the utility function for the criteria is the weight (relative importance) of the criteria. One way to get such a number is to ask the relevant stakeholders.

[3] Planning poker is a popular Agile technique for estimated relative efforts required for developing use stories. In it, each member of a team selects a numbered card that represents relative effort. These cards are kept private until each member has selected a card. Then all cards are displayed. Discussion about why estimates might be different ensues and the poker process is repeated until convergence is achieved.

For example, consider our Speed Demon Treadmill. For key system functions, we'll consider two: (i) downloading a video from the library to play and (ii) running an exercise protocol.

What are the assessment criteria of interest? We'll use three: manufacturing cost, usability, and durability. Manufacturing cost we can estimate from the parts list. Durability can be estimated from the manufacturer's reported failure rate of their touch screen, membrane touch switches, and keyboards. Usability is a more personal, qualitative issue. To get numbers from that, we'll create three mock-ups—one with an iPad embedded in a hand-build platform running a simple custom app to simulate the touch screen, one with an older numeric keypad hobbled together from old parts in the lab, and one with a standard PC keyboard with an off-the-shelf waterproof flexible plastic skin, driving a PC with an LCD display. Care is taken to ensure that the form factor for the three is as close as possible so as not to skew the results for reasons unrelated to what we're trying to evaluate. Then we'll ask our gym rats on our system engineering team to rate, on a scale of 0–10, the usability of selecting and downloading a video and selecting and enabling an exercise protocol.

We must also decide on the relative importance of each of these criteria. In discussions with the stakeholders, we've identified the weight for cost to be 0.3, the weight for usability to be 0.5, and the weight for durability to be 0.2.

We also identify a constraint that the manufacturing cost should not exceed $500, no matter what.

Constructing the analysis is a simple enough task. Using (made-up) numbers for this simple example, we find that the cost of using a suitable touch screen is $220. Simply building up a set of membrane switches to construct a flat keyboard comes to $50 plus the cost of an LCD screen of $70, for a total of $120. Using a standard keyboard, skin, and LCD screen comes to $95. If we construct a linear utility curve with the highest cost resulting in an assessment of 0 and the lowest cost with an assessment value of 10, we obtain a straight line with a slope of -0.08 and a y intercept of 17.6. Thus our assessment rankings are 0, 8, and 10 for touch screen, membrane switch, and standard keyboard solutions, respectively.

Durability ratings can be had from the specific manufacturers but it should be noted that not all gym dwellers are kind to their devices. In this case, the touch screen durability is rated at 500,000 presses, the membrane switches are rated to 5,000,000 presses and our standard keyboard is rated to 50,000,000 presses. If we construct a line with 500,000 being 0 on the scale and 50 million being 10 gives us a line with a slope of 2.02×10^{-7} and a y intercept of -0.101. We can use this as our utility curve for this objective function, giving us a score of 0 for the touch screen, 1 for the membrane switches, and 10 for the standard keyboard.

Our usability scores tell a different story. We asked the team to rank three solutions on a usability scale from 0 to 10. We then averaged the scores to get 1.5 for the keyboard, 7 for

Table 6.1: Simple trade study.

	Criteria and weights			
	Cost	Usability	Durability	
Candidate solution	0.30	0.50	0.20	Candidate weighted score
Touch screen	0.00	10.00	0.00	5.00
Membrane switches	8.00	7.86	1.00	6.53
Keyboard	10.00	0.00	10.00	5.00

the membrane keys, and 8.5 on the touch screen. We again linearly normalize the values to get a range of 0–10, giving us scores of 0 for the keyboard, 7.857 for the membrane keys, and 10 for the touch screen.

The results are summarized in Table 6.1. The table shows the weights at the top of the criteria columns and the values of the assessment for the criteria in the cells. The sum in the far right column performs a cross product sum of the assessment values times the relative weights for each of the candidate solutions. The membrane switches solution fared better overall even though it didn't score the best on any of the individual criteria.

6.3.2 The High-Fidelity Way

The other approach, on which we will spend the rest of the chapter, is to use parametric diagrams to represent the criteria, weights, and constraints. This approach is a bit more work than the simple approach above but is not only higher fidelity, it also scales up to more complex situations far better.

SysML provides parametrics diagrams to represent constraints and mathematical relations between model elements. We did a (very) brief discussion of parametric diagrams in Chapter 3. In my opinion, being able to represent the constraints and quantitative relationships is a good thing, but the killer app is when you can automatically solve and optimize values with tooling. Some people refer to this as "executable parametric diagrams" but it is not execution in the computer science sense[4]; I will refer to it as "evaluable parametric diagrams" for this reason.

[4] In computer science to "execute an algorithm" means to walk through the algorithm step by step and perform operations. The same is true of activity diagrams and state machines. What we represent in constraints and mathematical expressions are relations that can be evaluated (or solved or optimized) in many different orders. In the expression $Y = 10X^2 + 11X + 3$ can be solved for Y by plugging in a value for X but it can also be solved for X by plugging in a value for Y.

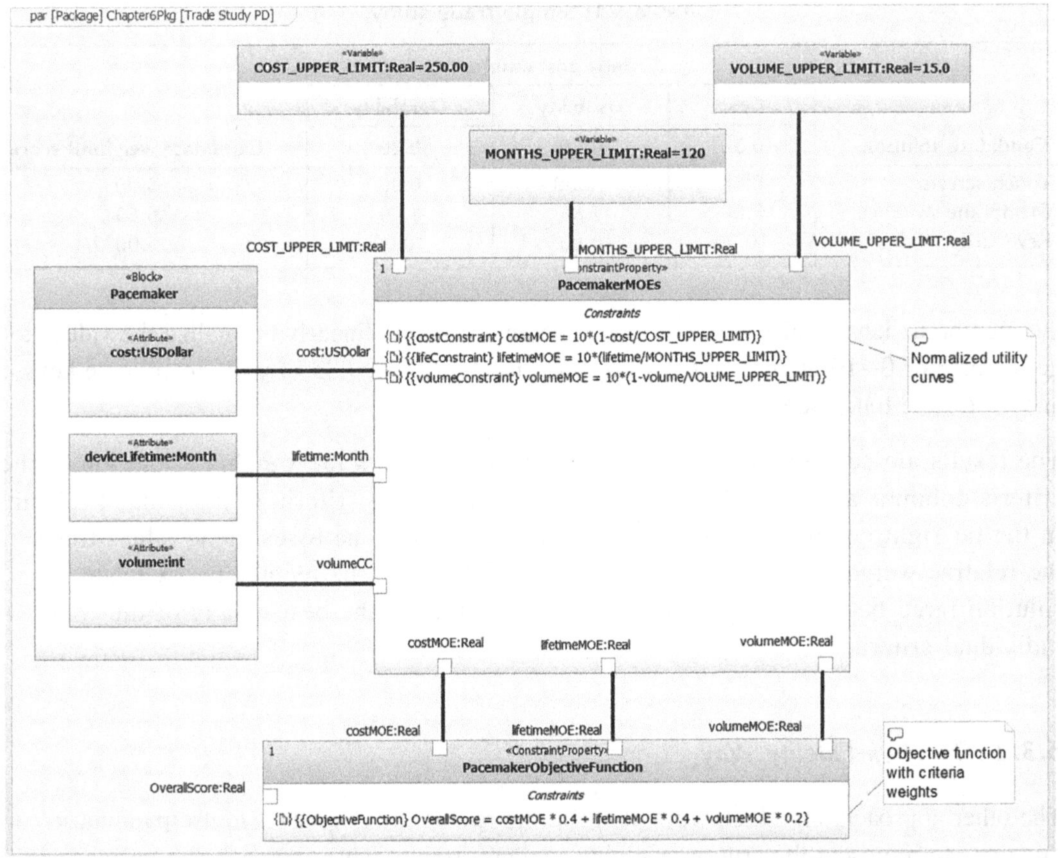

Figure 6.3
Pacemaker objective function and MOEs.

In this process, we'll typically make a number of parametric diagrams to analyze important system properties but for trade studies the key one usually looks something like Figure 6.3.

This figure contains two constraint properties. The first, `PacemakerMOEs`, looks at three criteria—cost, device life expectancy, and size (device volume) and defines utility curves for each. The utility functions are all normalized to an upper value so that 10 is the best possible score and 0 is the worst. The upper limits are defined at the top of the figure in variables. We can ask the PCE tool to plot the utility curves, resulting in Figure 6.4. As you should expect, lower values for cost and volume give better MOE values while higher numbers for device life expectancy give higher MOE values.

At the bottom of Figure 6.3, we see the constraint property `ObjectiveFunction` which shows the `OverallScore` for a given pacemaker design as the weighted sum of its three MOEs. The weights are directly represented as real numbers—0.4 for cost, 0.4 for device life

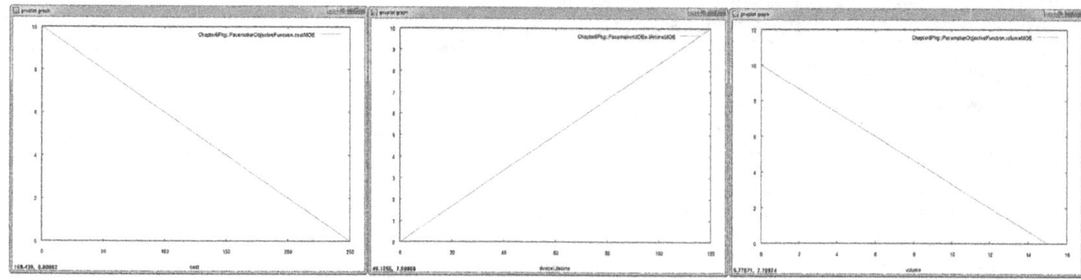

Figure 6.4
Plotted pacemaker utility curves.

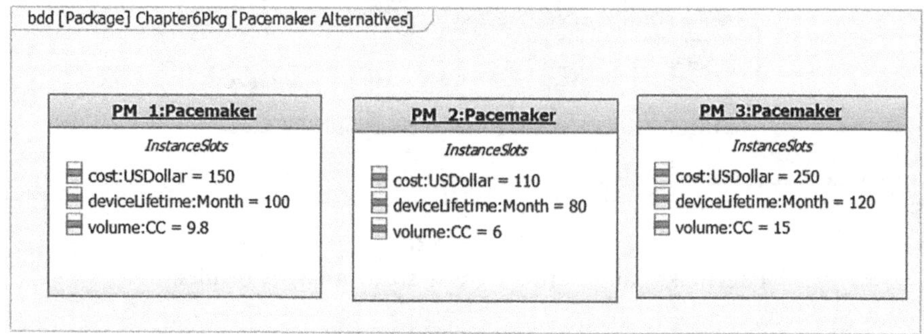

Figure 6.5
Pacemaker alternatives as instance specifications.

expectancy, and 0.2 for volume[5] and these represent the relative criticality of each factor to the determination of the optimal result.

From this parametric model, we can evaluate alternative designs. Three sample designs are presented in Figure 6.5 as *instance specifications.* We see from Figure 6.3 that the Pacemaker block has three relevant values for this trade determination—`cost`, `deviceLifetime`, and `volume`. When we create instance specifications, we can assign specific values to those attributes (called *instance slots* in this context) to be used by the PCE tool to compute the MOEs and the overall score of the objective function. Where do these attribute values come from? They might be known *a priori*, estimated, or even calculated from other parametric diagrams.

Running the PCE tool to evaluate the three pacemaker alternatives results in three overall scores (Figures 6.6–6.8). The first alternative has a resulting overall score of 5.63, the second has an overall score of 6.11, and the third alternative has an overall score of 4.00.

[5] Again, the weights are normalized in this usage.

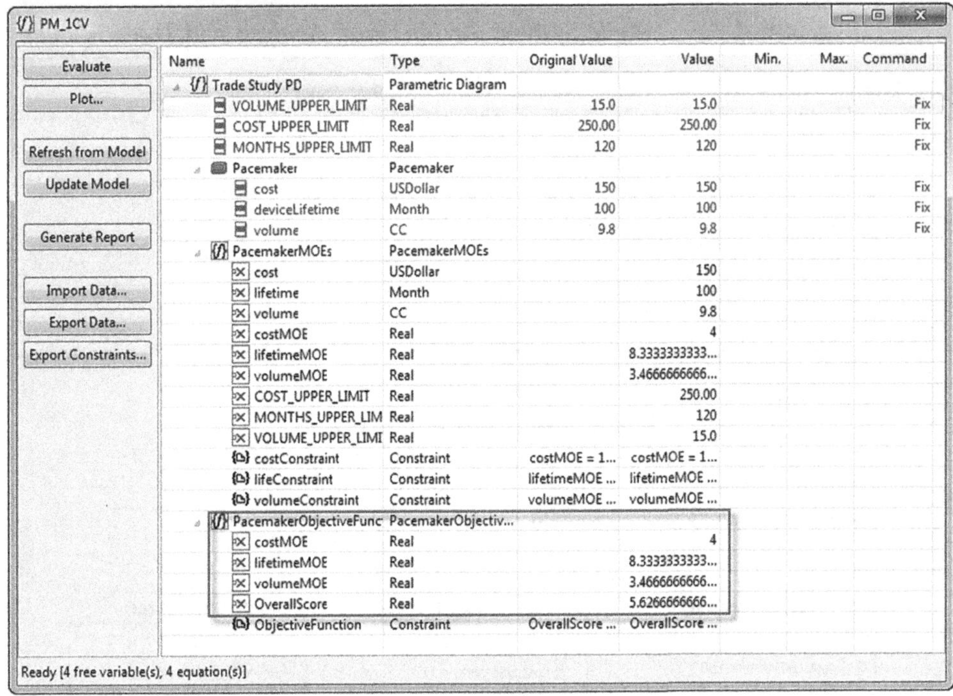

Figure 6.6
Pacemaker alternative 1 trade study analysis results.

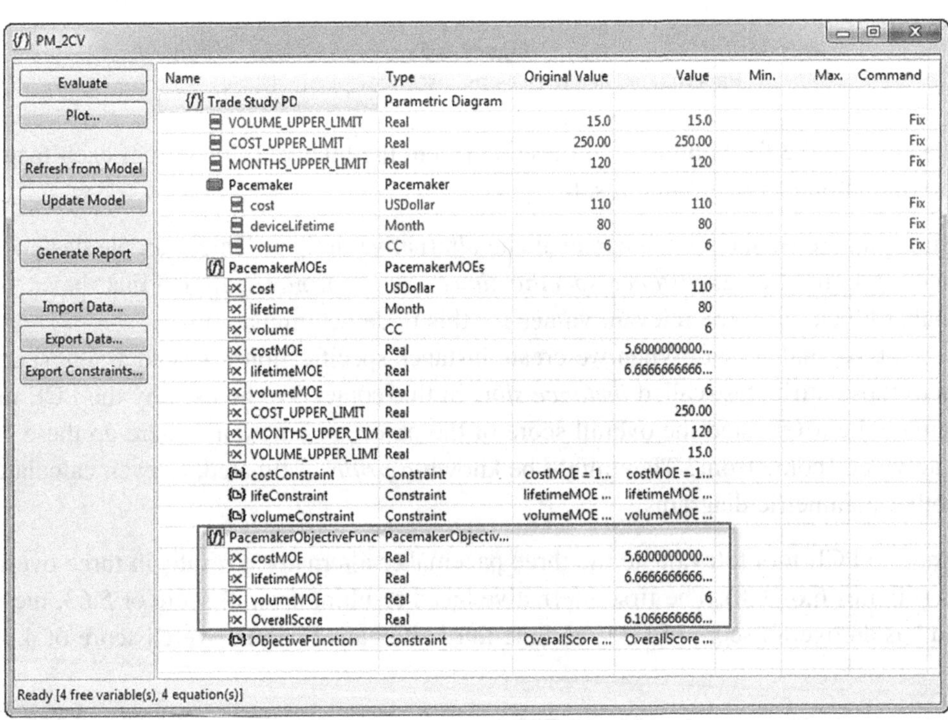

Figure 6.7
Pacemaker alternative 2 trade study analysis results.

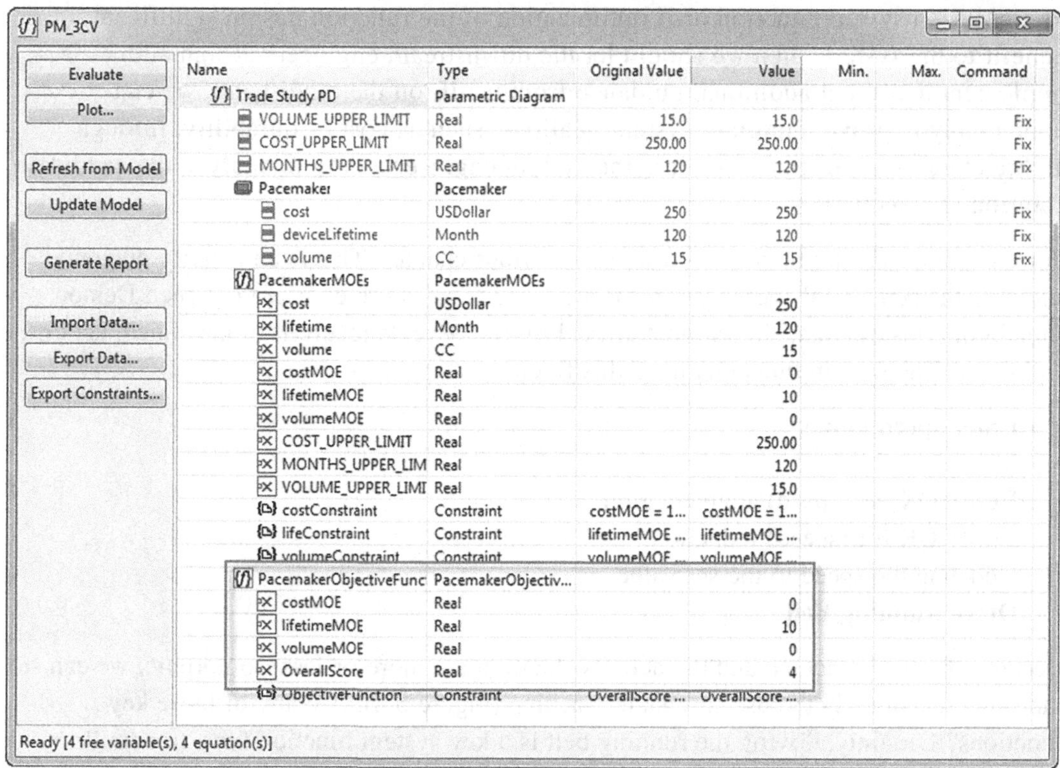

Figure 6.8
Pacemaker alternative 3 trade study analysis results.

Design alternative 2 is the overall winner and is selected as it best optimizes the weighted sum of the MOEs.

So that is a summary of the approach. Let's now get into it in a bit more detail.

6.4 Identify Key System Functions (and Properties)

Key system functions are crucially important behaviors performed by the system that can benefit from optimization. Since we are using an iterative, agile approach to systems engineering, we will generally only consider system functions that are a part of the use cases under current consideration. By this point, we've already created both activity diagrams and state machines for the use cases of concern. The system functions are the "high-level actions" within those behavioral specifications.

From the list of all such system functions, we must identify the key system functions. In this context, *a system function is "key" if the system can significantly benefit from architectural optimization of that function.* After all, if there is only one reasonable way to architect a system function or if optimization of the function has no significant benefit to the system, then we should let the downstream engineers design and implement it without additional guidance from us. If, on the other hand, we can appreciably improve important system qualities, such as cost or durability, through architectural optimization, then it is the system engineer's duty to analyze the candidate solution architectures.

For example, consider Figure 5.5 from the previous chapter. This is an activity diagram showing the behavioral specification for the `Speed Control` use case of the Speed Demon Treadmill. This diagram shows three critical things—events received or generated, actions, and flows. The system functions from this figure are:

- **Enter speed value**,
- Verify speed value,
- Verify OK for (speed) augmentation,
- Verify OK for (speed) reduction,
- Updating the speed to the set value,
- **Drive Running Belt**.

Because the state machine and the activity diagram are more-or-less isomorphic, we can see the same functions in the use case state machine (Figure 5.8). Are any of these key functions? Certainly, driving the running belt is a key system function for a treadmill. Arguably, the way that values are entered by the athlete (for augmentation or reduction of speed, for example) is another.

For the T-Wrecks example, let's consider the use cases `Move Joint` and `Proximity Detect`. For `Move Joint`, we can look at either the activity diagram (Figure 5.15) or the state machine (Figure 5.20). The identified system functions are (suggested key functions are shown in **bold**):

- Initialize Joint,
- Monitor joint pressure (implicit—the Produce Joint Pressure action is actually performed by the Pilot but our system must sense the pressure and deliver the signal to the system to determine how to move the joint),
- Compute Angular Torque,
- **Apply Coronal Torque**,
- **Apply Transverse Torque**,
- **Apply Sagittal Torque**,
- **Produce Movement**,
- Monitor Inertial Load (again, implicit as the Generate Inertial Load is "done" by the environment),
- Monitor joint—monitors the joint positions.

The T-Wrecks `Proximity Detect` use case activity diagram (Figures 5.39–5.42) and state machine (Figures 5.44 and 5.45) provide a rich set of system functions, including (suggested key functions again in **bold**):

- Enable proximity detect system,
- **Scan environment**,
- Identify objects,
- Characterize object,
- Apply object rejection filter,
- Proximity system health check,
- Configure proximity detection,
- Get start position (for the scanning emitter),
- **Position emitter**,
- Update Position,
- Build environment map,
- Construct Edges Map,
- Identify objects as contiguous edge sets.

The system functions involved in identifying and characterizing objects in the environment are certainly crucial (and interesting!) but they are not *key* by the narrow definition we are using here. They are algorithmically rich and will be designed and implemented by a combination of our AI and computer vision subject matter experts, aided by the software developers. However, the functions of scanning and positioning the scanner are definitely key and highly likely to benefit from optimization.

As mentioned previously, we might also want to look for other key system properties that are not represented as system functions. An example of a nonbehavioral system property is how much the system weighs or what color we paint it. Unless the system changes color dynamically, color is a static property and not a behavior. It is true that weight may influence a system function, such as in the weight of the limbs for the T-Wrecks system: everything else being equal, lighter is better for that system, but weight is not so much of a concern for the treadmill—unless we want to load it onto a Orbital Sciences rocket to take one up to the International Space Station on the COTS[6] program; then we'd care *a lot*. The point is, some properties of a system that we might want to optimize might not affect *any* system functions but still be worthwhile targets for optimization.

Common properties that fall into this category include:

- weight,
- cost,

[6] Commercial Orbital Transportation Services.

- assembly time,
- time to market,
- safety (no sharp edges on our treadmill!),
- heat generated,
- power used.

Of course, sometimes these properties *are* relevant to system functions but not always.

6.5 Define the Candidate Solutions

In this task, we look at each key system function we've identified and examine potential design realization. Should the front panel for the Speed Demon Treadmill be metal or molded plastic? Should it use a touch screen, membrane keys, or a traditional industrial keyboard? Should it be purchased as COTS[7] or should we manufacture it? What—if any—design constraints are placed upon the realization of the system function? Are there general system constraints or optimization criteria that should be applied to this specific system function or property?

As we address these (and similar) questions, we'll construct a list of viable alternative realizations. If any are nonviable,[8] they are immediately discarded. Then we are left with a list of viable alternatives to analyze to find the best overall solution.

6.5.1 Speed Demon Candidate Solutions

For the Speed Demon Treadmill key system functions, we will analyze Enter Speed Value and Drive Running Belt functions. Here are some candidate solutions:

Enter Speed Value candidate solutions

- Touch screen display with a custom-molded display (outsourced). Cost $220. Durability 500,000 presses. Usability from our study 8.5.
- Membrane keys in a custom-molded panel with embedded LCD (in-sourced). Cost $120. Durability 5,000,000 presses. Usability 7.0.
- Industrial grade keyboard with LCD in constructed panel (in-sourced). Cost $95. Durability 50,000,000 presses. Usability 1.5.

Drive Running Belt candidate solutions have different combinations of horsepower and RPM, with horsepower typically ranging from 2.0 to 4.0 hp and RPM rating from 3500 to 5000 RPM.

[7] Commercial Off The Shelf.

[8] Such as too expensive, too unreliable, uncertifiable, or physically impossible.

Generally speaking, treadmills are rated on the basis of their horsepower (hp) but the ability to deliver torque at low speeds is more important than total power. Even within horsepower ratings, there are continuous, peak, and duty horsepower. To simplify the discussion, we will only consider continuous duty horsepower, as we intend this treadmill for heavy-use environments, such as gyms. The mathematical relation between power and torque is given by Equation (6.1) (horsepower as a function of torque and RPM), where torque units are ft-pound and RPM units are revolutions per minute. So, for a given horsepower, lower RPM means higher torque. The result of higher torque is significantly less jerk[9] and less wear (therefore, longer life) on the motor. This is particularly true at low treadmill speeds where speed must be low but load is high. In fact, load is often lowest at high running speeds because the athlete both propels himself forward by pushing the running belt backwards and their weight is completely off the treadmill for some period of time during each stride. Neither of these phenomena occurs at walking speeds.

$$\mathrm{hp} = \frac{\mathrm{Torque} \times \mathrm{RPM}}{5252} \tag{6.1}$$

The motor solutions we'll look at include four potential solutions

- Solution 1: Drive motor rated at 2.5 hp and 3500 RPM with a cost of $150 and a reported mean time between failures (MTBF) of 2000 h.
- Solution 2: Drive motor rated at 3.0 hp and 4500 RPM with a cost of $250 and a reported MTBF of 3000 h.
- Solution 3: Drive motor rated at 4.0 hp and 4000 RPM with a cost of $300 and a reported MTBF of 3500 h.
- Solution 4: Drive motor rated at 3.5 hp and 3800 RPM with a cost of $500 and a reported MTBF of 6000 h.

6.5.2 T-Wrecks Candidate Solutions

We can also look at our T-Wrecks system key functions for that analysis as well. For the key system functions highlighted above, we detect that we need to focus on the approach for scanning the environment (Scan Environment and Position Emitter functions) and for applying torque and producing movement (Apply Coronal Torque, Apply Transverse Torque, Apply Sagittal Torque, and Produce Movement functions).

For the scanning functions case, possible solutions include the use of ultrasonic emissions (sonar) and light emission (lidar[10]).

Let's talk a little bit about the technologies in the candidate solutions.

---

[9] I don't mean obnoxious gym denizens. *Jerk* is the rate of change of acceleration over time. It manifests as a noticeably, well *jerky,* treadmill experience. And nobody likes that.

[10] Light Detection and Ranging.

6.5.2.1 Ultrasonic

The design under consideration generates 42 kHz sound wave. Operational range is 20 cm (7.9 inches) to 7.6 m (25 feet) range with a resolution of 1 cm with a 10 Hz rate. Low cost ($2.00 per emitter/sensor pair) but narrow beam focus (9°) means several (on the order of 40) will need to be deployed for adequate coverage. Each emitter and sensor assembly weighs 100 g.

6.5.2.2 Lidar scanning unit

The lidar technology proposed here is an infrared (1000 nm) micropulsed laser source directed by a rotating mirror. Because scanning must include 360° around the system (azimuth) and from the ground to slightly above the height of the system (elevation), multiple lidars, using slightly different frequencies must generally be used. Because of the near-distance measurements required, very close objects may be difficult to range accurately due to the very short time to return so triangulation will be used. Because of its high speed, when coupled with a fast-moving rotating mirror and fast CCD camera, the entire region can be painted and map constructed very quickly (0.25 s). Relative speed can be determined by Doppler shift of the light signal. The system under consideration is commercially available, with an operational range of 0.5–50 m (accuracy 2 cm) with 0.08° of azimuth resolution and 27° elevation range. The unit weighs 29 lbs (13.1 kg) and is expensive ($60,000).

Note: Using this technology introduces eye safety concerns (See? Dependability analysis is a concern throughout product development!) and this solution is rated for Class 1 (eye-safe) usage.

6.5.2.3 Lidar rangefinder

This is a fixed lidar unit with a single fixed up with rotating mirror, so at least four such units will be required. It provides a range of 0.5–20 m, with an angular resolution of 0.25° and a distance resolution of 1.75 cm. Individual weight is 1.1 kg, requires 0.35 s to perform a scan and each unit cost $5000.

The other functions of concern at this point for the T-Wrecks system have to do with the generation of movement at a joint. Candidate technologies include:

- Electric motor—produces mechanical movement through the interaction of the motor's magnetic field and the winding currents.
- Electro-hydraulic actuators—this kind of system contains sealed liquid actuators solely powered by electrical power. This reduces the size of a central fluid reservoir and the number of fluid pathways throughout the system (Figure 6.9).

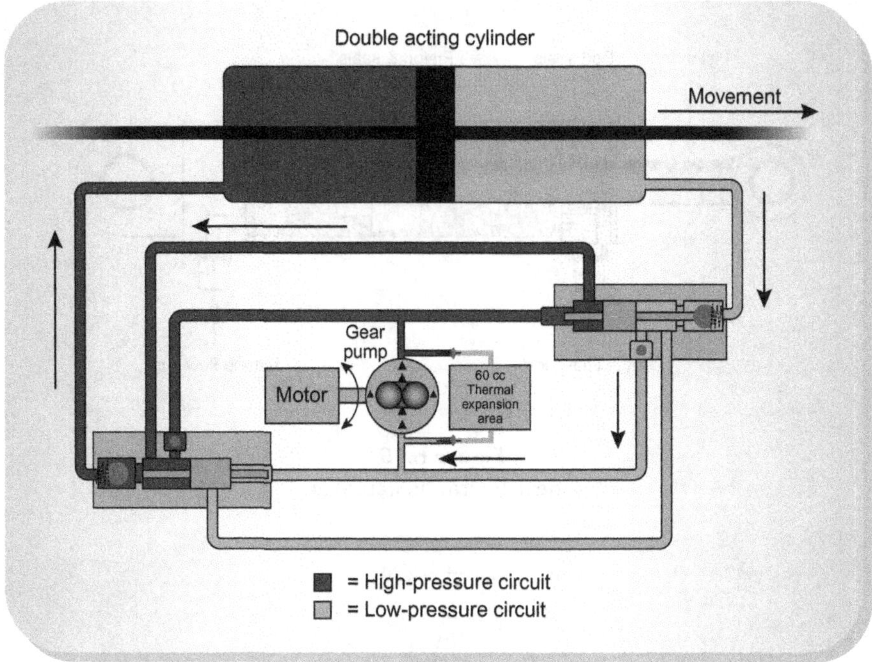

Figure 6.9
Electro-hydraulic actuator.

- Linear hydraulic actuator uses reversible pressures to drive a piston (Figure 6.10).
- Geared hydraulic motor—this device converts hydraulic pressure into torque and angular displacement by driving fluid through a gear system (Figure 6.11). This candidate solution uses a central fluid reservoir to drive all movements.
- Pneumatic actuator—this device converts energy stored in the form of pressure from compressed air into mechanical motion. This works much like the hydraulic actuator except that gas, rather than fluid, is used, and that gas is normally vented into the environment as movement is performed. This means that a replaceable reservoir of compressed gas is needed. On the other hand, other than valve control, no other power source need be provided to support movement. The system weight will include the weight of the compressed gas cylinder, since the system must be mobile and self contained.

Note that the joints must be movable in forward and backward directions in each of the joint's planes of motion (most joints will have a single plane). This can be done by having a motor that can selectively apply force in both directions or by having a pair of motors, one for each direction. Hydraulic actuators can be made that apply pressures on either side of the piston pressure plate and electric motors can be made reversible. Pneumatic actuators are generally only capable of applying force in one direction.

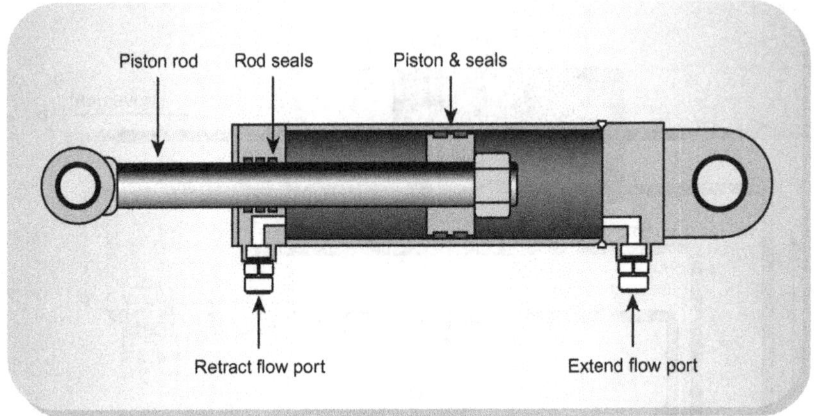

Figure 6.10
Linear hydraulic actuator.

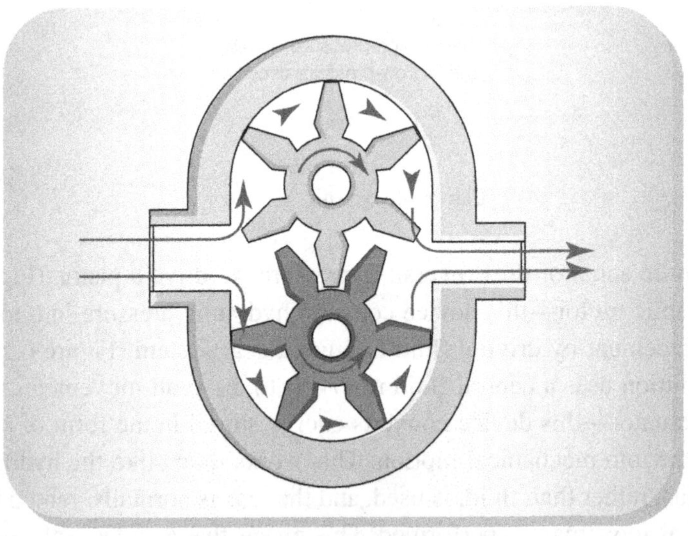

Figure 6.11
Geared hydraulic actuator.

For the T-Wrecks system, we'll need one (or possibly two) motor for each joint, so on the order of 10 such motors. Each will need to be able to lift and carry on the order of 3000 kg (depending on the joint), which includes 1500 kg load plus the weight of the system and pilot. For example, to hold a 1500-kg weight with two arms means that each shoulder joint will have to be able to lift around 800 kg (including the weight of the arm itself). If you consider the length of the arm (say 3 feet), this means the motor in the shoulder joint must be able to generate about 9921 lb ft of torque (3307 lbs $\times$ 3 feet) and to do so in, say 2 s, requires 14.2 hp. At the knee joint, the system will have to raise 1500 kg (total weight of 3000 kg divided by two) in the same timeframe, requiring about 28 hp.

Our candidate solutions will use appropriately sized motors for each of the 10 joints but will use the same technology across the solution. Minimum solution needs will have to be examined during the analysis to determine the required power ratings for each of the joints.

- Solution 1: Direct current electric motors. Response time for a standard 10 cm movement is 0.30 s. Durability of the solution is given as a MTBF of 40,000 h.
- Solution 2: Electro-hydraulic actuators. Response time for a standard 10 cm movement is 0.33 s. The MTBF for this solution is 60,000 h.
- Solution 3: Pneumatic actuators. Response time for a standard 10 cm movement is 0.10 s. The MTBF for this solution (including compressed air tubing) is 8000 h.

6.6 Perform the Architectural Trade Study

The preparatory work is done. At this point, we have a good idea of what we need to examine. The trade study will decide the evaluation criteria and their relative importance, construct the utility curves, compute the MOEs, and make the determination.

6.6.1 Define the Assessment Criteria

The assessment criteria are measures by which we judge "goodness" of the solution. The best way to identify the assessment criteria is to poll the stakeholders as they will all have ideas of what constitutes "good" from their point of view. Ideally, the list can be boiled down to a relatively small number of criteria—potentially up to a dozen in some cases—that can all be agreed upon by the stakeholders.

As well as the assessment criteria *per se*, you must also define the technique that will be used to perform the assessment: will it be done using the manufacturer's specifications? User opinions from a poll? A usability study with mock up devices? Measurements made on samples hand-made in the lab?

6.6.1.1 Speed Demon

The first point of concern is the user interface panel. In this case, we're going to use three assessment criteria: cost, durability, and usability. The first will be estimated from the parts list. The second will be determined from the manufacturer's specifications on the parts. The third will be done with a usability study on hand-made mockups added onto old model treadmill platforms.

The second point is the movement of the treadmill running belt. Here the assessment criteria are cost (from the manufacturer's published OEM cost price list), durability (from manufacturer's spec sheets), and torque (calculated from manufacturer's spec sheets providing horsepower and RPM).

6.6.1.2 T-Wrecks

The first concern for the architectural analysis was the technology to be used for proximity detection scanning. In this case the criteria are manufacturing cost, near-range accuracy, angular accuracy, weight, and response time. Cost, again, will be estimated by looking at the parts list. Near-range accuracy will be measured in the lab from manufacturer's samples. Response time will be estimated by looking at the time required to perform a complete scan of the environment around the system (internal computation time will be ignored as it is presumed to be approximately equal for all solutions). Angular accuracy and weight will be obtained from manufacturer's specifications.

For joint movement, we have four criteria: cost, weight, response time, and reliability. We will use information from the manufacturer for these key parameters although some calculation may be required.

6.6.2 Assign Weights to the Criteria

Just as polling the stakeholders to reach consensus on the set of criteria is a good idea, asking them to rank the relative importance of the criteria is also a good approach. Normally, this is done by ranking the importance of each criterion in the set on a scale of 0–10 (unnormalized). An issue is that you may have stakeholders who report that every criterion is of importance 10. You may also find that with many criteria 10 doesn't give you enough fidelity. A solution is to ask the stakeholders to provide numbers normalized so that they add up to 100.

We then either work with the stakeholders to reach a consensus or we can average their inputs. Then we normalize the weights so that they sum up to a fixed value (we've been using 1.0 here but any value can be used).

In this case we'll use the weights shown in Table 6.2.

For the T-Wrecks system, we'll use the weights in Table 6.3.

6.6.3 Define the Utility Curve for Each Criterion

In the previous discussions, we used straight lines for the utility functions. That is certainly most common, but it is possible to have other kinds of curves used. In this case, we'll use straight lines for all the criteria, normalized from 0 to 10 except for response time, which we'll weight using an exponential function.

Table 6.2: Speed Demon assessment criteria table.

Speed Demon assessment criteria weights			
Function/feature	**Criterion**	**Means of determination**	**Weight**
User interface panel	Cost	Estimated from parts list	0.30
	Durability	Estimated from manufacturer's specs	0.20
	Usability	Determined from usability study	0.50
Movement	Cost	Estimated from parts list	0.40
	Durability	Estimated from manufacturer's specs	0.20
	Torque	Calculated from manufacturer's specs	0.40

Table 6.3: T-Wrecks assessment criteria weights.

T-Wrecks assessment criteria weights			
Function/feature	**Criterion**	**Means of determination**	**Weight**
Proximity scanning	Cost	Use manufacturer's data	0.10
	Weight	Use manufacturer's data	0.20
	Near range accuracy	Measured in lab from samples	0.30
	Angular accuracy	Taken from manufacturer's spec	0.30
	Response time	Calculation based on manufacturer's data	0.10
Joint movement	Cost	Use manufacturer's data	0.1
	Weight	Use manufacturer's data	0.05
	Response time	Use manufacturer's data	0.2
	Durability	Use manufacturer's data	0.65

Table 6.4: Speed Demon utility curves.

Speed Demon assessment criteria weights		
Function/feature	**Criterion**	**Utility curve**
User interface panel	Cost	$\text{CostMOE} = -0.08 \times \text{cost} + 17.6$
	Durability	$\text{DurabilityMOE} = 2.0210^{-7} \times \text{Durability} - 0.101$
	Usability	$\text{UsabilityMOE} = 1.429 \times \text{Usability} - 2.1429$
Belt movement	Cost	$\text{CostMOE} = -\text{Cost}/35 + 14.28$
	Durability	$\text{DurabilityMOE} = \text{Durability}/400 - 5$
	Torque	$\text{TorqueMOE} = 30{,}303(\text{hp}/\text{RPM}) - 20.30$

Thus, the following Speed Demon utility curves are defined in Table 6.4 from the numbers given in the solution description and then normalized as discussed.

For the T-Wrecks solution, for both cost and weight, we have multiple parts of different sizes, and so must add up the attributes of the parts, together with any singular system properties, to determine the solution cost and weight. For response time, we will assume that we can run multiple scanning systems simultaneously (by using different frequencies, perhaps) so that the response times used will be the response times of individual emitter/

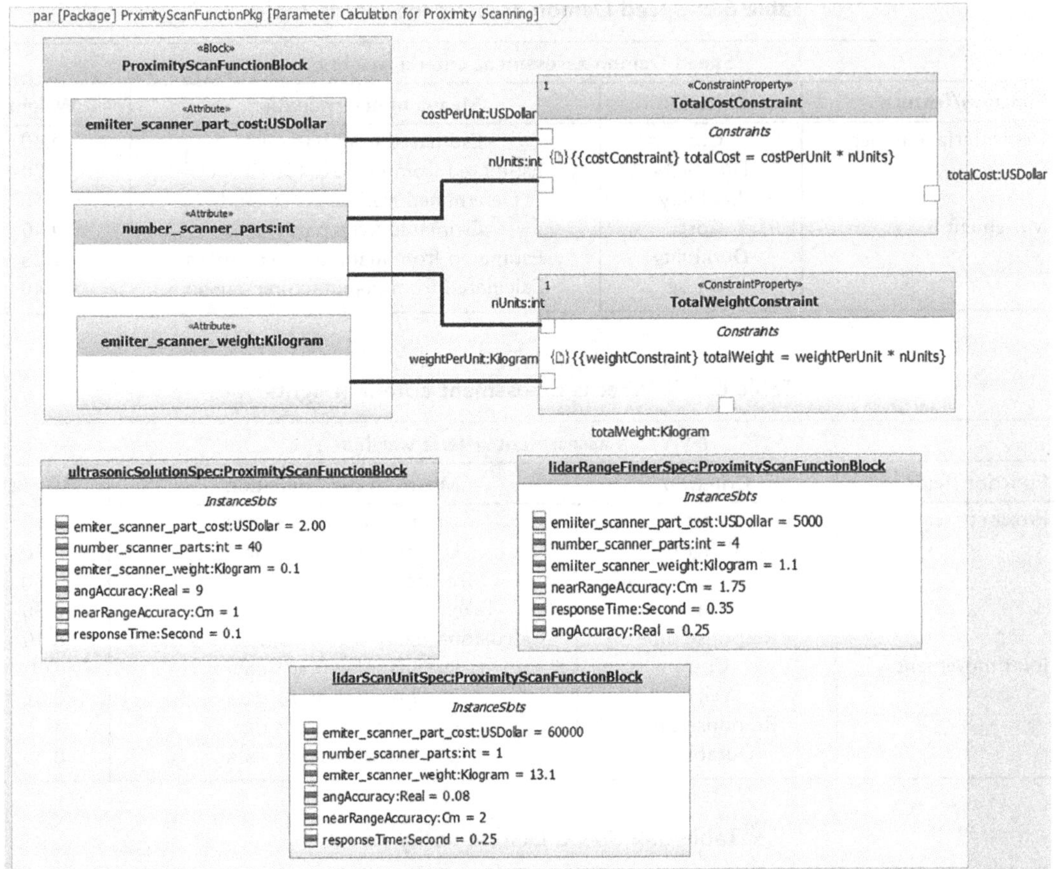

Figure 6.12
Parametric diagram for computing cost and weight for proximity scanning.

sensor units. The parametric diagram showing the calculation (as well as the three solution instance specifications) is shown in Figure 6.12.

I constructed three constraint views (one for each solution) and calculated the total cost and weight for each solution: ultrasonic—$80.00 and 4 kg, lidar scanning unit—$60,000.00 and 13.1 kg, lidar rangefinder—$20,000.00 and 4.4 kg. We can use these figures to construct the linear utility curves for cost and weight (see Table 6.6). Finally, we'll use the exponential curve in Equation (6.2) (utility curve for proximity scan response time) that gives both an exponential curve and (approximately) scale from 0 for the poorest to 10 for the best from among the candidate solutions for both scan and joint movement response times.

$$\text{ResponseTimeMOE} = 10 - \frac{e^{20 \times \text{ResponseTime}}}{110} \tag{6.2}$$

Table 6.5: Weights and costs for joint movement trades.

		Solution 1		Solution 2		Solution 3	
		Electric motor		Electro-hydraulic		Pneumatic	
Joint	**# Units required**	**Weight**	**Cost**	**Weight**	**Cost**	**Weight**	**Cost**
Shoulder	2	3.50	$250.00	5.10	$420.00	2.50	$180.00
Elbow	2	2.00	$175.00	4.20	$375.00	1.60	$120.00
Wrist	2	2.00	$175.00	4.20	$375.00	1.60	$120.00
Hip	2	4.00	$300.00	9.00	$700.00	3.00	$230.00
Knee	2	3.50	$250.00	8.00	$600.00	2.50	$180.00
Ankle	2	3.00	$225.00	7.50	$550.00	2.00	$150.00
Back	1	3.50	$250.00	7.50	$550.00	2.20	$180.00
Torso	1	2.50	$200.00	5.10	$420.00	1.75	$100.00
Central Unit	1	0.00	–	0.00	–	28.00	$600.00
Totals		**24.00**	**$1825.00**	**50.60**	**3990.00**	**45.15**	**1860.00**

Table 6.6: T-Wrecks utility curves.

T-Wrecks assessment criteria weights		
Function/feature	**Criterion**	**Utility curve**
Proximity scanning	Cost	psCostMOE = −1.67 × 10^{-4} × psTotalCost + 10.01
	Weight	psWeightMOE = −1.10 × psTotalWeight + 14.40
	Near range accuracy	NRAccuracyMOE = −10 × accuracy + 20
	Angular accuracy	angAccuracyMOE = −1.121 × AngAccuracy + 10.09
	Response time	psResponseTimeMOE = 10-exp(20 × responseTime)/110
Joint movement	Cost	CostMOE = −0.0462 × jmTotalCost + 18.43
	Weight	WeightMOE = −jmTotalWeight × 0.3759 + 22.389
	Response time	rtResponseTimeMOE = 10-exp(20 × responseTime)/110
	Durability	DurabilityMOE = MTBF/5200 − 1.538

For the costs of the different joint movement solutions, I constructed Table 6.5 to add up the costs, rather than a parametric diagram since the math was easy enough. These values are used to construct the linear normalized utility curves in Table 6.6.

6.6.4 Assign MOEs to Candidate Solutions

Now that we have the criteria, their weights, and the utility curves, we can construct the parametric diagrams to compute the MOEs of our selected criteria. The first one, computed manually at the start of the chapter, is shown in Figure 6.13. As before, evaluating the parametric constraints for the three solution candidates yields a best score for Solution 2 (membrane keys with LCD display).

Figure 6.14 looks at the trades for the four potential solutions. Note that we use a constraint property to compute torque from horsepower and RPM; this is an example of making

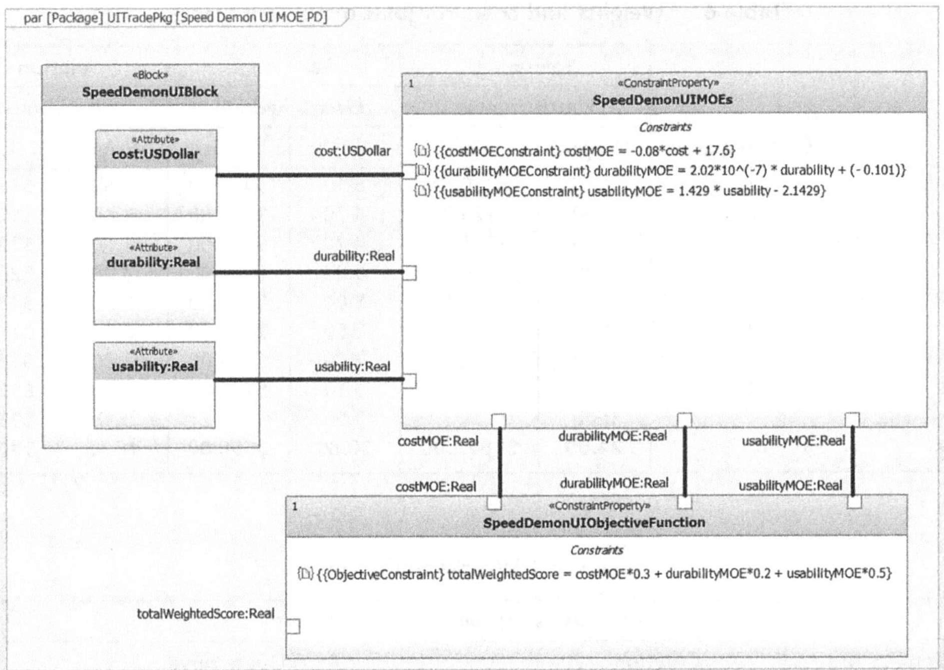

Figure 6.13
Calculating Speed Demon UI trades.

common conversions and calculations into reusable building blocks. Doing the math results in total weighted scores for Solution 1 (5.54), Solution 2 (3.16), Solution 3 (7.035), and Solution 4 (5.042). This makes Solution 3, the 4.0 hp, 4000 RPM drive motor, the best solution evaluated.

The analysis of the trades is done in much the same way for the T-Wrecks. Figure 6.15 shows the parametric diagram for computing the proximity scan MOEs. The two constraint properties in the upper right of the diagram sum of the costs and (physical) weights of the component pieces to feed into the `ProximityScanMOEs` constraint property. The output of these MOEs (cost, weight, near accuracy, angular accuracy, and response time) are then fed into the `ObjectiveFunctionCP` constraint property to compute the total weighted score for the solution being examined. This is where the weighting factors (scaled importance) of the assessment criteria are applied to compute the overall total.

For the last trade study, we'll calculate the MOEs and the total weighted score of for the joint movement solutions (Figure 6.16).

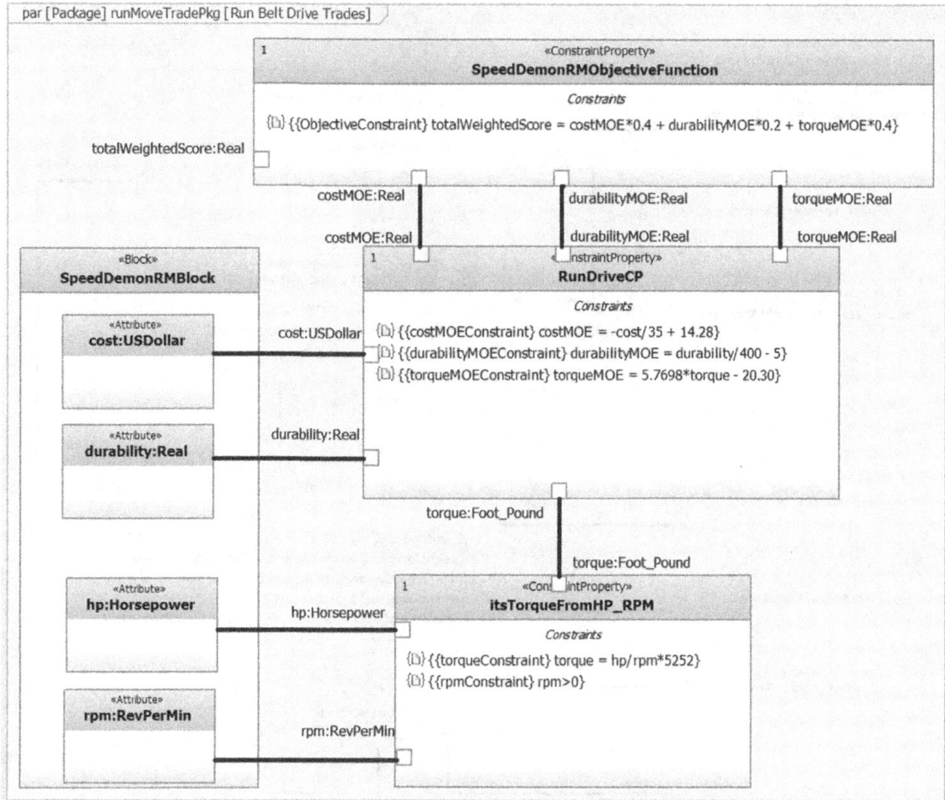

Figure 6.14
Calculating Speed Demon run belt drive trades.

6.6.5 Determine the Solution

Having now done the math, we can select the best solutions we examined. For the Speed Demon Treadmill, Table 6.7 shows the total weighted scores for the candidate solutions, with the best score highlighted (Table 6.8 for the T-Wrecks system).

You can see that some of the solutions, though widely different in values, have similar total weighted scores. The ultrasonic solution just barely beat the lidar rangefinder and the electro-hydraulic actuator barely beat the electric motor solution. When the values are close, the objective function is highly sensitive to the weighting values. If the weight criteria had a weighting factor of 0.1 instead of 0.05 (and the durability weight simultaneous reduced from 0.65 to 0.6), then the electric motor solution would have emerged victorious.

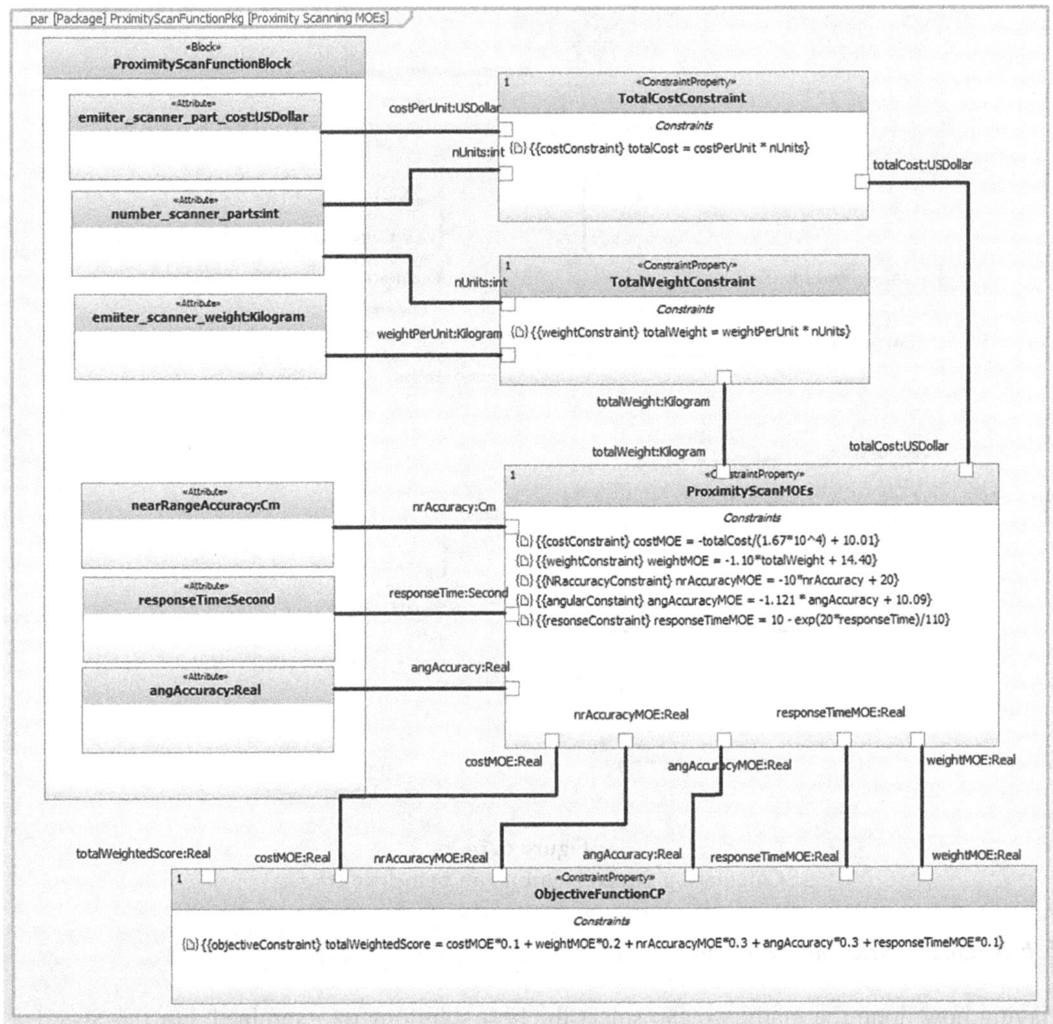

Figure 6.15
Calculating T-Wrecks proximity scan trades.

6.7 Merge the Solutions into the Systems Architecture

It is important not only to merge the solutions from analysis of different key system functions and use cases but also to merge with architectural decisions made in previous iterations. Generally, this is not difficult but sometimes the solutions that emerge from looking at different system properties end up in conflict. For example, what if we have selected a composite material for the T-Wrecks casing from a previous iteration but we find that we need a metal casing (because of sheer strength) to attach our electro hydraulic

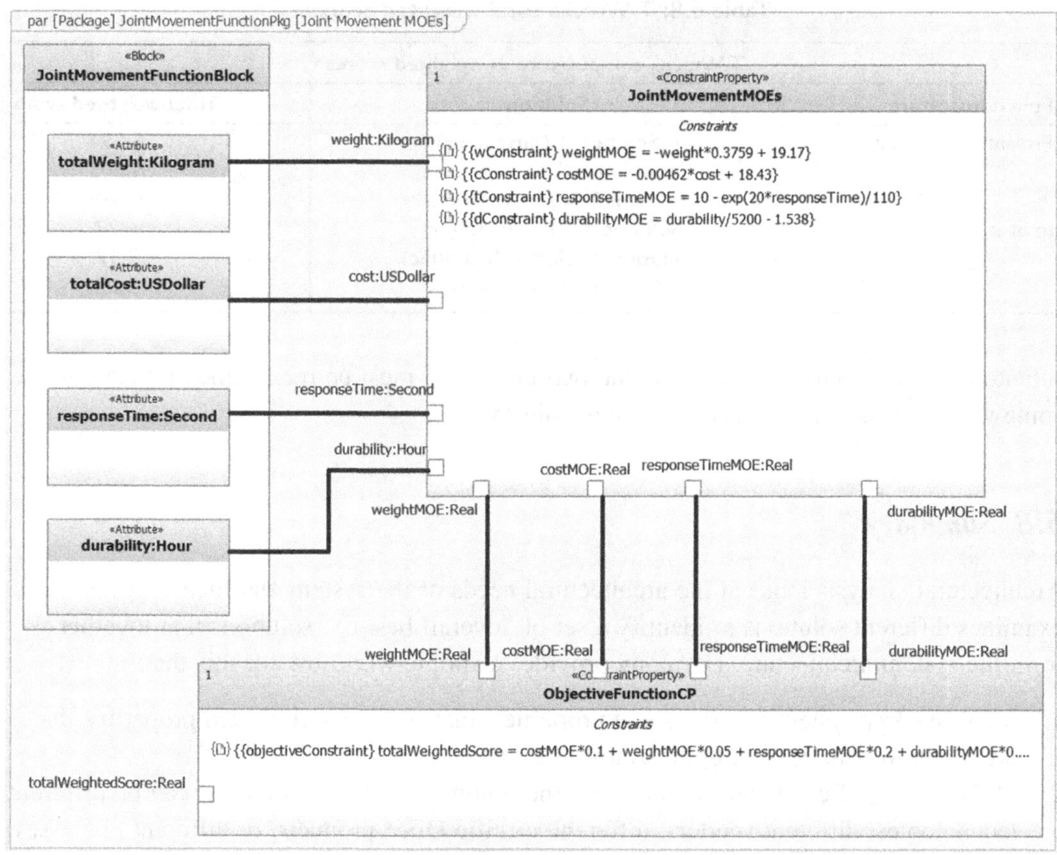

Figure 6.16

Calculating T-Wrecks joint movement trades.

Table 6.7: Speed Demon total weight scores.

Speed Demon computed total weighted scores		
Function/feature	**Solution**	**Total weighted score**
User interface panel	Solution 1 (Touch screen)	5.00
	Solution 2 (membrane)	**6.51**
	Solution 3 (keyboard)	3.18
Belt movement	Solution 1 (2.5 hp, 3500 rpm)	4.54
	Solution 2 (3 hp, 4500 rpm)	3.32
	Solution 3 (4.0 hp, 4000 rpm)	**7.03**
	Solution 4 (3.5 hp, 3800 rpm)	5.04

Table 6.8: T-Wrecks total weighted scores.

T-Wrecks computed total weighted scores		
Function/feature	**Solution**	**Total weighted score**
Proximity scanning	**Solution 1 (ultrasonic)**	**6.994**
	Solution 2 (lidar scan unit)	4.505
	Solution 3 (lidar rangefinder)	6.489
Joint movement	Solution 1 (electric motors)	6.77
	Solution 2 (electro-hydraulic)	**7.17**
	Solution 3 (pneumatic)	3.08

actuators? When such conflicts arise, the two properties must be reexamined together to come up with a satisfactory and consistent solution.

6.8 Summary

Architectural analysis looks at the architectural needs of the system and then suggests and examines different solutions to identify a set of "overall best fit" solutions that together form the system architecture. Harmony provides a simple workflow for this that:

1. Identifies key system functions and properties, that is, essential system properties that are likely to benefit from optimization.
2. Defines a set of candidate solutions for those concerns. These solutions can be different technologies, different vendors, different specific OEM products, or different processes.
3. Performs a trade study for each of the properties of concern.
   a. Define the assessment criteria—what does good "smell like"? Low cost? Low weight? Highly usable? Low power? High strength? Highly durable? Fast response? Usually several criteria are selected for solution evaluation.
   b. Assign weights to the criteria, based on their criticality to the system success.
   c. Define a utility curve for each criterion—this is usually a straight line normalized to provide the value 10 for the best of the candidate solutions and 0 for the worst, but other curves are possible.
   d. Assign MOEs to each of the solutions for each of the criteria. What does it cost? How fast is it? How much does it weigh? What is its MTBF? With this value, apply the utility curve to get the MOE score of the solution with respect to that criterion.
   e. Determine the weights by computing an objective function that applies the determined criteria weights times the MOE score of the solution against that criteria and then adds them up for all the criteria.
4. Merges the results of the trade study into a proposed architecture. Generally easy, this is usually additive. However, on rare occasions, results may be in conflict. When this

occurs, the conflicting solutions will need to be assessed together with the same analysis process we've described here.

Of course, remember that we're agile here, so we won't consider all system functions and properties in any single iteration. If system functions or properties appear correlated, then it is best to consider them together in the same iteration. If they are clearly independent, then they can be dealt within different iterations.

6.9 Moving On

At this point in the iteration, we have stakeholder and system requirements for a number of use cases. We've look at some key system properties and examined alternative architectural approaches and selected what appears to be the best one. The next step is to actually create and detail that architecture. And that's what we'll talk about in the next chapter.

References

[1] Maxima. A computer algebra system. Available from: <http://maxima.sourceforge.net/>.
[2] Planning Poker. Available from: <http://en.wikipedia.org/wiki/Planning_poker>.
[3] M. Cohn, Agile Estimation and Planning, Prentice Hall, Englewood Cliffs, NJ, 2005.

CHAPTER 7

Agile Systems Architectural Design

Chapter Outline

7.1 Objectives

The purpose of architectural design in the systems engineering workflow is two-fold. First, we want to identify the largest-scale pieces of the system, their responsibilities, and their (logical) interfaces. This includes allocation of requirements to the subsystems and, as necessary, derivation of subsystem-level requirements. Secondly, we want to support the decomposition of the system to support allocation of these subsystems to independent multidisciplinary downstream engineering teams. And—to be clear—we want to do this in such a way that the independently developed subsystems will integrate together incrementally with a minimum of fuss and effort.

7.1.1 So . . . What's a Subsystem?

On one hand, a *subsystem* can be thought of as a "major component of a larger system." While fine as far as it goes, it doesn't provide much in the way of guidance for identifying and characterizing such elements.

INCOSE[1] has this to say about subsystems [1]:

> No man is an island. Systems, businesses and people must be integrated so that they interact with one another. Integration means bringing things together so they work as a whole. Interfaces between subsystems must be designed. Subsystems should be defined along natural boundaries. Subsystems should be defined to minimize the amount of information to be exchanged between the subsystems. Well-designed subsystems send finished products to other subsystems. Feedback loops around individual subsystems are easier to manage than feedback loops around interconnected subsystems. Processes of co-evolving systems also need to be integrated. The consequence of integration is a system that is built and operated using efficient processes.

[1] International Council on Systems Engineering.

To complicate the issue, some people talk about different kinds of subsystems, such as "conceptual" (highly abstract groupings of system functions and data), "logical" (more refined groupings of system functions and data that are independent of physical boundaries), and "physical" (integrated combinations of hardware and software that implement system functions and properties). In complex situations, it may indeed make sense to have a subsystem divided into multiple layers of abstraction (e.g., conceptual, logical, and physical) with allocations from the more abstract to the more concrete. However, for most systems, my experience is that physical subsystems offer the most benefit and they will *always* need to be identified, so we will focus this chapter on physical subsystems alone.

We will use the following definition of a subsystem here:

> Subsystem: An integrated interdisciplinary collection of system components that together form the largest-scale pieces of a system. It is a key element in the subsystem and component architecture of the system.

Good subsystems have a set of common properties:

- They implement a coherent set of requirements and a small number of related system functions and properties
- The components within the subsystem are tightly coupled but only loosely coupled with components outside the subsystem
- They generally integrate multiple disciplines (e.g., mechanical, hydraulic, pneumatic, electronic, software, optical) within the subsystem itself
- They provide a small number of relatively simple interfaces to other subsystems and to elements outside the system
- They are created by a common, interdisciplinary team with close working relationships
- They form a run-time packaging of system components that doesn't do much work per se, but delegates responsibility to internal components and may aid in their coordination.

Physical subsystems are generally implemented with components from different engineering disciplines, but while the disciplines are different the components are generally tightly coupled. For example, an automotive braking subsystem will contain mechanical (brake pedal, braking pads), hydraulic (pistons, o-rings, pump, fluid reservoir), electronic (ECU,[2] pedal position, wiring), and software (ABS[3]) components. Physical subsystems are often

---

[2] Electronic Control Unit.

[3] Anti-Lock Braking System.

maintained or upgraded as a unit (and in aerospace are often referred to as LRUs[4]). Logical subsystems, on the other hand, often map to multiple physical subsystems and a physical subsystem may even contain multiple logical subsystems.

Large subsystems are often themselves decomposed into sub-subsystems, although we generally just continue to call them subsystems.

Note: subsystems are *not* packages. Packages are model organizational units and exist only at *design time*. Subsystems are organizational units for parts that will be implemented and so subsystem instances exist as real-world elements at run-time.

In SysML, a subsystem is just a usage of a block. You can add a «subsystem» stereotype if you find that clarifies your model (I often do). In fact, one of the most important diagrams—which can be either a block definition or an internal block diagram—is what I call a subsystem diagram. This diagram is a usage of a block diagram whose mission is to portray some (or all) aspects of the subsystem architecture.

It should also be pointed out that while subsystems are a key aspect of architecture, they are not the *only* important aspect of architecture. The Harmony process identifies five key views of architecture, of which, the Subsystem and Component view is one.

7.1.2 Key Architectural Views

There are many definitions for the term *architecture* even as it applies to systems. We also have people talking about conceptual, logical, and physical levels of abstraction with regards architecture and again we will focus on the physical architecture in this book. ISO[5] defines logical architecture as:

> The logical architecture of a system is composed of a set of related technical concepts and principles that support the logical operation of the system. It includes a functional architecture, a behavioral architecture, and a temporal architecture [2].

The same source goes on to define physical architecture in terms of the logical architecture:

> A *physical* architecture is an arrangement of physical elements (system elements and physical interfaces) which provides the design solution for a product, service, or enterprise, and is intended to satisfy logical architecture elements and system requirements. It is implementable through technologies [2].

[4] Line Replaceable Units.

[5] International Organization for Standardization (yeah I know the letters are out of order....).

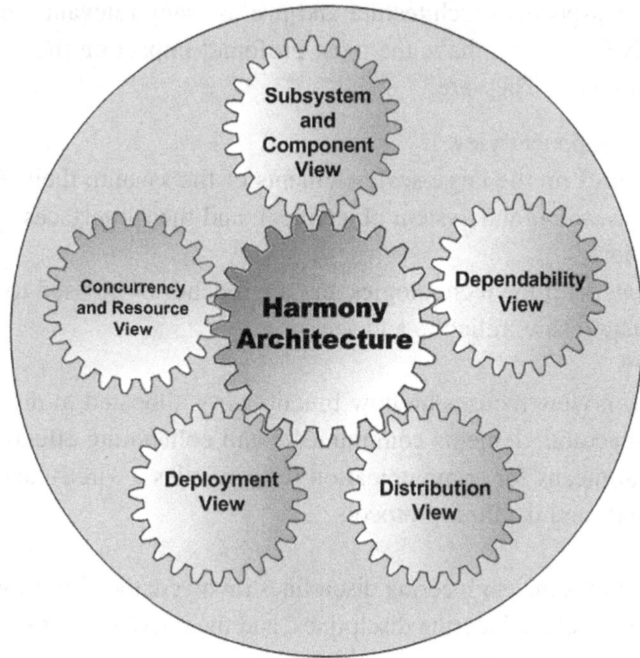

Figure 7.1
Harmony five key views of architecture.

This definition is fine but doesn't include guidance to developing architectures. So I'll add my own, which will drive our discussion in this chapter:

> Architecture: An integrated set of large-scale design decisions that implements system requirements in an optimized way.

Three aspects of this definition warrant special attention. The first is that to be considered architecture, it focuses on large-scale design decisions. Small, localized design decisions are, of course, important, but are not architectural because of their local impact and scope. The second point is that architecture is really about optimization, as we discussed in the previous chapter. A *good* architecture is one that implements the requirements in an optimal[6] way. In general, we try to achieve optimality through the application of design patterns, which are "generalized optimal solutions to recurring design problems" [3–5]. The third aspect is that the architecture is an integration of design decisions. The Harmony process identifies five key views of architecture (Figure 7.1).

[6] By *optimal*, in this sense, I mean that the solution has been optimized against the weighted set of design assessment criteria.

While there are many aspects to architecture and just as many relevant viewpoints, my experience is that five key views have the most profound impact on the system structure, behavior, and performance. They are:

- Subsystem and component view
  This view focuses on the large-scale elements of the system, their responsibilities (i.e., requirements, roles, and system objectives), and their interfaces.
- Dependability view
  This view deals with the technologies and approaches to be used to ensure the system is adequately safe, reliable, and secure.
- Distribution view
  The distribution view focuses on how functionality allocated to disparate and/or distributed architectural elements communicate and collaborate effectively. This includes physical means for communication (e.g., wireless, wired), and application, network, transport, and datalink protocols.
- Deployment view
  This view identifies the engineering disciplines involved, the allocation of requirements to elements in different engineering disciplines, and the interfaces between them.
- Concurrency and resource view
  This view concentrates on the identification, scheduling, and allocation of concurrent processes, performance analysis, and the robust sharing of resources among those processes. This is mostly a software-centric architectural view and so won't be discussed in this book.

A systems architecture is the sum of architectural design decisions made in *all* (and possibly more) the above views. Each view has its own vocabulary, technologies, and design patterns. In this chapter, we'll focus mostly on the Subsystem and Component View, with minor emphasis on the Dependability and Distribution views. The Deployment View will be discussed in the next chapter, as we hand off the system specifications to downstream engineering.

7.2 Architectural Design Workflow

Figure 7.2 shows the workflow for systems architectural design.

As before, I'll give a brief description of these tasks before getting into it all in earnest.

7.2.1 Identify Subsystems

This task is all about identifying these large-scale subsystem blocks and ensuring that they have a coherent set of responsibilities. This process is often started by grouping system functions together and reasoning about their congruence, coupling, and feasibility.

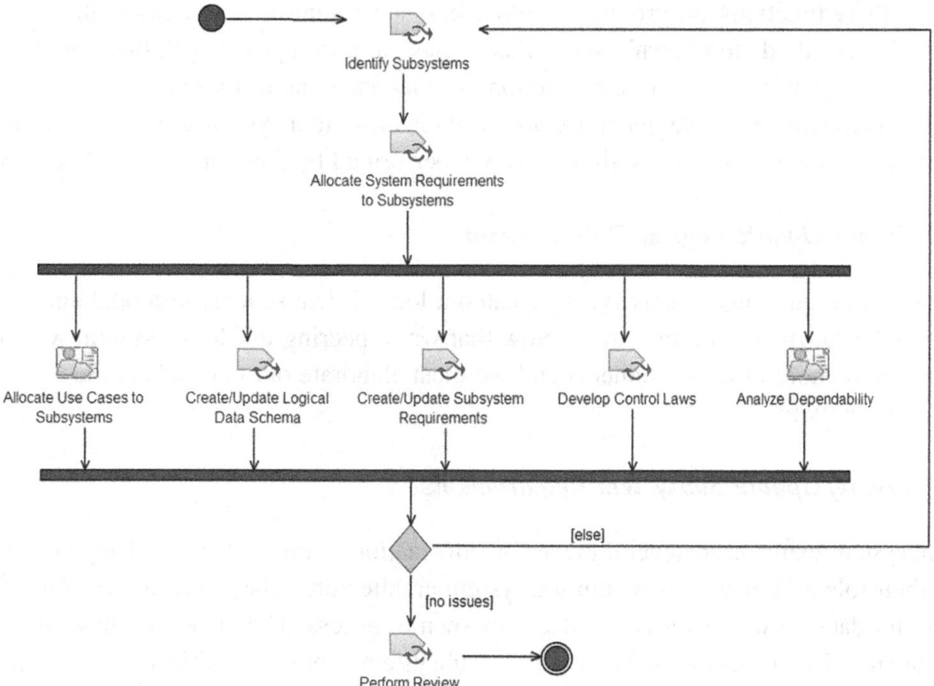

Figure 7.2
Architectural design workflow.

7.2.2 Allocate System Requirements to Subsystems

This is the first stab at allocation of system requirements. There are three cases to be considered: requirements that are sufficiently low-level to be directly allocated to a single subsystem; requirements that are simultaneously allocated to multiple (or all) subsystems; requirements that must be decomposed into subsystem-level requirements which may then be allocated. In general, the "system" per se doesn't do anything; its constituent subsystems do all the heavy lifting, so most requirements will end up either being allocated to a single subsystem or being decomposed and the derived requirements are then allocated to a single subsystem.

The next set of tasks and activities is performed in parallel. This doesn't mean they can't be done sequentially or by the same team, but it means that we don't care in principle in which order they are performed, and often it is best if the concurrent tasks cross-pollenate each other.

7.2.3 Allocate Use Cases to Subsystems

There are two viable approaches to use case allocation. The first, which I like to call "bottom up", allocated system functions and operations from the requirements model for a use case to appropriate subsystems. Once that is done for the set of system use cases in the iteration, these functions are grouped together into subsystem-level use cases. In the second flow, which is called "top down", system use cases are decomposed with the «include» relation, along with relevant system functions so that each one of these is allocated to only a single subsystem. What we generally *do not do* is allocate a system use case to a single subsystem. A system use case is almost always performed by a collaboration of subsystems.

7.2.4 Create/Update Logical Data Schema

In the system requirements activity, we created a logical data schema to model and understand data, flows, and resources. Now that we're peering inside the system we will identify many more of these elements and we must elaborate our data schema to accommodate them.

7.2.5 Create/Update Subsystem Requirements

The subsystem teams need several pieces of information to do their work. They need to know their role and interfaces within the system architecture. They need to know the data schema for data, flows, or resources that they own or access. They need to know their requirements. This task details the last. Each subsystem needs a specification of its specific subsystem requirements allocated or created in the other steps, and structured in a way that they can consume. For some, this will be creation of a textual document which contains their requirements (organized, of course, primarily by subsystem use cases). For others, it might be a DOORS requirements database. For some it might be a SysML model exported to them containing their requirements elements.

7.2.6 Develop Control Laws

Many, if not most, control laws, will be implemented within the confines of a single subsystem. This is because of the temporal restrictions and the tightly coupled nature of such algorithms. However, some control laws may span multiple subsystems and this task identifies, characterizes, and creates/allocates requirements for those. Such control laws must be dealt with here because they will profoundly affect the interfaces between the subsystems and therefore fall within the system purview.

7.2.7 Analyze Dependability

Because we are adding technologic solutions, decompositions, and allocations to our system specifications, we must analyze the updated specifications for their impact on the system dependability. This generally results in additional requirements to ensure the safety, reliability, and security of the system. For example, if, based on our trade study, we opt for a battery-powered engine for a car, we add safety concerns over electrocution and toxic chemical release; or, if we select a diesel engine, we have the safety concerns for fire and explosion. Selection of specific technologies adds dependability concerns that are not otherwise present for the system and we must ensure that we continue to meet our dependability goals.

7.2.8 Perform Review

As before, we will verify the completeness and correctness of our model preferentially with model execution and/or formal mathematics. Nevertheless, we still want to gain the benefit of both syntactic and semantic review of our models with quality assurance personnel and subject matter experts (respectively). We also generally want to disseminate design knowledge amongst our team members to improve its consistency and ensure that nothing important was missed.

7.3 Identify Subsystems

Given that a subsystem is a coherent system architectural element, we want to be able to identify the set of such elements that covers all of the system needs. Given that we're working incrementally, we may already have a set of subsystems, which may need augmentation. Alternatively, if this is not the first time we've built such a system, we may want to use the subsystem architecture of an existing fielded system. Or, we may need to create an initial subsystem set during the first iteration. In general, although we focus on the use cases of concern within the given iteration, there is nothing wrong with looking ahead a bit to ensure that the solution we propose will scale as we add more capability to our specification.

The set of steps we perform to identify the subsystems is very straightforward.

For each use case:

- Identify system functions and important data sets and resources
- Group sets of these features (functions, data, and resources) together based on commonality
- Specify the groups as subsystems
- Identify subsystem features that must be exposed to peer subsystems or to external actors
- Group exposed subsystem features into interfaces
- Draw the subsystem architecture diagram
- "Play" through scenarios from the system use cases to convince yourself that they can all be satisfied with the proposed set of subsystems.

Identify system functions and important data sets and resources

Remember, these use cases group together many system functions. System functions show up as actions on the use case activity, state, or sequence diagrams. We may also identify data sets exposed through the system interfaces or that are implied by those interfaces. For example, an MRI scanner is likely to have an image (data) as well as important image metadata. An oxygen supply system is likely to have an oxygen source (resource).

Group sets of these features (functions, data, and resources) together based on commonality

One of the key criteria for a good subsystem is commonality. Commonality might be in terms of materiel managed, design technology, services around a resource or data set, system purpose (such as manage safety), or security or safety level.

A system function may itself be too complex to be usefully allocated to a single subsystem and require decomposition down to sub-functions that may be allocated. The same is true of data sets, particularly when they are composed of elements from different sources or modalities.

Specify the groups as subsystems

The different sets of features are candidate subsystems. Ideally, each candidate subsystem's responsibility can be easily described in one or two sentences.

Identify subsystem features that must be exposed to peer subsystems

Interfaces are specifications of control, data, or materiel flow among (usually between) subsystems. Interfaces can be *provided* (by the subsystem to other system elements) or *required* (by the subsystem from some other element). Note that provided/required services do not imply information or materiel flow direction. A provided service can have data flowing in (such as with a service parameter) or out (such as a return value).

Group-exposed subsystem features into interfaces

Good interfaces expose essential information but do not expose internal subsystem design choices. We will use proxy ports to identify connection points, and interface blocks to specify what flows across them. Control messages will be modeled as SysML events, discrete data, and materiel flows will be modeled as parameters on those events, and continuous data and materiel flows will be modeled as flow properties.

Draw the subsystem architecture diagram

Create one—or possibly more—block diagram that depicts the subsystem, their connections and their interfaces. In my experience, this diagram(s) is the most used diagram created by the systems engineers.

"Play" through scenarios from the use cases to convince yourself that they can all be satisfied with the proposed set of subsystems

Look at some key scenarios from the use cases of interest for the iteration and convince yourself that they can be supported by the proposed set of subsystems. For each interaction between the subsystems as they collaborate, does it have the knowledge, resources, and ability to satisfy requests made of it? This is just a preliminary check, as in the subsequent activities, the ports and interfaces will be refined in detail.

Let's look at our system examples and see what emerges as candidate subsystem architectures.

7.3.1 Speed Demon Subsystems

Because this treadmill is meant to be a high-end workhorse treadmill for use by everyone from casual walkers and joggers to elite athletes, the industrial design team got together and sketched out the exterior view concept (Figure 7.3).

The most notable thing about the treadmill is the very large (70 cm wide by 150 cm tall) curved LCD display. This display provides both the workout display information but also plays movies, including race videos. At the bottom of the screen is a 50 × 70 cm kick guard to prevent damage to the display. The running deck itself is slightly curved to encourage optimal placement of the runner within the treadmill structure.

The next figure (Figure 7.4) shows the proposed set and placement of the control keys, which are positioned on the treadmill arms, close to the display. The left arm controls the program selection and treadmill control. It also sports a waterproof USB connector for the athlete data card. The right arm holds the media controls which allow the athlete to select, play, and control the playing of videos and music. It provides an iPod™ connector and a headphone jack.

While interesting and informative, the industrial design of the treadmill doesn't directly impact the identification of subsystems. It does help with their visualization, which is why it's included. Now, let's think about the system functions that we want to support and how we might group them. We've looked at a couple of different use cases for the Speed Demon Treadmill in some detail and we've more casually mentioned a few others. Table 7.1 shows the functions and resources we've identified or think might be relevant for the system. I've put the use cases and functions that we've identified in bold in Table 7.1 and the ones we're "looking ahead for consideration"[7] in italic text.

Grouping these functions into cohesive units leads us to a potential subsystem architecture, as shown in Figure 7.5. This figure shows the 14 proposed subsystems as blocks within a block definition diagram, although block instances are shown so that all subsystem connections can be displayed.

[7] Which means we're making "informed guesses" for them at this point.

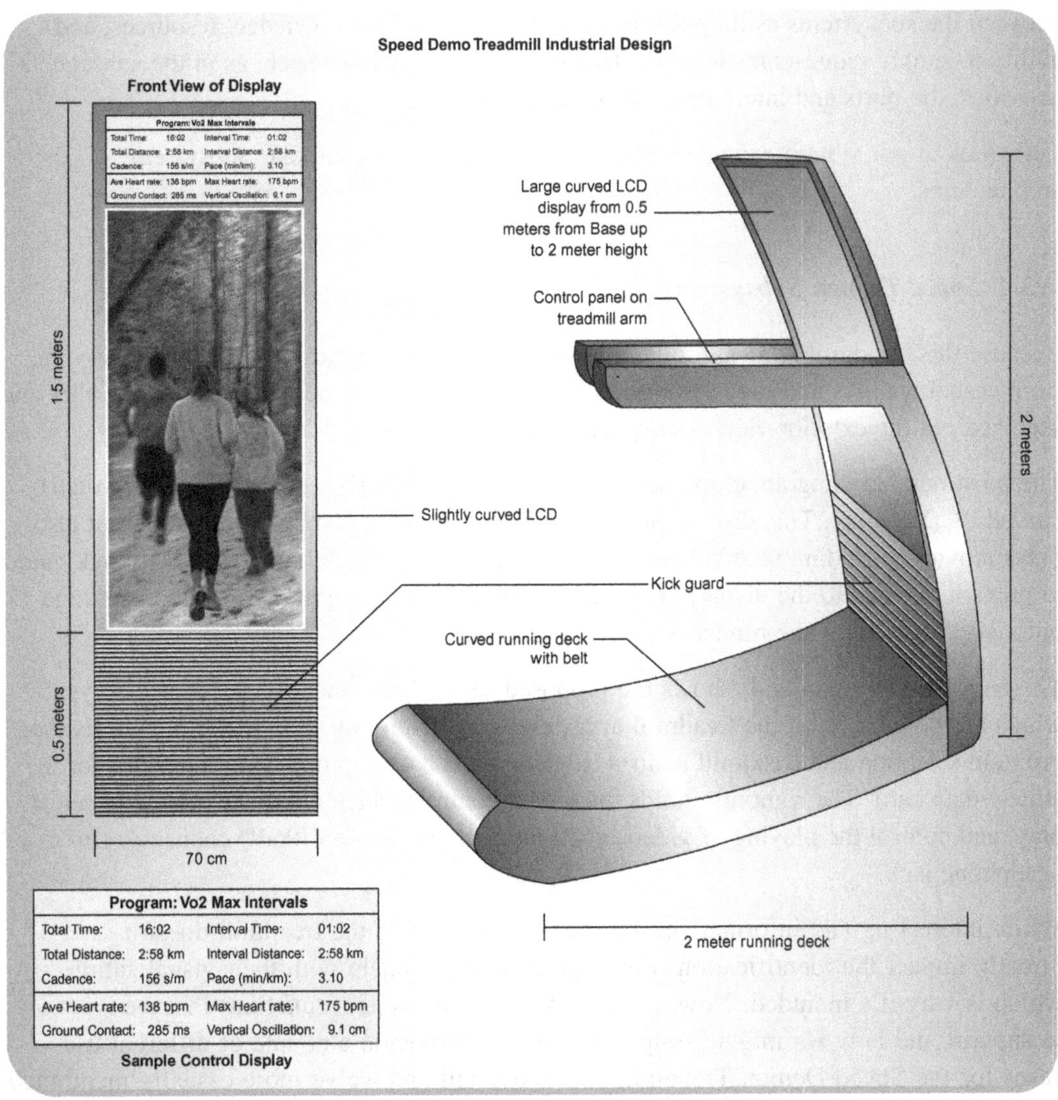

Figure 7.3
Speed Demon exterior view design concept.

Ports (proxy ports, although the stereotype is elided from the diagram) are used for dynamic connections. These are connections that exchange messages, control, or flows during system usage. Compositions show the aggregation nesting among the block types; for example, the `Frame` block (the instance on the diagram is labeled `itsFrame`) contains parts of the block types `Deck`, `LeftUpright`, `RightUpright`, `CenterUpright`, `LeftArmAssembly`, and `RightArmAssembly`. Associations indicate static mechanical connections (elements fastened together). For example, the `Deck` fastens to the `LeftUpright`, `RightUpright`, and `CenterUpright`.

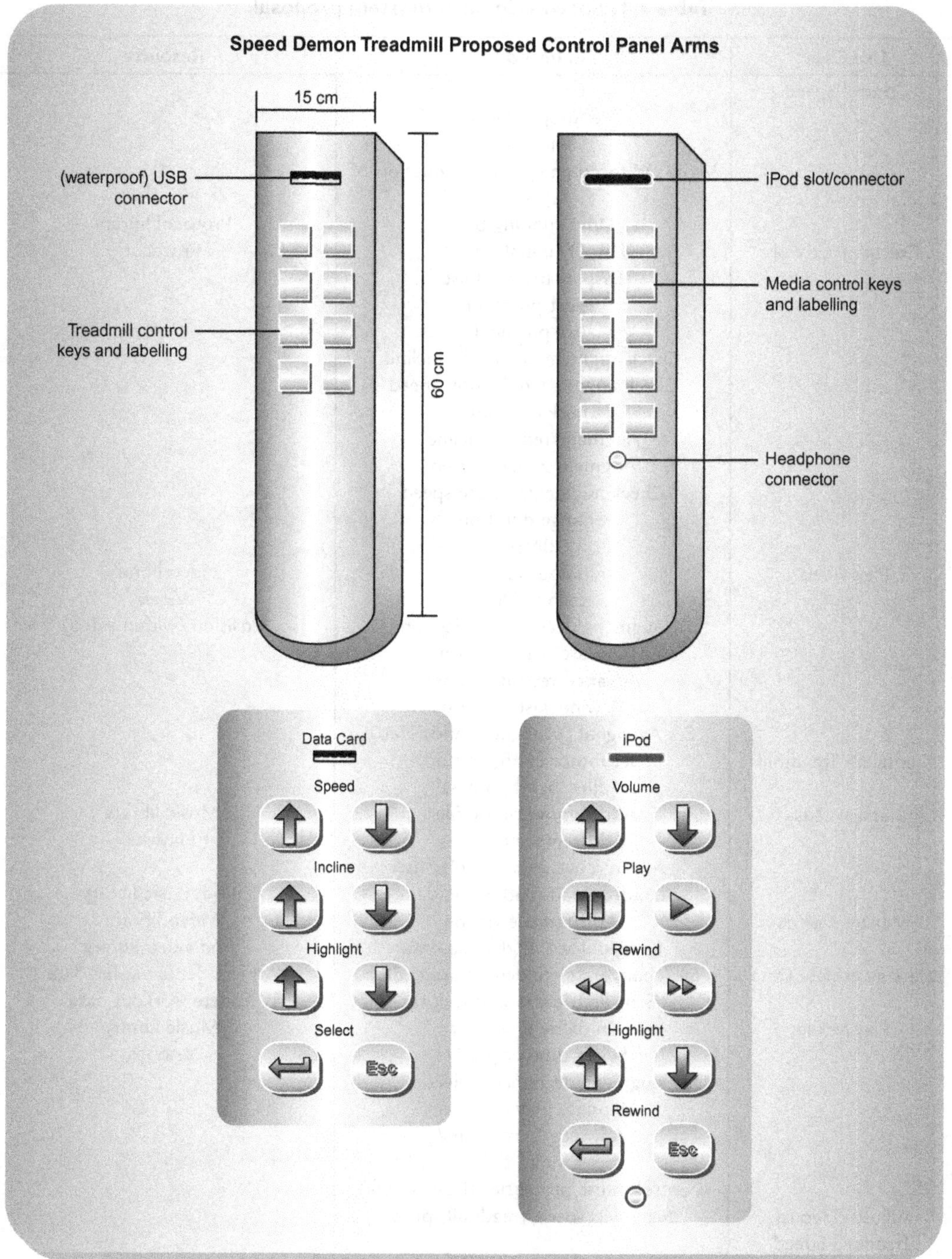

Figure 7.4
Speed Demon proposed control panel layout.

Table 7.1: Speed Demon subsystem proposal.

Use Case	Function	Resource
Control Speed	Enter speed	
	Verify speed value	
	Set speed	
	Verify OK for augmentation/reduction of speed	
	Drive running belt	Protocol library
Execute Protocol	Display initial screen	Protocol
	Display protocol list	
	Select protocol	
	Run protocol	
	Check augment/reduction incline	
	Check augment/reduction speed	
	Check duration	
	Augment/reduce incline	
	Augment/reduce speed	
	Check augment/reduce speed	
	Change duration	
	Beep	
Play Video	Initialize video list	Video library
	Select video	Video
	Augment/decrement selection	Position (within video)
	Update play position	
	Advance/retreat chapter	
	Rewind/fast forward	
	Set AV signal (play audio and video)	
Configure Treadmill	Set motor configuration	
	Adjust belt tightness	
Manage Music	Add/remove music files	Music library
	Add/remove playlists	Playlists
	Add/remove music to play list	
	Load/unload iPod music data	iPod music library
Manage Videos	Add/remove videos	Video library
	Load/unload iPod video data	iPod video library
Manage Athlete Data	Set/change athlete demographic data	Athlete demographic data
	Store/retrieve workout data	Athlete workout data
Play Music	Initialize music list	Music library
	Select tune or playlist	settings
	Augment/decrement selection	
	Update play position	
	Advance/retreat tune	
	Set audio signal	
	Control music properties (bass, treble)	
Adjust Video to Treadmill Speed	Set video speed/treadmill speed	
Define Protocol	Add/remove protocol	
	Add/remove interval	
	Configure interval time/elevation/speed	

(Continued)

Table 7.1: (Continued)

Use Case	Function	Resource
Manage Protocols	Add/remove protocol	
	Reorder protocol list	
Monitor Athlete	Identify/select athlete	Athlete workout data
	Monitor heart rate	
	Monitor cadence	
	Compute ground contact time	
	Computer vertical oscillation	
	Compute Vo_2 max estimate	
Control Elevation	Augment/reduce elevation	
Run Factor-Defined Protocol	Select protocol	
	Execute/stop protocol	
Execute Pre-planned Protocol	Select protocol	
	Execute/stop protocol	
Race	Configure race time/distance	Remote treadmill connect data
	Connect with remote treadmill	Remote treadmill time history performance data
	Display remote racer data	Remote racer data
	Run/stop race	
	Display race data	
	Disconnect with remove treadmill	
	Store/retrieve race data	

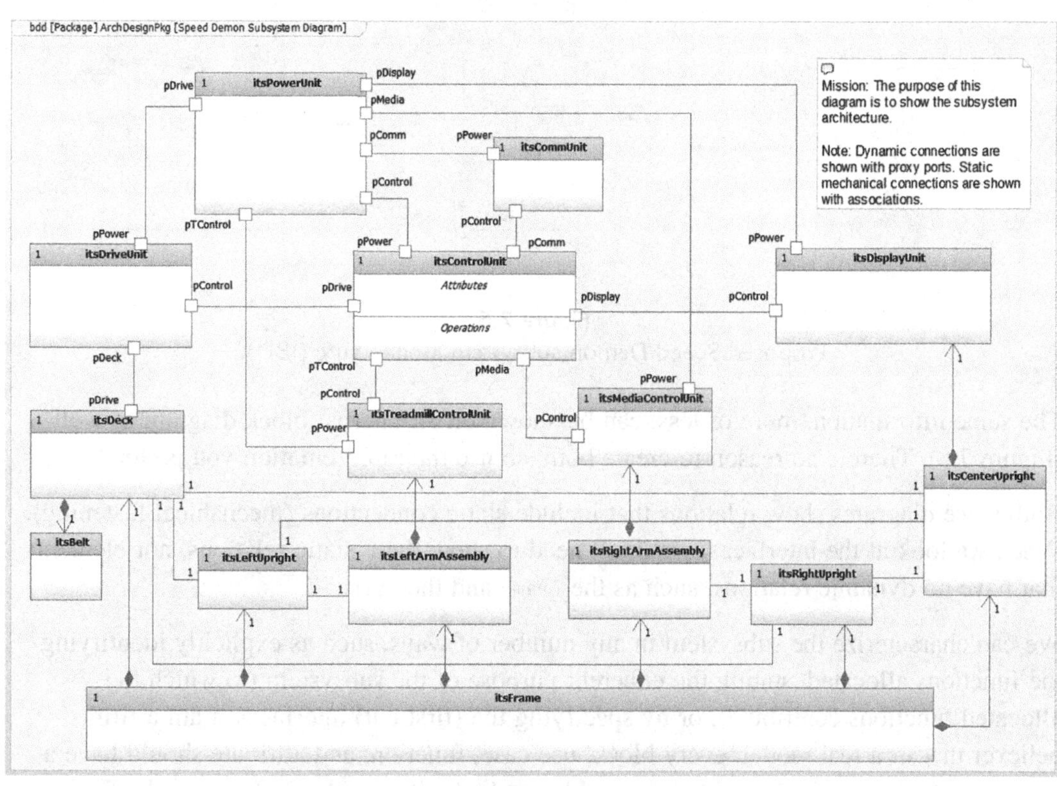

Figure 7.5
Proposed Speed Demon subsystem architecture (BDD).

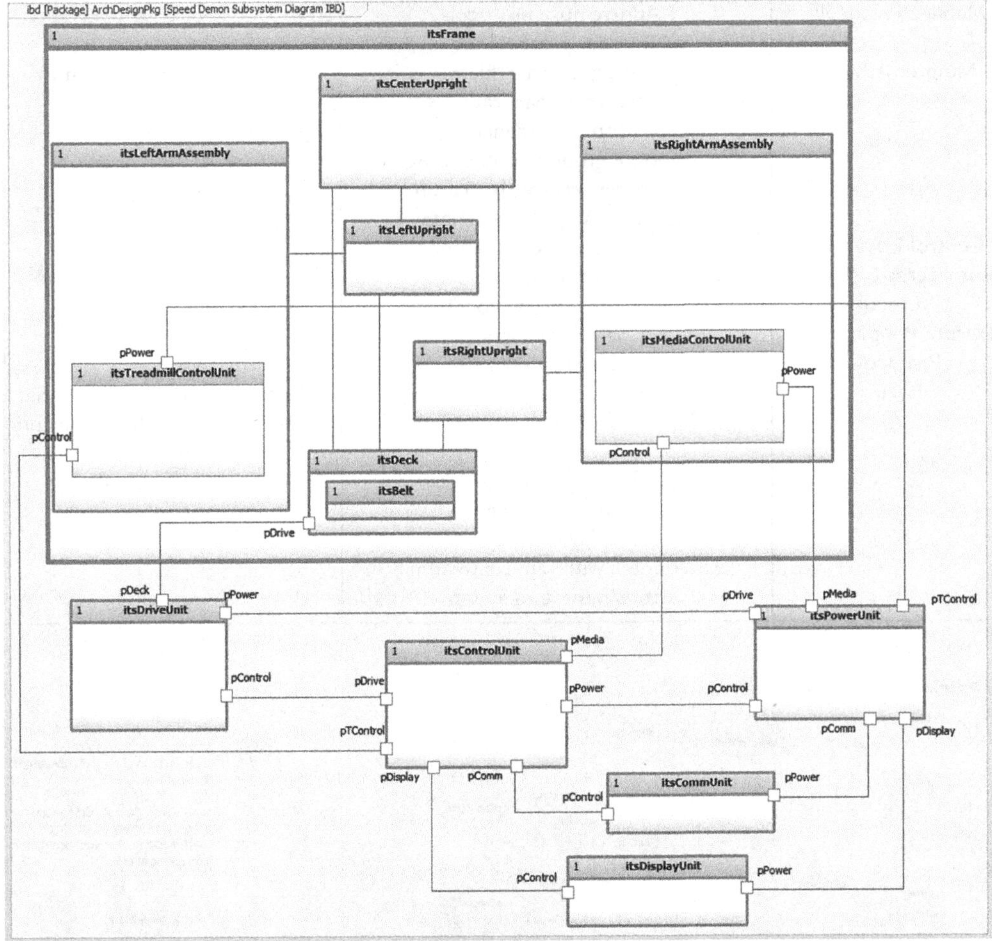

Figure 7.6
Proposed Speed Demon subsystem architecture (IBD).

The same information, more or less, can be shown on an internal block diagram as well (Figure 7.6). There's no reason to create both, so use the representation you prefer.

Both these diagrams show relations that include static connections (mechanical fastening). When we look at the interfaces, we don't need to show these static relations, nor elements that have no dynamic relations, such as the `Frame` and the `Belt`.

We can characterize the subsystem in any number of ways, such as explicitly identifying the functions allocated, stating the coherent purpose of the subsystem (to which the allocated functions contribute), or by specifying the (first cut) interfaces. I am a firm believer that in a real model, every block, use case, function, and attribute should have at least a brief description as to what it provides and why it provides it. I usually let the

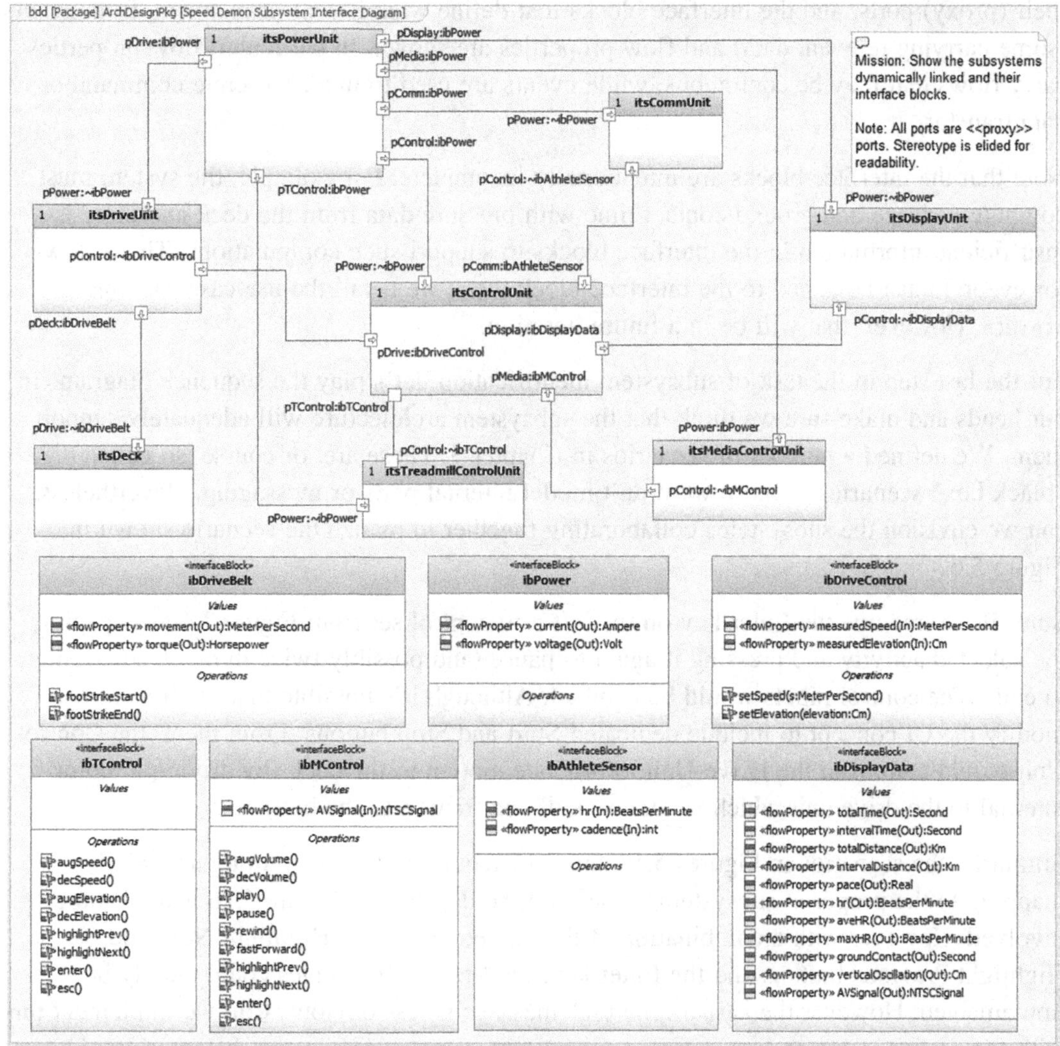

Figure 7.7
Speed Demon first cut subsystem interface blocks.

design detail of the element explain the *how*, unless the *how* is particularly complex. It is usually far more difficult to discern the *why*.[8]

The next thing we want to do is to begin to define the first-cut interfaces (or, in this case, interface blocks, since we are using proxy ports). Figure 7.7 shows the relevant subsystems,

---

[8] I remember reviewing someone's assembly code some years ago where the comments were things like "Put the value 5 in the Accumulator" to "document" a line of code like "LD A, 5". That is a completely useless comment! I'd much rather read about "Why the number 5" and "Why the accumulator."

their (proxy) ports, and the interface blocks that define what is sent or received. Both events (some carrying relevant data) and flow properties are shown. In particular, flow properties carry flows that may be continuous, while events are used to model discrete command or data transfer.

Note that the interface blocks are intentionally incomplete. For example, the system must compute cadence and ground contact time with pressure data from the deck and there is insufficient information in the interface blocks to support such computations. These flows (or events) must be added to the interface block when we detail the use case `Monitor Athlete`. However, that will be in a future iteration.

For the last step in the task of subsystem identification, let's play the sequence diagrams in our heads and make sure we think that the subsystem architecture will adequately support them. We defined a number of scenarios in Chapter 5. These are, of course, so-called "black box" scenarios because we didn't model internal parts or messaging. Nevertheless, can we envision the subsystems collaborating together to realize the scenario shown in Figure 5.6?

Sure. If we imagine the Enter key on the left arm control set from Figure 7.4 as engaging the selected activity and pressing it again to pause (and possibly twice in quick succession to end). The control inputs would be handled. Although it's possible that we'll want to modify the UI concept to include dedicated Start and Stop buttons. From there, the Control Unit would command the Drive Unit to produce motion to the deck (by driving a motor internal to the drive unit which is "connected" via friction to the belt).

Similarly, the scenarios in Figures 5.10 and 5.11 require only a very straightforward mapping to the proposed subsystems. The scenario depicted in Figure 5.26 is a bit more involved. However with a combination of the Athlete using the Highlight Next and Highlight Previous buttons and the Enter key, the first few messages could clearly be implemented. However the `setDuration(60)` message is less obvious. Can we implement this with the `Speed Augment` and `Speed Decrement` buttons or must we support the entering of a numeric value directly? We can go back to our stakeholders and discuss the pros (direct entry of a desired speed) and the cons (more complex UI, increased cost).

One of the key ideas of agile methods is to involve the stakeholders frequently to identify and resolve these kinds of issues. A common problem in more traditional systems engineering environments is that stakeholders are only involved at the very beginning and end of the process. This means they are not available to steer the project when questions, such as this, come up. Involving the stakeholder means that they are more likely to get what they want at the end.

A common concern with respect to increasing stakeholder involvement is "requirements creep." That is, in the name of "providing feedback", what some stakeholders might do is to actually add additional requirements. It is true that *does* happen and it is also true that it's not *necessarily* a bad thing. What is important is to clearly identify that they are *new* requirements, estimate the impact (cost, effort, release date, quality, etc.) and then judge whether or not the benefits of the suggested additions justify their impact. If deeper thinking on the part of the stakeholder makes the system more usable, then it may very well be the best outcome.

7.3.2 T-Wrecks Subsystems

The T-Wrecks system is quite a bit more complex than even our top-end treadmill. Of course, with the T-Wrecks system there are some "natural boundaries" for subsystems, notably the limbs, torso, and head. They don't *have* to be subsystems, but it is a natural way to decompose the system. On the other hand, having body segments as subsystems, doesn't address other system functions that don't naturally fit into the body-moving-part decomposition strategy, such as providing power, sensing the environment (proximity scan), system health monitoring, self test, and so on.

One could even take a different strategy altogether and use a strategy that cut across the body segments. For example, one might envision a "movement subsystem" which moves all the limbs and is physically distributed across the system. Some might even use such a strategy to develop logical subsystems and then use limbs as the physical subsystems and have a set of mapping rules for tracing between the two levels of architecture abstraction.

In this example, I'll go ahead and use body segments as the most obvious set of subsystems and layer on top of that subsystems for managing system-wide functions, such as proximity scanning and subsystems for dedicated purposes, such as system coordination.[9] The proposed architecture is shown in Figure 7.8.

There are a couple of things to note in Figure 7.8. First, note that there are four relations from `T_Wrecks` to `LimbAssembly`. I could have modeled these relations with a single composition with a multiplicity of four. However, when each part has a distinctive role, I prefer to use singular relations (and when the parts all fulfill the same role, I use plural multiplicity). Second, the diagram shows multiple levels of decomposition. For example, `T_Wrecks` contains the `TorsoAssembly`, which in turn contains the `CoordinationSubsystem`. Lastly, the diagram contains a comment that contains a hyperlink (see the underlined text in the figure). This is a common method for improving model navigation—adding explicit hyperlinks that, when clicked, take you to a related view or element.

[9] The functions of the other subsystem are fairly obvious but this subsystem has the responsibility for overall computation, balancing, and multi-limb coordinated movement.

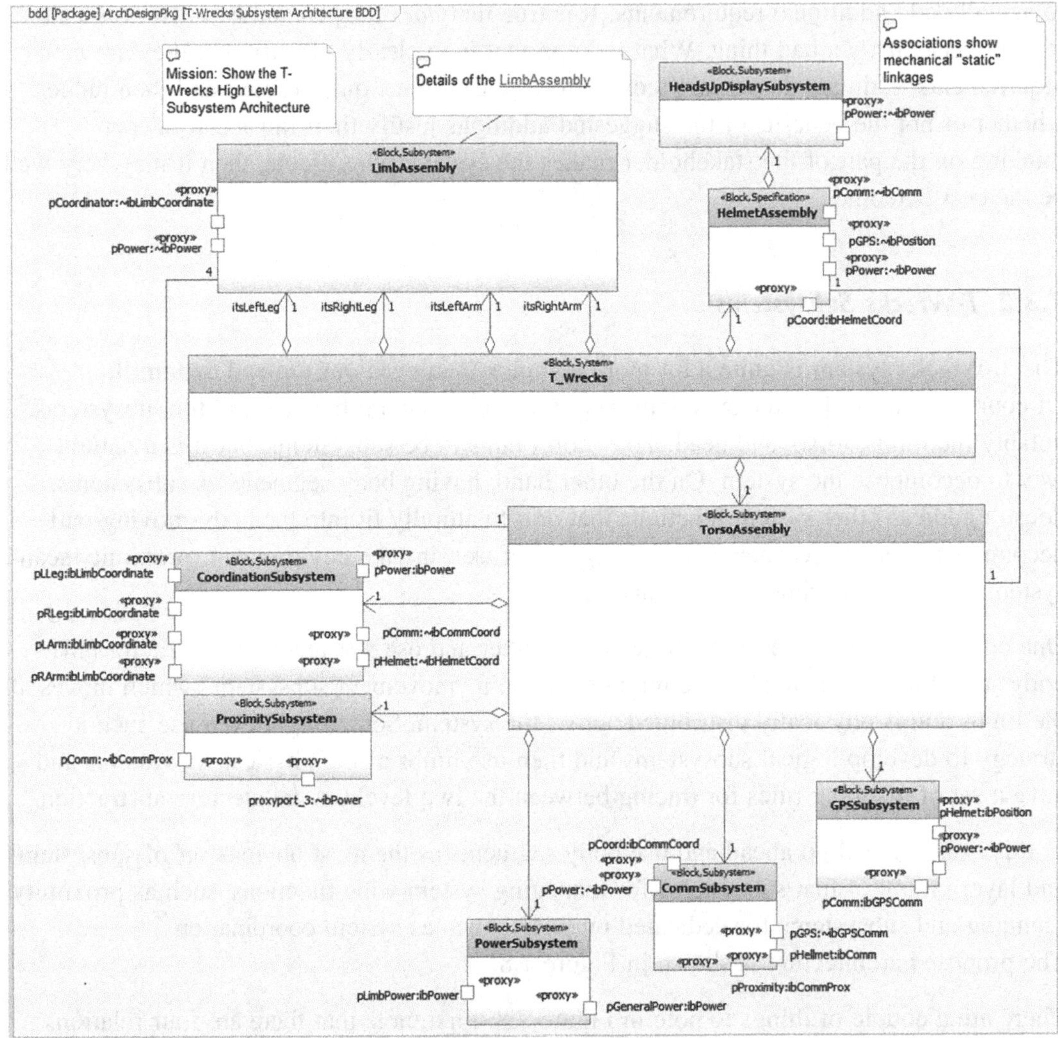

Figure 7.8
T-Wrecks proposed subsystem architecture.

The associations in the figure show static mechanical and/or electrical cabling linkages. For links across which flows traverse—whether they are software, energy, or materiel—we will use ports.

The `LimbAssembly` models four different limbs. Whether to model the limbs as different instances of a single block or as different blocks is an interesting one. If they were identical, there would be no question; they would be different instances of the same block. However, not only are arms different than legs, both arms and legs have *chirality* (handedness) and so are *not* identical. They may have the same electro-hydraulic actuators and the same software, but they differ, if nothing else, *mechanically* and in their layout. For this reason, in Figure 7.8,

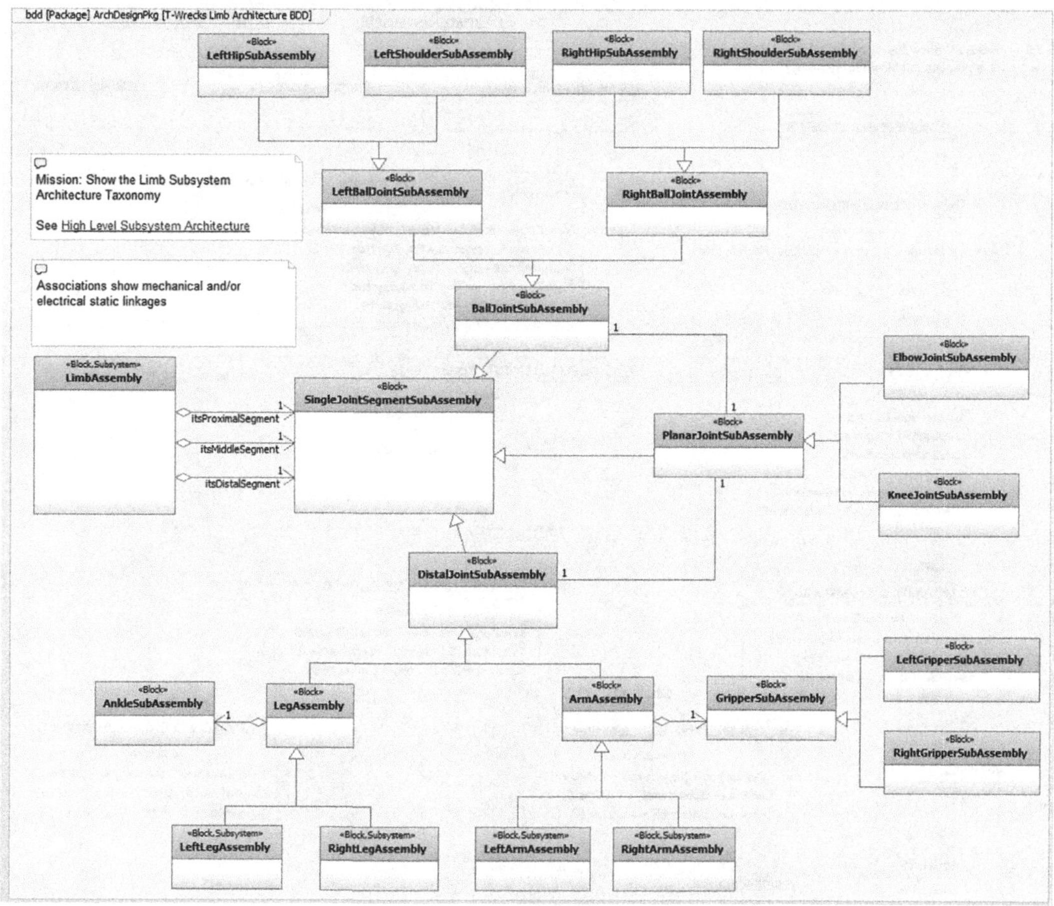

Figure 7.9
T-Wrecks Limb Architecture taxonomy.

I've modeled the limbs as a block, but elsewhere in the model (follow the hyperlink in the model to Figure 7.9), I specialized that block into `LegAssembly` and `ArmAssembly` as well as decomposed these blocks into subassemblies, which have their own specialized subtypes.

This is a (slightly) advanced modeling technique in that it allows use to think about the system at different levels of abstraction. The system contains four limbs—`itsLeftLeg`, `itsRightLeg`, `itsLeftArm`, and `itsRightArm`. Each of these is an instance of `LimbAssembly`, consisting of three (specialized) `SingleJointSubAssemblies`. Think about that. It means that `itsLeftLeg` is a specialized kind of `LimbAssembly` (specifically, one that is a `LeftLegAssembly` and contains parts of type `AnkleSubAssembly`, `KneeJointSubAssembly`, and `LeftHipSubAssembly`). It's important to remember that a `LeftLegAssembly` *is ultimately a usage of* `LimbAssembly`, and that a `LeftHipSubAssembly` *is ultimately a type of* `BallJointSubAssembly`. That means that if a

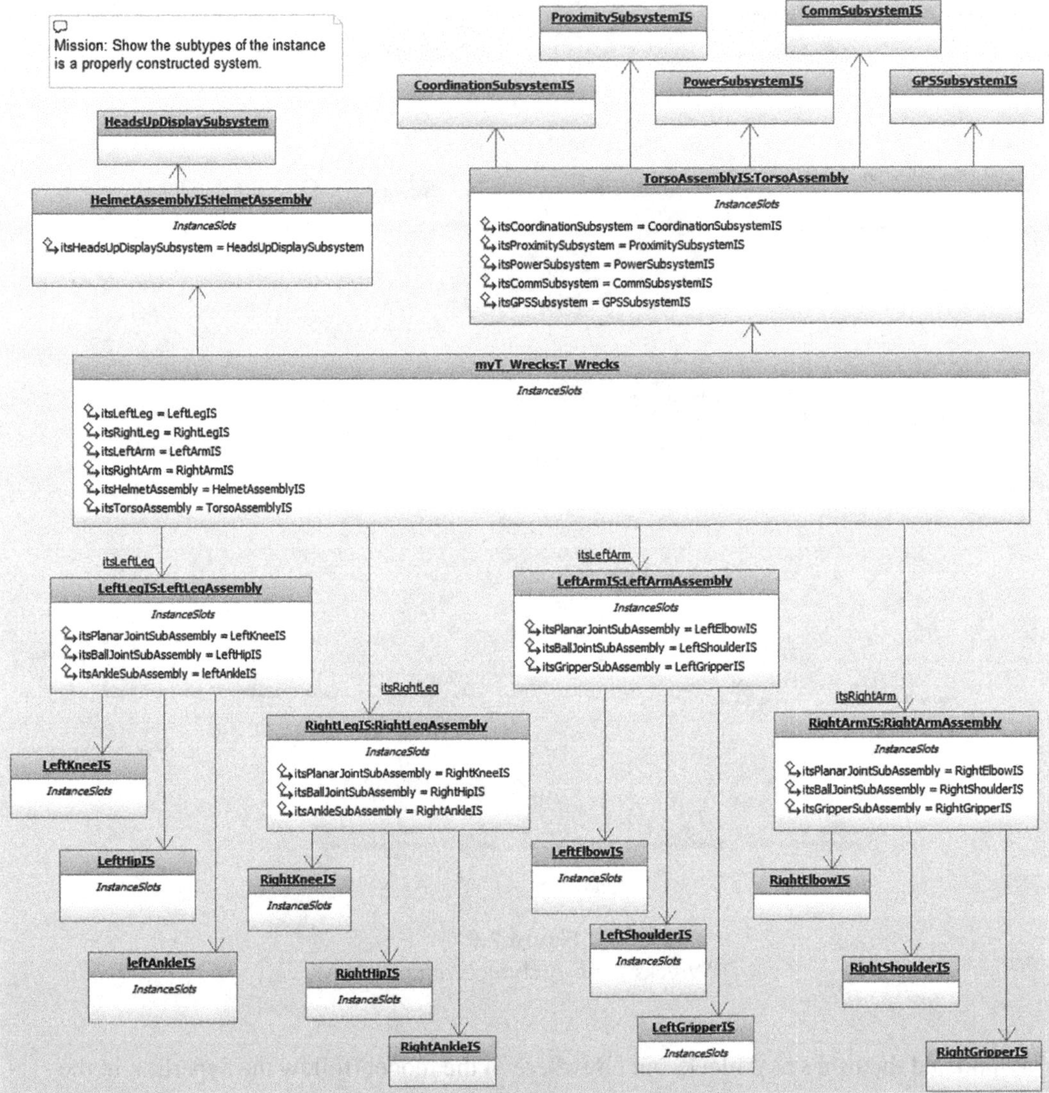

Figure 7.10
T-Wrecks Instance Specification Assembly diagram.

`LegAssembly` contains a `BallJointSubAssembly`, then a `LeftLegAssembly` can contain a `LeftHipSubAssembly` as the same internal part. This is a powerful way of reasoning about the system architecture, but it doesn't come naturally to everyone. It is, however, worth some effort to master.

It is with that context that I say that Figure 7.10 is completely compatible with the previous two diagrams. The former show the blocks (that is to say, *types*) and Figure 7.10 shows the particular instance specifications typed by those blocks in a specific configuration. In particular, while the `T_Wrecks` block has four compositions with the abstract block `LimbAssembly`, we see that they are implemented with instances named `LeftLegAssembly`, `RightLegAssembly`, `LeftArmAssembly`, and `RightArmAssembly` rather than some random assortment that might include three left legs and a right arm.

Notice that we've not added ports and interfaces to the T-Wrecks architecture just yet. We'll flesh them out as we walk though the rest of the chapter.

7.4 Allocate System Requirements to Subsystems

Once we've got an architecture, we can start allocating requirements to it. For some requirements, that means nothing more than a simple allocation and SysML provides a relation just for that. For others, multiple subsystems must collaborate in some way to realize the requirement, and that means that requirement must be decomposed into derived requirements that can be allocated to a single subsystem. There may also be some "cross-cutting requirements" that apply equally to many subsystem (such as "Coding must be done in MISRA C" or "The system must comply with The Electronic Product Radiation Control Provisions of the FDA 21 CFR 1020.33"). Since we're doing an incremental, iterative approach, we'll do requirements allocation on a relatively small number of requirements at a time. However, as the architecture evolves, we'll need to revisit past allocations to make sure that the allocations still make sense.

Why do this? It is important for the subsystem teams to know, clearly and completely, what is expected of the subsystems they are tasked to create. To do this they need four basic types of information: the properties their subsystem is required to have (static, dynamic, and dependability), the architectural framework into which their subsystem must fit, the interfaces they must provide to others, and the interfaces they can rely on from others. The first item we normally think of as requirements and the last three are aspects of what we normally consider architecture (sometimes known as *design requirements* or what DO-178 refers to as "low-level requirements" [6]).

The most common way to represent this information is in a *requirement x subsystem* table, but it can also be done graphically on requirements diagrams, by annotating requirements in a requirements database, or even by creating separate requirements databases for each subsystem. What is important is to have traceability so that:

- from the subsystem perspective, the team can easily identify all their requirements while not being burdened with the requirements for all the other subsystems
- from a system perspective, the lead engineer can ensure that all requirements are allocated

- from a test perspective, the testing team can identify what they need to test and where it is allocated
- from a dependability perspective, the impact the architecture and allocation decisions have on the safety, reliability, and security of the system.

7.5 Allocate Use Cases to Subsystems

This step is optional for very simple subsystems. If the subsystem has a total of 10 requirements, then creating use cases to organize them is a waste of effort. However, when the subsystems are themselves complex, this step provides the same crucial value of organizing requirements for the subsystems as it does for the system as a whole.

As you can see in Figure 7.11, there are two different workflows for this. The left which I call *bottom-up*, allocates the primitive elements (subsystem functions, messages, and flows) to the subsystem and then aggregates them into subsystem-level use cases. This is particularly useful when the subsystems are relatively simple so that there are only a few to

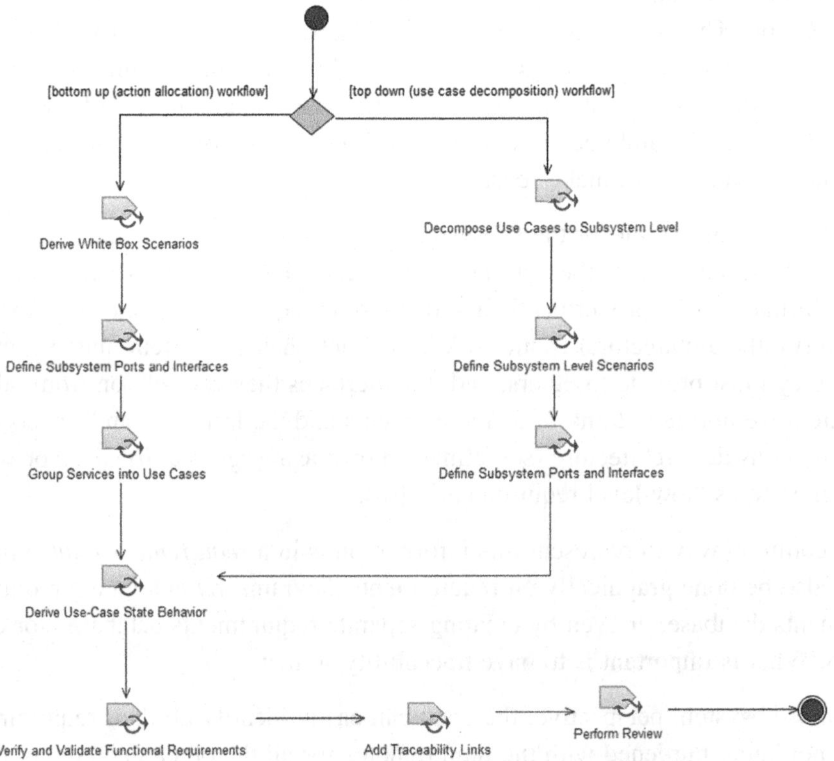

Figure 7.11
Allocate use cases to subsystems workflow.

a few dozen elements to be considered. The right workflow, known as *top-down* works best for complex subsystems which may have several dozen to hundreds of subsystem functions, messages, and flows.

Following the allocation of use cases to the subsystem, the use cases are separately analyzed using essentially the same techniques we applied to the system-level use cases. The good news is that each of the subsystem-level use cases is simpler than the system-level use cases. The less-good news is that there tends to be a great deal more of them. The total complexity of the system grows somewhat because we are drilling down and uncovering details that weren't visible before.

7.5.1 Bottom-Up Allocation

This workflow takes the primitive elements produced as a part of the system use case analysis—messages, system functions, and flows—and then allocates them to one of the subsystems identified in a previous step (see Section 7.3). Many of these system functions can be directly allocated to a subsystem but many will require decomposition first. Once the elements are allocated to the subsystem, the subsystem interfaces can be elaborated to support the necessary internal system interactions. Within the subsystems themselves, the requirements, functions, messages, and flows can be aggregated together into subsystem-level use cases.

7.5.1.1 Derive white box scenarios

Black box scenarios are among the key work products for system-level use case analysis (see Sections 5.5.1.3, 5.5.2.2, and 5.5.3.3). By "black box", we do not mean that the system is inscrutable.; we mean that we can't see inside to the system's internal structure or inner workings. In the black box view, we can characterize the nature of the input–output control and data transformations performed by the system but we can't tell how those transformations were performed or what internal parts played roles in those transformations. At this point, however, we can see those internal parts, at least to the subsystem level and we can map out the interactions among the subsystems that perform these interactions. The behavior within the subsystems is now the black box level, but the interactions among the subsystems are well within our sight.

Lifeline vertical decomposition will be a key technique to move from the system black box to white box view. If you remember from Figure 3.24, a lifeline in a sequence diagram can represent a set of collaborating elements (shown in Figure 3.25). In this context, where we had the system or system use case lifeline in our use case scenarios, we will decompose it into a set of collaborating subsystems to drill down inside the system architecture.

7.5.1.2 Define subsystem ports and interfaces

As we did at the system level, we'll use proxy ports and interface blocks to characterize the connections between the subsystem. In our scenarios from the previous step, we identified events, messages, and flows between pairs of subsystems. Wherever there is an interaction between a pair of subsystems, a port will be added to each to support it; wherever there is an event, message, or flow between subsystems, that element will be added to the interface block defining the relevant port.

Just as in the system-level analysis, we will create an execution context in which the use case and the actors are represented with blocks, with connectors linking together the block instances via their ports. This execution context will support the verification and validation of our subsystem-level use cases.

7.5.1.3 Group services into use cases

Back in Chapter 4, I introduced the creation of use cases to cluster requirements—in that case, for stakeholder requirements. We refined that approach a bit in Chapter 5 where we dealt with system requirements. Here, we will do much the same but at the subsystem level and on a per-subsystem basis. One difference here is, of course, the level of decomposition; at this level requirements are specific to the subsystem. The other difference is that we have more than just requirements to allocate. We also have events, messages, and flows from the system requirements analysis. Of course, these elements are not independent. There are relations between requirements and the elements that represent them in our scenarios, but the relations may be complex. A given requirement may be represented by multiple events, data, and flows and a given event or flow may represent multiple requirements. Nevertheless they are related, and this simplifies the allocation.

7.5.2 Top-Down Allocation

While the bottom-up approach takes small primitive pieces and constructs the subsystem-level use case from them, the top-down approach decomposes the use cases into subsystem-level use cases and allocates them to the subsystems. My experience is that this approach works better for large and complex systems than the bottom-up approach. Both approaches end up in the same place—subsystems are specified with a set of use cases and each of those use cases has allocated subsystem-level requirements, with scenarios, activity flows, state behavior, events, messages, actions (subsystem functions), and flows.

7.5.2.1 Decompose use cases to subsystem level

This task takes each system-level use case and, in turn, decomposes it into a set of subsystem-level use cases. This is done on (new) use case diagrams defined for that purpose. The key relation is the «include» relation between use cases. You may remember from Chapter 4 that the «include» relation is a stereotype of dependency that represents containment. That is the larger use case contains the included use case.

In my use case modeling, I use the «include» relation in only a few situations:

1. Create a use case abstraction/containment hierarchy for large systems[10] (system complexity management)
2. Decompose a large complex use case into smaller, more approachable use cases (use case complexity management)
3. Extract a smaller capability that can be reused by different use cases (reuse)
4. Allocate a portion of a system-level use case to a subsystem (allocation).

In this case, we're focused on the last—decomposing system use cases into a set of subsystem use cases such that all the system use case requirements are allocated to the subsystems.

For example, if we look at the partial set of use cases for an aircraft in Figure 7.12, we see the use of the «include» to relate three levels of abstraction of use cases. In the next figure (Figure 7.13), we take one of these and use the «include» relation to decompose the `Control Attitude` use case to allocate subsystem-level use cases to the aircraft architecture.

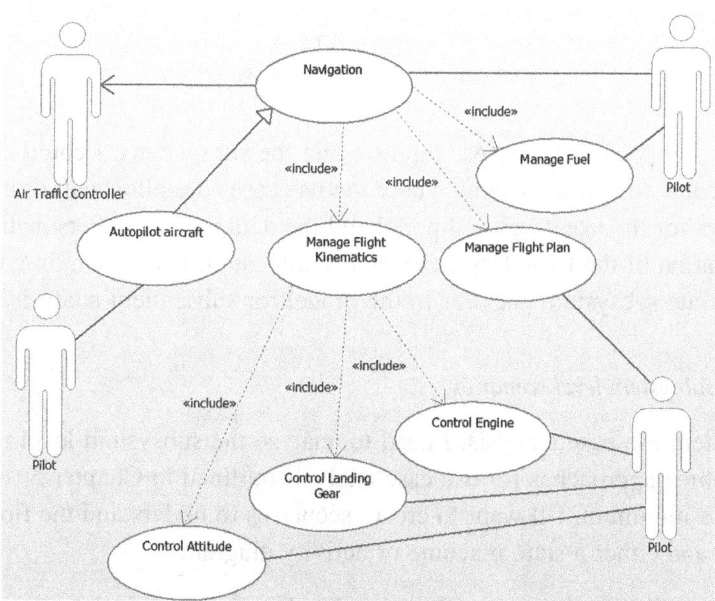

Figure 7.12
Partial set of use cases for an aircraft.

[10] It was very difficult to manage a flat organization of several hundred use cases – an appropriate number for a large system such as an aircraft (see Figure 4.2). But by creating 2–4 levels of abstraction we can create an organizational schema for managing such a large number of use cases.

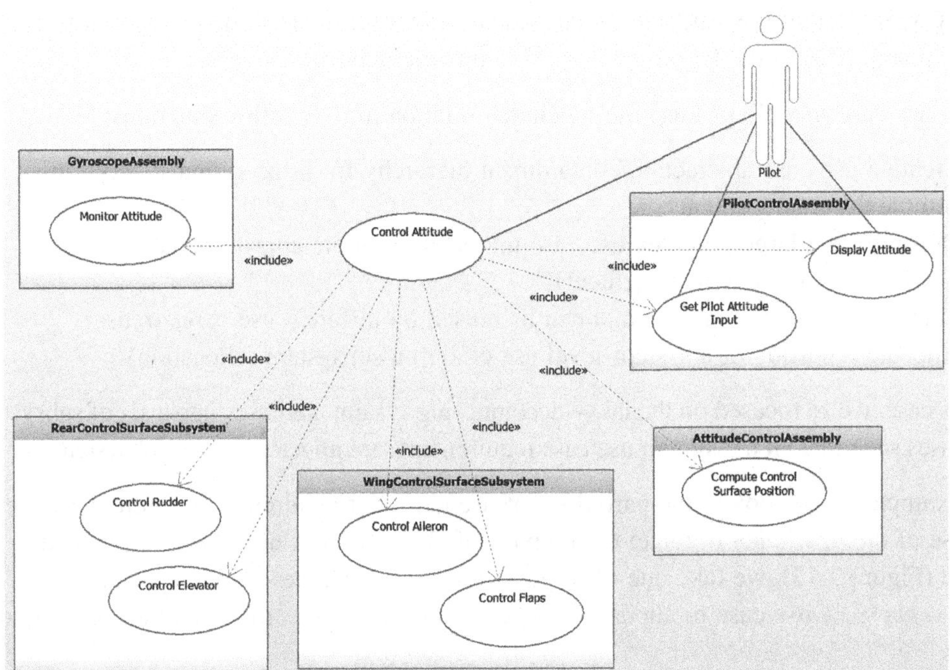

Figure 7.13
Use case allocation to subsystems.

In the figure, I used "boundary boxes" representing the subsystems. I could have equally well used «allocate» relations to show where the use cases are allocated, or even created AllocatedTo tags for the use cases and populated the data that way. Personally, I like the ease of visualization of the boundary boxes. Once allocated, I will then drag the use cases into the appropriate subsystem package in the model for subsequent analysis.

7.5.2.2 Define subsystem-level scenarios

Just as with system use case analysis, I need to analyze the subsystem-level use cases. I can use any of the three approaches for use case analysis outlined in Chapter 5 (refer to Figure 5.1). At a minimum, I'll want to create scenarios to understand the flows represented by the use case and either a state machine or activity diagram.

One thing that is different about the subsystem-level use case analysis is that the actors may not be system actions; they are more likely to be peer subsystems. Peer subsystems look like actors from a given subsystem's perspective. To model this, I use the stereotype «internal» on the actor to make it clear that the actor is internal to the system but external to the subsystem scope of the analysis. Just like in the system-level analysis, I'll create special limited versions of the «internal» actors for use in the analysis.

Care must be taken to ensure that the subsystem-level scenarios are consistent with the system-level scenarios and that you can trace between them in a straightforward way. The simplest way to do this is to use the lifeline decomposition approach discussed earlier.

7.5.2.3 Define subsystem ports and interfaces

As with the bottom-up approach, I'll need to define ports whenever two subsystems have an interaction and interfaces to specify what flows across them. Again, I'll mostly use proxy ports and interface blocks for this. Remember that we construct an execution context block diagram with the internal actors and subsystem use case represented as blocks. These blocks contain the ports typed by the interfaces and support verification and validation via execution.

7.5.3 Common Tasks

At this point, the two workflows join and continue in the same way. Regardless of whether you took the bottom-up or the top-down approach, you have use cases at the subsystem level, («internal») actors identified, and events, messages, and flows specified in the interactions. Now, we must verify and validate our understanding of the subsystem level use cases.

7.5.3.1 Derive use case state behavior

Executable use case models are the best way to ensure that we properly understand the requirements and to identify requirements that are missing, incorrect, or in conflict. For the most part, we'll support this execution with state-driven behavior but activity diagrams can be used as well. We'll construct an execution context and state machine for every subsystem-level use case that we analyze. Each of these state machines will generally be much simpler than the system-level state machines so the analysis for each use case will usually go faster.

7.5.3.2 Verify and validate functional requirements

Execution of the model allows exploration of the requirements and "what if" scenarios for abnormal values, unexpected sequences, and so on. Stakeholders can be exposed to the executing model in structured discussions to ensure proper understanding of the requirements and their consequences by the stakeholders and system engineers alike.

7.5.3.3 Add traceability links

Once the use case model and requirements stabilize, trace links can be added. While they can be added earlier, unstable requirements result in throwing away the work needed to create the links, so I like to wait until a good agreement and understanding of the requirements represented by the use case is achieved.

At this level, subsystem requirements will be allocated to use cases (which are traceable links) and also trace back to their system requirement origins. The subsystem use cases and its features (functions, data, events, and flows) will trace back to their source system-level use case work products.

7.5.3.4 Perform review

As with all system engineering work products, the use case model and its various features and related model elements are typically reviewed.

7.5.4 Speed Demon Subsystem Use Case Allocation Example

For the Speed Demon example, we will follow the bottom-up approach to allocation of a system use case to the subsystem architecture. We'll start with Scenario 1 of the `Execute Protocol` use case (Figure 5.26). Specifically we'll do the following

1. Create a package to hold the white box scenarios within the functional analysis package used for the `Execute Protocol` use case (which you'll remember was `FAPkg::ucExecuteProtocolPkg`). We'll name this nested package `FAPkg::ucExecuteProtocolPkg::ucEPWBPkg`. It is typical to put the white box scenarios in a package nested within the package used for the system functional analysis of the use case.
2. Copy (not move) the scenario to the nested package. We want to copy it because we'll be modifying it in the next step.
3. Select the lifeline corresponding to the use case (`ucExecuteProtocol`) and add a nested sequence diagram.[11] In this case, I'll name the diagram `ucExecuteProtocol Scenario 1 WB Details`, but the name isn't crucial.
4. You now have an empty sequence diagram. Drag the block `aEP_Athlete` onto the diagram. This is the system actor and it will be a part of the scenario.[12]
5. For each message on the original sequence diagram, either direct it to a subsystem lifeline (and you'll have to drag the subsystem from the `ArchDesignPkg` as you need them), or you'll have to decompose the message into pieces that can be so allocated.
6. If the subsystem receiving the message needs to collaborate with other subsystems to perform the required service, add messages, events, and flows among the subsystems to represent that part of the collaboration.
7. Get the next message from the original sequence diagram.
8. Repeat from step 5 until done.
9. When complete, add any events, messages, and flows used on the diagram that don't appear in the subsystem interfaces to the appropriate interface blocks.

---

[11] In Rhapsody, double-click on the lifeline to open the Features dialog, and then click on the Decomposed dropdown box and Add New decomposed diagram. In other tools, use the appropriate gestures to add a sequence diagram to hold the internal sequence for this use case scenario.

[12] You can drag all the actor blocks used in the original scenario but, in this case, there is only one. You can also use the System Boundary lifeline. This is useful when you have many actor blocks, as this special lifeline represents "all elements not otherwise explicitly shown in the diagram."

Consider the very first message on the sequence diagram (Figure 5.26). It's a message from the use case labeled `displayInitialScreen`. Ok, this is going to come from the `DisplayUnit` subsystem but how does it know to do that? What is likely is that the `ControlUnit` subsystem has completed its initialization and power on sequence and it instructs the `DisplayUnit` to display its initial screen. Further, that message is not currently in the interface block `ibDisplayData` so it will have to be added.

The next message, `requestProtocolList`, comes from the Athlete. The `TreadmillControlUnit`, affixed to the `LeftArmAssembly` (see Figure 7.5) provides buttons for treadmill-related user commands and the `MediaControlUnit`, part of the `RightArmAssembly`, provides media-related buttons. Since this is a treadmill operation-related command, let's use the buttons on the `TreadmillControlUnit`, specifically the `highligtPrev`, `highlightNext`, and `enter` messages to make the request. This is a case where at the high level, the system gets one command (`requestProtocolList`) but at a lower level, we see that it is composed of multiple messages.

To more easily understand this, we'll have our UI team mock up the initial screen (Figure 7.14). You can see the first item, *Perform a Manual Workout*, is highlighted and the second item is the one we want in this scenario. To send the appropriate message, the Athlete will need to press the `highlightNext` and `enter` keys on the treadmill control unit. In response to the first, the `DisplayUnit` will highlight the second item in the list. In respond to the second, the system will display the protocol list.

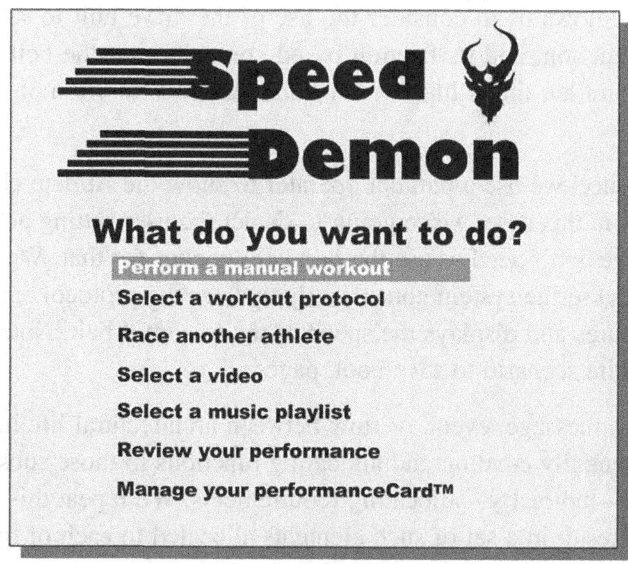

Figure 7.14
Speed Demon initial screen.

The protocol list comes from more than one source. Generally available protocols are held within the `ControlUnit` subsystem and athlete-specific ones are stored on the data card. The `ControlUnit` must construct the list and give it to the `DisplayUnit` when requested. This list is then formatted and displayed for the athlete.

The Athlete must then select the desired protocol (in this case, they will select the first protocol in the list for simplicity). The Athlete then sets the duration to run the protocol (to 60 min from the starting default of 30 min) and then runs it. This completes the top part of the scenario. The rest of the scenario consists of running the protocol. This is captured in Figure 7.15; note the use of a reference sequence diagram for the actual running of the protocol at the bottom of the figure.

Note that you can see how the internal subsystems collaborate in Figure 7.15 to produce the system-level behavior depicted in Figure 5.26. Note that this identifies (newly) derived requirements for the subsystems. For example, the `ControlUnit` must be able to construct a protocol list from two sources and the `TreadmillControlUnit` must be able to read stored protocols from the Athlete's data card. In the parallel Create/Update Subsystem Requirements task, these requirements will be added to the list of allocated requirements for the relevant subsystems.

Now, let's detail the referenced sequence diagram. In the original diagram, we didn't depict any specific protocol but left an unspecified referenced sequence diagram. In this case, we'll actually provide a specific protocol; 10-min warm up, then hard–easy intervals (5 min at fast pace followed by 5 min at Recovery Pace), followed by a 10-min warm down.[13] This allows us to consider the use of the drive unit to set running speed as a part of the interaction, and its friction-based connection to the belt on the treadmill deck. In parallel, the Athlete will up the fast pace to 7.0 mph during the second interval.

In the original sequence, we use a parallel operator to show the Athlete changing the treadmill speed. But in this case, we're going to depict the user setting at a particular point in the sequence so we don't need to use the parallel operator for that. We do need to use a parallel operator because the system concurrently updates the protocol and interval elapsed times and also measures and displays the speed of the treadmill belt. Note that Figure 7.16 doesn't show the entire scenario to save book pages.

Each time we draw a message, event, or flow between architectural lifelines in the sequence diagram, we are essentially creating and allocating functions to those subsystems, refining their interfaces, and—indirectly—allocating requirements. We repeat this white box scenario analysis to result in a set of such elements allocated to each of the subsystems.

[13] One of my favorite treadmill workouts. Just sayin'.

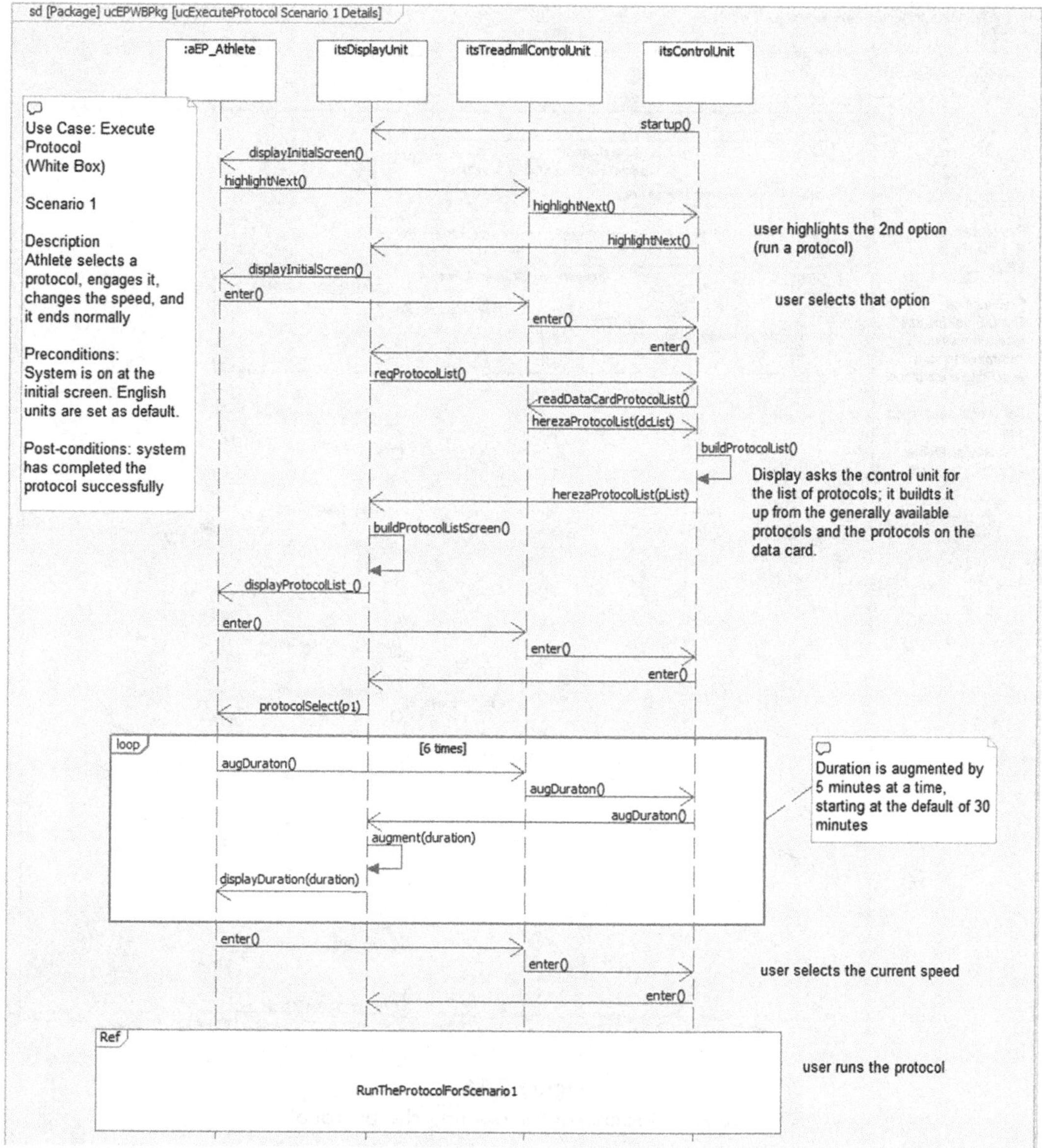

Figure 7.15
White box scenario.

Once this is done for the set of system use cases within the iteration, we can examine each subsystem in turn to identify useful cluster-related services, functions, flows, and requirements that will constitute the subsystem-level use cases. Where there is a small set of elements allocated to a subsystem, we might skip the identification of use cases entirely. For example, the `PowerUnit` subsystem of the treadmill doesn't really do many different

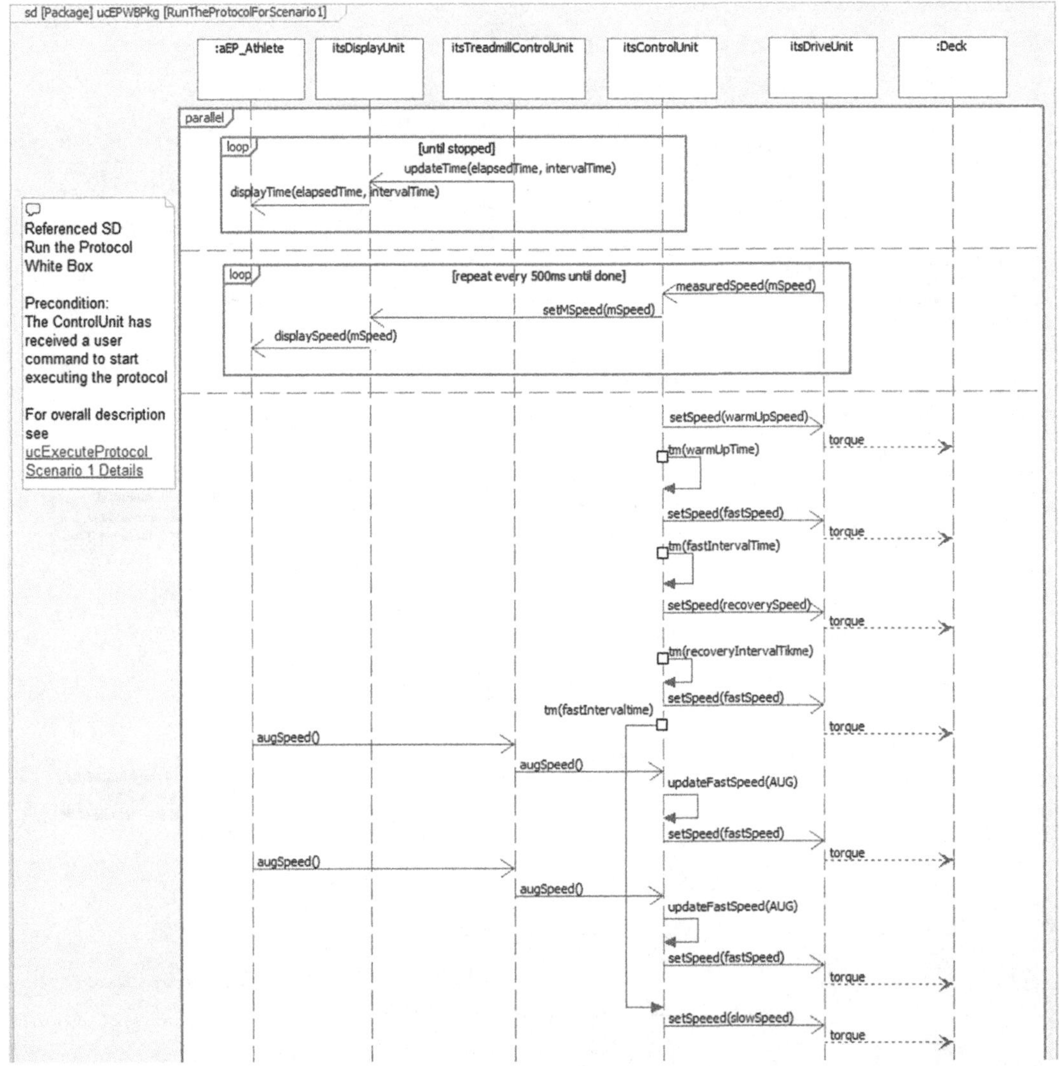

Figure 7.16
Referenced scenario for running the protocol.

things. It might provide services such as adapting input voltage and generating appropriate output voltage and current to power the Speed Demon electronic systems. Even though the `PowerUnit` may contain elements of different engineering disciplines—such as electronic, mechanical, and software—if the behavior is insufficiently complex to warrant creating use cases, we won't do it. We'll just allocate the requirements directly to the subsystem.

Compare the complexity of the `PowerUnit` with the range of behaviors supported by the `ControlUnit` or the `DisplayUnit` subsystems. Figure 7.17 shows the (ultimate) use case set for

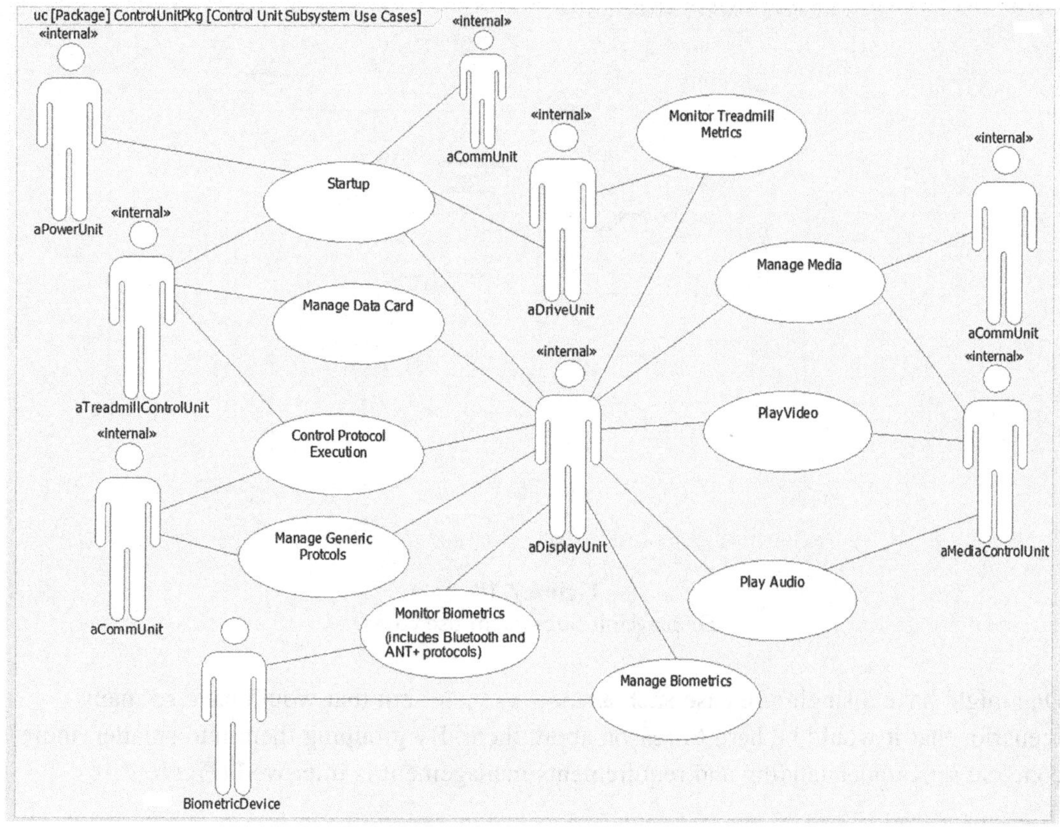

Figure 7.17
ControlUnit Subsystem use cases.

the `ControlUnit` subsystem. Note that some of these use cases will be derived from system use cases not yet explored—such as starting the system (including orchestrating the power on built in test), managing media files, and playing audio. Note the use of «internal» actors representing the peer subsystems and that the names of these actors are prefaced with an "a" to distinguish them from the actual subsystems of the (mostly) same name. In fact, the `ControlUnit` only directly connects to one system-level actor—Biometric Device which might be a heart rate sensor or running power meter.

The scope of these use cases is entirely within the `ControlUnit` subsystem, even if there are use cases with similar names allocated to other subsystems.

The `DisplayUnit` only has use-case-relevant connections to the `ControlUnit` (direct) and the Athlete (implied). However, since it provides the primary means by which the Athlete interacts with the system (along with the `ControlUnit`-mediated Athlete inputs via the `TreadmillControlUnit` and `MediaControlUnit`), it has a number of interesting use cases.

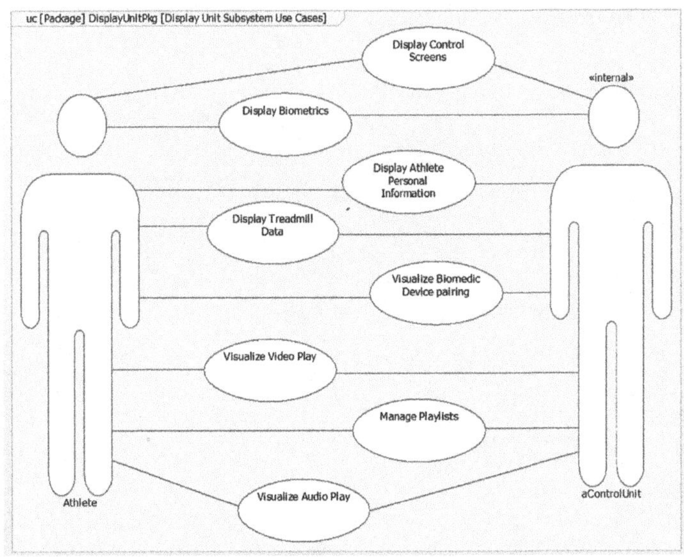

Figure 7.18
DisplayUnit Subsystem use cases.

One might have a single use case such as `Display Stuff`, but that would have so many scenarios that it would be hard to reason about them. By grouping them into smaller, more coherent sets, understanding and requirements management is improved (Figure 7.18).

7.5.5 T-Wrecks Subsystem Use Case Allocation Example

For the T-Wrecks example, we'll use the top-down use case decomposition flow from Figure 7.11. That is, we'll take our system use cases and use the «include» relations to decompose each into subsystem-level use cases. We've already done a little bit of this; in the original use case diagram (Figure 4.7), we identified a `Walk` use case which included the `Move Limb` use case, which in turn included the `Move Joint` use case. The `Walk` use case is really system level, which the `Move limb` use case maps well to the `LimbAssembly` subsystem and the `Move Joint` use case maps well to the various limb subassemblies (such as `ElbowJointSubAssembly`, `AnkleSubAssembly`, and `GripperSubAssembly`). What we didn't show in that case was the mapping to the multiplicity of subsystems (impossible, since we hadn't decided on the architecture then). Figure 7.19 shows the identification and allocation of subsystem-level use cases from the `Walk` system-level use case.

Because of the similarities among the `LimbAssembly` instances (they are not *quite* identical but close), it makes sense for a single downstream engineering team to design all of them. We can allocate the `Move Limb` and `Move Joint` use cases to the appropriate subsystems and sub-subsystems and let the design team tailor the specifics as needed for the different instances.

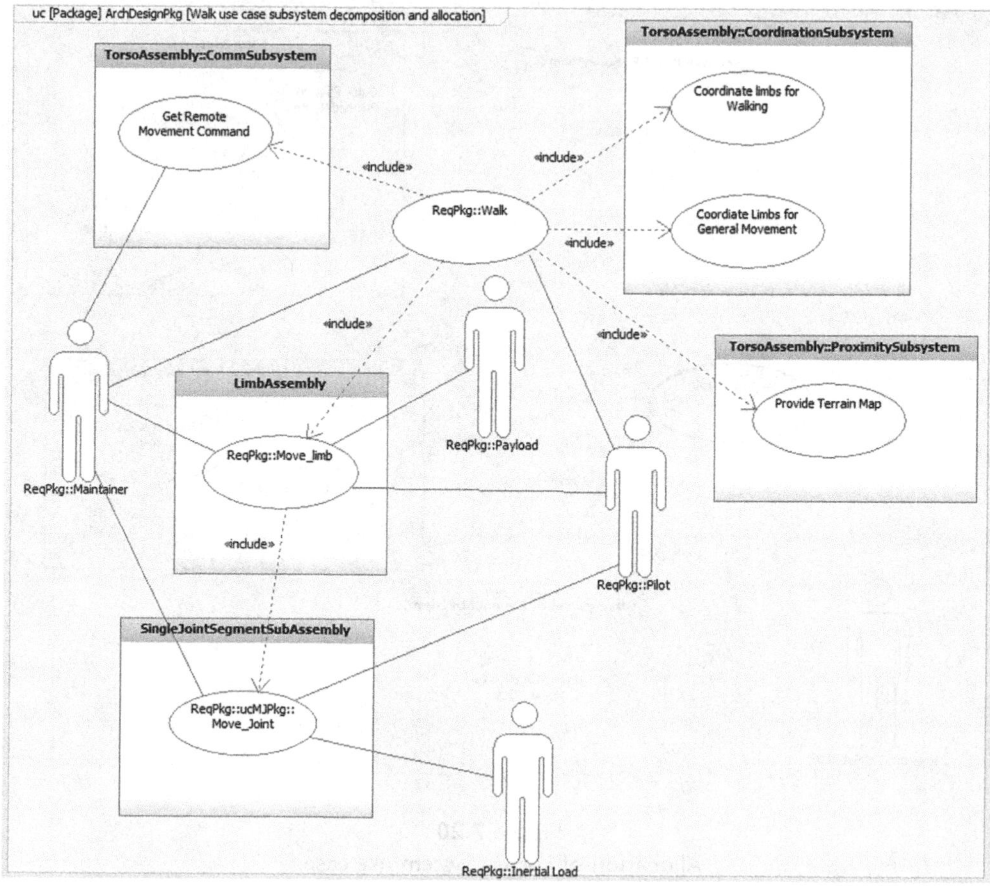

Figure 7.19
Allocation of Walk System use case.

Because the allocation of the use cases depends as much on the architecture as it does the system-level use case, the use case diagram showing the decomposition is placed into the ArchDesignPkg. This allows the Req package to remain innocent of internal system detail.

The `Locate` use case (see Section 5.5.3.5) is another use case that can be profitably decomposed using this technique. You will recall that this use case specifies the requirements for locating the system using a GPS, and includes information display to the Pilot, route planning and navigation, as well as periodic location reports sent to the home office. The allocation is shown in Figure 7.20. In case you think the allocation of responsibilities odd, the `GPSSubsystem` is solely dedicated to GPS location but computation related to route planning and map management is allocated to the general computing facilities located within the `TorsoAssembly`.

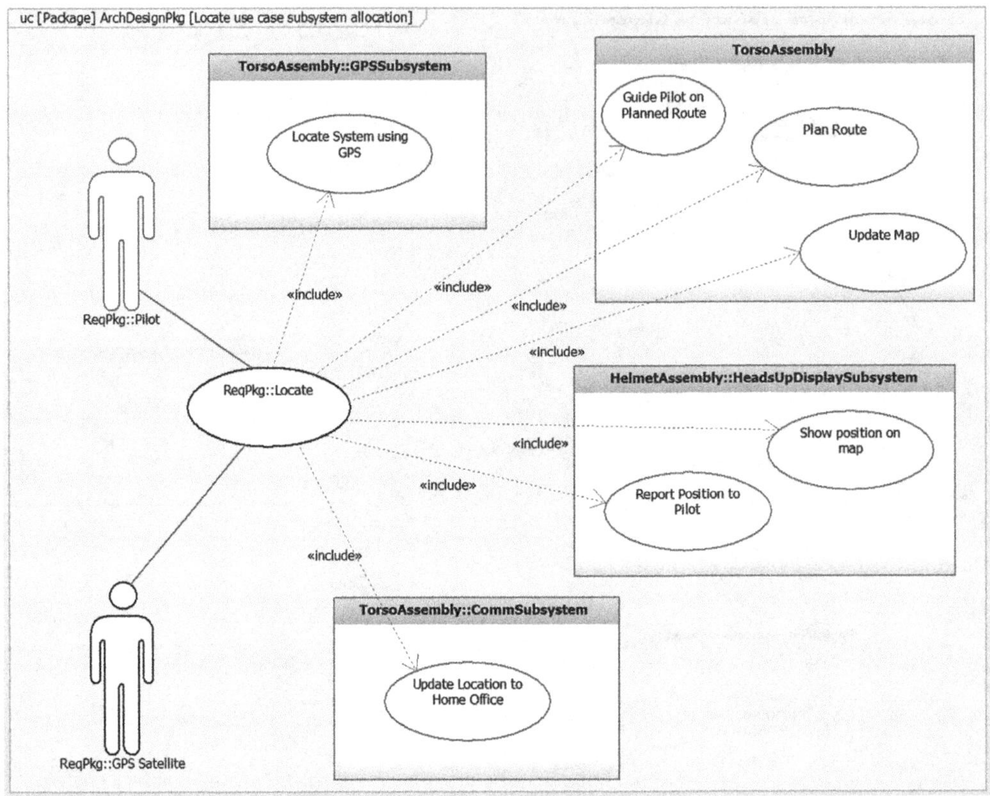

Figure 7.20
Allocation of Locate System use case.

As we do this for all system-level use cases under consideration in the iteration, we end up with a set of use cases allocated to each subsystem (including some requirements allocated directly to simple subsystems). At that point, the same techniques used in Chapter 5 for analyzing system use cases are applied here at the subsystem level. To be clear, this is done for *all* subsystem use cases derived from the system use cases under consideration. Because there is typically a "fan-out" factor of 2–8, that sounds like a lot of work, but each of the subsystem-level use cases is simpler than the system use case. Developing all the subsystem use cases will usually be more work than the system use cases but it isn't quite as bad as it sounds. The result of this fan out is that each subsystem has a specification of use cases—linked to subsystem-level requirements, a set of requirements for each subsystem, and an interface specification for each subsystem. That's the key set of data handed off to the downstream engineering subsystem teams for further development.

Just as we did for the system itself, for each subsystem we will create one or more use case diagrams, and perform functional analysis on those use cases to ensure we identified all the services and flows in the interfaces and properly allocated requirements. For example, Figure 7.21 shows the derived use cases allocated to the `Coordination` subsystem and Figure 7.22 shows the use cases for the `Limb Assembly` subsystem. Each of these will have a set of requirements allocated to it and undergo the same kind of functional analysis we performed for system use cases back in Chapter 5. Also notice that the actors shown are not only the system actors but also the peer subsystems with which the subsystem in question interacts. I've prepended "a" and appended "_ss" at the end of the actor name to clearly identify these elements as "internal" actors—subsystems which from this point of view are considered to be actors.

To provide an example, let's consider the `Coordinate limbs for Walking` use case, derived from the system use case `Walk` and allocated to the subsystem `CoordinationSubsystem`. Remember that the `Walk` use case is all about remote control. Under normal Pilot usage, the Pilot "commands" movement by applying pressure with his or her limbs and their cerebellum and motor cortex ultimately provides the coordination. However, the system can also be controlled remotely and to do so, it performs simple coordinated movements such as walking, sitting, standing, raising both arms, and so on.

Inside the `Coordination` Subsystem specification package (in this model it is `ArchPkg::ArchDesignPkg::CoordinateSSPkg` specifically) we will put the use case, the related subsystem requirements, and the use case functional analysis. This package will be handed off to the team responsible, as described in Chapter 8 at the end of the systems engineering iteration.

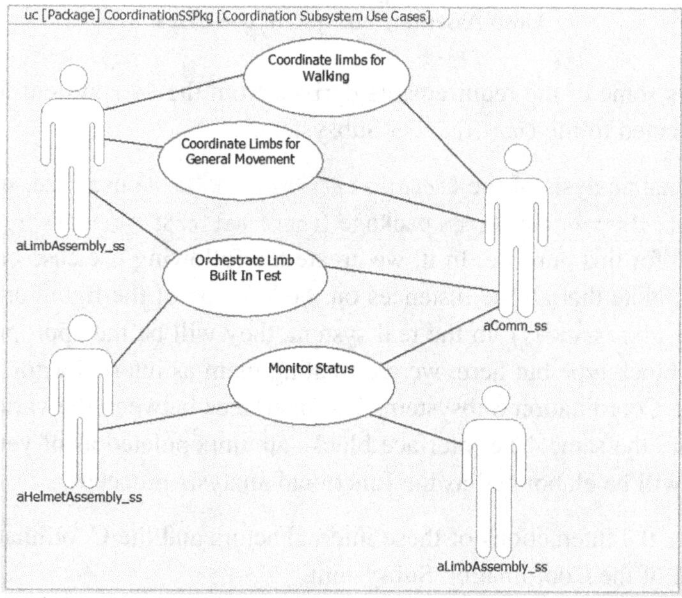

Figure 7.21
Coordination Subsystem use cases.

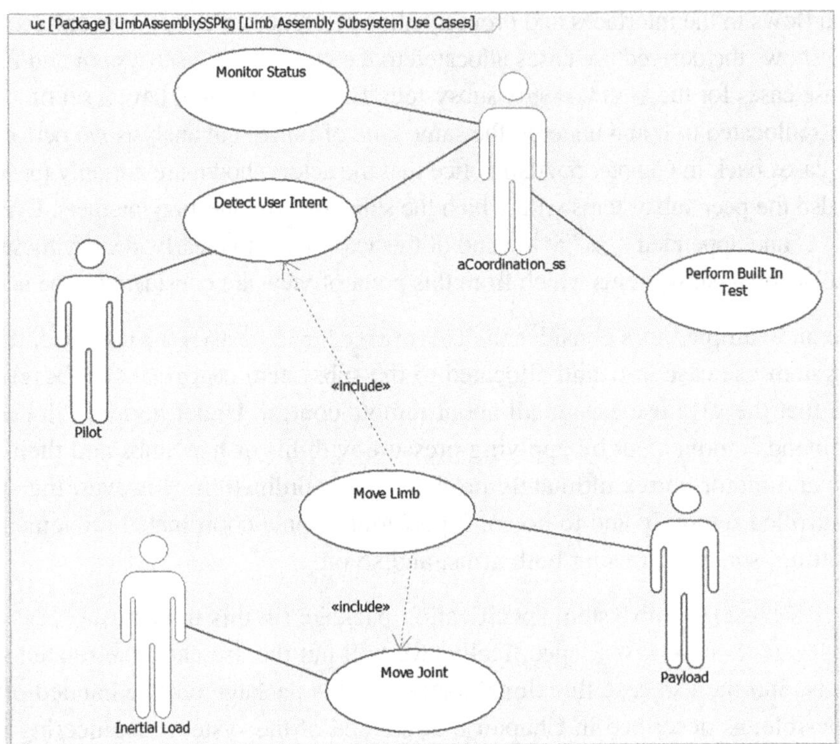

Figure 7.22
Limb Assembly Subsystem use cases.

Figure 7.23 shows some of the requirements derived from the `Walk` system-level requirements allocated to the `Coordination` Subsystem.

To do the functional analysis of the `Coordinate Limbs for Walking` use case, we'll create a package in the `Coordination Subsystem` package (`CoordinationSSPkg::FAPkg::CoLimbWalkingPkg`) for this purpose. In it, we create the following use case context diagram (see Figure 7.24). Note that all the instances on the left side of the figure are of the same block type (`aCLFW_LimbAssembly`). In the real system, they will be the appropriate subtypes of the `LimbAssembly` block type but here, we are treating them as internal actors from the perspective of the Coordination Subsystem. The interfaces between the various limbs and the use case are all the same. The interface blocks are unpopulated as of yet, but the flows, events, and data will be elaborated as the functional analysis proceeds.

Figure 7.25 shows the interactions of these internal actors and the Coordinate Limbs for Walking use case of the Coordination Subsystem.

Figure 7.26 shows the corresponding state machine for the use case. It accounts for the scenario in Figure 7.25 and others not shown.

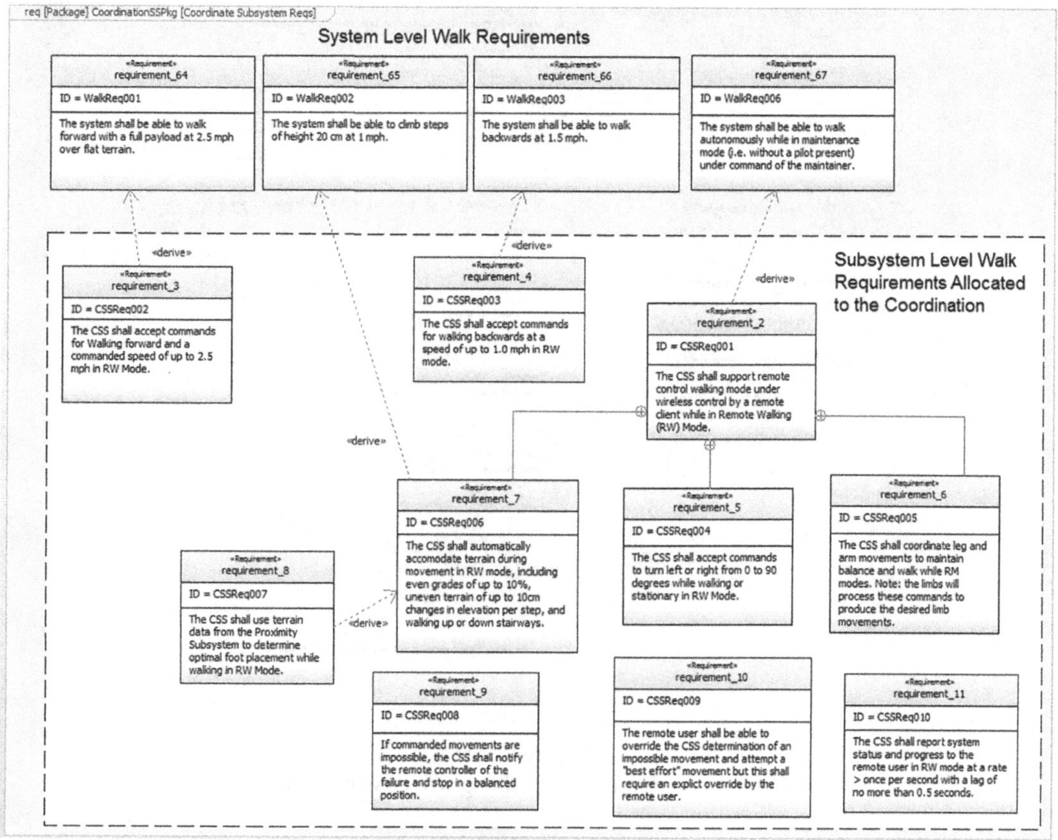

Figure 7.23
Coordination Subsystem Walk-related requirements.

7.6 Create/Update Logical Data Schema

Back in Section 5.6, I talked about creating a logical data schema during requirements specification. I mentioned that this is perhaps not the best name, because this includes the type taxonomy for things other than data, such as materiel and energy flows. Nevertheless, the name is common enough that we'll stick with it.

The point of defining the logical data schema is to reason about the properties of data and flows in the system, including valid and reasonable ranges, bandwidth, fidelity, and accuracy. The physical data schema—something I'll discuss in the next chapter—will have to define the actual means by which data and flows are exchanged, but here, we're still concerned about their logical characteristics.

The data schema in Chapter 5 focused on the exchange of flows between the system and its associated actors. However, now we are defining the internal architecture and subsystems

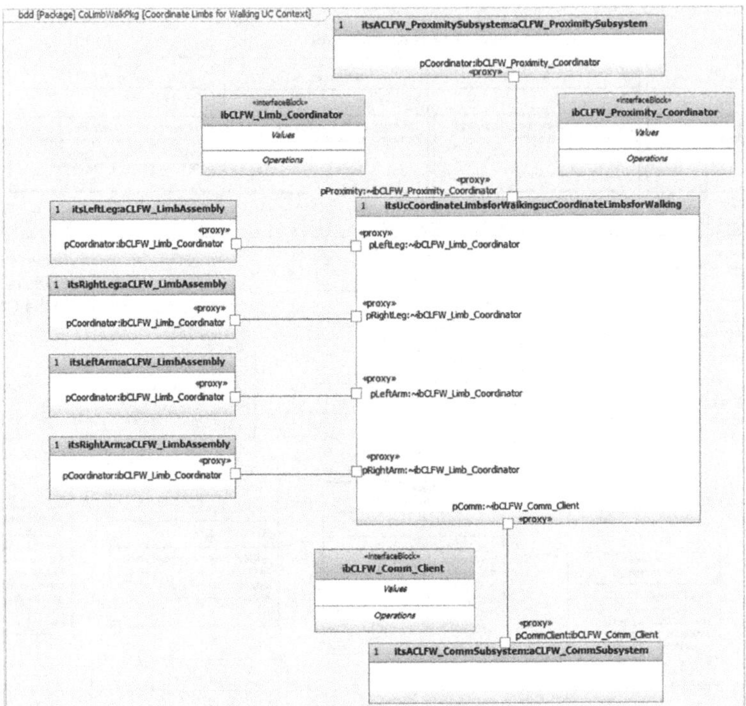

Figure 7.24
Coordinate Limbs for Walking use case context.

and those have data and flows exchanged between them as well. That is the reason that we are revisiting and elaborating the data schema during architectural design. The goal here is that every data or flow item defined in an internal or external subsystem interface is characterized in terms of extent, accuracy, and fidelity, as well as possibly in terms of units, (logical) subtypes, availability, and so on.

7.6.1 Speed Demon Treadmill Example

What new data or flows have been added in our exploration of the Speed Demon architecture? Here's a brief list:

- Protocol
- Protocol List
- Workout duration
  - Protocol execution duration
  - Elapsed time
  - Interval time

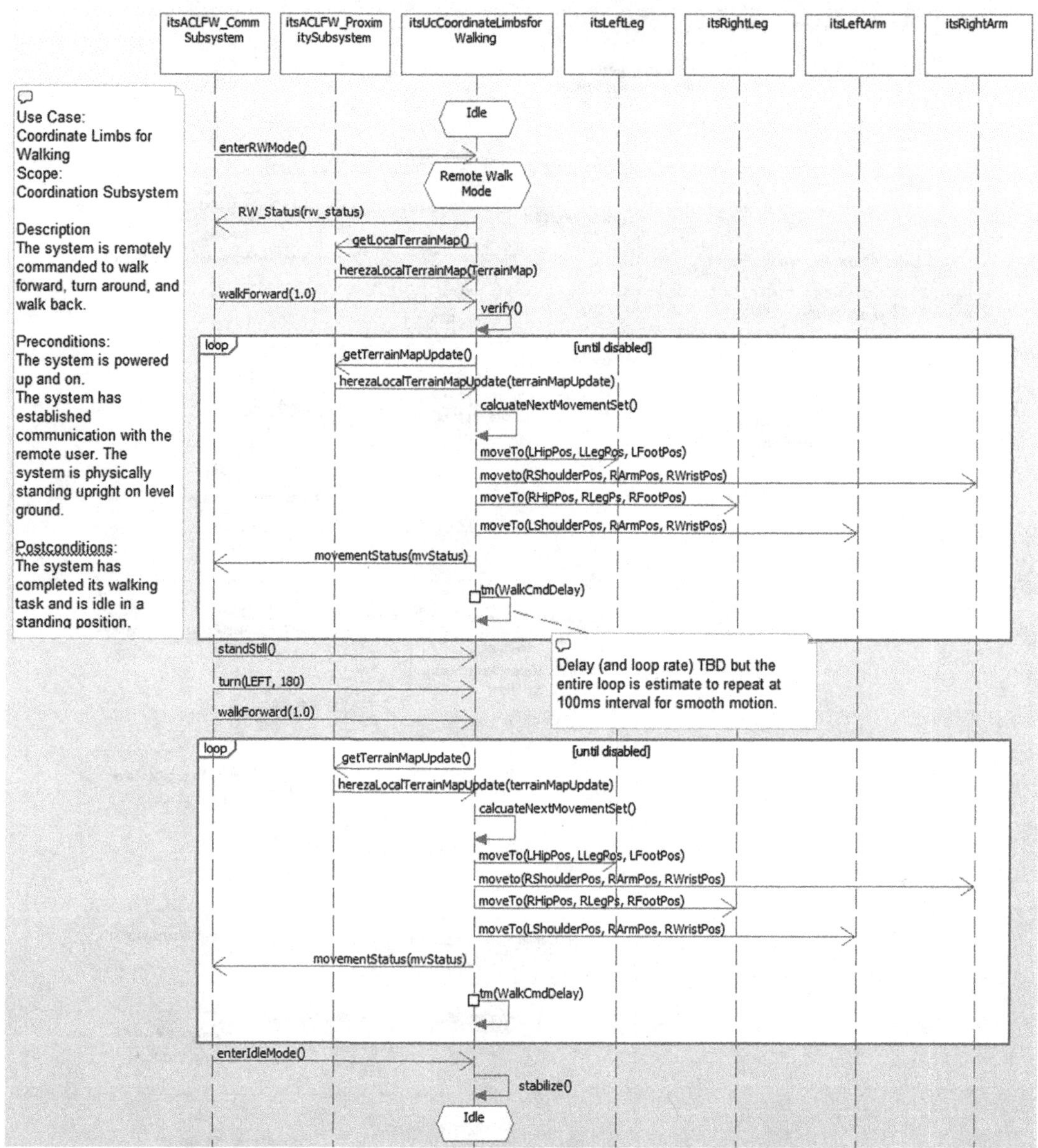

Figure 7.25
Walking scenario 1.

- Speed
- Torque.

It is important to remember that the purpose of this work is to characterize the logical properties of the data and not their internal physical representation. Consider the data type Protocol. What can we say about its logical characteristics?

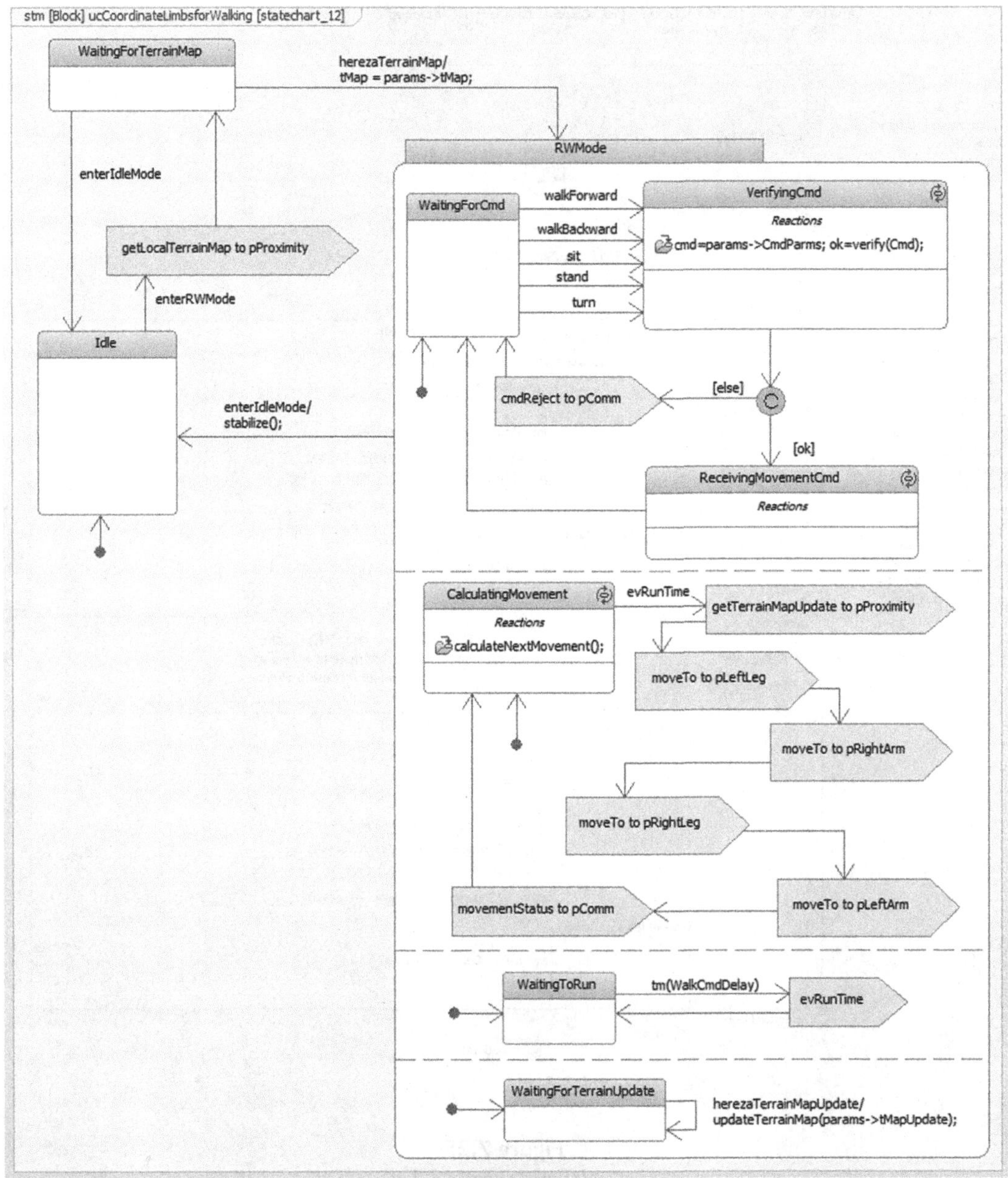

Figure 7.26
Coordinate limbs for walking use case statemachine.

First, a protocol consists of a set of intervals. Each interval consists of a measured value, a termination condition, and elevation. A "measured value" might be treadmill speed (most common), distance, heart rate, or output power. A termination condition could be an elapsed duration (most common), attained distance, heart rate value, achieved work value (such as calories burned).

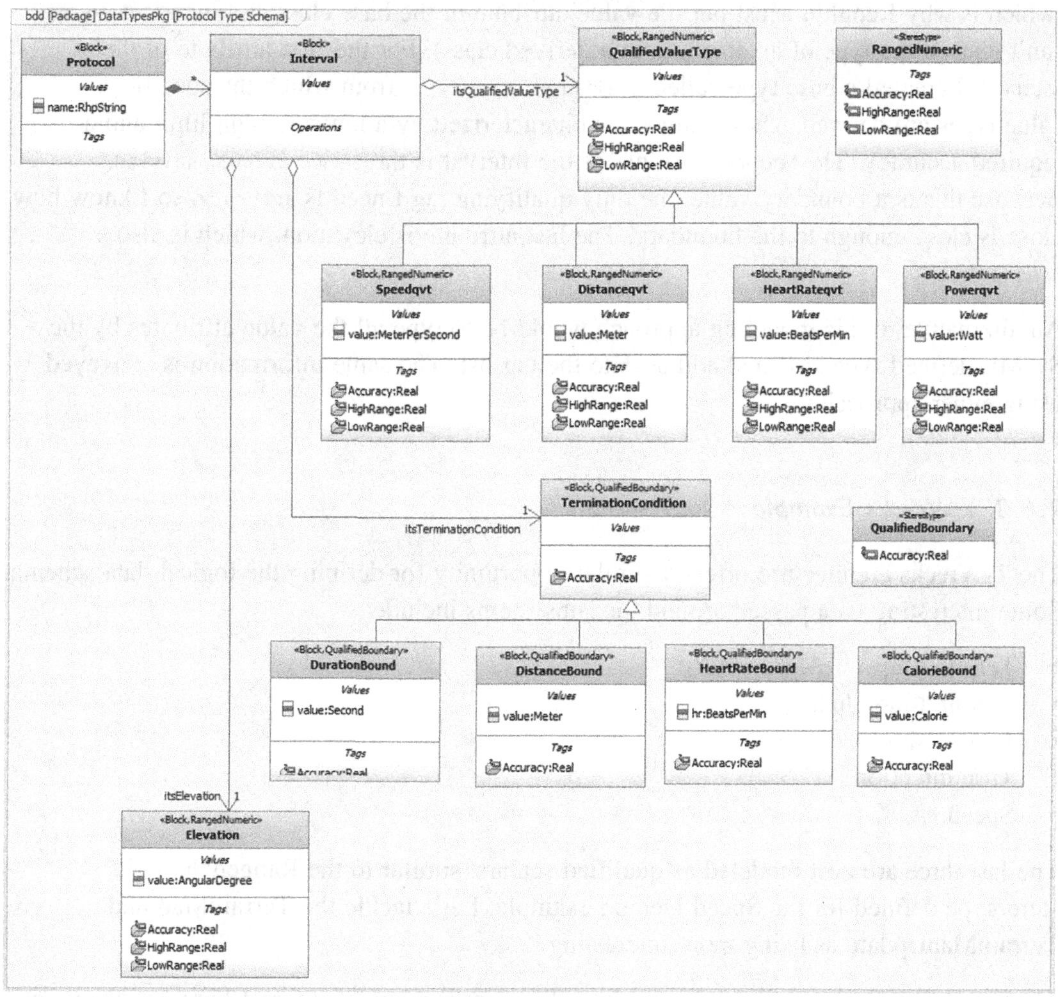

Figure 7.27
Protocol Logical Data Schema.

These are the logical properties of a protocol—things that it *must* contain to be valid. Whether the set of intervals is stored as an array or linked list is irrelevant to our current concern, as is whether speed is stored as scaled integers or IEEE floating point values.

Figure 7.27 shows the logical data schema for the Protocol type. There are a number of useful ways to model this. In this case, I've added two stereotypes—`RangedNumeric` and `QualifiedBoundary`—and added appropriate tags to hold the appropriate numeric metadata. In each subclass, I've added a `value` attribute but typed it appropriately for the subtype (which is why I couldn't just put the value attribute in the base class and inherit it—you can't change the type of an attribute in a derived class). For the first attribute of the interval, I created a base type called `Qualified Value Type`, from which the specific value types are derived. These values are characterized by a low and high limit and a required accuracy. The second attribute of the interval is the `Termination Condition`. Because this is a boundary value, the only qualifying tag I need is `accuracy`, so I know how close is close enough to the boundary. The last attribute is elevation, which is also a `RangedNumeric`.

An alternative to this modeling approach would be to type all the value attributes by the SysML defined type `Real` and add `Unit` to the tag list. The same information is conveyed using either approach.

7.6.2 T-Wrecks Example

The T-Wrecks architecture offers a similar opportunity for defining the logical data schema. Some interesting data passed around the subsystems include:

- Terrain Map
- Terrain Map Update
- Joint position
- Turn direction
- Speed.

The last three are best modeled as qualified scalars, similar to the RangedNumeric stereotype defined for the Speed Demon example. Let's tackle the TerrainMap and TerrainMapUpdate as being more interesting.

There are many ways to model map data. Two approaches of interest here are absolute references—that is, placing the map origin outside of the system itself—and relative references—that is, mapping everything from the original of a point on the system. Local terrain maps differ from absolute in that they are not mapped using a GPS map but are dynamically determined from active system sensors. For this reason, we'll use a relative mapping scheme, meaning that some location on the exoskeleton itself will be used as the origin for the map, and by "local" we mean that we are only concerned about objects within a finite distance of that origin. As the system moves through the terrain, the origin will be displaced and new data, particularly at the approaching boundaries of the system, will be added. This latter data set will constitute the Map Update. The logical data schema for this is shown in Figure 7.28. Are there more efficient representations of this information? Possibly, but optimality is not our concern here—correctness is.

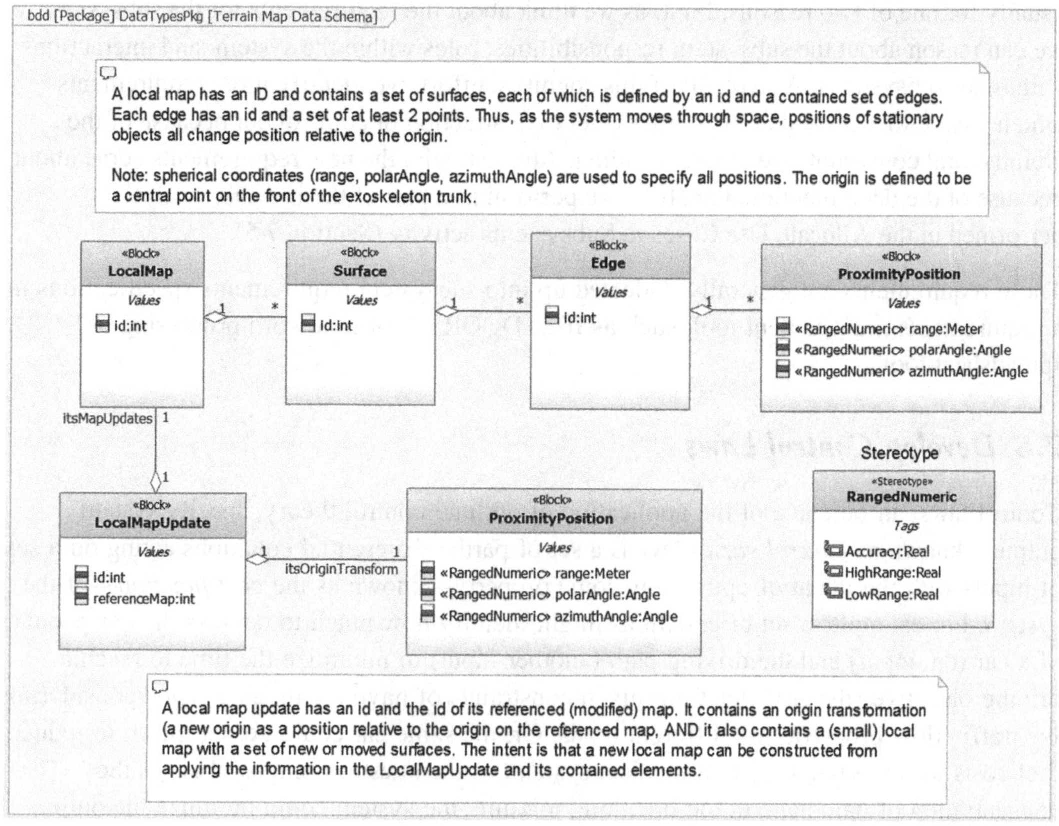

Figure 7.28
T-Wrecks Local Map Data Schema.

7.7 Create/Update Subsystem Requirements

Back in Section 7.4, we allocated system requirements to subsystems. For all the requirements in the use case under consideration each requirement is handled in one of several ways:

1. It may be directly allocated to a single subsystem
2. Because it applies to the interaction of more than one subsystem, it may be decomposed into derived requirements, each of which is allocated to a single subsystem
3. Because it applies equally to more than one subsystem, it may be allocated to more than one subsystem, each of which is required to meet and verify it.

Later, in Section 7.5, we created subsystem-level use cases to bring order to these requirements.

In this section, we reason about the adequacy of the requirements being allocated and identify new subsystem requirements for each of the use cases. These requirements come about usually for one of two reasons. First, as we think about the requirements for the subsystem, we can reason about the subsystem responsibilities, roles within the system, and interactions with other subsystems. As a result of this cognitive effort, we identify more requirements which were either missed at the higher level of abstraction or come about because of the architectural constraints we are now adding. Alternatively, the new requirements come about because of the deep functional analysis we perform as a part of the use case analysis performed in the Allocate Use Cases to Subsystems activity (Section 7.5).

These requirements are generally collected up into subsystem requirements specifications in a requirements management tool, such as IBM DOORS™, or in a word processing or spreadsheet tool.

7.8 Develop Control Laws

Control laws, an outcome of the application of optimal control theory, specify system outputs (known as *control variables*) as a set of partial differential equations acting on a set of inputs with the intent of optimizing some property—known as the *cost function*—of the system. For example, a set of equations might identify how much to depress the gas pedal of a car (the input) and the driving path (another input) to minimize the time to reach a driving objective (the cost function) given constraints of having enough gas and considering the traffic flow properties on different roads. Or, the same car could be optimized to reduce fuel costs for the same trip. In a medical system, as the anesthesiologist changes the concentration of halothane in the breathing mixture, the system could optimize the output flow of anesthetic to minimize the time to achieve the new set value or to minimize the cost of anesthetic drug usage. An elevator system, as it moves from floor to floor, can optimize the motive force applied to the elevator to minimize wear and tear on the motor and drive train while staying within customer comfort limits.

A detailed discussion of the development and representation of control laws is far, far outside of the scope of this book and we will leave it to other texts to describe the mathematics and implementation details. Of concern to us, however, is how we incorporate that information into our system engineering workflow. It is an important topic here for the control laws that span across multiple subsystems because it impacts the requirements and interfaces for those subsystems. For the most part, control laws fall within the confines of individual subsystems but there are often some that do not, and they then fall within the domain of the systems, as well as the control, engineer.

The steps for the systems engineer within the task *Develop Control Laws* task are:

- Identify the input variables. Often key input variables include set point values
- Select the domain in which to operate. Time, complex-s, and frequency are common domains in which to cast the control problem

- Identify the optimization criteria. Be clear about what the control law is trying to optimize
- Identify the optimization constraints. These include time, materiel, energy, and other constraints. Many control laws require severe time constraints to remain within stable regions in the control space
- Define the control laws. Define the mathematical transformations of inputs to outputs that optimize the desired system properties within the specified constraints
- Determine accuracy and fidelity constraints
- Perform error analysis. Error analysis looks at how errors are created, propagated, and multiply within the computation and affect the ability of the control law to achieve the desired optimization.

This work is normally performed by someone specifically trained in the mathematics and physics of the processes to be optimized, known as a *control engineer*. Although in principle this work can be done in activity diagrams, my experience is that many control engineers prefer to work in optimized tools such as MathWorks MATLAB™ or Simulink™ and link those models to the UML models. IBM Rhapsody™ provides a good interaction with Simulink, for example, and supports co-simulation and co-code generation.

Such models are often represented graphically (as they are in Simulink for example), especially when the optimization criteria is to minimize error between actual and commanded output. Figure 7.29 is a simple example of a typical control block diagram, this one created using the on-line tool Blockmesh.[14]

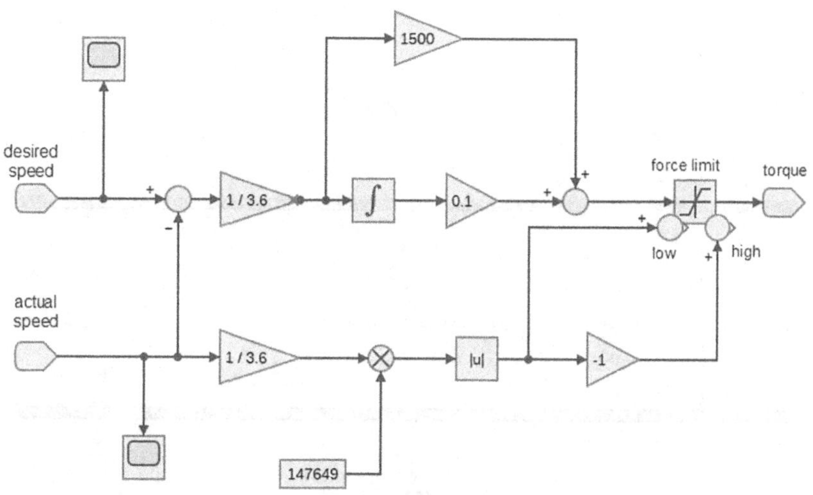

Figure 7.29
A simple example of a control block diagram.

[14] https://blockmesh.com/?main.

Once the control engineer has done their work on the control law, it must be allocated to the involved subsystems and the events and flows required for the control law enactment added to the subsystem interfaces. As in the data schema definition (see Section 7.6), the elements of the interface involved in the control laws should be characterized with constraints on timeliness, accuracy, and so on, so that they can meet the needs.

7.9 Analyze Dependability

The last activity we'll discuss in this chapter is Analyze Dependability. As mentioned earlier, dependability's primary aspects—safety, reliability, and security—must be considered throughout the systems development cycle. As we create the systems architecture, we make technical decisions that can negatively or positively impact our ability to depend upon the system. Figure 7.30 shows the three tasks that we perform to assess the impact of our architectural decisions. The outcome of this actually is commonly a set of new design-level requirements to ensure the system remains safe, reliable, and secure.

We will discuss these topics lightly here, having discussed them in more detail previously in Section 5.7. The same methods and techniques will be applied here, both at the subsystem and the system levels. The goal is ultimately systemic dependability but that levies requirements on the subsystems.

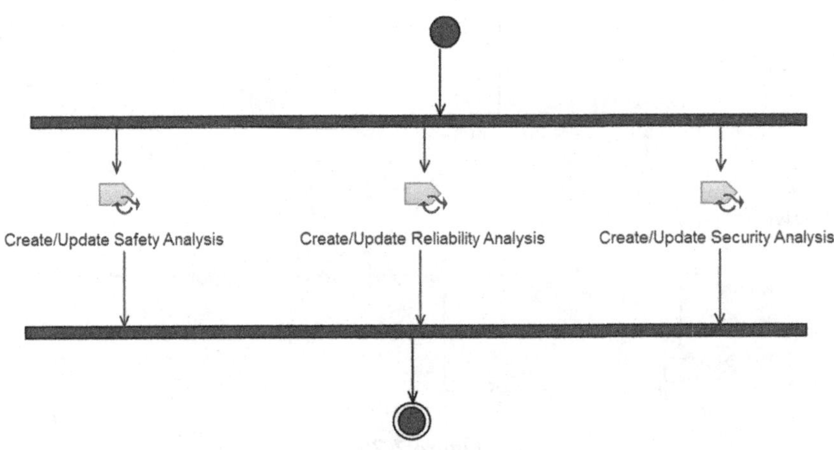

Figure 7.30
Analyze Dependability workflow.

7.9.1 Safety Analysis

The primary analytic technique here remains fault tree analysis. At the system level, we examine the existing FTAs in light of architectural decisions to see if there is any change necessary to maintain the same level of safety. We also look to see whether our technology decisions have introduced any new hazards with which we must deal. For example, adding a high-capacity battery in our technical solution might have introduced a hazard of electrocution or the selection of specific chemical processes might have introduced the opportunity for exposure to toxic materials. Although it is not (always) a requirement for a subsystem to be safe in isolation, it is common to repeat this analysis for each subsystem as well, just to ensure complete coverage. As before, the outcome of this analysis results in a hazard analysis. It is also common for both analysis and design hazard analyses to be separately maintained.

7.9.2 Reliability Analysis

Reliability analysis flows in two directions. From the system level, we require certain levels of reliability in subsystem functions so that system-level reliability can be achieved. These result in reliability requirements levied on the subsystems. From the bottom up, we may have begun the process of technology and device selection and these may have well-known reliability values. If known, we can compute the reliability of the subsystem services by analyzing the (known) reliability of component parts. If the resulting (bottom-up) reliability is inadequate for the need, this may result in additional design work to ensure adequate system reliability. As before, the FMEA is the most common tool for capturing and analyzing reliability.

7.9.3 Security Analysis

The techniques discussed Section 5.7.3 apply here as well. Besides looking at vulnerabilities added due to technical choices, we also look for additional assets, and want to anayze the system to ensure the security countermeasures remain adequate.

7.10 Summary

The theme for this chapter was the definition of the system architecture. The Harmony process identifies five key views of architecture:

- Subsystem and component view
- Distribution view
- Dependability view
- Deployment view
- Concurrency and resource view.

In systems engineering, we focus most strongly on the subsystem and component view but we begin to pay attention to the others as well. To achieve this, one of the most important things we do is to create a subsystem architecture, where subsystems are the largest-scale internal parts of the system. Requirements are allocated to these subsystems—including requirements that must be decomposed into derived requirements first—to clarify the roles and responsibilities of the subsystems.

Following that, there are a set of activities the system engineer performs in no particular order, including:

- Allocate use cases to subsystems
- Update logical data schema
- Update subsystem requirements
- Develop control laws
- Analyze dependability.

In Chapter 5, we used use case functional analysis as a key approach to understand the requirements and verify their adequacy. We do the same thing during architectural design for the subsystems. Unless a subsystem is quite simple, it can benefit from a thorough analysis of the requirements allocated to it. For this reason, we allocate use cases to the subsystems and then analyze them. The allocation can be done either top-down (by decomposing system use cases into included subsystem use cases) or bottom-up (allocating services, data, and flows to subsystems and grouping them up into subsystem use cases). In either case, the use cases are analyzed using the same techniques, including execution and simulation, which we applied to the system use cases.

As we perform the analysis, we create logical interfaces between the subsystems. These interfaces define services and flows into and out of the subsystems. The services and flows carry data or flow items and those must be understood and characterized. We do this in the *Create/Update Logical Data Schema* task.

Control laws are mathematical expressions that define how behavior and flows are controlled. At the heart of control laws is the need to provide optimal control. This is often done with specialized tools that provide the means to draw, simulate, and generate designs from those control laws. Almost all control laws will be scoped entirely within a subsystem, there are some that are not, and these must be dealt with when creating the systems architecture. The outcome of the control law analysis is a set of requirements allocated to the subsystems and addition of messages and flows to the subsystem interfaces.

Lastly, we must ensure the system remains safe, reliable, and secure as we make technical decisions. That is the function of the *Analyze Dependability* activity. We reapply the same basic techniques—FTA and hazard analysis for safety, FMEA for reliability, and threat analysis of security—but with newly revealed information about the technology and design inside the system.

At the end of this activity, we have specified a system architect that meets all the needs of the use cases analyzed so far. Of course, because we are doing this in an agile fashion, not all concerns have been dealt with until the last iteration is complete. Subsequent iterations add and factor the architecture as new stakeholder needs and system requirements are accounted for.

7.11 Moving On

The last chapter is on the hand off of systems engineering data to downstream engineering. Downstream engineering teams are cross-disciplinary teams organized around the subsystems and include software, electronic, and mechanical engineers. The hand off must take the systems engineering data and evolve the content to meet the needs of the downstream engineering teams and format it in such as way as to be useful. That is the subject of the last chapter of this book.

References

[1] <http://www.incose.org/practice/fellowsconsensus.aspx>.

[2] <http://sebokwiki.org/wiki/Logical_Architecture_(glossary)>. Adapted from ISO/IEC. 2010. Systems and Software Engineering, Part 1: Guide for Life Cycle Management. Geneva, Switzerland: International Organization for Standardization (ISO)/International Electrotechnical Commission (IEC), ISO/IEC 24748-1:2010.

[3] B.P. Douglass, Real-Time Design Patterns, Addison-Wesley, 2002.

[4] B.P. Douglass, Design Patterns for Embedded Systems in C, Elsevier Press, 2010.

[5] F. Buschmann, R. Meunier, H. Rohnert, P. Sommerlad, M. Stal, Pattern-Oriented Software Architecture Volume 1: A System of Patterns, Addison-Wesley, 1996.

[6] Software Considerations in Airborne Systems and Equipment Certification RTCA DO-178C (RTCA 2011).

CHAPTER 8

The Handoff to Downstream Engineering

Chapter Outline

8.1 Objectives

System engineers focus on system-level concerns by identifying stakeholder needs, defining system requirements, performing trade studies, and specifying system architecture. Their work guides the development, design, and implementation of internal system elements. These elements are created by experts in narrowly defined fields, including software, electronic, mechanical, hydraulic, pneumatic, optical, and control engineers. The objective of the activities presented in this chapter is to effectively convey the system engineering data to those engineers to support their work.

> The handoff to downstream engineering is a *process* not an event. The logical systems engineering data are evolved into physical engineering data so that they can be used by the downstream engineering, implementation, and verification teams.

8.2 The Handoff to Downstream Engineering Workflow

One of the most common questions I hear when consulting to MBSE teams is "How do I hand off specifications and engineering data to the downstream teams?" Interestingly, there isn't much published on this topic and it remains a weak point in many engineering organizations.

The Harmony process has an answer to this question that I've implemented in many customer projects. Figure 8.1 shows the workflow for the handoff to downstream engineering.

As before, I'll give a brief description of these tasks before getting into it all in earnest.

8.2.1 Gather Subsystem Specification Data

System engineers produce a lot of engineering data. In an MBSE approach, most of these data are in some or other model. If you follow the recommendations for model organization given earlier (see Section 3.3), then the information in the SysML model is already organized to facilitate the handoff to downstream engineering. Other engineers data held in other tools and other models must be gathered so that each of the subsystem teams understands where and how to access the information.

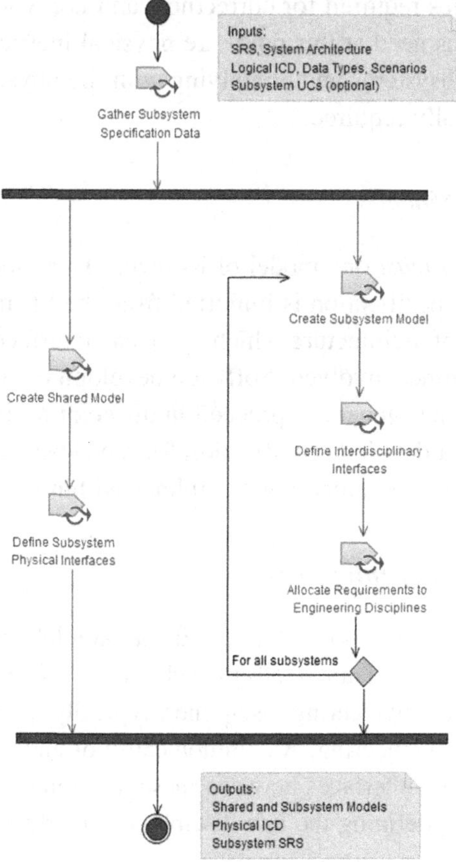

Figure 8.1
Handoff workflow.

8.2.2 Create the Shared Model

Information common to more than one subsystem must be placed into a repository accessible to all relevant subsystem teams. The purpose of the shared model is to provide a repository for engineering data—especially system and subsystem interfaces and flow item definitions and data type specifications used in those interfaces.

8.2.3 Define Subsystem Physical Interfaces

It has been repeatedly stressed that so far that the systems engineering interfaces and data/flow definitions have been *logical* in nature. That is, we have focused on the essential information and its properties required for correctness and not worried about optimality or format. What the subsystems need at this point are physical interfaces because they will be engineering the physical subsystems and complying with the physical interface specifications is fundamentally required.

8.2.4 Create Subsystem Model

Each subsystem will have *at least* one model of its own.[1] This model begins life as a skeletal framework and its specification is imported from the SE model. From there, it is elaborated into a deployment architecture which serves as interface specifications for the different engineering disciplines involved. Software development usually continues in the model but hardware disciplines generally proceed in different tooling. Nevertheless, the subsystem model serves as a detailed specification for the subsystem and source of data guiding the development for all engineering disciplines within the subsystem.

8.2.5 Define Interdisciplinary Interfaces

Requirements, subsystem interfaces, flow items, and data are defined in the handoff allocated to the subsystem team. Within the team itself, the subsystem will be created as an integrated set of elements from different engineering disciplines, typically including software, electronics, and mechanical engineering. A common cause of engineering failure is inadequate specification of the interfaces between these disciplines. This task addresses that point of failure by rigorously defining the interdisciplinary interfaces within the subsystem.

8.2.6 Allocation Requirements to Engineering Disciplines

In the previous chapter, we talked about how to allocate system requirements to subsystems. At the subsystem level, we must do the same to allocate requirements to the involved engineering disciplines. As before, some requirements may be directly allocated to an engineering discipline but many will require decomposition into derived requirements that can be addressed by the engineering discipline involved. Note that this task does not, in general, identify discipline-specific design elements but instead allocated requirements to the discipline. The engineers within the discipline are responsible for designing the elements for which they are in control.

None of the tasks involved in the handoff workflow are impenetrably complex or difficult to understand. They *are* however, real work that must be done to set up the subsystem teams for success.

[1] A large subsystem may consist of a collaboration of many models to manage complexity and access but there will always be at least one.

8.3 Gather Subsystem Specification Data

For the purpose of this task, there are two kinds of engineering data to gather for the handoff—data within the SysML model and other data of interest to the handoff. I'll address these two different sets of data separately in the following sections.

8.3.1 Gathering SysML Model Data

Back in Chapter 3, Figure 3.12 shows the recommended system engineering model organizational schema. The basic organization of information for the handoff is located with the architectural design package of the systems engineering model (Figure 8.2).

The data to be handed off is exclusively found in the Architectural Design Package (`ArchDesignPkg` in the figure). This package contains three uses of nested packages:

- SSnPkg
  There is one package here per subsystem. This package contains the requirements allocated to the subsystem, its subsystem-level use cases, and the functional analysis models for those use cases. Each subsystem model will import its corresponding subsystem specification package from the systems engineering model.

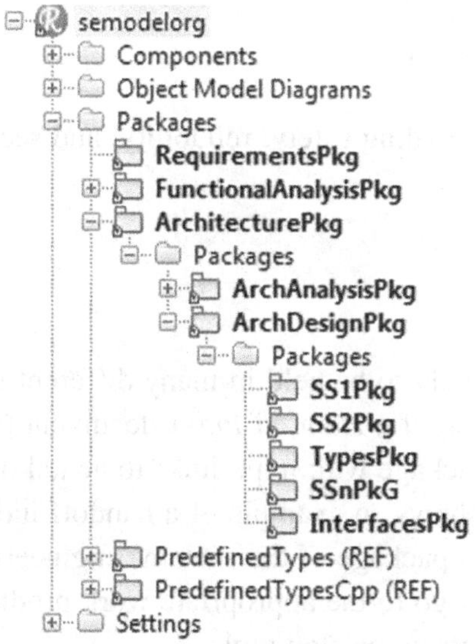

Figure 8.2
Model organization to support the handoff.

- InterfacesPkg

  This package contains the logical interfaces (including interface blocks) provided or required by those interfaces. Because this information inherently involves more than one architectural element, it will provide the basis for the physical interface definitions in the Shared Model. Depending upon its complexity, it may be subdivided into internal packages.
- TypesPkg

  This package contains the logical data types and flow item specifications used by the interfaces in the package above.

This organization is meant to ease the handoff of the information. Each subsystem team has a single place where it needs to go to get it's specification and the shared model has only two packages that it must import and adapt.

8.3.2 Gathering Other Engineering Data

The requirements, interfaces, and shared data schema form the primary sets of data that must be handed downstream. However, systems engineering may have a great deal of other data to be handed down as well, and much of these data may be in other formats and tools. This includes:

- process guidelines and standards,
- work product standards,
- project plan,
- project schedule and work items,
- certification plan,
- dependability analyses (including safety, reliability, and security analyses),
- performance analyses,
- test plans,
- trace data,
- configuration data.

Because this information is likely to be held in many different repositories, formats, and tools, I recommend the creation of a *Handoff Index* document (which can be a diagram in the subsystem specification package with hyperlinks to actual data) that links all of the data to be handed off. Figure 8.3 shows an example of a handoff index as a diagram to be found within the architectural design package of the systems engineering model. The underlined texts are hyperlinks that either go to the appropriate work product or area in the model or bring up the work product in its associated tool.

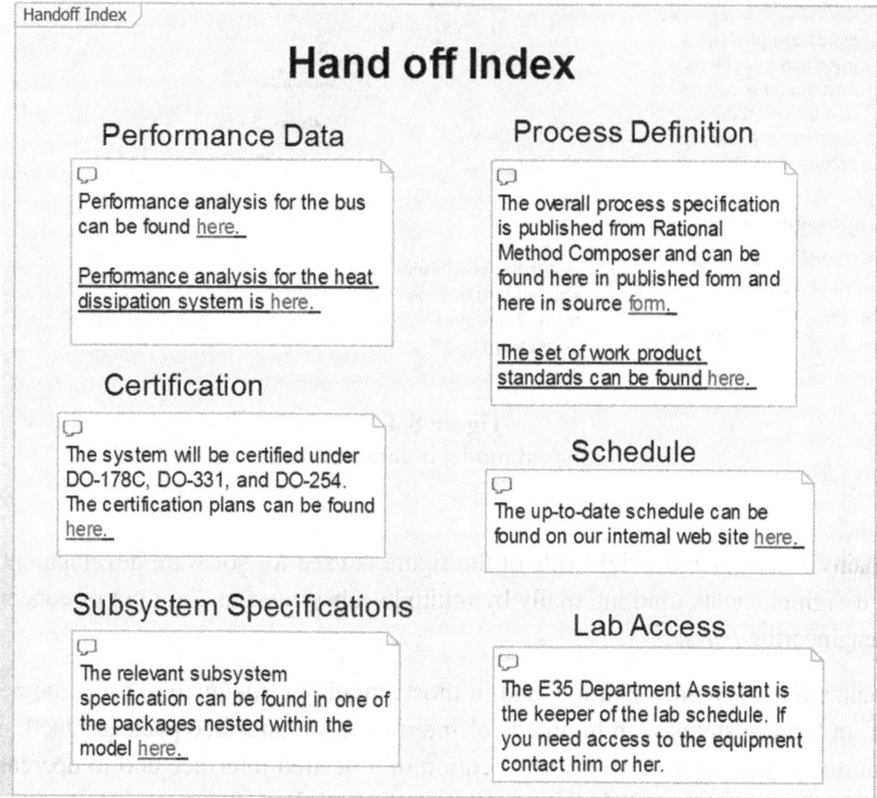

Figure 8.3
Handoff index.

8.4 Create the Shared Model

Along the left hand side of Figure 8.1, we see a flow that creates and then populates the Shared Model. To be clear, the purpose of the shared model is to hold engineering data common to more than one subsystem. In our context here, we mean physical interfaces and data/flow specifications.

8.4.1 Organizing the Shared Model

Figure 8.4 shows the recommended organization of the shared model.

The two packages of interest to us during the handoff are the Interfaces Package (`InterfacesPkg` in the figure) and the Common Types Package (`CommonTypesPkg` in the figure).

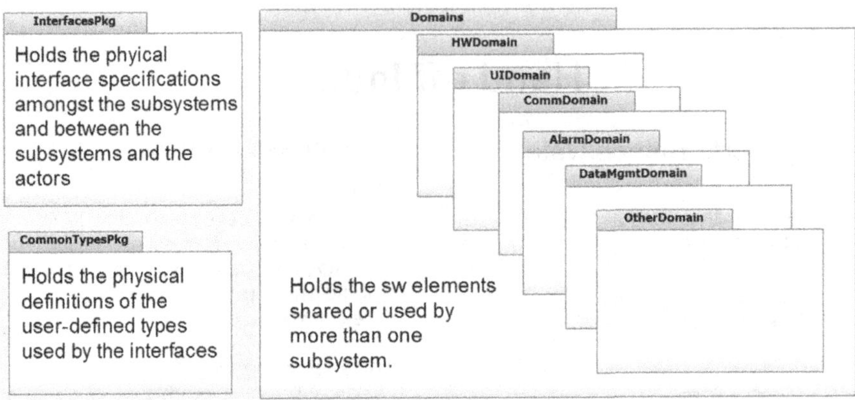

Figure 8.4
Shared model organization.

The Domains package on the right side of the figure is used for software development to hold software design elements used internally by multiple subsystems and are not of concern to systems engineering *per se*.[2]

This organizational schema is simple and in most situations, adequate to meet the need. However, in large systems with hundreds of interfaces, the interface package itself should contain nested packages to simplify the location of a desired interface and to decrease the dependency of subsystem models on information they don't actually need. In this more complex situation, I recommend that the Interface package contain a package for each subsystem. The subsystem interface package then only contains interfaces that are *provided* (and not referenced) by that subsystem. Thus, a given subsystem would only need to reference the interface packages for subsystems to which it connects.

Figure 8.5 shows a simple example for the decomposition of the shared model's interface package: one package for each subsystem (shown as `iSS1Pkg`, `iSS2Pkg`, and `iSSnPkg`), plus one additional one for the (generally rare) interfaces that are provided by more than one subsystem.

[2] A *domain*, in the Harmony process is a subject area with a common vocabulary—such as User Interface, Device I/O, or Alarm Management, and can be thought of as a usage for a package. Each domain contains many classes and types, and collaborations realizing use cases will contain classes from several different domains as well as context-specific elements. These packages in the shared model allow software developers a simple way to share software elements that might be reused in different subsystems. An example is a TCP (transmission control protocol) datagram class might be used in many different subsystems that are connected over an Ethernet network. Such a class would be put into a Communications domain in the shared model so that all subsystem teams can access it.

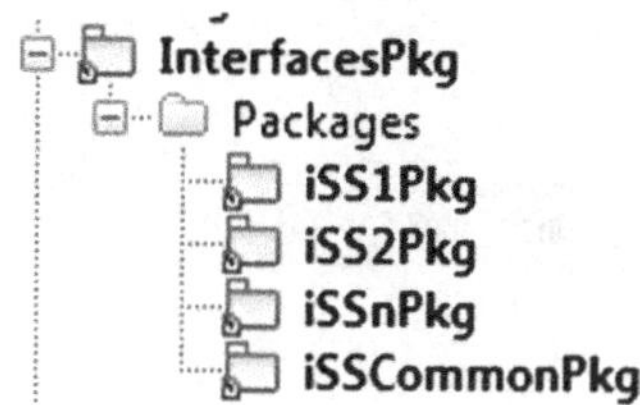

Figure 8.5
Packages nested within the Interface Package.

8.5 Define Subsystem Physical Interfaces

As a part of both the requirements definition and architectural design activities, we create interfaces. Some interfaces are between the system and elements in its environment, while others are between subsystems entirely within the system. However, these interfaces have been focused on essential properties—hence the term "logical interface" has been so far applied. Since we are preparing material to be handed over to downstream engineers that are going to define physical subsystems, we need to nail down the precise physical definition of the interfaces.

A question I often hear at this point is "but what if we get the interfaces wrong?"

I fully expect that, despite considerable effort we will employ to ensure the correctness of the interfaces, we will make mistakes. Even more than that, things that we cannot now foresee will change in the future. However, my experience is clear—it is crucial to define the interfaces as well as you can given the information you have now so that software, electronic, and mechanical engineers have a "known target" against which to design. These interfaces are put under configuration control in a known location for all interested parties to access. If (or rather, when) we discover some discrepancies or errors in the interfaces, we take the interface from configuration management, renegotiate the interface with all affected parties, and refreeze it in configuration management again. This will typically result in a small amount of rework but having the interfaces defined and under control keeps the entire team focused on the common system goal. Allowing interfaces to be undefined at the handoff is a common breakage point for many projects.

8.5.1 Creating Physical Specifications from Logical Specifications

The task of evolving the logical interface to a physical interface is work that requires both time and thought. In the systems engineering model, we have largely used interfaces or interface blocks to capture logical information without regard to the actual implementation. This frees us to reason about what services and flows we need, when we need them, and their properties. Subsystem teams, however, are building the actual subsystems and they

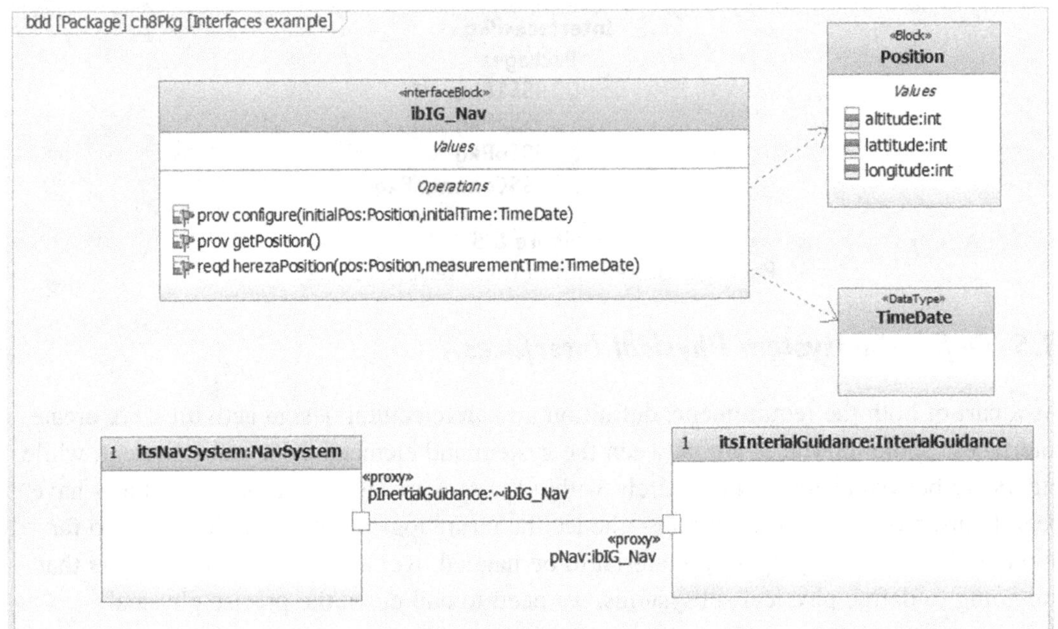

Figure 8.6
Logical interface example.

must provide and use physical interfaces. This task must therefore define those interfaces so that the subsystems who comply with them can be integrated together in the lab and in manufacturing.

Consider the logical interface between a Navigation subsystem and an Inertial Guidance subsystem, shown in Figure 8.6. This interface shows SysML events passed between two subsystems, two of which carry data. The idea is that the Inertial Guidance subsystem is initialized by sending the `configure` event that carries the initial position and time. Later, the Navigation system can send a `getPosition` event and the Inertial Guidance system responds by sending the Navigation system a `herezaPosition` event that carries current position and time of measurement. These logical events are control signals that can carry data via the interface block `ibIG_NAV`.

Now, let's us suppose that we are actually going to implement the connection between the subsystems with a 1553 bus. How should the subsystems interpret the interface definition in Figure 8.6?

The answer is that they shouldn't. There are too many ways for the two teams to implement the logical interface. What is needed is a physical interface definition. The 1553 bus protocol definition is defined by the 1978 US Department of Defense (DoD) standard [1]. The format used for transmission is shown in Figure 8.7.

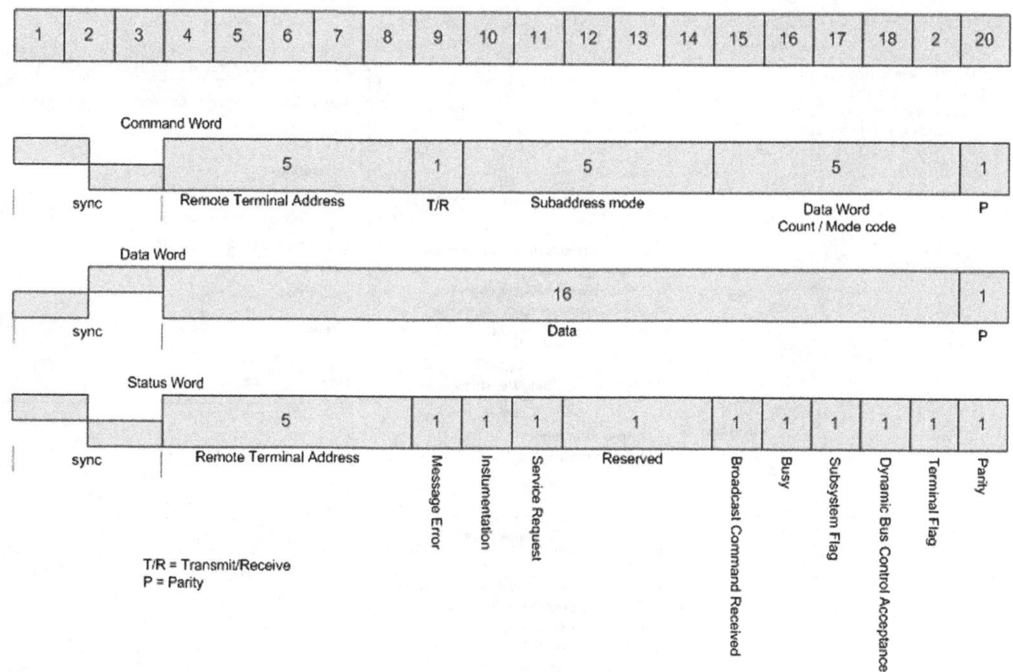

Figure 8.7
1153 Bus word format.

This interface can be realized in SysML or UML with a combination of blocks (or classes), stereotypes with tagged values, types, and definitions. Figure 8.8 shows that a Msg1553 contains three types of words. The first word is the `CommandWord1553` and it has a number of attributes, each of which is a «`bitfield`». The «`bitfield`» stereotype defines two tags. The first is the number of bits used to hold the value (`bitWidth`) and the second is the starting position of the bit field within the word. The second is zero or more `DataWord1553` blocks. The last is the `StatusWord`. The dialog box in the upper right-hand corner of the figure shows the values of the tags for the `subaddressMode` bit field within the `CommandWord1553` block. Also shown on the diagram is an enumerated type (with values shown in the accompanying comment) for important data words used as commands and responses. Finally, the diagram has a comment at the upper left that contains a hyperlink to the electronic and software standard that defines the interface.

We'll use tags more later, when we define the deployment architecture in Section 8.7.

For every interface we define, we must

- refine the logical service into a physical service,
- refine the data schema,
- refine the constraints,
- put the physical interface and data into the shared model.

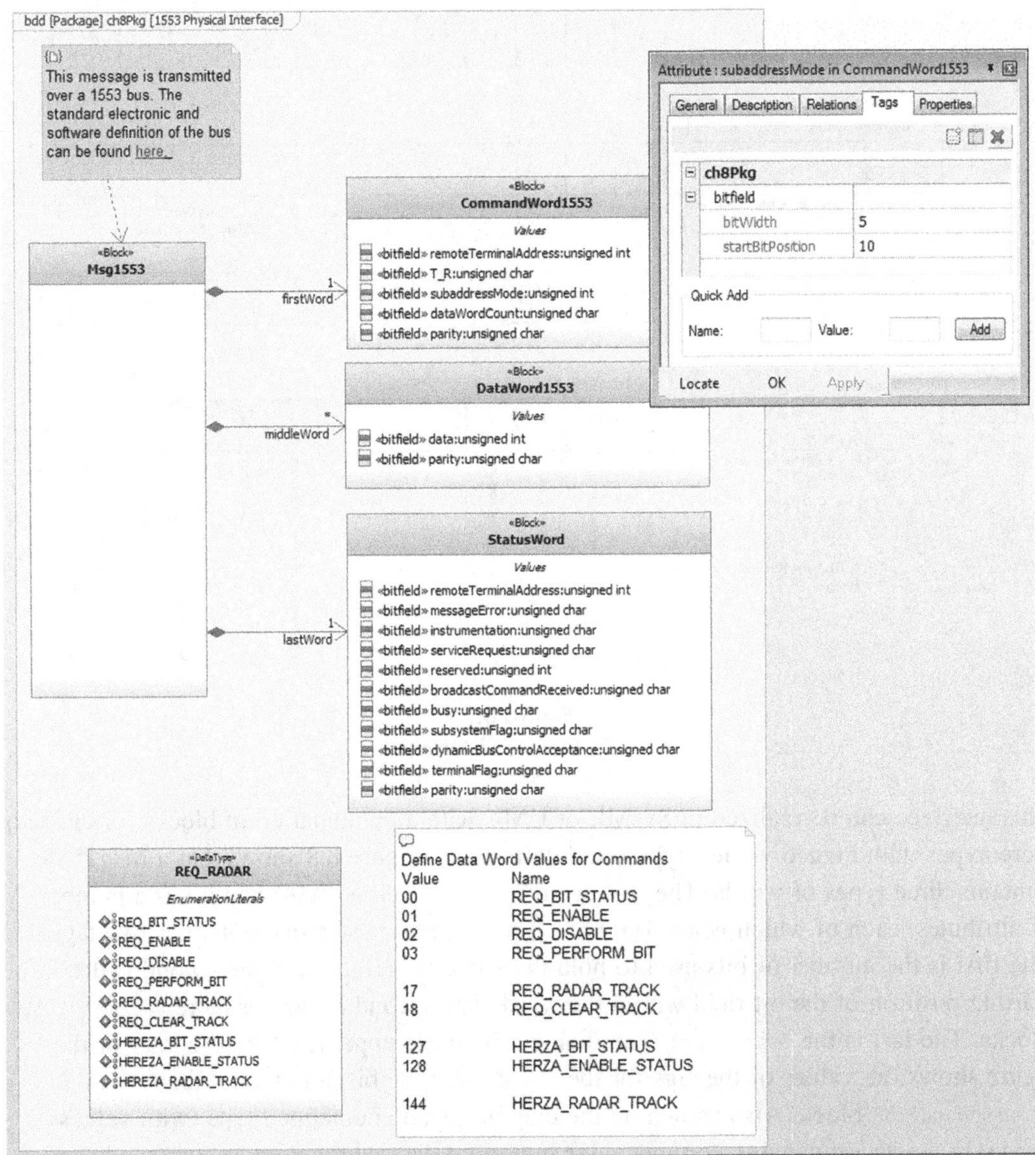

Figure 8.8
SysML physical interface.

Then, as mentioned, we create a configuration-controled interface baseline and we can have a review with all interested parties.

8.5.1.1 Refine the logical service into a physical service

An interface is a collection of services provided (or required) by an element. Each service should be defined in terms of:

- service name,
- description of functionality (data or control transformation performed),
- inputs and output data or flows,
- quality of service constraints (such as maximum performance time or reliability),
- underlying mechanism (e.g., 1553 bus, mechanical linkage, voltage level).

8.5.1.2 Refine the data schema

The physical data schema specifies how the logical properties of the logical data schema will be realized. In software, this generally comes down to the definition of types that specify the data down to the individual bit level, whether it is big endian or little endian, and so on. For materiel or energy flows, this may include the refinement of units, quantities, and ranges.

8.5.1.3 Refine the constraints

The logical constraints will certainly still hold, but often must be refined further in the physical interface. Additional constraints—due to the nature of the physical interface selected—may also be added.

8.5.1.4 Put the physical interface and data into the shared model

The shared model holds or references all the data necessary for the subsystem teams to understand the interaction well enough to built it or buy it. Just remember—poor interface specification is a leading cause of project failure!

8.5.2 Speed Demon Interface Example

Let's look at our treadmill model and refine some of the logical interfaces into the physical realm.

The key diagram to start the analysis is the architecture diagram (Figure 7.7). The relevant interfaces are shown in Figure 8.9.

The interface blocks there define the logical interfaces—the services and flows—between the subsystems. There are several kinds of interface types within these interfaces. `ibTControl`, `ibMControl`, and `ibDisplayData` are heavily biased towards small

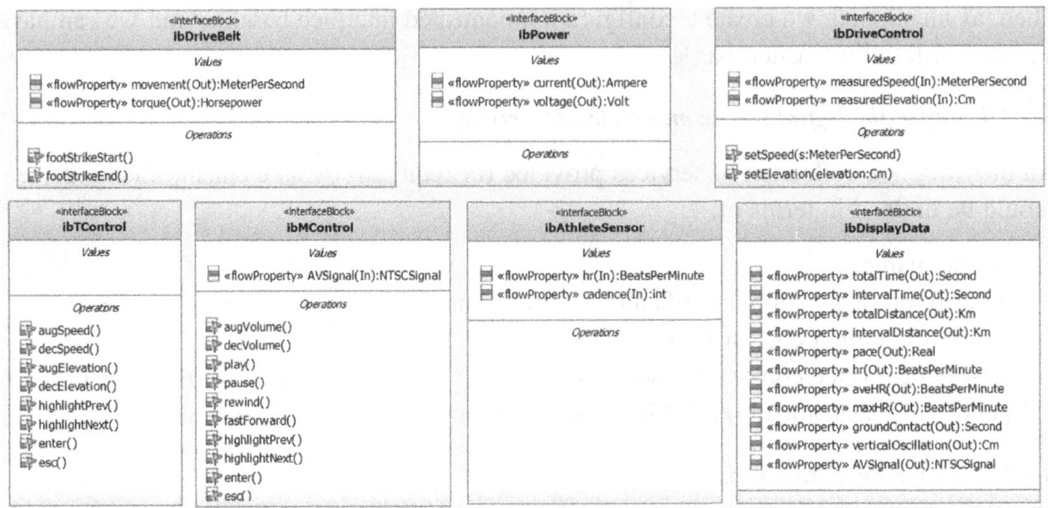

Figure 8.9
Speed Demon logical interfaces.

discrete values that must be exchanged. `ibMControl` and `ibDisplayData` also include an `AVsignal` to transmit video from the `MediaControlUnit` subsystem (via `theControlUnit` subsystem) to the `DisplayUnit` subsystem. `ibPower` is conducting electrical power from the power unit to the various subsystems. Although there is only a single interface block for power distribution, the different subsystems are very likely to have quite different power needs.

- The `MediaControlUnit`, for example, needs to control and stream video, requiring about 1 amp.
- The `DisplayUnit` must drive a rather large display—requiring a moderate amount of power, around 4 amps at 120 VAC.
- The `DriveUnit` must drive the 4000 RPM 4.0 hp motor to drive the drive belt—requiring relatively high power, around 45 amps at 120 VAC.

Based on this information, the physical interfaces for the treadmill will be realized in the following physical media:

- power
  - 120 VAC 45 amp high power interface for driving the drive belt motor,
  - 5 V DC 4 amp power bus for other subsystems,
- data
  - CAN bus using 11-bit headers for discrete data exchange,
- video
  - 1080p HDTV video.

Of course, in a real project we might use the tradeoff study methods outlined in Chapter 6 to evaluate different physical media, such as Ethernet versus CAN bus and NTSC versus HDTV 1080i versus HDTV 1080p. We'll just assume that was done.

The CAN bus is an interesting choice. It uses a multimastered bit-dominance protocol to handle transmission collisions and excels at transmitting small data packets. It is widely used in automobiles because of its speed (1 Mbit/s), robustness, and low cost. You can even select the headers to provide a priority transmission scheme. I've deployed it in medical systems to great advantage. A downside to the CAN bus is that it only provides 8 bytes for data delivery. It can be used to send large volumes of data by disassembling the data sets into small network packets and reassembling at the receiver side but it excels when the data come naturally in small elements. The 11-bit header can be used to identify the message content and that is the strategy we will use here.

Figure 8.10 shows the base types for the specific interface definitions. I've defined a stereotype bitmap that provides a tag to specify the bit width of the value in the CAN bus message type. The `PowerBusInterface` has attributes defining the power type (AC or DC), the amps, and the voltage. The HDTV interface just refers to the standard to which the system designers must comply as there is little benefit to replicating a specification that already exists.

Now we can specify the specific interfaces. Figure 8.10 showed specific interfaces for the power interfaces using interface specifications. This is in contrast to the approach used in Figure 8.8, which used a block diagram and a comment to identify the different field values (including the values for the specific command bytes). These two approaches are shown as alternatives that are both possible. In the Figure 8.8 situation, the complexity of the 1553 bus message made the block diagram with comment approach a bit simpler than using instance specifications, while the example in Figure 8.10 was arguably simpler with instance specifications. Both, however, are possible.

Also shown in Figure 8.10 are the values for the `bitWidth` tag for some of the attributes of the `CANBusMsg` block. This tag is present for all attributes stereotyped with the «bitmap» stereotype. The comments display the value in those tags by de-referencing the hyperlink added into the comment. We can see, for example, that the `StartOfFrame` is 1 bit wide, while the `id` field is 11 bits wide. All the fields are so defined in the model, but not all are shown here on the diagram.

We used instance specifications to define the values for the fields for the power interfaces. For the bus messages, we also know *some* of the bit values (such as the 11-bit header (which is the same as the command ID)) for the `IntervalTime` message. Other fields, such as the particular value of the data being sent or the computed message CRC (cyclic redundancy check), won't be known until run-time. Figure 8.11 shows the messages for the services provided for the `ibDisplayData` interface block.

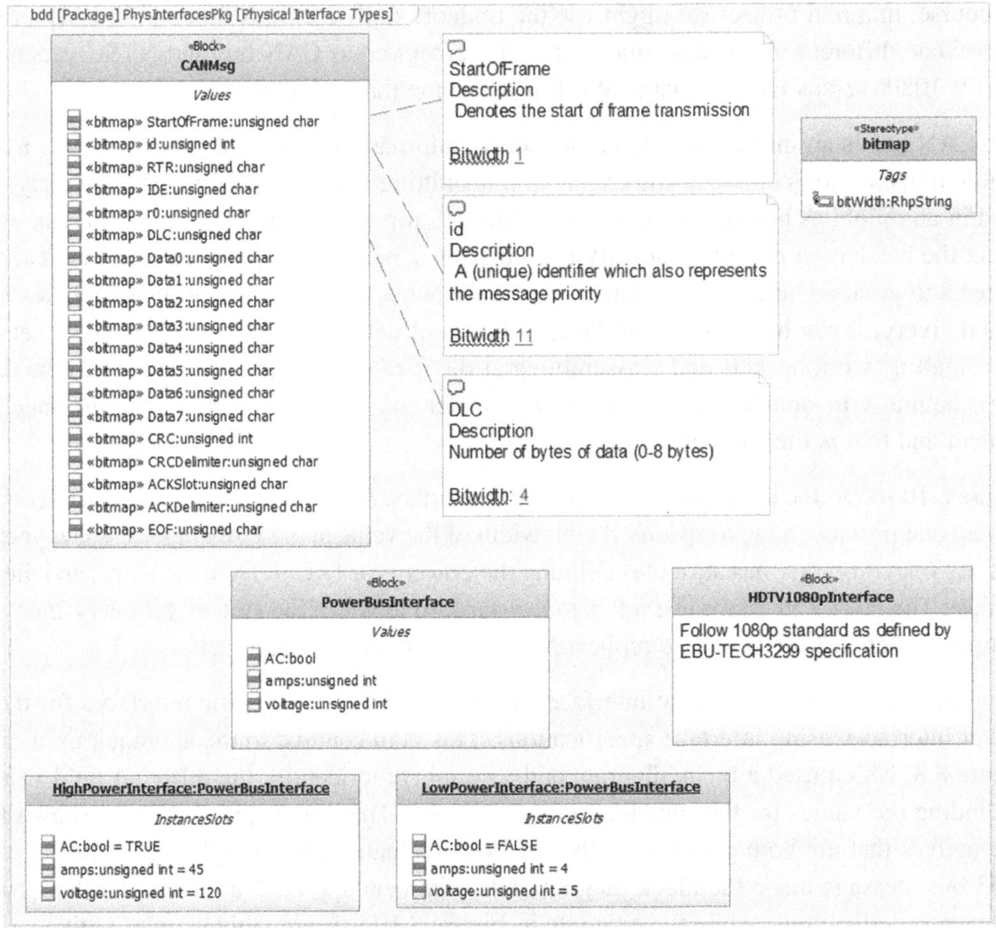

Figure 8.10
Speed Demon physical interface types.

This can be repeated for all interfaces in the Speed Demon architecture. Of course the physical interfaces and data types are put into the shared model.

8.5.3 T-Wrecks Interface Example

For the T-Wrecks example, I'll just look at the `Coordination` subsystem in detail. The other physical subsystem interfaces would be developed in the same fashion. Figure 8.12 shows a block definition diagram used to show the interfaces of a single subsystem, a usage I refer to as a *subsystem interface diagram.* In this case, it shows the logical interfaces for the `Coordination` subsystem. I like this diagram usage because a separate diagram is drawn for each subsystem and clearly identifies the interfaces supported or required by that subsystem at a glance.

bdd [Package] PhysInterfacesPkg [DisplayData Physical Interfaces]

Data Messages for ibDisplayData interface block using instance specifications. All values are 2 byes, unsigned integer, Big Endian format. Except for Pace which is 4 byte IEEE real.

totalTimeMsg:CANMsg

InstanceSlots

«bitmap» StartOfFrame:unsigned char = 1
«bitmap» id:unsigned int = 100
«bitmap» RTR:unsigned char = 0
«bitmap» IDE:unsigned char = 0
«bitmap» r0:unsigned char = 0
«bitmap» DLC:unsigned char = 2
«bitmap» EOF:unsigned char = 127
«bitmap» ACKDelimiter:unsigned char = 1
«bitmap» ACKSlot:unsigned char = 1
«bitmap» CRCDelimiter:unsigned char = 1

IntervalTimeMsg:CANMsg

InstanceSlots

«bitmap» StartOfFrame:unsigned char = 1
«bitmap» id:unsigned int = 101
«bitmap» RTR:unsigned char = 0
«bitmap» IDE:unsigned char = 0
«bitmap» r0:unsigned char = 0
«bitmap» DLC:unsigned char = 2
«bitmap» EOF:unsigned char = 127
«bitmap» ACKDelimiter:unsigned char = 1
«bitmap» ACKSlot:unsigned char = 1
«bitmap» CRCDelimiter:unsigned char = 1

TotalDistanceMsg:CANMsg

InstanceSlots

«bitmap» StartOfFrame:unsigned char = 1
«bitmap» id:unsigned int = 102
«bitmap» RTR:unsigned char = 0
«bitmap» IDE:unsigned char = 0
«bitmap» r0:unsigned char = 0
«bitmap» DLC:unsigned char = 2
«bitmap» EOF:unsigned char = 127
«bitmap» ACKDelimiter:unsigned char = 1
«bitmap» ACKSlot:unsigned char = 1
«bitmap» CRCDelimiter:unsigned char = 1

IntervalDistanceMsg:CANMsg

InstanceSlots

«bitmap» StartOfFrame:unsigned char = 1
«bitmap» id:unsigned int = 103
«bitmap» RTR:unsigned char = 0
«bitmap» IDE:unsigned char = 0
«bitmap» r0:unsigned char = 0
«bitmap» DLC:unsigned char = 2
«bitmap» EOF:unsigned char = 127
«bitmap» ACKDelimiter:unsigned char = 1
«bitmap» ACKSlot:unsigned char = 1
«bitmap» CRCDelimiter:unsigned char = 1

PaceMsg:CANMsg

InstanceSlots

«bitmap» StartOfFrame:unsigned char = 1
«bitmap» id:unsigned int = 104
«bitmap» RTR:unsigned char = 0
«bitmap» IDE:unsigned char = 0
«bitmap» r0:unsigned char = 0
«bitmap» DLC:unsigned char = 4
«bitmap» EOF:unsigned char = 127
«bitmap» ACKDelimiter:unsigned char = 1
«bitmap» ACKSlot:unsigned char = 1
«bitmap» CRCDelimiter:unsigned char = 1

HRMsg:CANMsg

InstanceSlots

«bitmap» StartOfFrame:unsigned char = 1
«bitmap» id:unsigned int = 105
«bitmap» RTR:unsigned char = 0
«bitmap» IDE:unsigned char = 0
«bitmap» r0:unsigned char = 0
«bitmap» DLC:unsigned char = 2
«bitmap» EOF:unsigned char = 127
«bitmap» ACKDelimiter:unsigned char = 1
«bitmap» ACKSlot:unsigned char = 1
«bitmap» CRCDelimiter:unsigned char = 1

AveHRMsg:CANMsg

InstanceSlots

«bitmap» StartOfFrame:unsigned char = 1
«bitmap» id:unsigned int = 106
«bitmap» RTR:unsigned char = 0
«bitmap» IDE:unsigned char = 0
«bitmap» r0:unsigned char = 0
«bitmap» DLC:unsigned char = 2
«bitmap» EOF:unsigned char = 127
«bitmap» ACKDelimiter:unsigned char = 1
«bitmap» ACKSlot:unsigned char = 1
«bitmap» CRCDelimiter:unsigned char = 1

MaxHRMsg:CANMsg

InstanceSlots

«bitmap» StartOfFrame:unsigned char = 1
«bitmap» id:unsigned int = 107
«bitmap» RTR:unsigned char = 0
«bitmap» IDE:unsigned char = 0
«bitmap» r0:unsigned char = 0
«bitmap» DLC:unsigned char = 2
«bitmap» EOF:unsigned char = 127
«bitmap» ACKDelimiter:unsigned char = 1
«bitmap» ACKSlot:unsigned char = 1
«bitmap» CRCDelimiter:unsigned char = 1

GroundContactTimeMsg:CANMsg

InstanceSlots

«bitmap» StartOfFrame:unsigned char = 1
«bitmap» id:unsigned int = 108
«bitmap» RTR:unsigned char = 0
«bitmap» IDE:unsigned char = 0
«bitmap» r0:unsigned char = 0
«bitmap» DLC:unsigned char = 2
«bitmap» EOF:unsigned char = 127
«bitmap» ACKDelimiter:unsigned char = 1
«bitmap» ACKSlot:unsigned char = 1
«bitmap» CRCDelimiter:unsigned char = 1

VerticalOscillationMsg:CANMsg

InstanceSlots

«bitmap» StartOfFrame:unsigned char = 1
«bitmap» id:unsigned int = 109
«bitmap» RTR:unsigned char = 0
«bitmap» IDE:unsigned char = 0
«bitmap» r0:unsigned char = 0
«bitmap» DLC:unsigned char = 2
«bitmap» EOF:unsigned char = 127
«bitmap» ACKDelimiter:unsigned char = 1
«bitmap» ACKSlot:unsigned char = 1
«bitmap» CRCDelimiter:unsigned char = 1

«Block»
HDTV1080pInterface

Follow 1080p standard as defined by EBU-TECH3299 specification

Figure 8.11
Display data interface services.

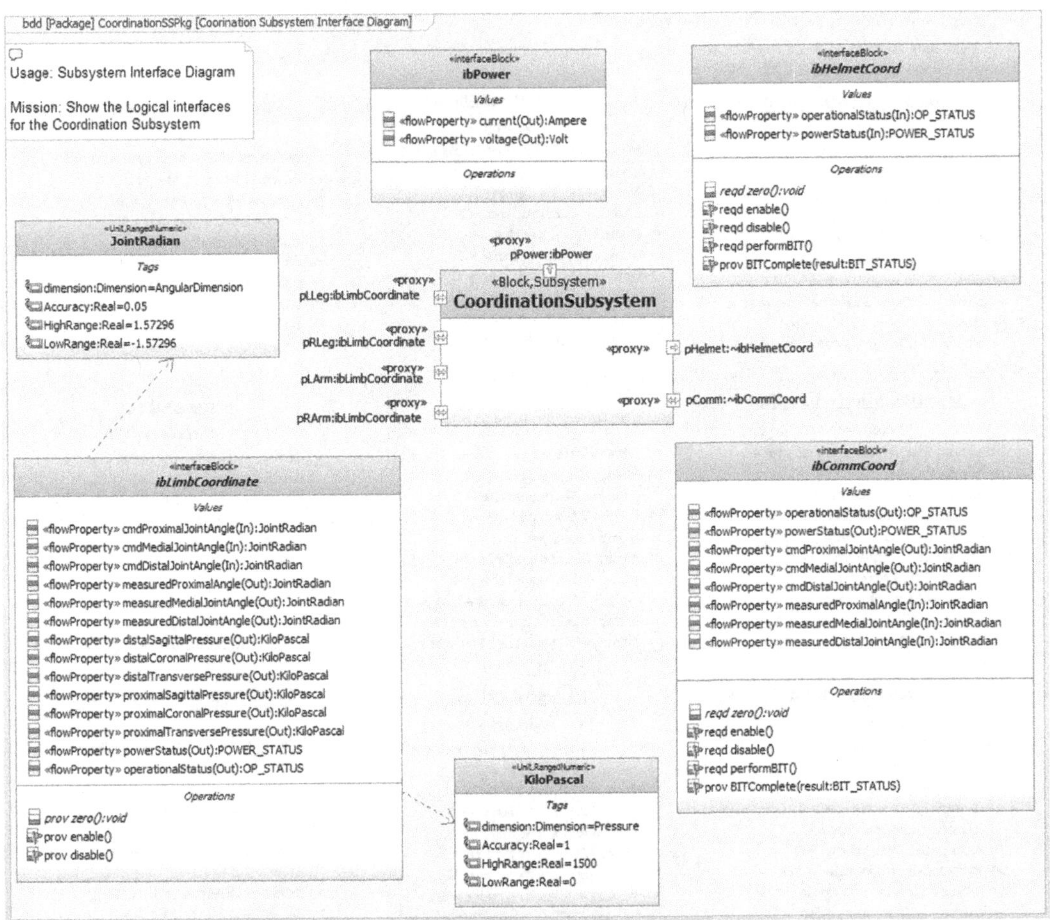

Figure 8.12
Coordination subsystem interface diagram.

Notice the use of directional features (flow, operations, and events) in the interface blocks in the figure. To keep the direction straight, I've used the naming convention for the interface blocks ib<source><target>. If a feature is provided by <source> it will be an `in` flow or `prov` operation or reception in the interface block. Flows going to <target> are indicated as `out` and operations and receptions invoked on the target are shown as `reqd`. You can also see that I've added a couple of units (JointRadian and KiloPascal) with range and accuracy specifications to clarify the data we need to move around the system.

Figure 8.12 shows the logical interfaces for the `Coordination` subsystem. Here in the handoff activity, we must convert these to physical interface and data specifications. A common communication protocol used in robotics (a closely related field to our system) is DeviceNet.[3] Since DeviceNet is a network protocol that uses the CAN bus as the physical layer, much of the discussion we had around the Speed Demon Treadmill also applies here. To save trees, we won't show all the messages as instance specifications, but we will show some interesting ones.

It makes sense to group some data elements together into command and response messages for the `Coordination` subsystem. Let's group together the three joint angles (proximal, medial, and distal) into one message for commanded joint and another for measured joint angles. We must also decide on the bit representation. Figure 8.12 shows the units as radians with a required accuracy of 0.05 radians. If we use 100 times the angle and round to the nearest integer, the values can be stored in a small integer (range −157 to 157) and the required representational accuracy to meet the needs and it can be stored in 2 bytes. All three angles can be stored in 6 bytes, which is less that our maximum 8-byte payload for the DeviceNet bus message.

The pressures come from the limb sensors and indicate the amount of pressure being exerted by the pilot; the `Coordination` subsystem interprets this as a signal to move the limb segment in the corresponding direction with a speed and force proportional to the amount of pressure. The pressure exerted by the pilot is bound to be within the limits of 0 and 1500 kPa (roughly 217 psi). Since we have nine of these pressures at a time (three dimensions and three joints), this requires 18 bytes to transmit. We could break this up into multiple CAN data link messages at the network layer (requiring disassembly at the transmission side and reassembly at the receiver side), or we can just transmit three separate messages from each limb, one for each limb segment. We would also like to be able to identify the limb and the joint for which these data are being sent. To that end, we add a 1-byte limb ID (0 = right arm, 1 = left arm, 2 = right leg, 3 = left leg) and a 1-byte joint ID (0 = proximal, 1 = medial, 2 = distal).

We will also combine power status and operational status together in a single message. BIT (built in test) status and errors codes will be combined into another message called ErrorStatus. BIT status is represented as a 16-bit set, which allows for separately reporting the results as pass (1) or fail (0) for up to 16 tests. Error Status is an enumerated type (ERROR_CODE), shown with a single defined enumeration value (NO_ERROR) but as potential errors are uncovered, this enumerated list will be extended. Using two bytes for Error Status allows for up to 65,536 error messages to be encoded. Figure 8.13 shows these messages as instance specifications of the CANMsg block.

[3] DeviceNet is a master–slave protocol owned by Open DeviceNet Vendor Association (ODVA) that uses the CAN bus specification as the physical layer and can have up to 64 communication nodes on the network [2].

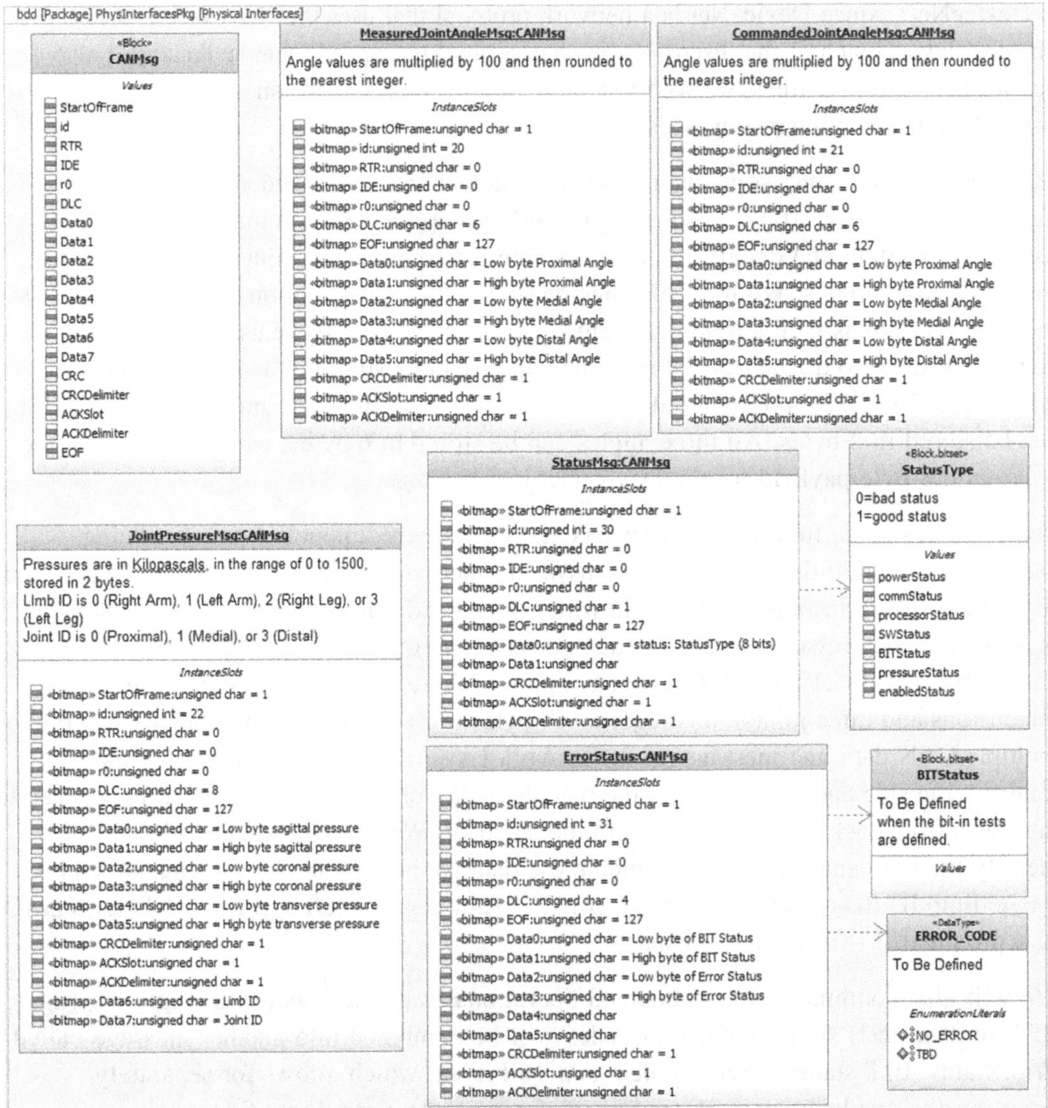

Figure 8.13
Messages for Coordinate subsystem.

8.6 Create Subsystem Model

In parallel with the creation of the shared model, we must also create a separate subsystem model for each subsystem. The recommended organization for the subsystem model is shown in Figure 8.14. The software-specific packages are of interest only to the software developers since that is where they will put in their software requirements analysis, software architecture, and software design. We won't discuss those topics here,

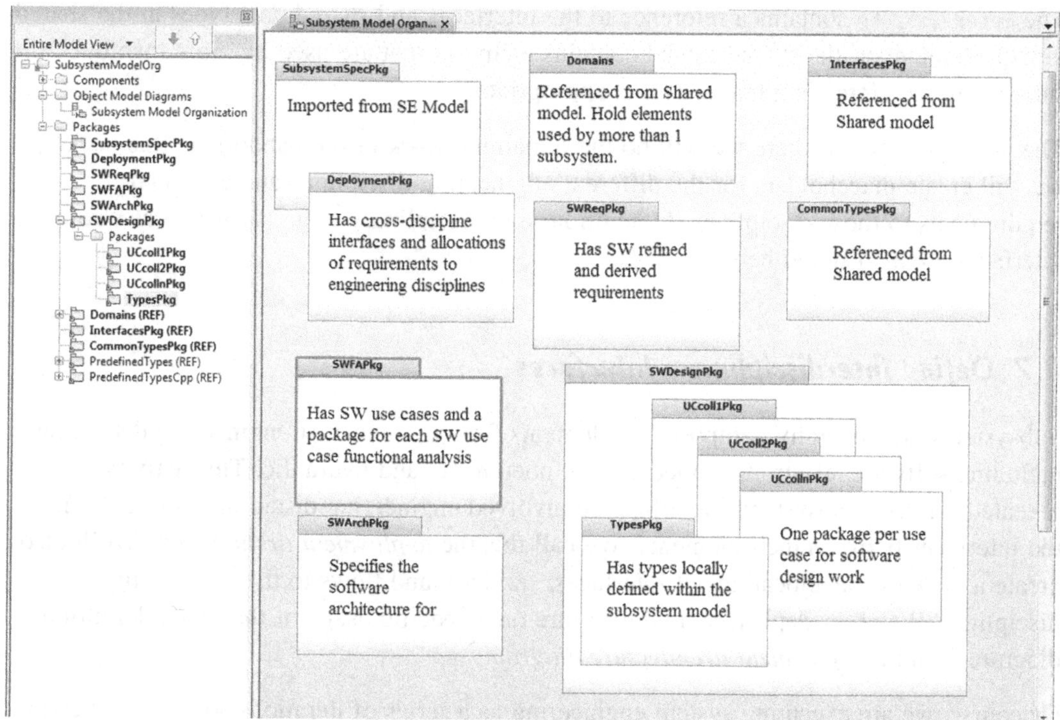

Figure 8.14
Subsystem model organization.

and in fact, we can let the software developers add the packages they need later, as they need them. Readers interested in the software development topics can consult other works, such as Ref. [3] for more detail.

In this book, we will focus on the packages used to specify the subsystem itself, and not just the software. These include the following packages:

- `SubsystemSpecPkg`,
- `InterfacesPkg`,
- `DeploymentPkg`.

The SubsystemSpecPkg is imported (as a copy) from the `ArchPkg->ArchDesignPkg` package of the systems engineering model. As discussed in Chapter 7, there is one package per subsystem, and it contains the requirements, use cases, and functional analyses of that subsystem. We can copy it into the subsystem model as it forms the primary part of its specification.[4]

[4] Some people prefer to use the package *by reference* from the systems engineering model rather than *by copy*. Both can work, but I prefer the *by copy* approach so that if the system engineers continue work on it, the subsystem specification doesn't change until the subsystem team explicitly loads the latest copy (which they might do in response to a work item). Intermediate work done by systems engineers remain invisible to the subsystem team until explicitly imported. That is not the case if the current status of the systems model is merely referenced.

The `InterfacesPkg` contains a reference to the interfaces and shared data types in the shared model. Remember, the shared model contains elements that are used by more than one subsystem, so referencing that model is appropriate.

The `DeploymentPkg` is where we will do the remaining work of the handoff. In this package, we will create placeholders for the different engineering disciplines and allocated requirements to those disciplines. In addition, interdisciplinary (e.g., software–electronics) interfaces are also stored here.

8.7 Define Interdisciplinary Interfaces

Subsystems are generally composed of elements from a number of engineering disciplines, including software, electronics, mechanical, pneumatic, and hydraulic. This activity, repeated for each subsystem, identifies the involved engineering disciplines and specifies the interfaces between their elements. We call this the *deployment architecture.* We'll also create a view of the allocations of interfaces, services, and flows to the engineering disciplines. We show deployment architecture on a specific usage of the block definition diagram, I call a *deployment architecture diagram.*[5]

Or course, we are executing system engineering as a series of iterations so we only need to consider the interfaces necessary to support the new features added in the current iteration. This means that we will elaborate (and possibly refactor) the interfaces for each subsystem during each iteration.

It is important to understand that even though specifying the interdisciplinary interfaces allows the different engineers to go off and do their work more-or-less independently, these interfaces are still likely to change and evolve. Since these interfaces are parts of the model, they will be under configuration management and they can be "thawed" and renegotiated among the pertinent players when it becomes necessary. However, my experience is that avoiding an early interface definition is a mistake and leads to long integration times and significant downstream rework. Having a known target for the interfaces has proven to be important.

It is common to represent the set of all elements from a single engineering discipline as a single block in this deployment view. Interfaces between the disciplines can be specified and elucidated without concerns about the internal design of contributions each of those disciplines makes to the subsystem design. In addition, it is a place to allocate discipline-specific requirements (see Section 8.8).

[5] The deployment architecture diagram (DAD) should not be confused with a standard UML "deployment diagram" which is the most useless of the UML diagrams because it is so "dumbed down." In contrast, a DAD is a far richer representation.

These interfaces will serve as specifications for the engineers so they know what to design for and against. As before, we'll use tags to clarify interface details.

8.7.1 Speed Demon Example: Control Unit Subsystem Interface Specification

Although more diagrams would be drawn for the actual deployment architecture, only two are shown here to illustrate the approach. Figure 8.15 shows the deployment architecture of the Speed Demon Control Unit subsystem. In this case, three distinct interface blocks are shown for the interface between the software and the electronics within that subsystem. Because of the richness of the interfaces, they were divided into interfaces for the Drive Unit, the Treadmill Control, and for the Media Control subsystems. The services and values are stereotyped; this adds tagged values (metadata) to the services and flows to characterize the data. That characterization is shown in Figure 8.16 for the drive-related interface block (`ibCU_SW_EE_Drive`).

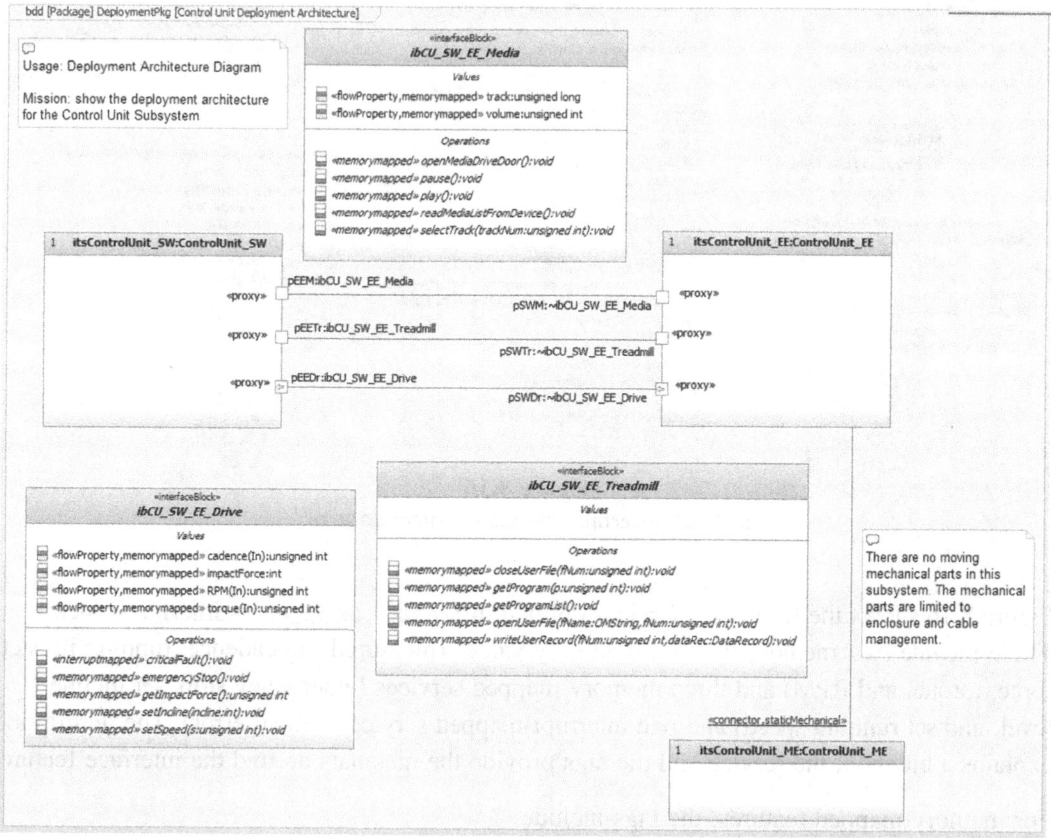

Figure 8.15
Control Unit deployment architecture.

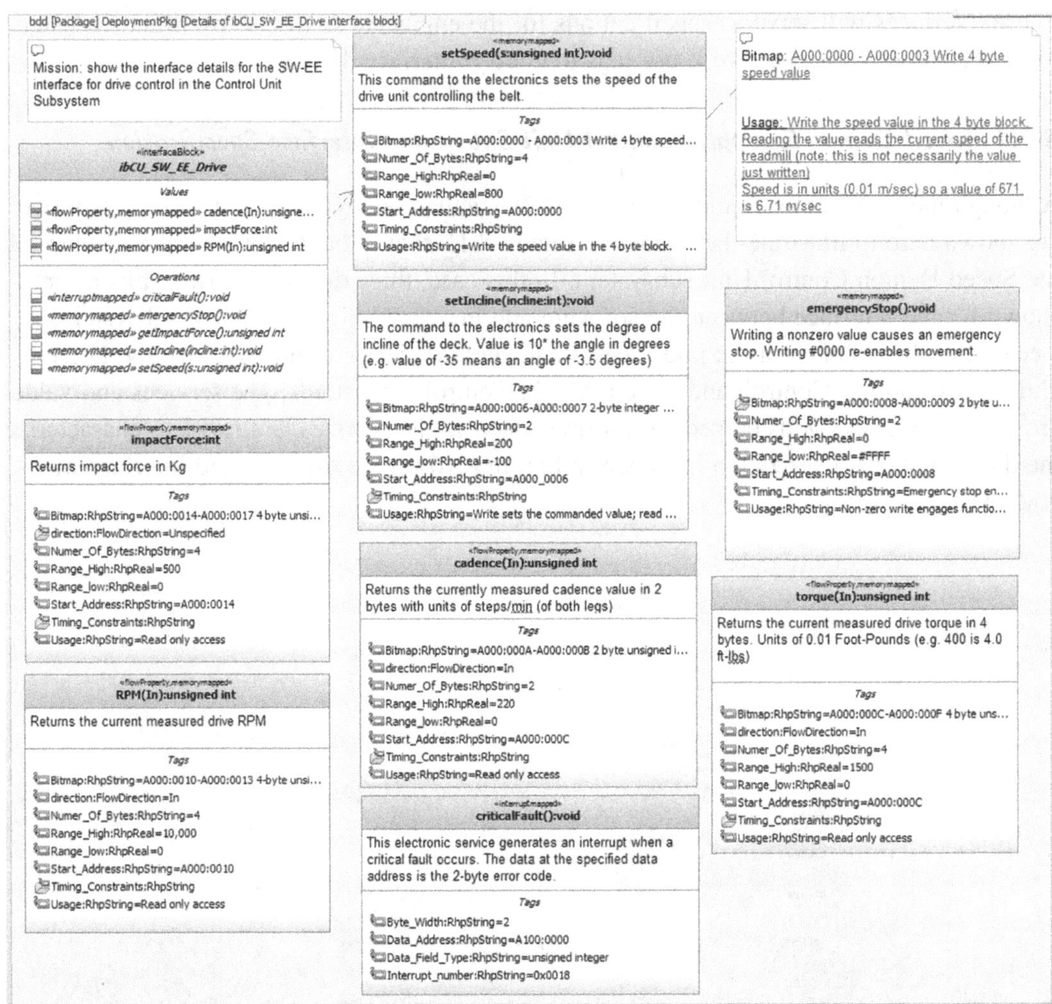

Figure 8.16
SW–EE interface details for drive control.

Figure 8.16 shows the flows and services defined in the ibCU_SW_EE_Drive interface block. These include four memory-mapped read-only values (measured run cadence, running impact force, torque, and RPM) and three memory-mapped services (emergency stop, set incline level, and set running speed) and one interrupt-mapped service (critical error). The description explains a bit about the service and the tags provide the metadata around the interface feature.

For memory-mapped features, the tags include

- Bitmap: a description of the bit mapping of the data field.
- Direction (for flow only): In (in this case to the SW) or Out (in this case, to the electronics).

- Number of bytes: the byte-width of the data register.
- Range High: highest expected value.
- Range Low: lowest expected value.
- Start Address: starting address of the data register.
- Timing constraints: read or write timing, if applicable.
- Usage: an explanation of the usage of the flow or service.

The interrupt-mapped service sports a different set of descriptive tags:

- Byte width: number of bytes of any associated data.
- Data address: where to read data associated with the interrupt.
- Data field type: data type of the data to be found at the data address.
- Interrupt number: the index of the interrupt for the ISR.

Of course, other tags can be added when there are metadata to be represented.

These interdisciplinary interface specifications provide guidance for both disciplines. On one hand, it tells the software developers how to invoke the services and get or set data manipulated by the hardware. On the other hand, it tells the electronics engineers how the software will send commands and share information with the hardware.

Figure 8.16 uses the *display options* feature of Rhapsody to expose the description and tags for the interface block features. For the `setSpeed` service, an associated comment is shown that uses hyperlinks to display some of the tagged values that are too long to show in their entirety within the normal box notation.

8.7.2 T-Wrecks Example

As described in the previous chapter, the T-Wrecks system has a rich architecture. We'll focus here on the deployment architecture of just two of the subsystems—the `Coordination` subsystem and the `Limb Assembly` subsystem.

8.7.2.1 The Coordination subsystem

The deployment architecture for the `Coordination` subsystem is very straightforward (Figure 8.17). As before, the only mechanical interface between the electronics and the mechanical parts is enclosure and cabling. The only interesting interface between the software and the electronics is the CAN bus interface.

The interface block `ibSE_EE_CAN` defines the interface between the software and the electronics. There are two buffers, one for incoming messages (`rxBuffer`) and one for messages to transmit (`txBuffer`). Each of these is of type `CAN_Buffer`. The 10-byte buffer bit map is defined in the tag `Bitmap` (shown in the associated comment, via hyperlink).

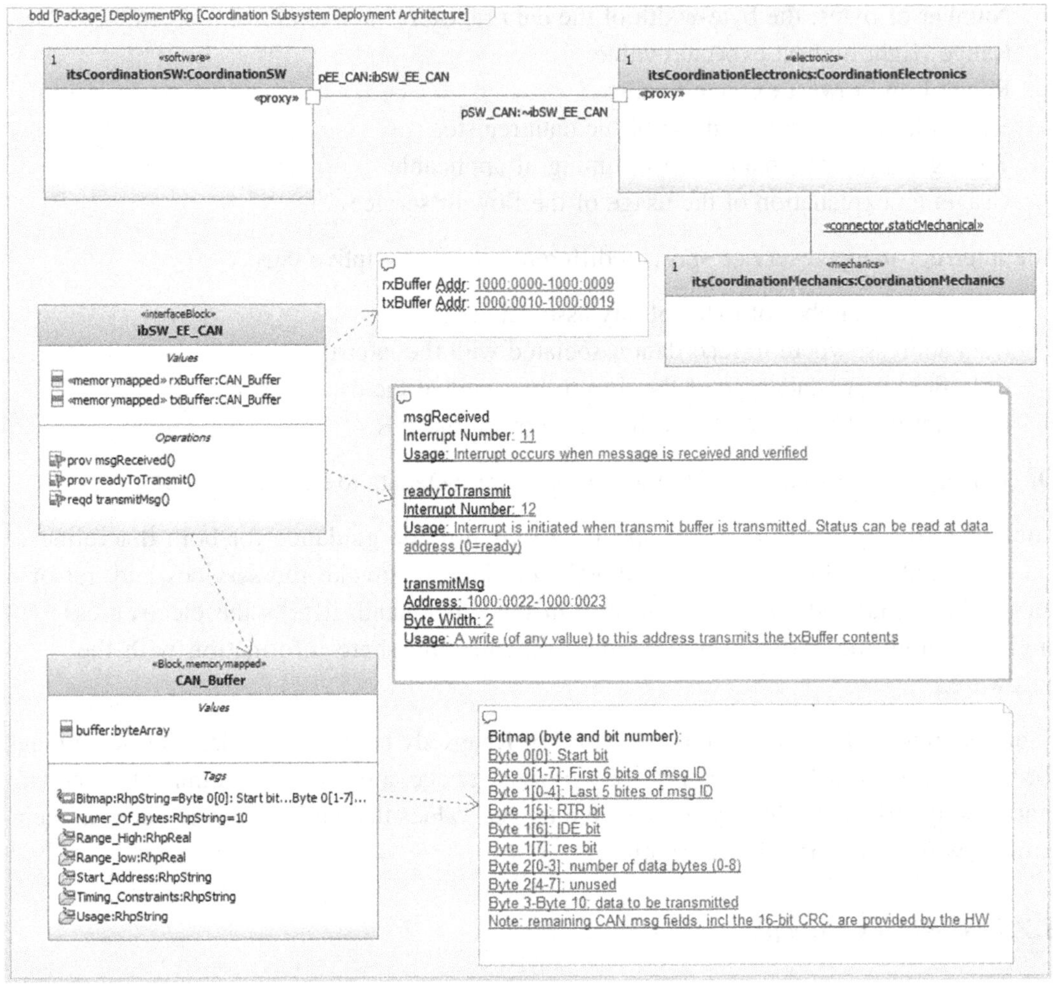

Figure 8.17
Coordination subsystem deployment architecture.

Note that the remain bits, including the 16-bit CRC, the CRC Delimiter bit, the ACK Slot bit, the ACK Delimiter bit, and the End of Frame 7 bits needn't be provided by the software as they will be produced by the hardware.

Besides the buffers, there are three services, all represented as event receptions. The first two—`msgReceived` and `readyToTransmit`—are both interrupt mapped. This means that the hardware will generate an interrupt that the software must capture. The `msgReceived` interrupt signals when a complete message has been received and its CRC verified. The `readyToTransmit` interrupt occurs after the hardware has completed a transmission and is ready to send the next message. The event `transmitMsg` is memory-mapped; writing any value to the specified address tells the hardware to transmit the message in `txBuffer`.

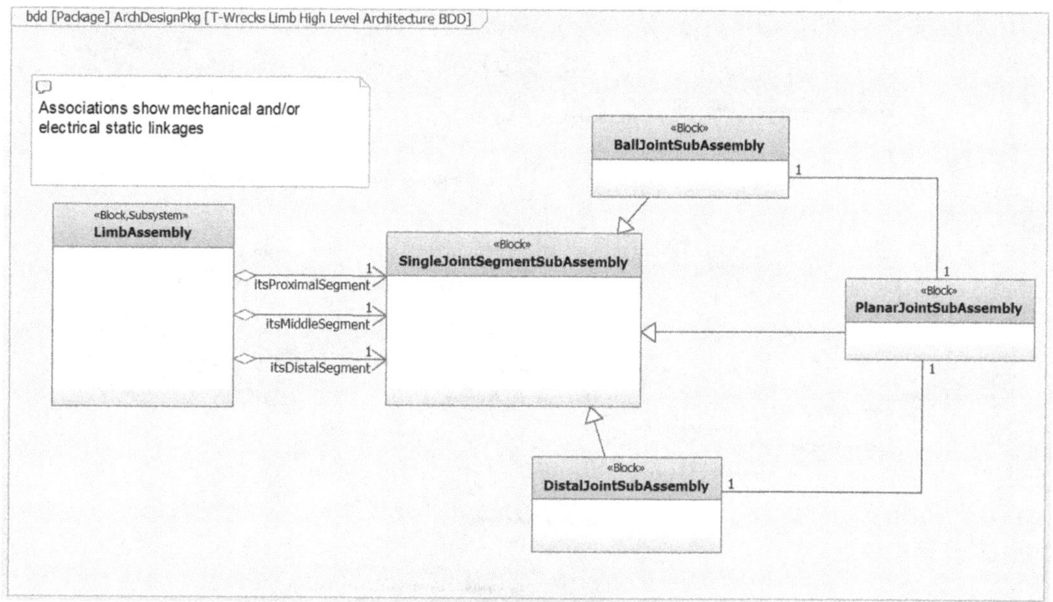

Figure 8.18
Limb Assembly high-level architecture.

8.7.2.2 The Limb Assembly subsystem

We're talking about this subsystem like it's just one thing, but remember, due to both chirality and limb type there are four distinct variants of this subsystem in each T-Wrecks instance. Despite the subtle differences in the (mostly mechanical) aspects, the subsystems are far more alike than they are different so we can use the same deployment architecture for all.

The `Limb Assembly` subsystem already has a high-level architecture as shown in Figure 8.18 (based on Figure 7.9). Each of the blocks in the figure must be decomposed into its constituent discipline-specific aspects. This process is simplified somewhat because the `BallJointSubAssembly`, `PlanarJointSubAssembly`, and `DistalJointAssembly` are all specialized forms of the more generic `SingleJointSubAssembly`. For this reason, we will create a single deployment architecture diagram that includes just the `LimbAssembly` and the `SingleJointSegmentSubAssembly`.

Figure 8.19 shows the high-level deployment architecture of the `Limb Assembly` subsystem. In addition to the software, electronic, and mechanical aspects of the limb assembly itself, we also see the three subassemblies, the Ball Joint (proximal), the Planar Joint (medial), and the Distal subassemblies. There are a few noteworthy features in the diagram.

First, there are two separate connections of the limb assembly software aspect to the limb assembly electronic aspects. One is to support communications with the other subsystems

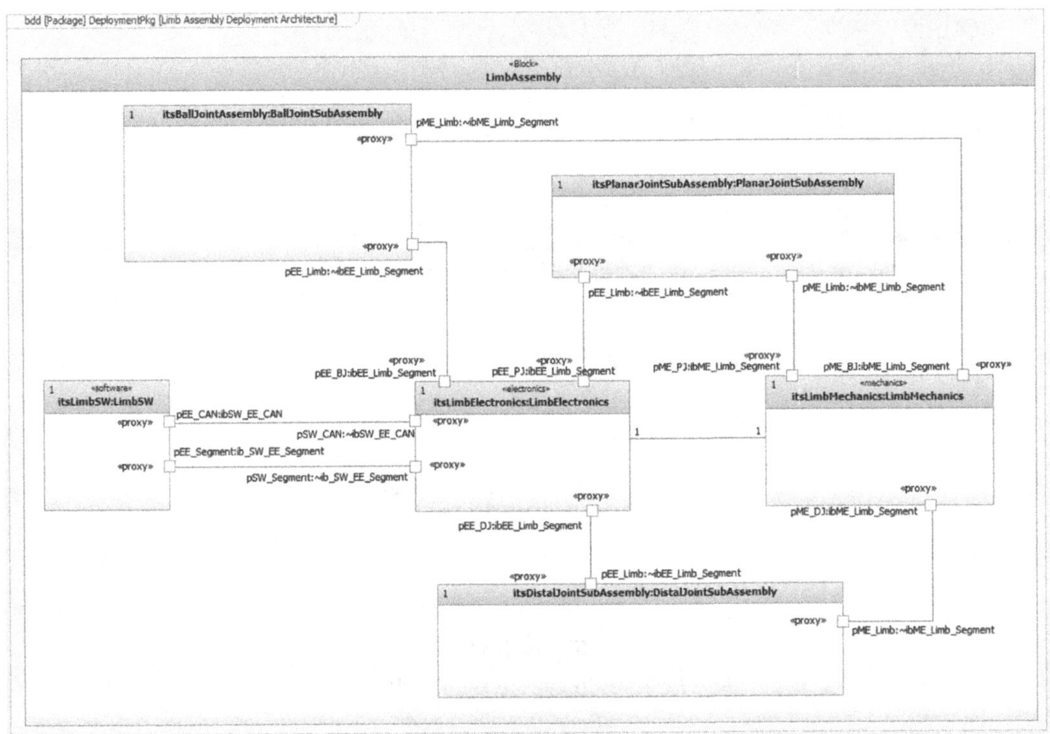

Figure 8.19
Limb Assembly high-level deployment architecture.

over the DeviceNet (CAN) bus. The other is to interface with the limb segments. However, the limb segments don't contain any software so all the communication will take place using electronic and mechanical means.

Second, as before, the only connections between the electronics and the mechanical aspects in the limb assembly *per se* are enclosure and cabling, so an association (rather than a port-based connection) is used.

Third, there are electronic–electronic and mechanical–mechanical connections that are behavioral (they pass information, signals, or energy) between the limb assembly *per se* and the limb segment parts. These will not be the subject of discussion here because they do not cross discipline boundaries. We'll let the electronic engineers work out the electronic-only interfaces and the mechanical engineers work out the mechanical-only interfaces.

Lastly, there is a deployment architecture for the limb segment parts but it is not shown in Figure 8.19 for simplicity. The details for the generic `SingleJointSegmentSubAssembly` (of which the parts are all subtypes) are shown in Figure 8.21.

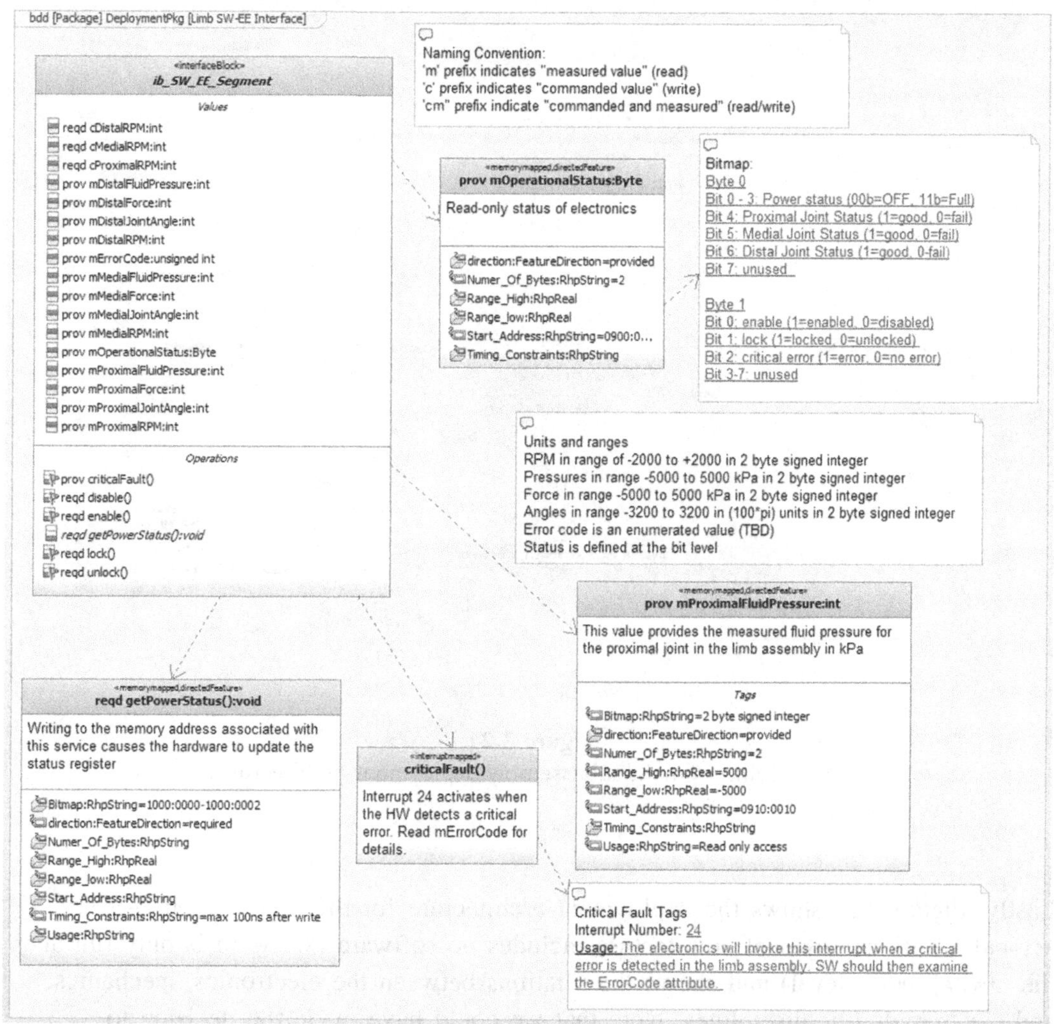

Figure 8.20
SW—electronics interface for the Limb Assembly segment control.

The interface block for the limb segment control and management is shown in Figure 8.20. Details for some of the elements are shown in the diagram. Comments add additional information, including the naming convention, and the units and ranges of values. `prov` features are features read by the SW and `reqd` fields are those written by the software. Most of the features are memory-mapped. There is a `criticalFault` interrupt that is generated by the hardware when appropriate. The software interrupt service routine is expected to read the `mErrorCode` register to get the details on the error that occurs (the error codes are TBD (to be defined) at this point).

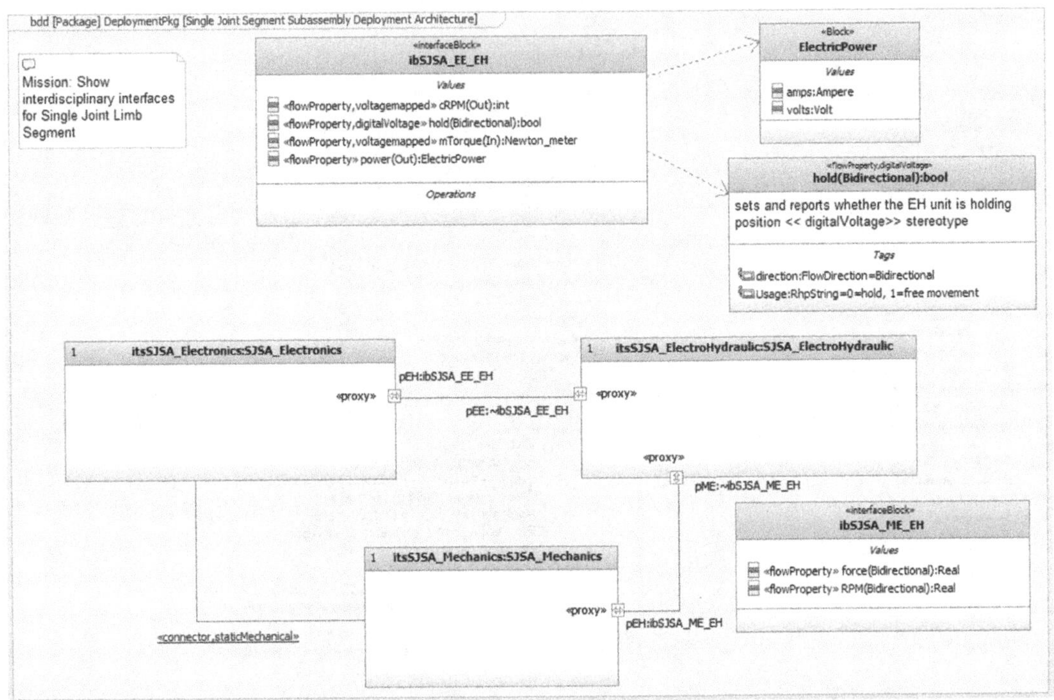

Figure 8.21
Single Joint segment subassembly deployment architecture.

Lastly, Figure 8.21 shows the deployment architecture for the `Single Joint Segment Assembly`. This deployment architecture includes no software (software is only run at the `Limb Assembly` level) and shows the relations between the electronics, mechanics, and electrohydraulic disciplines. Note that we could have made the decision to decompose the electrohydraulic aspects into component electronic and hydraulic (mechanical) aspects but did not because we will be receiving these systems as OEM (orginial equipment manufacturer) components. The electronic–electrohydraulic interface is mostly a matter of passing (in the form of electronic signals) electronic information and power to the electrohydraulic unit. The electronic–mechanical interface is, as before, limited to enclosure and cabling. The mechanical–electrohydraulic interface focuses on the transfer of mechanical energy from the electrohydraulic unit to the mechanical arm. This might be realized in many different ways, including using gears, belts, or even tension cables. How the energy is transferred is a matter of mechanical design and not a topic of interest here.

8.8 Allocation Requirements to Engineering Disciplines

The last task in the handoff workflow (other than a review of the engineering data by interested stakeholders) is the allocation of subsystem requirements to the engineering disciplines. Some subsystem requirements will be realized in a single discipline, so those are easy. Many, however, will require decomposition into discipline-specific derived requirements before they can be allocated.

It is important to remember that we are doing *agile* systems engineering and we organize our requirements around use cases. Therefore, this activity is performed in the context of an iteration that includes a subsystem of the system and subsystem use cases. That means that in each system engineering iteration, one or a small number of use cases will be considered at a time. Only those requirements in the use cases currently under consideration will be addressed in any given iteration. That means, this activity is done, essentially, a use case at a time, with most use cases deferred to a different iteration.

The allocation must be clear to all concerned parties and be traceable back to subsystem or system requirements and forward to the associated engineering discipline. This can be accomplished in a number of ways. "Clone-and-own" (copy the requirement from the generic subsystem requirements package to a package specific to the discipline) is common and easy but leads to maintenance issues when problems are discovered. Trace links, implemented with the SysML «trace» or «Satisfy» relations, are a good way. Adding discipline-specific stereotypes (such as «software» or «electronic») to the requirements works as well. Trace links are the most common.

Once each engineering discipline knows (1) the interfaces to other associated engineering disciplines and (2) their specific requirements, then the discipline-specific engineering can begin in earnest.

8.8.1 Speed Demon Example

For the Speed Demon example, we'll look at the requirements for the `Control Protocol Execution` use case for the `Control Unit` subsystem. The subsystem requirements allocated to this use case are shown in Figures 8.22 while Figure 8.23 shows the allocation of requirements to engineering disciplines.

8.8.2 T-Wrecks Example

For the T-Wrecks example, let's use the `Move Joint` use case of the `Limb Assembly`. Table 8.1 shows the requirements allocated to the subsystem during the system architecture activity.

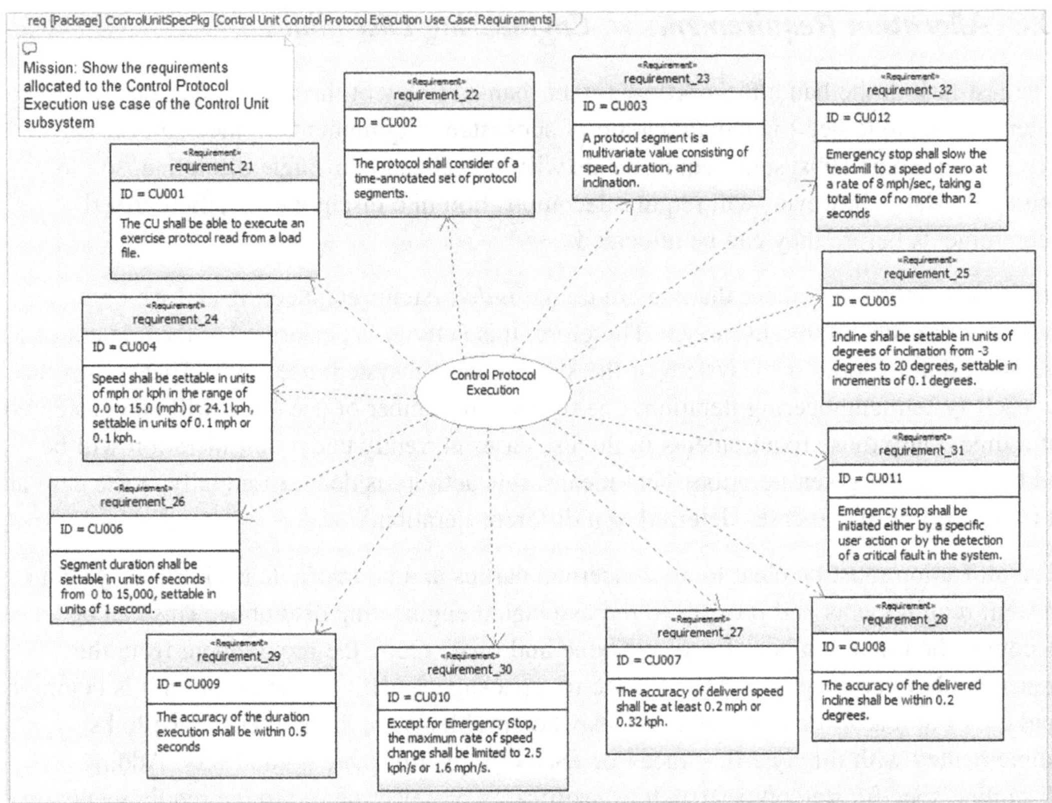

Figure 8.22
Requirements for the Control Unit Control Protocol Execution use case.

Most of the requirements in Table 8.1 must be satisfied by the collaboration of multiple disciplines. For example, requirement LA020 must be satisfied by the electronics (don't deliver power to the motor on start up, accept software commands to enable/disable movement), the electrohydraulic system (lock the start up position), and the limb assembly software (process commands to enable or disable joint movement). As a part of the engineering discipline requirements allocation process, we must derive these more detailed requirements so that the different engineers are clear about the work they must do. Figure 8.24 shows how some of the discipline-specific requirements are derived from five of the requirements allocated to the subsystem Move Joint use case. There are other diagrams as well (not shown) that focus on arm-specific, leg-specific,

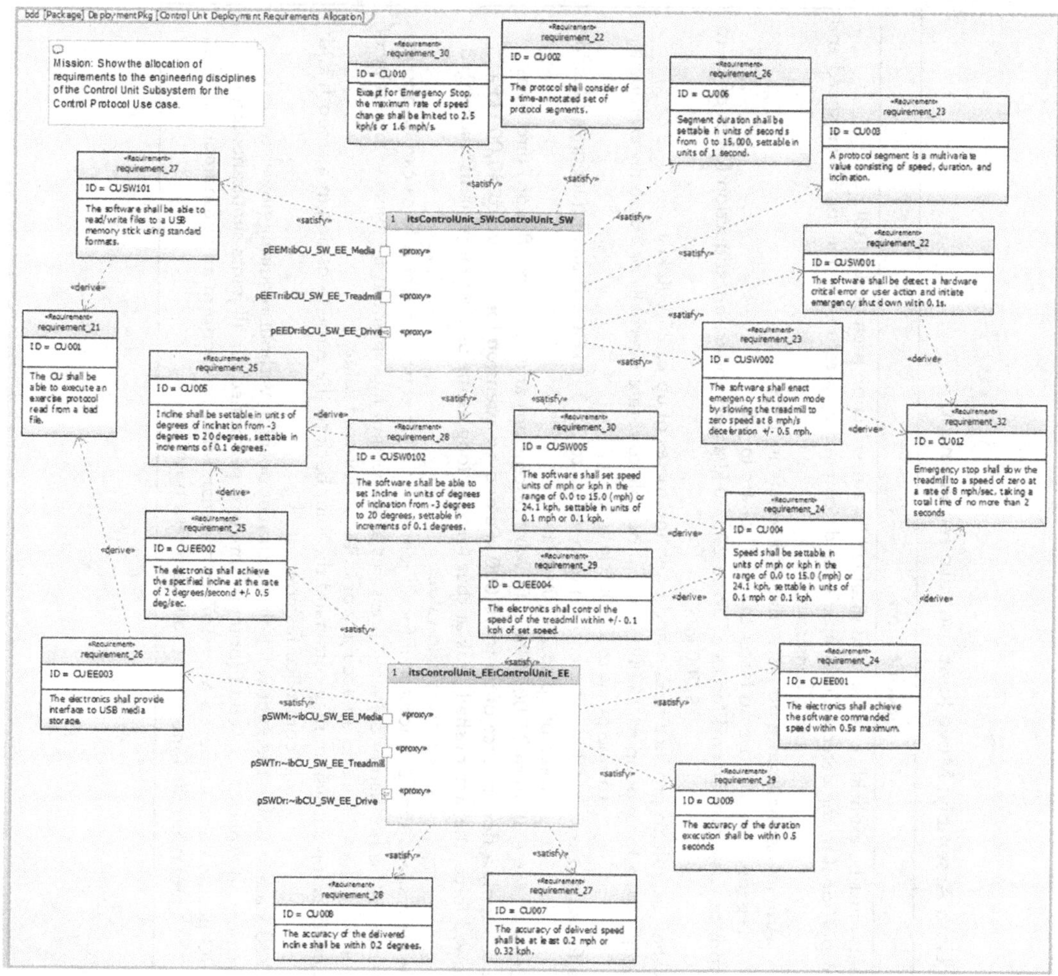

Figure 8.23
Allocation of Control Protocol Execution requirements to disciplines.

and other subsystem-level requirements. Each of the derived requirements is stereotyped with the discipline to which it is allocated—«software», «electronics», «mechanics», or «electrohydraulics».

Once this is done, we have a set of discipline-specific requirements. We can represent this by generating a textual specification, showing them in discipline-specific tables, or showing them diagrammatically. Figure 8.25 shows one format for this information—a table of requirements that includes their discipline stereotype.

Table 8.1: Limb Assembly: Move Joint use case requirements.

ID	Specification
LA020	Movement of the joint must be explicitly enabled and disabled by a user action (default DISABLED)
LA021	Force applied at a joint shall be proportional to the detected user intent (as determined by pressure) within maximum speed and force constraints
LA022	Arm joints shall move no faster than 90° of arc in 1.0 s
LA023	Leg joints shall move no faster than 90° of arc in 1.5 s
LA024	Shoulder joints shall be able to produce forward/rearward forces of up to 20,000 kPa and abduction/adduction forces of up to 15,000 kPa
LA025	Elbow joints shall be able to produce flexion and extension forces of up to 25,000 kPa
LA026	Arm grapplers shall be able to grip with a force of up to 25,000 kPa and be able to rotate internally or externally exerting a torque of up to 20,000 kPa
LA027	Hip joints shall be able to exert a forward/rearward (flexion/extension) force of up to 35,000 kPa and an abduction/adduction force of up to 25,000 kPa
LA028	Knee joints shall be able to deliver a force of up to 35,000 kPa in forward (extension) and rearward (flexion) directions
LA029	The angle joint shall be able to supply a flexion force of up to 10,000 kPa and an extension force of up to 40,000 kPa
LA030	If a joint reaches its maximum allowed force, the system shall peak at that force as long as the user intent remains unchanged or increases in value
LA031	Delivered pressure and joint movement speed shall be monitored for all joints and all directions in which force can be applied
LA032	The Pilot (or maintenance engineer) shall be notified of delivered pressures and speed of movement at all joints with a delay of no more than 0.5 s and an accuracy of ±4% of delivered value
LA033	If a joint fault is detected, the Coordination subsystem may command the joint back to the zeroed position in a smooth and controlled fashion
LA035	All joints shall support a LOCKed state in which the joint will hold its current position without requiring power to do so. UNLOCKING a joint shall require an explicit user action (note: this may be performed for all joints simultaneously)
LA036	All joints will have a defined ZERO position and support a MoveToZero command that will perform an autonomous smooth and controlled movement to regain zero position

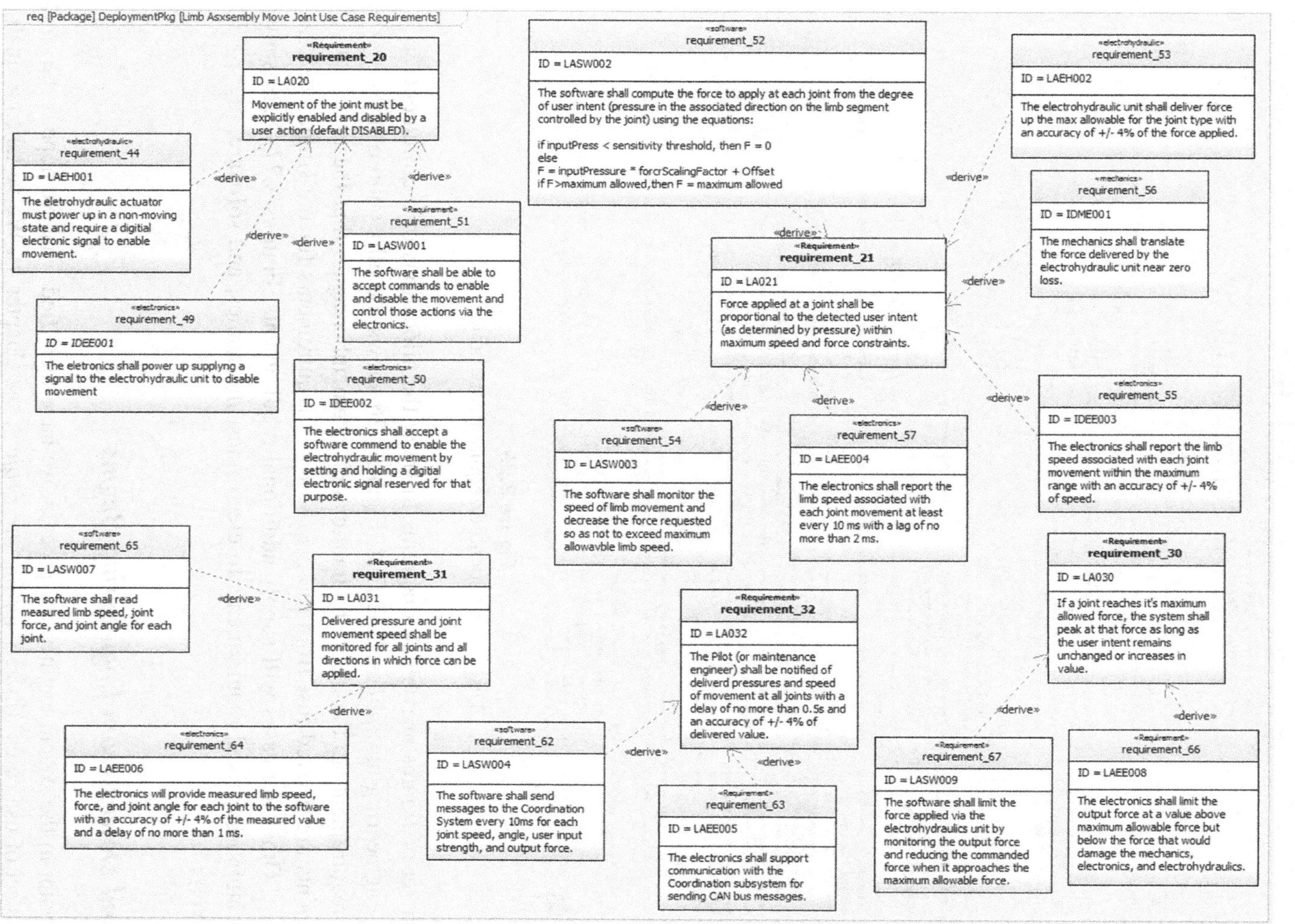

Figure 8.24
Discipline-specific requirements for Move Joint use case.

ID	Stereotypes	Specification
LASW031	software in DeploymentPkg	The joint software shall be able to lock the joint in its current position or unlock the joint based on commands received from the Coordination subsystem.
LASW030	software in DeploymentPkg	If joint software detects a joint fault, it shall notify the Coordination system of the fault and attempt to lock the limb in its current position. Note: The Coordination system may send subsequent commands to override the fault or to zero the joint.
LASW021	software in DeploymentPkg	The software shall prevent the hip joint from exerting more than 35,000 kPA in flexion and extension or more than 25,000 kPa in abduction and adduction.
LASW020	software in DeploymentPkg	The hip sw shall be able to deliver force in flexion and extension of up to 35,000 kPa and up to 25,000 kPa for abduction and adduction.
LASW020	software in DeploymentPkg	The knee sw shall not specify a force of greater than 35,000 kPa; if the force limit is reached, the software shall reduce the delivered force to ensure it remains within range.
LASW019	software in DeploymentPkg	The ankle software shall be able to deliver a force from 0 to 40,000 kPa in extension and 10,000 in flexion.
LASW018	software in DeploymentPkg	The knee joint softwar shall be able to set the delivered force up to 35,000 kPa in both flexion and extension.
LASW017	software in DeploymentPkg	Leg joint sw shall control the leg limb movement so as not to exceed 90 degrees of arc in less than 1.5 seconds.
LASW012	software in DeploymentPkg	The arm joint software shall be able to monitor the speed of the arm jont segments and control them so that they do not exceed 90 degrees of arc in 1.0 seconds.
LASW009		The software shall limit the force applied via the electrohydraulics unit by monitoring the output force and reducing the commanded force when it approaches the maximum allowable force.
LASW007	software in DeploymentPkg	The software shall read measured limb speed, joint force, and joint angle for each joint.
LASW004	software in DeploymentPkg	The software shall send messages to the Coordination System every 10ms for each joint speed, angle, user input strength, and output force.
LASW003	software in DeploymentPkg	The software shall monitor the speed of limb movement and decrease the force requested so as not to exceed maximum allowavble limb speed.
LASW002	software in DeploymentPkg	The software shall compute the force to apply at each joint from the degree of user intent (pressure in the associated direction on the limb segment controlled by the joint) using the equations: if inputPress < sensitivity threshold, then F = 0 else F = inputPressure * forcrScalingFactor + Offset if F>maximum allowed,then F = maximum allowed
LASW0016	software in DeploymentPkg	The software shall be able to control the elbow joint force up to 25,000 kpa with a resolution of at least 100 kPa.
LASW0015	software in DeploymentPkg	The elbow software shall be able to read the monitored joint position, speed, and force.
LASW0014	software in DeploymentPkg	The gripper software shall be able to control the gripping force up to 25,000 kPa
LASW001		The software shall be able to accept commands to enable and disable the movement and control those actions via the electronics.
LAME031	mechanics in DeploymentPkg	The mechancs will provide the ability to UNLOCK a locked joint.
LAME030	mechanics in DeploymentPkg	The joint mechanics shall provide a LOCK mode, commanded by the electronics, that freezes the joint in its current position without requiring power to sustain.
LAME023	mechanics in DeploymentPkg	The hip mechanics shall be able to deliver a force up to 35,000 kPa with less than 1% limb material flexion.
LAME022	mechanics in DeploymentPkg	The ankle mechanics shall be able to deliver a continuous force up to 40,000 kPa with less than 1% material flexion.
LAME021	mechanics in DeploymentPkg	The knee mechanics shall be able to deliver a limb movement with a force of up to 35,000 kPa with less than 1% limb flexion.
LAME020	mechanics in DeploymentPkg	The leg mechanics shall support leg movement up to 90 degrees of arc in 1.5 seconds.
LAME012	mechanics in DeploymentPkg	The elbow mechanics shall be able to deliver a force from the electrohydraulic unit up to 25,000 kPa with less than 1% material flexion.
LAME011	mechanics in DeploymentPkg	The gripper mechanics shall be able to translate a force from the electrohydraulics of up to 25,000 kPa with less than 1% material flexion.
LAME010	mechanics in DeploymentPkg	The shoulder joint mechanics shall be able to deliver 20,000 kPa in any direction with less then 1% flexion in the limb.
LAEH032	electrohydraulic in DeploymentPkg	The joint electrohydraulics shall support a LOCK mode which freezes the joint position without requiring additional power to hold the position.
LAEH021	electrohydraulic in DeploymentPkg	The hip electrohydraulics shall be able to deliver up to 35,000 kPa for flexion and extension and up to 25,000 kPa in abduction and adduction.
LAEH020	electrohydraulic in DeploymentPkg	The ankle electrohydraulics shall be able to deliver a force from 0 to 40,000 kPa.
LAEH019	electrohydraulic in DeploymentPkg	The knee electrohydraulics shall be able to deliver force from 0 to 35,000 kPa in knee flexion and extension.
LAEH017	electrohydraulic in DeploymentPkg	The elbow electrohydraulics shall be able to deliver a force of up to 25,000 kPa.
LAEH015	electrohydraulic in DeploymentPkg	The gripper electroydraulics shall be able to deliver a gripping force of up to 25,000 kPa with a resolutin of at least 10 kPa and and accuracy of +/- 4% of commanded value.
LAEH010	electrohydraulic in DeploymentPkg	The arm joint electohydraulics shall support rotational speed 90 degrees in 1.0 seconds.
LAEH002	electrohydraulic in DeploymentPkg	The electrohydraulic unit shall deliver force up the max allowable for the joint type with an accuracy of +/- 4% of the force applied.
LAEH0014	electrohydraulic in DeploymentPkg	The shoulder electrohydraulics shall be able to deliver up to 20,000 kPa in forward/readward directions and 15,000 kpA in abduction/adduction direction.
LAEH001	electrohydraulic in DeploymentPkg	The eletrohydraulic actuator must power up in a non-moving state and require a digitial electronic signal to enable movement.
LAEE032	electronics in DeploymentPkg	The joint electronics will accept software commands to LOCK or UNLOCK a joint.

Figure 8.25

Discipline-allocated requirements table.

The next set of figures uses block diagrams to show the allocations of requirements to specific engineering disciplines. The first, Figure 8.26 shows the allocation of the derived requirements to the electrohydraulics unit. Remember again that these requirements are derived just from the `Limb Assembly` requirements for the single use case `Move Joint`. Other use cases will supply additional requirements. Figures 8.27–8.29 show the allocation of derived requirements to electronics, mechanics, and software, respectively.

8.9 And Downstream Engineering Begins

At this point in the system engineering process, we have identified what we hope is the complete set of use cases[6] (in activity *Initiate Project*; see Chapter 4). We've taken a small

[6] Remember, that because we have an iterative approach, it is easy to add use cases later, if needed.

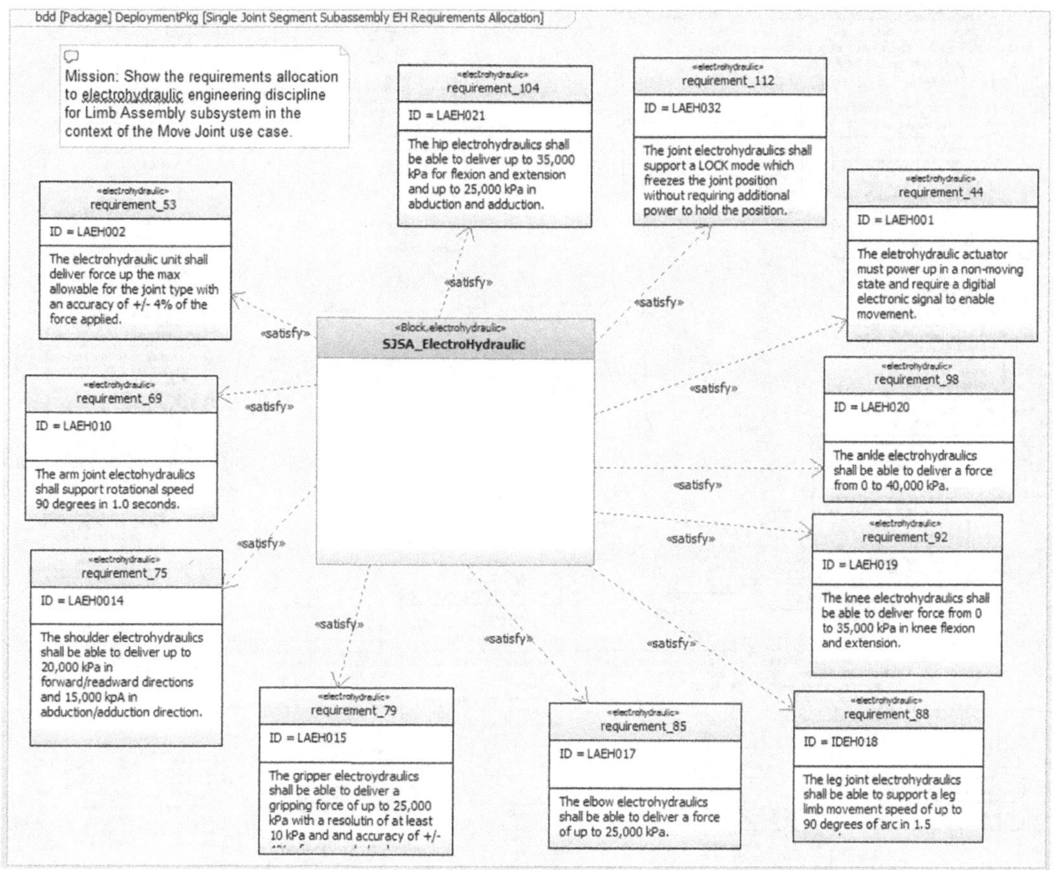

Figure 8.26
Allocation of requirements to electrohydraulics.

number of these and identified the stakeholder needs and requirements (in activity *Define Stakeholder Requirements*; see Chapter 4). Then we took these statements of stakeholder need and identified what the system must do, the system requirements (in the activity System Requirements Definition and Analysis; see Chapter 5). We analyzed these by constructing executable models. We constructed data and flow schema to understand the flow of information, materiel, and energy. We began the process of dependability analysis, including the analysis of safety, reliability, and security and these tasks resulted in additional system requirements. We even started developing the system verification plan.

In the next activity, we looked at trade studies and used parametric analysis to determine the optimal architectural and technical solutions to our system needs (in activity *Architectural Analysis*; see Chapter 6). Based on this information, we then created a system architecture. This consisted primarily of identifying subsystem, allocating responsibilities, requirements and use cases to them, defining their interfaces, and refining both the data and

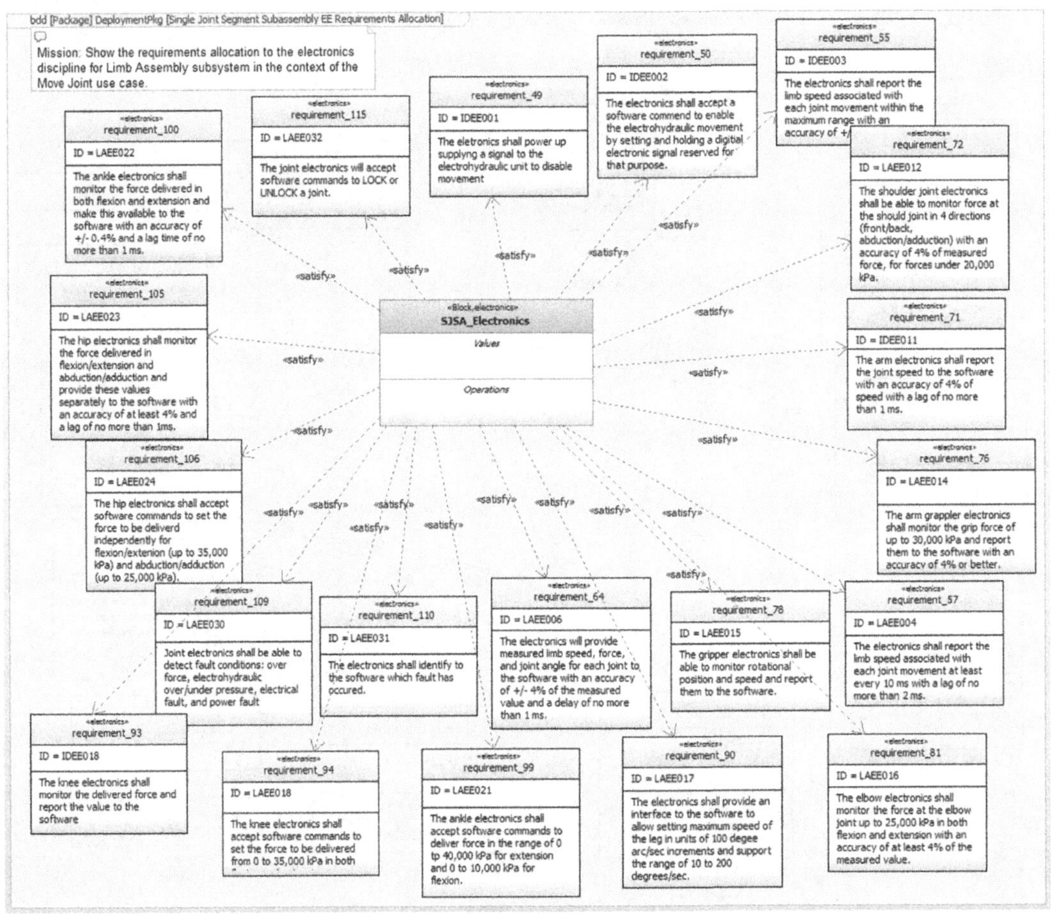

Figure 8.27
Allocation of requirements to electronics.

flow schema and the dependability analyses (in activity *Architectural Design*; see Chapter 7). Finally, in this chapter, we prepared for the handoff to downstream engineering. This consisted of creating a shared model for the (physical) interfaces, data, and flows that are used by more than one subsystem and creating a subsystem model for each identified subsystem. The subsystem model is created initially by importing its specification from the systems engineering model and referencing its interfaces in the shared model. We then created the deployment architecture, defining the interfaces between the engineering disciplines and allocating requirements to them.

At this point, the subsystem model can be handed off to the subsystem team for further development. That development can be agile and incremental, as described in Ref. [3], or it can follow a more traditional process, if desired.

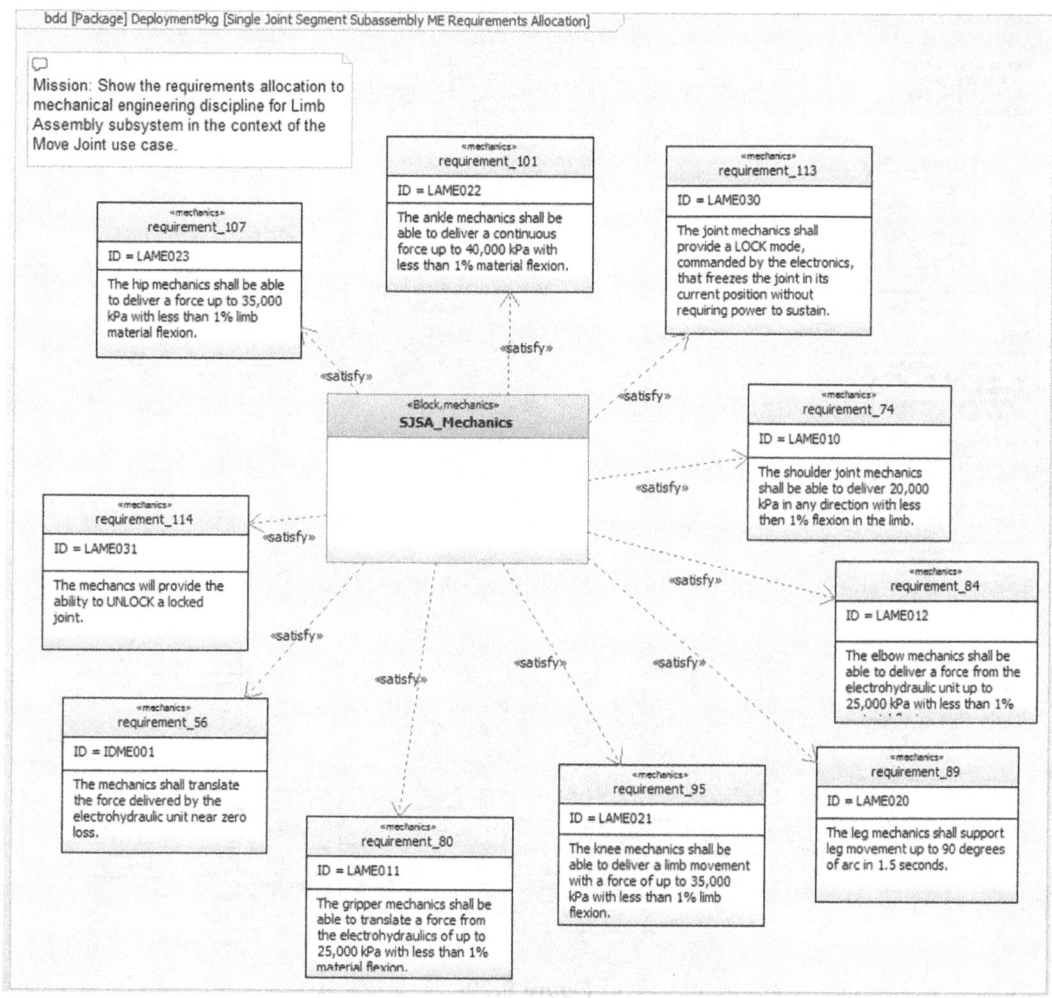

Figure 8.28
Allocation of requirements to mechanics.

8.10 And System Engineering Continues . . .

Because we deal with only a few use cases during each iteration, once we handoff to downstream engineering, systems engineering activities can continue focusing on the next set of features, capabilities, risks, and use cases. If any issues are identified in downstream engineering, they will result in work items that systems engineers will address in a future iteration. In general, this will happen less frequently than in a more traditional process because of the effort we've spent using model-based systems engineering to create verifiably correct models and specifications. Nevertheless, it is expected that there may be some omissions or some assumptions or requirements will change over time; they always do.

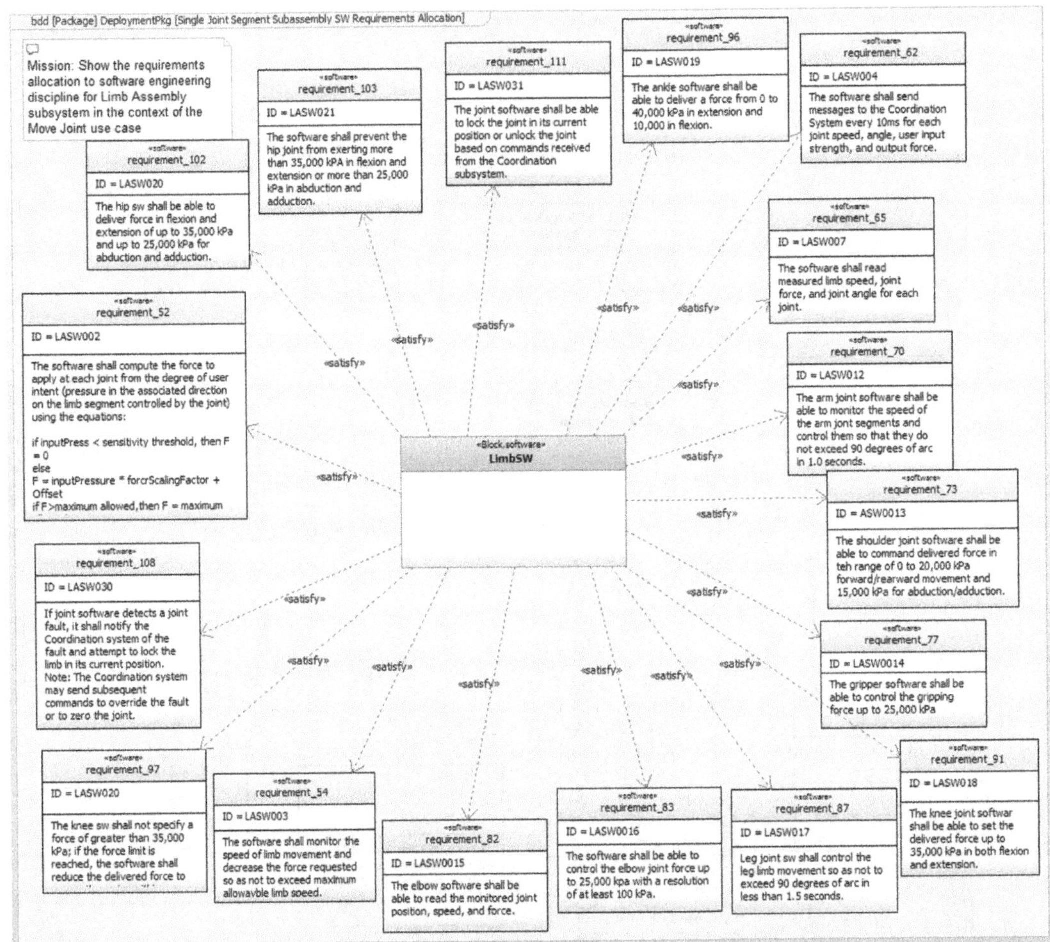

Figure 8.29
Allocation of requirements to software.

References

[1] US Department of Defense, 1978. MIL-STD-1553B Aircraft Internal Time Division Command/Response Multiplex Data Bus.

[2] DeviceNet Technology Overview. Available from: <http://www.odva.org/Home/ODVATECHNOLOGIES/DeviceNet/DeviceNetTechnologyOverview/tabid/72/Default.aspx>.

[3] B.P. Douglass, Real-Time Agility, Addison-Wesley, Reading, MA, 2009.

Appendix A: T-Wrecks Stakeholder Requirements

Project Overview

The T-Wrecks™ is a heavy loader exoskeleton system for use in moving heavy payloads of up to 1500 Kg at walking speeds and lighter loads at jogging speeds. The system is intended for industrial, warehouse, ship loading, and military use. It is equipped with instrument panels at the pilot's hands and both a heads up display (HUD) and a small LCD display on the inner arm. It can accommodate pilots from 5 feet to 6 feet 5 inches in height and has an endurance (without load) of over 36 hours without recharge and 12 hours at full load.

T-Wrecks High Level Use Cases

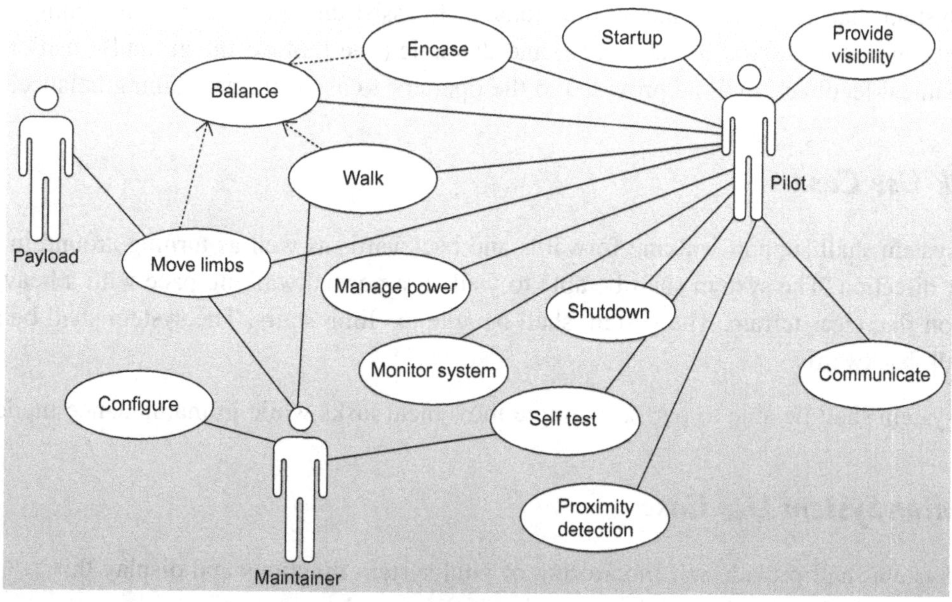

Figure A.1
T-Wreaks high level uses cases.

General Requirements

The system shall be an exoskeleton for industrial, warehouse, ship loading, military and factory operation. It shall support heavy industrial loads while at walking speeds and medium loads at jogging speeds. The operator shall be able to control it easily while performing normal operations of picking up and dropping off loads, and conveying them at various speeds on varied terrain. It shall be operational in all weather conditions found within the continental United States and western Europe. It shall be able to handle loads across rugged terrain, including shallow swamp.

Encase Use Case

The system shall encase a normal size male operator. The system shall firmly and comfortably encase the user permitting comfortable entry, exit, and operation of the vehicle. The system shall not overburden the user's body and loads of any weight shall not vary the mechanical stress on the user. The system shall support and emergency escape procedure to allow rapid exit in an emergency. The system shall protect the user in the event of a crash or toppling of the vehicle.

Balance Use Case

The system shall provide balancing functionality to assist the operator in maintaining stability in both static (both feet placed) and dynamic (one foot off the ground) positions. Mechanical feedback shall be provided to the operator to assist in maintaining balance.

Walk Use Case

The system shall support walking forwards and backwards as well as turning around in either direction. The system shall be able to walk at a normal walking pace with a heavy load on flat, clear terrain. The system shall be able to climb stairs. The system shall be able to walk backwards.

The system shall be able to perform simple movement tasks while in maintenance mode.

Monitor System Use Case

The System shall provide self monitoring of vital system functions and display this information to the user, in addition to saving it to internal storage.

Usable external rear and side views shall be provided to the user.

Move Limbs Use Case

The system shall respond to user's limb movement to control movement of the exoskeletal limbs. This limb response will be proportional to the muscular effort and range performed by the user.

The system shall be able to lift and transport heavy loads at walking speed, even with the arms fully extended in front holding a load.

The exoskeleton shall be able to rotate at the waist easily to both sides even while under load.

Loads may be picked up with mechanical grippers on the ends of the arms that are controlled by the user, mimicking the orientation and position of his or her hands. The force applied by the grippers shall be proportional to the force applied by the user but shall be adequate to pick up and grip heavy loads.

The exoskeletal legs, arms, and shoulders shall mimic the mobility of the user's legs, arms, and shoulders, respectively. It shall be possible to lock the limb position so that it requires no effort on the part of the user to maintain a position indefinitely.

The system shall be able to sit or stand and transition between the two positions even with a moderate load.

Manage Power Use Case

The system shall be to provide power for continuous operation of 36 hours without load and 12 hours with heavy load. This system shall be rechargeable from a standard wall outlet in a standard workday.

The system shall provide the user with estimate time of power remaining.

Startup Use Case

The system shall initiate a set of built in tests when it is first powered up and continuation of operation is contingent upon successful completion of those tests. When the tests are passed, a visual indication shall be provided to the user.

System communication and lighting functions shall be provided quickly during start up.

Self Test Use Case

The self test shall test all vital systems at system start up.

The outcomes of the start up tests will be stored for later retrieval.

If the maintenance tool is connected during start up, the system will go into a maintenance mode that allows access to configuration and maintenance features.

Provide Visibility Use Case

The system shall provide front and back lighting. The front lighting shall be adequate for pilot navigation at night. Other lighting shall identify the system activity to bystanders during operation at night, including protruding elements such as grippers, head, and feet.

The system shall sound an tone audible to bystanders in a noisy environment when the system is backing up.

Monitor System Use Case

The system shall monitor the health of its internal systems and report identified problems both to the user and to the internal error log.

Shutdown Use Case

Normal "Park" model positions the system in a standard upright position for pilot entry and exit.

The system shall provide an emergency shutdown that locks the position of all limbs.

Proximity Detection Use Case

The system shall be able to detect stationary and moving objects within the vicinity of the system and to alert the user when a collision is possible or likely.

Configure Use Case

The system shall be configurable by a trained maintenance engineer. The sensitivity of the system to operator movement shall be adjustable. The maintenance engineer shall be able to download and manage error and action logs of the system for off line analysis. The system shall be accessible by a standard laptop, although it is expected that custom software may need to be written.

Communicate Use Case

The system shall provide cell phone service and communication for the operator using commercial cell phone services. This shall include both initiating and receiving calls as well as transmission of system data, where appropriate. In addition, in the event of an accident, the system shall be able to initiate and complete a 911 emergency response request call without an action on the part of the user.

The system shall provide video chat capability of the cell phone network.

The system shall provide GPS information for position, location identification, and map planning.

Appendix B: T-Wrecks System Requirements

The T-Wrecks™ is a heavy loader exoskeleton system for use in moving heavy payloads of up to 1500 kg at walking speeds and lighter loads at jogging speeds. The system is intended for industrial, warehouse, ship loading, and military use. It is equipped with instrument panels at the pilot's hands and both a heads up display (HUD) and a small LCD display on the inner arm. It can accommodate pilots from 5 feet to 6 feet 5 inches in height and has an endurance (without load) of over 36 h without recharge and 12 h at full load.

T-Wrecks High Level Use Cases

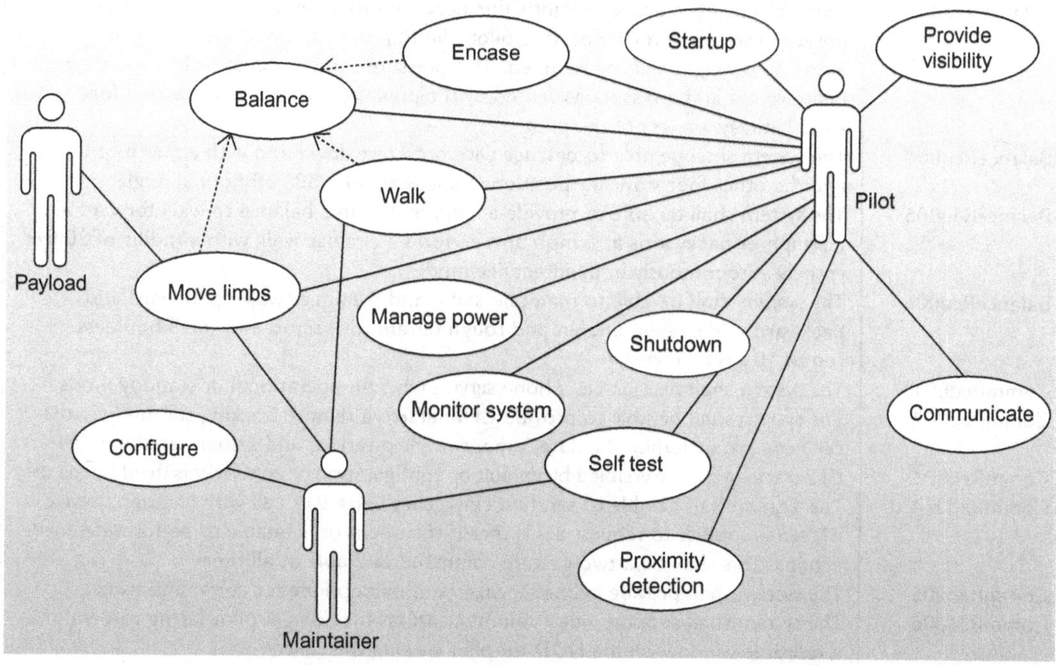

Figure A.1
T-Wreaks high level use cases.

Requirements Table (Initial Set)

ID	Specification
AOverview001	The T-Wrecks™ is a heavy loader exoskeleton system for use in moving heavy payloads of up to 1500 kg at walking speeds and lighter loads at jogging speeds. The system is intended for industrial, warehouse, ship loading, and military use. It is equipped with instrument panels at the pilot's hands and both a HUD and a small LCD display on the inner arm. It can accommodate pilots from 5 feet to 6 feet 5 inches in height and has an endurance (without load) of over 36 h without recharge and 12 h at full load
AOverviewReq002	The system shall operate in temperature ranges from −40°C to +50°C
AOverviewReq003	The system shall be able to operate submerged up to the top of the hip joint for an indefinite period of time (i.e., as long as power is available)
AOverviewReq003	The system shall be able to operate in low and high humidity environments including rain and snow
AOverviewReq004	The system shall not provide electrical current (> 1 mA for alternate current or >5 mA direct current) in direct contact with the pilot body, without engaging current-limiting countermeasures
BalanceReq001	While ON, the system shall attempt to remain in a static balance when not moving, whether with one leg down or two, by adjusting the position of various limbs and weight distribution
BalanceReq002	While ON and moving, the system shall attempt to maintain balance by adjusting stride length, direction, foot position, and weight distribution to maintain balance and a smooth stride
BalanceReq003	While balancing is active, weight shifts necessary to maintain balance shall result in pressure exerted to the associated pilot's limb, proportional to the degree of automated weight shifting required. This pressure can be overcome by increasing pilot-exerted limb pressure as sensed by the pressure sensors; this is added for kinesthetic awareness of the pilot
BalanceReq004	The system shall be able to balance with both feet down and with either foot down and the other foot statically positioned anywhere in a 30° off normal angle
BalanceReq005	The system shall be able to provide adequate dynamic balance to walk forward at 2.5 mph or backwards at 1 mph and perform a circular walk with a radius of 20 feet entirely autonomously in maintenance mode
BalanceReq006	The system shall be able to maintain static and dynamic (walking forward and backward) balance on uneven and rough terrain with scrub and small boulders (up to 10 cm diameter)
CommRed001	The system shall provide cell phone service when in operational or standby mode
CommRed002	The system shall be able to provide GPS data to a remote tracking station over the cell network, including the date, time, current position, and system serial number
CommRed003	GPS tracking can be enabled by default by configuration or enabled/disabled by the user
CommRed004	The system shall be able to send an emergency voice 911 call with location, device ID, serial number to request assistance if the operator is unable to perform detailed actions. This shall be a two-gesture command available at all times
CommReq005	The system shall provide helmet speaker and microphone for communication
CommReq006	The system shall support video communications including a pilot-facing camera and a resizable window on the HUD for pilot viewing the caller
ConfigReq001	The maintenance personnel shall be able to configure the system properties while the system is in standby mode
ConfigReq002	The maintainer shall be able to configure GPS tracking to be active on power up

(*Continued*)

(Continued)

ID	Specification
ConfigReq003	The maintainer shall be able to set the default sensitivity of the pressure sensors
ConfigReq004	The maintainer shall be able to download and clear the error and performance logs of the system
ConfigReq005	The maintainer shall be able to reconfigure the system by plugging in the maintenance system into the system diagnostic port. This action shall cause the system to go into configuration mode
ConfigReq006	Configuration mode shall support remote movement commands (in place of pressure sensor input) and the setting of all default system parameters
EncaseReq001	The system shall be adjustable to fit pilots ranging in size from 5 feet tall to 6 feet 5 inches
EncaseReq002	The system shall automatically adjust to conform the user to the pilot position
EncaseReq005	The system shall put no weight-bearing stress on the pilot due to payload or system frame
EncaseReq006	The system shall provide an Emergency Release function that will raise the HUD and release any restraints to enable emergency exit from the system
EncaseReq006	The system shall provide cushioning for the pilot torso and head (via helmet) able to withstand the system toppling over and landing on a hard surface without serious injury to the pilot
EncaseReq008	The system shall resist crushing force on the pilot head and torso such that the system with pilot may be placed in any position (including prone and supine) with minimal force on the torso and head that will not restrict breathing
MonitorReq001	The system shall provide continuous monitoring of vital system functions and display status to the pilot
MonitorReq002	The system shall provide a rear-facing camera and a user display option to display the rear view, spanning an angle of 30° to 120° off normal
MonitorReq003	The system shall provide left- and right-facing wide-angle visualization for the pilot to see their surroundings
MoveReq001	The system shall respond to pressure from the pilot's limbs by attempting to move the corresponding machine limb in the same direction and orientation
MoveReq002	The system shall respond to pressure sensors from the pilot only when the system is enabled to move
MoveReq003	When enabled for movement, the system shall apply force proportional to the pressure from the user's limb as detected via pressure sensors up to the maximum allowed force
MoveReq005	The system proportional response to limb pressure shall be configurable during off-line system configuration (for default settings) and during start up (for current use)
MoveReq006	System limb movement shall respond with a latency of no more than 10 ms
MoveReq007	System maximum limb movement range shall be such to support 75% of normal human limb movement
MoveReq008	Limb movement is only available in normal operational mode OR when in standby mode and the operator has explicitly selected emergency override
MoveReq009	The system shall have a minimal carrying capacity of 1500 kg payload at 2.5 mph walking speed
MoveReq010	The system arms shall be able to maintain a payload at full forward limb extension of 1200 kg
MoveReq011	The system shall provide force-assisted torso twisting to 90° left and right while carrying its maximum capacity

(Continued)

(Continued)

ID	Specification
MoveReq012	The system shall provide grippers on the end of its arms, activated by the pressure sensors on the pilot's hands when inserted into the distal gripper gloves
MoveReq013	The grippers shall open and close and apply pressure proportional to the pilot pressure applied
MoveReq014	The grippers shall be able to optionally maintain a constant pressure set by the pilot's hands when activated with a right-handed thumb switch in the gripper glove. This switch shall enable and disable the constant pressure applied by the grippers
MoveReq015	The grippers shall be able to pronate to +30° and to supinate to +60°, as indicated by the pressure sensors monitoring the pilot's hands and wrists
MoveReq016	The legs shall flex in the sagittal plane in three joints: hip, knee, and foot
MoveReq017	The arms shall flex in the sagittal plane at three joints: shoulder, elbow, and hand
MoveReq018	The hip joint shall provide movement in the frontal and transverse planes to support walking and turning
MoveReq019	The shoulder joint shall provide movement in the frontal and transverse planes to facilitate flexible movement to pick up and deposit payloads
MoveReq020	The gripper shall provide rotational movement, similar to the pilot wrist movement
MoveReq021	The gripper shall have a span of 60 cm and be able to grip an item 25 cm in diameter with a gripping force of up to 600 kg
MoveReq022	The system shall provide pilot and maintainer control for fully automated sit down function
MoveReq023	The system shall provide fully automated stand mode from sitting, supine, and prone positions, available to pilot or maintainer
MoveReq024	The system shall be able to, with bending at the knees and hips, pick up a payload weighing at least 1000 kg and return to a standing position
MoveReq025	The system shall be able to raise a load of at least 500 kg overhead and indefinitely support the weight over the pilot's head and maintain static balance
MoveReq026	The system shall be able to bend at the knee joint to +100° but shall not be able to hyperextend beyond −2°
MoveReq028	The system shall be able to bend at the ankle from nominal position (+90°) to +120° (dorsiflexion) to +10° (plantar flexion)
MoveReq028	The system shall be able to bend at the hip joint in the sagittal plane from +90° (forward) to −50° (backwards)
MoveReq029	The system shall be able to move the wrist joint to +90° (flexion), −60° (extension), −20° (radial deviation), and −30° (ulnar deviation)
MoveReq030	The system shall be able to flex the elbow from 0° (full extension) to +120° (flexion)
MoveReq031	The system shall provide a flexible shoulder joint that shall be able to reach straight over the pilot's head with free motion within the bounds of fully flexed (+180°) and fully at the side (0°) and behind (−10°) in the sagittal plane and in the frontal plane from at the sides (0°) to fully overhead (+180°) and in the transverse plane from the midline of the pilot's torso (−20°) to fully at the side (+90°)
PowerReq001	The system shall be able to provide 50 kWh capacity to power movement and system services
PowerReq002	The system shall alert the user with a warning when the capacity of the battery is at or below 5 kWh and an urgent warning when the capacity falls to 2 kWh or below
PowerReq002	The system shall be able to recharge from a standard 220 V wall supply from full drained to fully charged in 8 h
PowerReq003	The system shall provide the user with a continuous display of capacity in kWh and estimated remaining operational time in hh:mm:ss

(*Continued*)

(Continued)

ID	Specification
PowerReq005	The remaining power display shall be updated at least every 5 min when more than 1 h estimated time remains, every minute when less than 1 h estimated time remains, and every second when less than 5 min estimated time remain
PowerReq006	The battery shall weigh no more than 80 kg
Proximity001	The system shall be able to detect objects with which current movement pattern will result in a collision. Such a detection shall be highlighted in a wireframe view in the pilot HUD and provide a repeating alert tone to the pilot
ShutdownReq001	The system shall provide an option to go into a Park mode (feet 10 cm apart, arms at the sides) to the pilot during the shutdown step
ShutdownReq002	The system shall provide an emergency shutdown option at all times that freezes the system limbs in their current position and enters Standby mode
Startup006	If the diagnostics port is plugged into a maintenance system during start up, the system shall power up into Standby mode
StartupReq001	The system shall initiate a power on self test when first activated by the user or when powered up from a powered down state
StartupReq002	The status of power on test shall be reported to the pilot during execution
StartupReq003	Successful completion of the power on self tests shall result in a green READY light and enablement of all system functions
StartupReq004	The system shall provide communications and lighting functions within 1 s of power application and in Standby mode
StartupReq005	If the system fails power on test, it shall enter Standby mode with a Power On Self Test Flight light lit
TestReq001	The system shall perform a diagnostic self test during system start up and only provide movement capability if the self tests pass
TestReq002	The success or failure of the power on self test shall be displayed in the pilot's display, along with any identified error codes, ordered by criticality
TestReq003	Any identified self test failures shall be logged for later retrieval
TestReq004	Self test history shall be available to the system maintenance staff over a (wired plug) diagnostic link
TestReq005	Power on self test shall verify, at minimum, proper pressure on any hydraulic systems, computer node health checks, communication link check, internal communication link checks, battery status, internal temperature, and pilot limb pressure sensors
VisibilityReq001	The system shall provide flood lights under on—off control to optionally illuminate the area in front
VisibilityReq002	The system shall provide side lights of a lesser strength than the front flood lights to illuminate the areas on the sides of the system, under the control of the pilot
VisibilityReq004	The system will provide low-power amber safety lighting for the feet and hands of the system, under the control of the user
VisibilityReq005	The system will annunciate a back up tone when the system is walking backwards
VisibilityReq006	The lights shall be available in normal operating mode and in Standby mode
VisibilityReq007	The system shall provide always-on safety red lighting for the rear of the system, at low, middle, and top positions
WalkReq001	The system shall be able to walk forward with a full payload at 2.5 mph over flat terrain
WalkReq002	The system shall be able to climb steps of height 20 cm at 1 mph
WalkReq003	The system shall be able to walk backwards at 1.5 mph
WalkReq006	The system shall be able to walk autonomously while in maintenance mode (i.e., without a pilot present) under command of the maintainer

Index

Note: Page numbers followed by "*f*" and "*t*" refer to figures and tables, respectively.

B

C

T

U